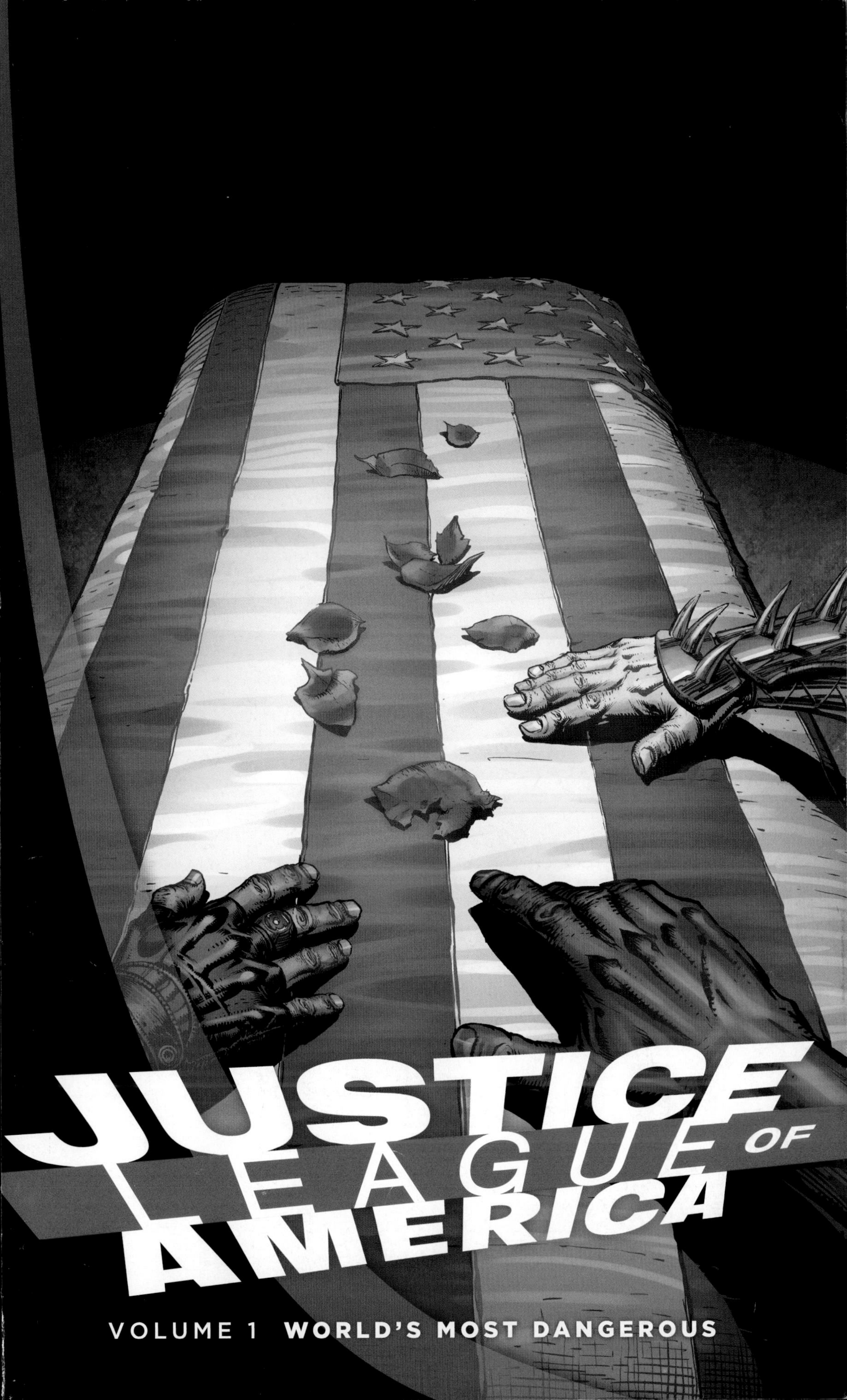

JUSTICE LEAGUE OF AMERICA

VOLUME 1 WORLD'S MOST DANGEROUS

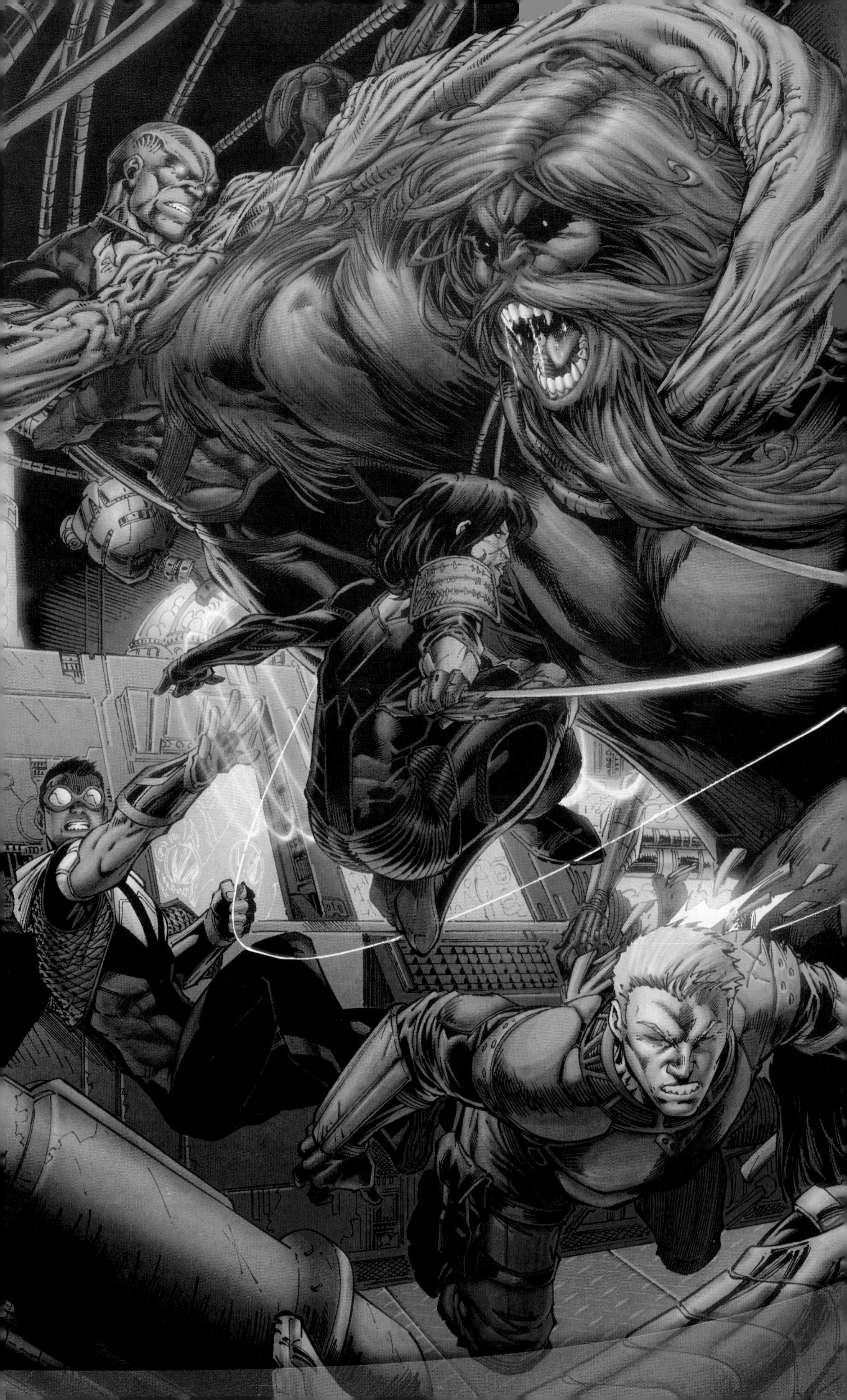

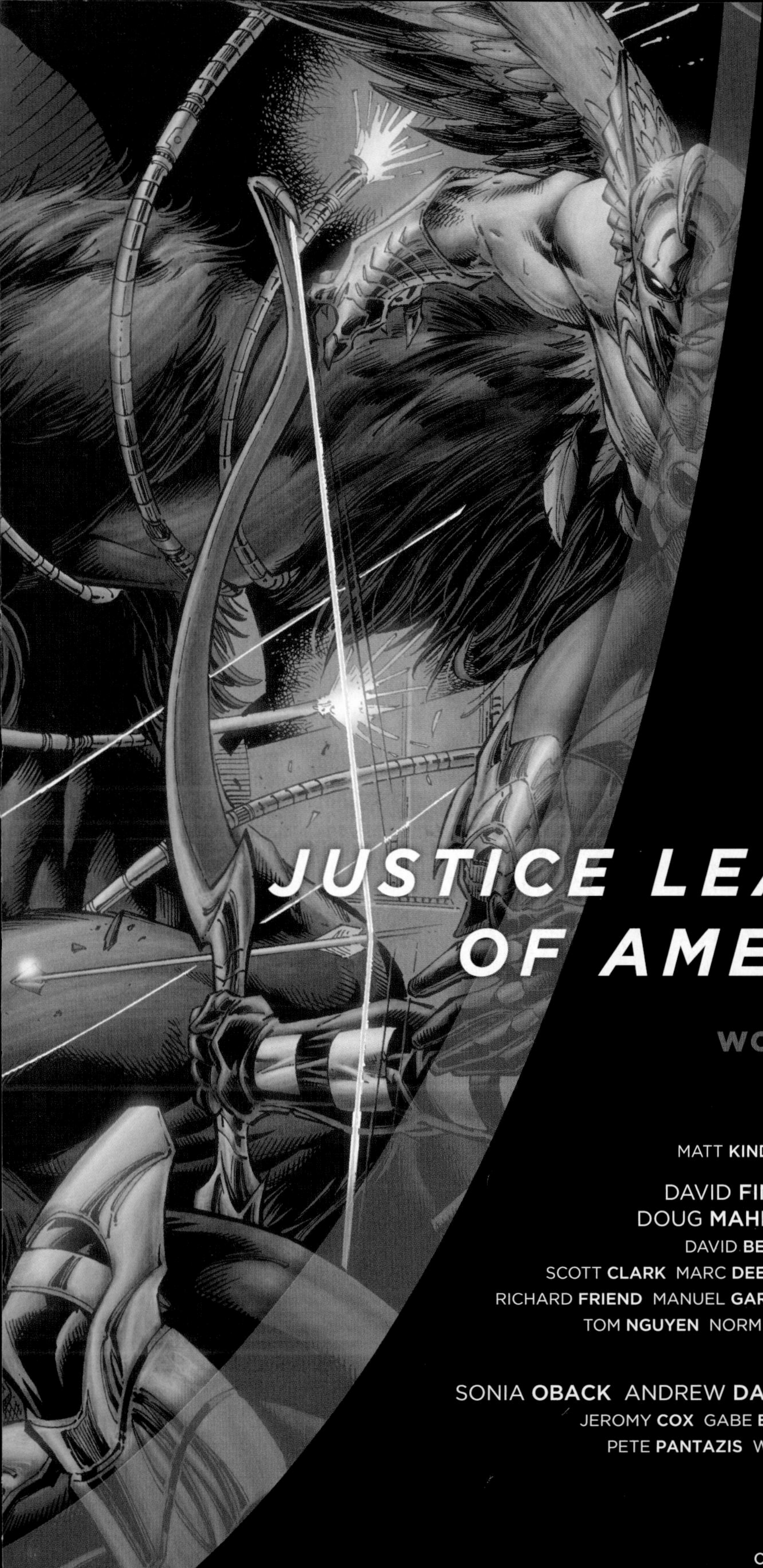

JUSTICE LEAGUE OF AMERICA

VOLUME 1

WORLD'S MOST DANGEROUS

GEOFF **JOHNS**
MATT **KINDT** JEFF **LEMIRE** writers

DAVID **FINCH** BRETT **BOOTH**
DOUG **MAHNKE** CHRISTIAN **ALAMY**
DAVID **BEATY** KEITH **CHAMPAGNE**
SCOTT **CLARK** MARC **DEERING** RAUL **FERNANDEZ**
RICHARD **FRIEND** MANUEL **GARCIA** ANDRES **GUINALDO**
TOM **NGUYEN** NORM **RAPMUND** ROBIN **RIGGS**
WALDEN **WONG** artists

SONIA **OBACK** ANDREW **DALHOUSE** JEFF **CHANG**
JEROMY **COX** GABE **ELTAEB** NATHAN **EYRING**
PETE **PANTAZIS** WIL **QUINTANA** colorists

ROB **LEIGH** letterer

DAVID **FINCH**
collection cover artist

SUPERMAN created by JERRY **SIEGEL** & JOE **SHUSTER**
By special arrangement with the Jerry Siegel family

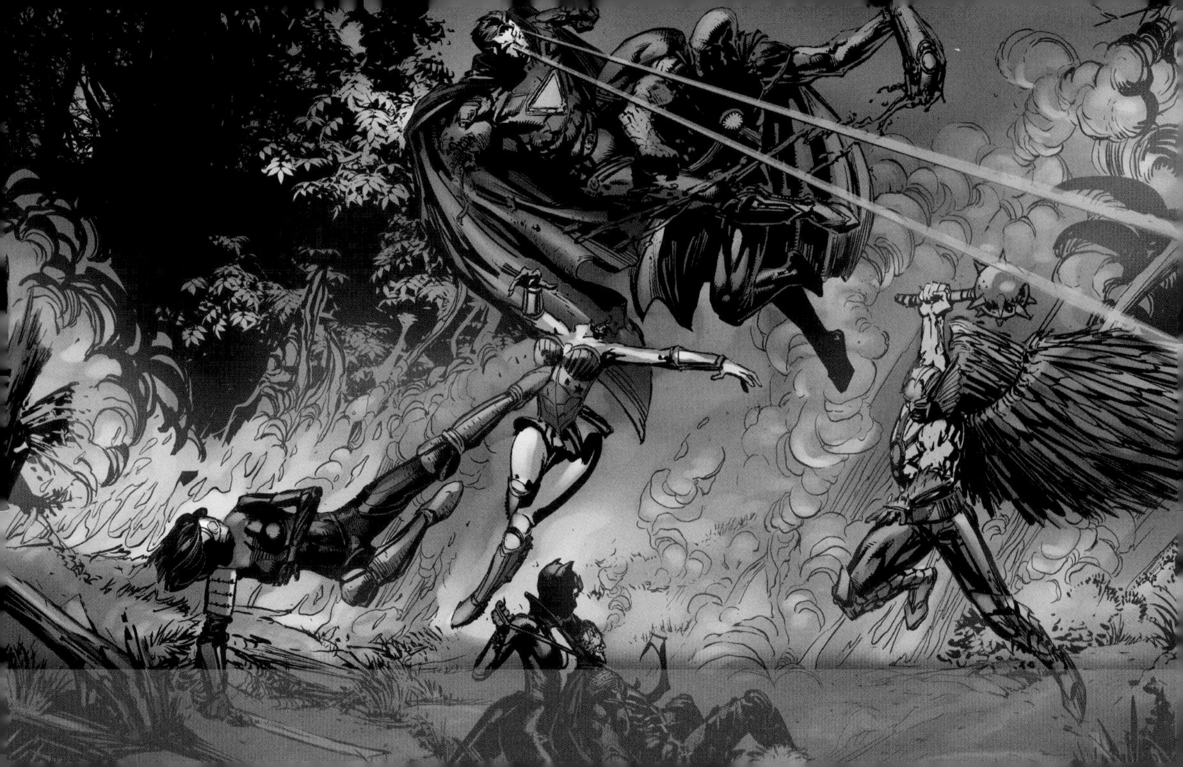

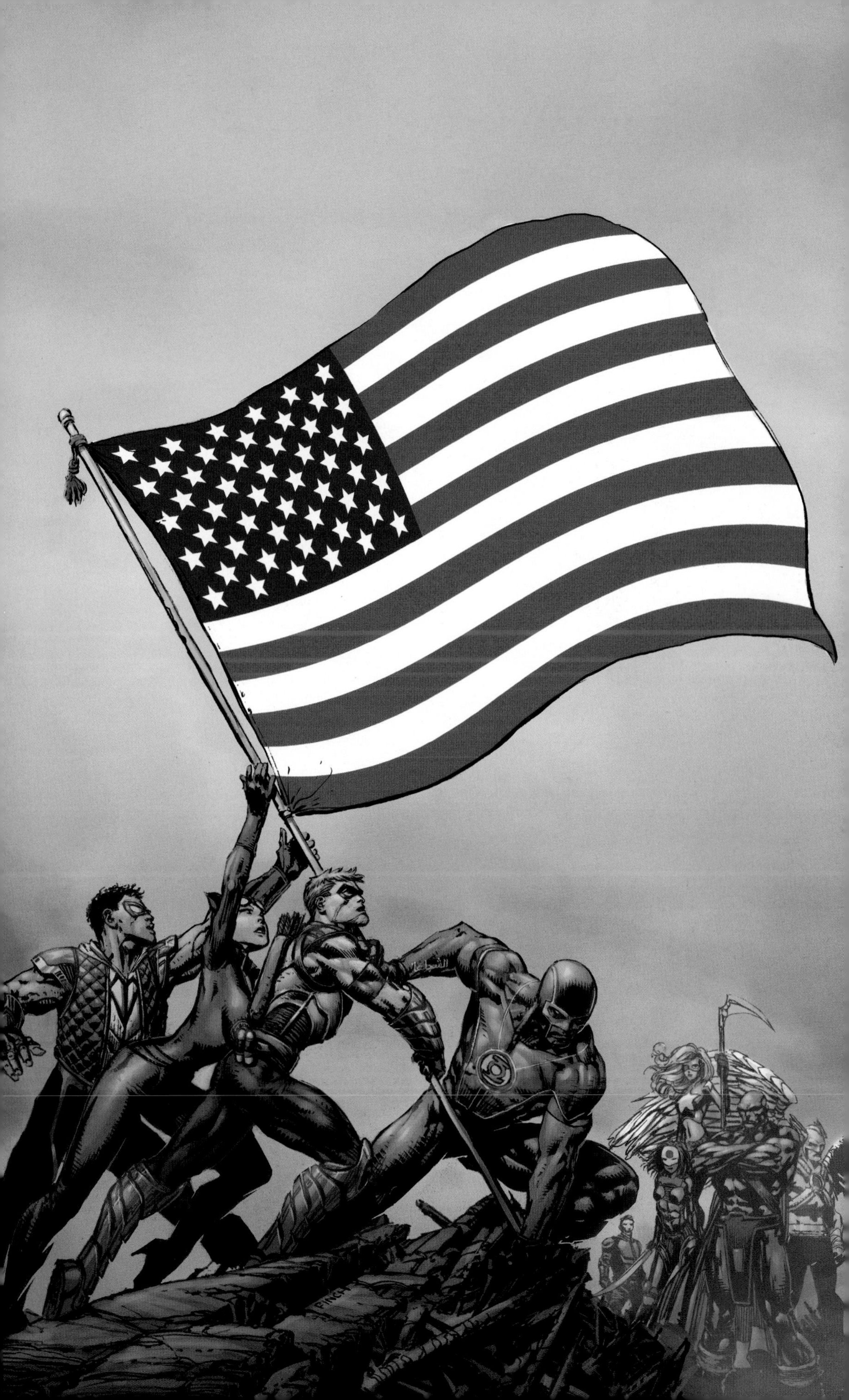
FINCH

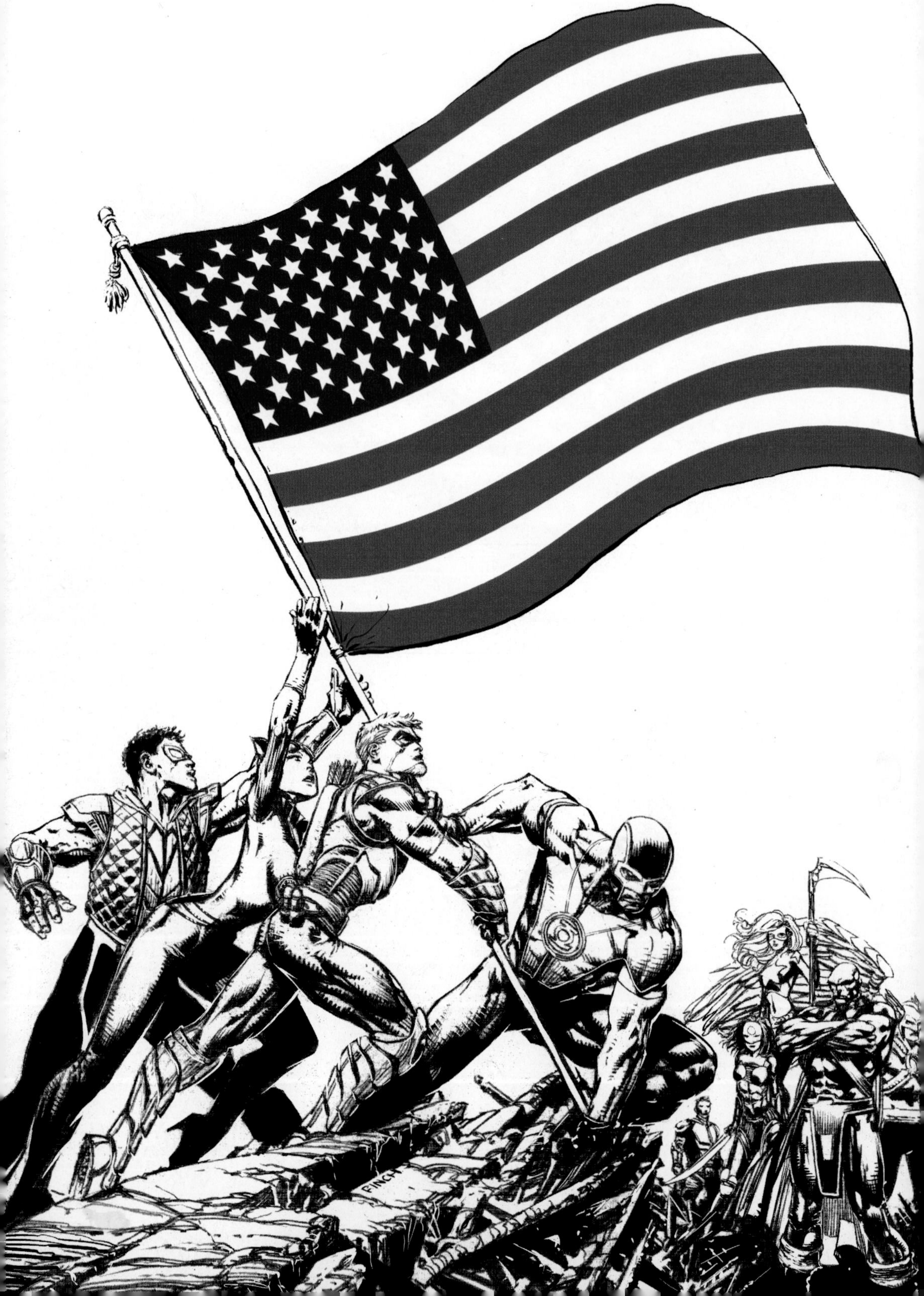
FINCH

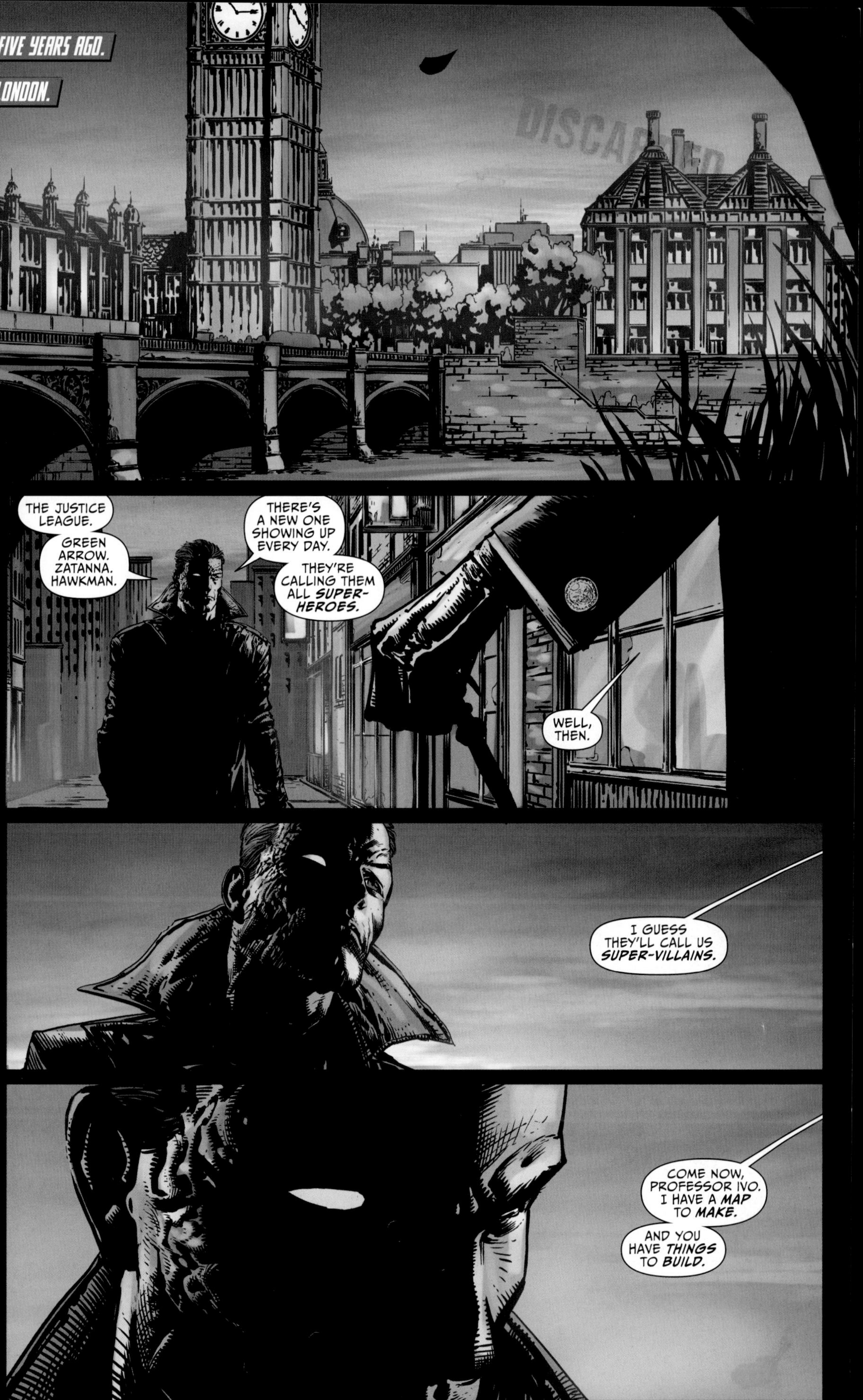
FIVE YEARS AGO.
LONDON.
THE JUSTICE LEAGUE.
GREEN ARROW. ZATANNA. HAWKMAN.
THERE'S A NEW ONE SHOWING UP EVERY DAY.
THEY'RE CALLING THEM ALL SUPER-HEROES.
WELL, THEN.
I GUESS THEY'LL CALL US SUPER-VILLAINS.
COME NOW, PROFESSOR IVO. I HAVE A MAP TO MAKE.
AND YOU HAVE THINGS TO BUILD.

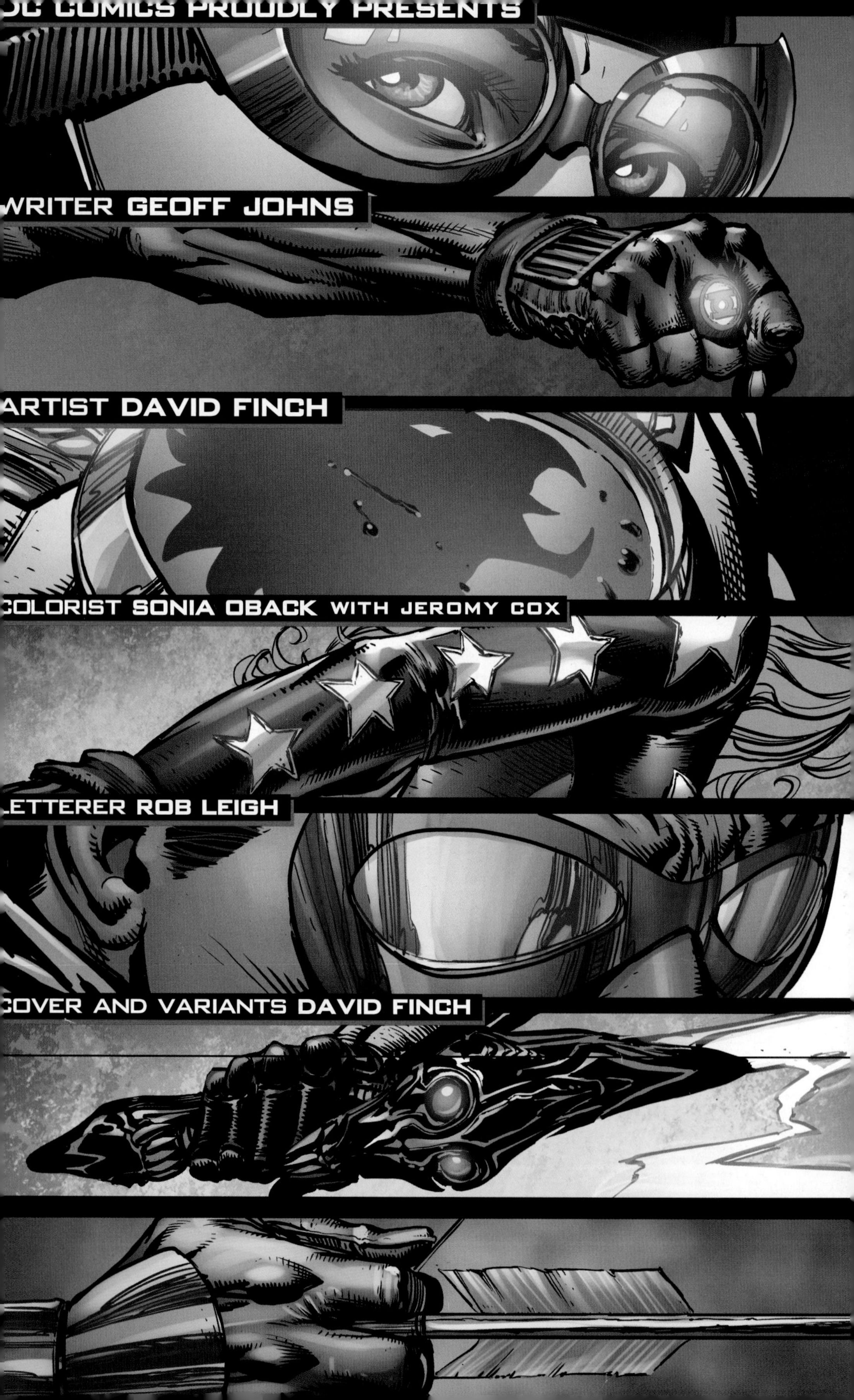
DC COMICS PROUDLY PRESENTS
WRITER GEOFF JOHNS
ARTIST DAVID FINCH
COLORIST SONIA OBACK WITH JEROMY COX
LETTERER ROB LEIGH
COVER AND VARIANTS DAVID FINCH

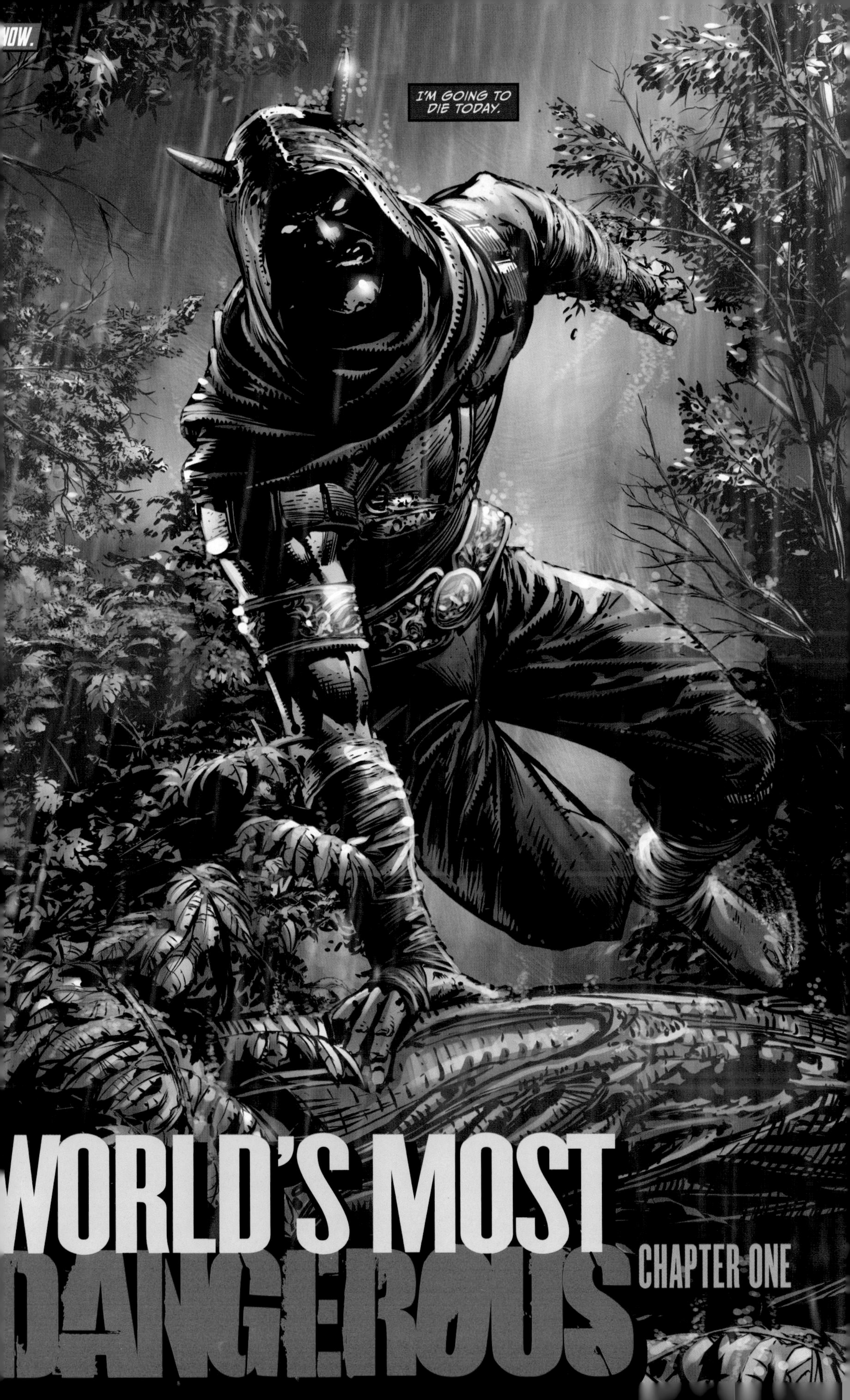
NOW.
I'M GOING TO DIE TODAY.
WORLD'S MOST DANGEROUS
CHAPTER ONE

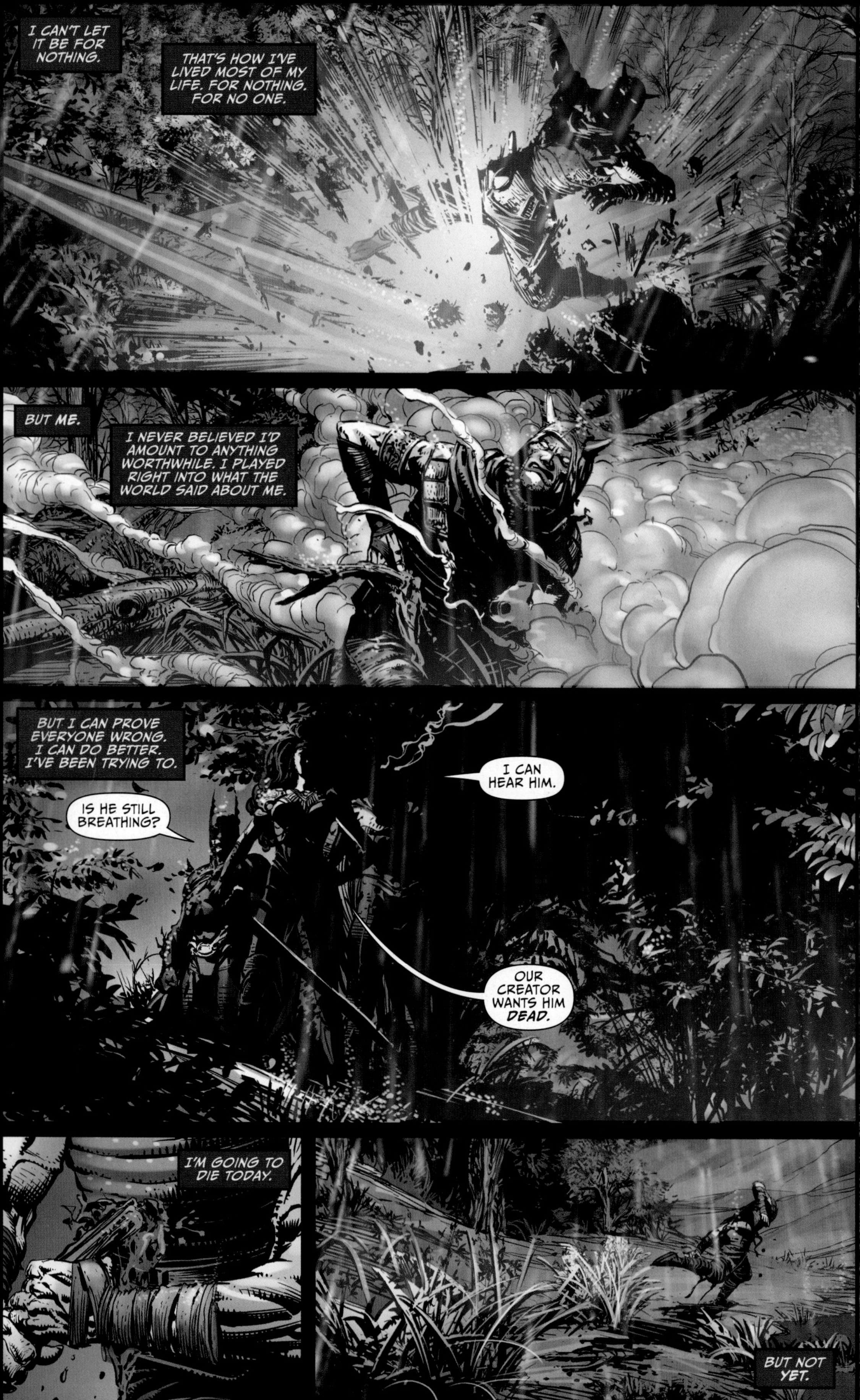
I CAN'T LET IT BE FOR NOTHING.
THAT'S HOW I'VE LIVED MOST OF MY LIFE. FOR NOTHING. FOR NO ONE.
BUT ME.
I NEVER BELIEVED I'D AMOUNT TO ANYTHING WORTHWHILE. I PLAYED RIGHT INTO WHAT THE WORLD SAID ABOUT ME.
BUT I CAN PROVE EVERYONE WRONG. I CAN DO BETTER. I'VE BEEN TRYING TO.
IS HE STILL BREATHING?
I CAN HEAR HIM.
OUR CREATOR WANTS HIM DEAD.
I'M GOING TO DIE TODAY.
BUT NOT YET.

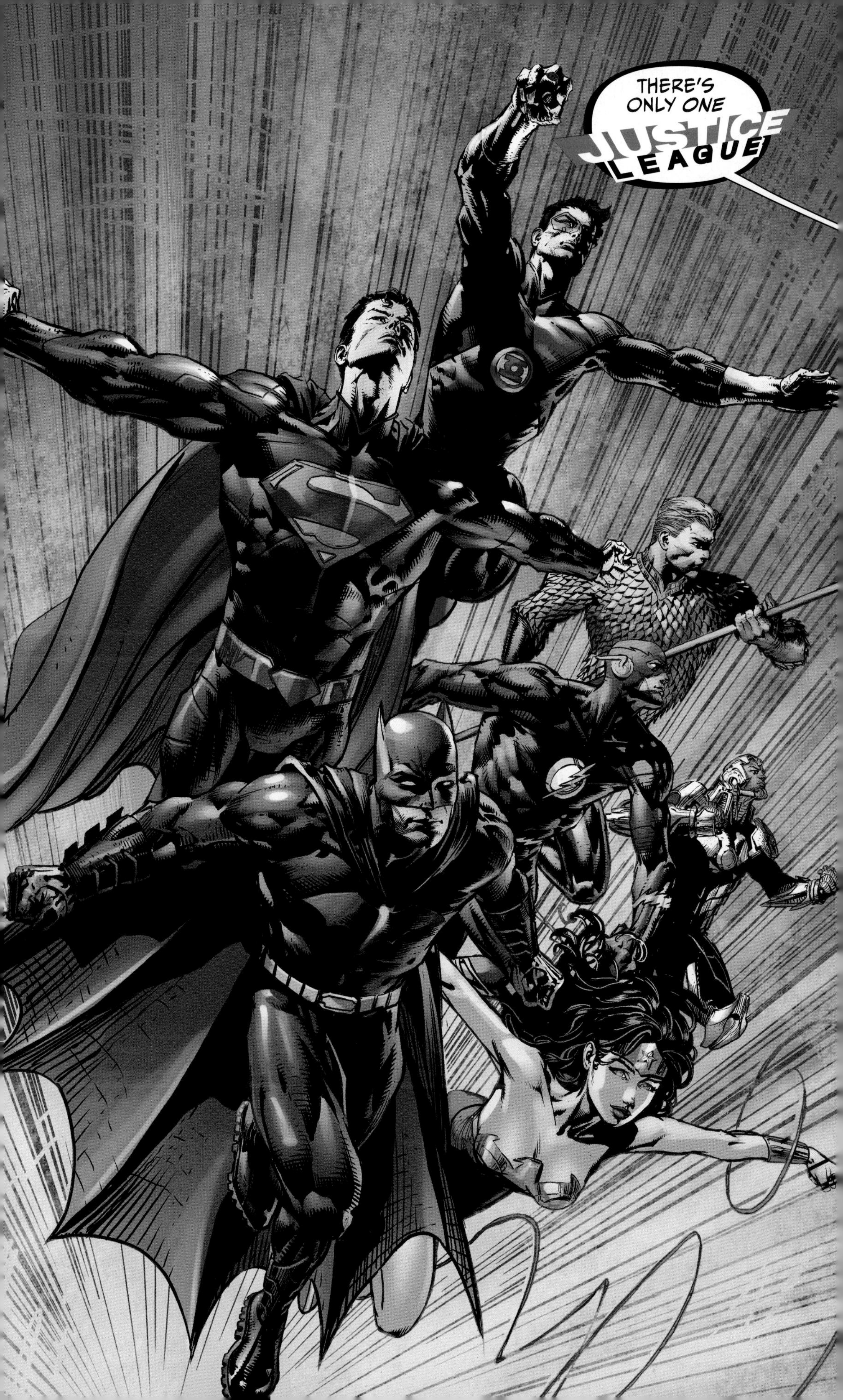
THERE'S ONLY ONE JUSTICE LEAGUE

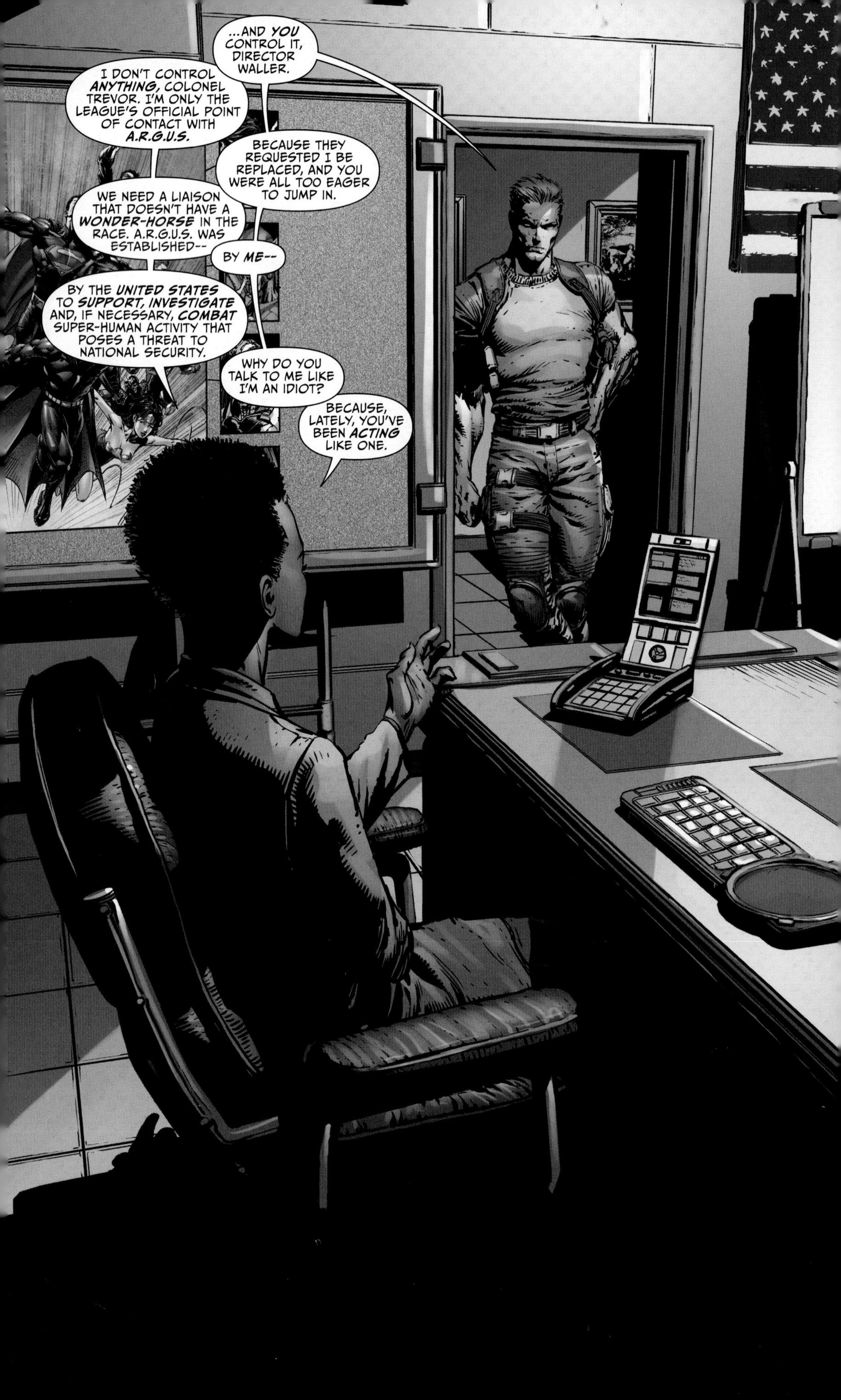
I DON'T CONTROL ANYTHING, COLONEL TREVOR. I'M ONLY THE LEAGUE'S OFFICIAL POINT OF CONTACT WITH A.R.G.U.S.
...AND YOU CONTROL IT, DIRECTOR WALLER.
BECAUSE THEY REQUESTED I BE REPLACED, AND YOU WERE ALL TOO EAGER TO JUMP IN.
WE NEED A LIAISON THAT DOESN'T HAVE A WONDER-HORSE IN THE RACE. A.R.G.U.S. WAS ESTABLISHED--
BY ME--
BY THE UNITED STATES TO SUPPORT, INVESTIGATE AND, IF NECESSARY, COMBAT SUPER-HUMAN ACTIVITY THAT POSES A THREAT TO NATIONAL SECURITY.
WHY DO YOU TALK TO ME LIKE I'M AN IDIOT?
BECAUSE, LATELY, YOU'VE BEEN ACTING LIKE ONE.

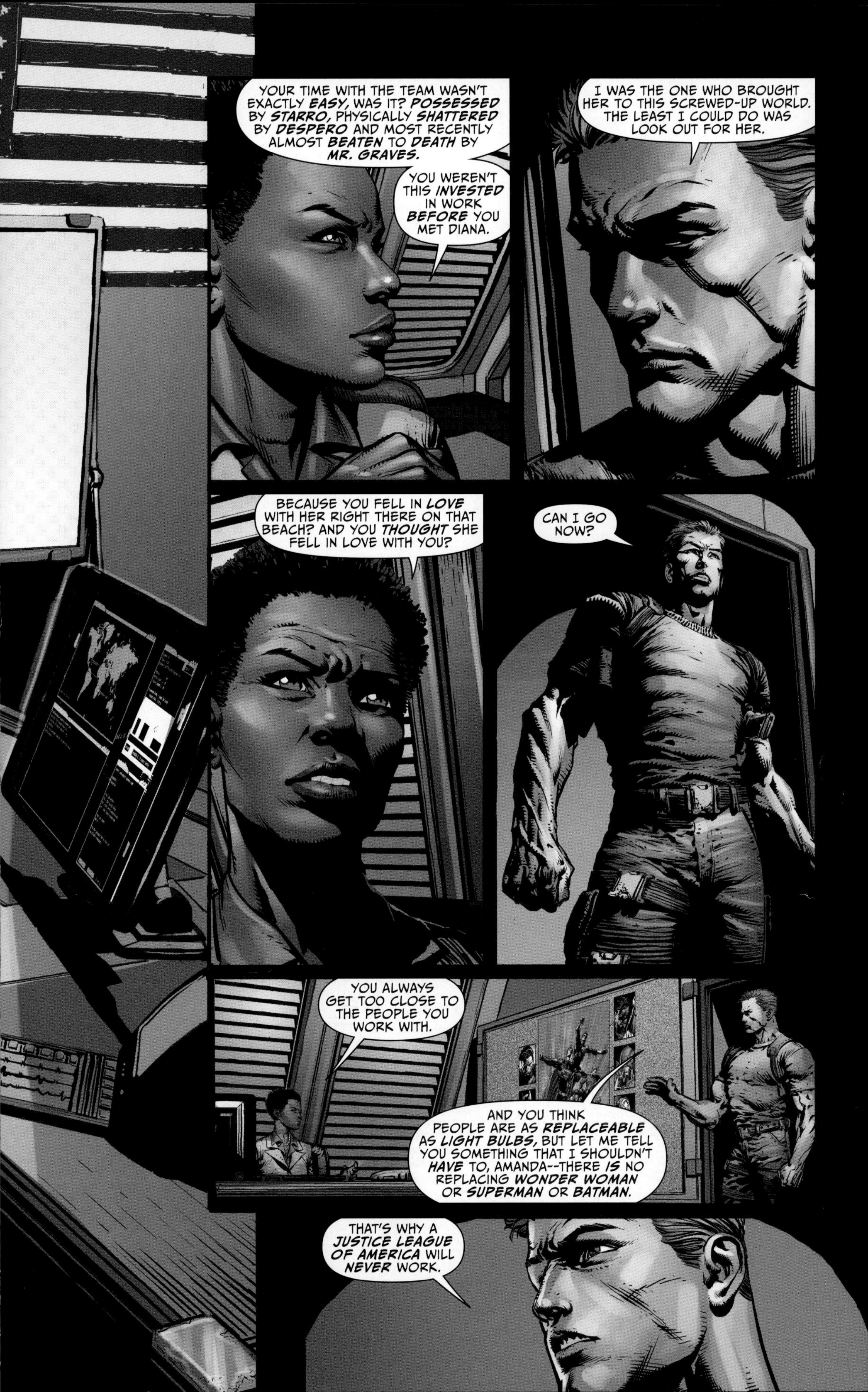
YOUR TIME WITH THE TEAM WASN'T EXACTLY EASY, WAS IT? POSSESSED BY STARRO, PHYSICALLY SHATTERED BY DESPERO AND MOST RECENTLY ALMOST BEATEN TO DEATH BY MR. GRAVES.
YOU WEREN'T THIS INVESTED IN WORK BEFORE YOU MET DIANA.
I WAS THE ONE WHO BROUGHT HER TO THIS SCREWED-UP WORLD. THE LEAST I COULD DO WAS LOOK OUT FOR HER.
BECAUSE YOU FELL IN LOVE WITH HER RIGHT THERE ON THAT BEACH? AND YOU THOUGHT SHE FELL IN LOVE WITH YOU?
CAN I GO NOW?
YOU ALWAYS GET TOO CLOSE TO THE PEOPLE YOU WORK WITH.
AND YOU THINK PEOPLE ARE AS REPLACEABLE AS LIGHT BULBS, BUT LET ME TELL YOU SOMETHING THAT I SHOULDN'T HAVE TO, AMANDA--THERE IS NO REPLACING WONDER WOMAN OR SUPERMAN OR BATMAN.
THAT'S WHY A JUSTICE LEAGUE OF AMERICA WILL NEVER WORK.

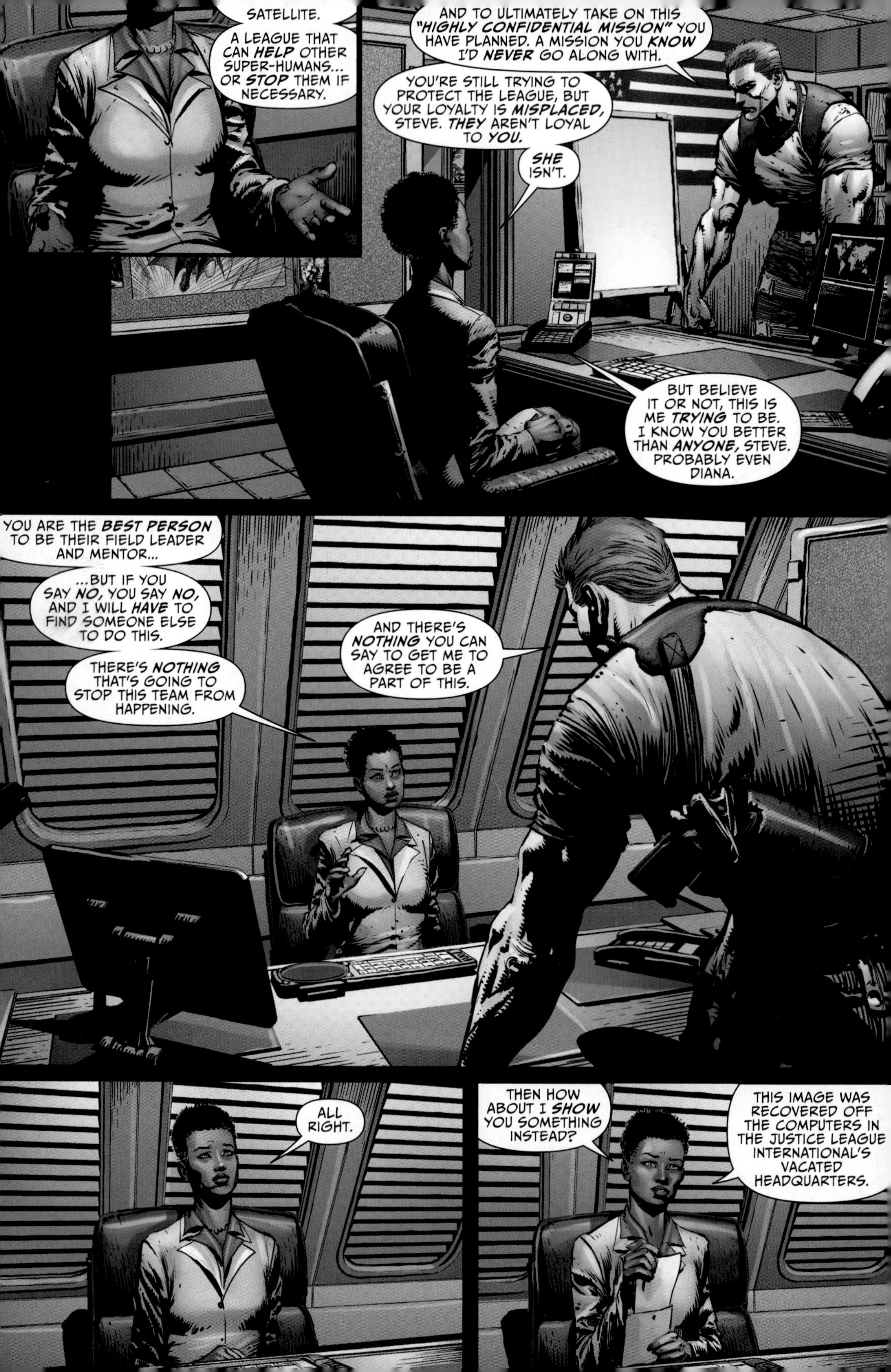
SATELLITE.
A LEAGUE THAT CAN HELP OTHER SUPER-HUMANS... OR STOP THEM IF NECESSARY.
AND TO ULTIMATELY TAKE ON THIS "HIGHLY CONFIDENTIAL MISSION" YOU HAVE PLANNED. A MISSION YOU KNOW I'D NEVER GO ALONG WITH.
YOU'RE STILL TRYING TO PROTECT THE LEAGUE, BUT YOUR LOYALTY IS MISPLACED, STEVE. THEY AREN'T LOYAL TO YOU.
SHE ISN'T.
BUT BELIEVE IT OR NOT, THIS IS ME TRYING TO BE. I KNOW YOU BETTER THAN ANYONE, STEVE. PROBABLY EVEN DIANA.
YOU ARE THE BEST PERSON TO BE THEIR FIELD LEADER AND MENTOR...
...BUT IF YOU SAY NO, YOU SAY NO, AND I WILL HAVE TO FIND SOMEONE ELSE TO DO THIS.
THERE'S NOTHING THAT'S GOING TO STOP THIS TEAM FROM HAPPENING.
AND THERE'S NOTHING YOU CAN SAY TO GET ME TO AGREE TO BE A PART OF THIS.
ALL RIGHT.
THEN HOW ABOUT I SHOW YOU SOMETHING INSTEAD?
THIS IMAGE WAS RECOVERED OFF THE COMPUTERS IN THE JUSTICE LEAGUE INTERNATIONAL'S VACATED HEADQUARTERS.

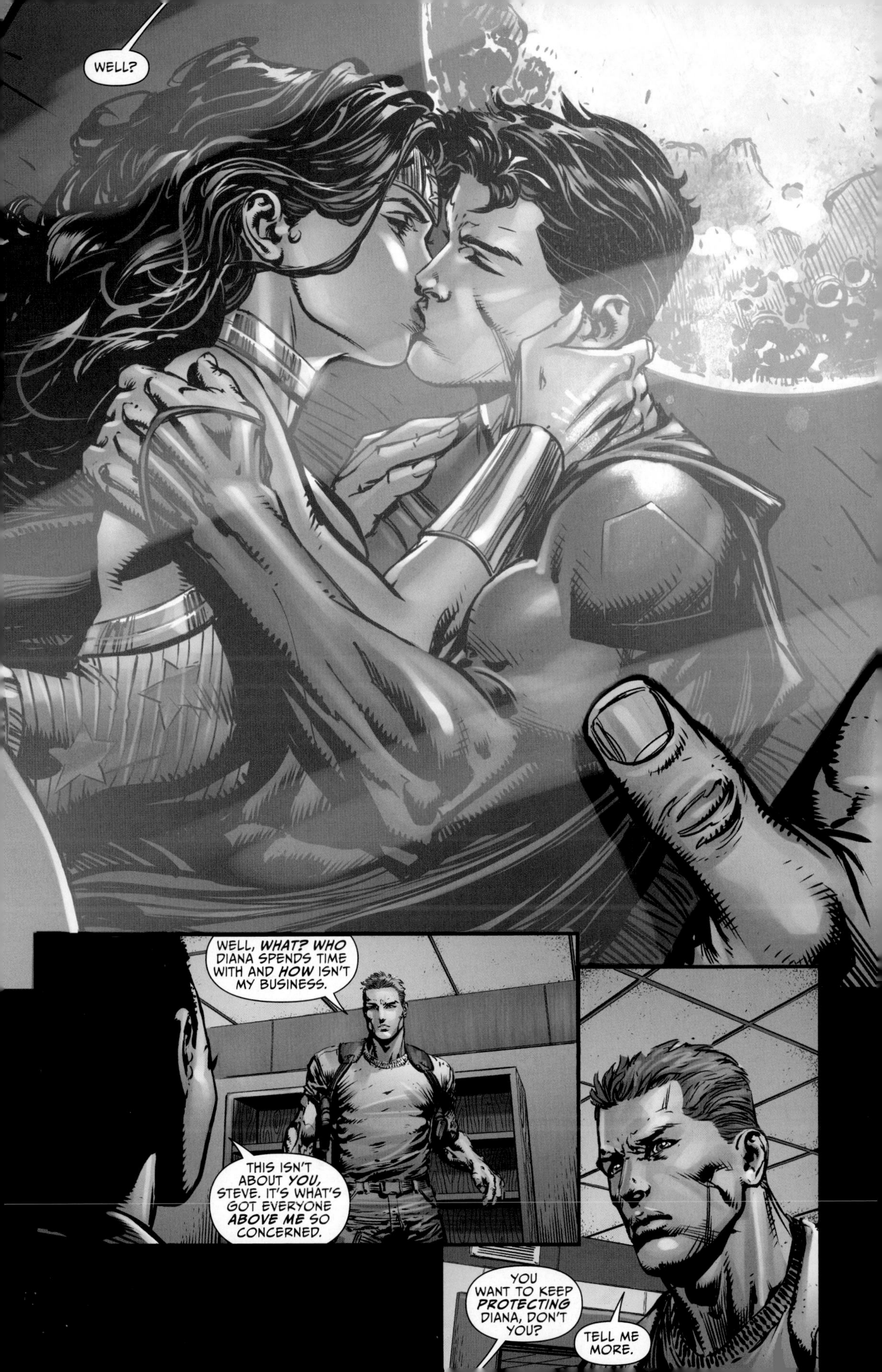
WELL?
WELL, WHAT? WHO DIANA SPENDS TIME WITH AND HOW ISN'T MY BUSINESS.
THIS ISN'T ABOUT YOU, STEVE. IT'S WHAT'S GOT EVERYONE ABOVE ME SO CONCERNED.
YOU WANT TO KEEP PROTECTING DIANA, DON'T YOU?
TELL ME MORE.

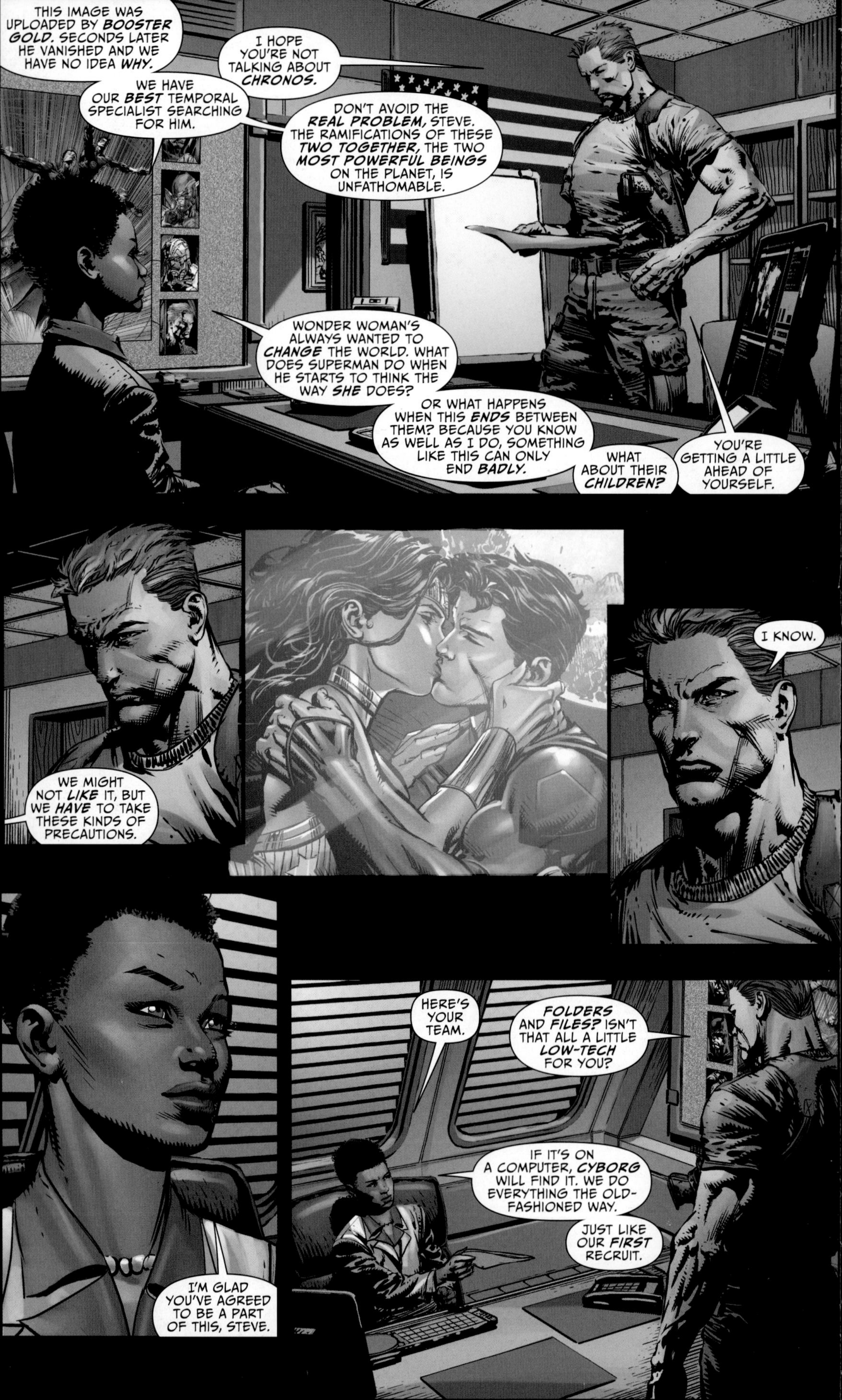

THIS IMAGE WAS UPLOADED BY BOOSTER GOLD. SECONDS LATER HE VANISHED AND WE HAVE NO IDEA WHY.
I HOPE YOU'RE NOT TALKING ABOUT CHRONOS.
WE HAVE OUR BEST TEMPORAL SPECIALIST SEARCHING FOR HIM.
DON'T AVOID THE REAL PROBLEM, STEVE. THE RAMIFICATIONS OF THESE TWO TOGETHER, THE TWO MOST POWERFUL BEINGS ON THE PLANET, IS UNFATHOMABLE.
WONDER WOMAN'S ALWAYS WANTED TO CHANGE THE WORLD. WHAT DOES SUPERMAN DO WHEN HE STARTS TO THINK THE WAY SHE DOES?
OR WHAT HAPPENS WHEN THIS ENDS BETWEEN THEM? BECAUSE YOU KNOW AS WELL AS I DO, SOMETHING LIKE THIS CAN ONLY END BADLY.
WHAT ABOUT THEIR CHILDREN?
YOU'RE GETTING A LITTLE AHEAD OF YOURSELF.
WE MIGHT NOT LIKE IT, BUT WE HAVE TO TAKE THESE KINDS OF PRECAUTIONS.
I KNOW.
I'M GLAD YOU'VE AGREED TO BE A PART OF THIS, STEVE.
HERE'S YOUR TEAM.
FOLDERS AND FILES? ISN'T THAT ALL A LITTLE LOW-TECH FOR YOU?
IF IT'S ON A COMPUTER, CYBORG WILL FIND IT. WE DO EVERYTHING THE OLD-FASHIONED WAY.
JUST LIKE OUR FIRST RECRUIT.

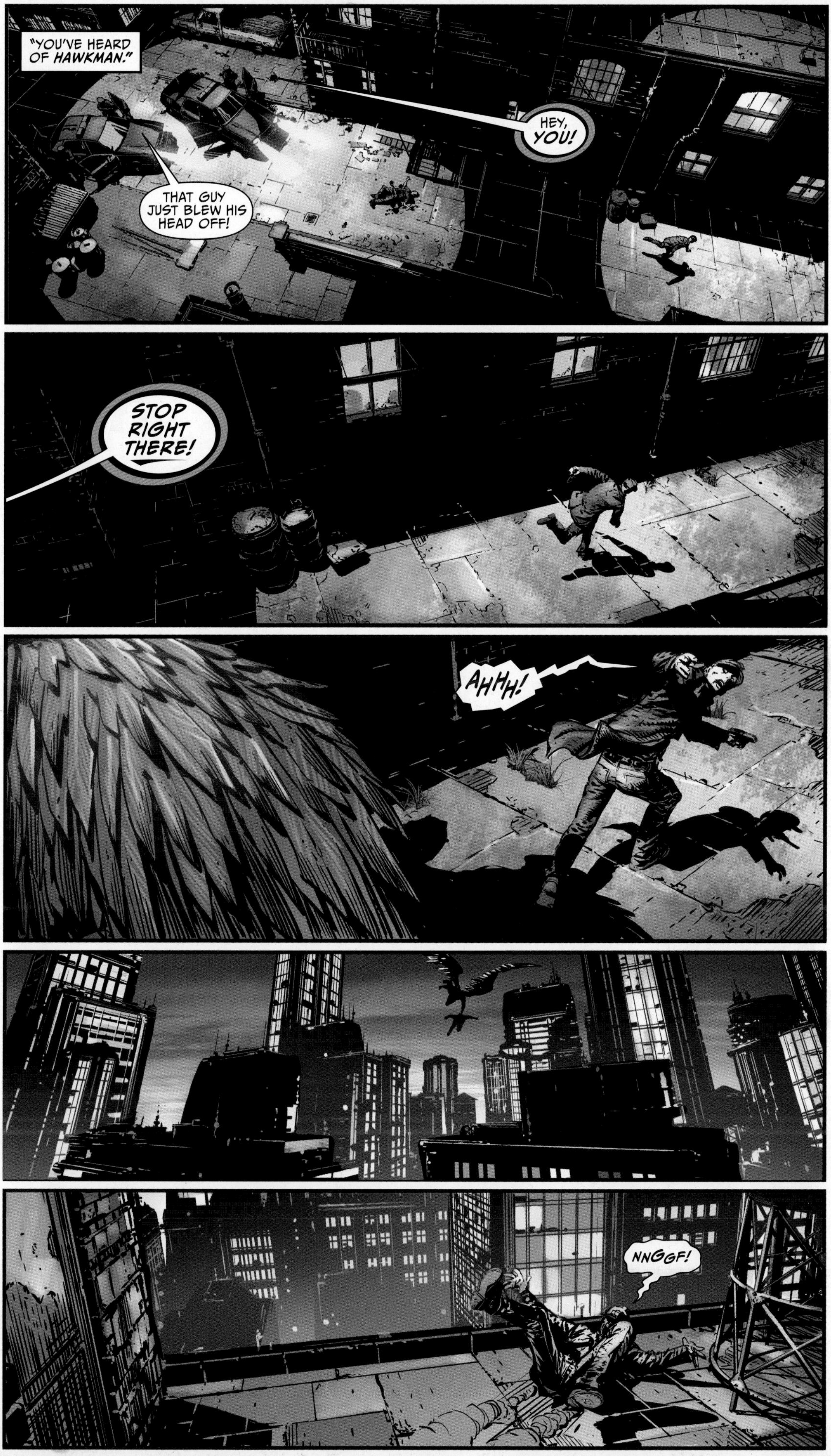
"YOU'VE HEARD OF HAWKMAN."
HEY, YOU!
THAT GUY JUST BLEW HIS HEAD OFF!
STOP RIGHT THERE!
AHHH!
NNGGF!

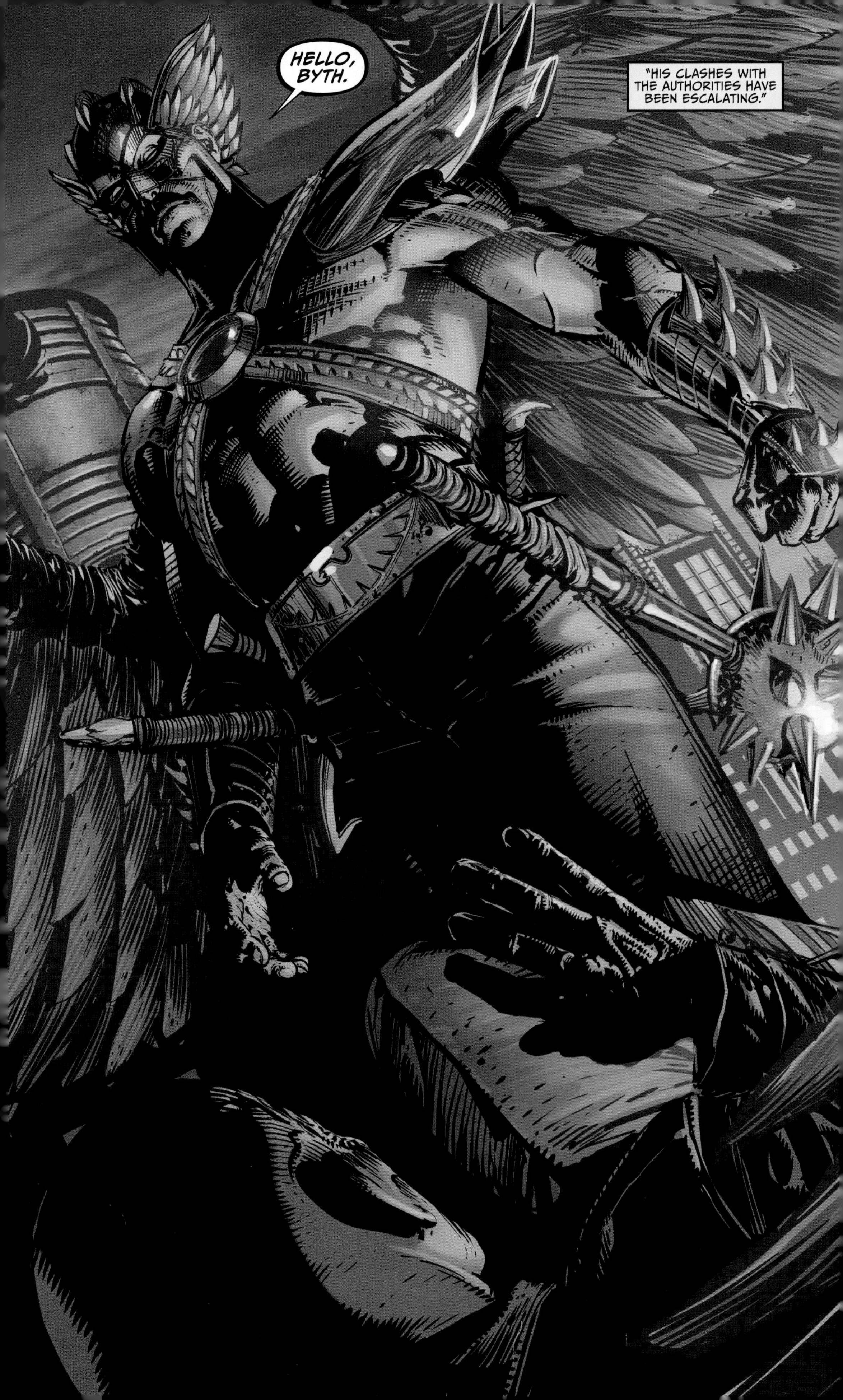
HELLO, BYTH.
"HIS CLASHES WITH THE AUTHORITIES HAVE BEEN ESCALATING."

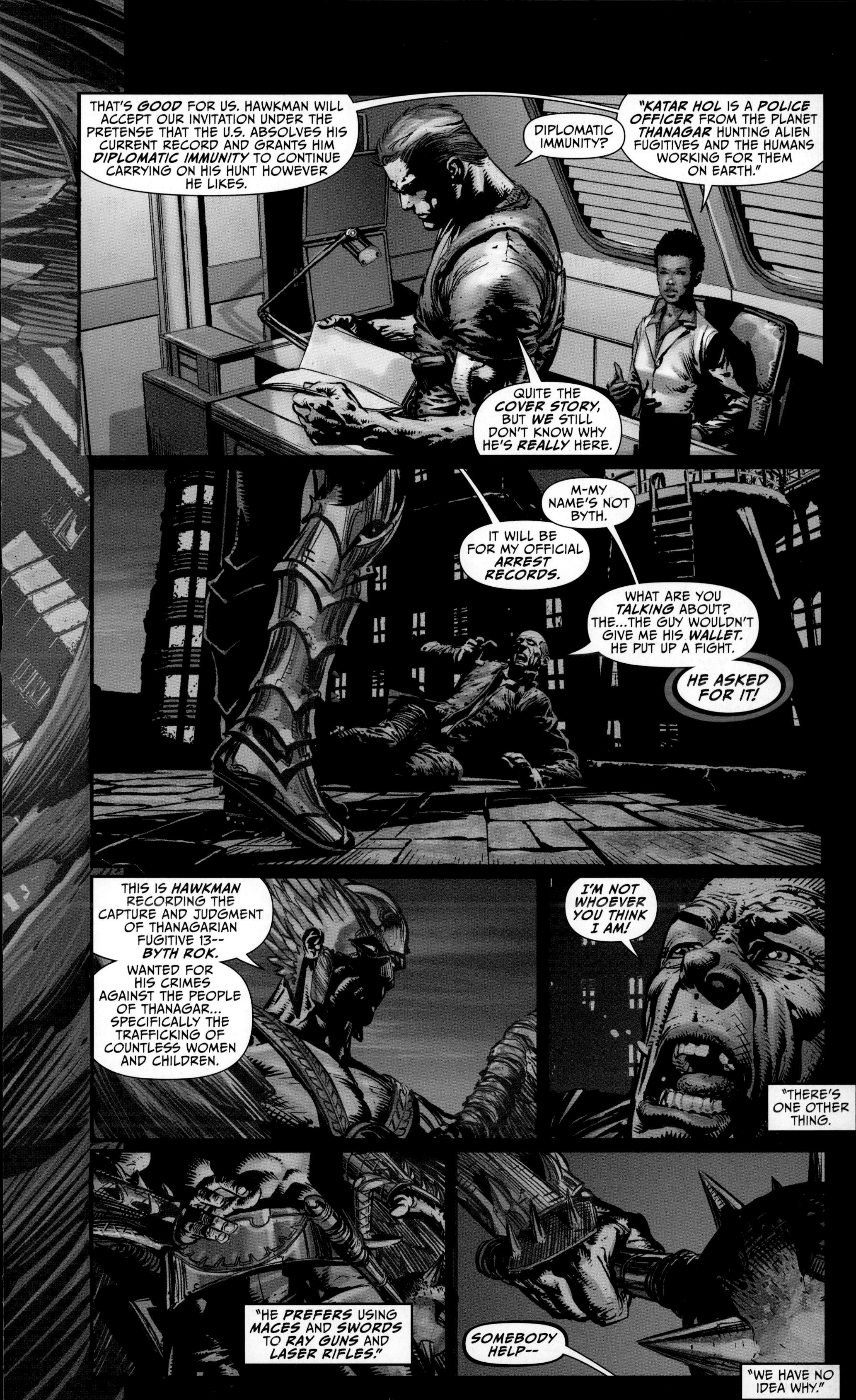

THAT'S GOOD FOR US. HAWKMAN WILL ACCEPT OUR INVITATION UNDER THE PRETENSE THAT THE U.S. ABSOLVES HIS CURRENT RECORD AND GRANTS HIM DIPLOMATIC IMMUNITY TO CONTINUE CARRYING ON HIS HUNT HOWEVER HE LIKES.
DIPLOMATIC IMMUNITY?
"KATAR HOL IS A POLICE OFFICER FROM THE PLANET THANAGAR HUNTING ALIEN FUGITIVES AND THE HUMANS WORKING FOR THEM ON EARTH."
QUITE THE COVER STORY, BUT WE STILL DON'T KNOW WHY HE'S REALLY HERE.
M-MY NAME'S NOT BYTH.
IT WILL BE FOR MY OFFICIAL ARREST RECORDS.
WHAT ARE YOU TALKING ABOUT? THE...THE GUY WOULDN'T GIVE ME HIS WALLET. HE PUT UP A FIGHT.
HE ASKED FOR IT!
THIS IS HAWKMAN RECORDING THE CAPTURE AND JUDGMENT OF THANAGARIAN FUGITIVE 13-- BYTH ROK.
WANTED FOR HIS CRIMES AGAINST THE PEOPLE OF THANAGAR... SPECIFICALLY THE TRAFFICKING OF COUNTLESS WOMEN AND CHILDREN.
I'M NOT WHOEVER YOU THINK I AM!
"THERE'S ONE OTHER THING.
"HE PREFERS USING MACES AND SWORDS TO RAY GUNS AND LASER RIFLES."
SOMEBODY HELP--
"WE HAVE NO IDEA WHY."

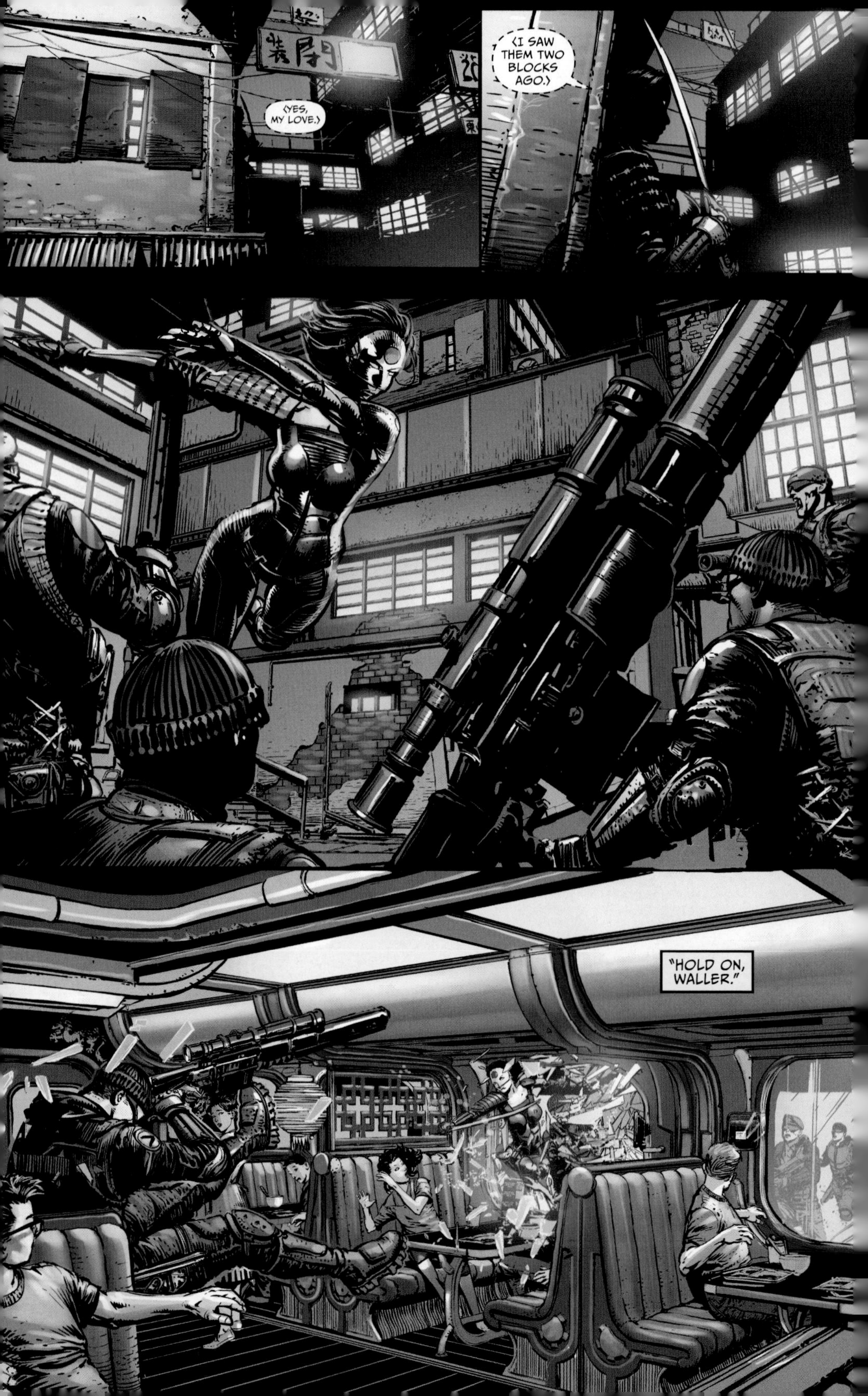
‹YES, MY LOVE.›
‹I SAW THEM TWO BLOCKS AGO.›
"HOLD ON, WALLER."

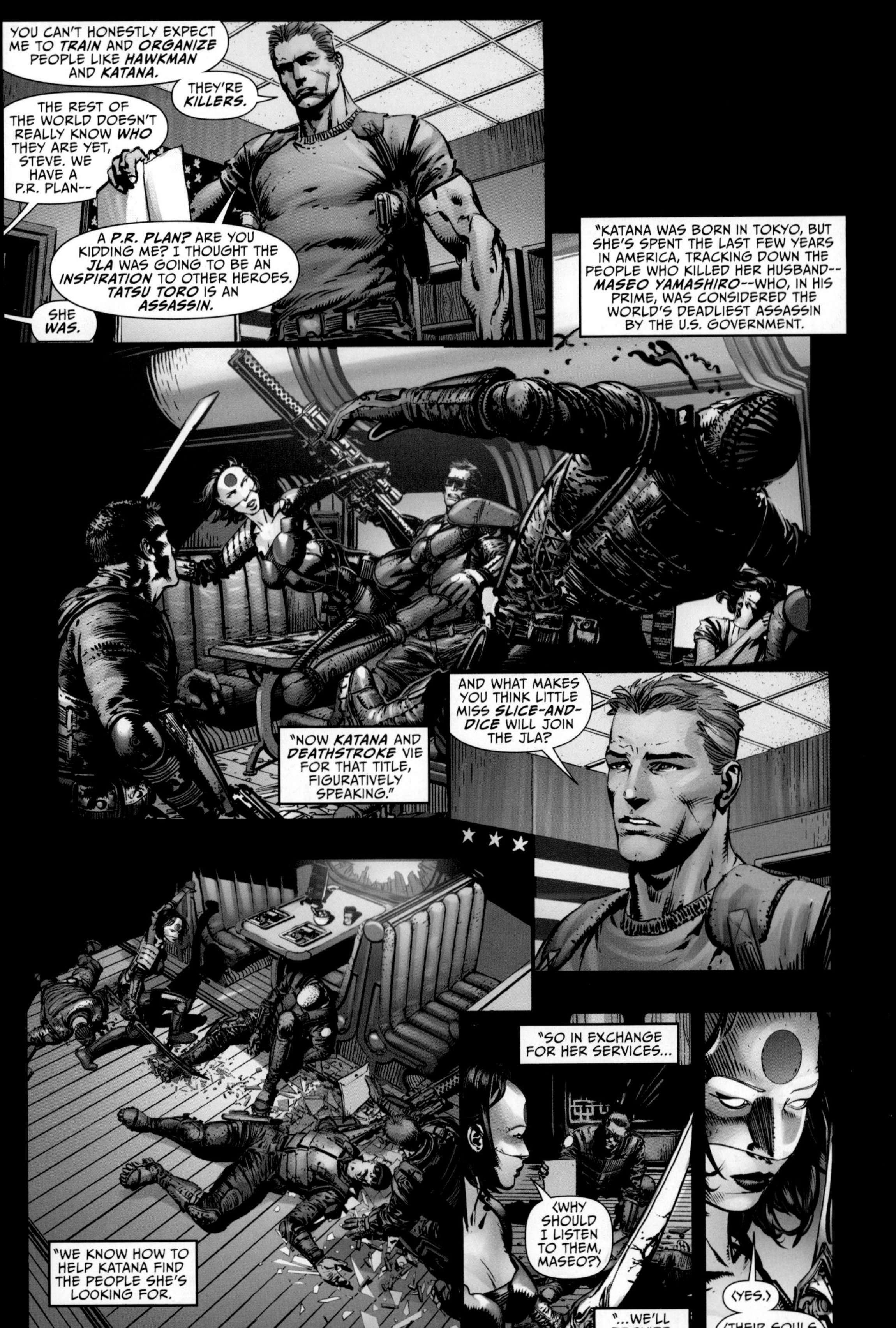

YOU CAN'T HONESTLY EXPECT ME TO TRAIN AND ORGANIZE PEOPLE LIKE HAWKMAN AND KATANA.
THEY'RE KILLERS.
THE REST OF THE WORLD DOESN'T REALLY KNOW WHO THEY ARE YET, STEVE. WE HAVE A P.R. PLAN--
A P.R. PLAN? ARE YOU KIDDING ME? I THOUGHT THE JLA WAS GOING TO BE AN INSPIRATION TO OTHER HEROES. TATSU TORO IS AN ASSASSIN.
SHE WAS.
"KATANA WAS BORN IN TOKYO, BUT SHE'S SPENT THE LAST FEW YEARS IN AMERICA, TRACKING DOWN THE PEOPLE WHO KILLED HER HUSBAND--MASEO YAMASHIRO--WHO, IN HIS PRIME, WAS CONSIDERED THE WORLD'S DEADLIEST ASSASSIN BY THE U.S. GOVERNMENT.
"NOW KATANA AND DEATHSTROKE VIE FOR THAT TITLE, FIGURATIVELY SPEAKING."
AND WHAT MAKES YOU THINK LITTLE MISS SLICE-AND-DICE WILL JOIN THE JLA?
"WE KNOW HOW TO HELP KATANA FIND THE PEOPLE SHE'S LOOKING FOR.
"SO IN EXCHANGE FOR HER SERVICES...
‹WHY SHOULD I LISTEN TO THEM, MASEO?›
"...WE'LL PROVIDE REVENGE."
‹YES.›
‹THEIR SOULS WILL BELONG TO YOU.›

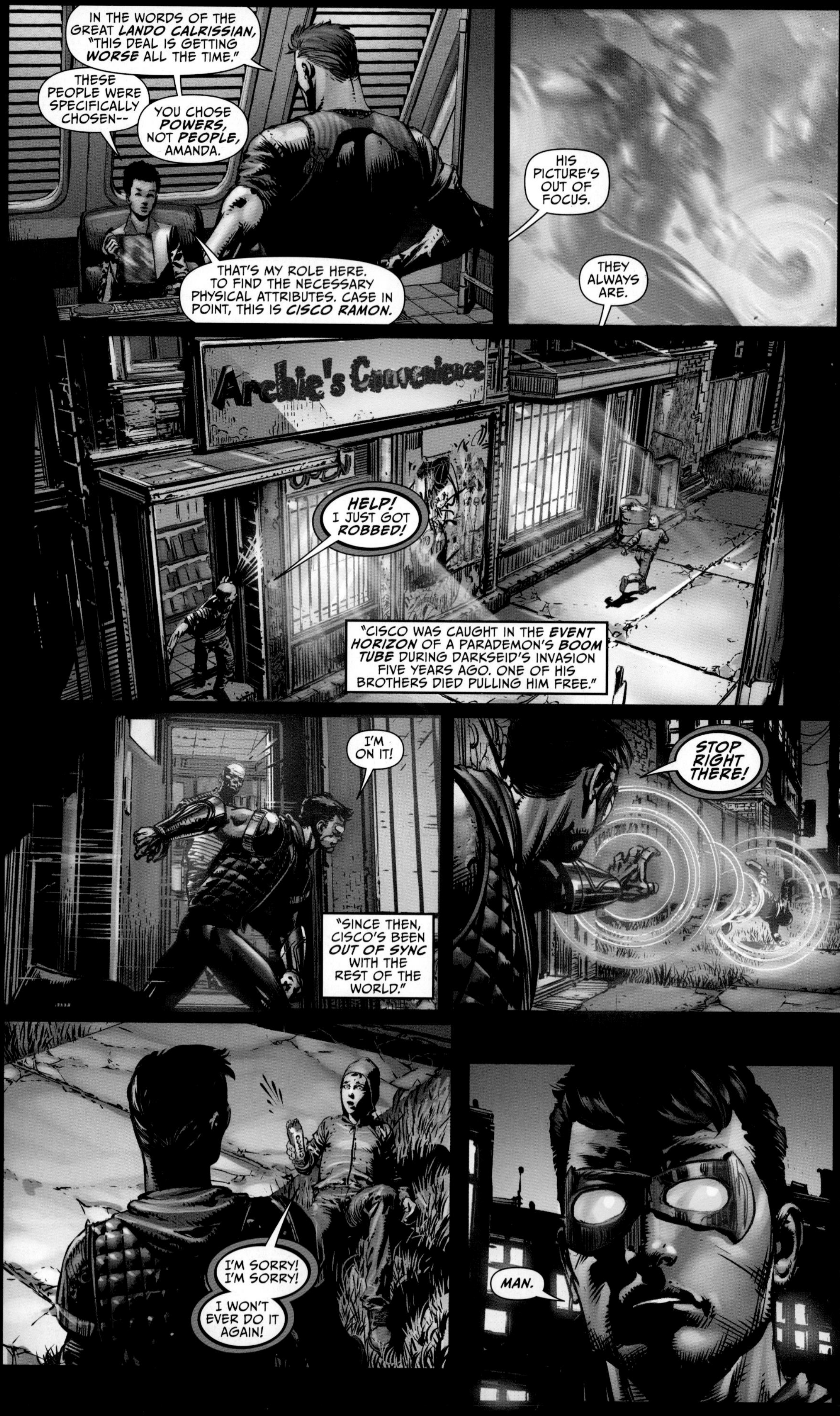
IN THE WORDS OF THE GREAT LANDO CALRISSIAN, "THIS DEAL IS GETTING WORSE ALL THE TIME."
THESE PEOPLE WERE SPECIFICALLY CHOSEN--
YOU CHOSE POWERS, NOT PEOPLE, AMANDA.
THAT'S MY ROLE HERE. TO FIND THE NECESSARY PHYSICAL ATTRIBUTES. CASE IN POINT, THIS IS CISCO RAMON.
HIS PICTURE'S OUT OF FOCUS.
THEY ALWAYS ARE.
Archie's Convenience
HELP! I JUST GOT ROBBED!
"CISCO WAS CAUGHT IN THE EVENT HORIZON OF A PARADEMON'S BOOM TUBE DURING DARKSEID'S INVASION FIVE YEARS AGO. ONE OF HIS BROTHERS DIED PULLING HIM FREE."
I'M ON IT!
"SINCE THEN, CISCO'S BEEN OUT OF SYNC WITH THE REST OF THE WORLD."
STOP RIGHT THERE!
I'M SORRY! I'M SORRY!
I WON'T EVER DO IT AGAIN!
MAN.

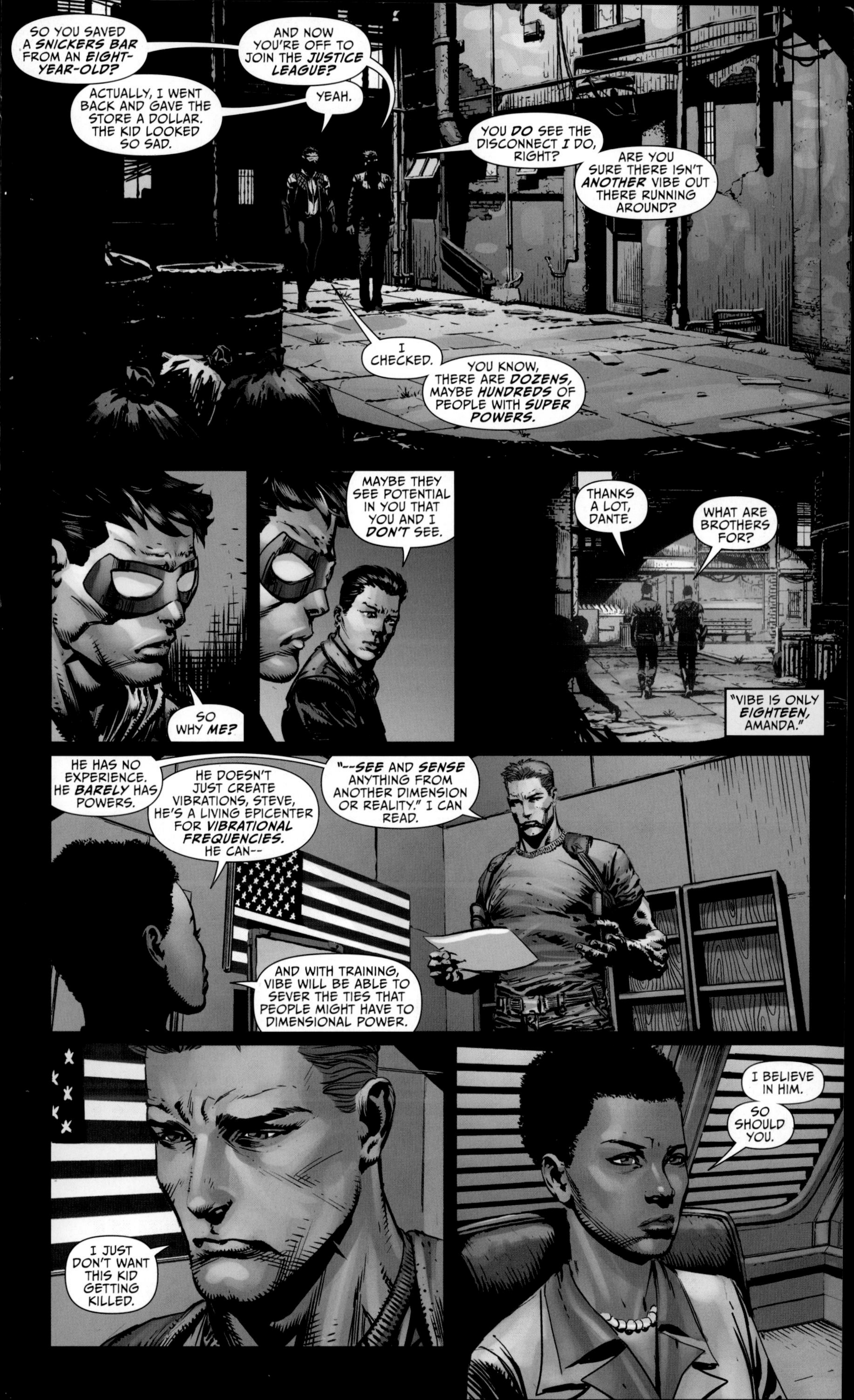

SO YOU SAVED A SNICKERS BAR FROM AN EIGHT-YEAR-OLD?
AND NOW YOU'RE OFF TO JOIN THE JUSTICE LEAGUE?
ACTUALLY, I WENT BACK AND GAVE THE STORE A DOLLAR. THE KID LOOKED SO SAD.
YEAH.
YOU DO SEE THE DISCONNECT I DO, RIGHT?
ARE YOU SURE THERE ISN'T ANOTHER VIBE OUT THERE RUNNING AROUND?
I CHECKED.
YOU KNOW, THERE ARE DOZENS, MAYBE HUNDREDS OF PEOPLE WITH SUPER POWERS.
SO WHY ME?
MAYBE THEY SEE POTENTIAL IN YOU THAT YOU AND I DON'T SEE.
THANKS A LOT, DANTE.
WHAT ARE BROTHERS FOR?
"VIBE IS ONLY EIGHTEEN, AMANDA."
HE HAS NO EXPERIENCE. HE BARELY HAS POWERS.
HE DOESN'T JUST CREATE VIBRATIONS, STEVE, HE'S A LIVING EPICENTER FOR VIBRATIONAL FREQUENCIES. HE CAN--
"--SEE AND SENSE ANYTHING FROM ANOTHER DIMENSION OR REALITY." I CAN READ.
AND WITH TRAINING, VIBE WILL BE ABLE TO SEVER THE TIES THAT PEOPLE MIGHT HAVE TO DIMENSIONAL POWER.
I JUST DON'T WANT THIS KID GETTING KILLED.
I BELIEVE IN HIM.
SO SHOULD YOU.

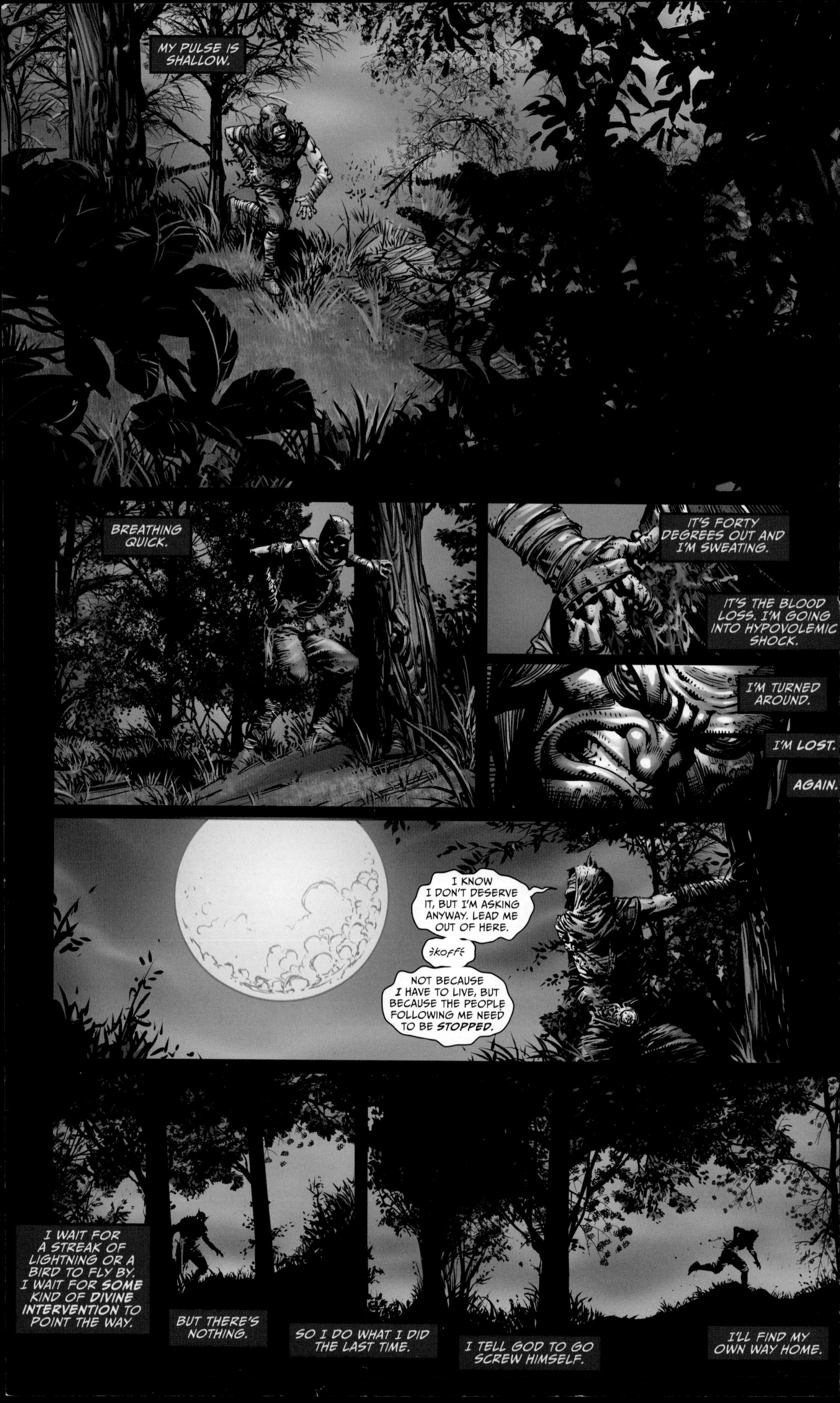

MY PULSE IS SHALLOW.
BREATHING QUICK.
IT'S FORTY DEGREES OUT AND I'M SWEATING.
IT'S THE BLOOD LOSS. I'M GOING INTO HYPOVOLEMIC SHOCK.
I'M TURNED AROUND.
I'M LOST.
AGAIN.
I KNOW I DON'T DESERVE IT, BUT I'M ASKING ANYWAY. LEAD ME OUT OF HERE.
koff
NOT BECAUSE I HAVE TO LIVE, BUT BECAUSE THE PEOPLE FOLLOWING ME NEED TO BE STOPPED.
I WAIT FOR A STREAK OF LIGHTNING OR A BIRD TO FLY BY. I WAIT FOR SOME KIND OF DIVINE INTERVENTION TO POINT THE WAY.
BUT THERE'S NOTHING.
SO I DO WHAT I DID THE LAST TIME.
I TELL GOD TO GO SCREW HIMSELF.
I'LL FIND MY OWN WAY HOME.

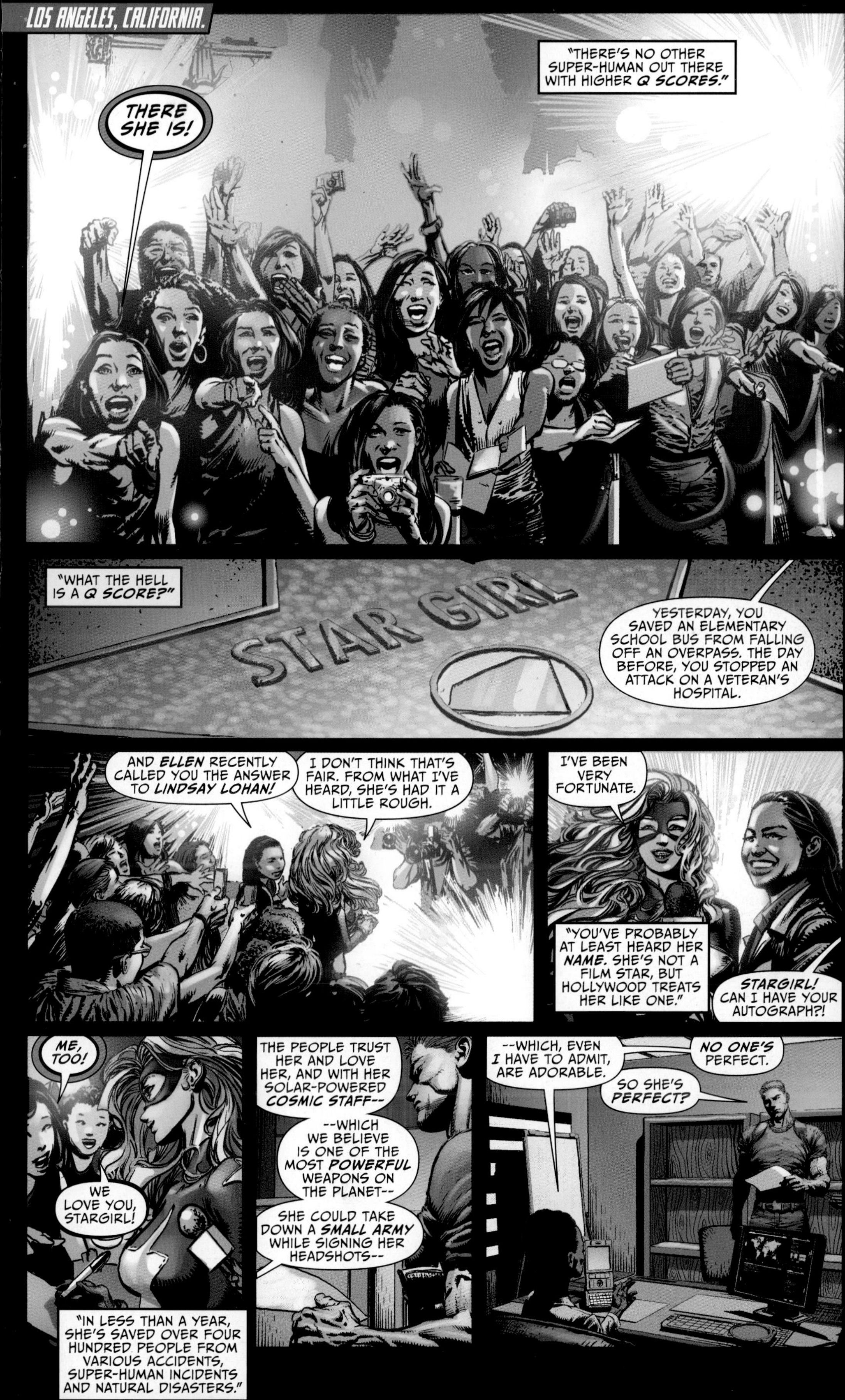
LOS ANGELES, CALIFORNIA.
"THERE'S NO OTHER SUPER-HUMAN OUT THERE WITH HIGHER Q SCORES."
THERE SHE IS!
"WHAT THE HELL IS A Q SCORE?"
STAR GIRL
YESTERDAY, YOU SAVED AN ELEMENTARY SCHOOL BUS FROM FALLING OFF AN OVERPASS. THE DAY BEFORE, YOU STOPPED AN ATTACK ON A VETERAN'S HOSPITAL.
AND ELLEN RECENTLY CALLED YOU THE ANSWER TO LINDSAY LOHAN!
I DON'T THINK THAT'S FAIR. FROM WHAT I'VE HEARD, SHE'S HAD IT A LITTLE ROUGH.
I'VE BEEN VERY FORTUNATE.
"YOU'VE PROBABLY AT LEAST HEARD HER NAME. SHE'S NOT A FILM STAR, BUT HOLLYWOOD TREATS HER LIKE ONE."
STARGIRL! CAN I HAVE YOUR AUTOGRAPH?!
ME, TOO!
WE LOVE YOU, STARGIRL!
"IN LESS THAN A YEAR, SHE'S SAVED OVER FOUR HUNDRED PEOPLE FROM VARIOUS ACCIDENTS, SUPER-HUMAN INCIDENTS AND NATURAL DISASTERS."
THE PEOPLE TRUST HER AND LOVE HER, AND WITH HER SOLAR-POWERED COSMIC STAFF--
--WHICH WE BELIEVE IS ONE OF THE MOST POWERFUL WEAPONS ON THE PLANET--
SHE COULD TAKE DOWN A SMALL ARMY WHILE SIGNING HER HEADSHOTS--
--WHICH, EVEN I HAVE TO ADMIT, ARE ADORABLE.
SO SHE'S PERFECT?
NO ONE'S PERFECT.

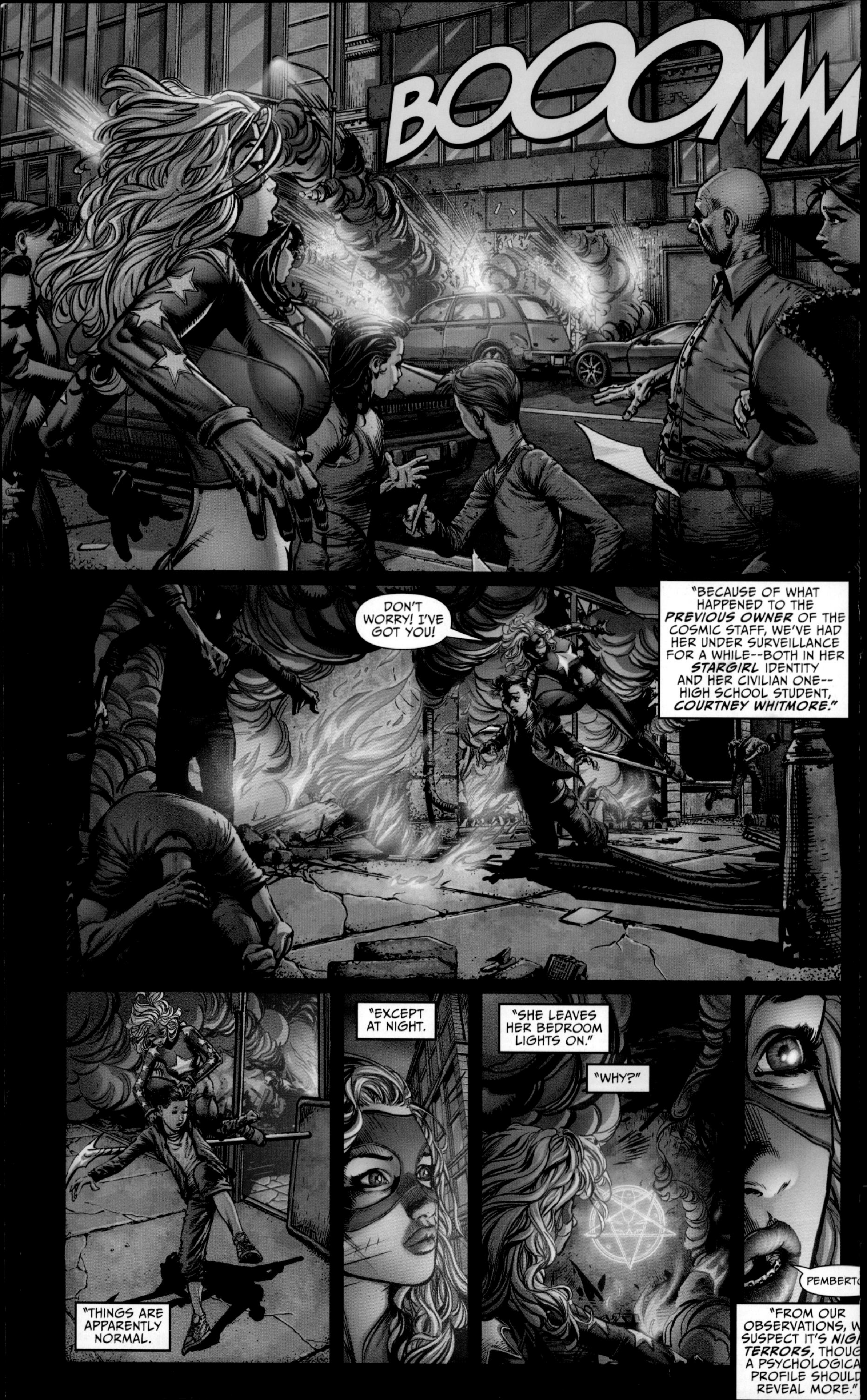
BOOOM
DON'T WORRY! I'VE GOT YOU!
"BECAUSE OF WHAT HAPPENED TO THE PREVIOUS OWNER OF THE COSMIC STAFF, WE'VE HAD HER UNDER SURVEILLANCE FOR A WHILE--BOTH IN HER STARGIRL IDENTITY AND HER CIVILIAN ONE--HIGH SCHOOL STUDENT, COURTNEY WHITMORE."
"THINGS ARE APPARENTLY NORMAL.
"EXCEPT AT NIGHT.
"SHE LEAVES HER BEDROOM LIGHTS ON."
"WHY?"
PEMBERT
"FROM OUR OBSERVATIONS, W SUSPECT IT'S NIG TERRORS, THOUG A PSYCHOLOGICA PROFILE SHOULD REVEAL MORE."

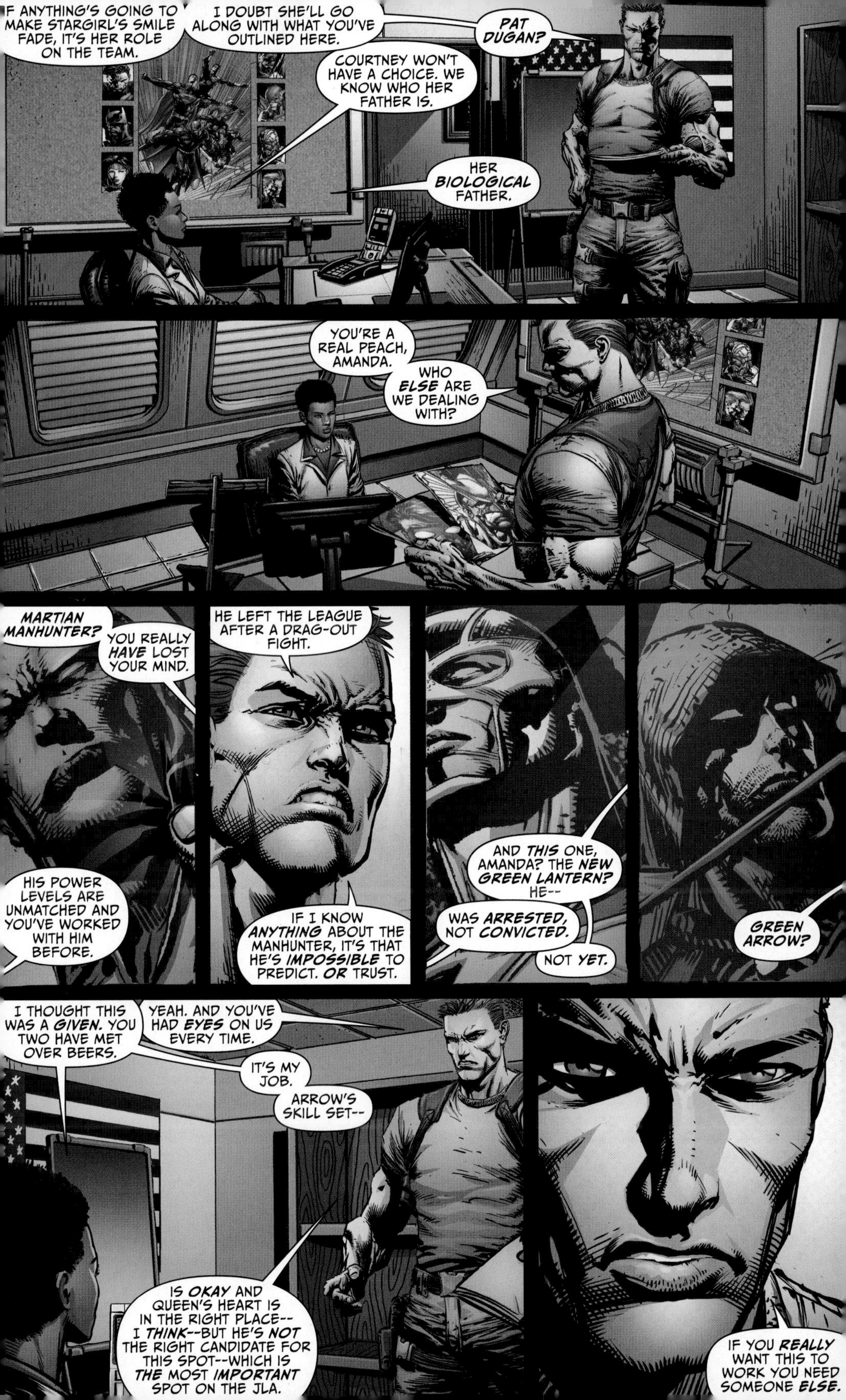
IF ANYTHING'S GOING TO MAKE STARGIRL'S SMILE FADE, IT'S HER ROLE ON THE TEAM.
I DOUBT SHE'LL GO ALONG WITH WHAT YOU'VE OUTLINED HERE.
PAT DUGAN?
COURTNEY WON'T HAVE A CHOICE. WE KNOW WHO HER FATHER IS.
HER BIOLOGICAL FATHER.
YOU'RE A REAL PEACH, AMANDA.
WHO ELSE ARE WE DEALING WITH?
MARTIAN MANHUNTER?
YOU REALLY HAVE LOST YOUR MIND.
HIS POWER LEVELS ARE UNMATCHED AND YOU'VE WORKED WITH HIM BEFORE.
HE LEFT THE LEAGUE AFTER A DRAG-OUT FIGHT.
IF I KNOW ANYTHING ABOUT THE MANHUNTER, IT'S THAT HE'S IMPOSSIBLE TO PREDICT. OR TRUST.
AND THIS ONE, AMANDA? THE NEW GREEN LANTERN? HE--
WAS ARRESTED, NOT CONVICTED.
NOT YET.
GREEN ARROW?
I THOUGHT THIS WAS A GIVEN. YOU TWO HAVE MET OVER BEERS.
YEAH. AND YOU'VE HAD EYES ON US EVERY TIME.
IT'S MY JOB.
ARROW'S SKILL SET--
IS OKAY AND QUEEN'S HEART IS IN THE RIGHT PLACE-- I THINK--BUT HE'S NOT THE RIGHT CANDIDATE FOR THIS SPOT--WHICH IS THE MOST IMPORTANT SPOT ON THE JLA.
IF YOU REALLY WANT THIS TO WORK YOU NEED SOMEONE ELSE.

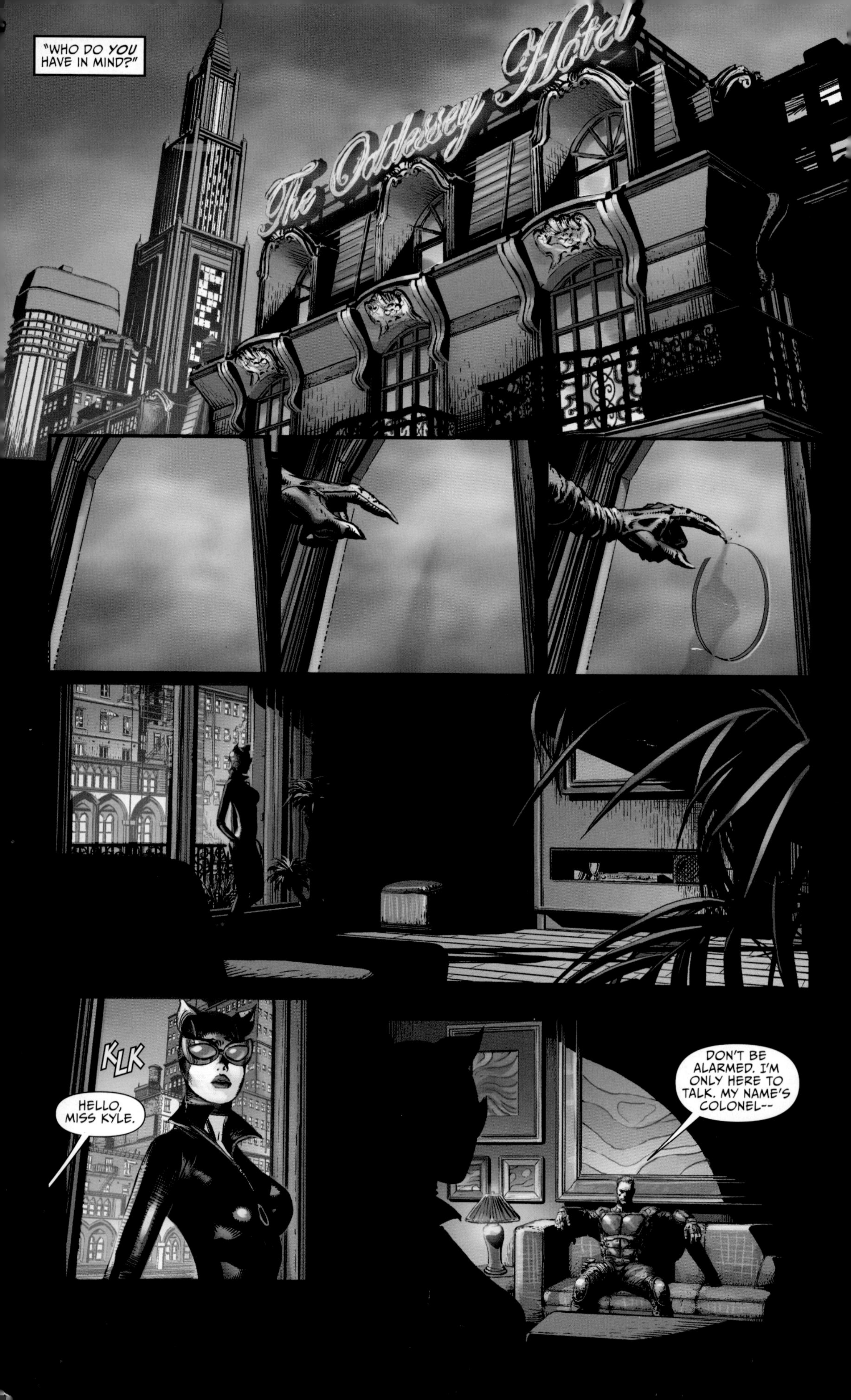
"WHO DO YOU HAVE IN MIND?"
The Oddessey Hotel
KLK
HELLO, MISS KYLE.
DON'T BE ALARMED. I'M ONLY HERE TO TALK. MY NAME'S COLONEL--

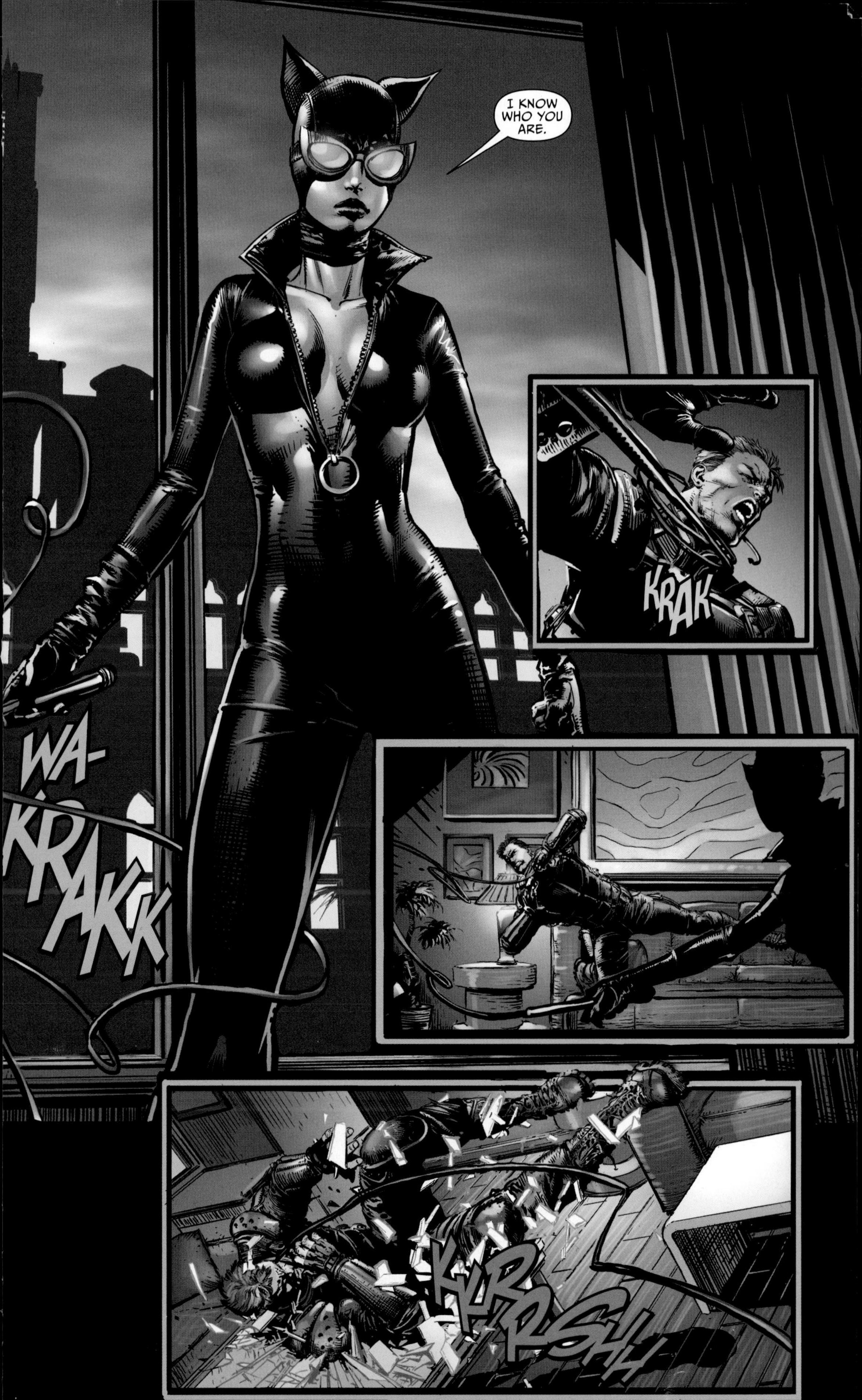
I KNOW WHO YOU ARE.
WA-KRAKK
KRAK
KRRSHH

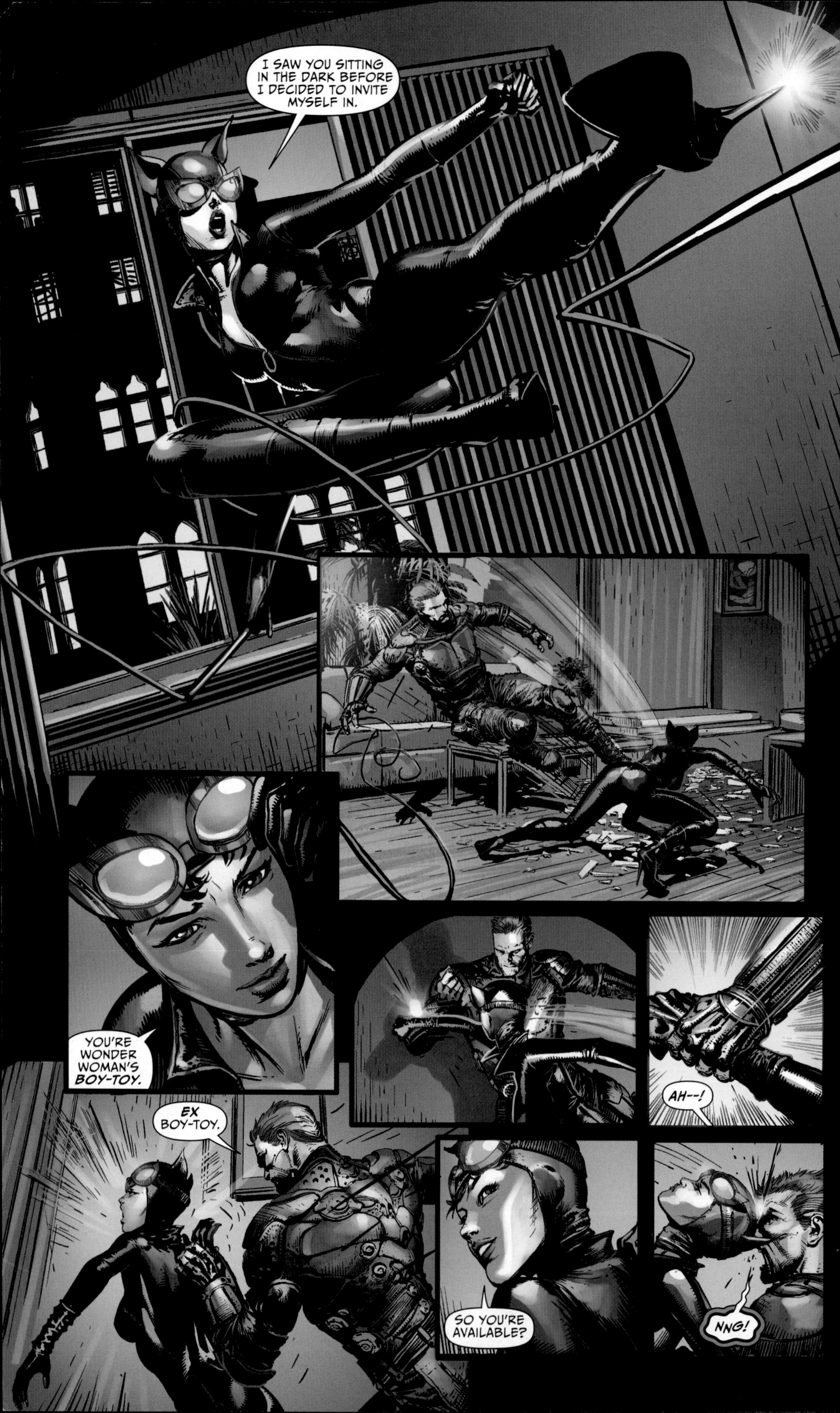
I SAW YOU SITTING IN THE DARK BEFORE I DECIDED TO INVITE MYSELF IN.
YOU'RE WONDER WOMAN'S *BOY-TOY.*
AH--!
EX BOY-TOY.
SO YOU'RE AVAILABLE?
NNG!

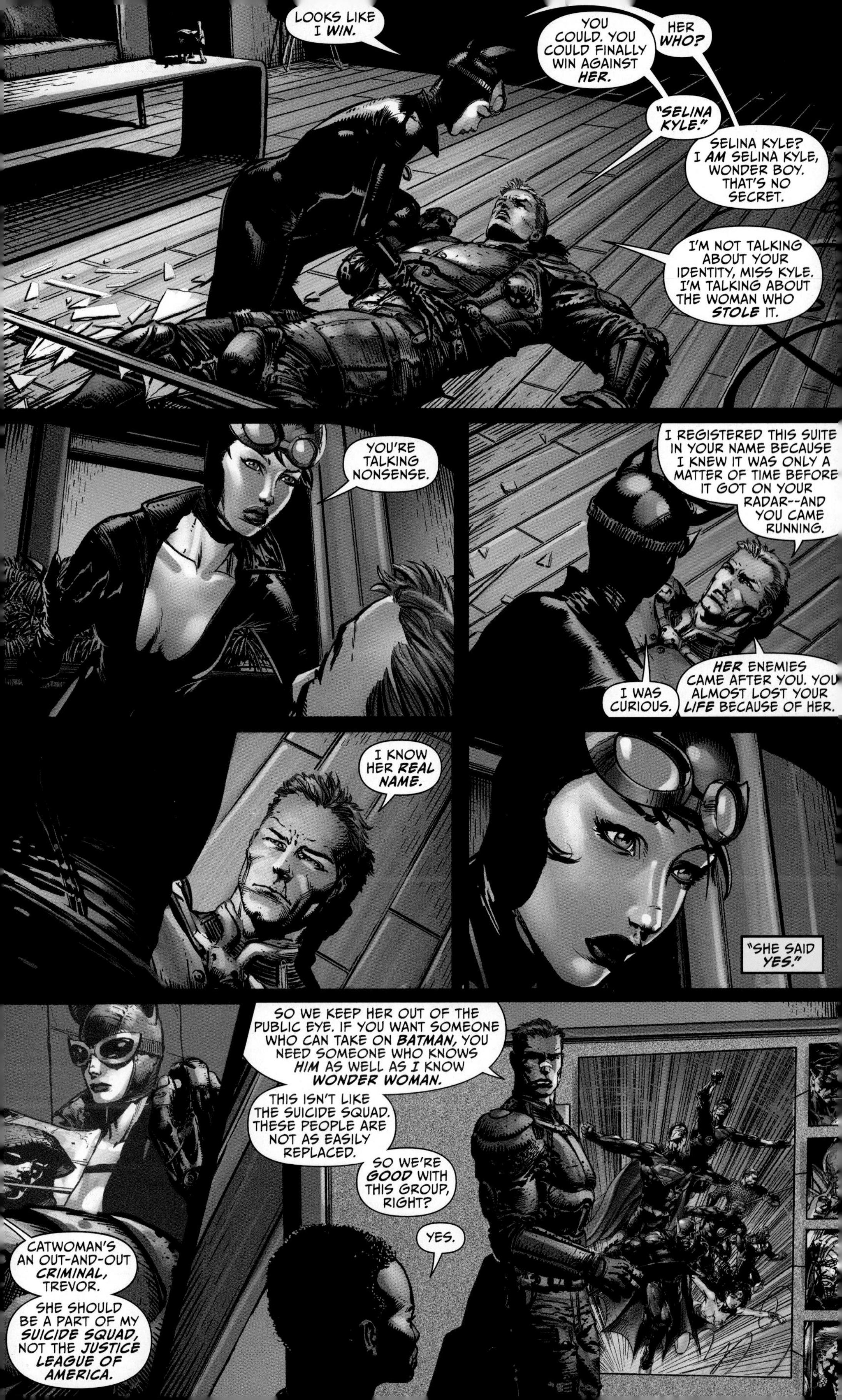
LOOKS LIKE I *WIN.*
YOU COULD. YOU COULD FINALLY WIN AGAINST *HER.*
HER *WHO?*
"SELINA KYLE."
SELINA KYLE? I *AM* SELINA KYLE, WONDER BOY. THAT'S NO SECRET.
I'M NOT TALKING ABOUT YOUR IDENTITY, MISS KYLE. I'M TALKING ABOUT THE WOMAN WHO *STOLE* IT.
YOU'RE TALKING NONSENSE.
I REGISTERED THIS SUITE IN YOUR NAME BECAUSE I KNEW IT WAS ONLY A MATTER OF TIME BEFORE IT GOT ON YOUR RADAR--AND YOU CAME RUNNING.
I WAS CURIOUS.
HER ENEMIES CAME AFTER YOU. YOU ALMOST LOST YOUR *LIFE* BECAUSE OF HER.
I KNOW HER *REAL NAME.*
"SHE SAID *YES.*"
CATWOMAN'S AN OUT-AND-OUT *CRIMINAL,* TREVOR.
SHE SHOULD BE A PART OF MY *SUICIDE SQUAD,* NOT THE *JUSTICE LEAGUE OF AMERICA.*
SO WE KEEP HER OUT OF THE PUBLIC EYE. IF YOU WANT SOMEONE WHO CAN TAKE ON *BATMAN,* YOU NEED SOMEONE WHO KNOWS *HIM* AS WELL AS *I* KNOW *WONDER WOMAN.*
THIS ISN'T LIKE THE SUICIDE SQUAD. THESE PEOPLE ARE NOT AS EASILY REPLACED.
SO WE'RE *GOOD* WITH THIS GROUP, RIGHT?
YES.

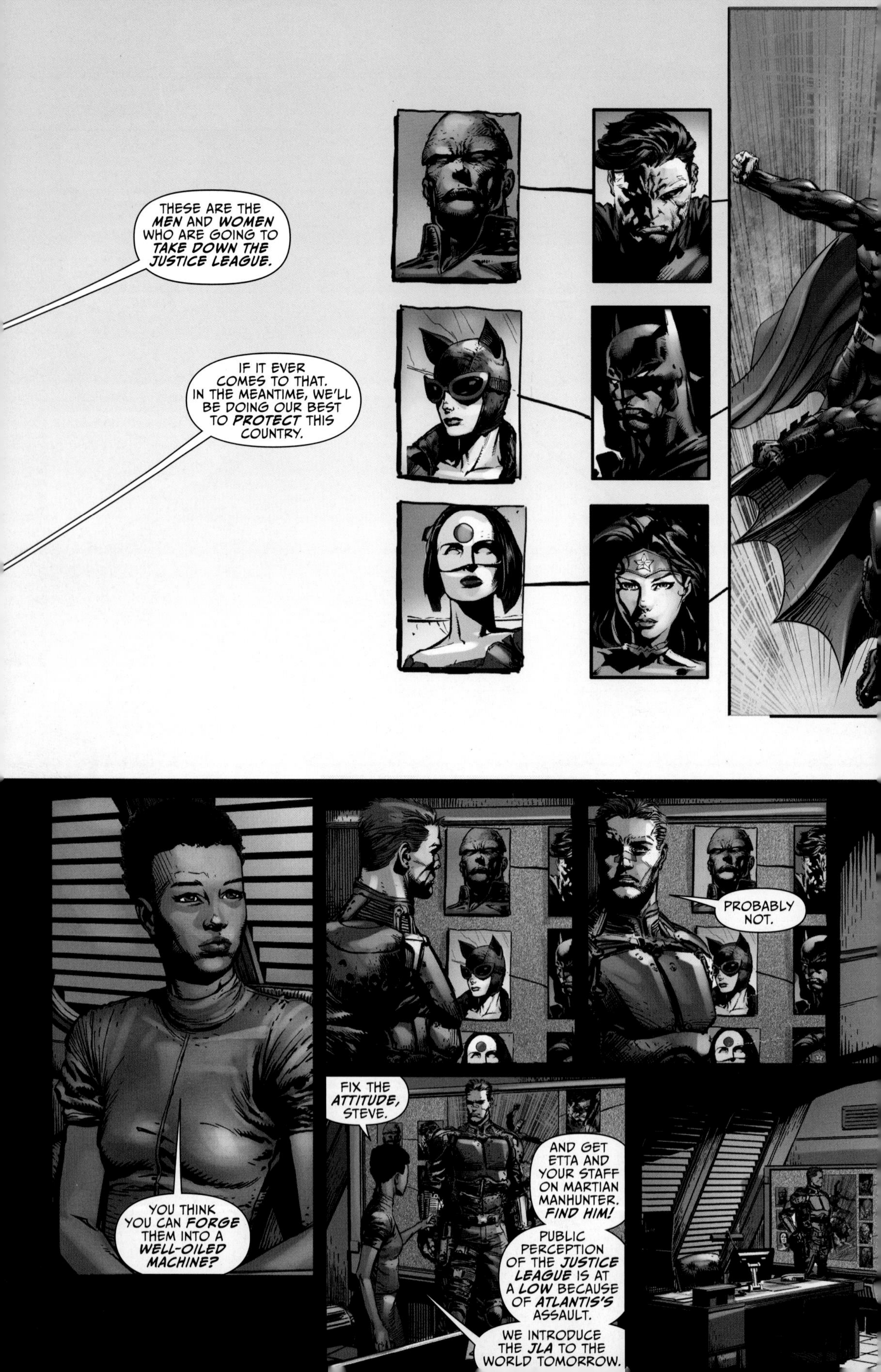
THESE ARE THE MEN AND WOMEN WHO ARE GOING TO TAKE DOWN THE JUSTICE LEAGUE.
IF IT EVER COMES TO THAT. IN THE MEANTIME, WE'LL BE DOING OUR BEST TO PROTECT THIS COUNTRY.
YOU THINK YOU CAN FORGE THEM INTO A WELL-OILED MACHINE?
PROBABLY NOT.
FIX THE ATTITUDE, STEVE.
AND GET ETTA AND YOUR STAFF ON MARTIAN MANHUNTER. FIND HIM!
PUBLIC PERCEPTION OF THE JUSTICE LEAGUE IS AT A LOW BECAUSE OF ATLANTIS'S ASSAULT.
WE INTRODUCE THE JLA TO THE WORLD TOMORROW.

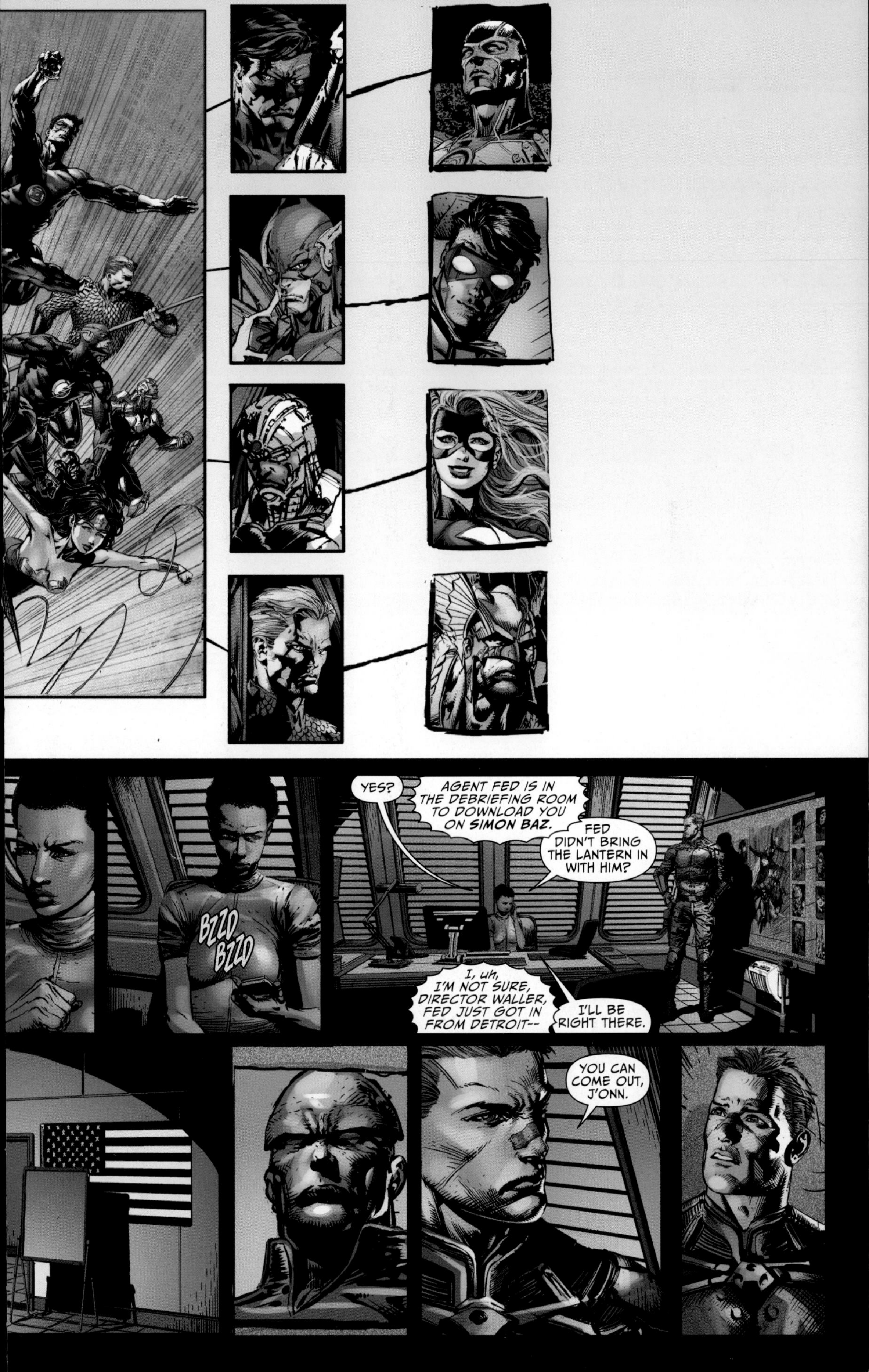
YES?
AGENT FED IS IN THE DEBRIEFING ROOM TO DOWNLOAD YOU ON SIMON BAZ.
FED DIDN'T BRING THE LANTERN IN WITH HIM?
I, uh, I'M NOT SURE, DIRECTOR WALLER, FED JUST GOT IN FROM DETROIT--
I'LL BE RIGHT THERE.
YOU CAN COME OUT, J'ONN.

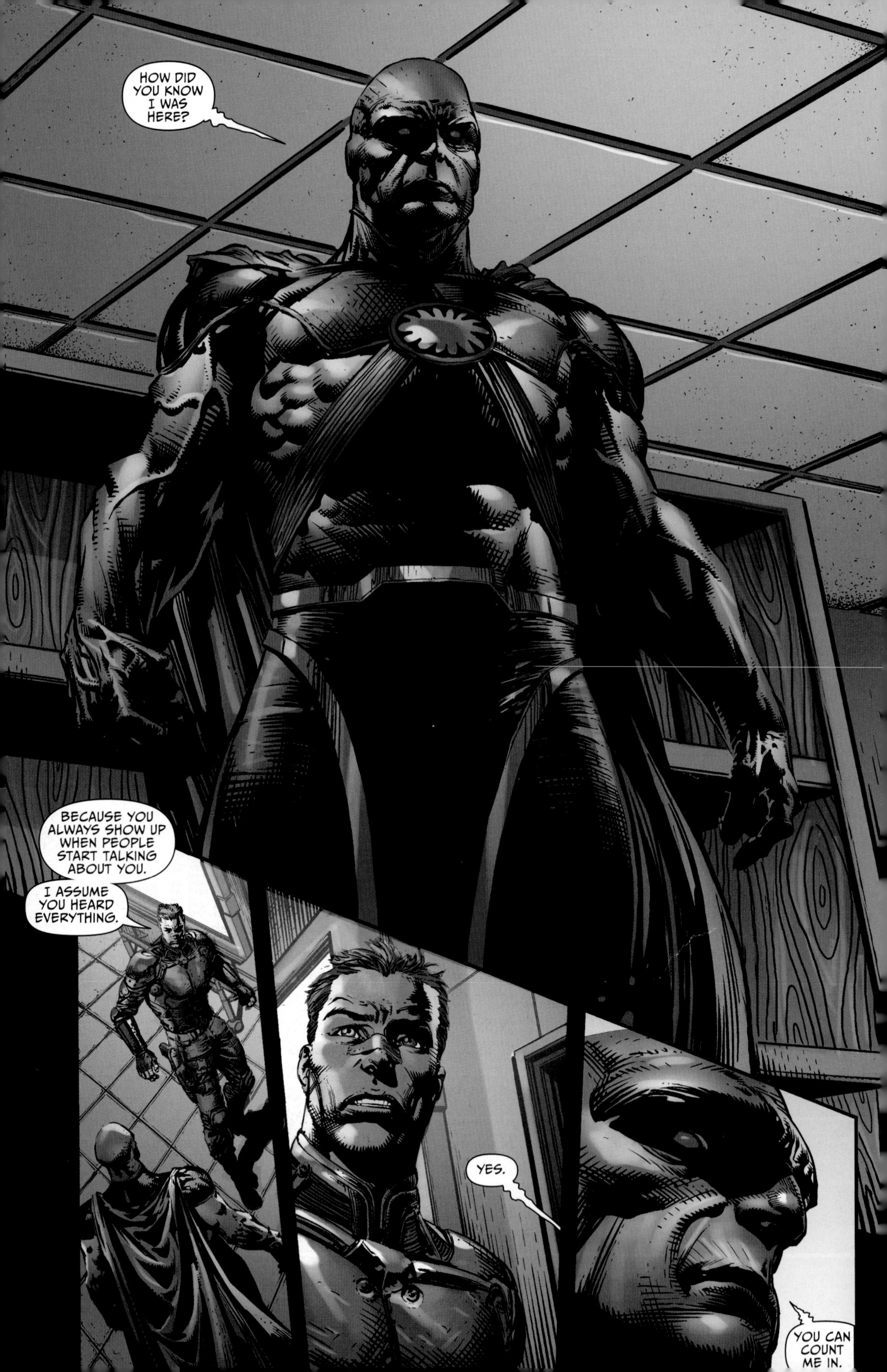
HOW DID YOU KNOW I WAS HERE?
BECAUSE YOU ALWAYS SHOW UP WHEN PEOPLE START TALKING ABOUT YOU.
I ASSUME YOU HEARD EVERYTHING.
YES.
YOU CAN COUNT ME IN.

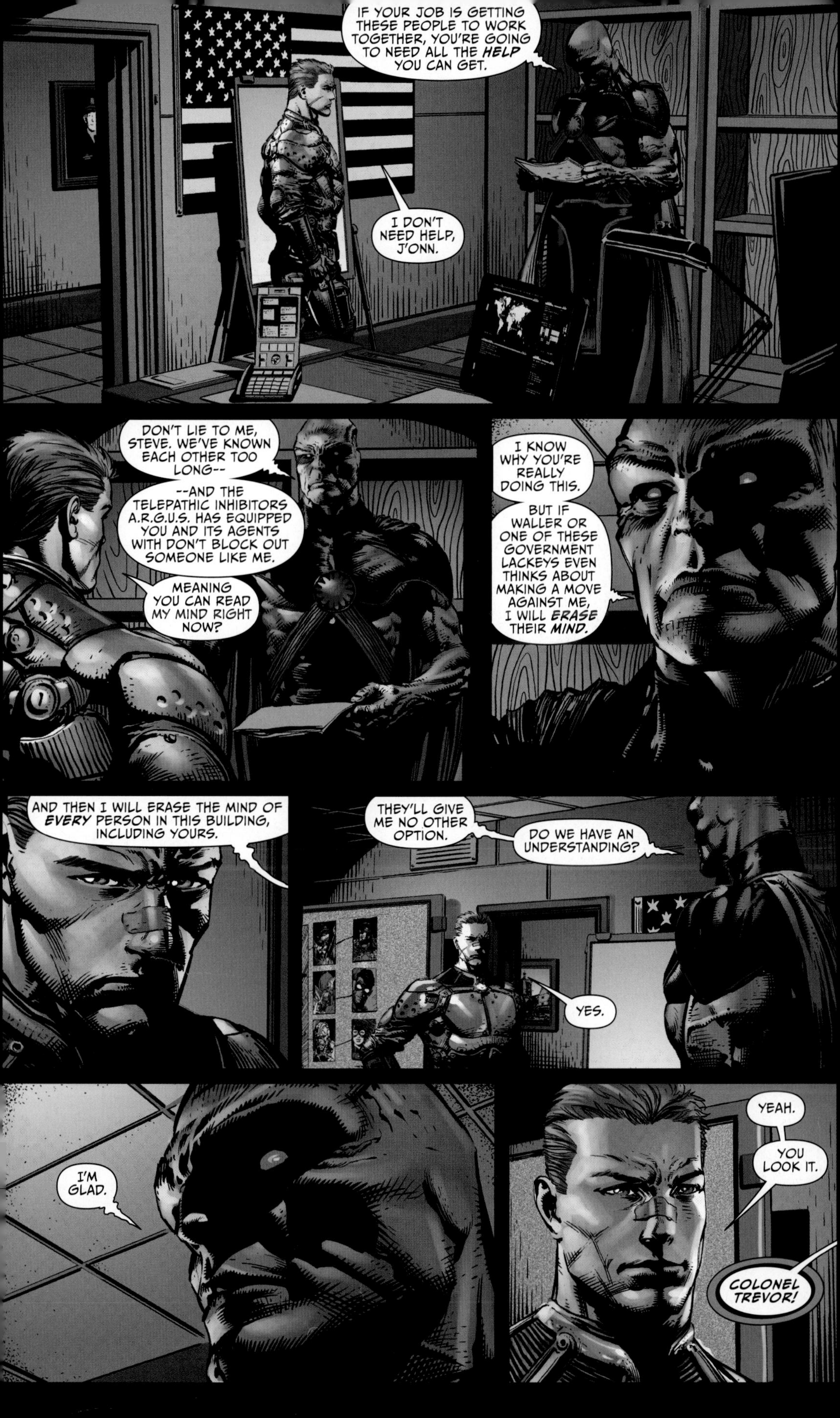
IF YOUR JOB IS GETTING THESE PEOPLE TO WORK TOGETHER, YOU'RE GOING TO NEED ALL THE HELP YOU CAN GET.
I DON'T NEED HELP, J'ONN.
DON'T LIE TO ME, STEVE. WE'VE KNOWN EACH OTHER TOO LONG--
--AND THE TELEPATHIC INHIBITORS A.R.G.U.S. HAS EQUIPPED YOU AND ITS AGENTS WITH DON'T BLOCK OUT SOMEONE LIKE ME.
MEANING YOU CAN READ MY MIND RIGHT NOW?
I KNOW WHY YOU'RE REALLY DOING THIS.
BUT IF WALLER OR ONE OF THESE GOVERNMENT LACKEYS EVEN THINKS ABOUT MAKING A MOVE AGAINST ME, I WILL ERASE THEIR MIND.
AND THEN I WILL ERASE THE MIND OF EVERY PERSON IN THIS BUILDING, INCLUDING YOURS.
THEY'LL GIVE ME NO OTHER OPTION.
DO WE HAVE AN UNDERSTANDING?
YES.
I'M GLAD.
YEAH.
YOU LOOK IT.
COLONEL TREVOR!

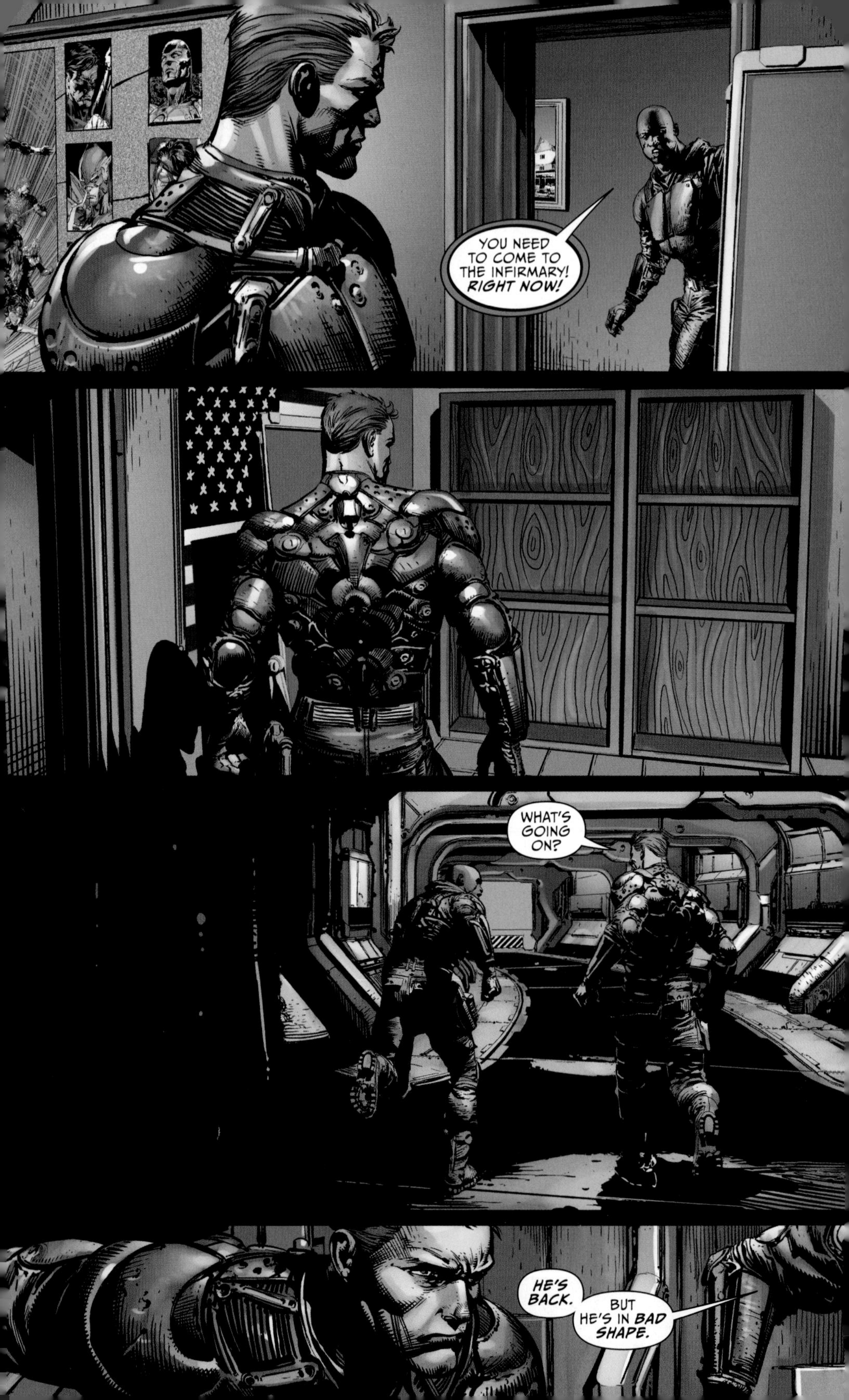
YOU NEED TO COME TO THE INFIRMARY! *RIGHT NOW!*
WHAT'S GOING ON?
HE'S BACK.
BUT HE'S IN *BAD SHAPE.*

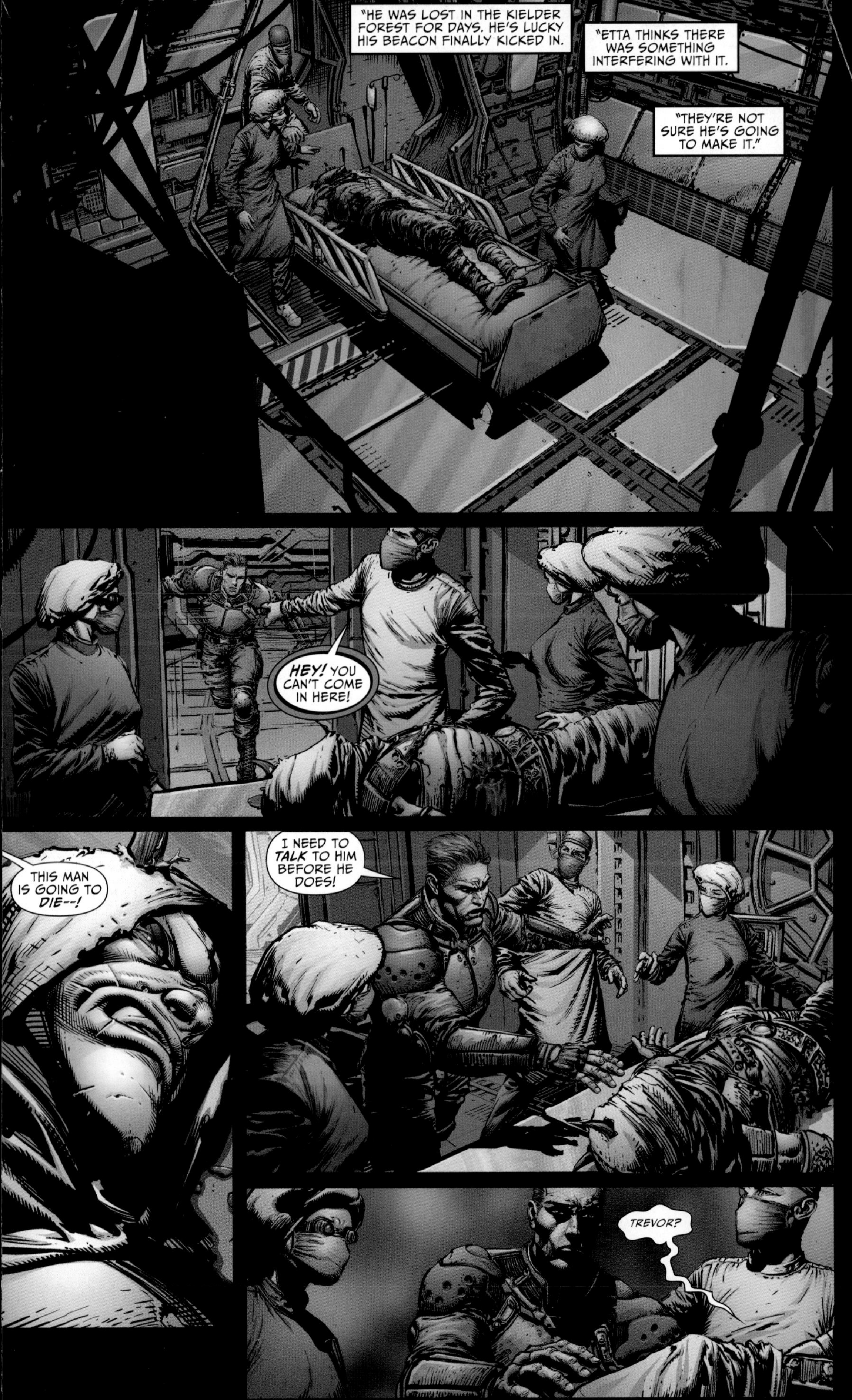
"HE WAS LOST IN THE KIELDER FOREST FOR DAYS. HE'S LUCKY HIS BEACON FINALLY KICKED IN.
"ETTA THINKS THERE WAS SOMETHING INTERFERING WITH IT.
"THEY'RE NOT SURE HE'S GOING TO MAKE IT."
HEY! YOU CAN'T COME IN HERE!
THIS MAN IS GOING TO DIE--!
I NEED TO TALK TO HIM BEFORE HE DOES!
TREVOR?

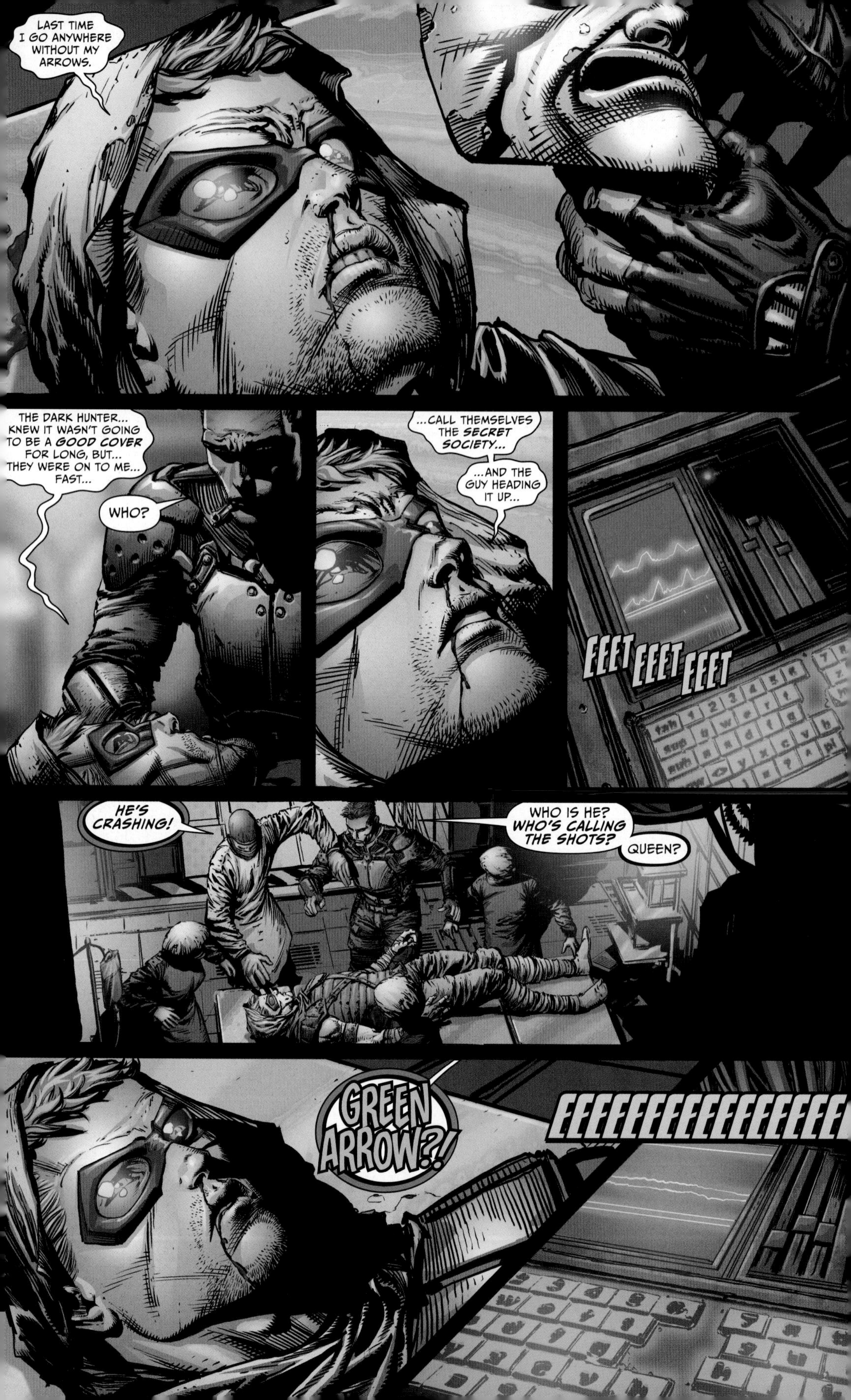
LAST TIME I GO ANYWHERE WITHOUT MY ARROWS.
THE DARK HUNTER... KNEW IT WASN'T GOING TO BE A *GOOD COVER* FOR LONG, BUT... THEY WERE ON TO ME... FAST...
WHO?
...CALL THEMSELVES THE *SECRET SOCIETY*...
...AND THE GUY HEADING IT UP...
EEET EEET EEET
HE'S CRASHING!
WHO IS HE? *WHO'S CALLING THE SHOTS?*
QUEEN?
GREEN ARROW?!
EEEEEEEEEEEEEEEE

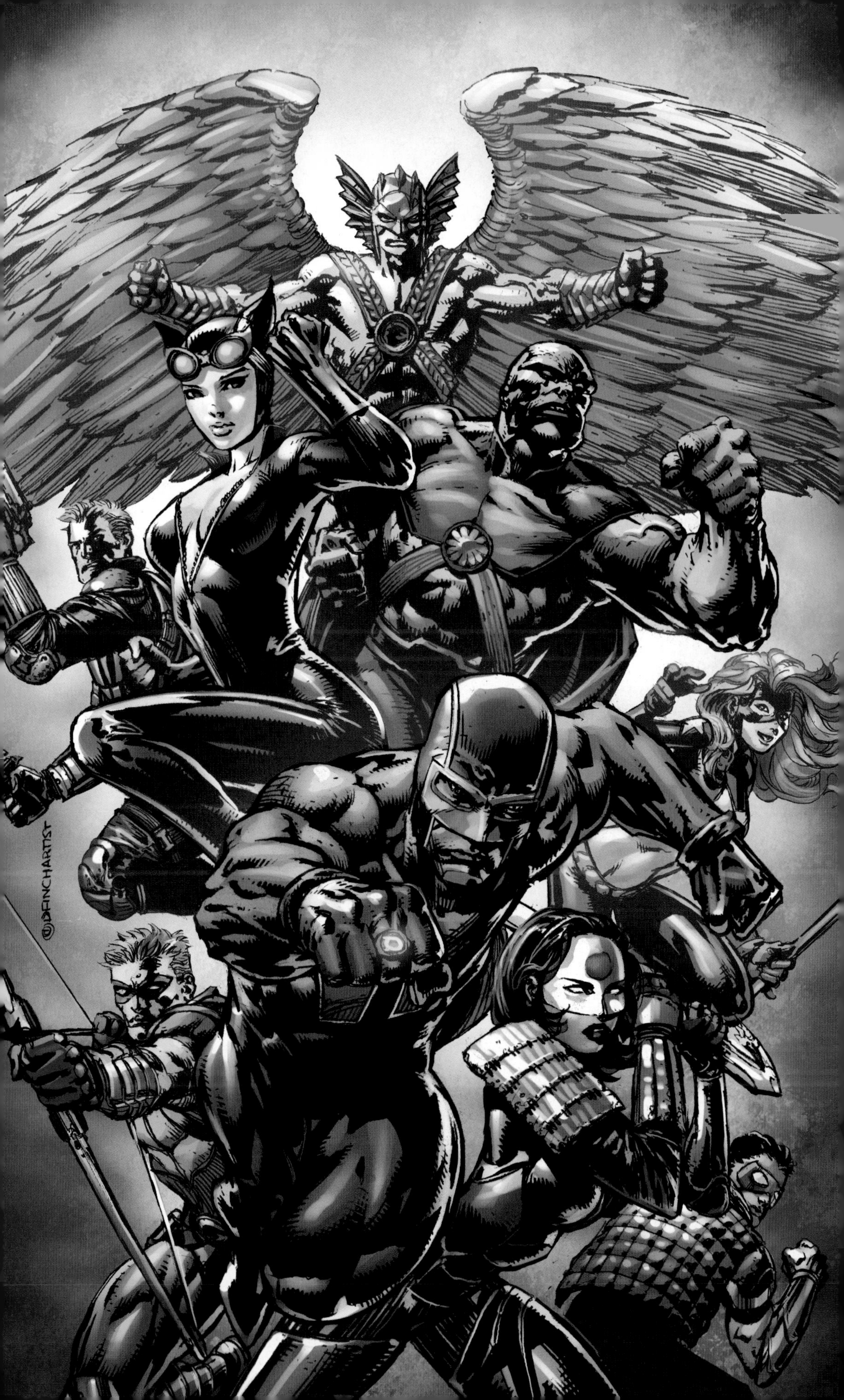
@DFINCHARTIST

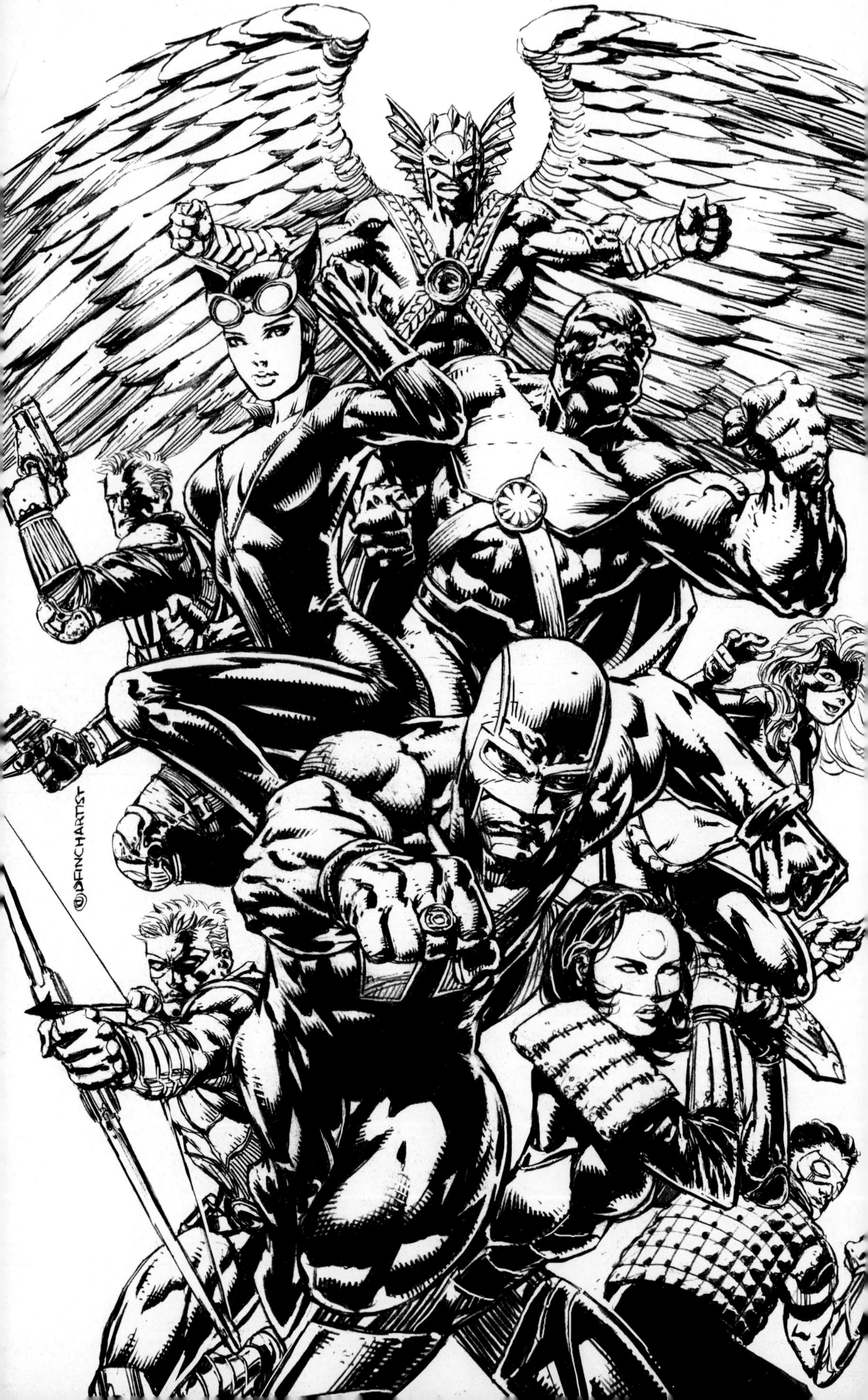
@DFINCHARTIST

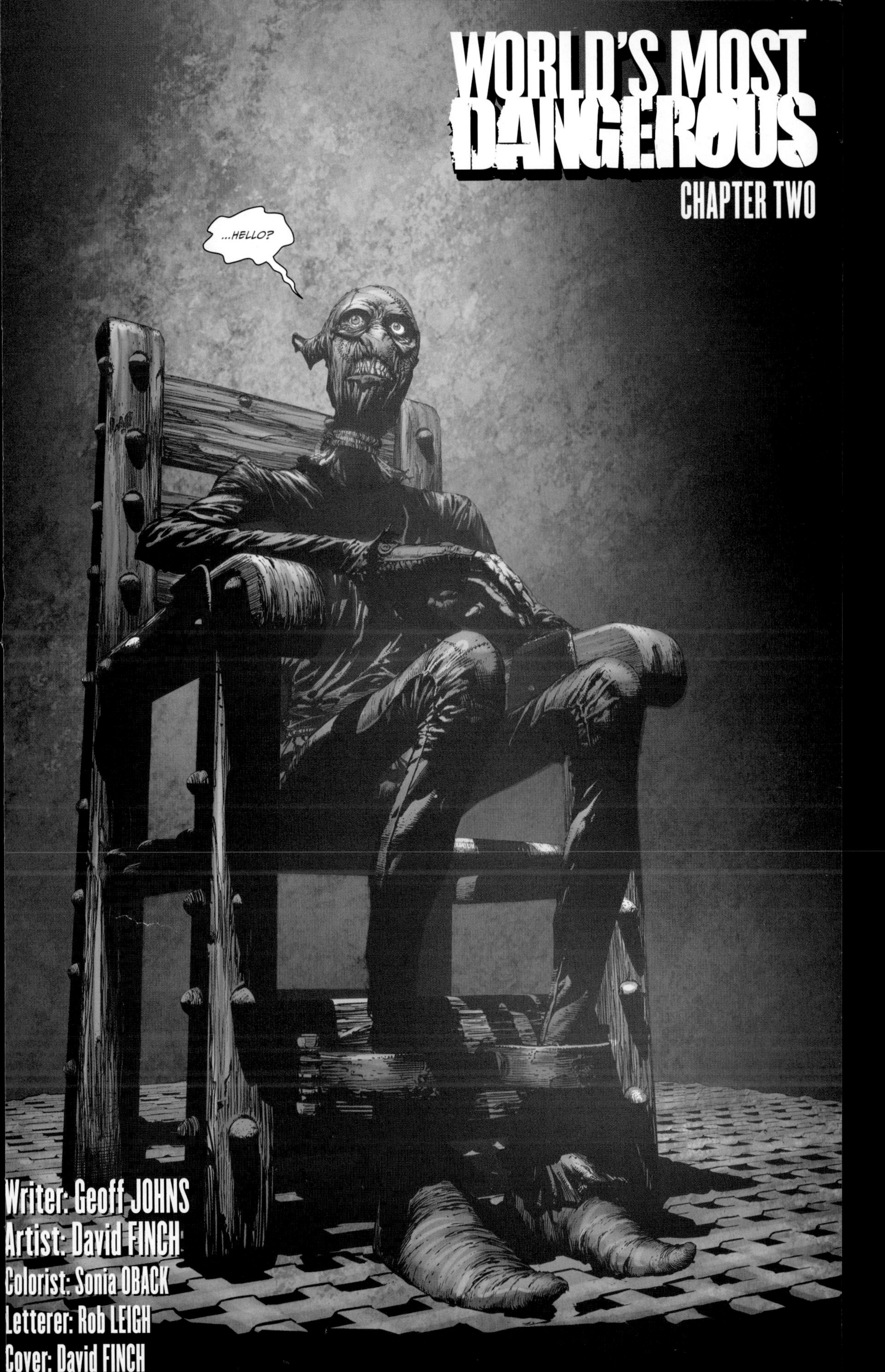
WORLD'S MOST DANGEROUS
CHAPTER TWO
...HELLO?
Writer: Geoff JOHNS
Artist: David FINCH
Colorist: Sonia OBACK
Letterer: Rob LEIGH
Cover: David FINCH

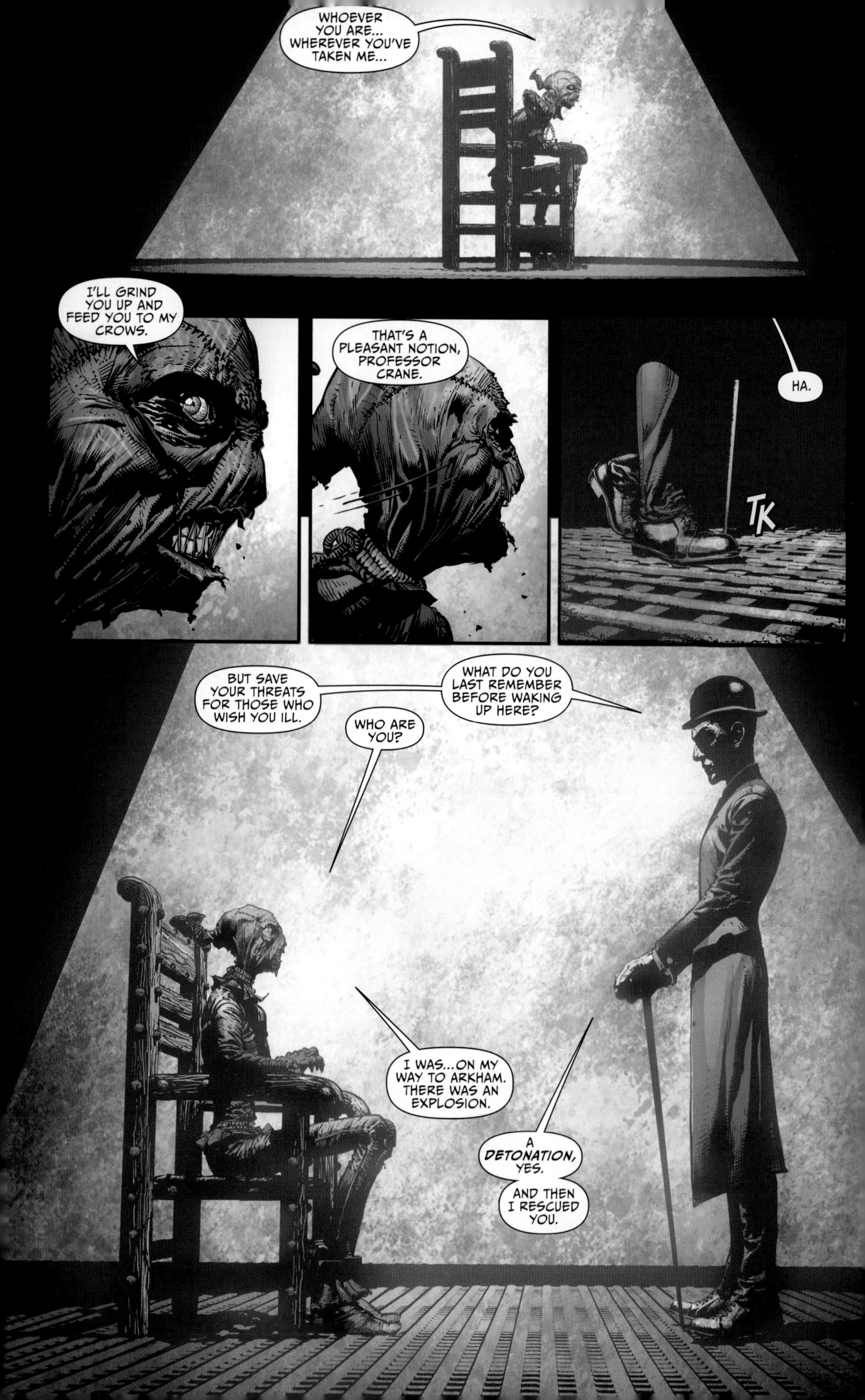
WHOEVER YOU ARE... WHEREVER YOU'VE TAKEN ME...
I'LL GRIND YOU UP AND FEED YOU TO MY CROWS.
THAT'S A PLEASANT NOTION, PROFESSOR CRANE.
HA.
TK
BUT SAVE YOUR THREATS FOR THOSE WHO WISH YOU ILL.
WHO ARE YOU?
WHAT DO YOU LAST REMEMBER BEFORE WAKING UP HERE?
I WAS...ON MY WAY TO ARKHAM. THERE WAS AN EXPLOSION.
A *DETONATION*, YES.
AND THEN I RESCUED YOU.

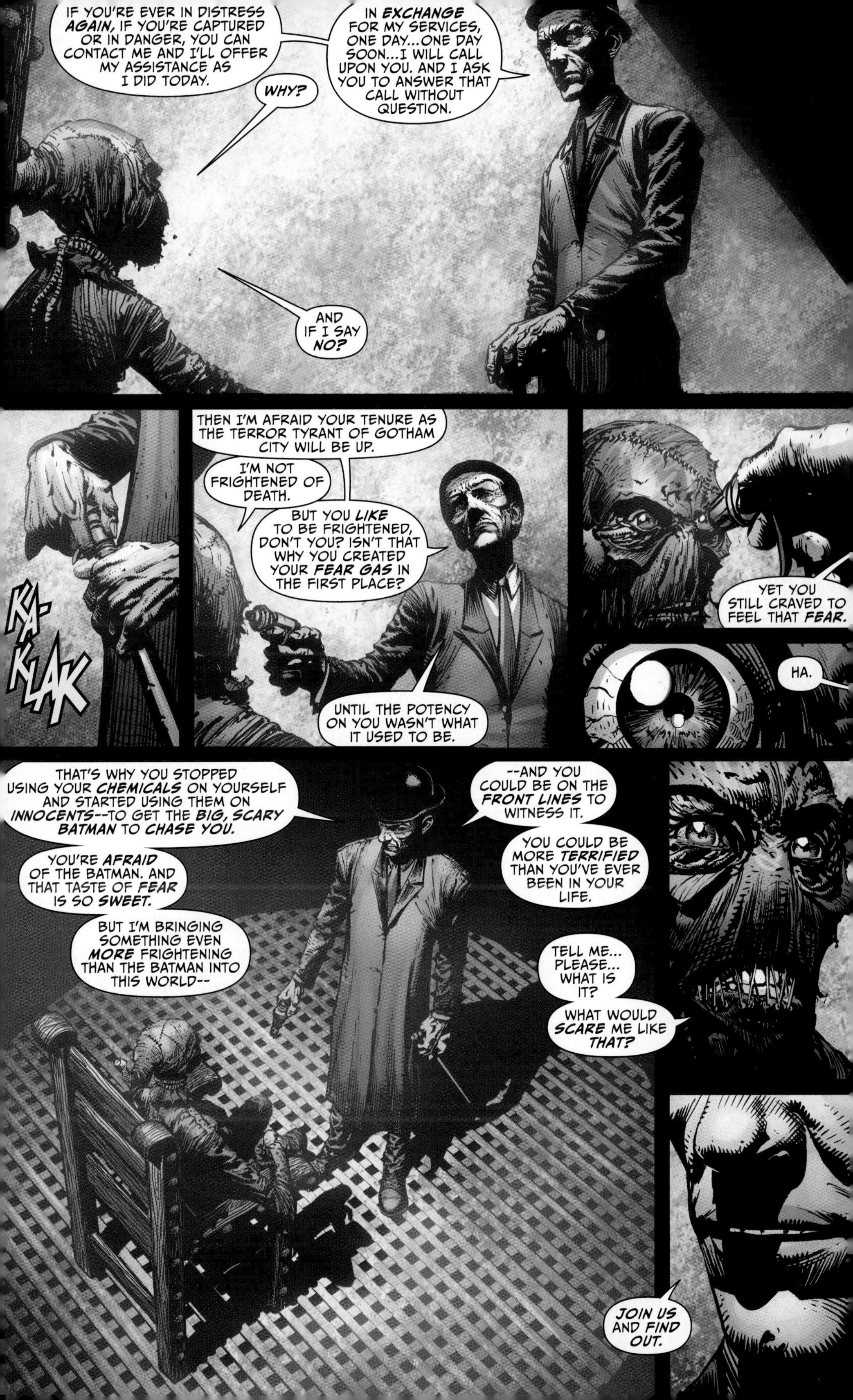
IF YOU'RE EVER IN DISTRESS AGAIN, IF YOU'RE CAPTURED OR IN DANGER, YOU CAN CONTACT ME AND I'LL OFFER MY ASSISTANCE AS I DID TODAY.
IN EXCHANGE FOR MY SERVICES, ONE DAY...ONE DAY SOON...I WILL CALL UPON YOU. AND I ASK YOU TO ANSWER THAT CALL WITHOUT QUESTION.
WHY?
AND IF I SAY NO?
KA-KLAK
THEN I'M AFRAID YOUR TENURE AS THE TERROR TYRANT OF GOTHAM CITY WILL BE UP.
I'M NOT FRIGHTENED OF DEATH.
BUT YOU LIKE TO BE FRIGHTENED, DON'T YOU? ISN'T THAT WHY YOU CREATED YOUR FEAR GAS IN THE FIRST PLACE?
UNTIL THE POTENCY ON YOU WASN'T WHAT IT USED TO BE.
YET YOU STILL CRAVED TO FEEL THAT FEAR.
HA.
THAT'S WHY YOU STOPPED USING YOUR CHEMICALS ON YOURSELF AND STARTED USING THEM ON INNOCENTS--TO GET THE BIG, SCARY BATMAN TO CHASE YOU.
YOU'RE AFRAID OF THE BATMAN. AND THAT TASTE OF FEAR IS SO SWEET.
BUT I'M BRINGING SOMETHING EVEN MORE FRIGHTENING THAN THE BATMAN INTO THIS WORLD--
--AND YOU COULD BE ON THE FRONT LINES TO WITNESS IT.
YOU COULD BE MORE TERRIFIED THAN YOU'VE EVER BEEN IN YOUR LIFE.
TELL ME... PLEASE... WHAT IS IT?
WHAT WOULD SCARE ME LIKE THAT?
JOIN US AND FIND OUT.

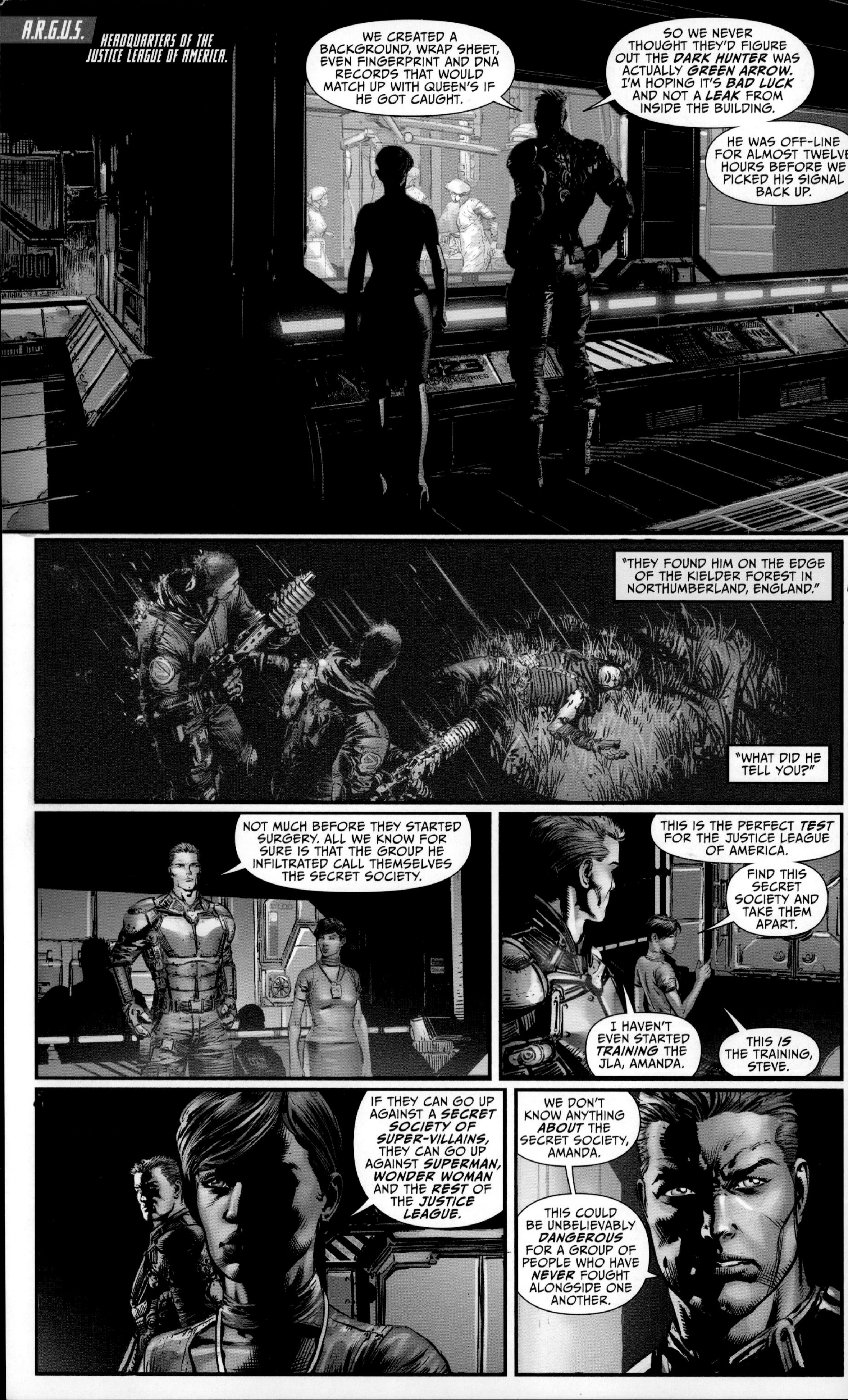
A.R.G.U.S.
HEADQUARTERS OF THE JUSTICE LEAGUE OF AMERICA.
WE CREATED A BACKGROUND, WRAP SHEET, EVEN FINGERPRINT AND DNA RECORDS THAT WOULD MATCH UP WITH QUEEN'S IF HE GOT CAUGHT.
SO WE NEVER THOUGHT THEY'D FIGURE OUT THE DARK HUNTER WAS ACTUALLY GREEN ARROW. I'M HOPING IT'S BAD LUCK AND NOT A LEAK FROM INSIDE THE BUILDING.
HE WAS OFF-LINE FOR ALMOST TWELVE HOURS BEFORE WE PICKED HIS SIGNAL BACK UP.
"THEY FOUND HIM ON THE EDGE OF THE KIELDER FOREST IN NORTHUMBERLAND, ENGLAND."
"WHAT DID HE TELL YOU?"
NOT MUCH BEFORE THEY STARTED SURGERY. ALL WE KNOW FOR SURE IS THAT THE GROUP HE INFILTRATED CALL THEMSELVES THE SECRET SOCIETY.
THIS IS THE PERFECT TEST FOR THE JUSTICE LEAGUE OF AMERICA.
FIND THIS SECRET SOCIETY AND TAKE THEM APART.
I HAVEN'T EVEN STARTED TRAINING THE JLA, AMANDA.
THIS IS THE TRAINING, STEVE.
IF THEY CAN GO UP AGAINST A SECRET SOCIETY OF SUPER-VILLAINS, THEY CAN GO UP AGAINST SUPERMAN, WONDER WOMAN AND THE REST OF THE JUSTICE LEAGUE.
WE DON'T KNOW ANYTHING ABOUT THE SECRET SOCIETY, AMANDA.
THIS COULD BE UNBELIEVABLY DANGEROUS FOR A GROUP OF PEOPLE WHO HAVE NEVER FOUGHT ALONGSIDE ONE ANOTHER.

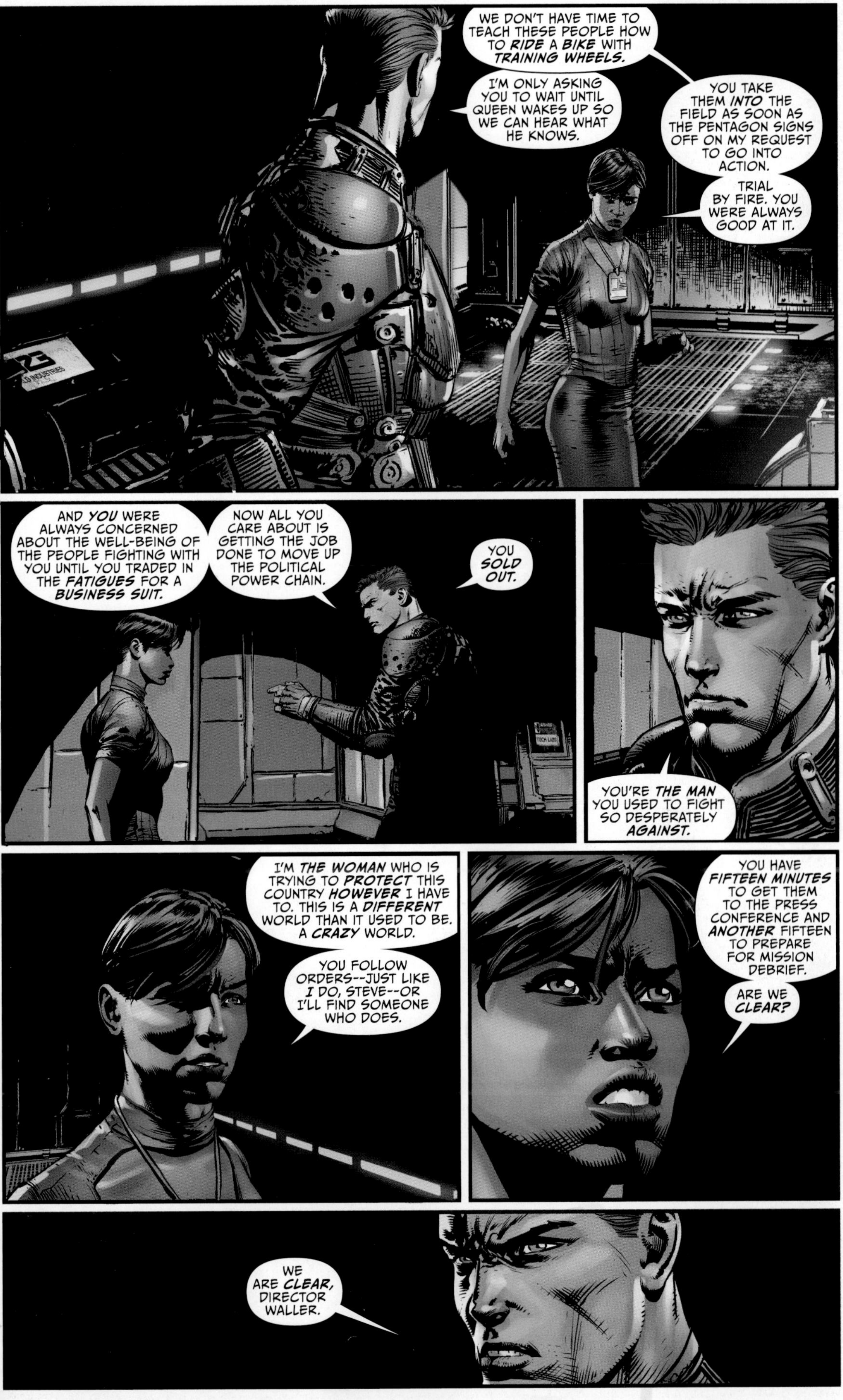

WE DON'T HAVE TIME TO TEACH THESE PEOPLE HOW TO RIDE A BIKE WITH TRAINING WHEELS.
I'M ONLY ASKING YOU TO WAIT UNTIL QUEEN WAKES UP SO WE CAN HEAR WHAT HE KNOWS.
YOU TAKE THEM INTO THE FIELD AS SOON AS THE PENTAGON SIGNS OFF ON MY REQUEST TO GO INTO ACTION.
TRIAL BY FIRE. YOU WERE ALWAYS GOOD AT IT.
AND YOU WERE ALWAYS CONCERNED ABOUT THE WELL-BEING OF THE PEOPLE FIGHTING WITH YOU UNTIL YOU TRADED IN THE FATIGUES FOR A BUSINESS SUIT.
NOW ALL YOU CARE ABOUT IS GETTING THE JOB DONE TO MOVE UP THE POLITICAL POWER CHAIN.
YOU SOLD OUT.
YOU'RE THE MAN YOU USED TO FIGHT SO DESPERATELY AGAINST.
I'M THE WOMAN WHO IS TRYING TO PROTECT THIS COUNTRY HOWEVER I HAVE TO. THIS IS A DIFFERENT WORLD THAN IT USED TO BE. A CRAZY WORLD.
YOU FOLLOW ORDERS--JUST LIKE I DO, STEVE--OR I'LL FIND SOMEONE WHO DOES.
YOU HAVE FIFTEEN MINUTES TO GET THEM TO THE PRESS CONFERENCE AND ANOTHER FIFTEEN TO PREPARE FOR MISSION DEBRIEF.
ARE WE CLEAR?
WE ARE CLEAR, DIRECTOR WALLER.

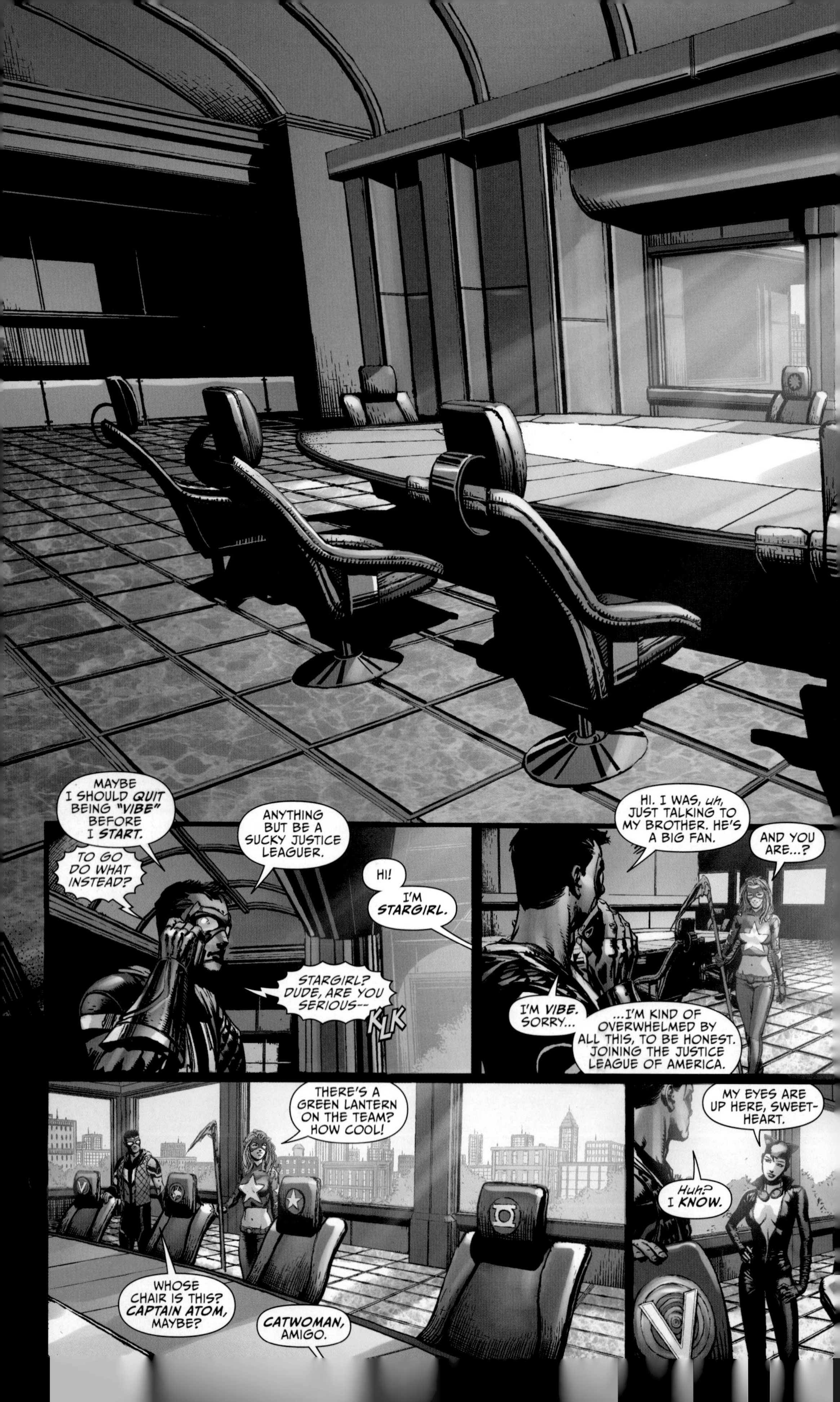

MAYBE I SHOULD QUIT BEING "VIBE" BEFORE I START.
TO GO DO WHAT INSTEAD?
ANYTHING BUT BE A SUCKY JUSTICE LEAGUER.
HI!
I'M STARGIRL.
STARGIRL? DUDE, ARE YOU SERIOUS--
KLK
HI. I WAS, uh, JUST TALKING TO MY BROTHER. HE'S A BIG FAN.
AND YOU ARE...?
I'M VIBE. SORRY...
...I'M KIND OF OVERWHELMED BY ALL THIS, TO BE HONEST. JOINING THE JUSTICE LEAGUE OF AMERICA.
THERE'S A GREEN LANTERN ON THE TEAM? HOW COOL!
WHOSE CHAIR IS THIS? CAPTAIN ATOM, MAYBE?
CATWOMAN, AMIGO.
MY EYES ARE UP HERE, SWEET-HEART.
Huh? I KNOW.

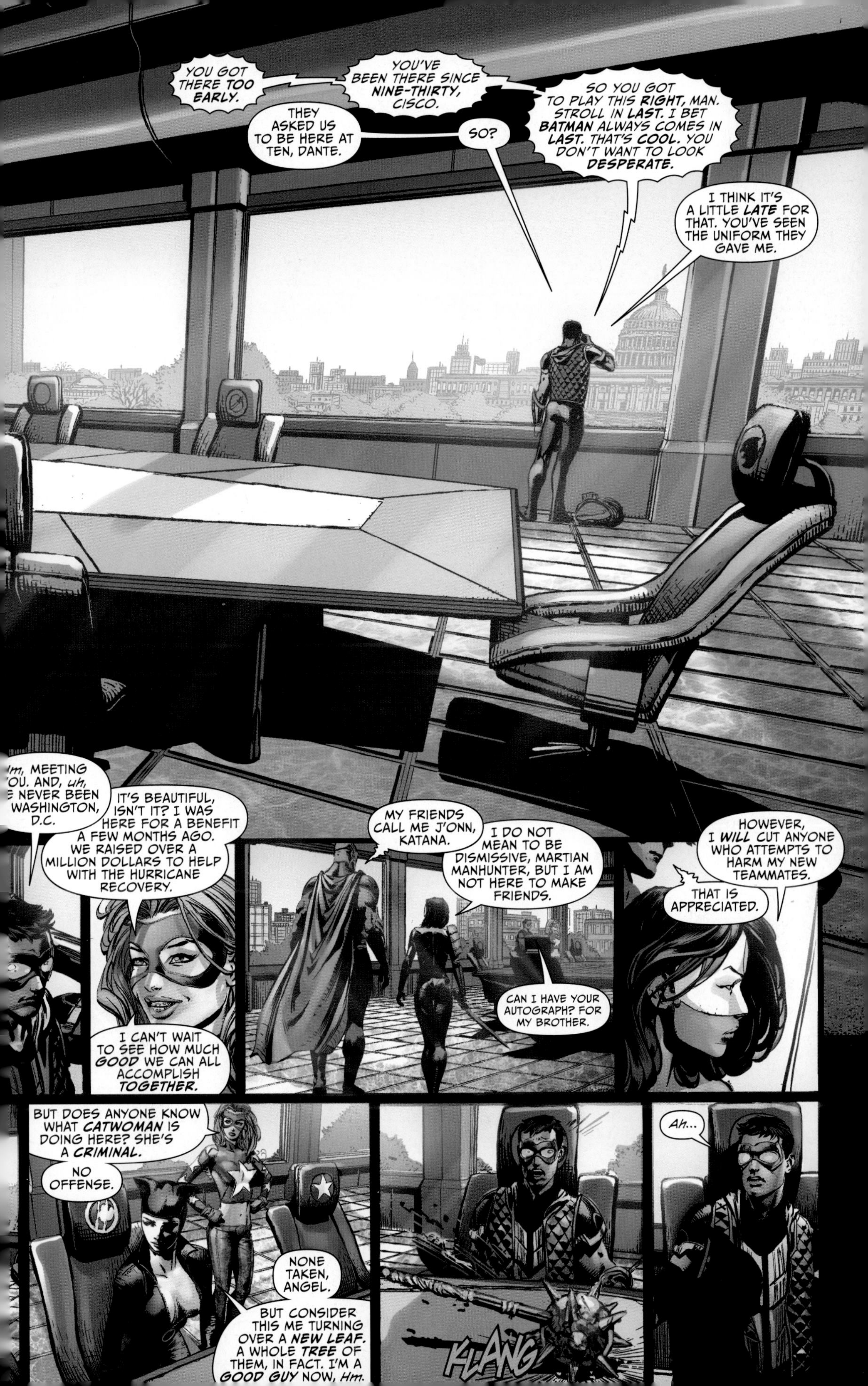
YOU GOT THERE TOO EARLY.
YOU'VE BEEN THERE SINCE NINE-THIRTY, CISCO.
THEY ASKED US TO BE HERE AT TEN, DANTE.
SO?
SO YOU GOT TO PLAY THIS RIGHT, MAN. STROLL IN LAST. I BET BATMAN ALWAYS COMES IN LAST. THAT'S COOL. YOU DON'T WANT TO LOOK DESPERATE.
I THINK IT'S A LITTLE LATE FOR THAT. YOU'VE SEEN THE UNIFORM THEY GAVE ME.
m, MEETING OU. AND, uh, E NEVER BEEN WASHINGTON, D.C.
IT'S BEAUTIFUL, ISN'T IT? I WAS HERE FOR A BENEFIT A FEW MONTHS AGO. WE RAISED OVER A MILLION DOLLARS TO HELP WITH THE HURRICANE RECOVERY.
I CAN'T WAIT TO SEE HOW MUCH GOOD WE CAN ALL ACCOMPLISH TOGETHER.
MY FRIENDS CALL ME J'ONN, KATANA.
I DO NOT MEAN TO BE DISMISSIVE, MARTIAN MANHUNTER, BUT I AM NOT HERE TO MAKE FRIENDS.
CAN I HAVE YOUR AUTOGRAPH? FOR MY BROTHER.
HOWEVER, I WILL CUT ANYONE WHO ATTEMPTS TO HARM MY NEW TEAMMATES.
THAT IS APPRECIATED.
BUT DOES ANYONE KNOW WHAT CATWOMAN IS DOING HERE? SHE'S A CRIMINAL.
NO OFFENSE.
NONE TAKEN, ANGEL.
BUT CONSIDER THIS ME TURNING OVER A NEW LEAF. A WHOLE TREE OF THEM, IN FACT. I'M A GOOD GUY NOW, Hm.
KLANG
Ah...

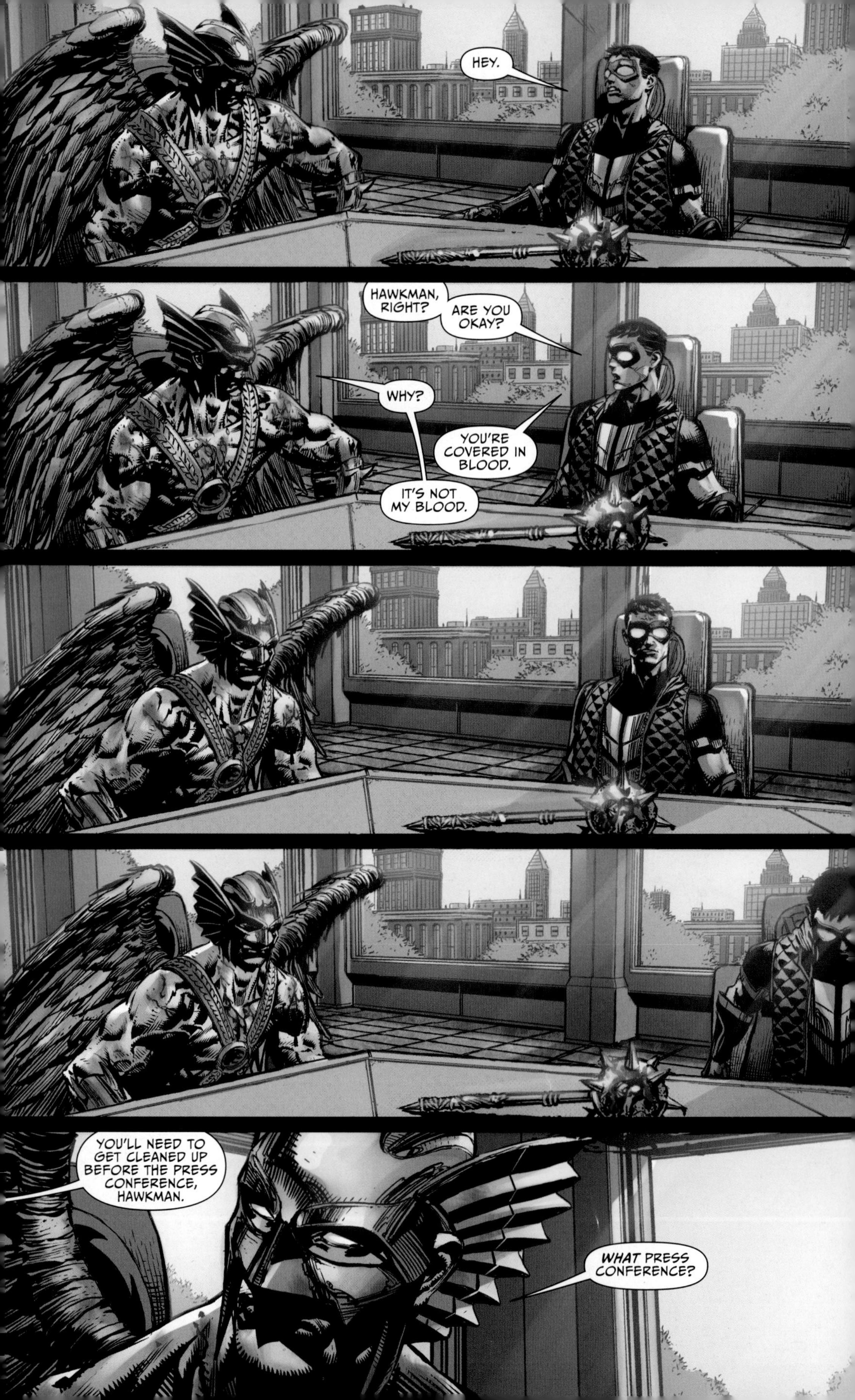
HEY.
HAWKMAN, RIGHT?
ARE YOU OKAY?
WHY?
YOU'RE COVERED IN BLOOD.
IT'S NOT MY BLOOD.
YOU'LL NEED TO GET CLEANED UP BEFORE THE PRESS CONFERENCE, HAWKMAN.
WHAT PRESS CONFERENCE?

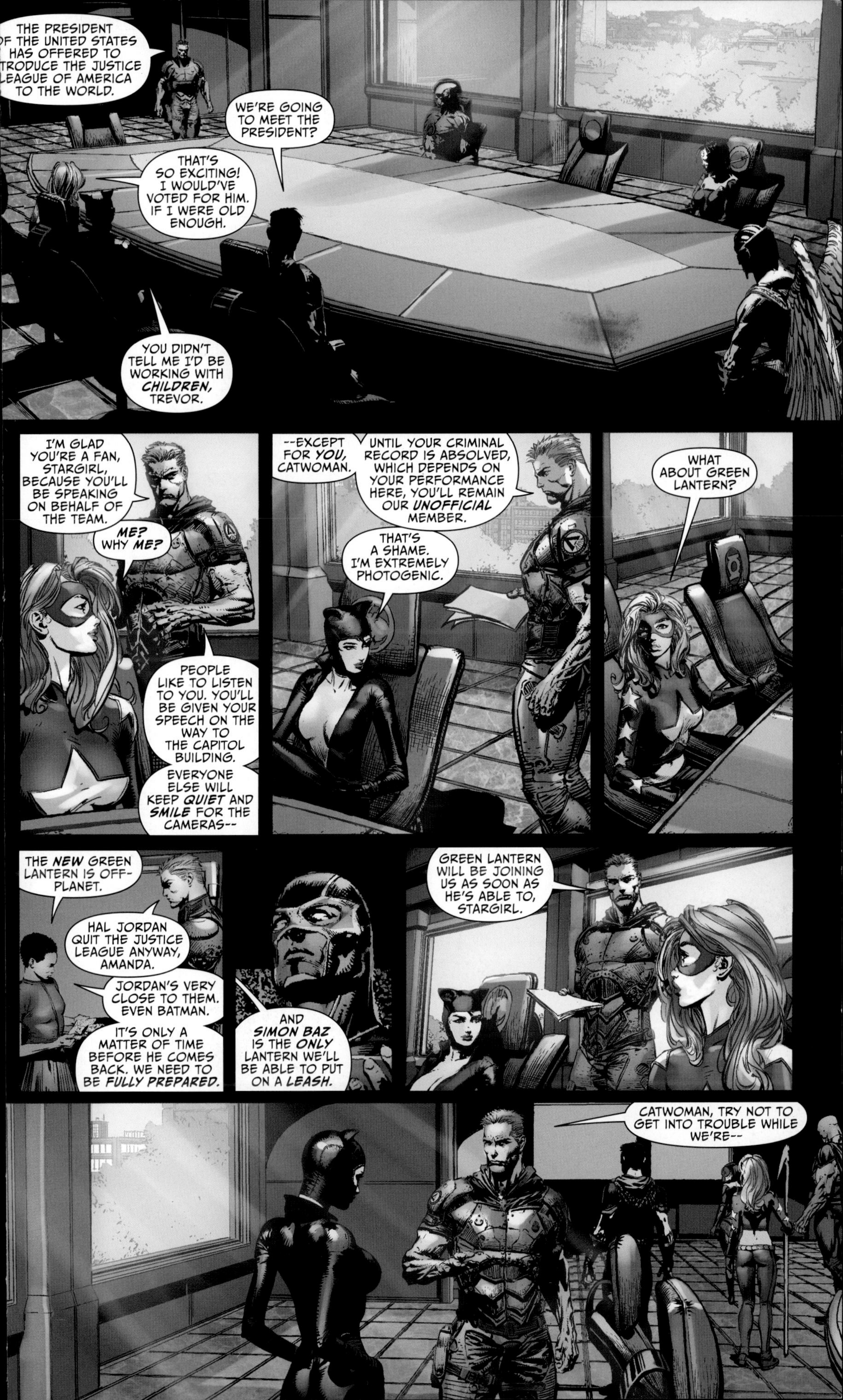
THE PRESIDENT OF THE UNITED STATES HAS OFFERED TO INTRODUCE THE JUSTICE LEAGUE OF AMERICA TO THE WORLD.
WE'RE GOING TO MEET THE PRESIDENT?
THAT'S SO EXCITING! I WOULD'VE VOTED FOR HIM. IF I WERE OLD ENOUGH.
YOU DIDN'T TELL ME I'D BE WORKING WITH *CHILDREN,* TREVOR.
I'M GLAD YOU'RE A FAN, STARGIRL, BECAUSE YOU'LL BE SPEAKING ON BEHALF OF THE TEAM.
ME? WHY *ME?*
PEOPLE LIKE TO LISTEN TO YOU. YOU'LL BE GIVEN YOUR SPEECH ON THE WAY TO THE CAPITOL BUILDING.
EVERYONE ELSE WILL KEEP *QUIET* AND *SMILE* FOR THE CAMERAS--
--EXCEPT FOR *YOU,* CATWOMAN.
UNTIL YOUR CRIMINAL RECORD IS ABSOLVED, WHICH DEPENDS ON YOUR PERFORMANCE HERE, YOU'LL REMAIN OUR *UNOFFICIAL* MEMBER.
THAT'S A SHAME. I'M EXTREMELY PHOTOGENIC.
WHAT ABOUT GREEN LANTERN?
THE *NEW* GREEN LANTERN IS OFF-PLANET.
HAL JORDAN QUIT THE JUSTICE LEAGUE ANYWAY, AMANDA.
JORDAN'S VERY CLOSE TO THEM. EVEN BATMAN.
IT'S ONLY A MATTER OF TIME BEFORE HE COMES BACK. WE NEED TO BE *FULLY PREPARED.*
AND *SIMON BAZ* IS THE *ONLY* LANTERN WE'LL BE ABLE TO PUT ON A *LEASH.*
GREEN LANTERN WILL BE JOINING US AS SOON AS HE'S ABLE TO, STARGIRL.
CATWOMAN, TRY NOT TO GET INTO TROUBLE WHILE WE'RE--

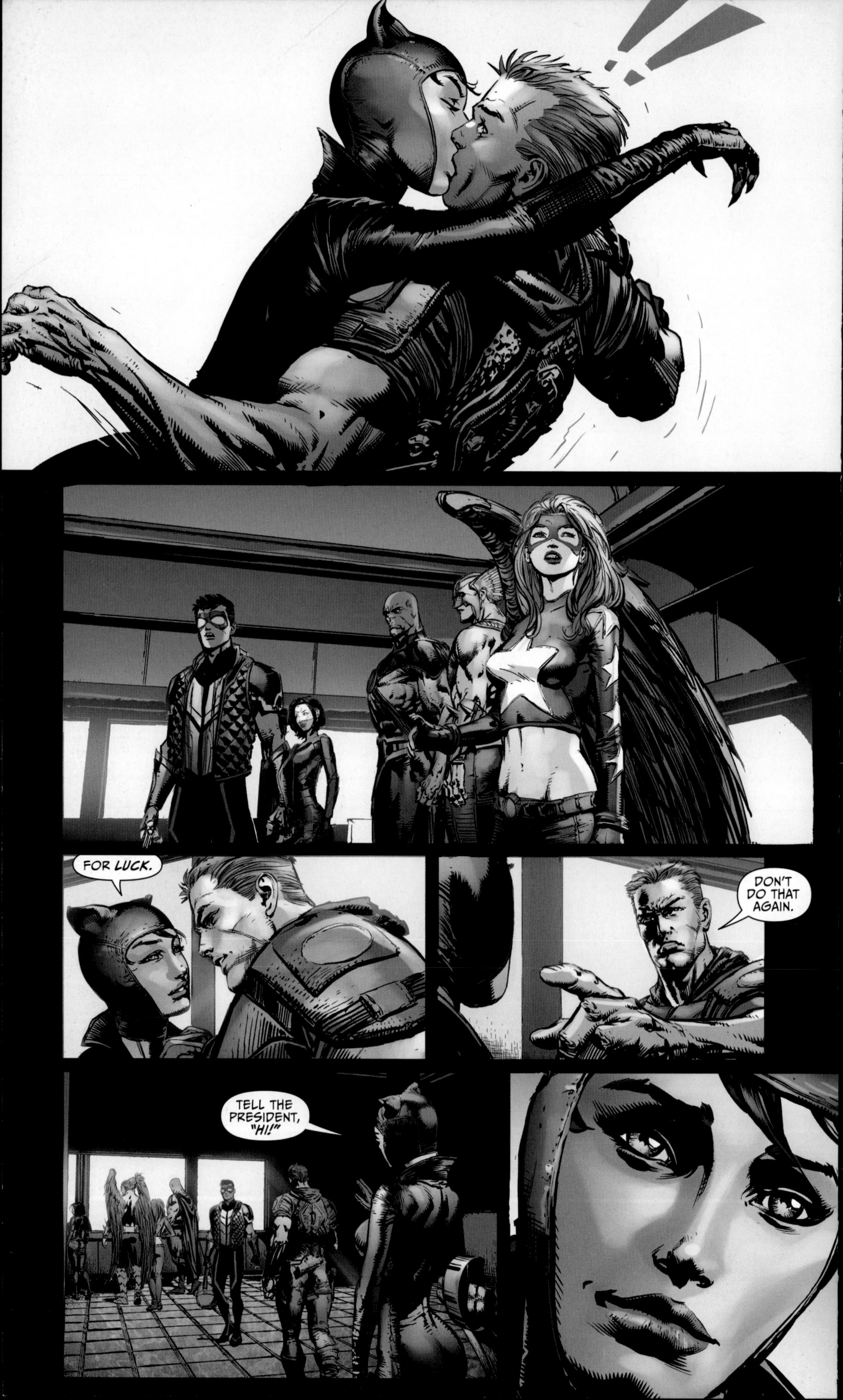
!!
FOR LUCK.
DON'T DO THAT AGAIN.
TELL THE PRESIDENT, "HI!"

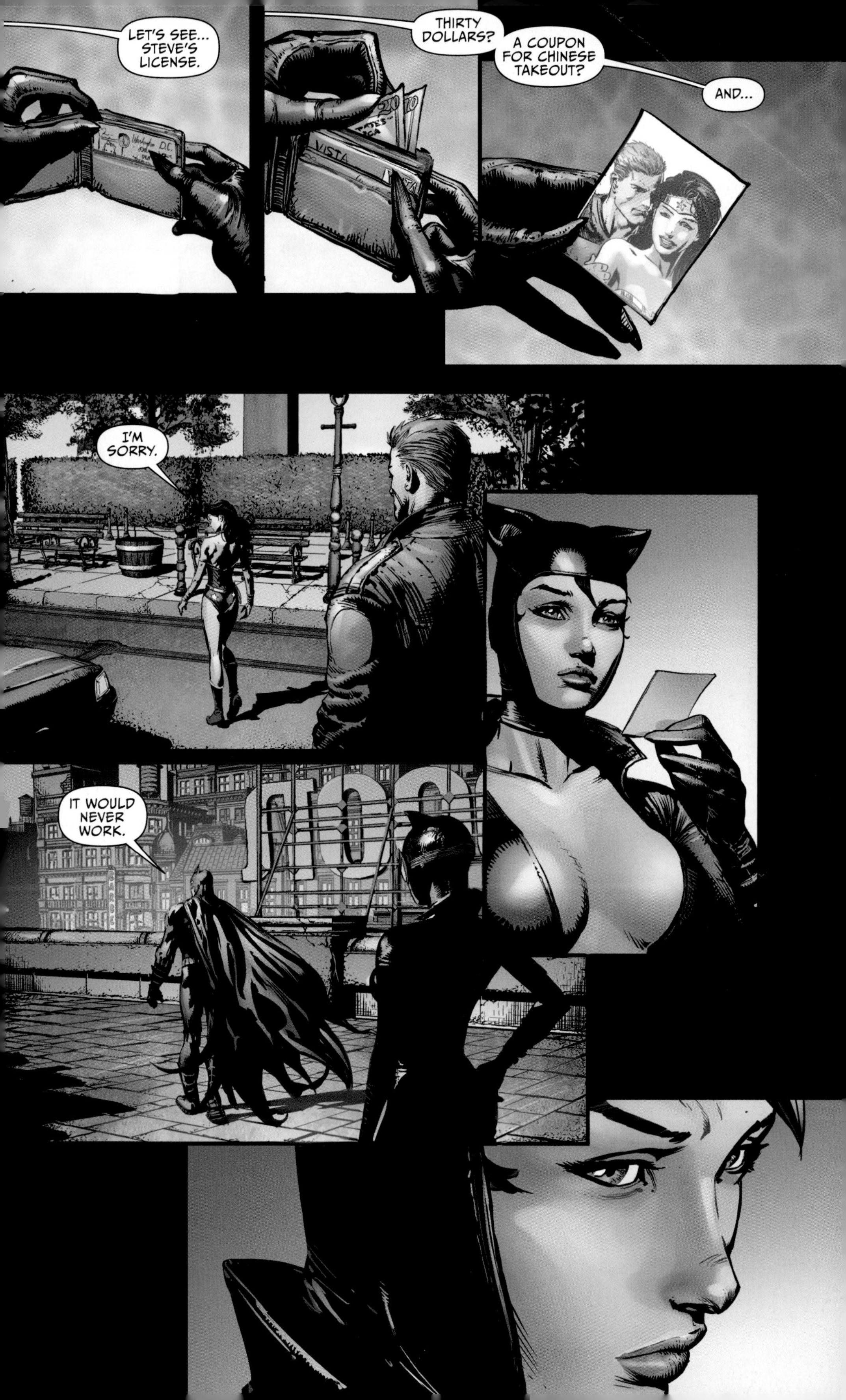
LET'S SEE... STEVE'S LICENSE.
THIRTY DOLLARS?
A COUPON FOR CHINESE TAKEOUT?
AND...
I'M SORRY.
IT WOULD NEVER WORK.

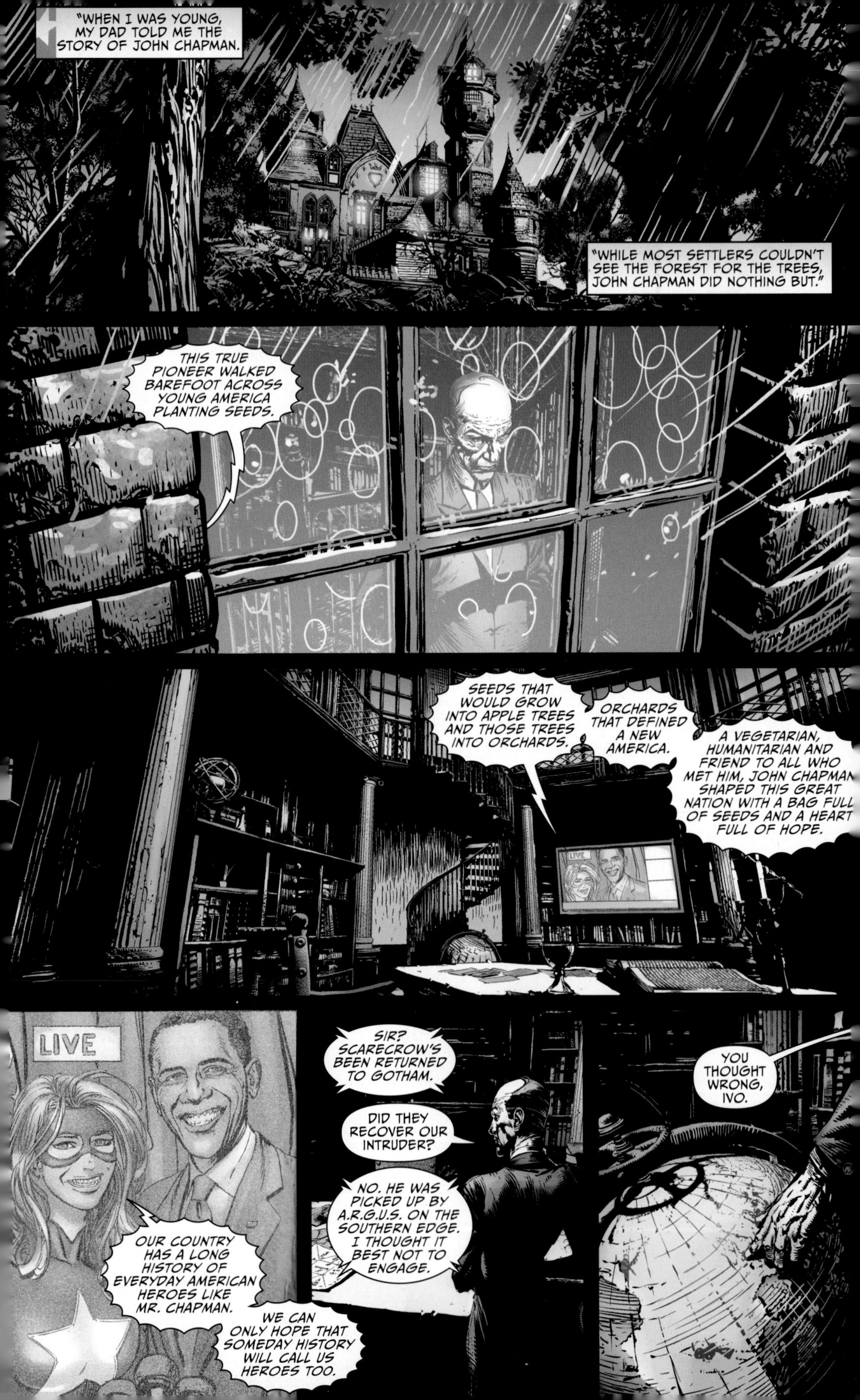
"WHEN I WAS YOUNG, MY DAD TOLD ME THE STORY OF JOHN CHAPMAN.
"WHILE MOST SETTLERS COULDN'T SEE THE FOREST FOR THE TREES, JOHN CHAPMAN DID NOTHING BUT."
THIS TRUE PIONEER WALKED BAREFOOT ACROSS YOUNG AMERICA PLANTING SEEDS.
SEEDS THAT WOULD GROW INTO APPLE TREES AND THOSE TREES INTO ORCHARDS.
ORCHARDS THAT DEFINED A NEW AMERICA.
A VEGETARIAN, HUMANITARIAN AND FRIEND TO ALL WHO MET HIM, JOHN CHAPMAN SHAPED THIS GREAT NATION WITH A BAG FULL OF SEEDS AND A HEART FULL OF HOPE.
LIVE
LIVE
OUR COUNTRY HAS A LONG HISTORY OF EVERYDAY AMERICAN HEROES LIKE MR. CHAPMAN.
WE CAN ONLY HOPE THAT SOMEDAY HISTORY WILL CALL US HEROES TOO.
SIR? SCARECROW'S BEEN RETURNED TO GOTHAM.
DID THEY RECOVER OUR INTRUDER?
NO. HE WAS PICKED UP BY A.R.G.U.S. ON THE SOUTHERN EDGE. I THOUGHT IT BEST NOT TO ENGAGE.
YOU THOUGHT WRONG, IVO.

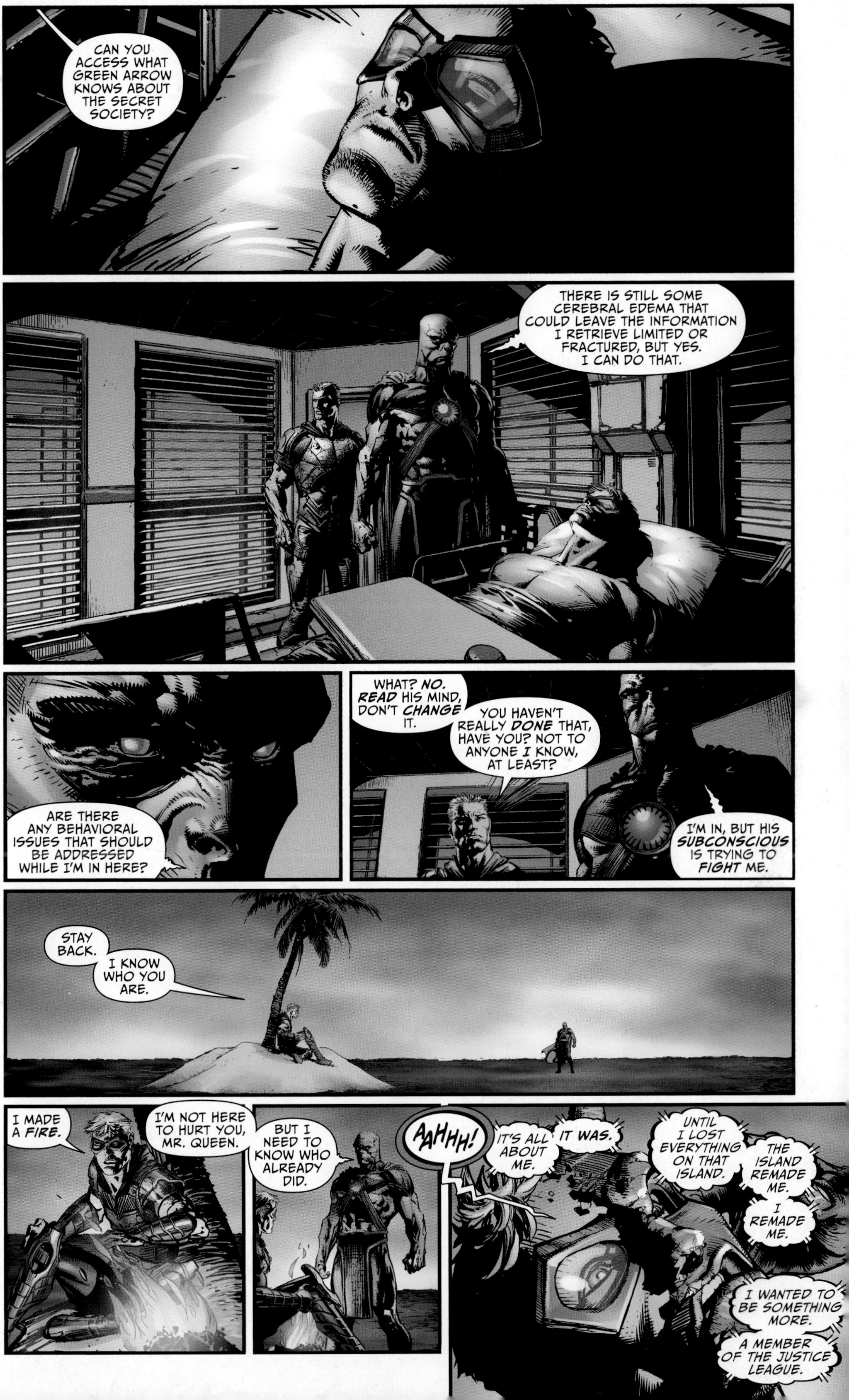

CAN YOU ACCESS WHAT GREEN ARROW KNOWS ABOUT THE SECRET SOCIETY?
THERE IS STILL SOME CEREBRAL EDEMA THAT COULD LEAVE THE INFORMATION I RETRIEVE LIMITED OR FRACTURED, BUT YES. I CAN DO THAT.
ARE THERE ANY BEHAVIORAL ISSUES THAT SHOULD BE ADDRESSED WHILE I'M IN HERE?
WHAT? NO. READ HIS MIND, DON'T CHANGE IT.
YOU HAVEN'T REALLY DONE THAT, HAVE YOU? NOT TO ANYONE I KNOW, AT LEAST?
I'M IN, BUT HIS SUBCONSCIOUS IS TRYING TO FIGHT ME.
STAY BACK.
I KNOW WHO YOU ARE.
I MADE A FIRE.
I'M NOT HERE TO HURT YOU, MR. QUEEN.
BUT I NEED TO KNOW WHO ALREADY DID.
AAHHH!
IT'S ALL ABOUT ME.
IT WAS.
UNTIL I LOST EVERYTHING ON THAT ISLAND.
THE ISLAND REMADE ME.
I REMADE ME.
I WANTED TO BE SOMETHING MORE.
A MEMBER OF THE JUSTICE LEAGUE.

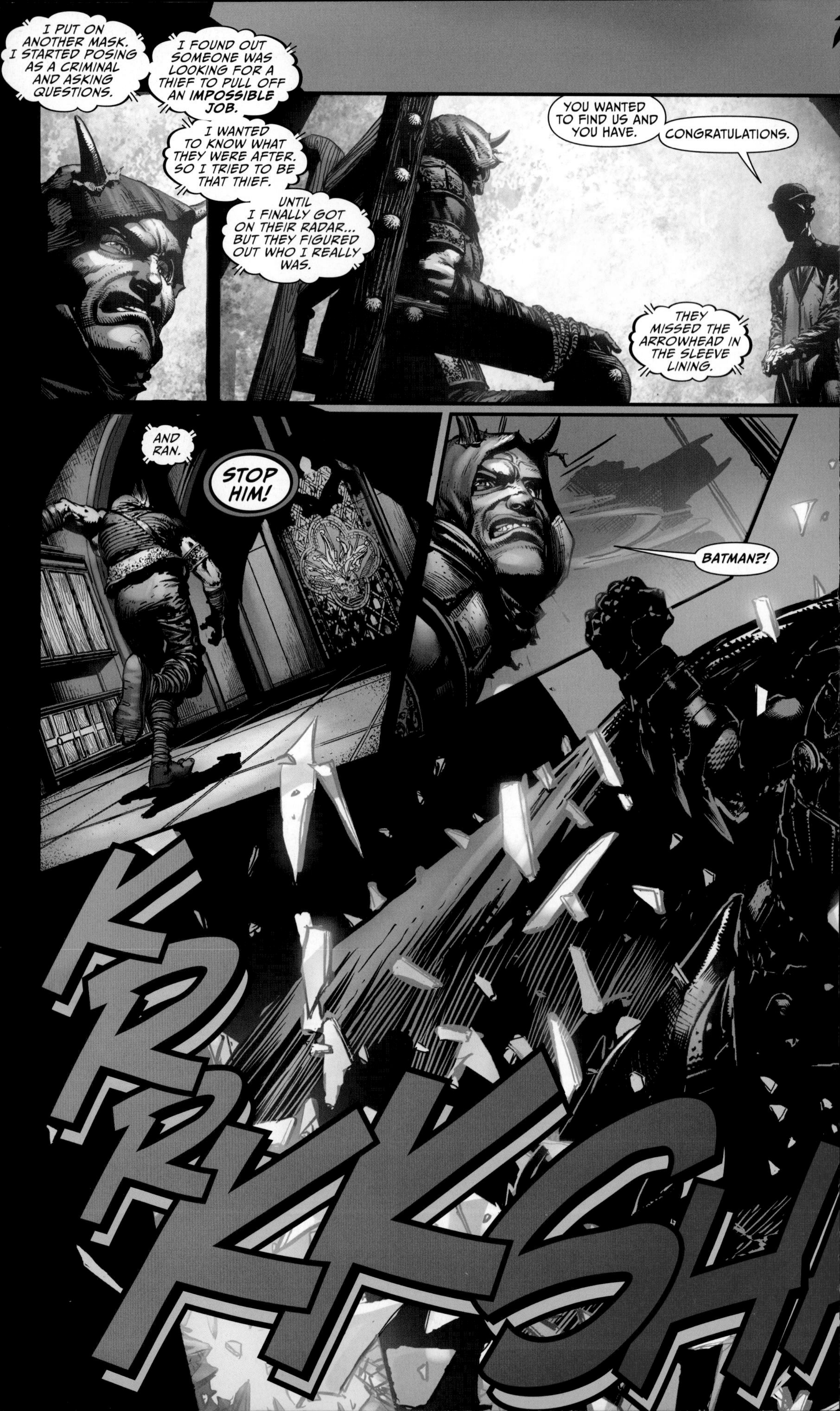
I PUT ON ANOTHER MASK. I STARTED POSING AS A CRIMINAL AND ASKING QUESTIONS.
I FOUND OUT SOMEONE WAS LOOKING FOR A THIEF TO PULL OFF AN **IMPOSSIBLE** JOB.
I WANTED TO KNOW WHAT THEY WERE AFTER. SO I TRIED TO BE THAT THIEF.
UNTIL I FINALLY GOT ON THEIR RADAR... BUT THEY FIGURED OUT WHO I REALLY WAS.
YOU WANTED TO FIND US AND YOU HAVE.
CONGRATULATIONS.
THEY MISSED THE ARROWHEAD IN THE SLEEVE LINING.
AND RAN.
STOP HIM!
BATMAN?!
KRRKKSH!

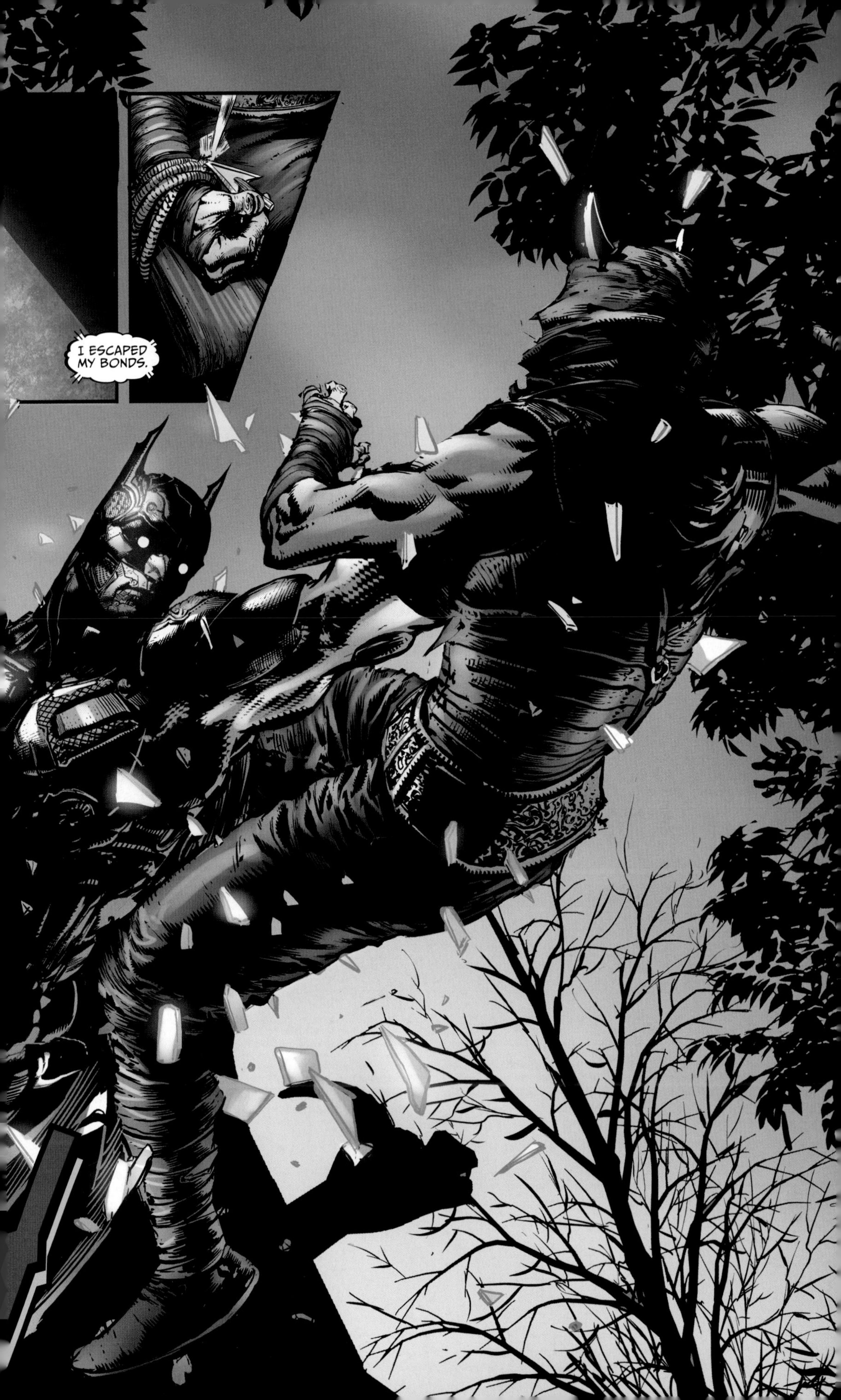
I ESCAPED MY BONDS.

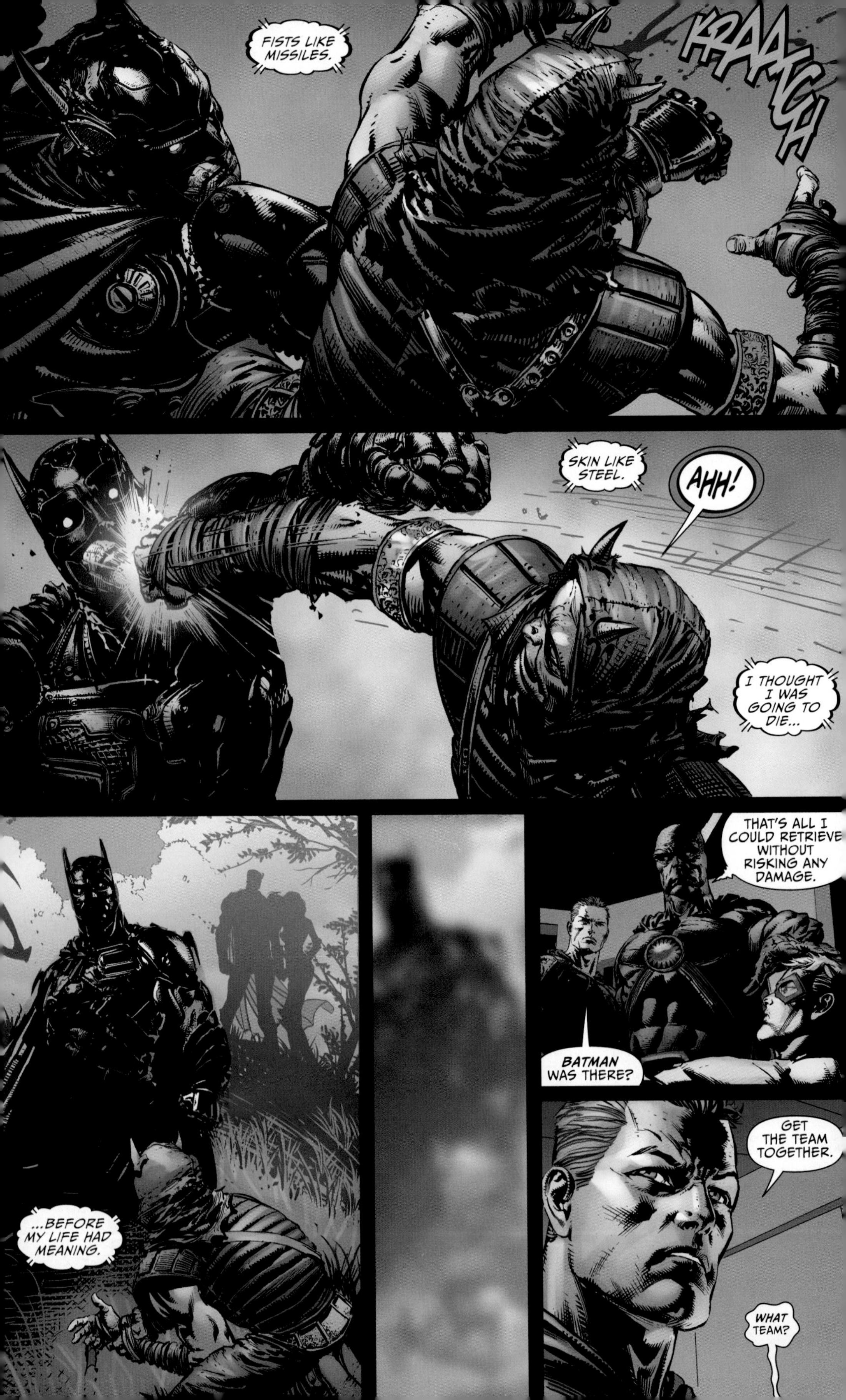
FISTS LIKE MISSILES.
KRAAAATCH
SKIN LIKE STEEL.
AHH!
I THOUGHT I WAS GOING TO DIE...
...BEFORE MY LIFE HAD MEANING.
THAT'S ALL I COULD RETRIEVE WITHOUT RISKING ANY DAMAGE.
BATMAN WAS THERE?
GET THE TEAM TOGETHER.
WHAT TEAM?

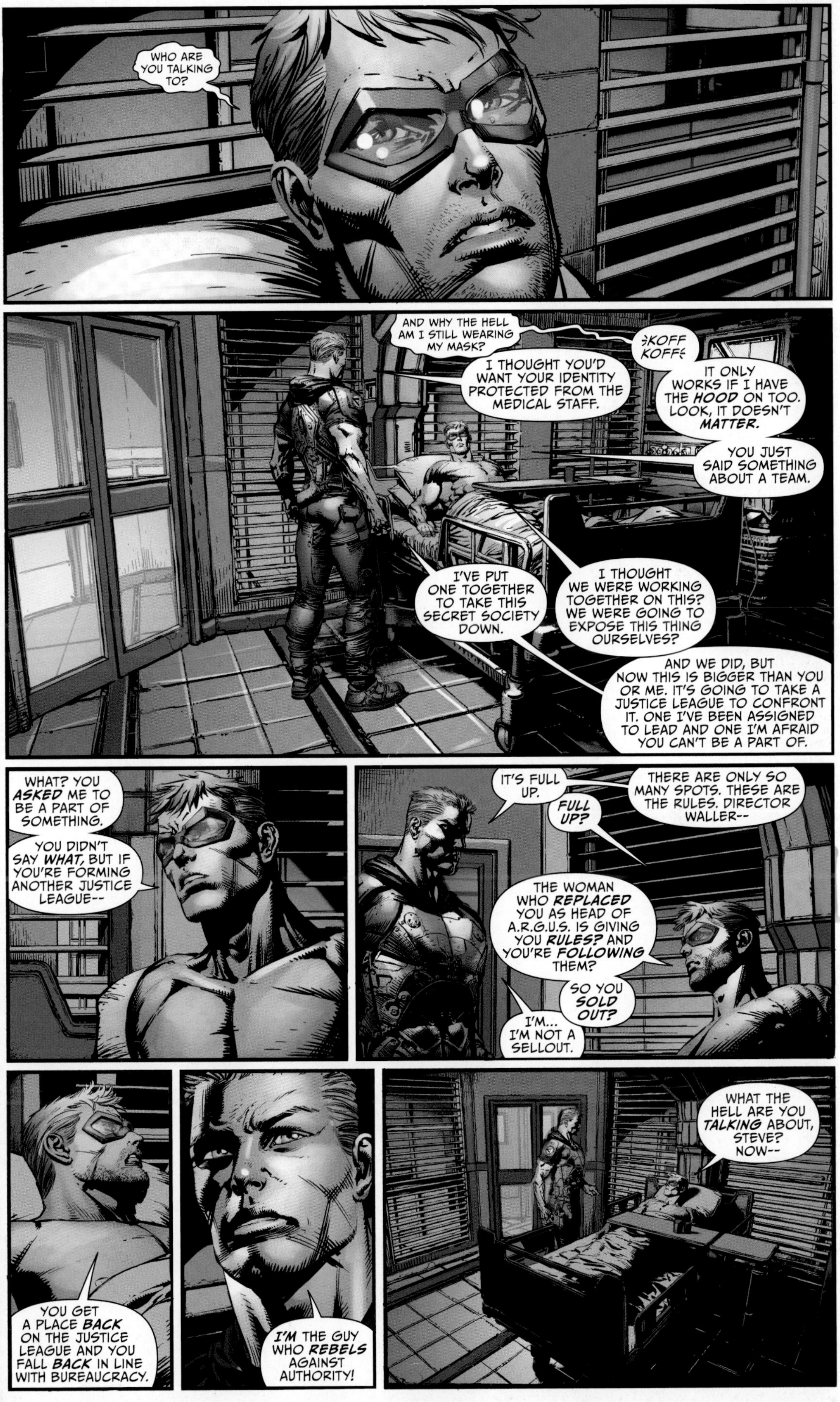

WHO ARE YOU TALKING TO?
AND WHY THE HELL AM I STILL WEARING MY MASK?
I THOUGHT YOU'D WANT YOUR IDENTITY PROTECTED FROM THE MEDICAL STAFF.
KOFF KOFF
IT ONLY WORKS IF I HAVE THE HOOD ON TOO. LOOK, IT DOESN'T MATTER.
YOU JUST SAID SOMETHING ABOUT A TEAM.
I'VE PUT ONE TOGETHER TO TAKE THIS SECRET SOCIETY DOWN.
I THOUGHT WE WERE WORKING TOGETHER ON THIS? WE WERE GOING TO EXPOSE THIS THING OURSELVES?
AND WE DID, BUT NOW THIS IS BIGGER THAN YOU OR ME. IT'S GOING TO TAKE A JUSTICE LEAGUE TO CONFRONT IT. ONE I'VE BEEN ASSIGNED TO LEAD AND ONE I'M AFRAID YOU CAN'T BE A PART OF.
WHAT? YOU ASKED ME TO BE A PART OF SOMETHING.
YOU DIDN'T SAY WHAT, BUT IF YOU'RE FORMING ANOTHER JUSTICE LEAGUE--
IT'S FULL UP.
FULL UP?
THERE ARE ONLY SO MANY SPOTS. THESE ARE THE RULES. DIRECTOR WALLER--
THE WOMAN WHO REPLACED YOU AS HEAD OF A.R.G.U.S. IS GIVING YOU RULES? AND YOU'RE FOLLOWING THEM?
SO YOU SOLD OUT?
I'M... I'M NOT A SELLOUT.
YOU GET A PLACE BACK ON THE JUSTICE LEAGUE AND YOU FALL BACK IN LINE WITH BUREAUCRACY.
I'M THE GUY WHO REBELS AGAINST AUTHORITY!
WHAT THE HELL ARE YOU TALKING ABOUT, STEVE? NOW--

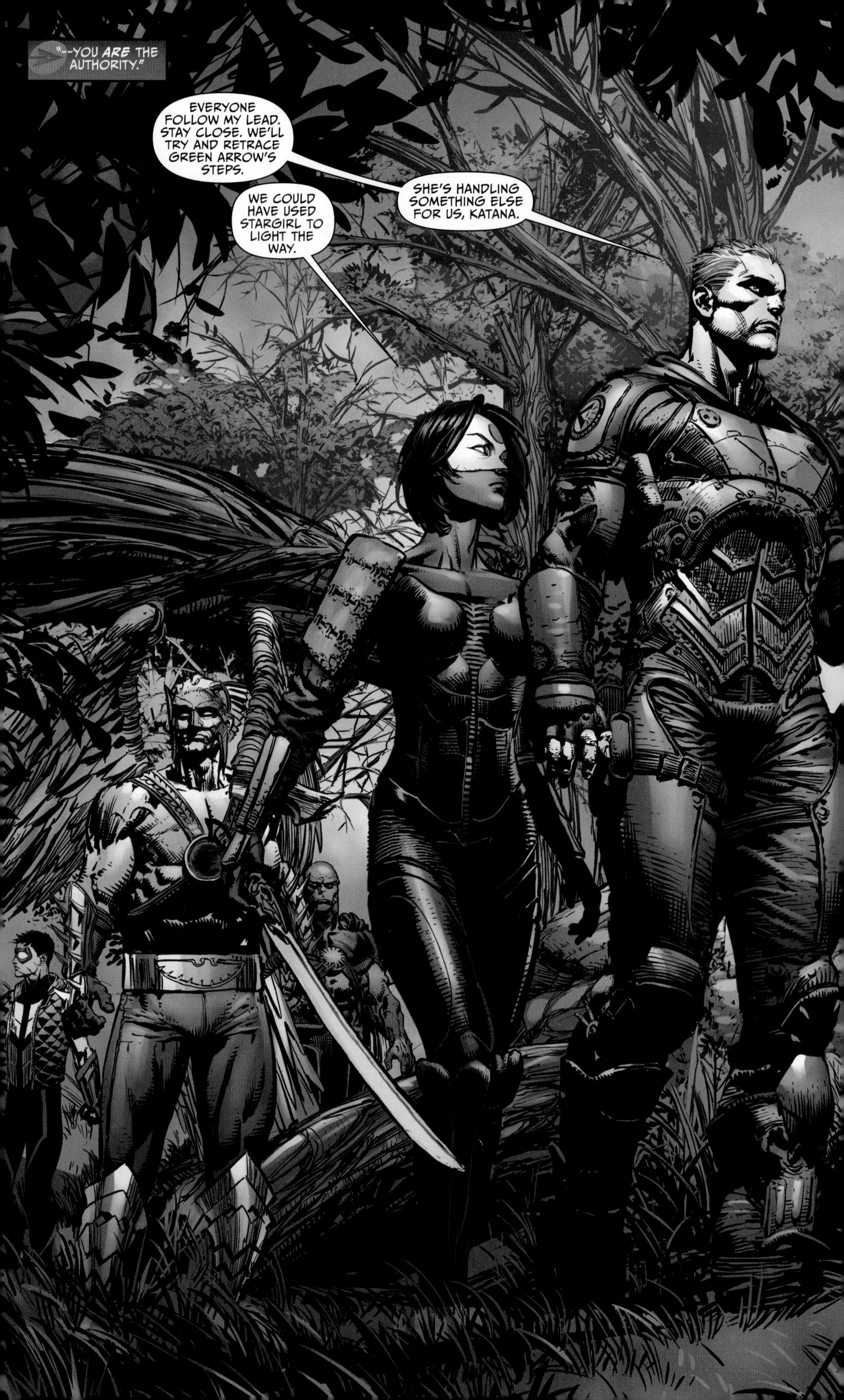
"--YOU ARE THE AUTHORITY."
EVERYONE FOLLOW MY LEAD. STAY CLOSE. WE'LL TRY AND RETRACE GREEN ARROW'S STEPS.
WE COULD HAVE USED STARGIRL TO LIGHT THE WAY.
SHE'S HANDLING SOMETHING ELSE FOR US, KATANA.

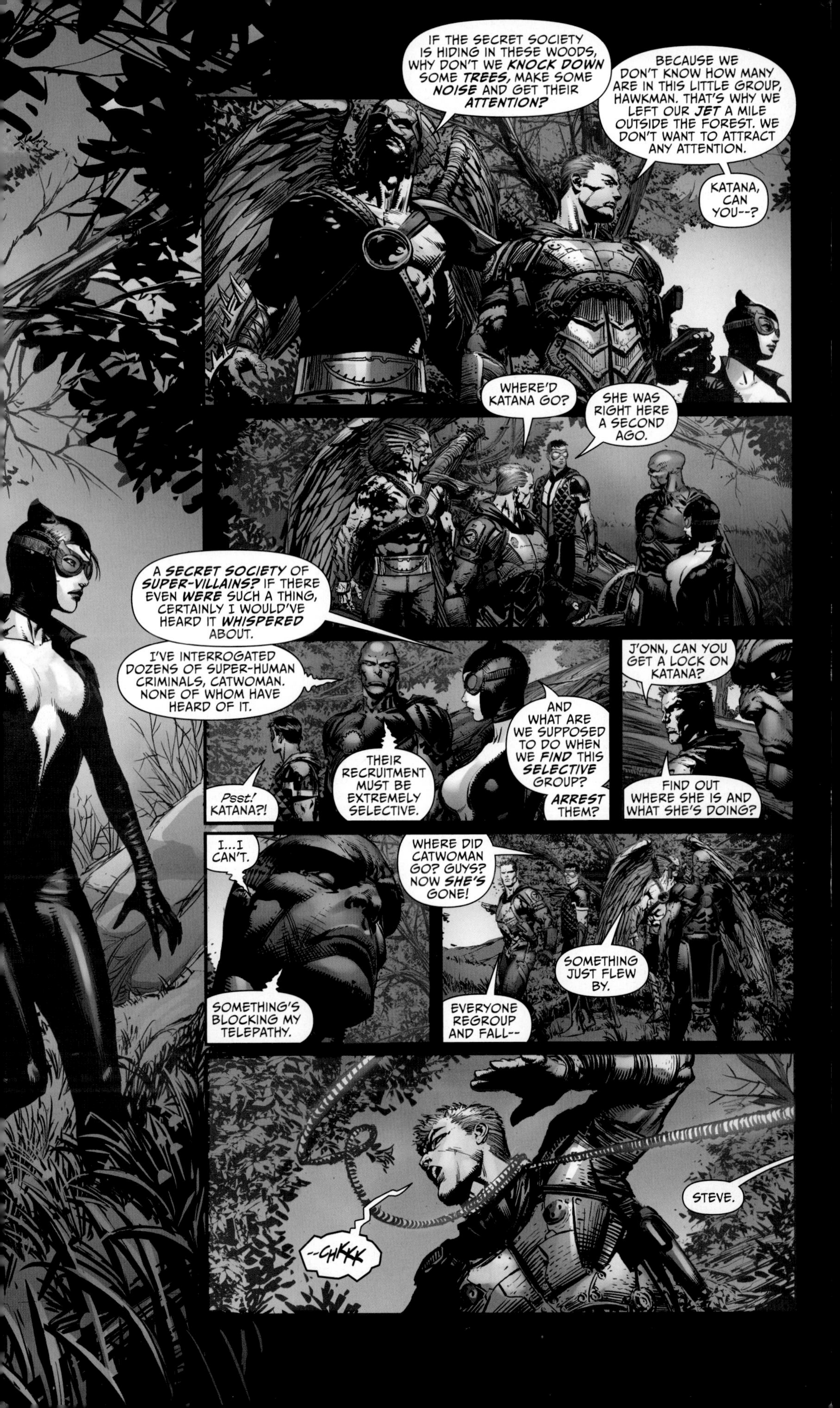
IF THE SECRET SOCIETY IS HIDING IN THESE WOODS, WHY DON'T WE KNOCK DOWN SOME TREES, MAKE SOME NOISE AND GET THEIR ATTENTION?
BECAUSE WE DON'T KNOW HOW MANY ARE IN THIS LITTLE GROUP, HAWKMAN. THAT'S WHY WE LEFT OUR JET A MILE OUTSIDE THE FOREST. WE DON'T WANT TO ATTRACT ANY ATTENTION.
KATANA, CAN YOU--?
WHERE'D KATANA GO?
SHE WAS RIGHT HERE A SECOND AGO.
A SECRET SOCIETY OF SUPER-VILLAINS? IF THERE EVEN WERE SUCH A THING, CERTAINLY I WOULD'VE HEARD IT WHISPERED ABOUT.
I'VE INTERROGATED DOZENS OF SUPER-HUMAN CRIMINALS, CATWOMAN. NONE OF WHOM HAVE HEARD OF IT.
Psst! KATANA?!
THEIR RECRUITMENT MUST BE EXTREMELY SELECTIVE.
AND WHAT ARE WE SUPPOSED TO DO WHEN WE FIND THIS SELECTIVE GROUP? ARREST THEM?
J'ONN, CAN YOU GET A LOCK ON KATANA?
FIND OUT WHERE SHE IS AND WHAT SHE'S DOING?
I...I CAN'T.
SOMETHING'S BLOCKING MY TELEPATHY.
WHERE DID CATWOMAN GO? GUYS? NOW SHE'S GONE!
EVERYONE REGROUP AND FALL--
SOMETHING JUST FLEW BY.
--CHKKK
STEVE.

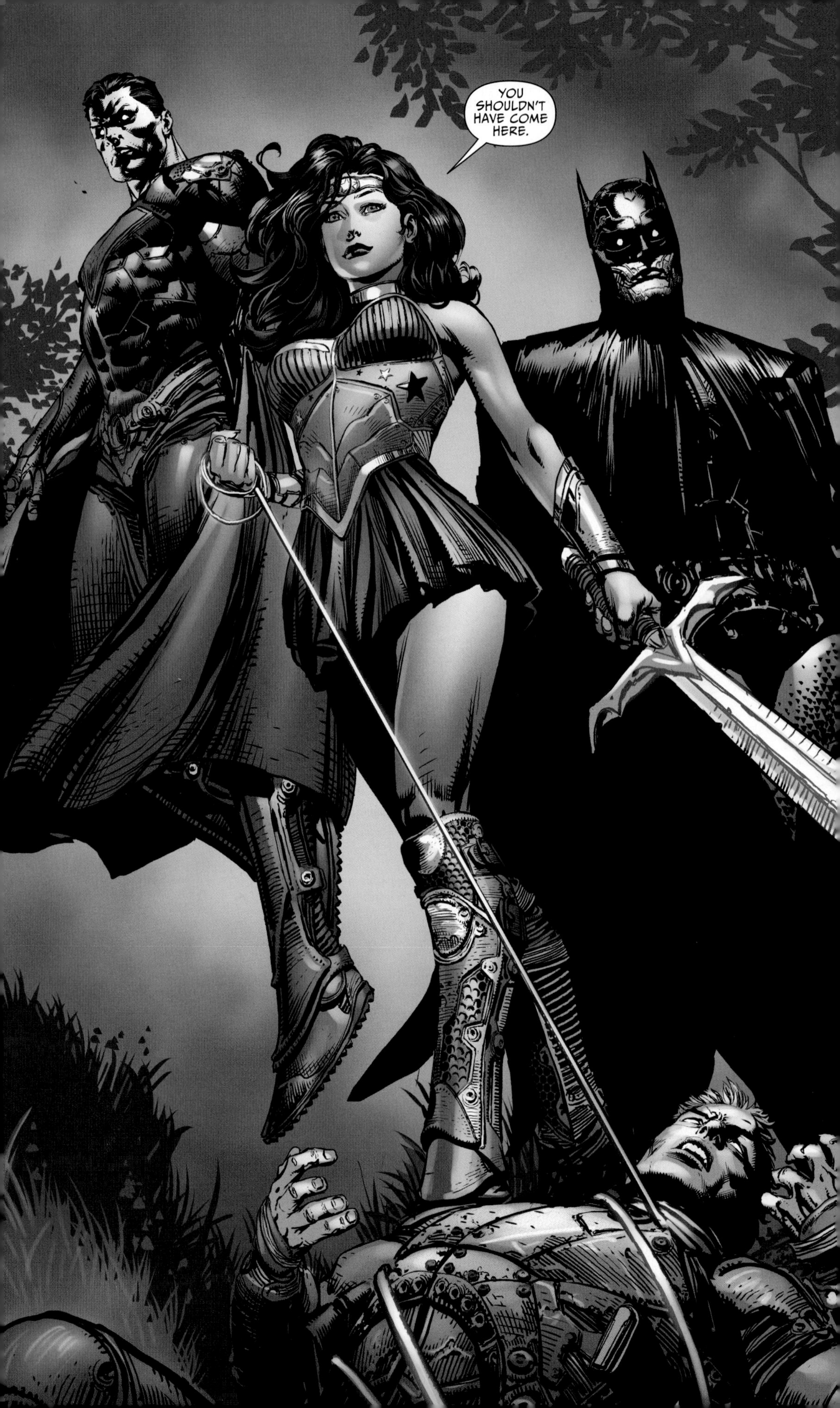
YOU SHOULDN'T HAVE COME HERE.

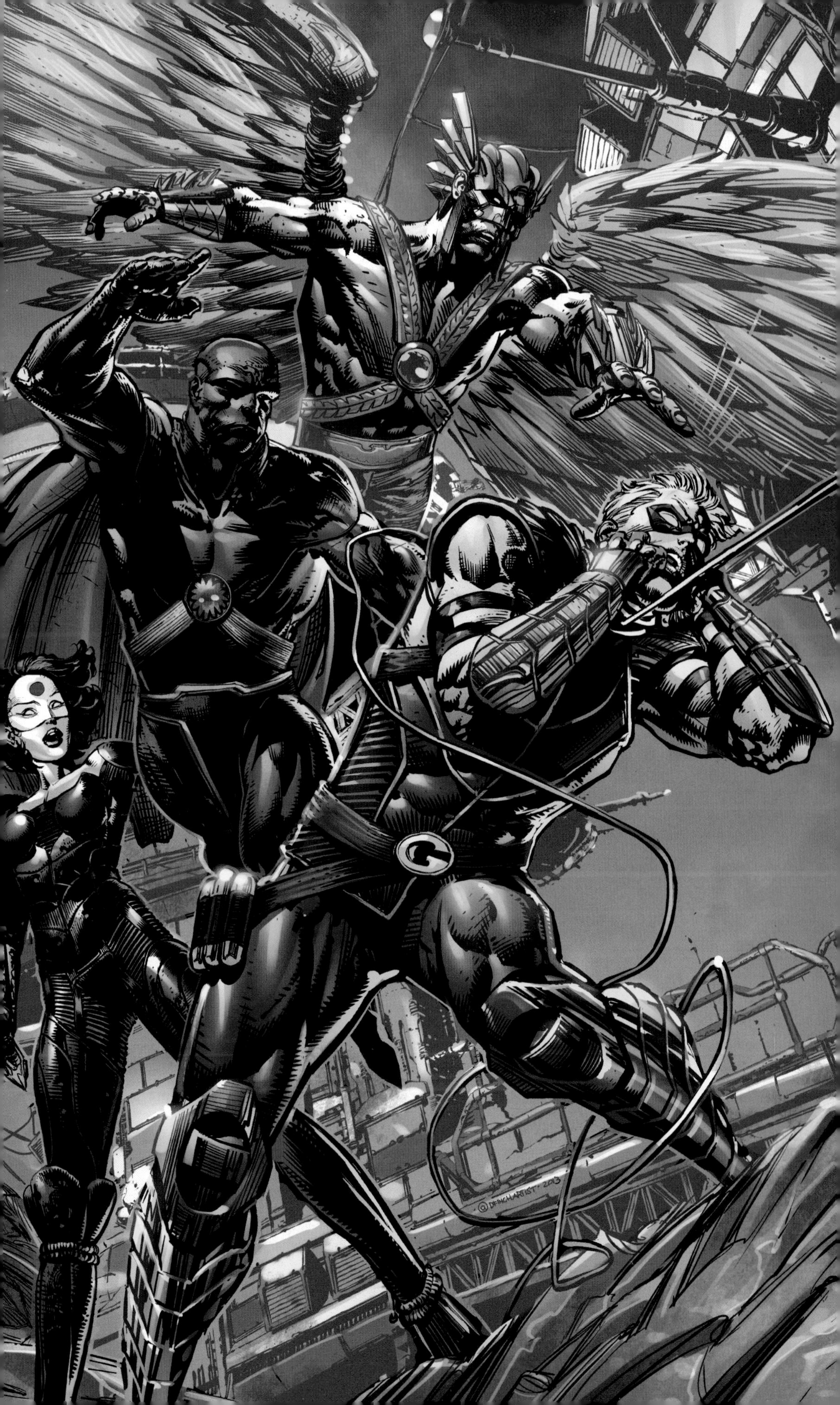

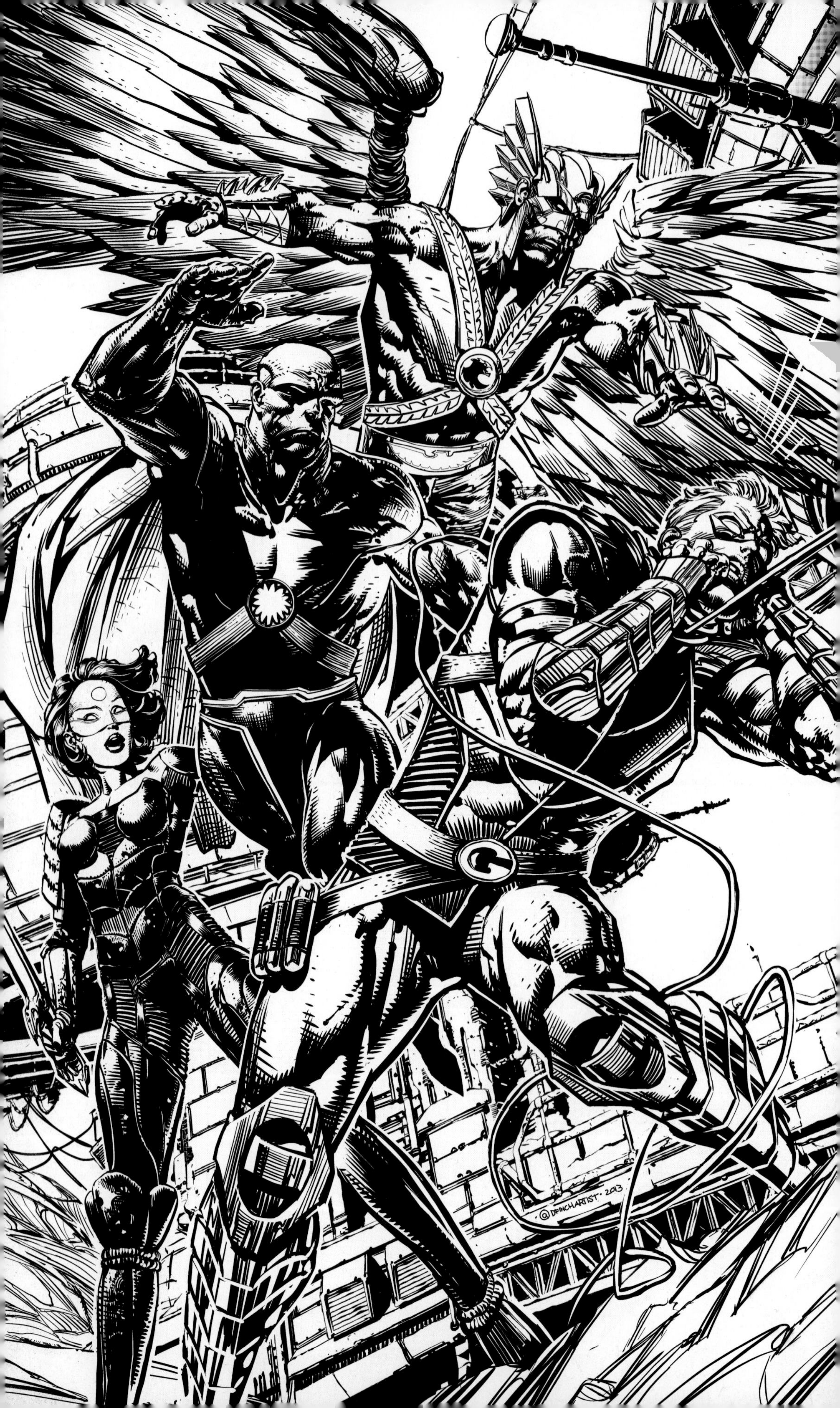
@DFINCHARTIST · 2013

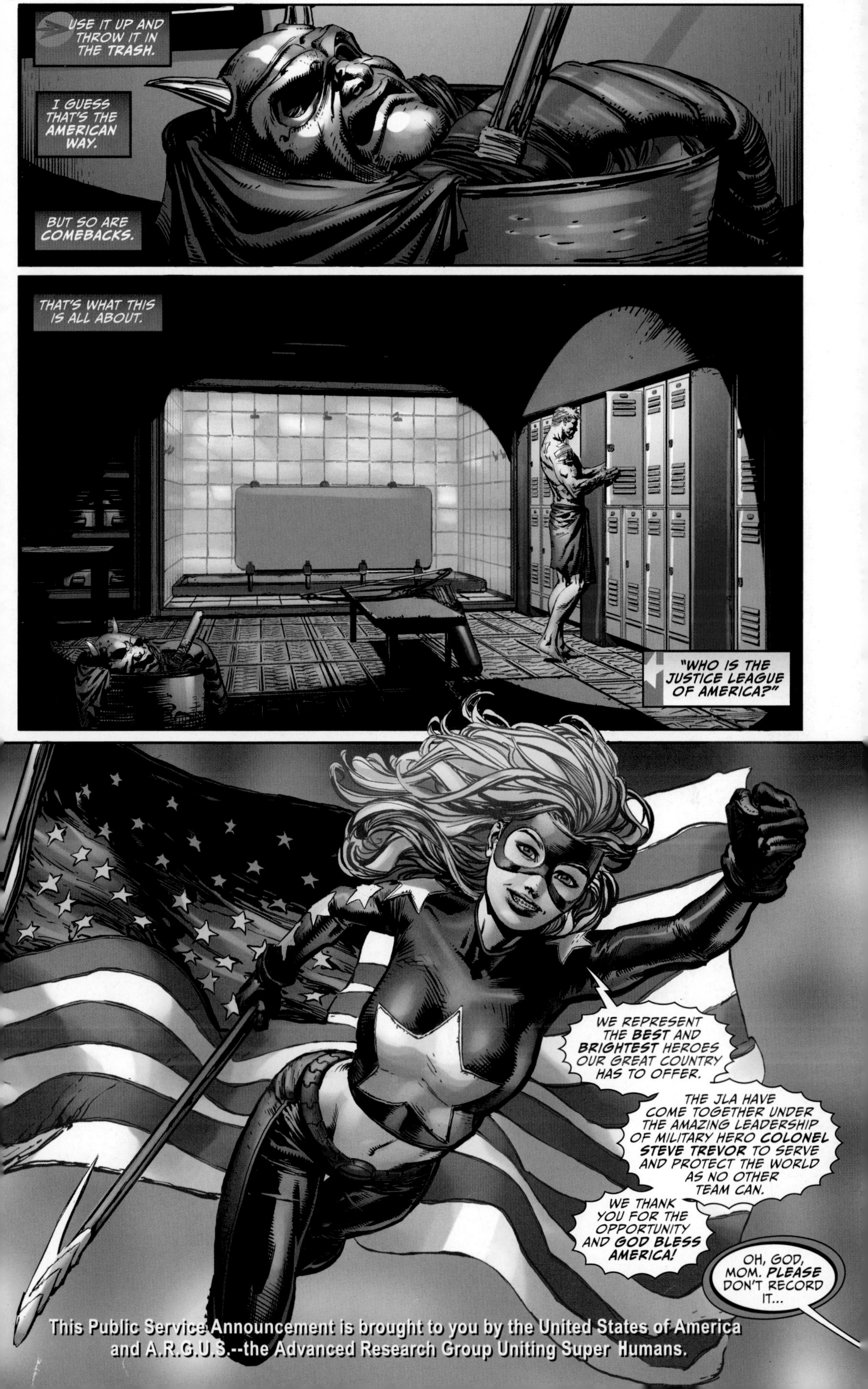

USE IT UP AND THROW IT IN THE TRASH.
I GUESS THAT'S THE AMERICAN WAY.
BUT SO ARE COMEBACKS.
THAT'S WHAT THIS IS ALL ABOUT.
"WHO IS THE JUSTICE LEAGUE OF AMERICA?"
WE REPRESENT THE BEST AND BRIGHTEST HEROES OUR GREAT COUNTRY HAS TO OFFER.
THE JLA HAVE COME TOGETHER UNDER THE AMAZING LEADERSHIP OF MILITARY HERO COLONEL STEVE TREVOR TO SERVE AND PROTECT THE WORLD AS NO OTHER TEAM CAN.
WE THANK YOU FOR THE OPPORTUNITY AND GOD BLESS AMERICA!
OH, GOD, MOM. PLEASE DON'T RECORD IT...
This Public Service Announcement is brought to you by the United States of America and A.R.G.U.S.--the Advanced Research Group Uniting Super Humans.

...IT SOUNDS SO *CANNED*.

NO, I DIDN'T *WRITE* IT.

YES, OF COURSE I HAVE THE *COSMIC STAFF*. I WON'T LET IT OUT OF MY SIGHT. EVEN IF SOMEONE *DID* GET HOLD OF IT, THE STAFF WOULDN'T...

...

BECAUSE THIS IS MY CHANCE TO HELP PEOPLE ON A WHOLE *OTHER* LEVEL. ISN'T THAT WHAT PAT'S ALWAYS LECTURING ME--

--LOOK...I'VE GOT TO GO, MOM.

TELL *YOU-KNOW-WHO* I'M FINE AND STOP WORRYING. I HEAR HIM BACK THERE. LOVE YOU TOO.

WE HAVE A FEW MORE HOURS OF PRESS INTERVIEWS SCHEDULED, STARGIRL. THESE ARE YOUR TALKING POINTS ON "THE BRIGHT FUTURE OF AMERICA."

FIRST YOU WRITE ME A *SPEECH* ABOUT *JOHNNY APPLESEED* AND NOW YOU HAND ME *TALKING POINTS* ON *AMERICA?*

I'M A PRETTY GOOD SPEAKER *WITHOUT* THESE, DIRECTOR WALLER, BUT I CAN'T USE THEM ANYWAY. COLONEL TREVOR'S ASKED US BACK TO THE JLA MEETING ROOM.

WE'RE GOING OUT ON MISSION.

THE LEAGUE ALREADY LEFT, STARGIRL.

WHAT? WHERE DID THEY GO?

SOMEPLACE TOO DANGEROUS FOR YOU.

TOO *DANGEROUS?*

IF SOMETHING *HAPPENED* TO STARGIRL OUT IN THE FIELD, IT WOULD BE A *P.R. DISASTER* FOR THE JLA.

I RISK MY LIFE *EVERY DAY*. I'M NOT STAYING HERE TO TALK TO REPORTERS.

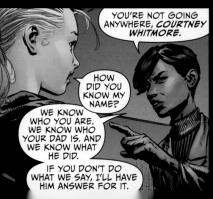

YES, YOU ARE. THAT'S YOUR ROLE ON THE TEAM. YOU'LL BE OUR FACE TO THE PUBLIC. YOU'LL ASSURE THE WORLD THE JLA IS EVERYTHING WE'VE SAID IT IS.

THEY'LL BELIEVE YOU.

I'M NOT A *CHEER-LEADER*, I'M AN *ACTIVE* MEMBER OF THE JLA.

IF *NOT*, I'M LEAVING.

YOU'RE NOT GOING ANYWHERE, *COURTNEY WHITMORE*.

HOW DID YOU KNOW MY NAME?

WE KNOW WHO YOU ARE. WE KNOW WHO YOUR DAD IS. AND WE KNOW WHAT HE DID.

IF YOU DON'T DO WHAT WE SAY, I'LL HAVE HIM ANSWER FOR IT.

SO *READ* THE DAMN TALKING POINTS.

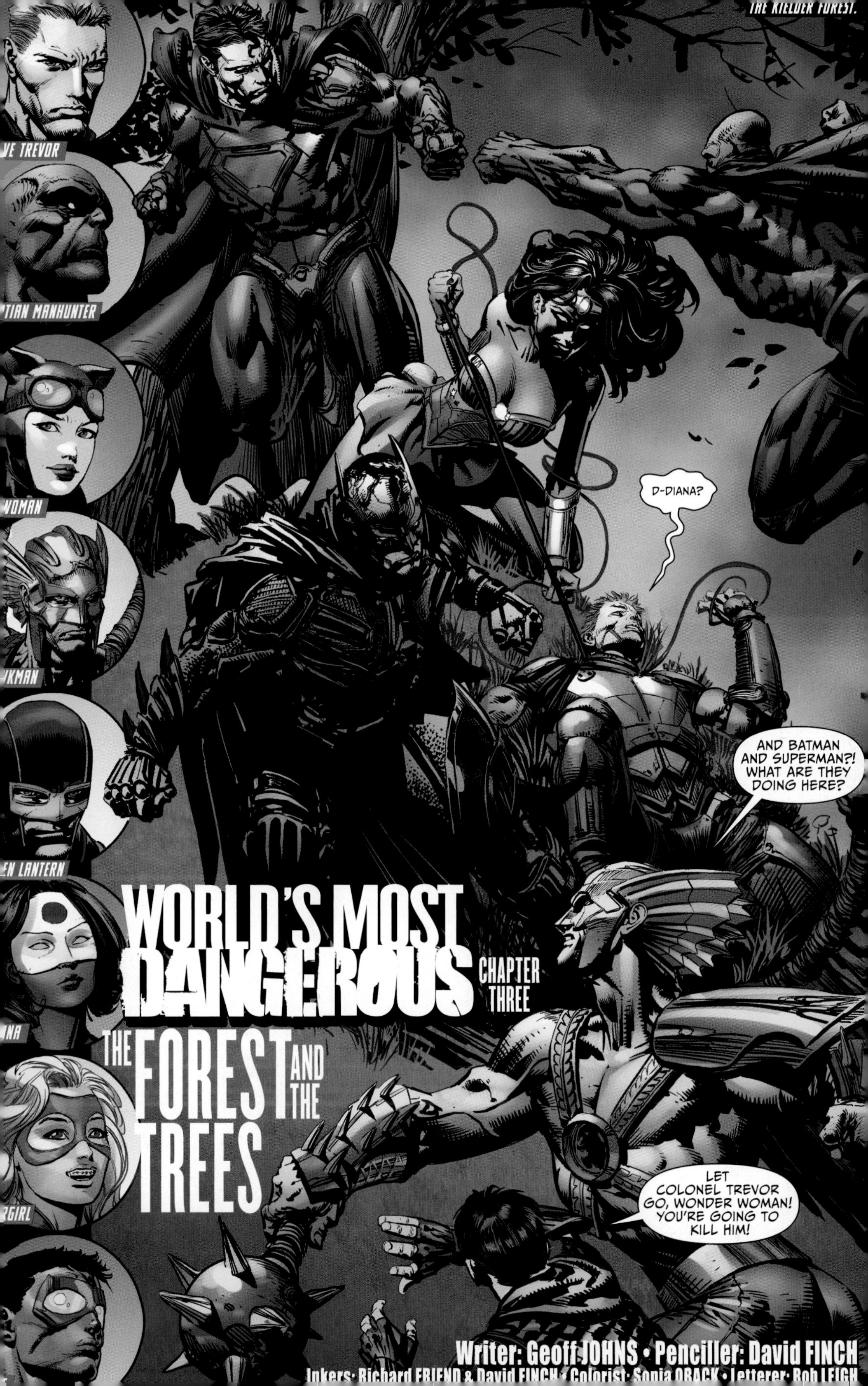
THE KIELDER FOREST.
D-DIANA?
AND BATMAN AND SUPERMAN?! WHAT ARE THEY DOING HERE?
LET COLONEL TREVOR GO, WONDER WOMAN! YOU'RE GOING TO KILL HIM!
WORLD'S MOST DANGEROUS
CHAPTER THREE
THE FOREST AND THE TREES
Writer: Geoff JOHNS • Penciller: David FINCH
Inkers: Richard FRIEND & David FINCH • Colorist: Sonia OBACK • Letterer: Rob LEIGH

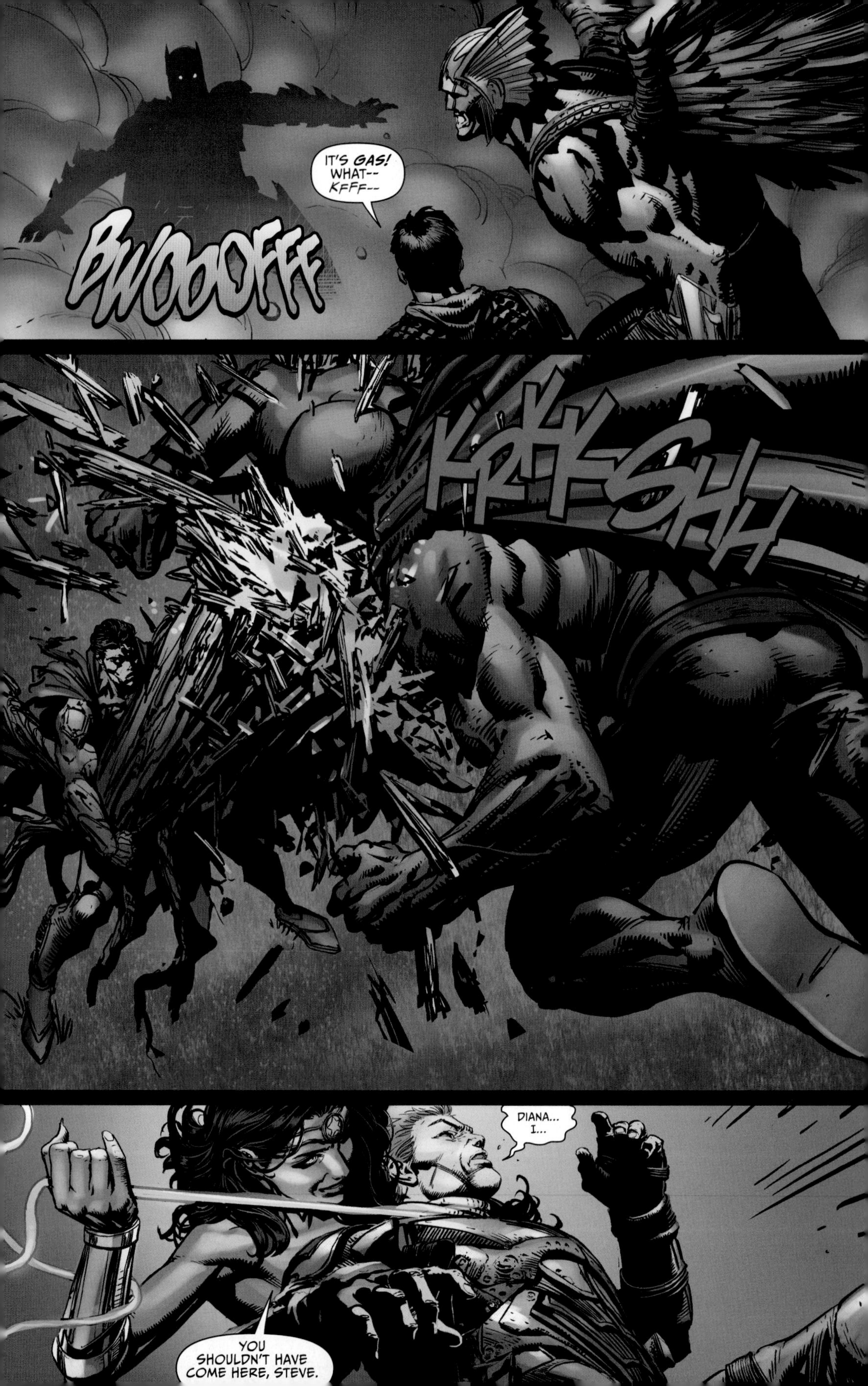
IT'S GAS! WHAT-- KFFF--
BWOOOFFF
KRKKSHH
DIANA... I...
YOU SHOULDN'T HAVE COME HERE, STEVE.

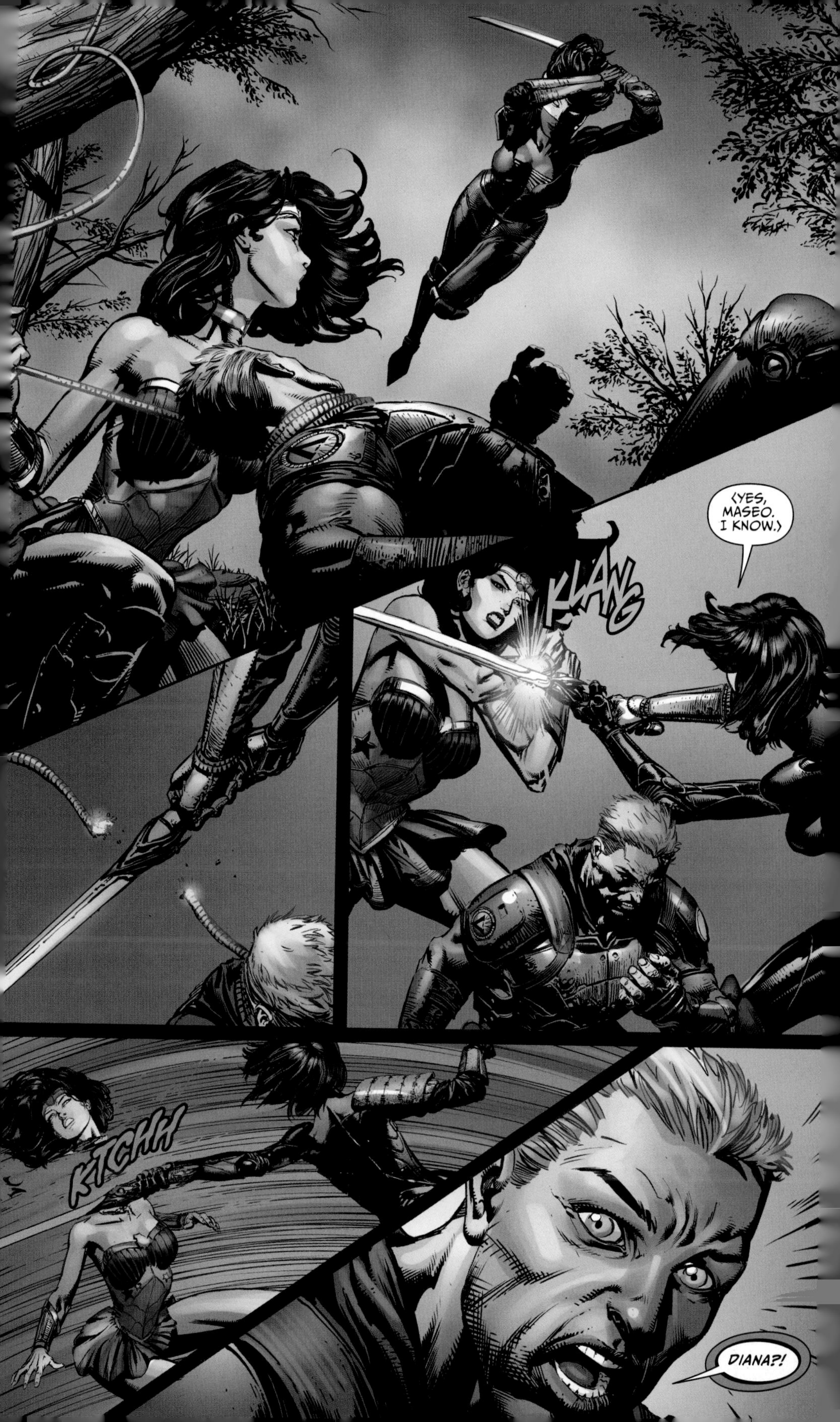
‹YES, MASEO. I KNOW.›
KLANG
KTCHH
DIANA?!

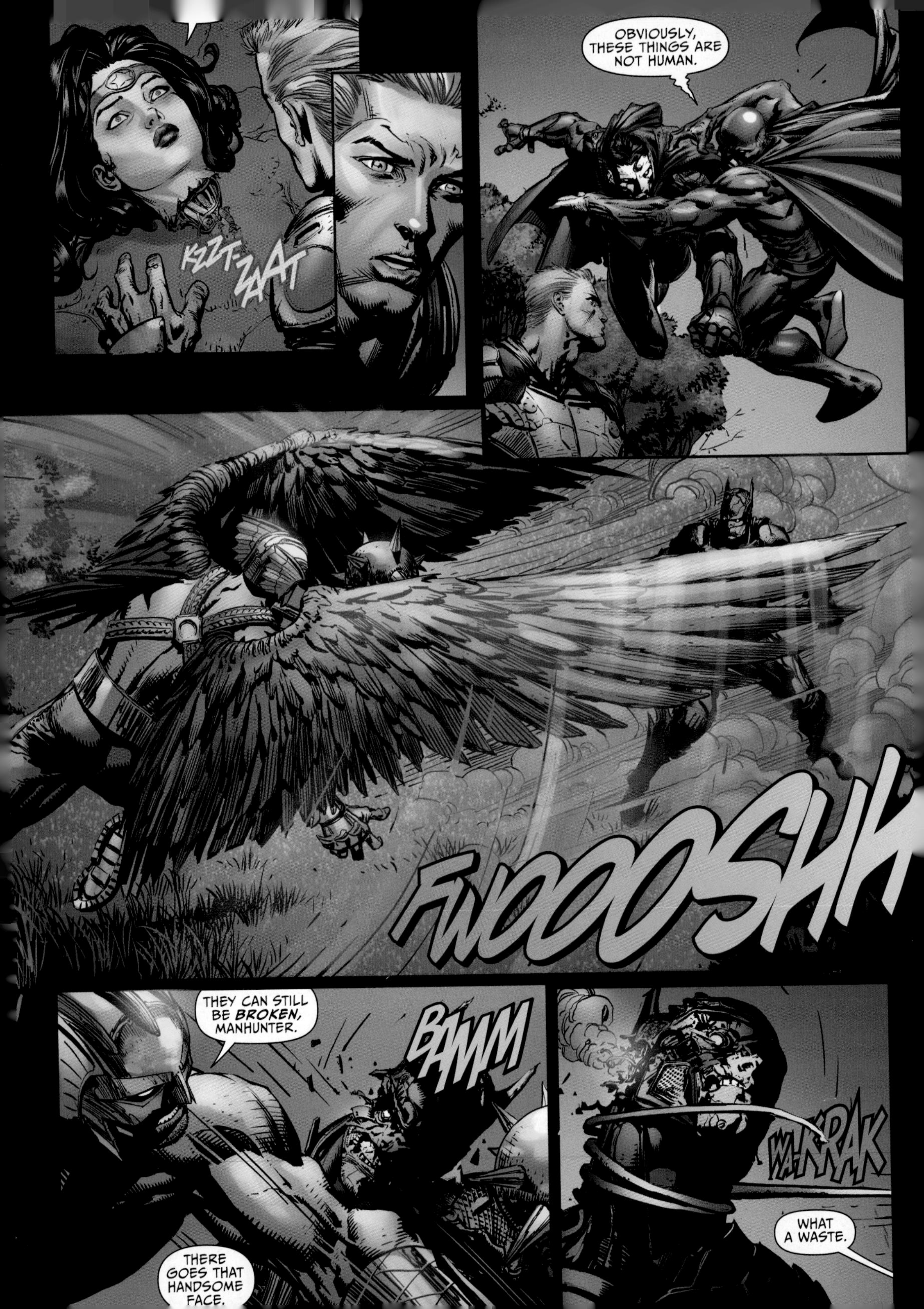
KZZT-ZAAT
OBVIOUSLY, THESE THINGS ARE NOT HUMAN.
FWOOOSHK
THEY CAN STILL BE *BROKEN*, MANHUNTER.
BAMM
THERE GOES THAT HANDSOME FACE.
WA-KRAK
WHAT A WASTE.

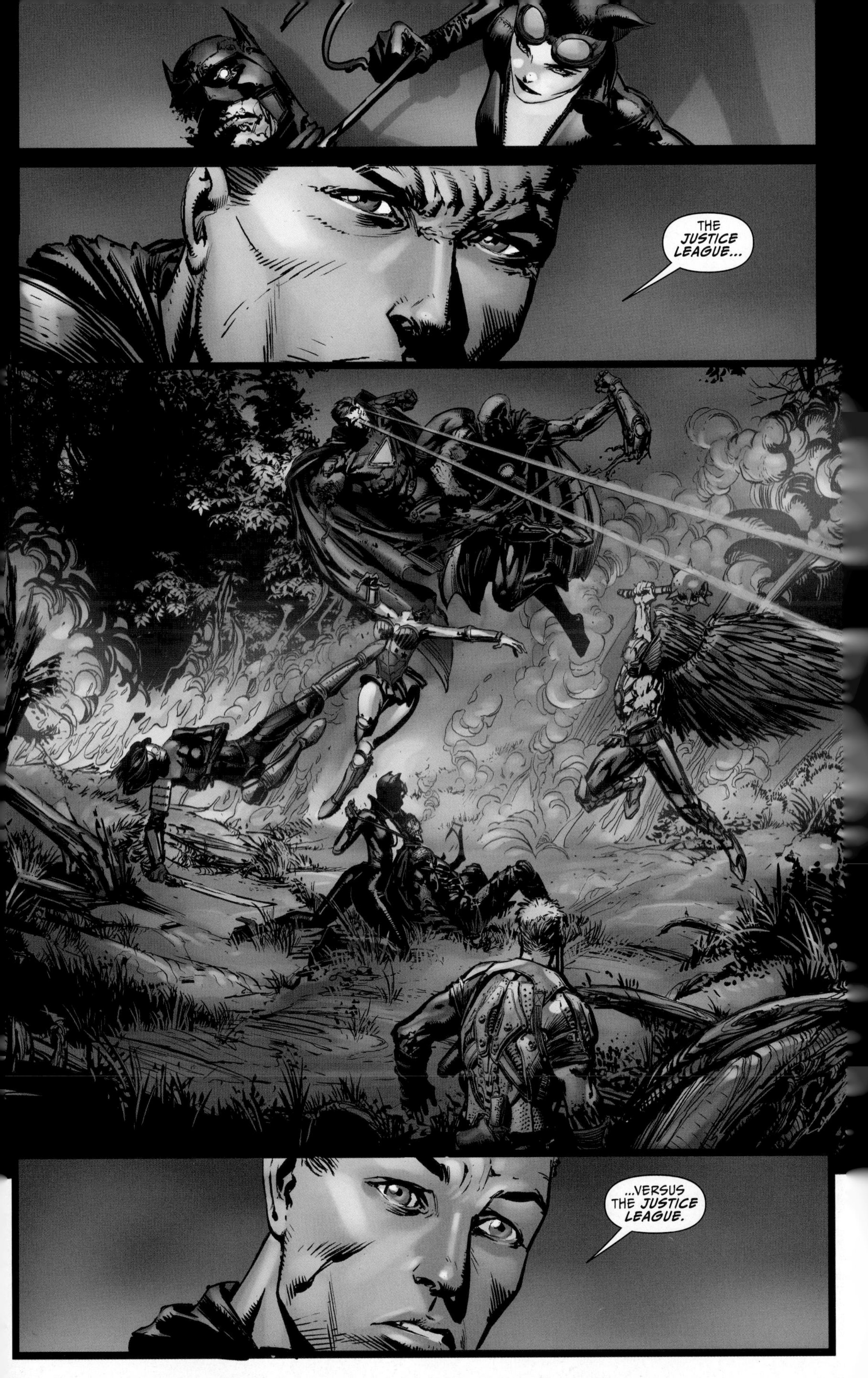
THE JUSTICE LEAGUE...
...VERSUS THE JUSTICE LEAGUE.

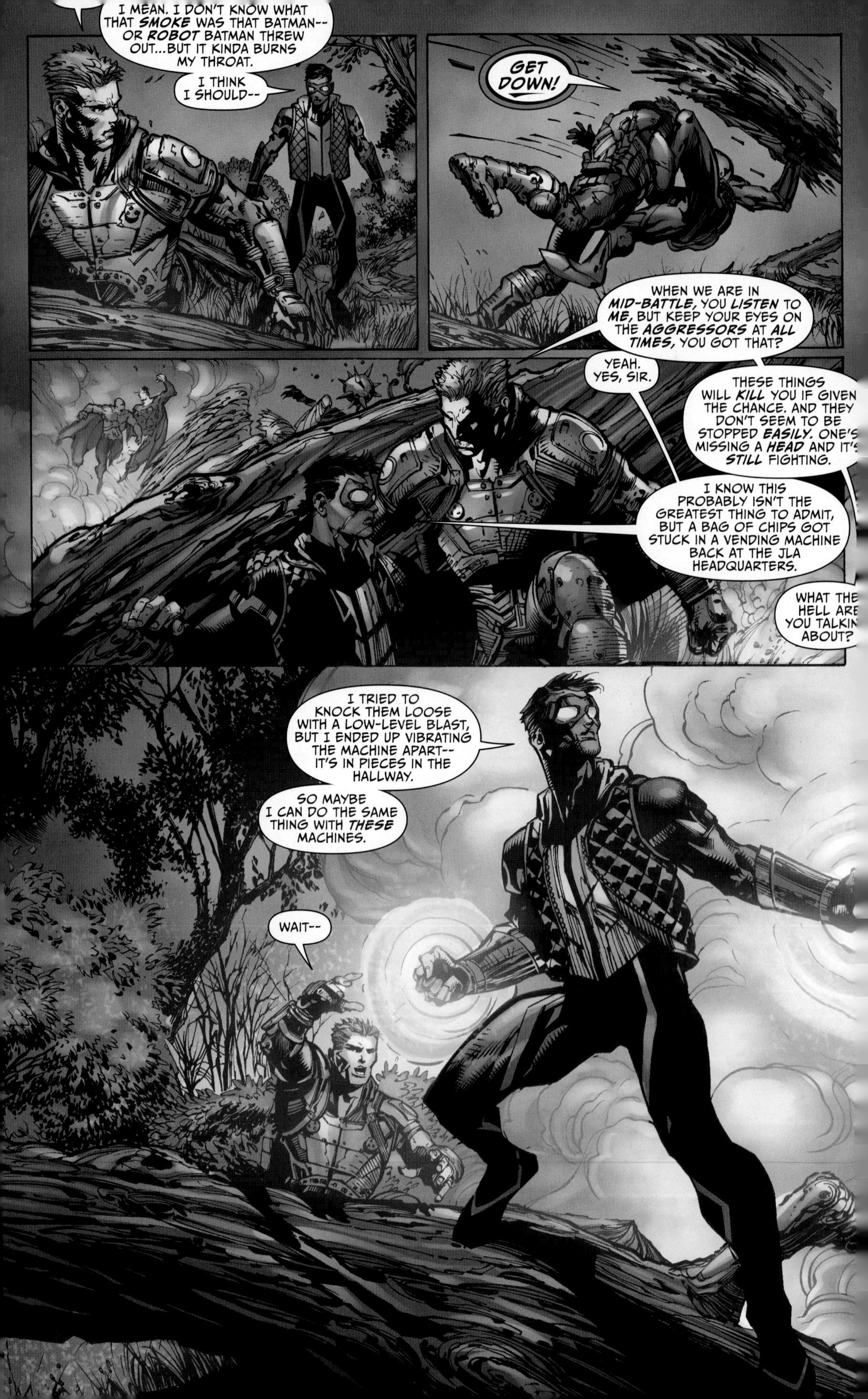
I MEAN. I DON'T KNOW WHAT THAT SMOKE WAS THAT BATMAN-- OR ROBOT BATMAN THREW OUT...BUT IT KINDA BURNS MY THROAT.
I THINK I SHOULD--
GET DOWN!
WHEN WE ARE IN MID-BATTLE, YOU LISTEN TO ME, BUT KEEP YOUR EYES ON THE AGGRESSORS AT ALL TIMES, YOU GOT THAT?
YEAH. YES, SIR.
THESE THINGS WILL KILL YOU IF GIVEN THE CHANCE. AND THEY DON'T SEEM TO BE STOPPED EASILY. ONE'S MISSING A HEAD AND IT'S STILL FIGHTING.
I KNOW THIS PROBABLY ISN'T THE GREATEST THING TO ADMIT, BUT A BAG OF CHIPS GOT STUCK IN A VENDING MACHINE BACK AT THE JLA HEADQUARTERS.
WHAT THE HELL ARE YOU TALKIN' ABOUT?
I TRIED TO KNOCK THEM LOOSE WITH A LOW-LEVEL BLAST, BUT I ENDED UP VIBRATING THE MACHINE APART-- IT'S IN PIECES IN THE HALLWAY.
SO MAYBE I CAN DO THE SAME THING WITH THESE MACHINES.
WAIT--

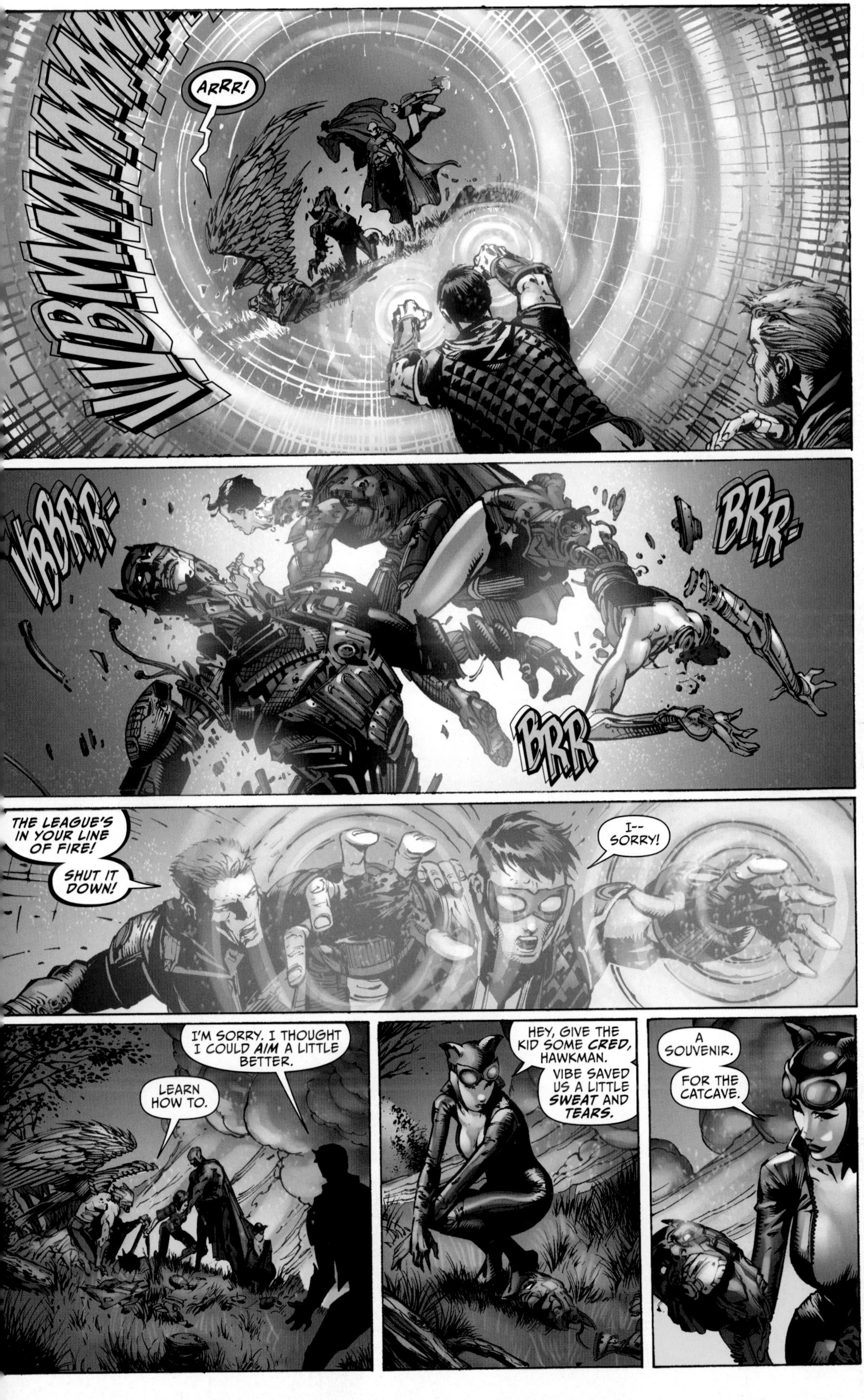

VVBMMMMMM
ARRR!
VBBRR-
BRR-
BRR
THE LEAGUE'S IN YOUR LINE OF FIRE!
SHUT IT DOWN!
I-- SORRY!
I'M SORRY. I THOUGHT I COULD AIM A LITTLE BETTER.
LEARN HOW TO.
HEY, GIVE THE KID SOME CRED, HAWKMAN.
VIBE SAVED US A LITTLE SWEAT AND TEARS.
A SOUVENIR.
FOR THE CATCAVE.

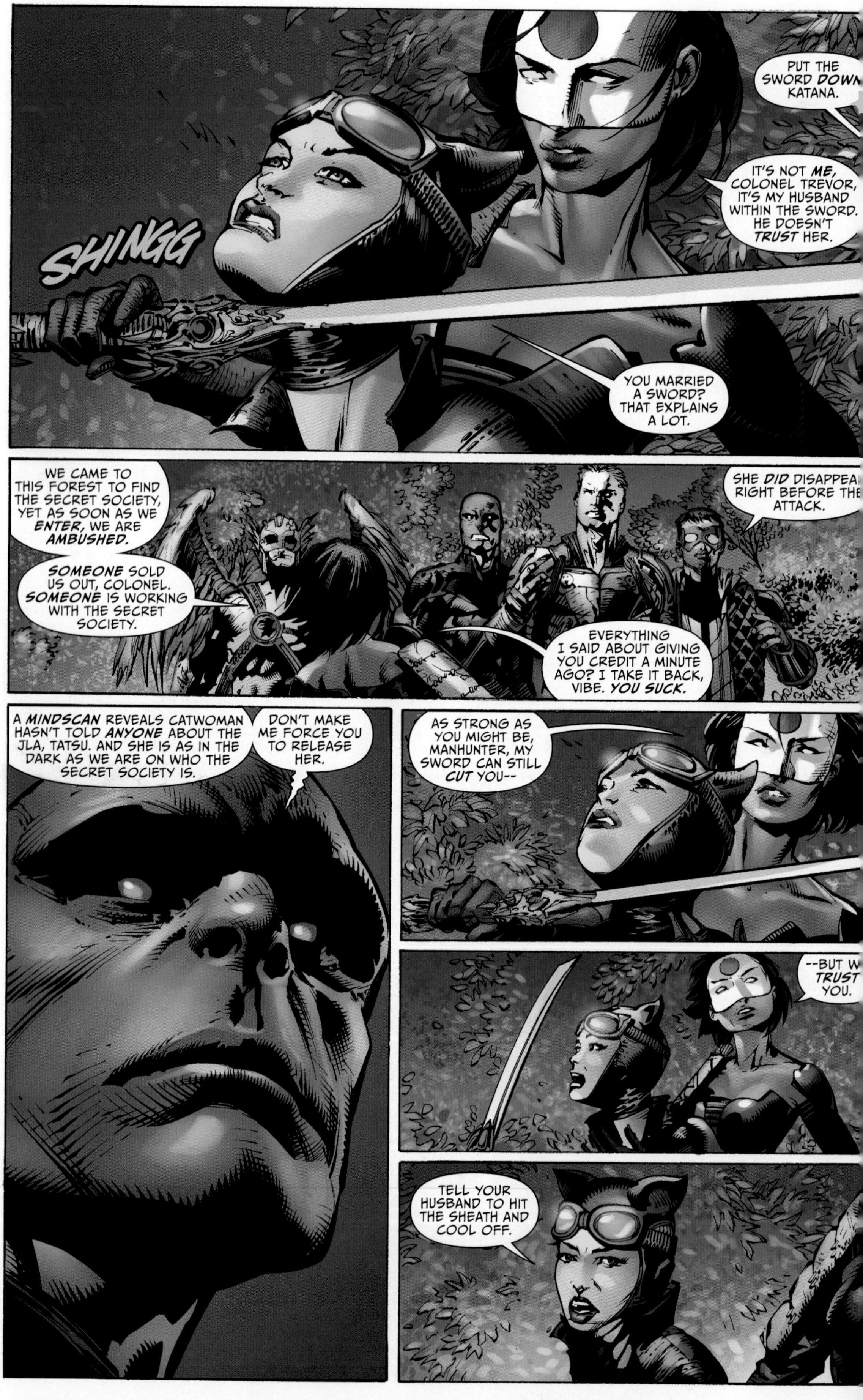
PUT THE SWORD DOWN KATANA.
IT'S NOT ME, COLONEL TREVOR, IT'S MY HUSBAND WITHIN THE SWORD. HE DOESN'T TRUST HER.
SHINGG
YOU MARRIED A SWORD? THAT EXPLAINS A LOT.
WE CAME TO THIS FOREST TO FIND THE SECRET SOCIETY, YET AS SOON AS WE ENTER, WE ARE AMBUSHED.
SOMEONE SOLD US OUT, COLONEL. SOMEONE IS WORKING WITH THE SECRET SOCIETY.
SHE DID DISAPPEA RIGHT BEFORE THE ATTACK.
EVERYTHING I SAID ABOUT GIVING YOU CREDIT A MINUTE AGO? I TAKE IT BACK, VIBE. YOU SUCK.
A MINDSCAN REVEALS CATWOMAN HASN'T TOLD ANYONE ABOUT THE JLA, TATSU. AND SHE IS AS IN THE DARK AS WE ARE ON WHO THE SECRET SOCIETY IS.
DON'T MAKE ME FORCE YOU TO RELEASE HER.
AS STRONG AS YOU MIGHT BE, MANHUNTER, MY SWORD CAN STILL CUT YOU--
--BUT W TRUST YOU.
TELL YOUR HUSBAND TO HIT THE SHEATH AND COOL OFF.

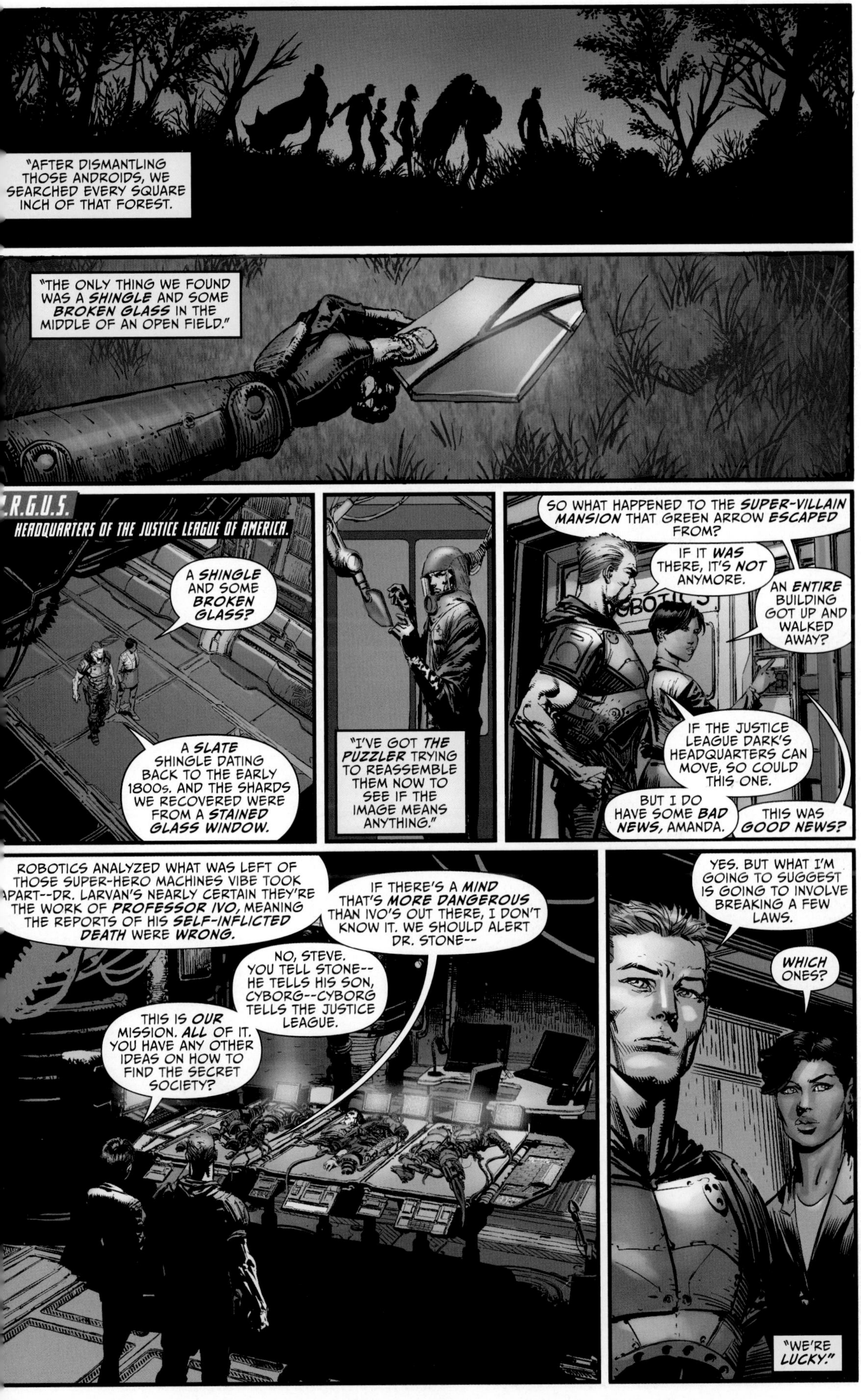
"AFTER DISMANTLING THOSE ANDROIDS, WE SEARCHED EVERY SQUARE INCH OF THAT FOREST.
"THE ONLY THING WE FOUND WAS A SHINGLE AND SOME BROKEN GLASS IN THE MIDDLE OF AN OPEN FIELD."
A.R.G.U.S.
HEADQUARTERS OF THE JUSTICE LEAGUE OF AMERICA.
A SHINGLE AND SOME BROKEN GLASS?
A SLATE SHINGLE DATING BACK TO THE EARLY 1800s. AND THE SHARDS WE RECOVERED WERE FROM A STAINED GLASS WINDOW.
"I'VE GOT THE PUZZLER TRYING TO REASSEMBLE THEM NOW TO SEE IF THE IMAGE MEANS ANYTHING."
SO WHAT HAPPENED TO THE SUPER-VILLAIN MANSION THAT GREEN ARROW ESCAPED FROM?
IF IT WAS THERE, IT'S NOT ANYMORE.
AN ENTIRE BUILDING GOT UP AND WALKED AWAY?
IF THE JUSTICE LEAGUE DARK'S HEADQUARTERS CAN MOVE, SO COULD THIS ONE.
BUT I DO HAVE SOME BAD NEWS, AMANDA.
THIS WAS GOOD NEWS?
ROBOTICS ANALYZED WHAT WAS LEFT OF THOSE SUPER-HERO MACHINES VIBE TOOK APART--DR. LARVAN'S NEARLY CERTAIN THEY'RE THE WORK OF PROFESSOR IVO, MEANING THE REPORTS OF HIS SELF-INFLICTED DEATH WERE WRONG.
IF THERE'S A MIND THAT'S MORE DANGEROUS THAN IVO'S OUT THERE, I DON'T KNOW IT. WE SHOULD ALERT DR. STONE--
NO, STEVE. YOU TELL STONE--HE TELLS HIS SON, CYBORG--CYBORG TELLS THE JUSTICE LEAGUE.
THIS IS OUR MISSION. ALL OF IT. YOU HAVE ANY OTHER IDEAS ON HOW TO FIND THE SECRET SOCIETY?
YES. BUT WHAT I'M GOING TO SUGGEST IS GOING TO INVOLVE BREAKING A FEW LAWS.
WHICH ONES?
"WE'RE LUCKY."

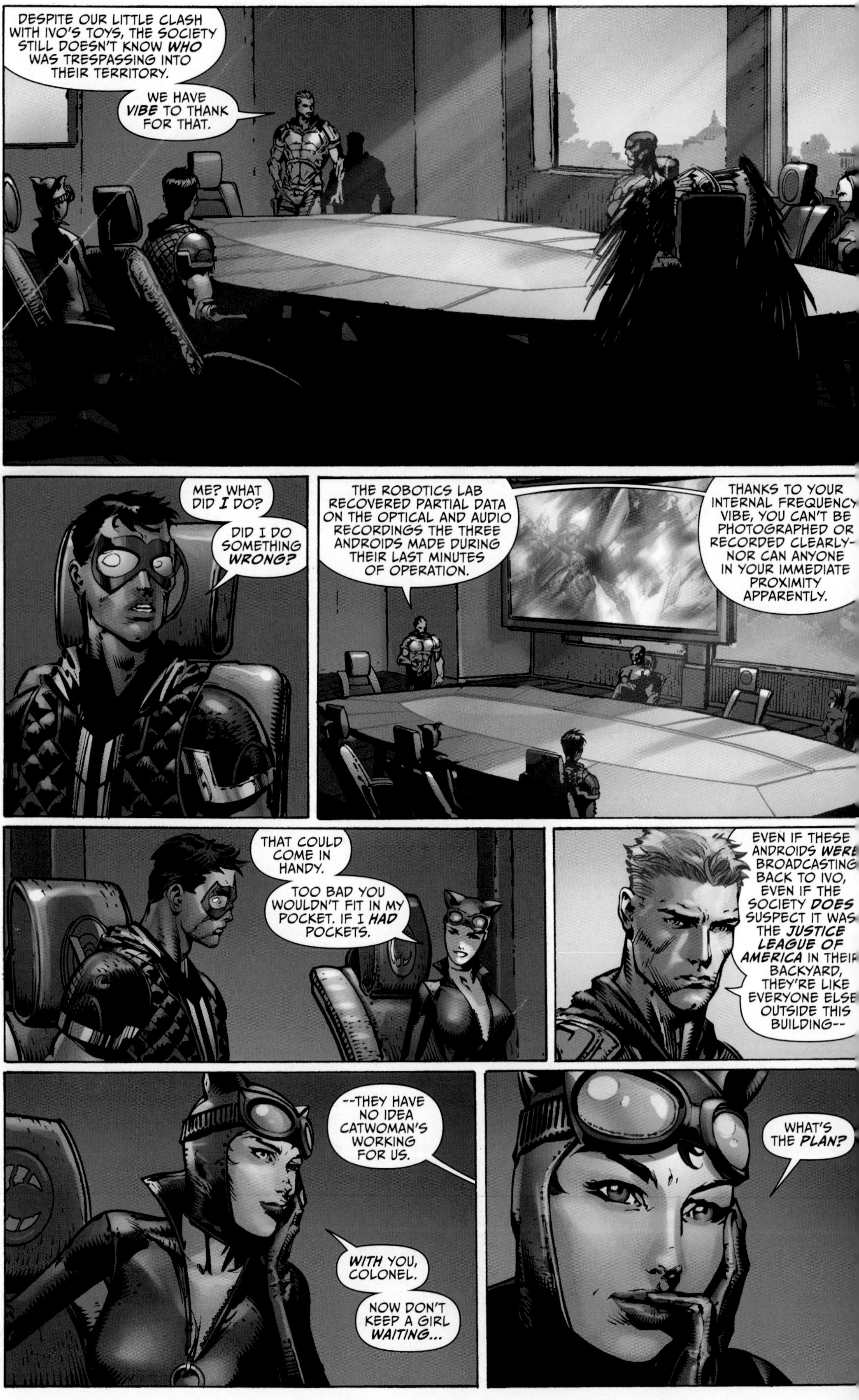

DESPITE OUR LITTLE CLASH WITH IVO'S TOYS, THE SOCIETY STILL DOESN'T KNOW *WHO* WAS TRESPASSING INTO THEIR TERRITORY.
WE HAVE *VIBE* TO THANK FOR THAT.
ME? WHAT DID *I* DO?
DID I DO SOMETHING *WRONG?*
THE ROBOTICS LAB RECOVERED PARTIAL DATA ON THE OPTICAL AND AUDIO RECORDINGS THE THREE ANDROIDS MADE DURING THEIR LAST MINUTES OF OPERATION.
THANKS TO YOUR INTERNAL FREQUENCY VIBE, YOU CAN'T BE PHOTOGRAPHED OR RECORDED CLEARLY-- NOR CAN ANYONE IN YOUR IMMEDIATE PROXIMITY APPARENTLY.
THAT COULD COME IN HANDY.
TOO BAD YOU WOULDN'T FIT IN MY POCKET. IF I *HAD* POCKETS.
EVEN IF THESE ANDROIDS *WERE* BROADCASTING BACK TO IVO, EVEN IF THE SOCIETY *DOES* SUSPECT IT WAS THE *JUSTICE LEAGUE OF AMERICA* IN THEIR BACKYARD, THEY'RE LIKE EVERYONE ELSE OUTSIDE THIS BUILDING--
--THEY HAVE NO IDEA CATWOMAN'S WORKING FOR US.
WITH YOU, COLONEL.
NOW DON'T KEEP A GIRL *WAITING...*
WHAT'S THE *PLAN?*

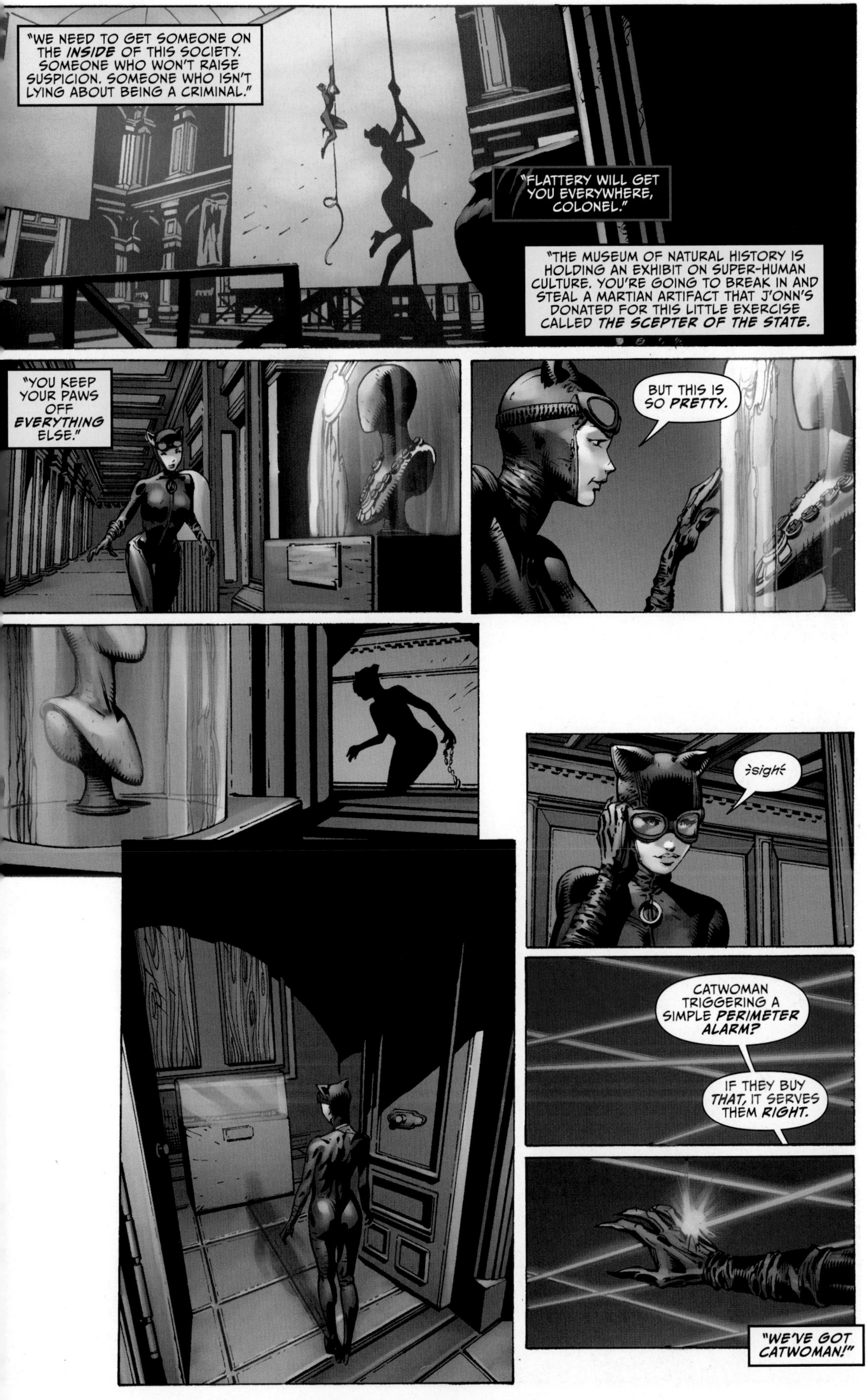

"WE NEED TO GET SOMEONE ON THE *INSIDE* OF THIS SOCIETY. SOMEONE WHO WON'T RAISE SUSPICION. SOMEONE WHO ISN'T LYING ABOUT BEING A CRIMINAL."
"FLATTERY WILL GET YOU EVERYWHERE, COLONEL."
"THE MUSEUM OF NATURAL HISTORY IS HOLDING AN EXHIBIT ON SUPER-HUMAN CULTURE. YOU'RE GOING TO BREAK IN AND STEAL A MARTIAN ARTIFACT THAT J'ONN'S DONATED FOR THIS LITTLE EXERCISE CALLED *THE SCEPTER OF THE STATE.*
"YOU KEEP YOUR PAWS OFF *EVERYTHING* ELSE."
BUT THIS IS SO *PRETTY.*
sigh
CATWOMAN TRIGGERING A SIMPLE *PERIMETER ALARM?*
IF THEY BUY *THAT,* IT SERVES THEM *RIGHT.*
"WE'VE GOT CATWOMAN!"

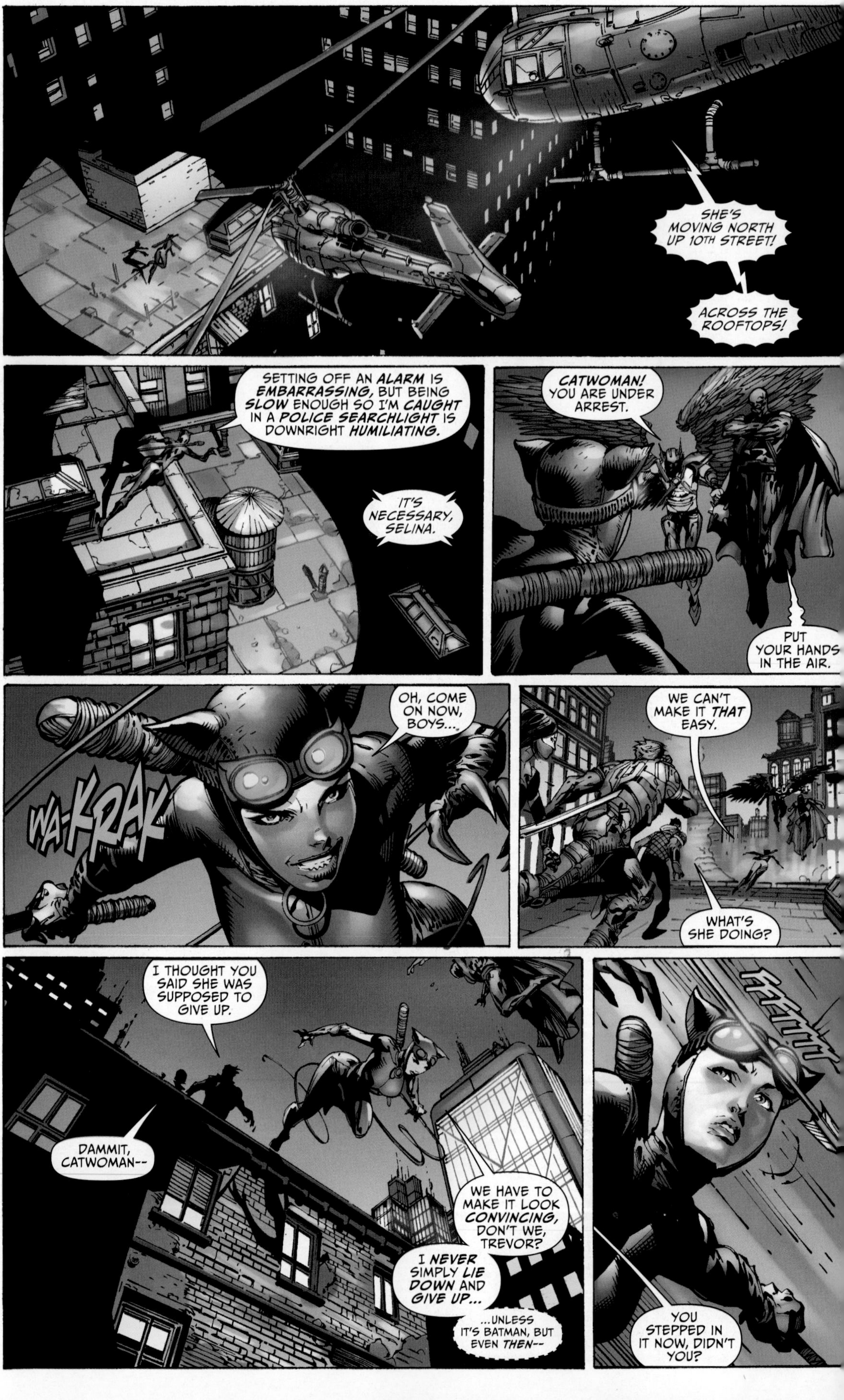
SHE'S MOVING NORTH UP 10TH STREET!
ACROSS THE ROOFTOPS!
SETTING OFF AN ALARM IS EMBARRASSING, BUT BEING SLOW ENOUGH SO I'M CAUGHT IN A POLICE SEARCHLIGHT IS DOWNRIGHT HUMILIATING.
IT'S NECESSARY, SELINA.
CATWOMAN! YOU ARE UNDER ARREST.
PUT YOUR HANDS IN THE AIR.
OH, COME ON NOW, BOYS...
WA-KRAK
WE CAN'T MAKE IT THAT EASY.
WHAT'S SHE DOING?
I THOUGHT YOU SAID SHE WAS SUPPOSED TO GIVE UP.
DAMMIT, CATWOMAN--
WE HAVE TO MAKE IT LOOK CONVINCING, DON'T WE, TREVOR?
I NEVER SIMPLY LIE DOWN AND GIVE UP...
...UNLESS IT'S BATMAN, BUT EVEN THEN--
YOU STEPPED IN IT NOW, DIDN'T YOU?

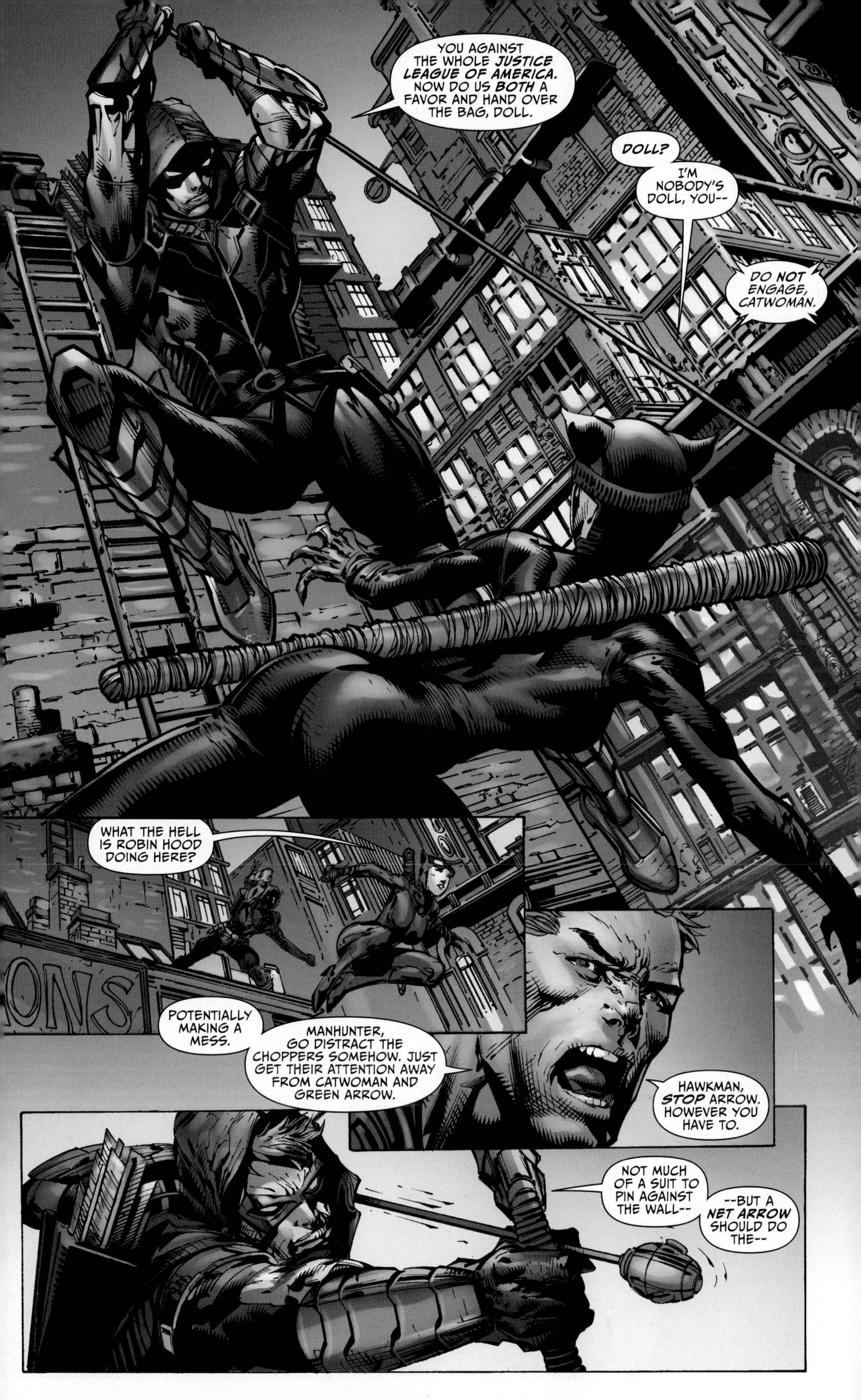
YOU AGAINST THE WHOLE *JUSTICE LEAGUE OF AMERICA.* NOW DO US *BOTH* A FAVOR AND HAND OVER THE BAG, DOLL.
DOLL?
I'M NOBODY'S DOLL, YOU--
DO *NOT* ENGAGE, CATWOMAN.
WHAT THE HELL IS ROBIN HOOD DOING HERE?
POTENTIALLY MAKING A MESS.
MANHUNTER, GO DISTRACT THE CHOPPERS SOMEHOW. JUST GET THEIR ATTENTION AWAY FROM CATWOMAN AND GREEN ARROW.
HAWKMAN, *STOP* ARROW. HOWEVER YOU HAVE TO.
NOT MUCH OF A SUIT TO PIN AGAINST THE WALL--
--BUT A *NET ARROW* SHOULD DO THE--

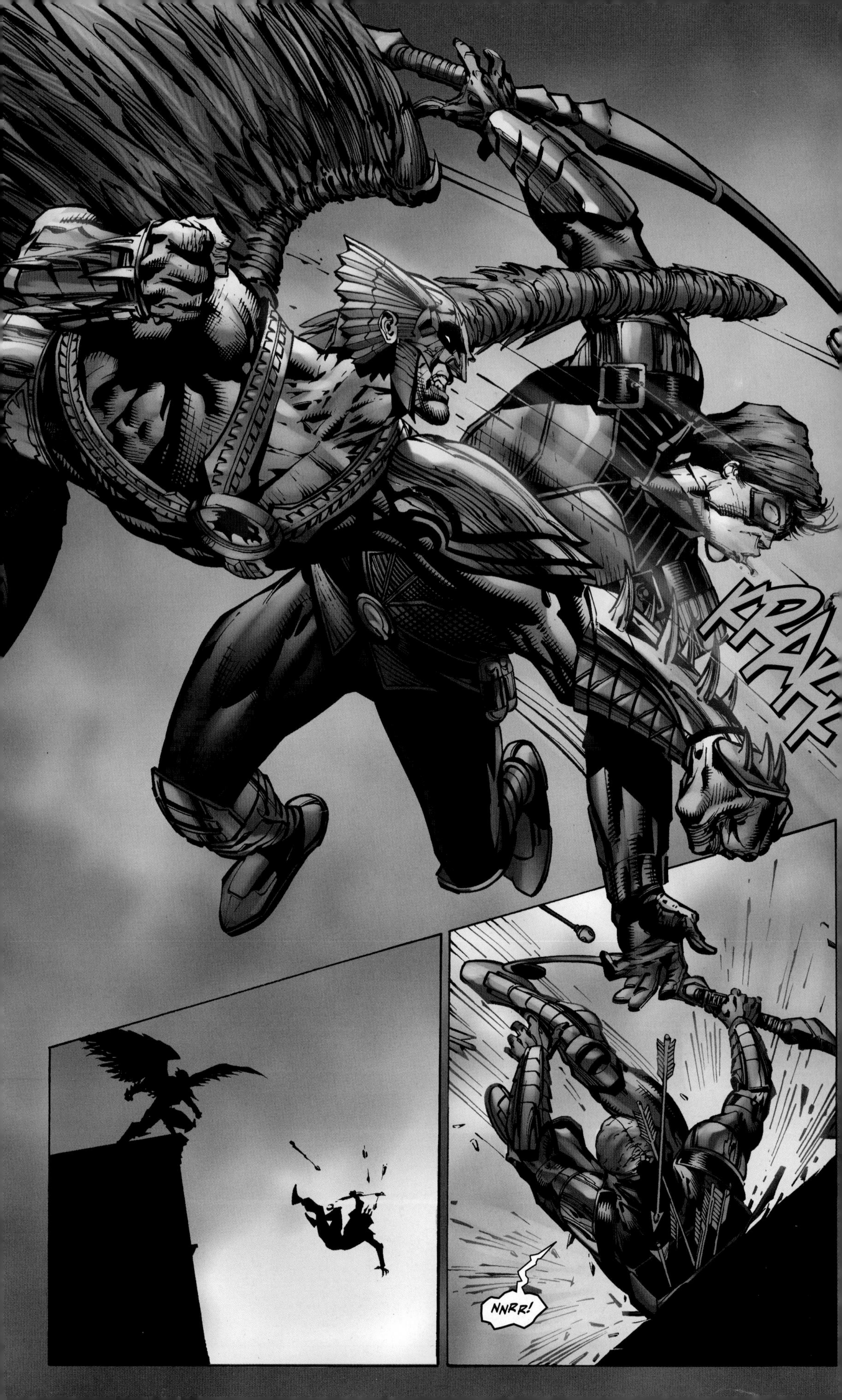
NNRR!

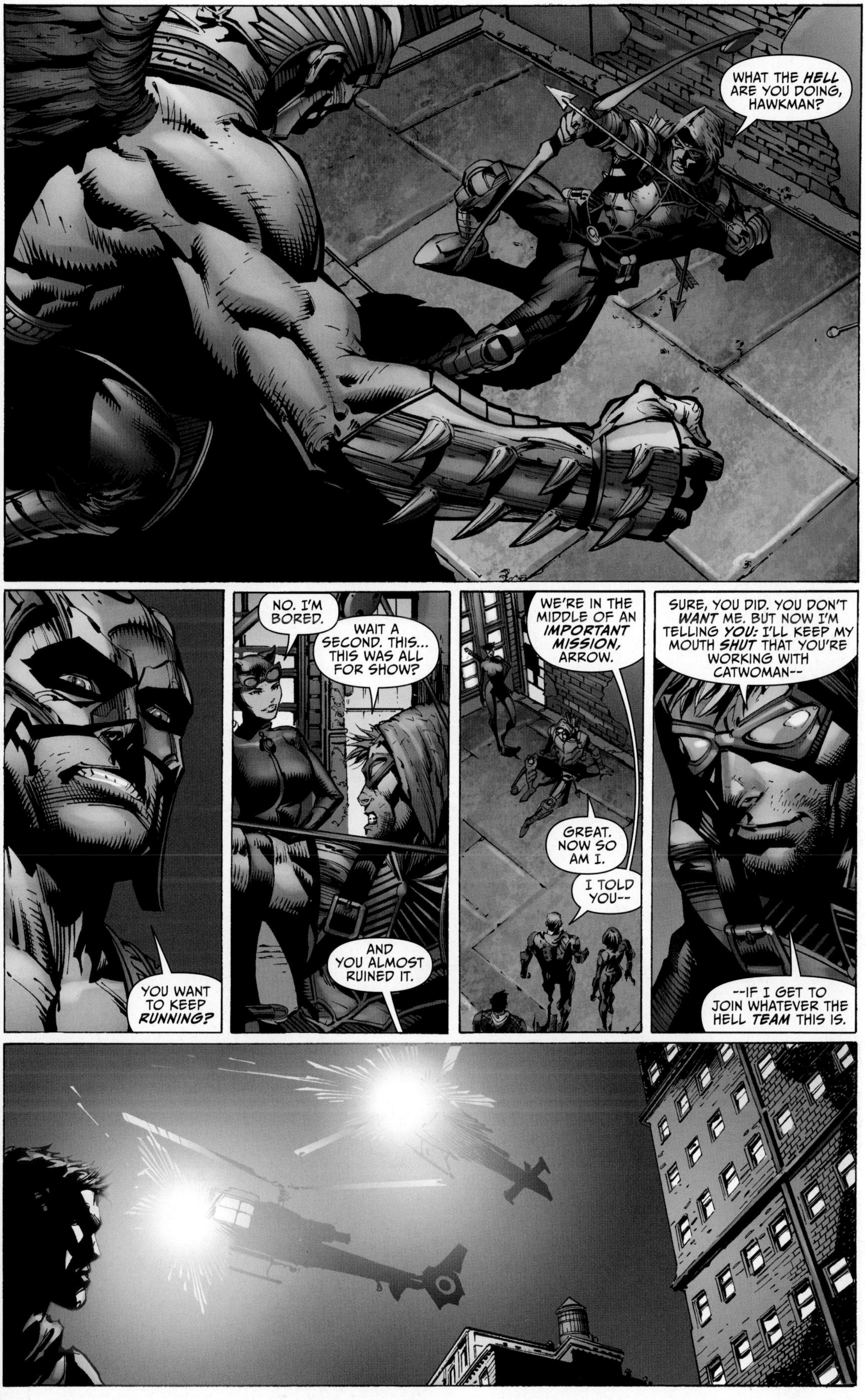
WHAT THE *HELL* ARE YOU DOING, HAWKMAN?
YOU WANT TO KEEP *RUNNING?*
NO. I'M BORED.
WAIT A SECOND. THIS... THIS WAS ALL FOR SHOW?
AND YOU ALMOST RUINED IT.
WE'RE IN THE MIDDLE OF AN *IMPORTANT MISSION,* ARROW.
GREAT. NOW SO AM I.
I TOLD YOU--
SURE, YOU DID. YOU DON'T *WANT* ME. BUT NOW I'M TELLING *YOU:* I'LL KEEP MY MOUTH *SHUT* THAT YOU'RE WORKING WITH CATWOMAN--
--IF I GET TO JOIN WHATEVER THE HELL *TEAM* THIS IS.

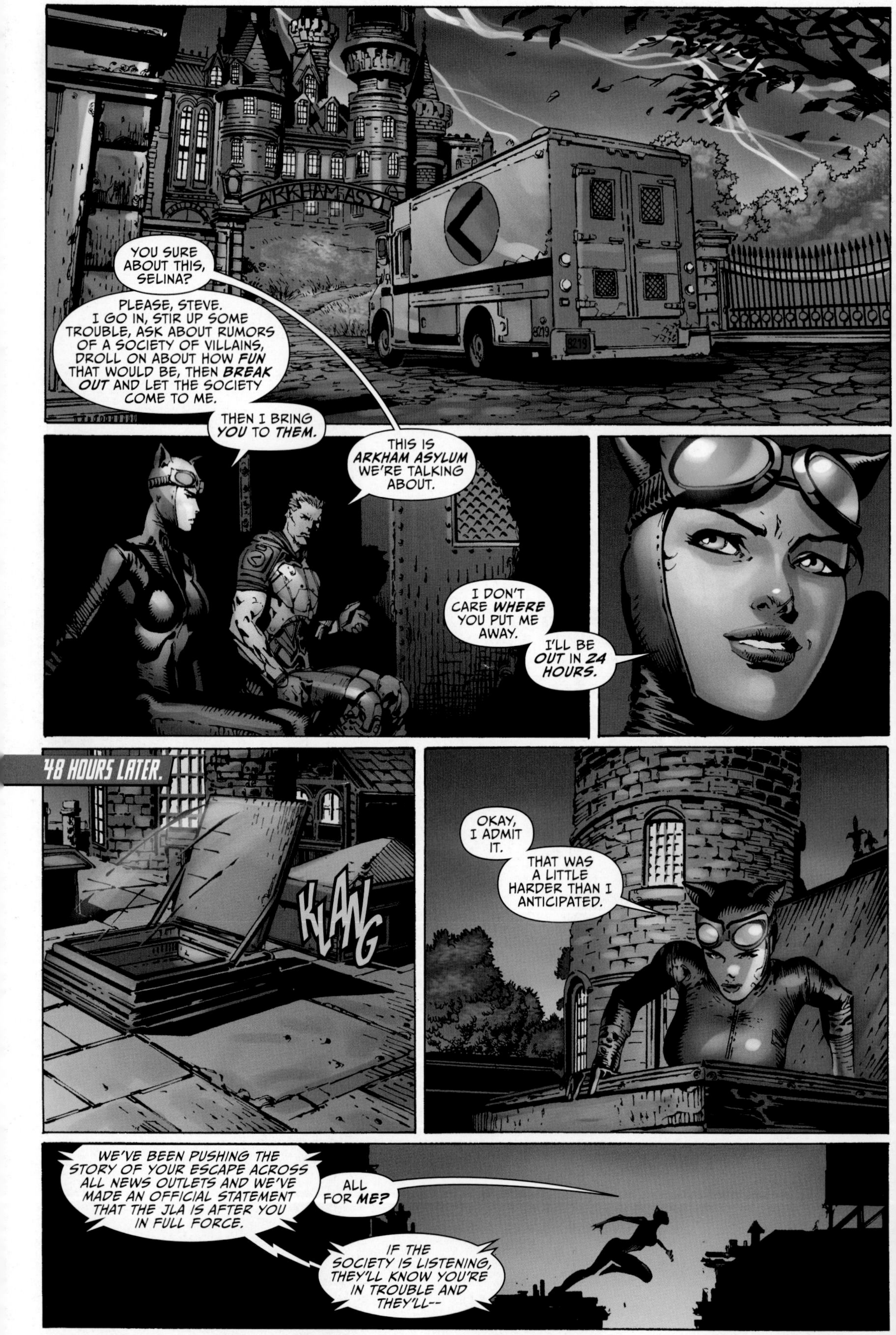
YOU SURE ABOUT THIS, SELINA?
PLEASE, STEVE. I GO IN, STIR UP SOME TROUBLE, ASK ABOUT RUMORS OF A SOCIETY OF VILLAINS, DROLL ON ABOUT HOW FUN THAT WOULD BE, THEN BREAK OUT AND LET THE SOCIETY COME TO ME.
THEN I BRING YOU TO THEM.
THIS IS ARKHAM ASYLUM WE'RE TALKING ABOUT.
I DON'T CARE WHERE YOU PUT ME AWAY.
I'LL BE OUT IN 24 HOURS.
48 HOURS LATER.
KLANG
OKAY, I ADMIT IT.
THAT WAS A LITTLE HARDER THAN I ANTICIPATED.
WE'VE BEEN PUSHING THE STORY OF YOUR ESCAPE ACROSS ALL NEWS OUTLETS AND WE'VE MADE AN OFFICIAL STATEMENT THAT THE JLA IS AFTER YOU IN FULL FORCE.
ALL FOR ME?
IF THE SOCIETY IS LISTENING, THEY'LL KNOW YOU'RE IN TROUBLE AND THEY'LL--

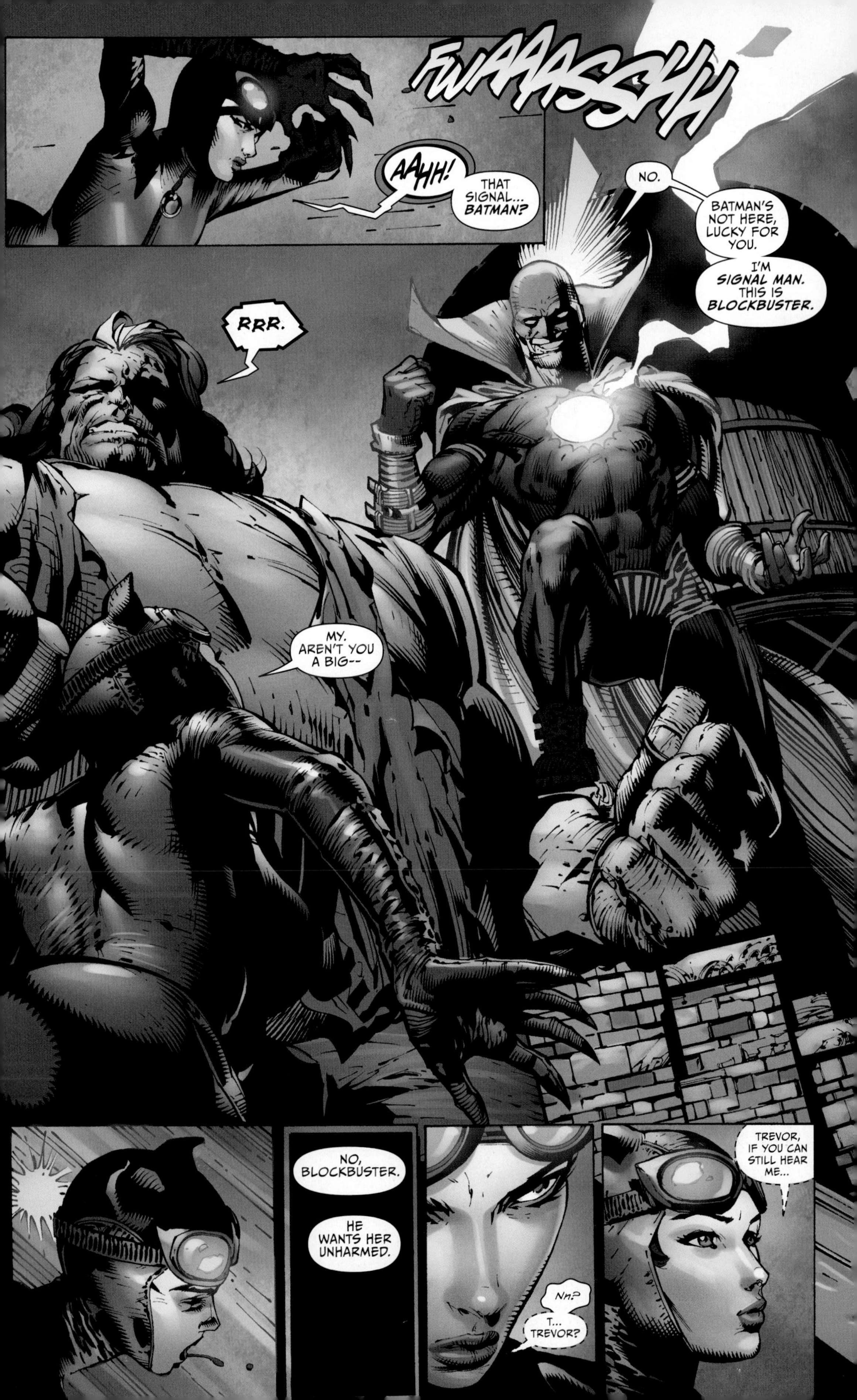
FWAAASSHH
AAHH!
THAT SIGNAL... BATMAN?
NO.
BATMAN'S NOT HERE, LUCKY FOR YOU.
I'M SIGNAL MAN. THIS IS BLOCKBUSTER.
RRR.
MY. AREN'T YOU A BIG--
NO, BLOCKBUSTER.
HE WANTS HER UNHARMED.
Nn?
T... TREVOR?
TREVOR, IF YOU CAN STILL HEAR ME...

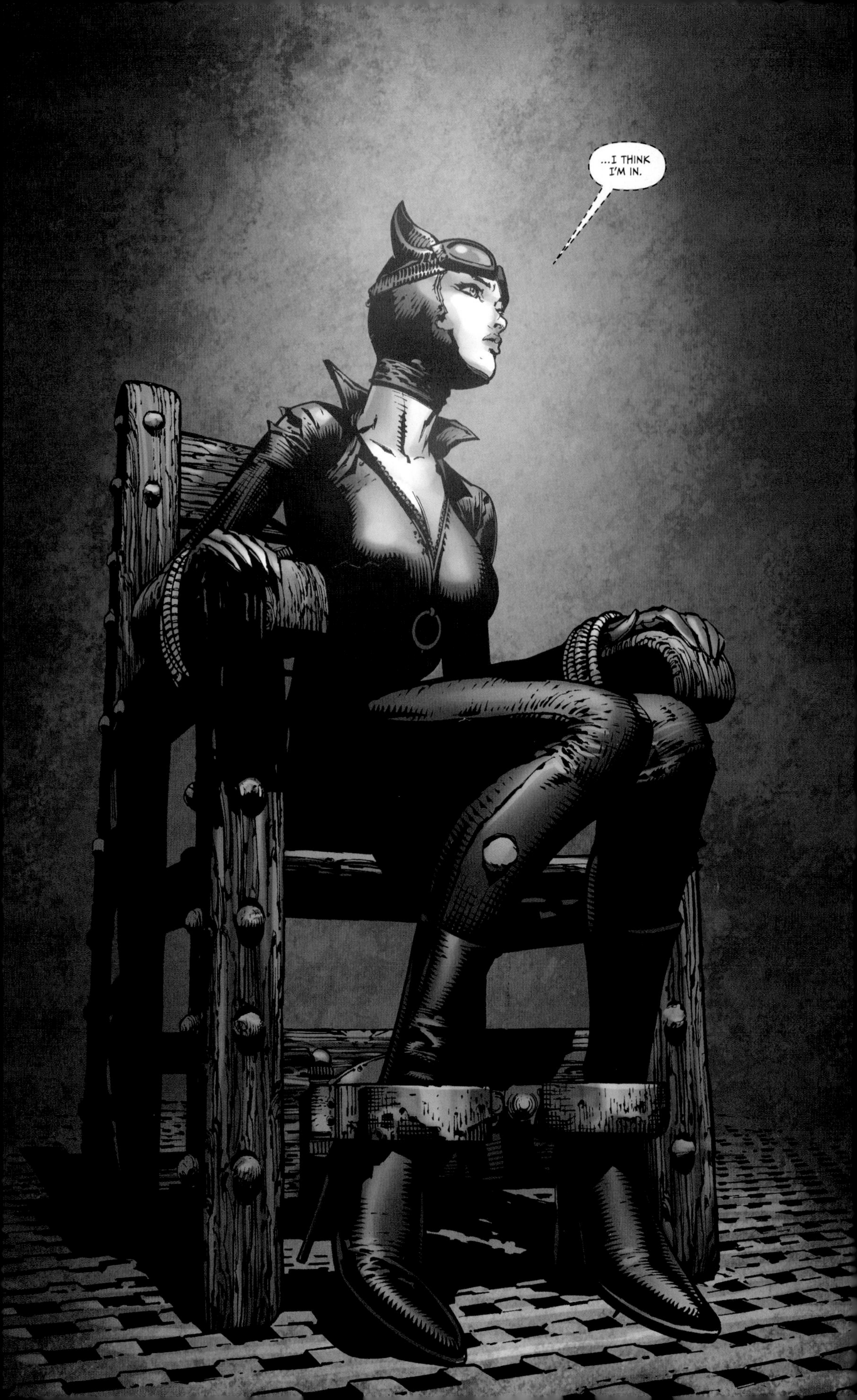
...I THINK I'M IN.

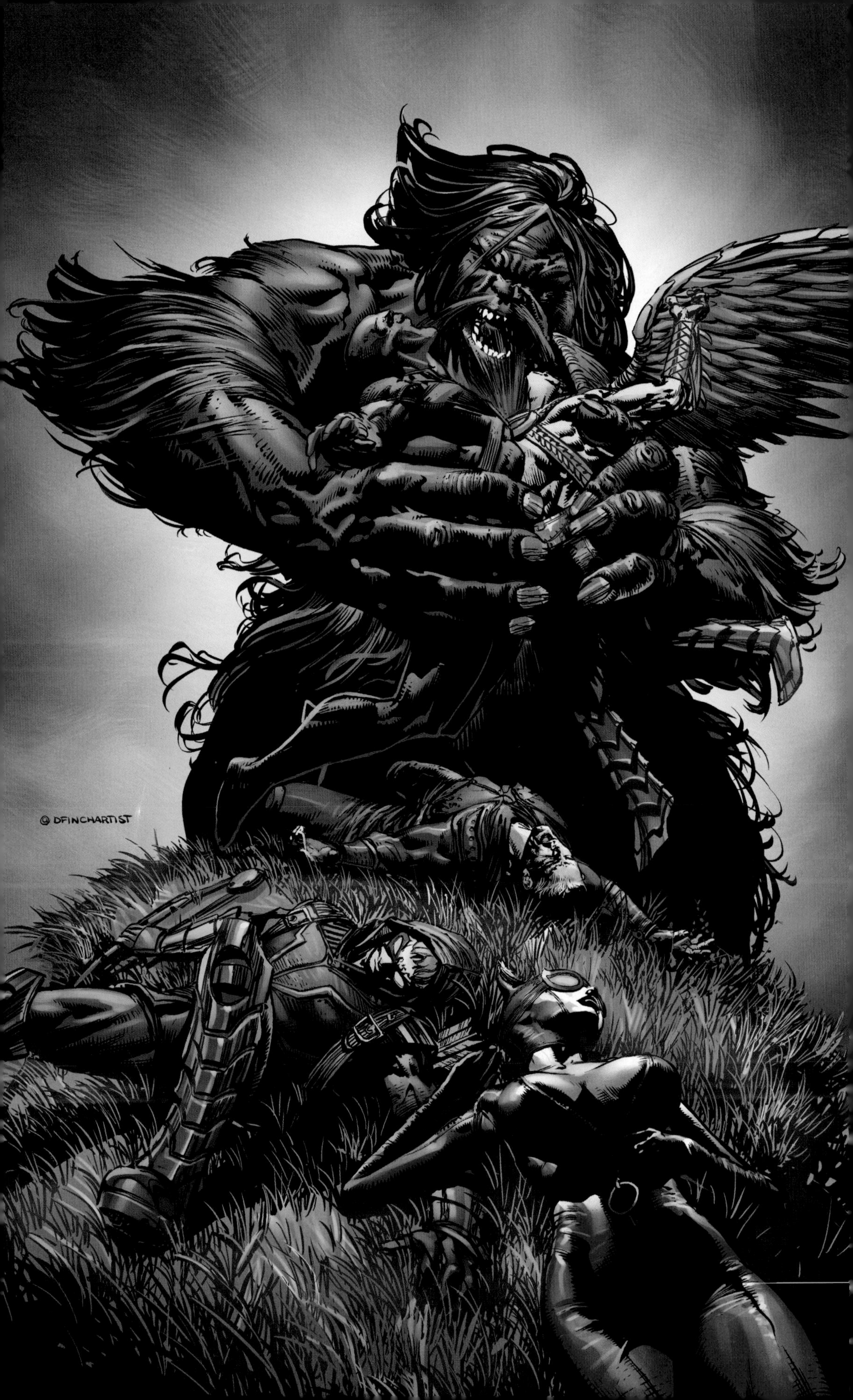
@ DFINCHARTIST

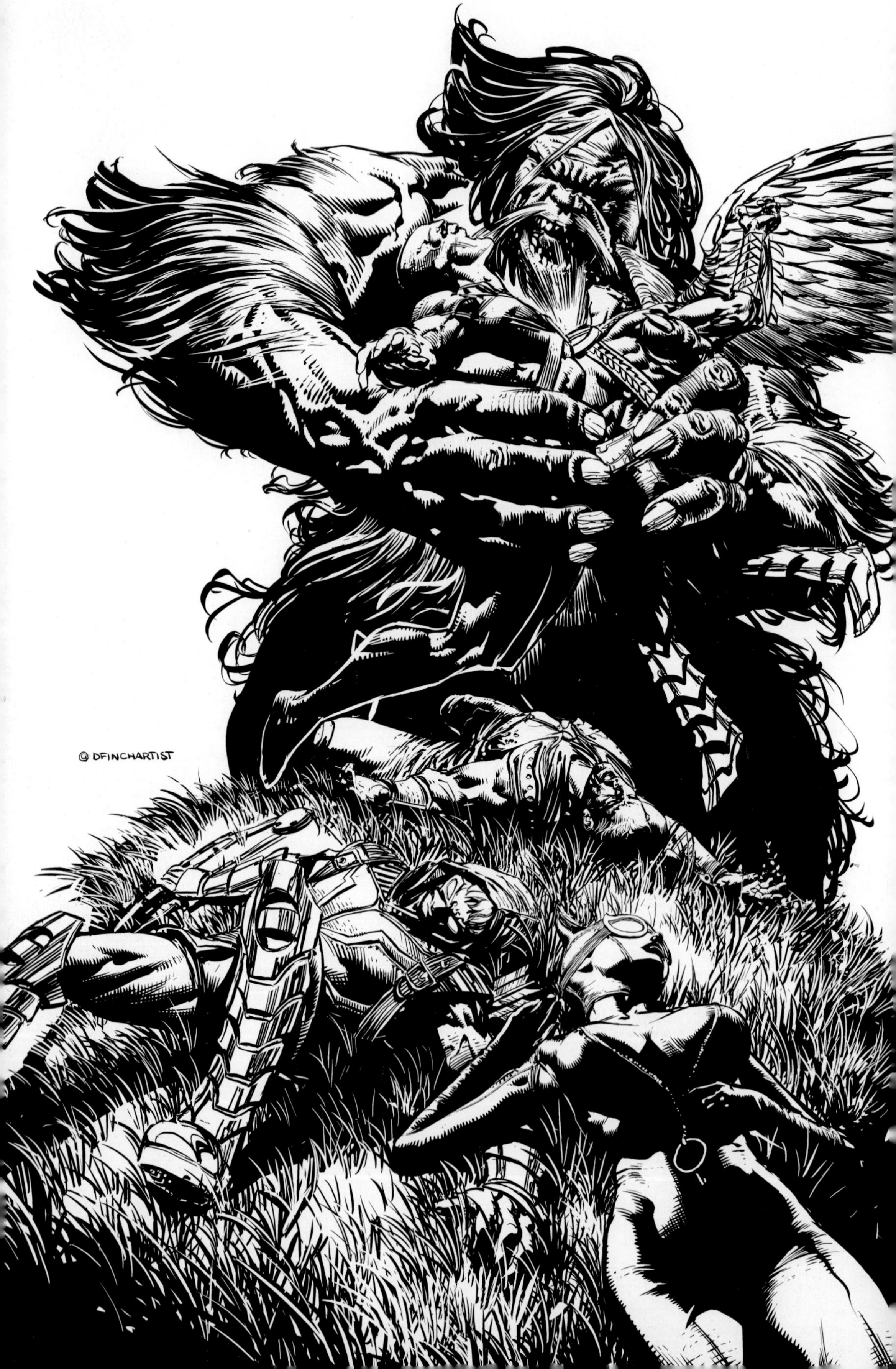
@DFINCHARTIST

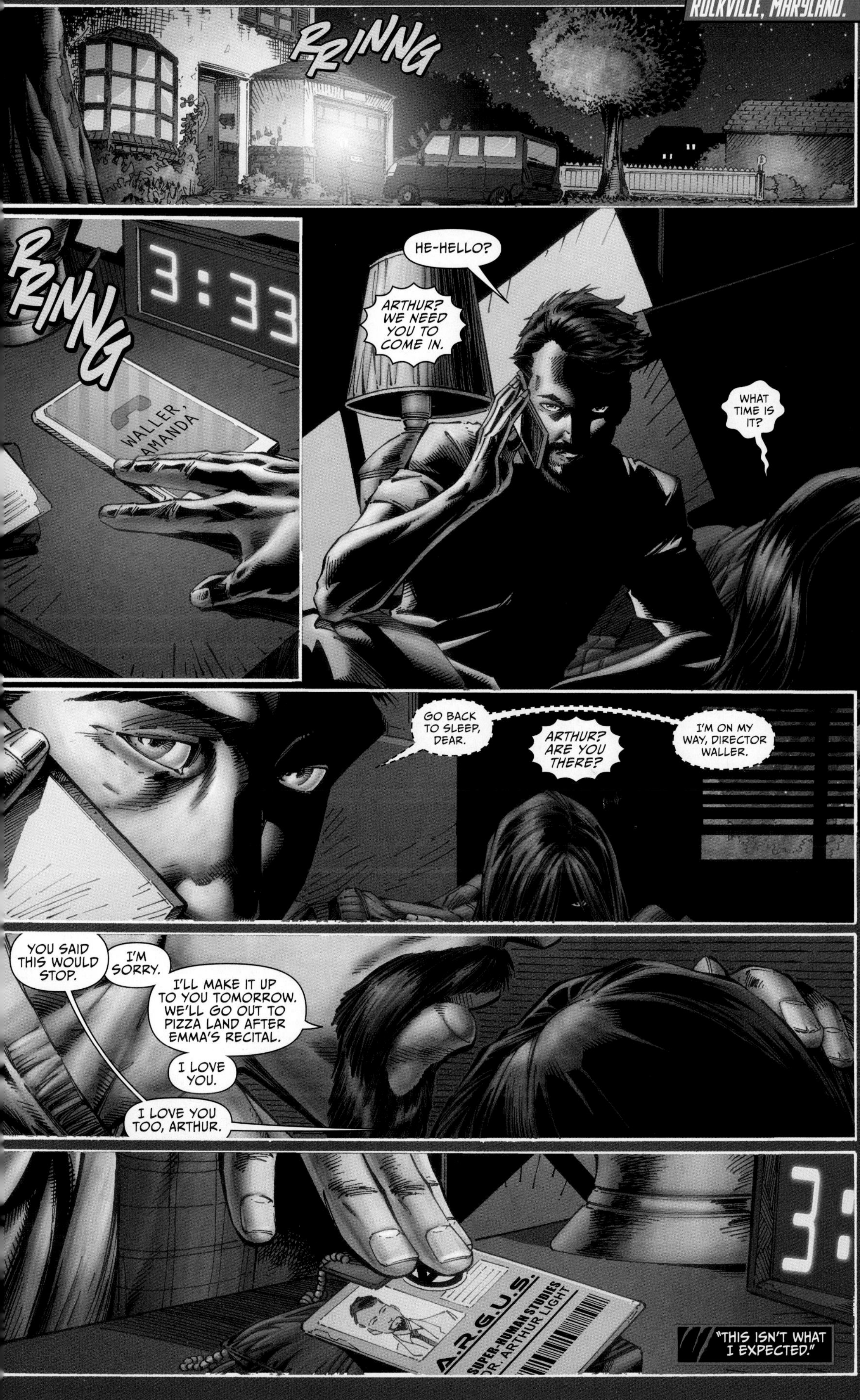
ROCKVILLE, MARYLAND.
RRINNG
RRINNG
3:33
WALLER, AMANDA
HE-HELLO?
ARTHUR? WE NEED YOU TO COME IN.
WHAT TIME IS IT?
GO BACK TO SLEEP, DEAR.
ARTHUR? ARE YOU THERE?
I'M ON MY WAY, DIRECTOR WALLER.
YOU SAID THIS WOULD STOP.
I'M SORRY.
I'LL MAKE IT UP TO YOU TOMORROW. WE'LL GO OUT TO PIZZA LAND AFTER EMMA'S RECITAL.
I LOVE YOU.
I LOVE YOU TOO, ARTHUR.
A.R.G.U.S.
SUPER-HUMAN STUDIES
DR. ARTHUR LIGHT
"THIS ISN'T WHAT I EXPECTED."

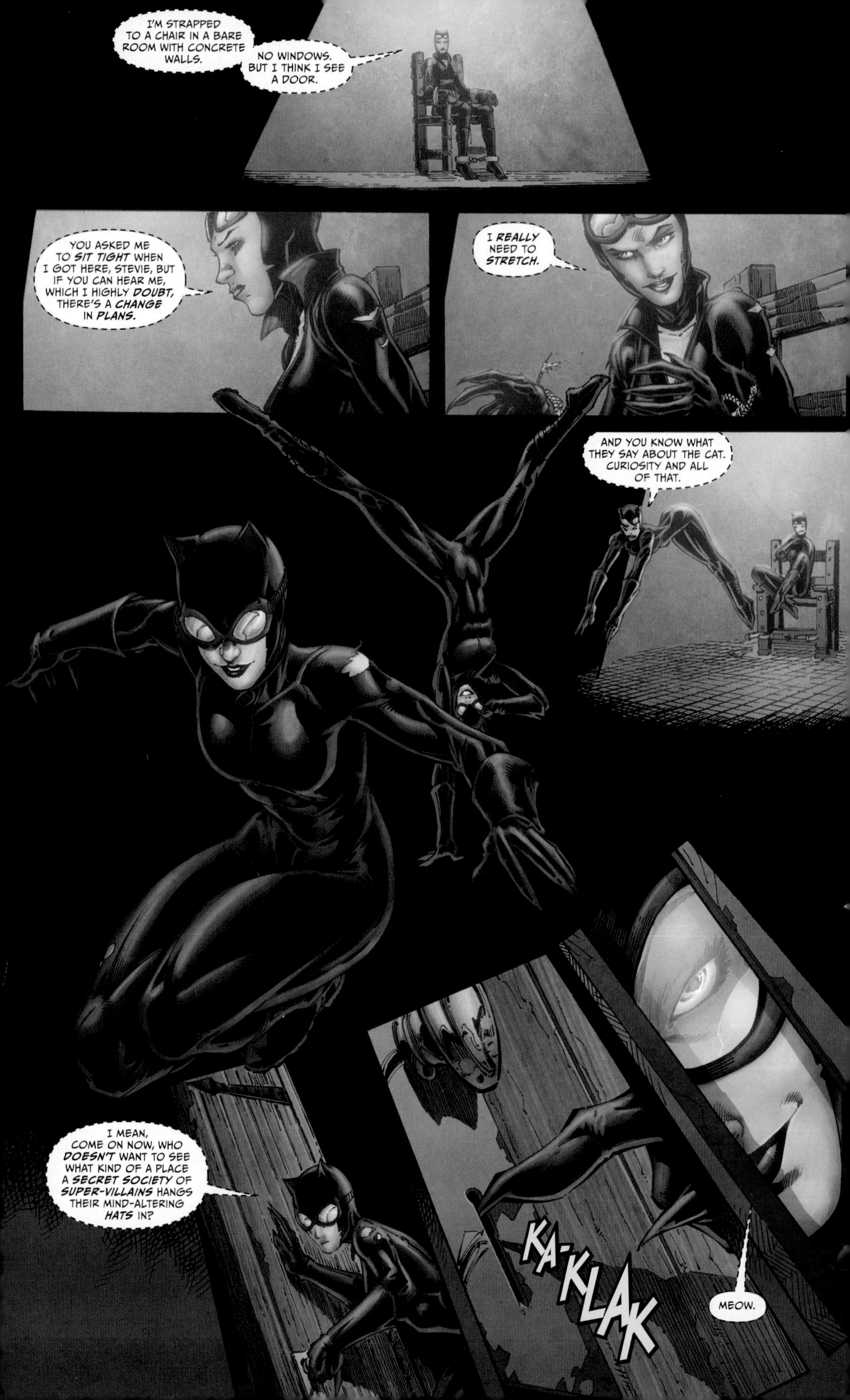
I'M STRAPPED TO A CHAIR IN A BARE ROOM WITH CONCRETE WALLS.
NO WINDOWS. BUT I THINK I SEE A DOOR.
YOU ASKED ME TO SIT TIGHT WHEN I GOT HERE, STEVIE, BUT IF YOU CAN HEAR ME, WHICH I HIGHLY DOUBT, THERE'S A CHANGE IN PLANS.
I REALLY NEED TO STRETCH.
AND YOU KNOW WHAT THEY SAY ABOUT THE CAT. CURIOSITY AND ALL OF THAT.
I MEAN, COME ON NOW, WHO DOESN'T WANT TO SEE WHAT KIND OF A PLACE A SECRET SOCIETY OF SUPER-VILLAINS HANGS THEIR MIND-ALTERING HATS IN?
KA-KLAK
MEOW.

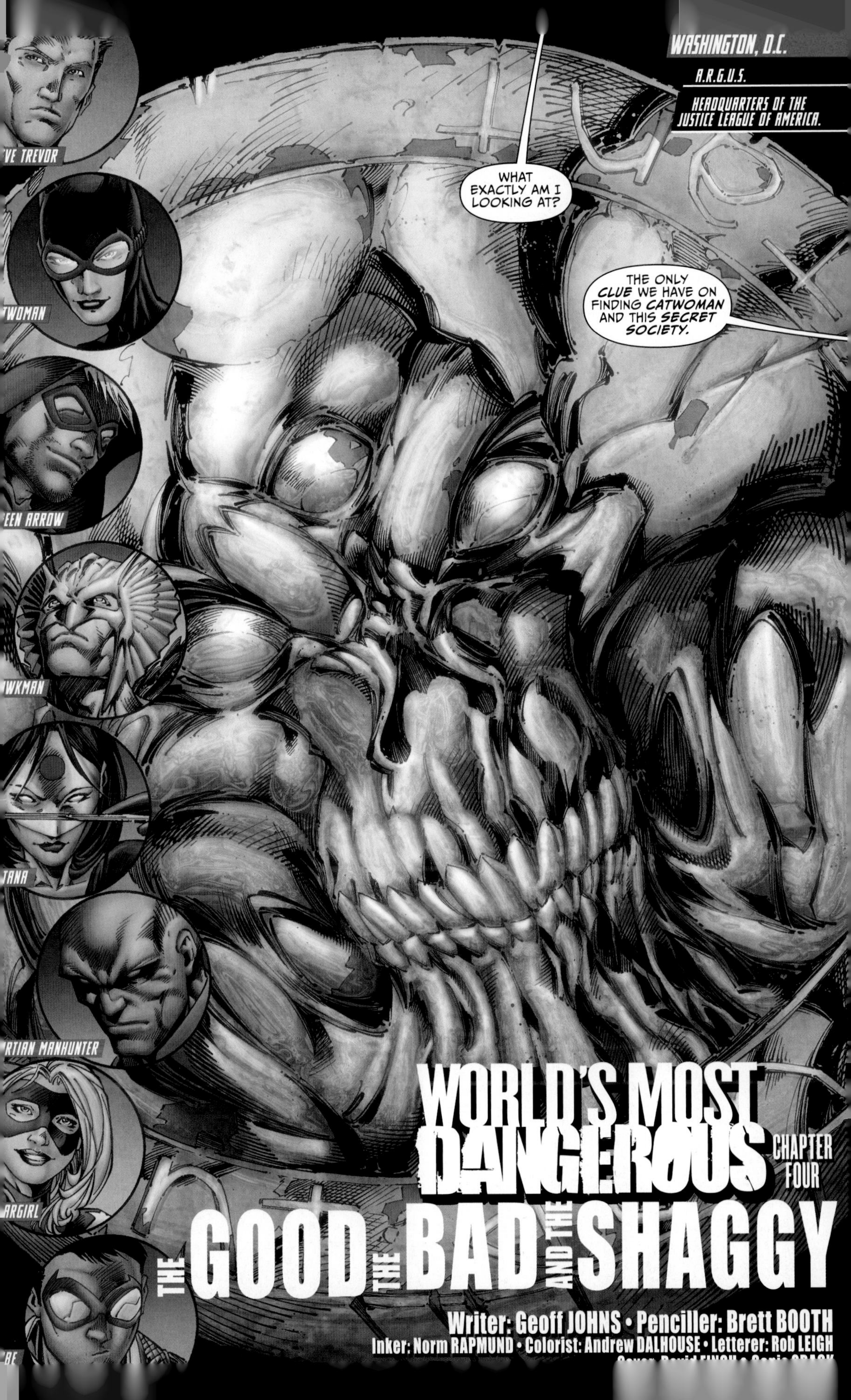
WASHINGTON, D.C.
A.R.G.U.S.
HEADQUARTERS OF THE JUSTICE LEAGUE OF AMERICA.
WHAT EXACTLY AM I LOOKING AT?
THE ONLY CLUE WE HAVE ON FINDING CATWOMAN AND THIS SECRET SOCIETY.
VE TREVOR
TWOMAN
EEN ARROW
WKMAN
TANA
RTIAN MANHUNTER
ARGIRL
BE
WORLD'S MOST DANGEROUS CHAPTER FOUR
THE GOOD THE BAD AND THE SHAGGY
Writer: Geoff JOHNS • Penciller: Brett BOOTH
Inker: Norm RAPMUND • Colorist: Andrew DALHOUSE • Letterer: Rob LEIGH

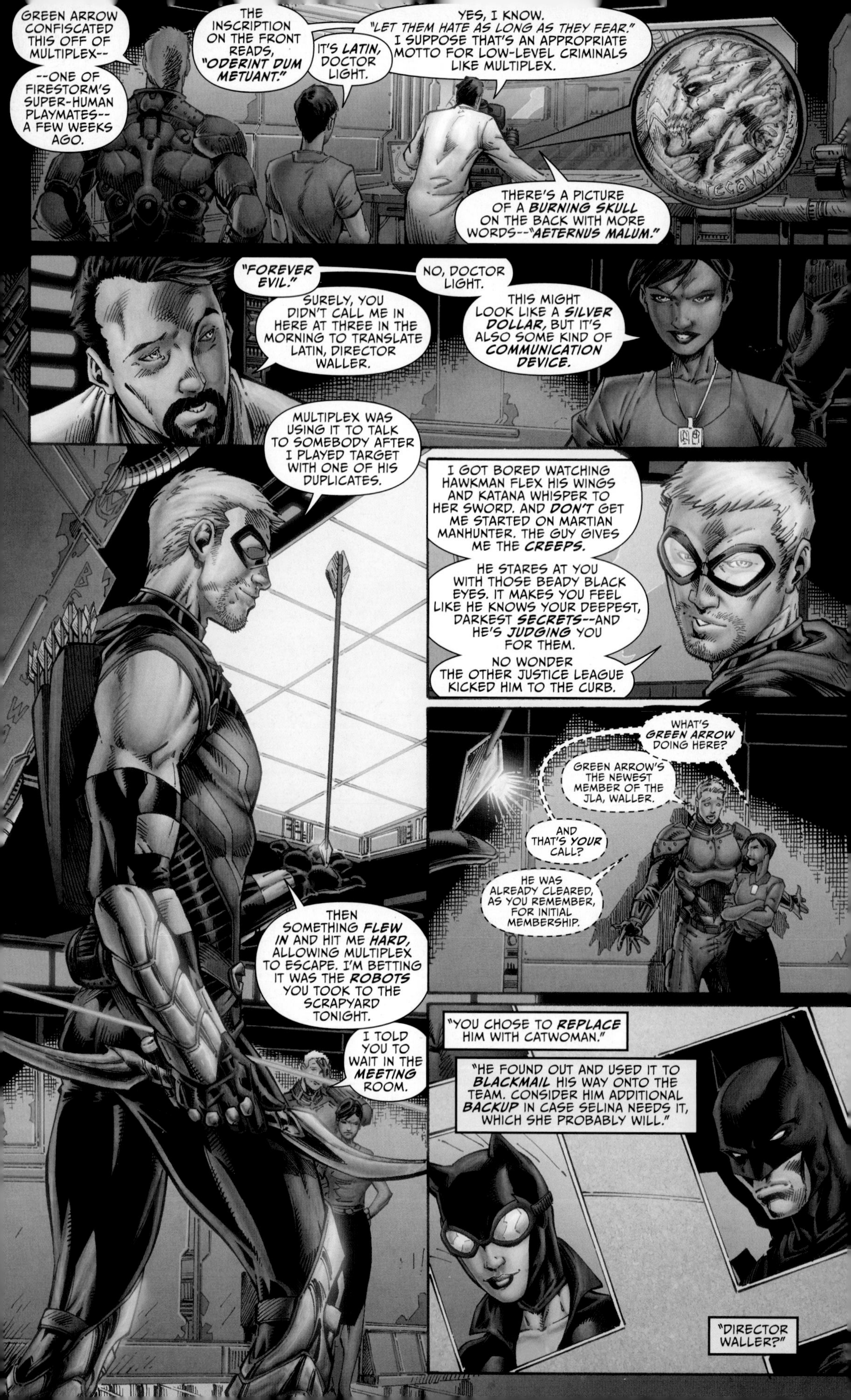

GREEN ARROW CONFISCATED THIS OFF OF MULTIPLEX--
--ONE OF FIRESTORM'S SUPER-HUMAN PLAYMATES--A FEW WEEKS AGO.
THE INSCRIPTION ON THE FRONT READS, "ODERINT DUM METUANT."
IT'S LATIN, DOCTOR LIGHT.
YES, I KNOW. "LET THEM HATE AS LONG AS THEY FEAR." I SUPPOSE THAT'S AN APPROPRIATE MOTTO FOR LOW-LEVEL CRIMINALS LIKE MULTIPLEX.
THERE'S A PICTURE OF A BURNING SKULL ON THE BACK WITH MORE WORDS--"AETERNUS MALUM."
"FOREVER EVIL."
SURELY, YOU DIDN'T CALL ME IN HERE AT THREE IN THE MORNING TO TRANSLATE LATIN, DIRECTOR WALLER.
NO, DOCTOR LIGHT.
THIS MIGHT LOOK LIKE A SILVER DOLLAR, BUT IT'S ALSO SOME KIND OF COMMUNICATION DEVICE.
MULTIPLEX WAS USING IT TO TALK TO SOMEBODY AFTER I PLAYED TARGET WITH ONE OF HIS DUPLICATES.
I GOT BORED WATCHING HAWKMAN FLEX HIS WINGS AND KATANA WHISPER TO HER SWORD. AND DON'T GET ME STARTED ON MARTIAN MANHUNTER. THE GUY GIVES ME THE CREEPS.
HE STARES AT YOU WITH THOSE BEADY BLACK EYES. IT MAKES YOU FEEL LIKE HE KNOWS YOUR DEEPEST, DARKEST SECRETS--AND HE'S JUDGING YOU FOR THEM.
NO WONDER THE OTHER JUSTICE LEAGUE KICKED HIM TO THE CURB.
WHAT'S GREEN ARROW DOING HERE?
GREEN ARROW'S THE NEWEST MEMBER OF THE JLA, WALLER.
AND THAT'S YOUR CALL?
HE WAS ALREADY CLEARED, AS YOU REMEMBER, FOR INITIAL MEMBERSHIP.
THEN SOMETHING FLEW IN AND HIT ME HARD, ALLOWING MULTIPLEX TO ESCAPE. I'M BETTING IT WAS THE ROBOTS YOU TOOK TO THE SCRAPYARD TONIGHT.
I TOLD YOU TO WAIT IN THE MEETING ROOM.
"YOU CHOSE TO REPLACE HIM WITH CATWOMAN."
"HE FOUND OUT AND USED IT TO BLACKMAIL HIS WAY ONTO THE TEAM. CONSIDER HIM ADDITIONAL BACKUP IN CASE SELINA NEEDS IT, WHICH SHE PROBABLY WILL."
"DIRECTOR WALLER?"

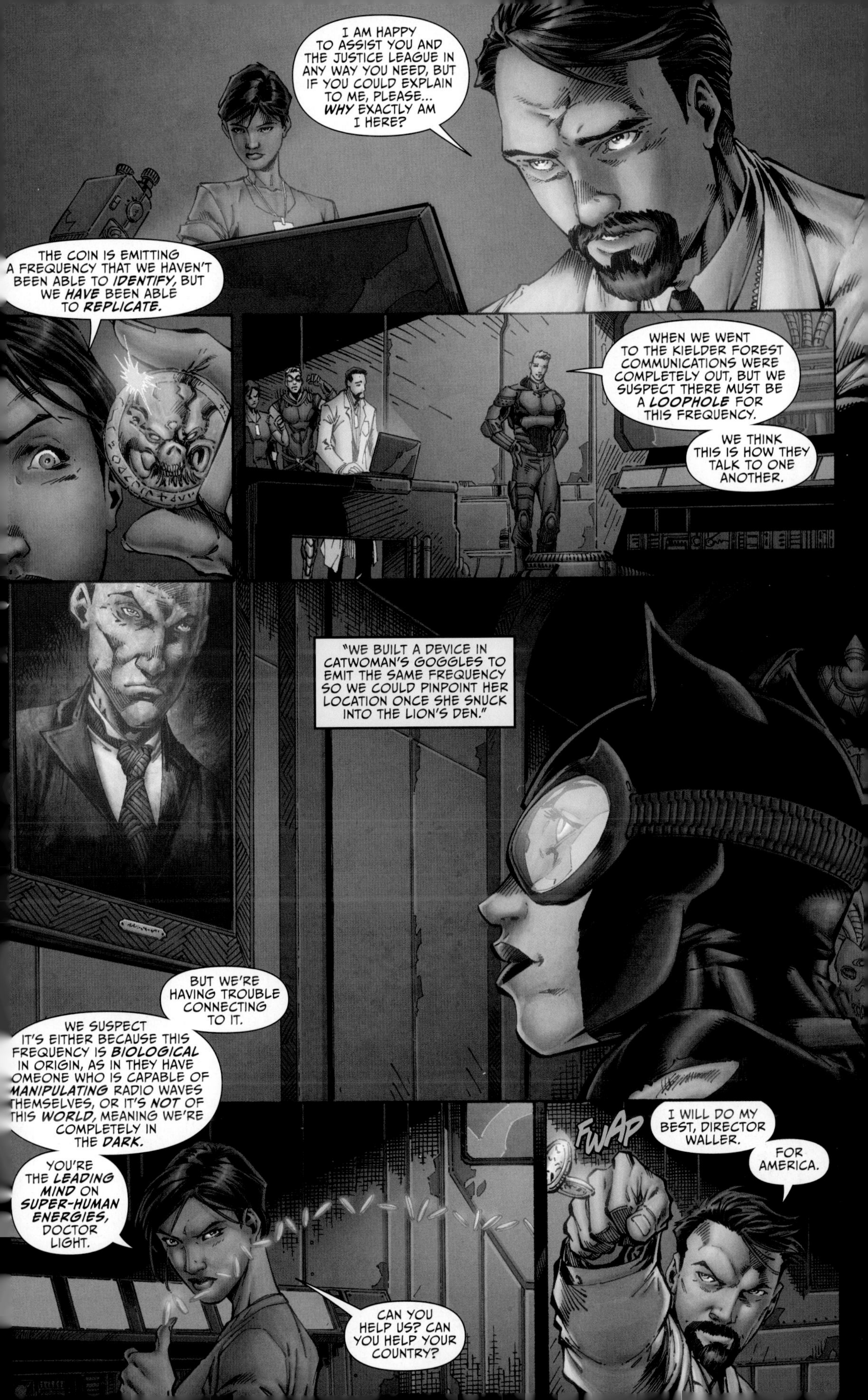

I AM HAPPY TO ASSIST YOU AND THE JUSTICE LEAGUE IN ANY WAY YOU NEED, BUT IF YOU COULD EXPLAIN TO ME, PLEASE... *WHY* EXACTLY AM I HERE?
THE COIN IS EMITTING A FREQUENCY THAT WE HAVEN'T BEEN ABLE TO *IDENTIFY,* BUT WE *HAVE* BEEN ABLE TO *REPLICATE.*
WHEN WE WENT TO THE KIELDER FOREST COMMUNICATIONS WERE COMPLETELY OUT, BUT WE SUSPECT THERE MUST BE A *LOOPHOLE* FOR THIS FREQUENCY.
WE THINK THIS IS HOW THEY TALK TO ONE ANOTHER.
"WE BUILT A DEVICE IN CATWOMAN'S GOGGLES TO EMIT THE SAME FREQUENCY SO WE COULD PINPOINT HER LOCATION ONCE SHE SNUCK INTO THE LION'S DEN."
BUT WE'RE HAVING TROUBLE CONNECTING TO IT.
WE SUSPECT IT'S EITHER BECAUSE THIS FREQUENCY IS *BIOLOGICAL* IN ORIGIN, AS IN THEY HAVE OMEONE WHO IS CAPABLE OF *MANIPULATING* RADIO WAVES THEMSELVES, OR IT'S *NOT* OF THIS *WORLD,* MEANING WE'RE COMPLETELY IN THE *DARK.*
YOU'RE THE *LEADING MIND* ON *SUPER-HUMAN ENERGIES,* DOCTOR LIGHT.
CAN YOU HELP US? CAN YOU HELP YOUR COUNTRY?
FWAP
I WILL DO MY BEST, DIRECTOR WALLER.
FOR AMERICA.

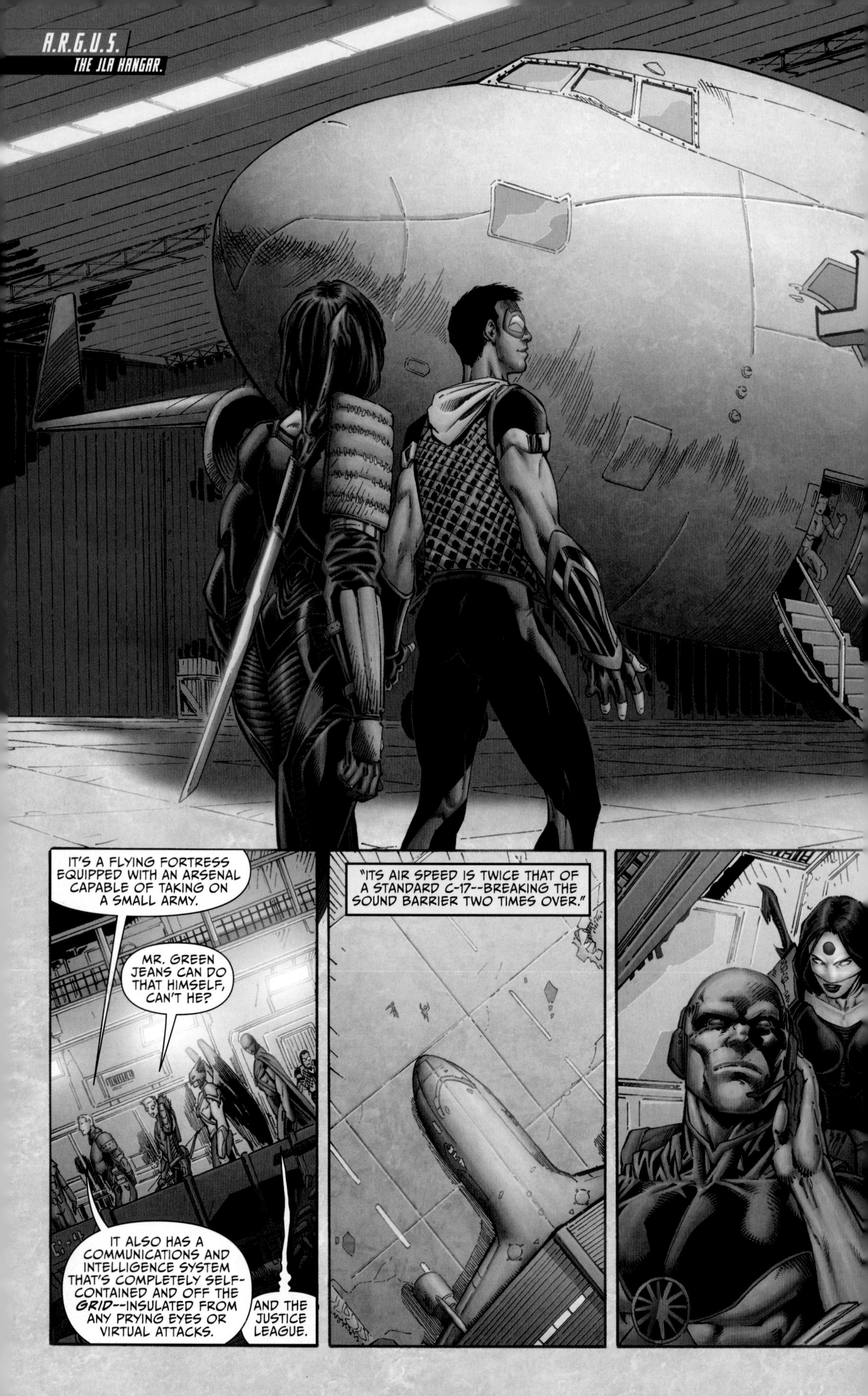
A.R.G.U.S.
THE JLA HANGAR.
IT'S A FLYING FORTRESS EQUIPPED WITH AN ARSENAL CAPABLE OF TAKING ON A SMALL ARMY.
MR. GREEN JEANS CAN DO THAT HIMSELF, CAN'T HE?
IT ALSO HAS A COMMUNICATIONS AND INTELLIGENCE SYSTEM THAT'S COMPLETELY SELF-CONTAINED AND OFF THE GRID--INSULATED FROM ANY PRYING EYES OR VIRTUAL ATTACKS.
AND THE JUSTICE LEAGUE.
"ITS AIR SPEED IS TWICE THAT OF A STANDARD C-17--BREAKING THE SOUND BARRIER TWO TIMES OVER."

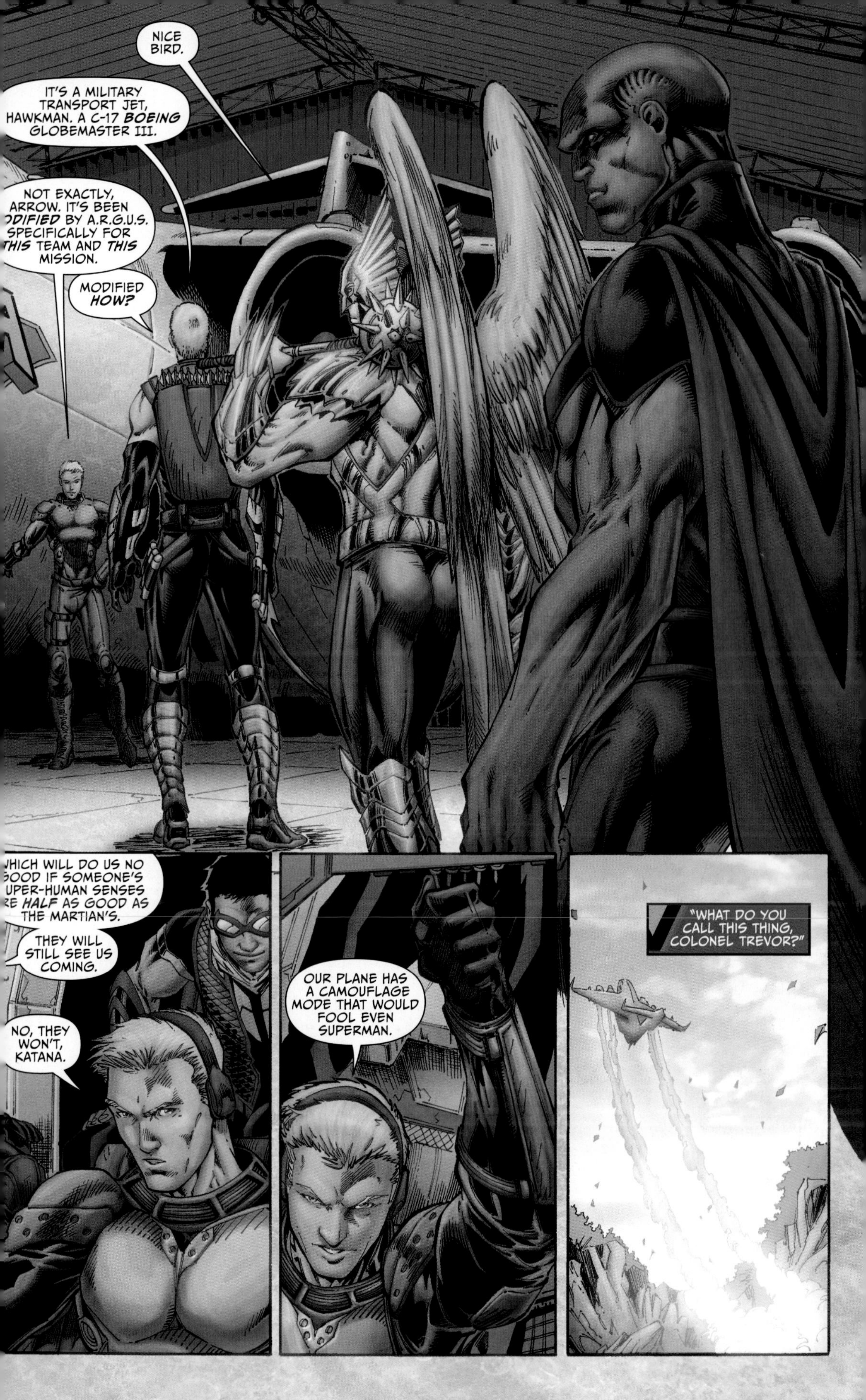

NICE BIRD.
IT'S A MILITARY TRANSPORT JET, HAWKMAN. A C-17 *BOEING* GLOBEMASTER III.
NOT EXACTLY, ARROW. IT'S BEEN ODIFIED BY A.R.G.U.S. SPECIFICALLY FOR *THIS* TEAM AND *THIS* MISSION.
MODIFIED *HOW?*
HICH WILL DO US NO GOOD IF SOMEONE'S UPER-HUMAN SENSES E *HALF* AS GOOD AS THE MARTIAN'S.
THEY WILL STILL SEE US COMING.
NO, THEY WON'T, KATANA.
OUR PLANE HAS A CAMOUFLAGE MODE THAT WOULD FOOL EVEN SUPERMAN.
"WHAT DO YOU CALL THIS THING, COLONEL TREVOR?"

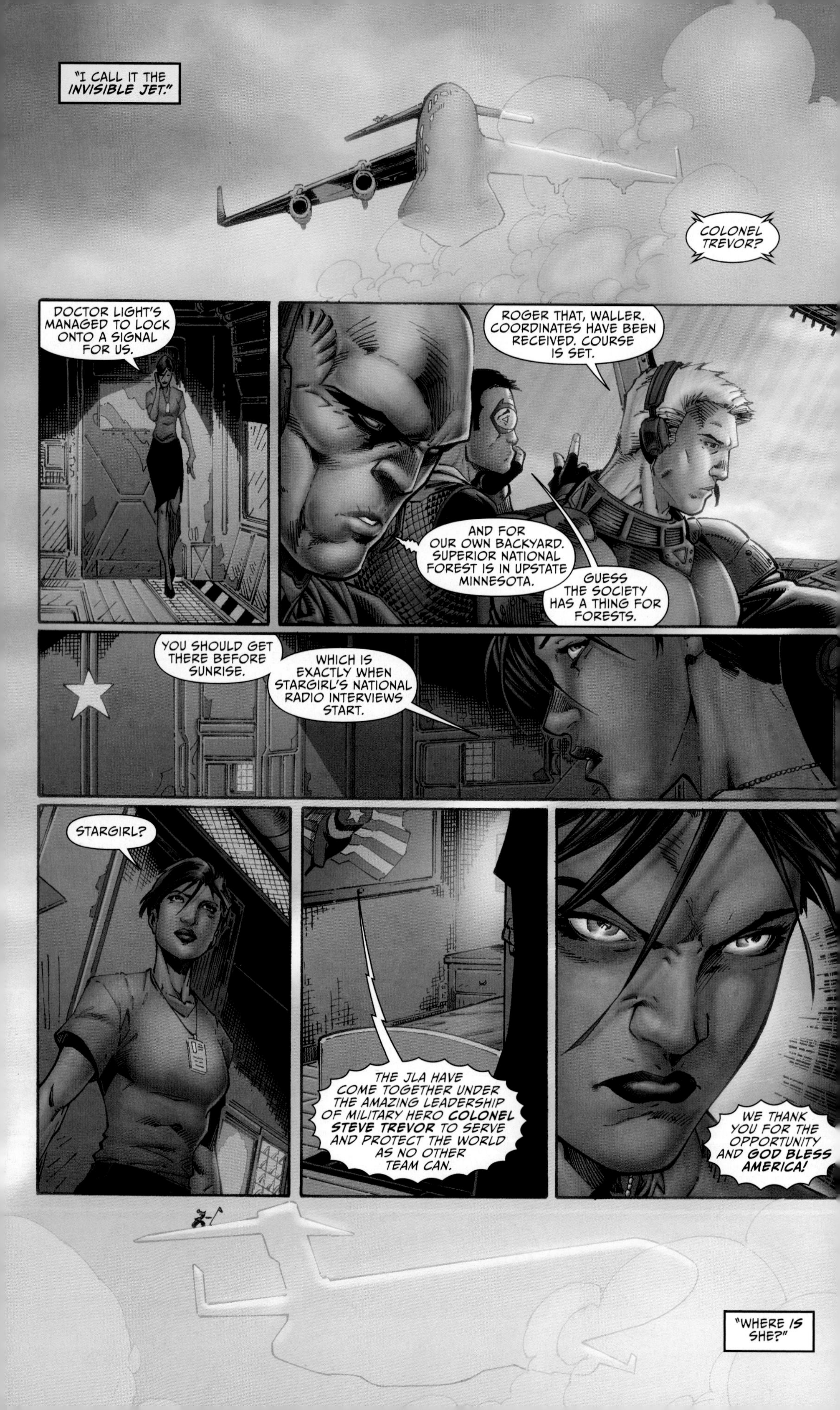

"I CALL IT THE *INVISIBLE JET*."
COLONEL TREVOR?
DOCTOR LIGHT'S MANAGED TO LOCK ONTO A SIGNAL FOR US.
ROGER THAT, WALLER. COORDINATES HAVE BEEN RECEIVED. COURSE IS SET.
AND FOR OUR OWN BACKYARD. SUPERIOR NATIONAL FOREST IS IN UPSTATE MINNESOTA.
GUESS THE SOCIETY HAS A THING FOR FORESTS.
YOU SHOULD GET THERE BEFORE SUNRISE.
WHICH IS EXACTLY WHEN STARGIRL'S NATIONAL RADIO INTERVIEWS START.
STARGIRL?
THE JLA HAVE COME TOGETHER UNDER THE AMAZING LEADERSHIP OF MILITARY HERO **COLONEL STEVE TREVOR** TO SERVE AND PROTECT THE WORLD AS NO OTHER TEAM CAN.
WE THANK YOU FOR THE OPPORTUNITY AND **GOD BLESS AMERICA!**
"WHERE *IS* SHE?"

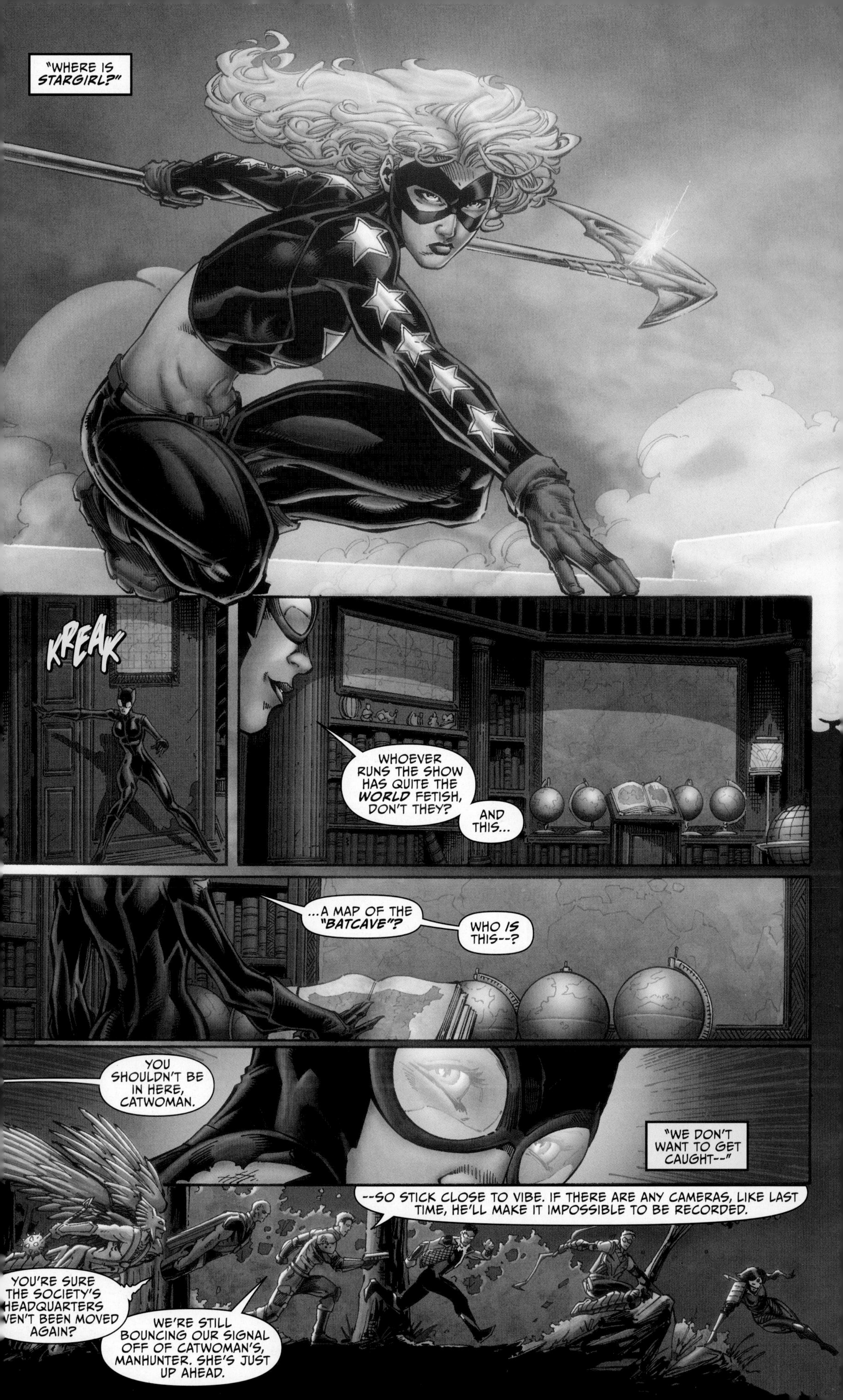
"WHERE IS STARGIRL?"
KREAK
WHOEVER RUNS THE SHOW HAS QUITE THE WORLD FETISH, DON'T THEY?
AND THIS...
...A MAP OF THE "BATCAVE"?
WHO IS THIS--?
YOU SHOULDN'T BE IN HERE, CATWOMAN.
"WE DON'T WANT TO GET CAUGHT--"
--SO STICK CLOSE TO VIBE. IF THERE ARE ANY CAMERAS, LIKE LAST TIME, HE'LL MAKE IT IMPOSSIBLE TO BE RECORDED.
YOU'RE SURE THE SOCIETY'S HEADQUARTERS HAVEN'T BEEN MOVED AGAIN?
WE'RE STILL BOUNCING OUR SIGNAL OFF OF CATWOMAN'S, MANHUNTER. SHE'S JUST UP AHEAD.

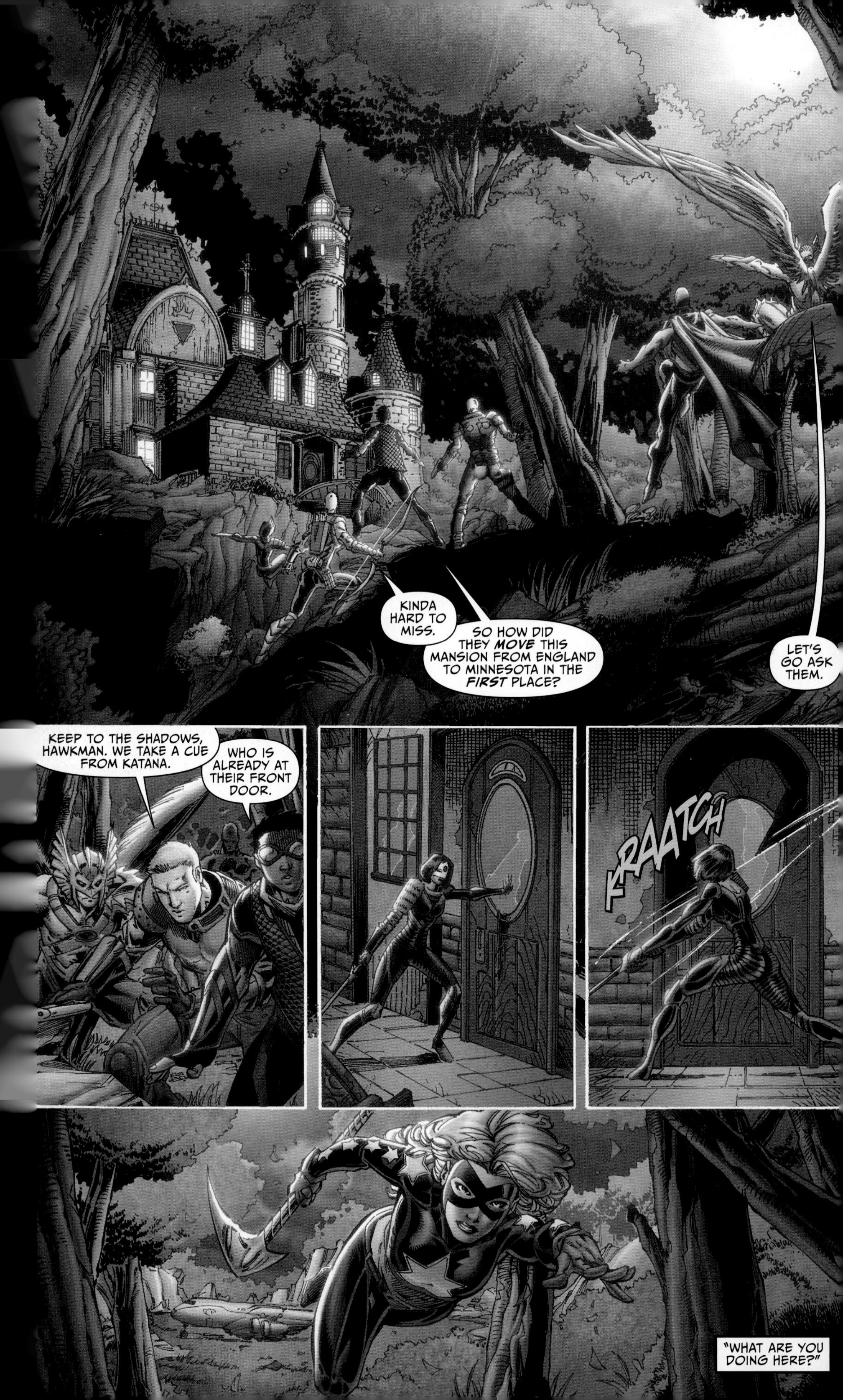

KINDA HARD TO MISS.
SO HOW DID THEY *MOVE* THIS MANSION FROM ENGLAND TO MINNESOTA IN THE *FIRST* PLACE?
LET'S GO ASK THEM.
KEEP TO THE SHADOWS, HAWKMAN. WE TAKE A CUE FROM KATANA.
WHO IS ALREADY AT THEIR FRONT DOOR.
KRAATCH
"WHAT ARE YOU DOING HERE?"

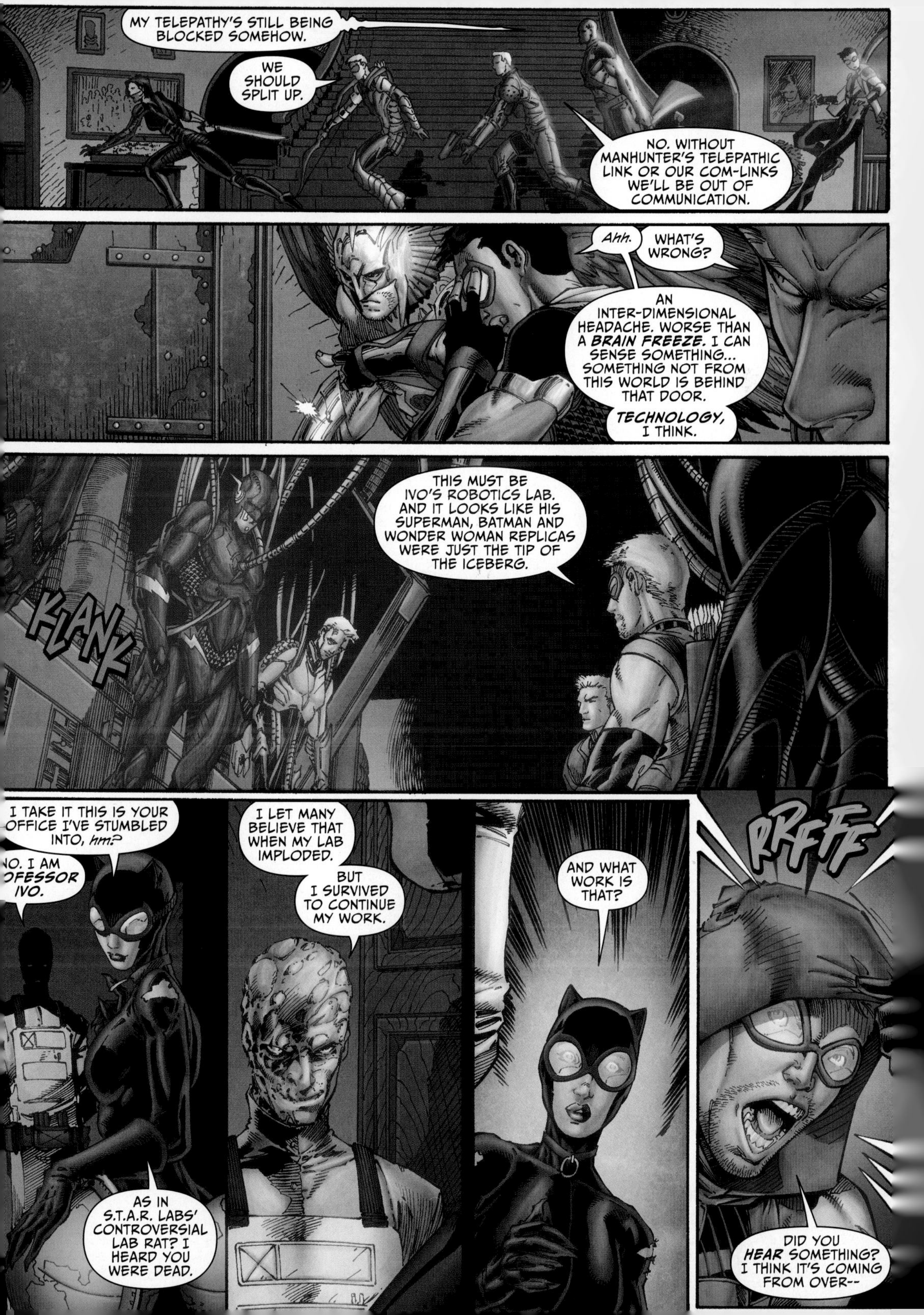
MY TELEPATHY'S STILL BEING BLOCKED SOMEHOW.
WE SHOULD SPLIT UP.
NO. WITHOUT MANHUNTER'S TELEPATHIC LINK OR OUR COM-LINKS WE'LL BE OUT OF COMMUNICATION.
Ahh.
WHAT'S WRONG?
AN INTER-DIMENSIONAL HEADACHE. WORSE THAN A ***BRAIN FREEZE.*** I CAN SENSE SOMETHING... SOMETHING NOT FROM THIS WORLD IS BEHIND THAT DOOR.
TECHNOLOGY, I THINK.
THIS MUST BE IVO'S ROBOTICS LAB. AND IT LOOKS LIKE HIS SUPERMAN, BATMAN AND WONDER WOMAN REPLICAS WERE JUST THE TIP OF THE ICEBERG.
KLANK
I TAKE IT THIS IS YOUR OFFICE I'VE STUMBLED INTO, *hm?*
NO. I AM ***OFESSOR IVO.***
AS IN S.T.A.R. LABS' CONTROVERSIAL LAB RAT? I HEARD YOU WERE DEAD.
I LET MANY BELIEVE THAT WHEN MY LAB IMPLODED.
BUT I SURVIVED TO CONTINUE MY WORK.
AND WHAT WORK IS THAT?
RRFFF
DID YOU ***HEAR*** SOMETHING? I THINK IT'S COMING FROM OVER--

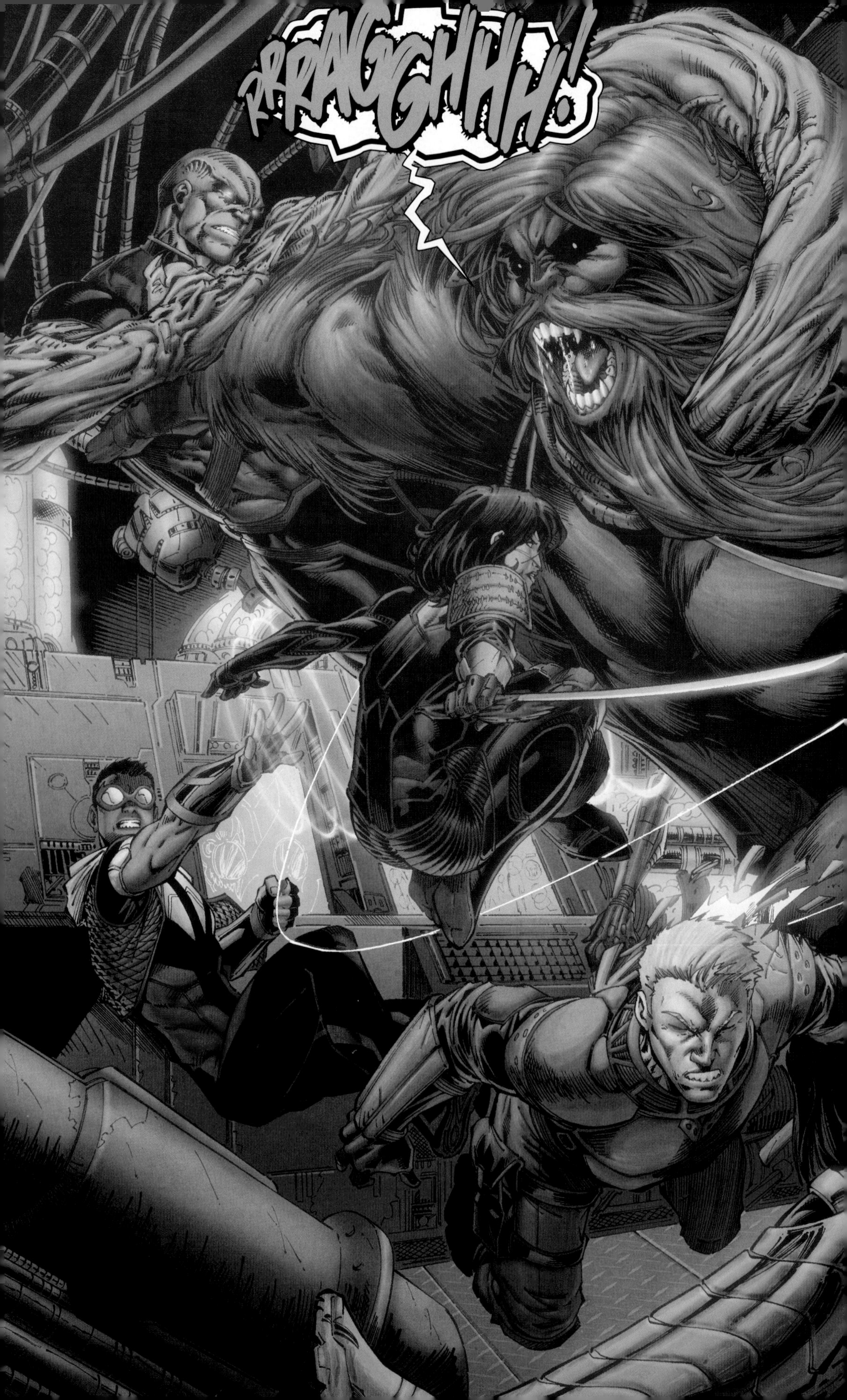
RRRAGGHHHH!

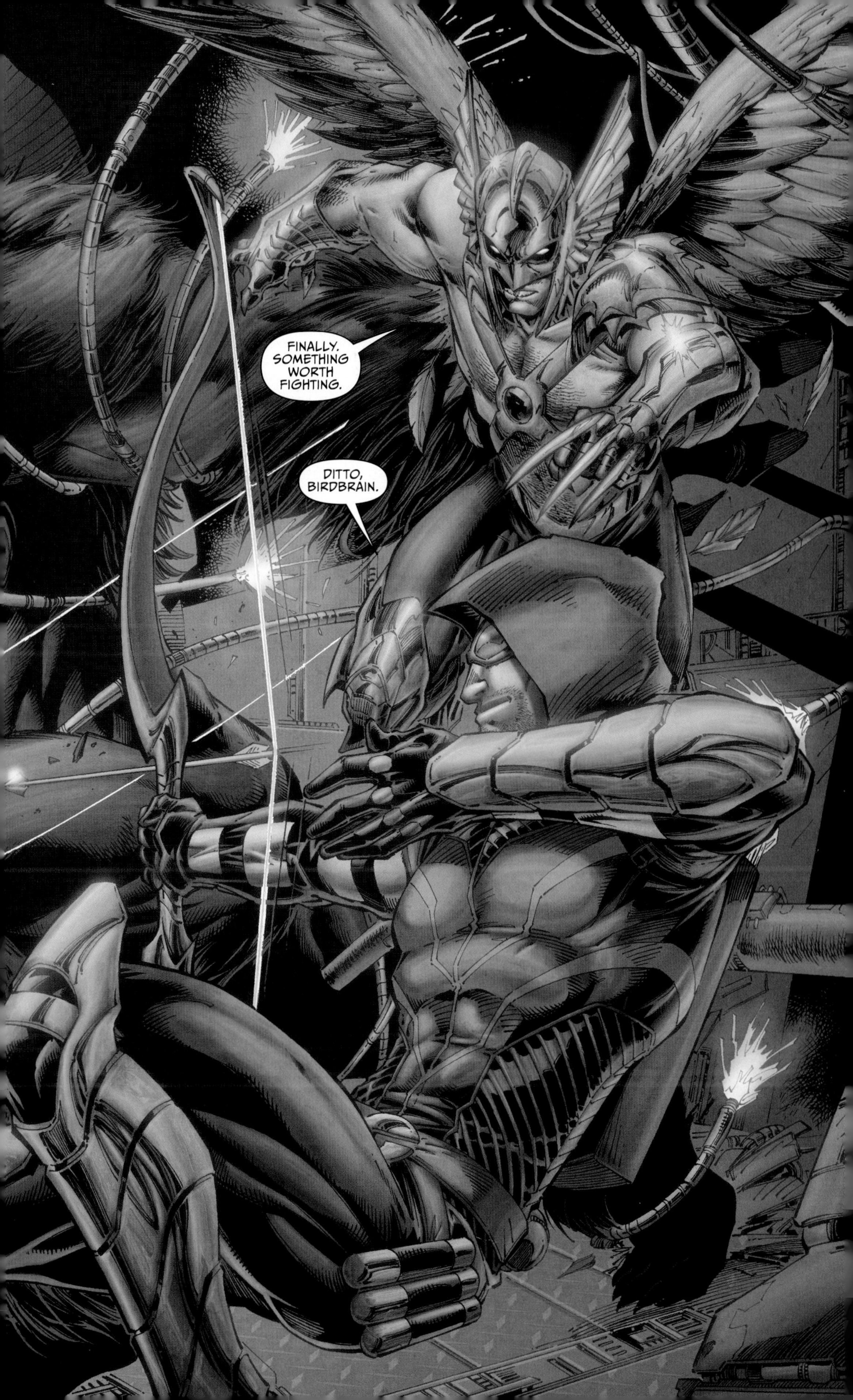
FINALLY. SOMETHING WORTH FIGHTING.
DITTO, BIRDBRAIN.

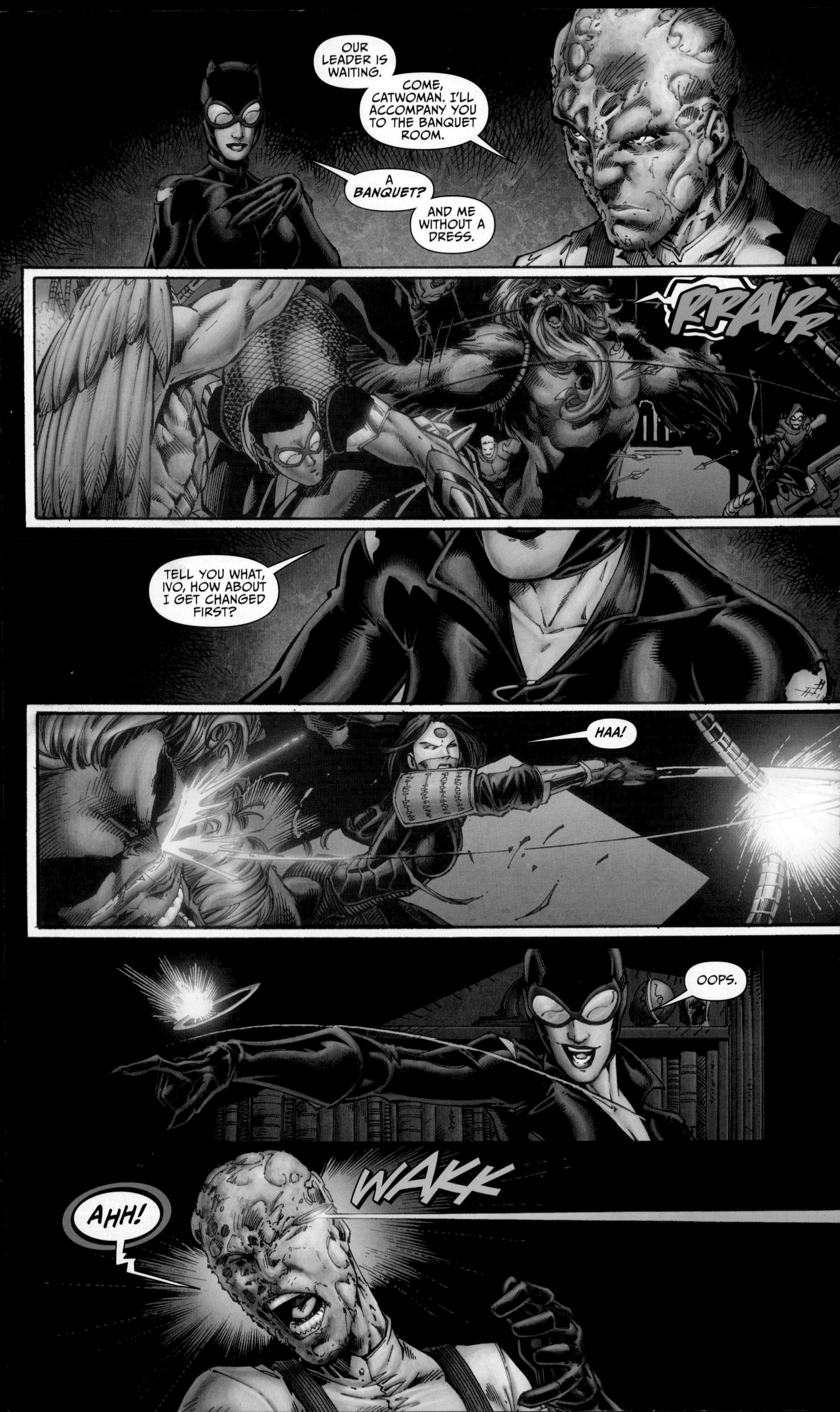

OUR LEADER IS WAITING.
COME, CATWOMAN. I'LL ACCOMPANY YOU TO THE BANQUET ROOM.
A *BANQUET?*
AND ME WITHOUT A DRESS.
RRAR
TELL YOU WHAT, IVO, HOW ABOUT I GET CHANGED FIRST?
HAA!
OOPS.
WAKK
AHH!

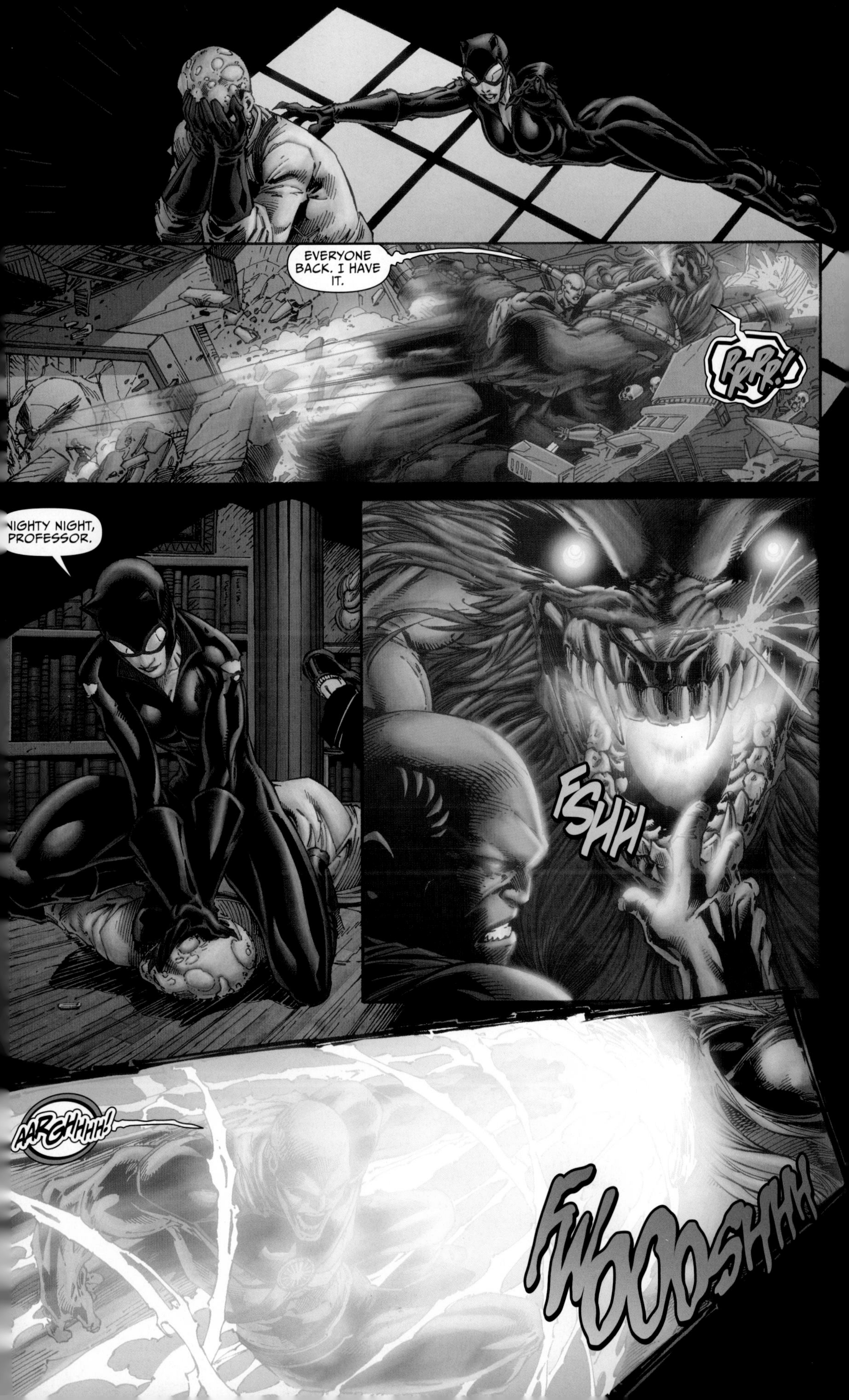
EVERYONE BACK. I HAVE IT.
RRRR!!
NIGHTY NIGHT, PROFESSOR.
FSHH
AARGHHHH!
FWOOOSHHH

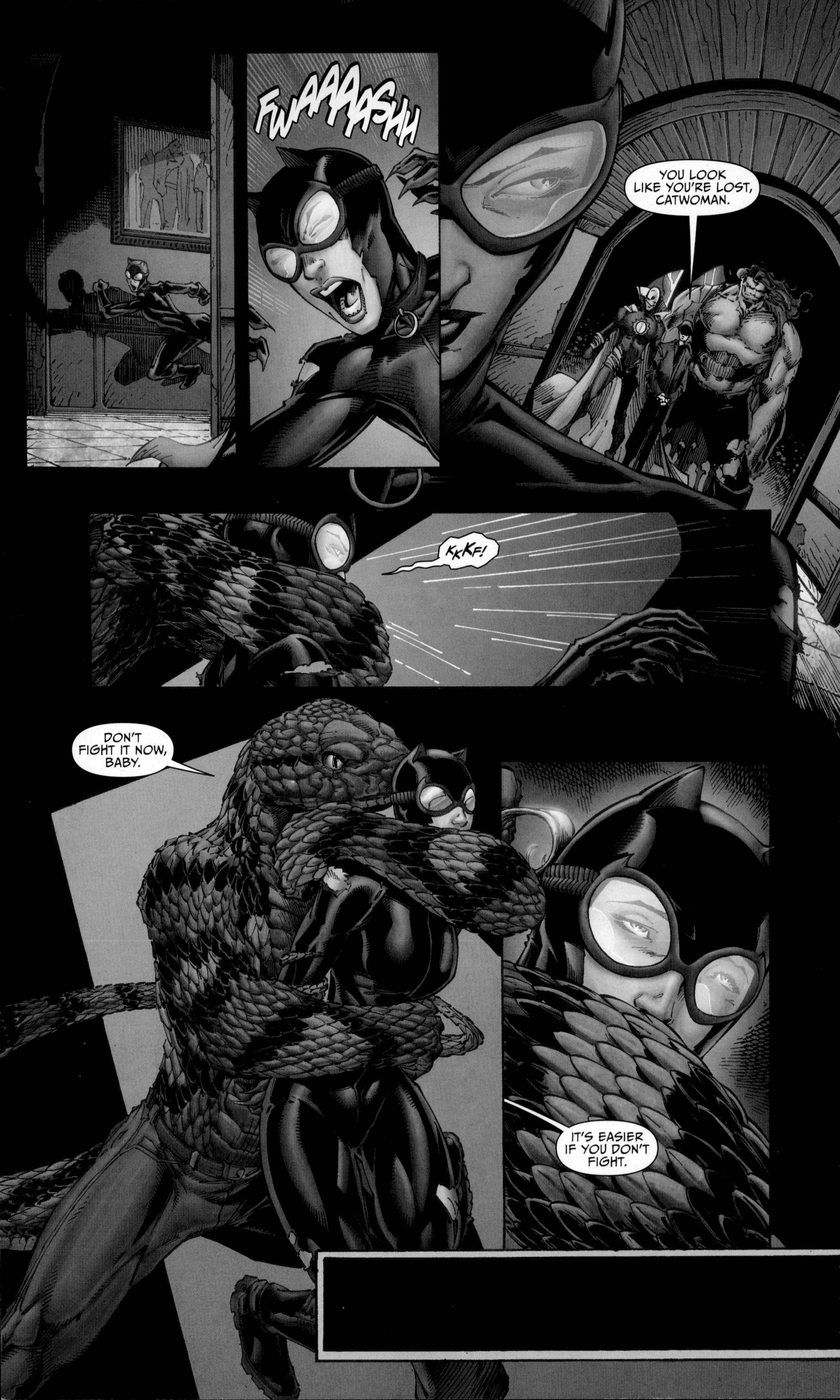
FWAAAASHH
YOU LOOK LIKE YOU'RE LOST, CATWOMAN.
KKKF!
DON'T FIGHT IT NOW, BABY.
IT'S EASIER IF YOU DON'T FIGHT.

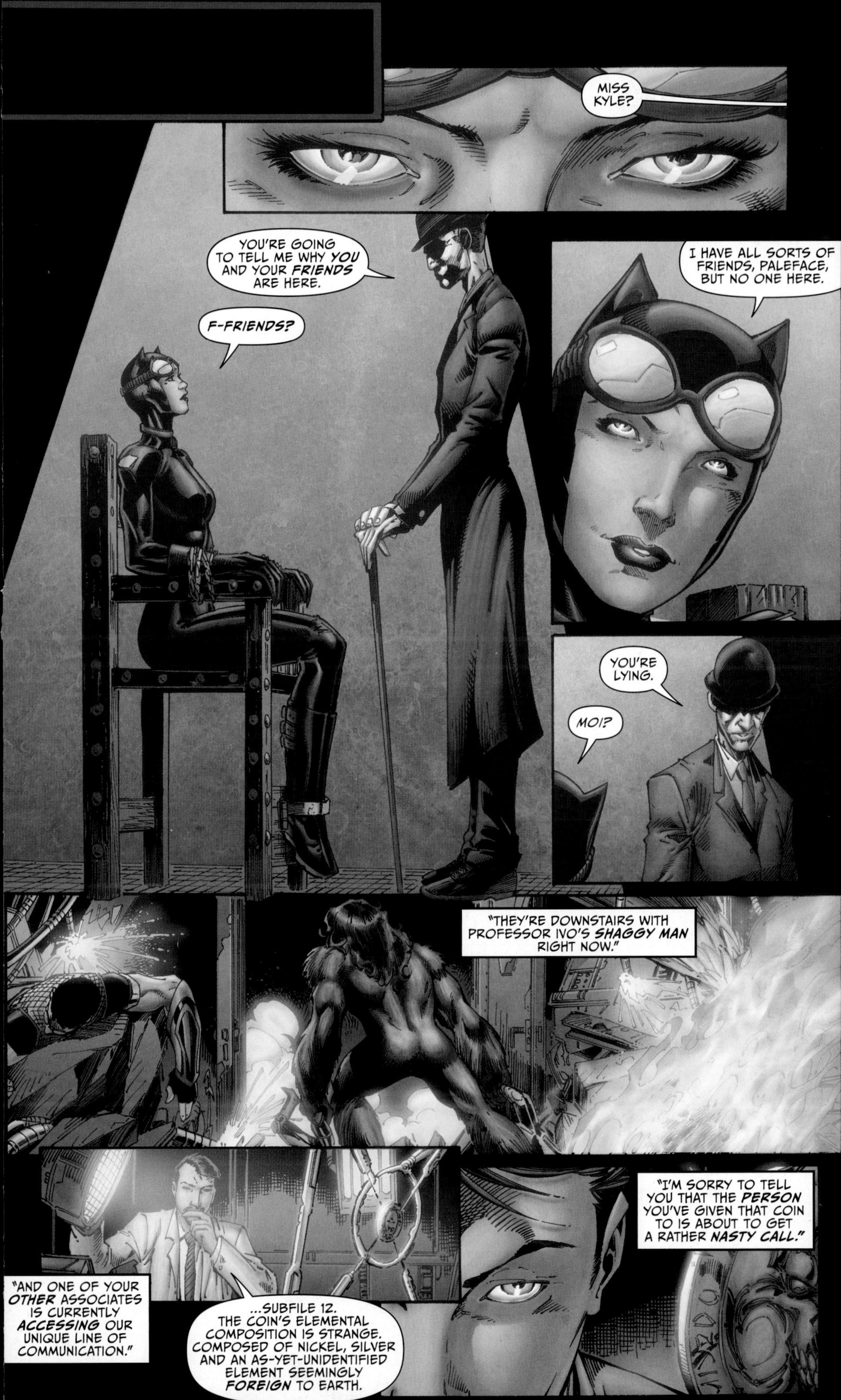
MISS KYLE?
YOU'RE GOING TO TELL ME WHY *YOU* AND YOUR *FRIENDS* ARE HERE.
F-FRIENDS?
I HAVE ALL SORTS OF FRIENDS, PALEFACE, BUT NO ONE HERE.
YOU'RE LYING.
MOI?
"THEY'RE DOWNSTAIRS WITH PROFESSOR IVO'S *SHAGGY MAN* RIGHT NOW."
"AND ONE OF YOUR *OTHER* ASSOCIATES IS CURRENTLY *ACCESSING* OUR UNIQUE LINE OF COMMUNICATION."
...SUBFILE 12. THE COIN'S ELEMENTAL COMPOSITION IS STRANGE. COMPOSED OF NICKEL, SILVER AND AN AS-YET-UNIDENTIFIED ELEMENT SEEMINGLY *FOREIGN* TO EARTH.
"I'M SORRY TO TELL YOU THAT THE *PERSON* YOU'VE GIVEN THAT COIN TO IS ABOUT TO GET A RATHER *NASTY CALL.*"

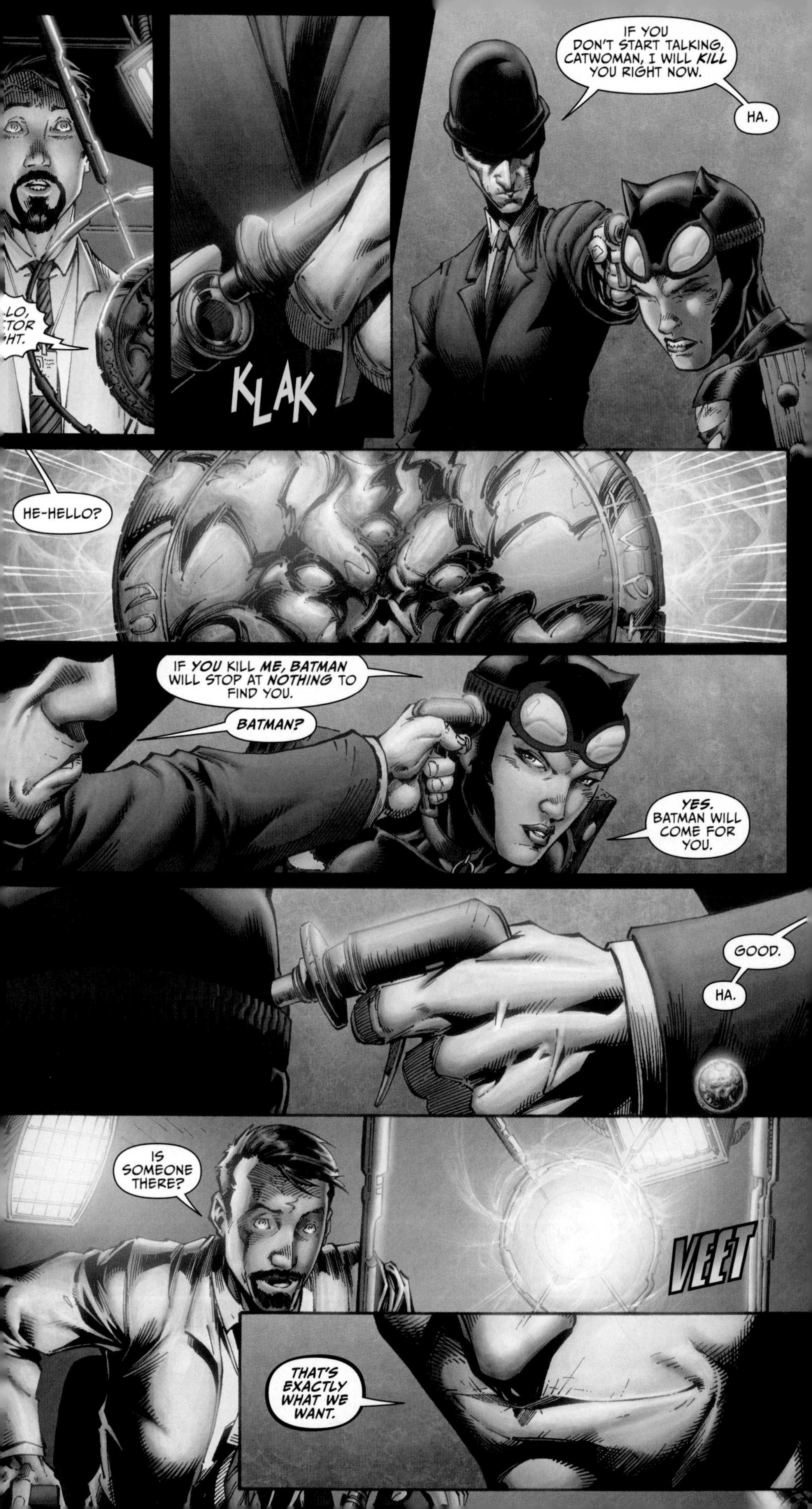
KLAK
IF YOU DON'T START TALKING, CATWOMAN, I WILL KILL YOU RIGHT NOW.
HA.
HE-HELLO?
IF YOU KILL ME, BATMAN WILL STOP AT NOTHING TO FIND YOU.
BATMAN?
YES. BATMAN WILL COME FOR YOU.
GOOD.
HA.
IS SOMEONE THERE?
VEET
THAT'S EXACTLY WHAT WE WANT.

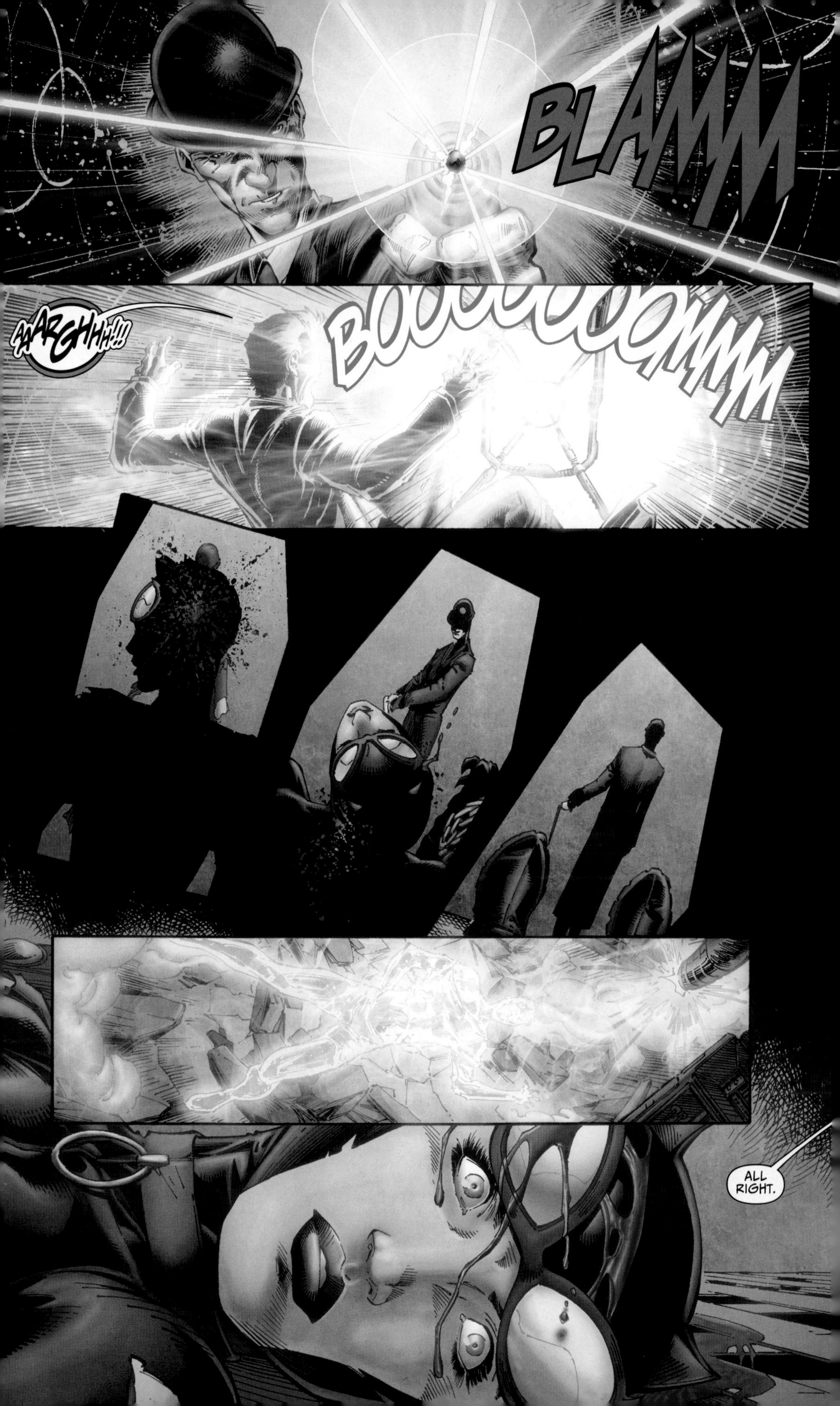
BLAMM
AAARGHHH!!!
BOOOOOOOMMM
ALL RIGHT.

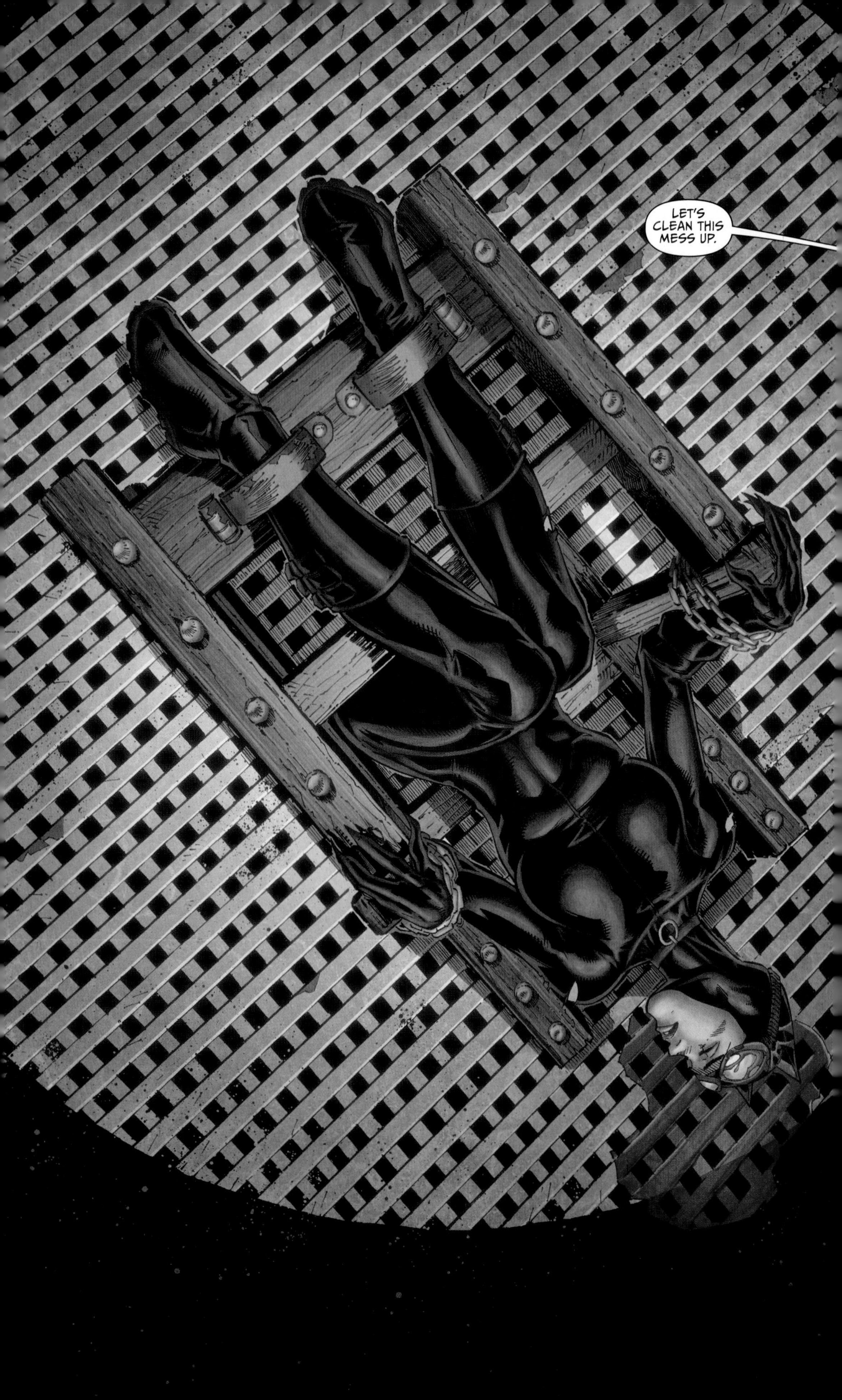
LET'S CLEAN THIS MESS UP.

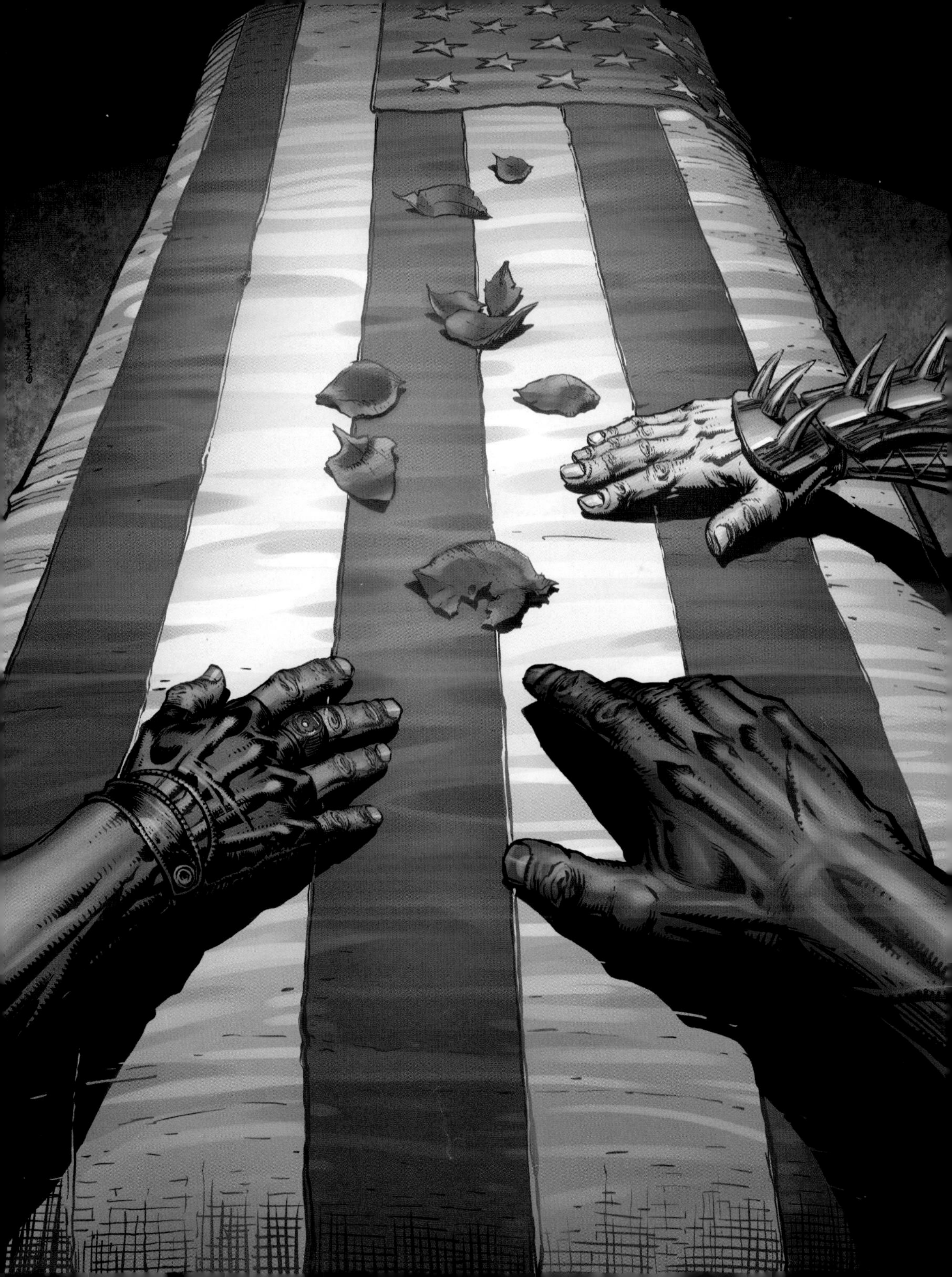

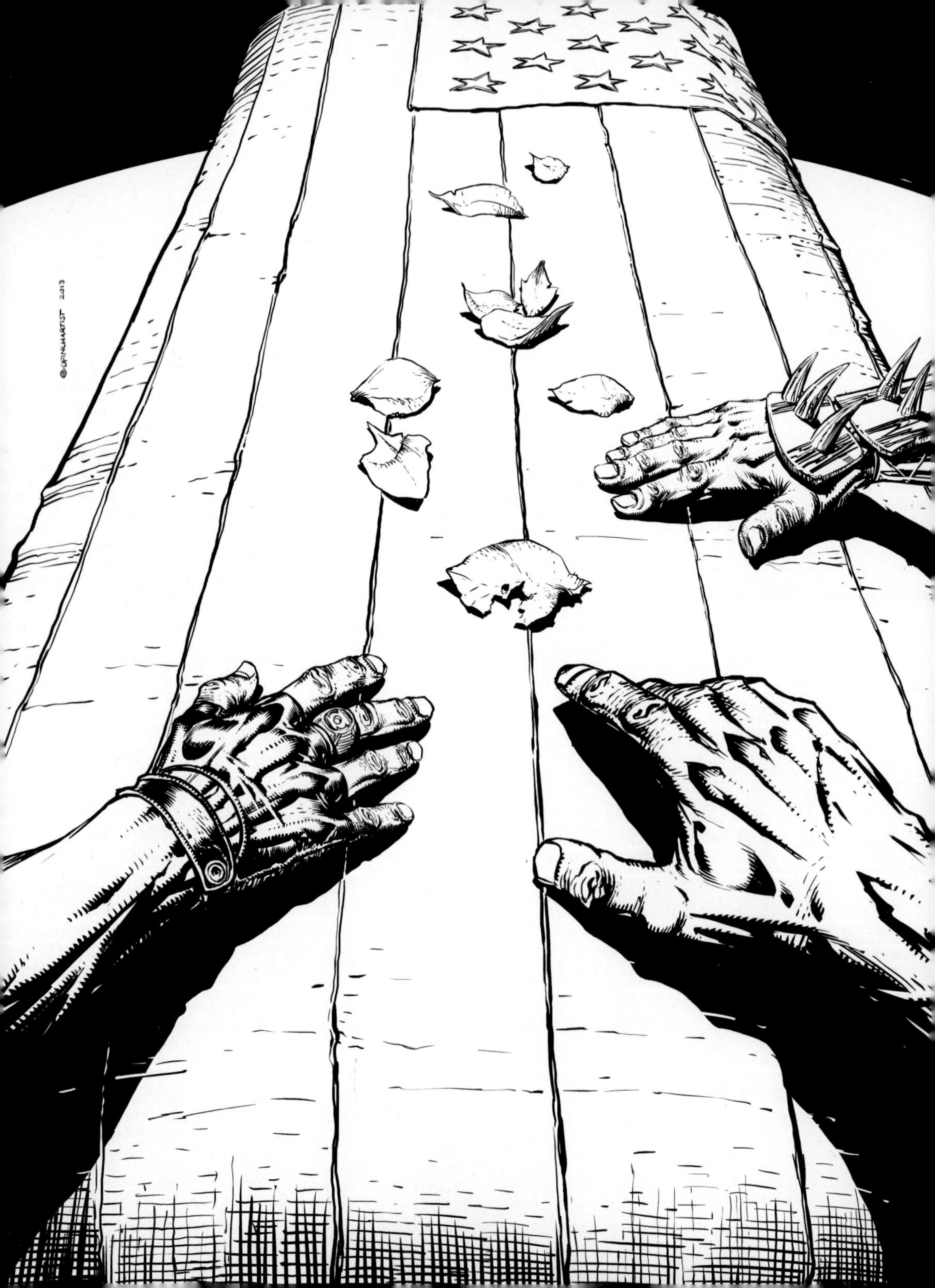
©DFINCHARTIST 2013

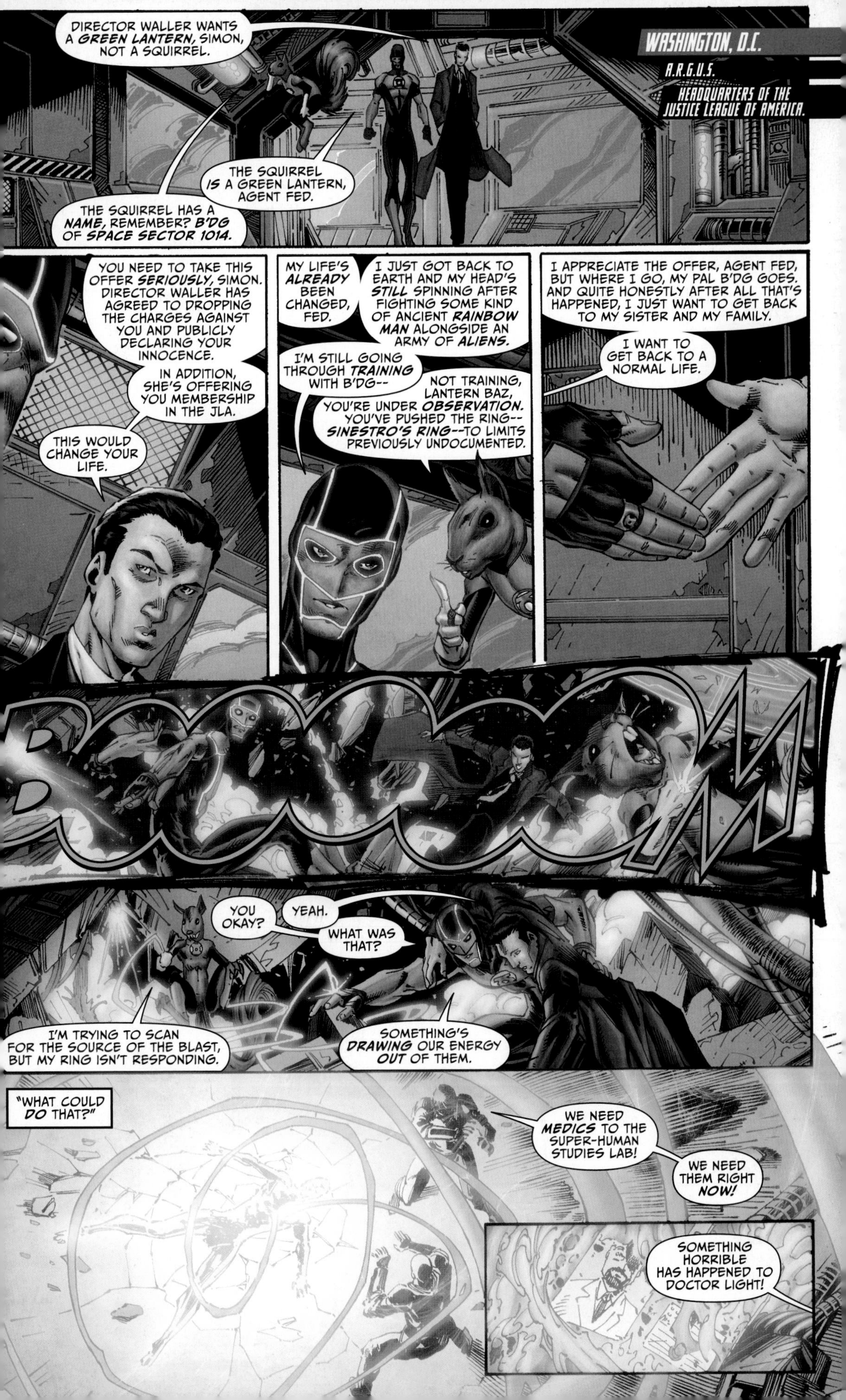
DIRECTOR WALLER WANTS A GREEN LANTERN, SIMON, NOT A SQUIRREL.
WASHINGTON, D.C.
A.R.G.U.S.
HEADQUARTERS OF THE JUSTICE LEAGUE OF AMERICA.
THE SQUIRREL IS A GREEN LANTERN, AGENT FED.
THE SQUIRREL HAS A NAME, REMEMBER? B'DG OF SPACE SECTOR 1014.
YOU NEED TO TAKE THIS OFFER SERIOUSLY, SIMON. DIRECTOR WALLER HAS AGREED TO DROPPING THE CHARGES AGAINST YOU AND PUBLICLY DECLARING YOUR INNOCENCE.
IN ADDITION, SHE'S OFFERING YOU MEMBERSHIP IN THE JLA.
THIS WOULD CHANGE YOUR LIFE.
MY LIFE'S ALREADY BEEN CHANGED, FED.
I JUST GOT BACK TO EARTH AND MY HEAD'S STILL SPINNING AFTER FIGHTING SOME KIND OF ANCIENT RAINBOW MAN ALONGSIDE AN ARMY OF ALIENS.
I'M STILL GOING THROUGH TRAINING WITH B'DG--
NOT TRAINING, LANTERN BAZ, YOU'RE UNDER OBSERVATION. YOU'VE PUSHED THE RING-- SINESTRO'S RING--TO LIMITS PREVIOUSLY UNDOCUMENTED.
I APPRECIATE THE OFFER, AGENT FED, BUT WHERE I GO, MY PAL B'DG GOES. AND QUITE HONESTLY AFTER ALL THAT'S HAPPENED, I JUST WANT TO GET BACK TO MY SISTER AND MY FAMILY.
I WANT TO GET BACK TO A NORMAL LIFE.
BOOOOOOM
YOU OKAY?
YEAH.
WHAT WAS THAT?
I'M TRYING TO SCAN FOR THE SOURCE OF THE BLAST, BUT MY RING ISN'T RESPONDING.
SOMETHING'S DRAWING OUR ENERGY OUT OF THEM.
"WHAT COULD DO THAT?"
WE NEED MEDICS TO THE SUPER-HUMAN STUDIES LAB!
WE NEED THEM RIGHT NOW!
SOMETHING HORRIBLE HAS HAPPENED TO DOCTOR LIGHT!

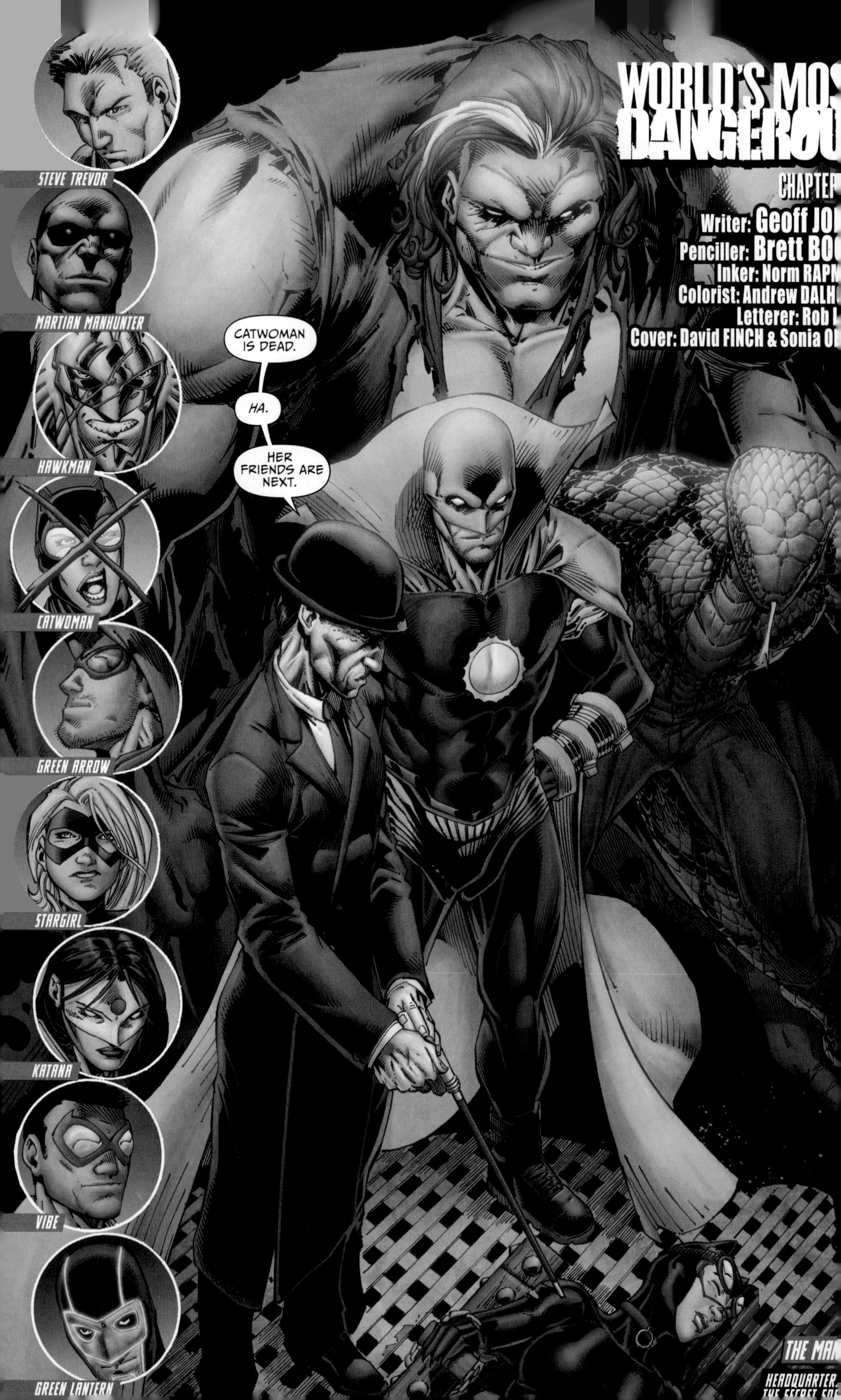
STEVE TREVOR
MARTIAN MANHUNTER
HAWKMAN
CATWOMAN
GREEN ARROW
STARGIRL
KATANA
VIBE
GREEN LANTERN
WORLD'S MOS
DANGEROU
CHAPTE
Writer: Geoff JO
Penciller: Brett BO
Inker: Norm RAPN
Colorist: Andrew DALH
Letterer: Rob
Cover: David FINCH & Sonia O
CATWOMAN IS DEAD.
HA.
HER FRIENDS ARE NEXT.
THE MAN
HEADQUARTER

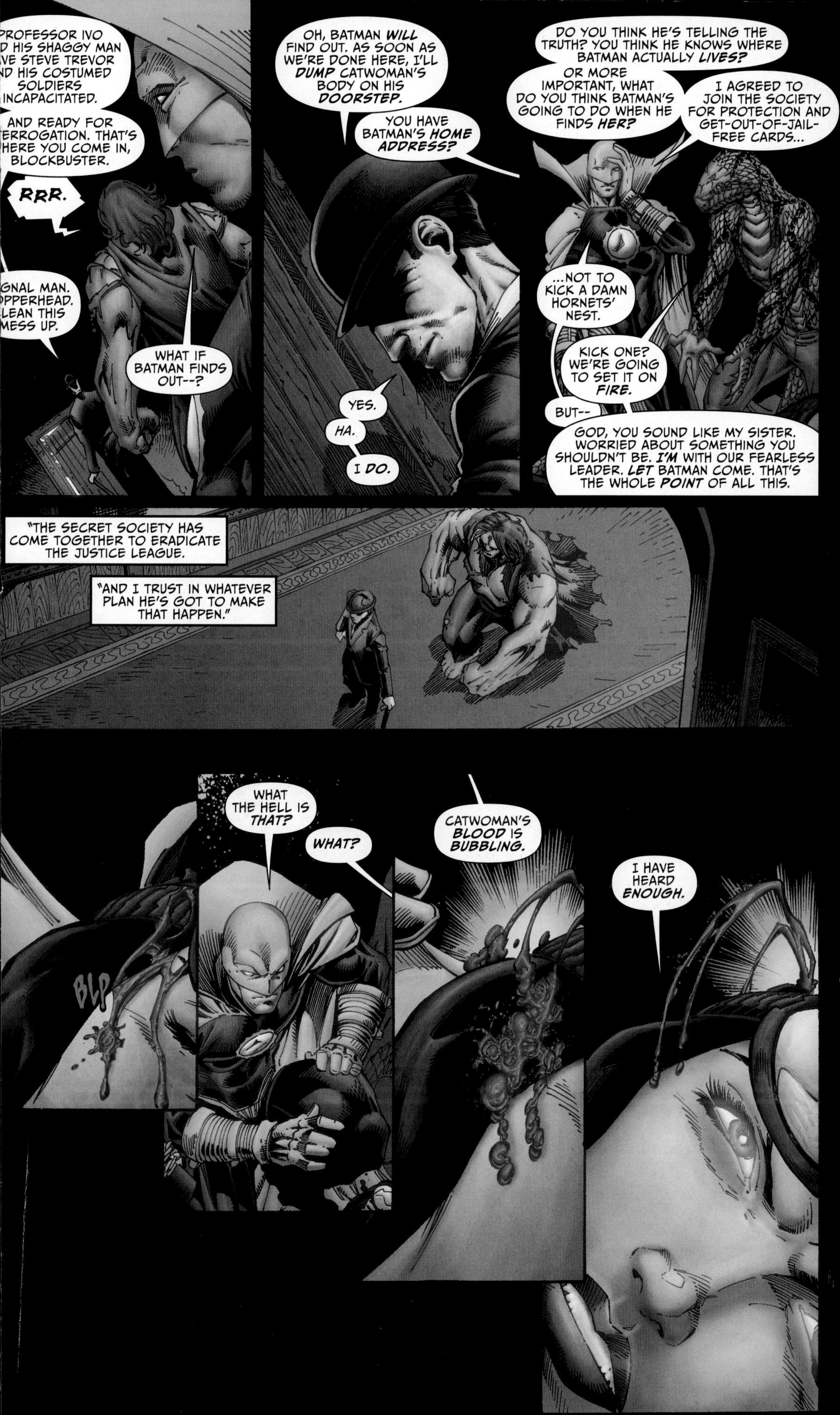

PROFESSOR IVO
D HIS SHAGGY MAN
VE STEVE TREVOR
ND HIS COSTUMED
SOLDIERS
INCAPACITATED.
AND READY FOR
TERROGATION. THAT'S
HERE YOU COME IN,
BLOCKBUSTER.
RRR.
GNAL MAN.
OPPERHEAD.
LEAN THIS
MESS UP.
WHAT IF BATMAN FINDS OUT--?
OH, BATMAN WILL FIND OUT. AS SOON AS WE'RE DONE HERE, I'LL DUMP CATWOMAN'S BODY ON HIS DOORSTEP.
YOU HAVE BATMAN'S HOME ADDRESS?
YES.
HA.
I DO.
DO YOU THINK HE'S TELLING THE TRUTH? YOU THINK HE KNOWS WHERE BATMAN ACTUALLY LIVES?
OR MORE IMPORTANT, WHAT DO YOU THINK BATMAN'S GOING TO DO WHEN HE FINDS HER?
I AGREED TO JOIN THE SOCIETY FOR PROTECTION AND GET-OUT-OF-JAIL-FREE CARDS...
...NOT TO KICK A DAMN HORNETS' NEST.
KICK ONE? WE'RE GOING TO SET IT ON FIRE.
BUT--
GOD, YOU SOUND LIKE MY SISTER. WORRIED ABOUT SOMETHING YOU SHOULDN'T BE. I'M WITH OUR FEARLESS LEADER. LET BATMAN COME. THAT'S THE WHOLE POINT OF ALL THIS.
"THE SECRET SOCIETY HAS COME TOGETHER TO ERADICATE THE JUSTICE LEAGUE.
"AND I TRUST IN WHATEVER PLAN HE'S GOT TO MAKE THAT HAPPEN."
BLP
WHAT THE HELL IS THAT?
WHAT?
CATWOMAN'S BLOOD IS BUBBLING.
I HAVE HEARD ENOUGH.

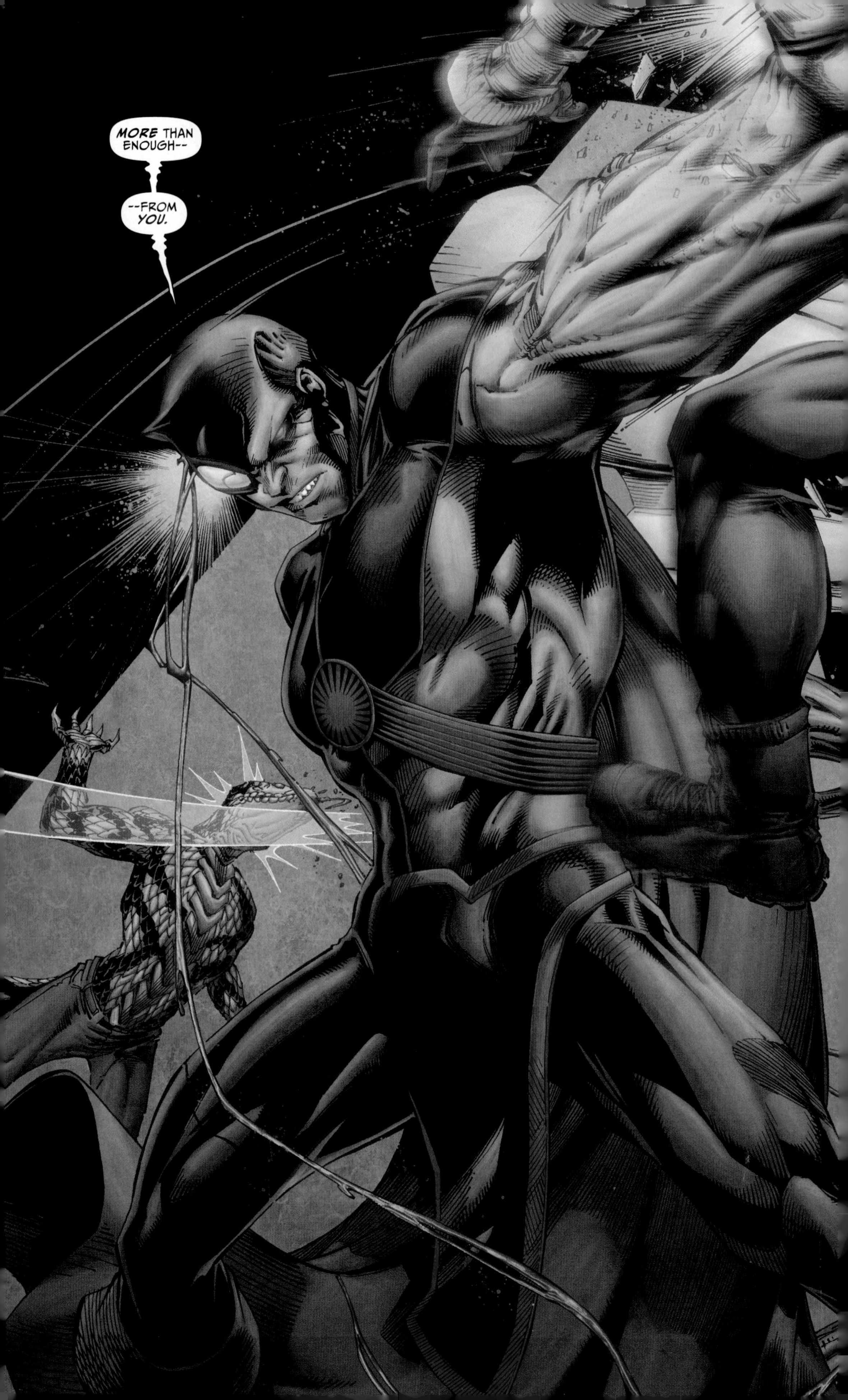
MORE THAN ENOUGH--
--FROM YOU.

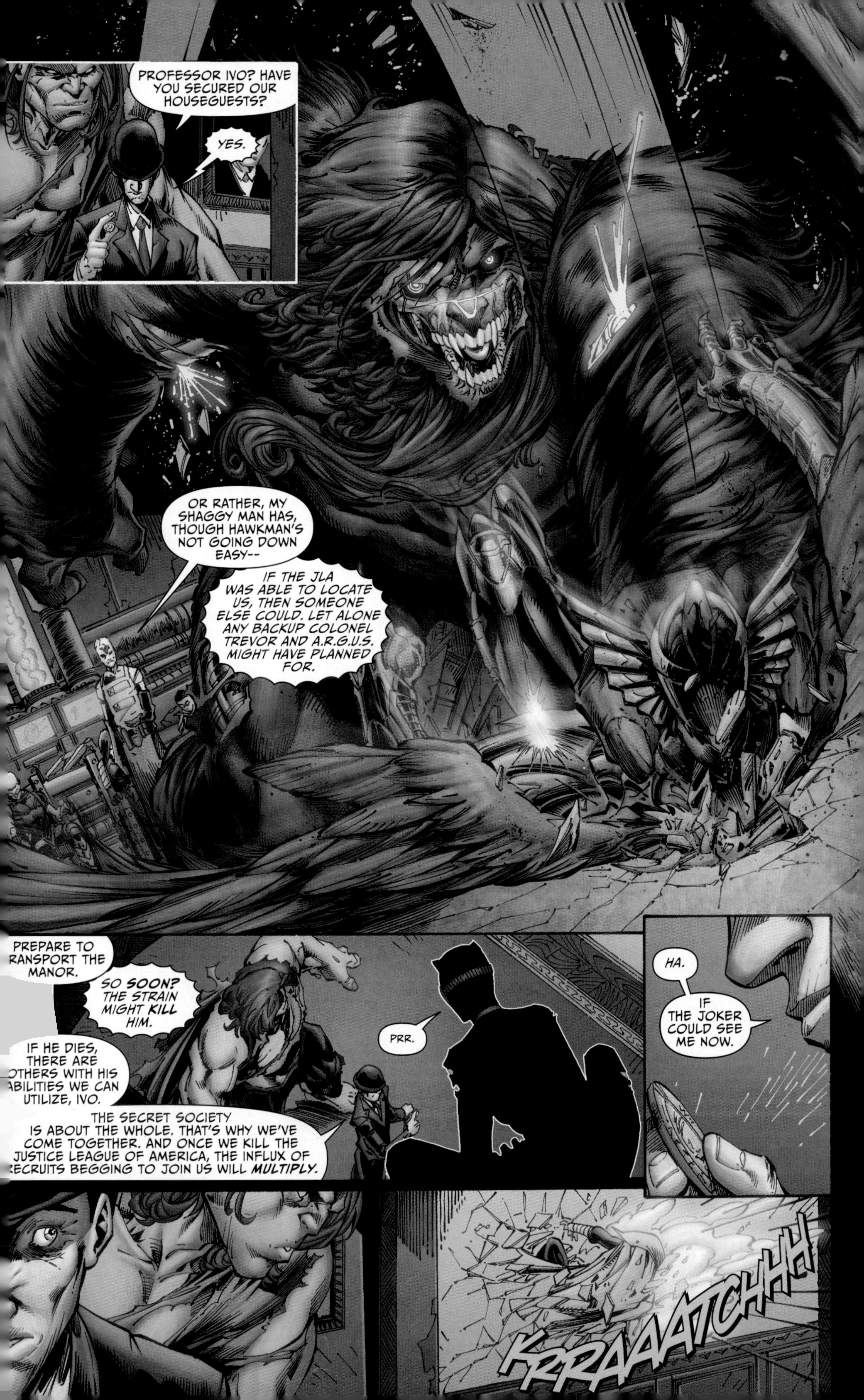
PROFESSOR IVO? HAVE YOU SECURED OUR HOUSEGUESTS?
YES.
OR RATHER, MY SHAGGY MAN HAS, THOUGH HAWKMAN'S NOT GOING DOWN EASY--
IF THE JLA WAS ABLE TO LOCATE US, THEN SOMEONE ELSE COULD. LET ALONE ANY BACKUP COLONEL TREVOR AND A.R.G.U.S. MIGHT HAVE PLANNED FOR.
PREPARE TO RANSPORT THE MANOR.
SO SOON? THE STRAIN MIGHT KILL HIM.
IF HE DIES, THERE ARE OTHERS WITH HIS ABILITIES WE CAN UTILIZE, IVO.
THE SECRET SOCIETY IS ABOUT THE WHOLE. THAT'S WHY WE'VE COME TOGETHER. AND ONCE WE KILL THE JUSTICE LEAGUE OF AMERICA, THE INFLUX OF RECRUITS BEGGING TO JOIN US WILL MULTIPLY.
PRR.
HA.
IF THE JOKER COULD SEE ME NOW.
KRRAAATCHHH

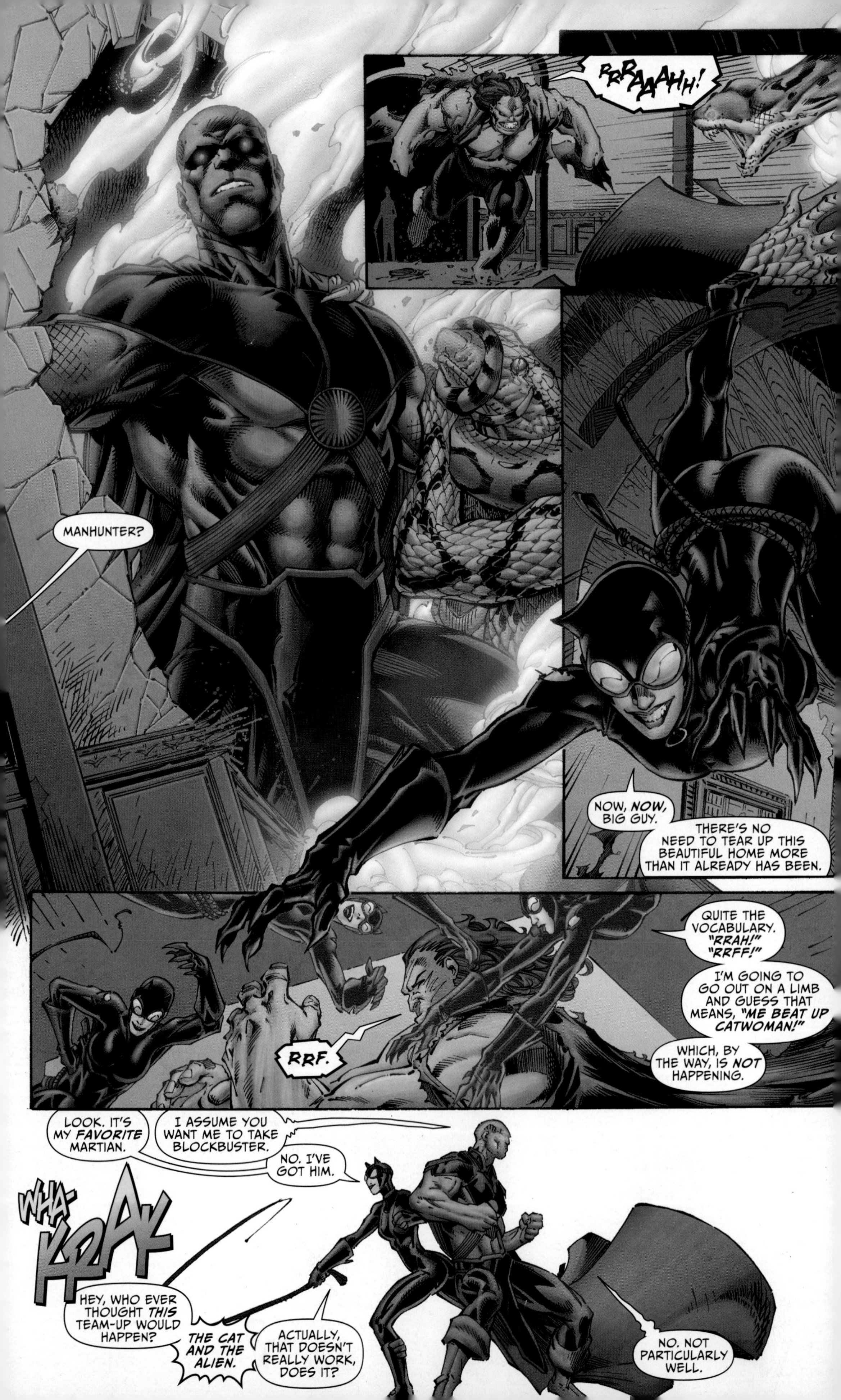
RRRAAAHH!
MANHUNTER?
NOW, NOW, BIG GUY.
THERE'S NO NEED TO TEAR UP THIS BEAUTIFUL HOME MORE THAN IT ALREADY HAS BEEN.
QUITE THE VOCABULARY. "RRAH!" "RRFF!"
I'M GOING TO GO OUT ON A LIMB AND GUESS THAT MEANS, "ME BEAT UP CATWOMAN!"
WHICH, BY THE WAY, IS NOT HAPPENING.
RRF.
LOOK. IT'S MY FAVORITE MARTIAN.
I ASSUME YOU WANT ME TO TAKE BLOCKBUSTER.
NO. I'VE GOT HIM.
WHA-KRAK
HEY, WHO EVER THOUGHT THIS TEAM-UP WOULD HAPPEN?
THE CAT AND THE ALIEN.
ACTUALLY, THAT DOESN'T REALLY WORK, DOES IT?
NO. NOT PARTICULARLY WELL.

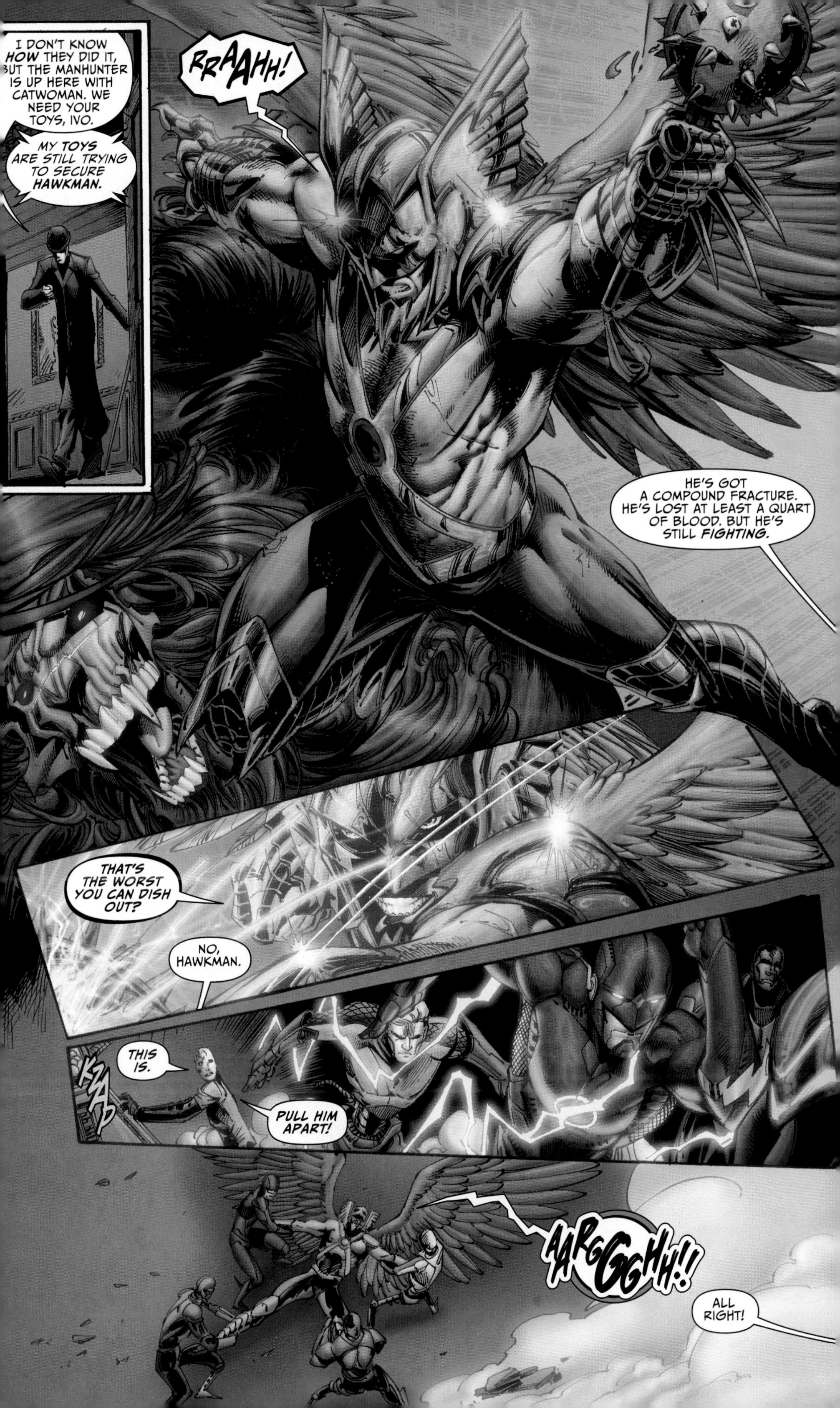
I DON'T KNOW HOW THEY DID IT, BUT THE MANHUNTER IS UP HERE WITH CATWOMAN. WE NEED YOUR TOYS, IVO.
MY TOYS ARE STILL TRYING TO SECURE HAWKMAN.
RRAAHH!
HE'S GOT A COMPOUND FRACTURE. HE'S LOST AT LEAST A QUART OF BLOOD. BUT HE'S STILL FIGHTING.
THAT'S THE WORST YOU CAN DISH OUT?
NO, HAWKMAN.
KZZAP
THIS IS.
PULL HIM APART!
AARGGGHH!!
ALL RIGHT!

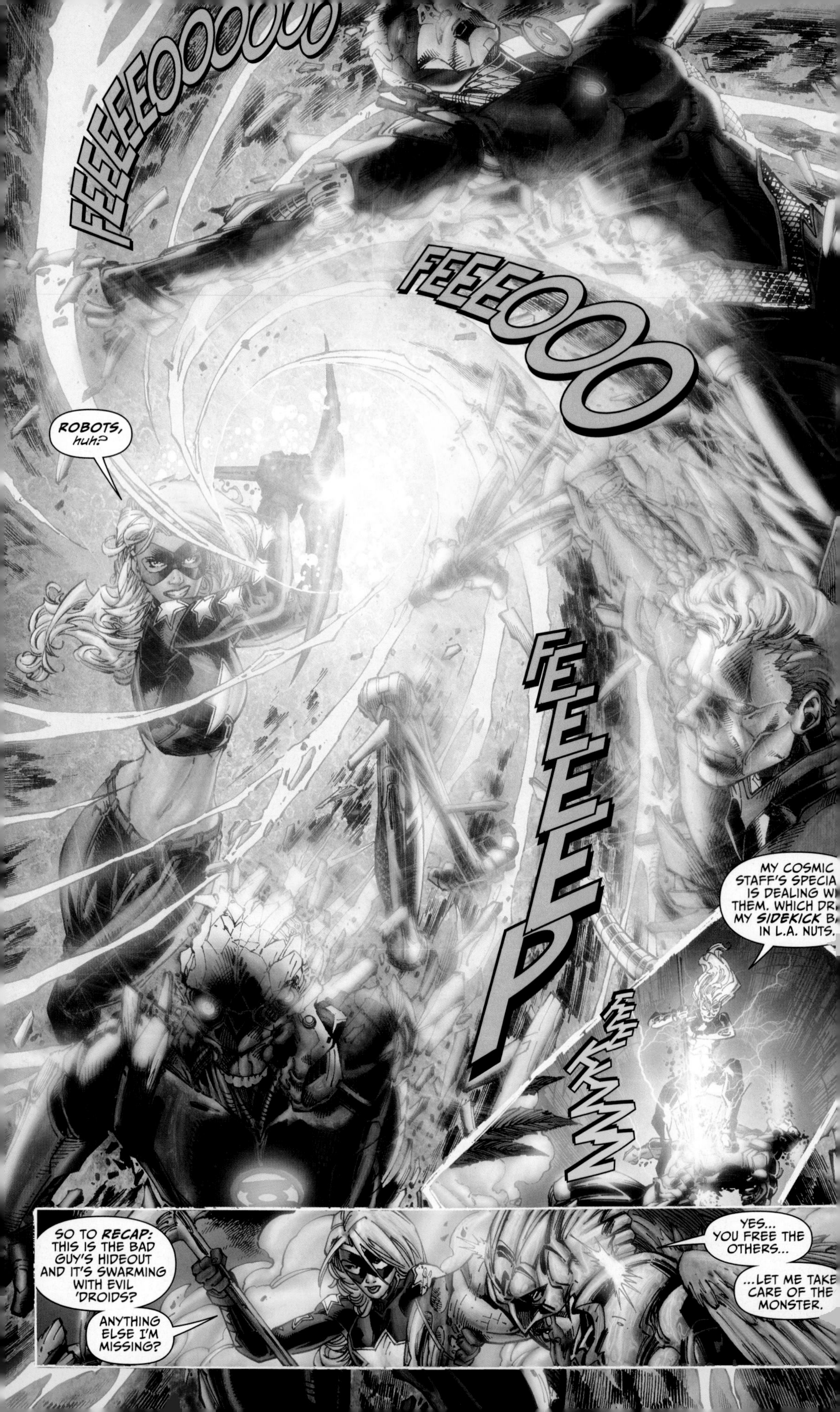
FEEEEEOOOOOOO
FEEEOOO
ROBOTS, huh?
FEEEEEEP
FEEKMM
MY COSMIC STAFF'S SPECIA IS DEALING W THEM. WHICH DR MY SIDEKICK B IN L.A. NUTS.
SO TO RECAP: THIS IS THE BAD GUY'S HIDEOUT AND IT'S SWARMING WITH EVIL 'DROIDS?
ANYTHING ELSE I'M MISSING?
YES... YOU FREE THE OTHERS...
...LET ME TAKE CARE OF THE MONSTER.

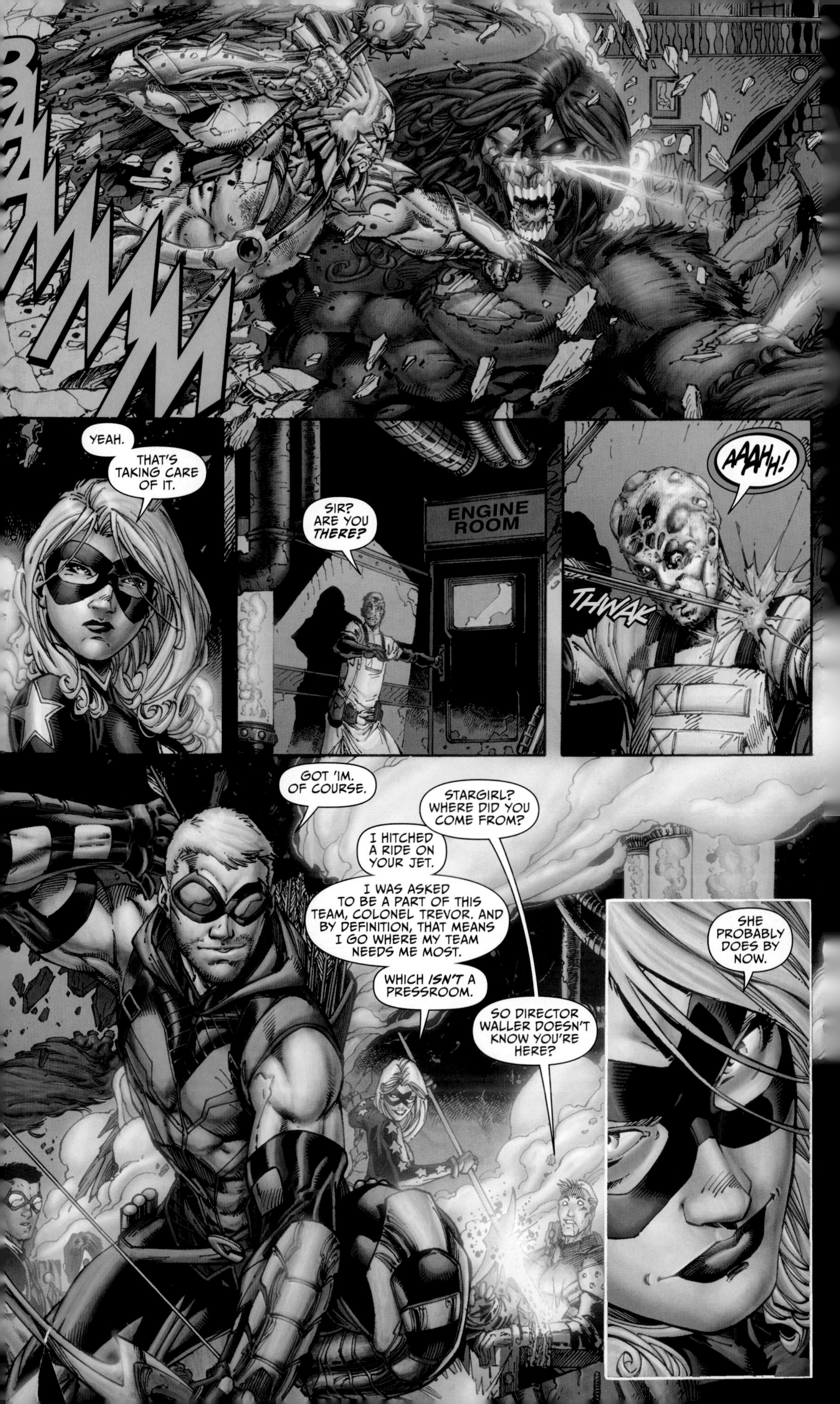
BRAAAMMM
YEAH.
THAT'S TAKING CARE OF IT.
SIR? ARE YOU *THERE?*
ENGINE ROOM
AAAHH!
THWAK
GOT 'IM. OF COURSE.
STARGIRL? WHERE DID YOU COME FROM?
I HITCHED A RIDE ON YOUR JET.
I WAS ASKED TO BE A PART OF THIS TEAM, COLONEL TREVOR. AND BY DEFINITION, THAT MEANS I GO WHERE MY TEAM NEEDS ME MOST.
WHICH *ISN'T* A PRESSROOM.
SO DIRECTOR WALLER DOESN'T KNOW YOU'RE HERE?
SHE PROBABLY DOES BY NOW.

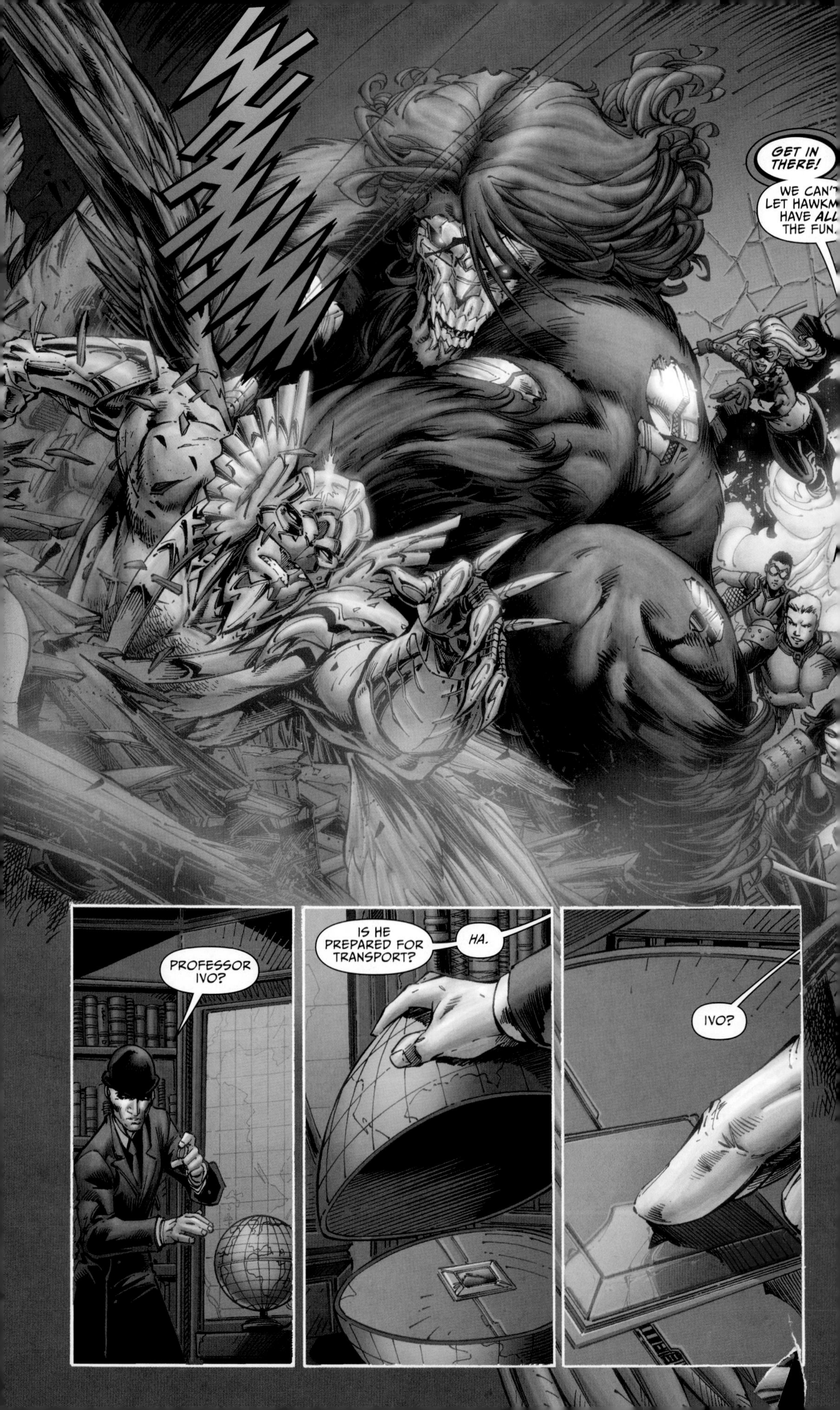
GET IN THERE!
WE CAN'T LET HAWKM HAVE ALL THE FUN.
PROFESSOR IVO?
IS HE PREPARED FOR TRANSPORT?
HA.
IVO?

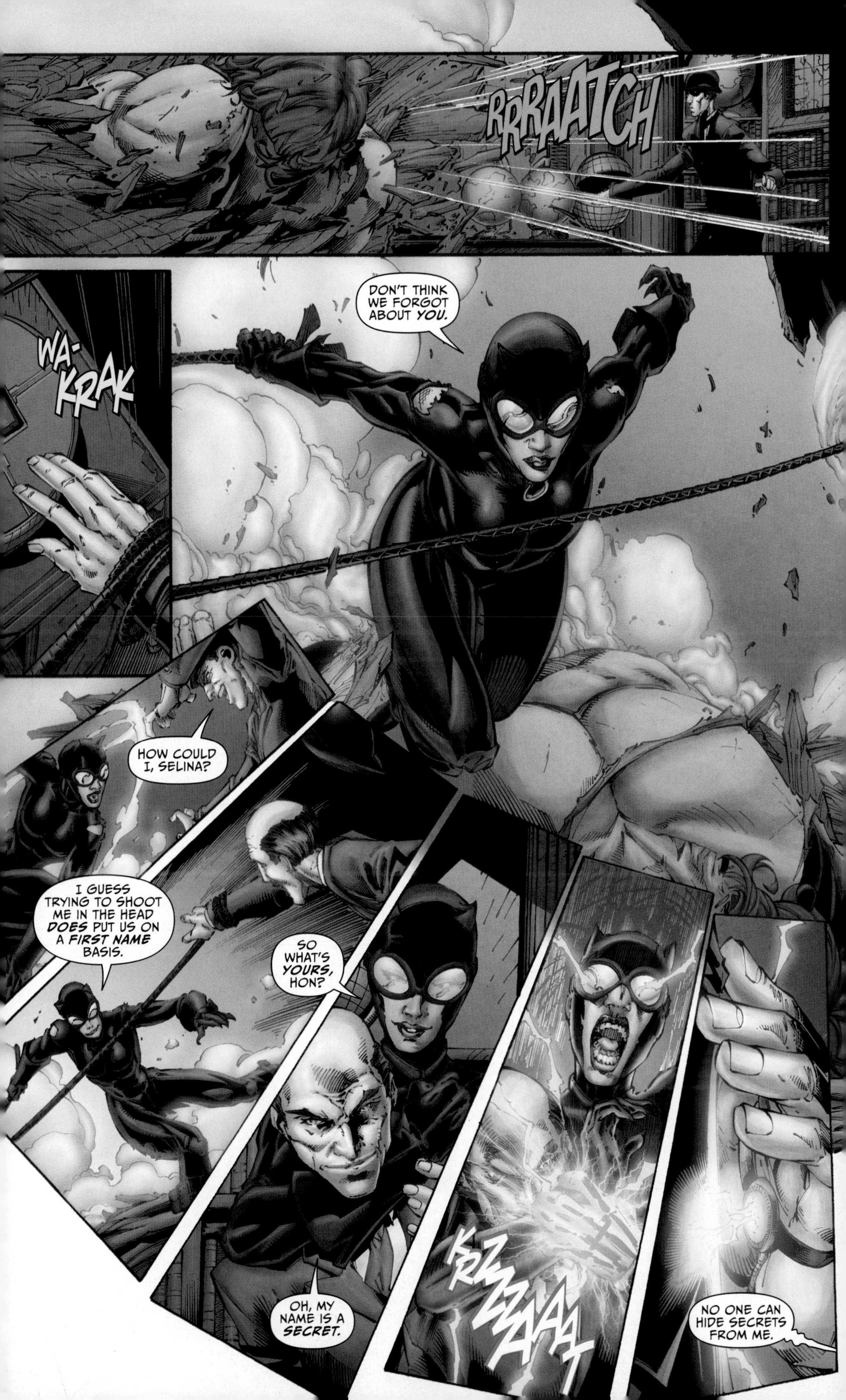
RRRAATCH
WA-KRAK
DON'T THINK WE FORGOT ABOUT YOU.
HOW COULD I, SELINA?
I GUESS TRYING TO SHOOT ME IN THE HEAD DOES PUT US ON A FIRST NAME BASIS.
SO WHAT'S YOURS, HON?
OH, MY NAME IS A SECRET.
KRZZZAAAK
NO ONE CAN HIDE SECRETS FROM ME.

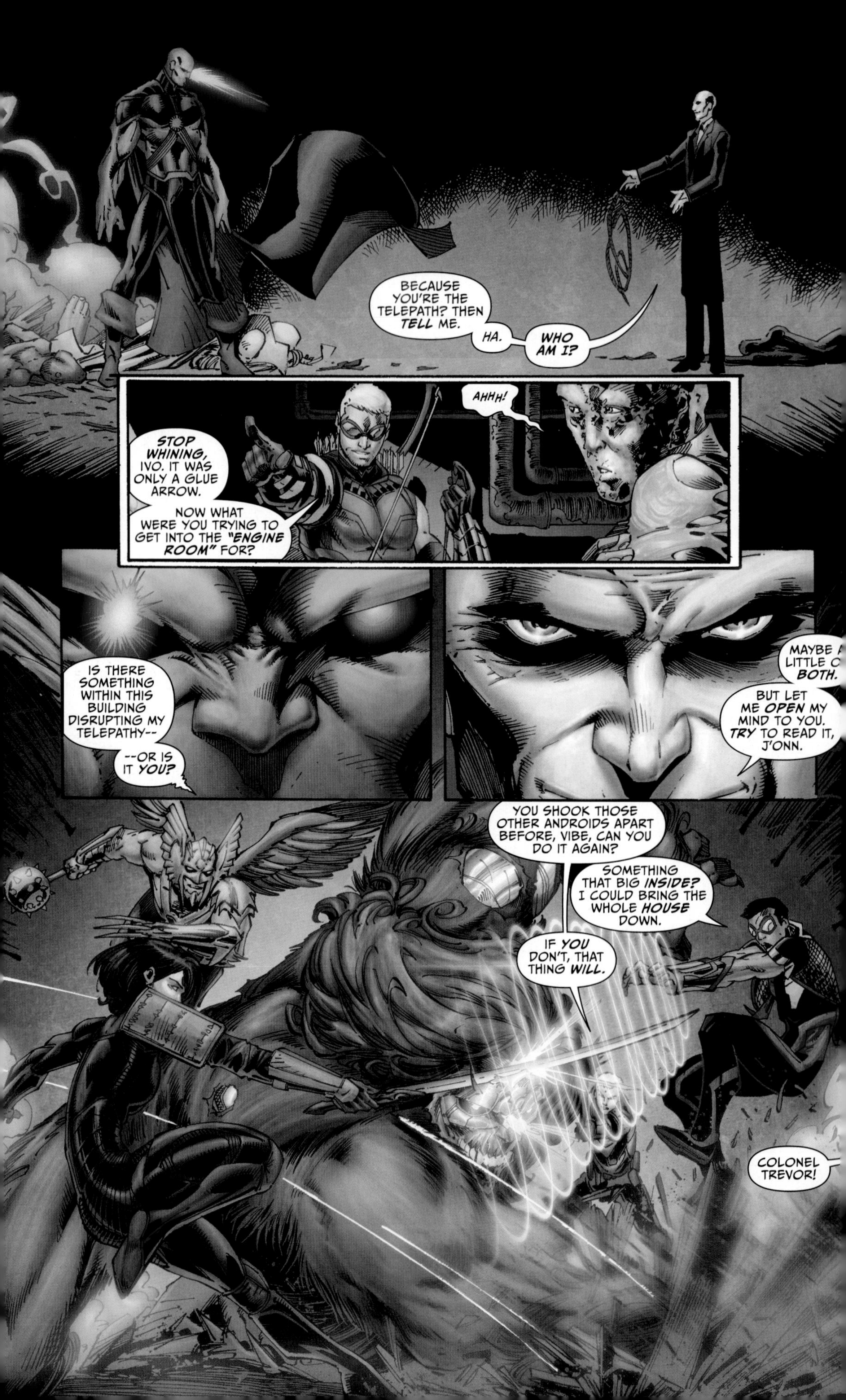
BECAUSE YOU'RE THE TELEPATH? THEN TELL ME.
HA.
WHO AM I?
AHHH!
STOP WHINING, IVO. IT WAS ONLY A GLUE ARROW.
NOW WHAT WERE YOU TRYING TO GET INTO THE "ENGINE ROOM" FOR?
IS THERE SOMETHING WITHIN THIS BUILDING DISRUPTING MY TELEPATHY--
--OR IS IT YOU?
MAYBE A LITTLE OF BOTH.
BUT LET ME OPEN MY MIND TO YOU. TRY TO READ IT, J'ONN.
YOU SHOOK THOSE OTHER ANDROIDS APART BEFORE, VIBE, CAN YOU DO IT AGAIN?
SOMETHING THAT BIG INSIDE? I COULD BRING THE WHOLE HOUSE DOWN.
IF YOU DON'T, THAT THING WILL.
COLONEL TREVOR!

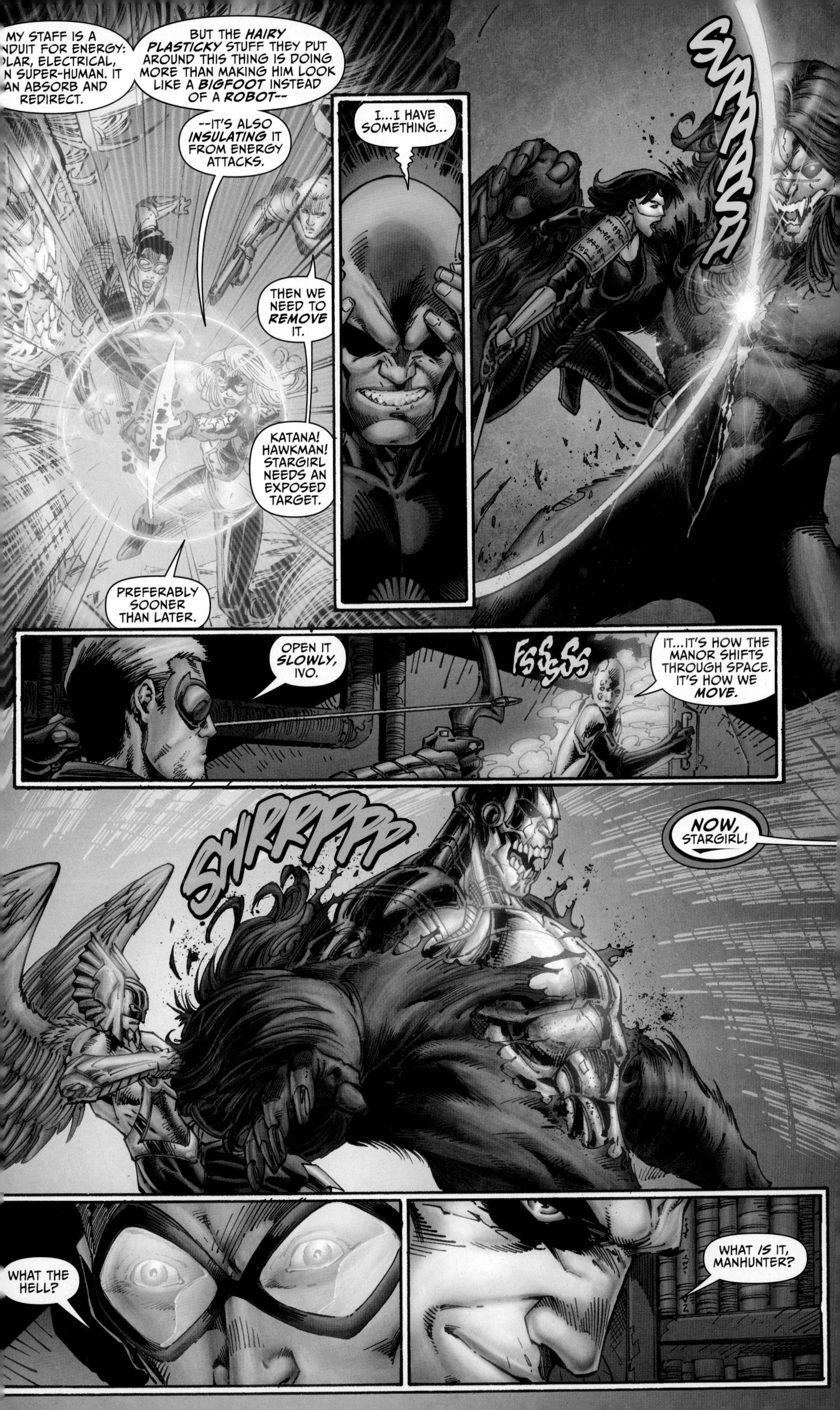
MY STAFF IS A
NDUIT FOR ENERGY:
OLAR, ELECTRICAL,
N SUPER-HUMAN. IT
AN ABSORB AND
REDIRECT.
BUT THE HAIRY PLASTICKY STUFF THEY PUT AROUND THIS THING IS DOING MORE THAN MAKING HIM LOOK LIKE A BIGFOOT INSTEAD OF A ROBOT--
--IT'S ALSO INSULATING IT FROM ENERGY ATTACKS.
THEN WE NEED TO REMOVE IT.
KATANA! HAWKMAN! STARGIRL NEEDS AN EXPOSED TARGET.
PREFERABLY SOONER THAN LATER.
I...I HAVE SOMETHING...
SLAAASH
OPEN IT SLOWLY, IVO.
FSSSSS
IT...IT'S HOW THE MANOR SHIFTS THROUGH SPACE. IT'S HOW WE MOVE.
SHRRRRR
NOW, STARGIRL!
WHAT THE HELL?
WHAT IS IT, MANHUNTER?

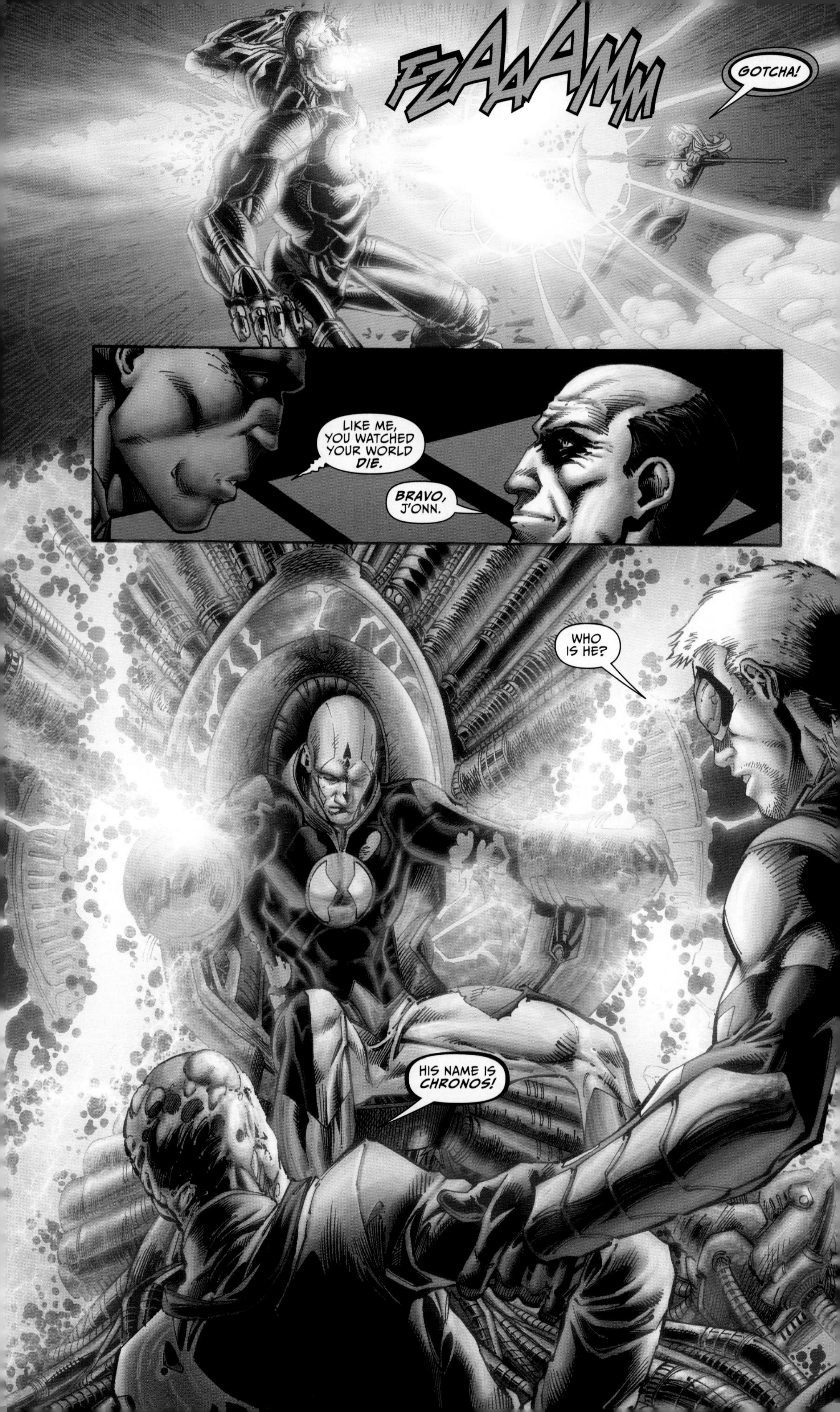
FZAAAMM
GOTCHA!
LIKE ME, YOU WATCHED YOUR WORLD DIE.
BRAVO, J'ONN.
WHO IS HE?
HIS NAME IS CHRONOS!

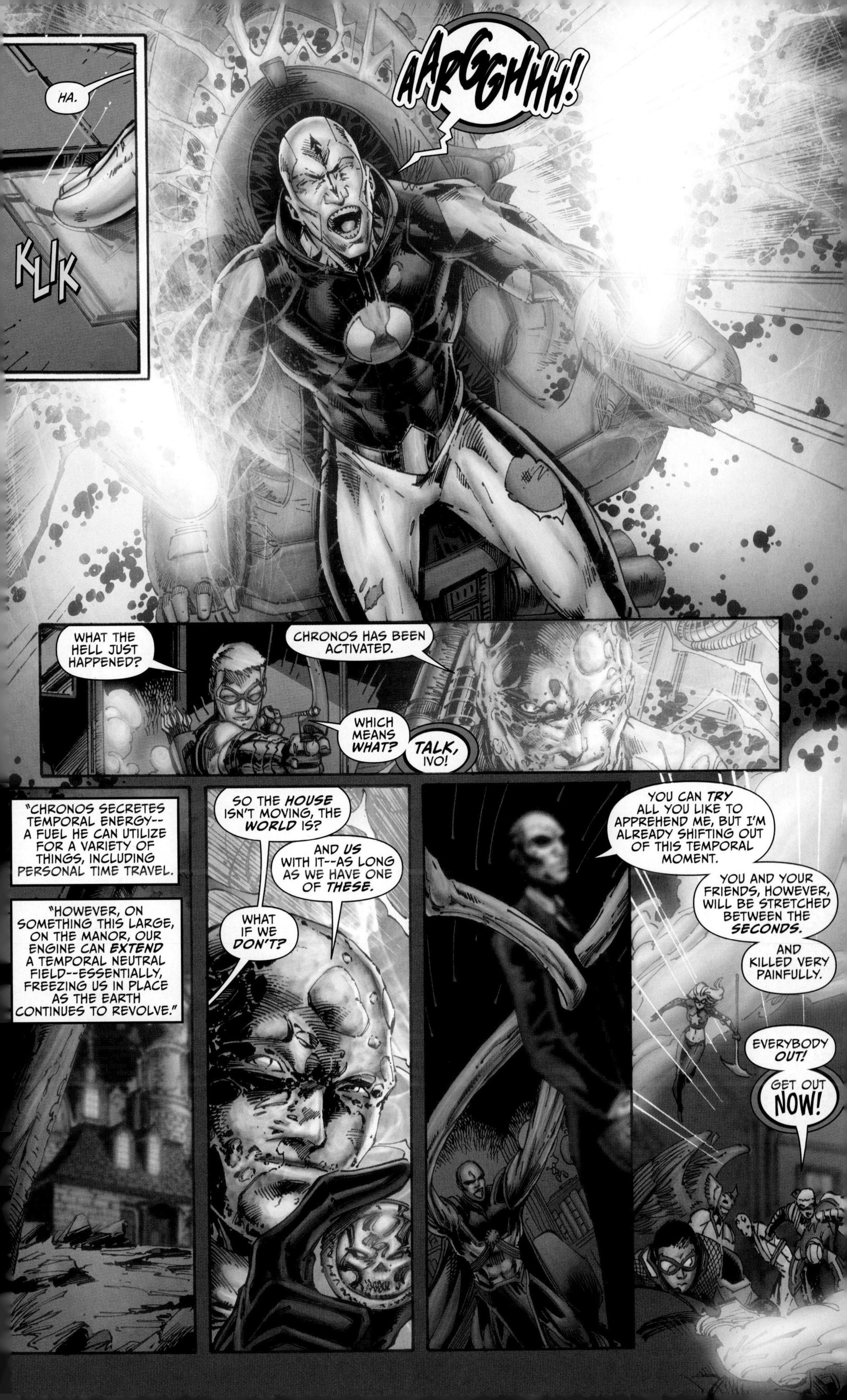
HA.
KLIK
AARGGHHH!
WHAT THE HELL JUST HAPPENED?
CHRONOS HAS BEEN ACTIVATED.
WHICH MEANS WHAT?
TALK, IVO!
"CHRONOS SECRETES TEMPORAL ENERGY-- A FUEL HE CAN UTILIZE FOR A VARIETY OF THINGS, INCLUDING PERSONAL TIME TRAVEL.
"HOWEVER, ON SOMETHING THIS LARGE, ON THE MANOR, OUR ENGINE CAN EXTEND A TEMPORAL NEUTRAL FIELD--ESSENTIALLY, FREEZING US IN PLACE AS THE EARTH CONTINUES TO REVOLVE."
SO THE HOUSE ISN'T MOVING, THE WORLD IS?
AND US WITH IT--AS LONG AS WE HAVE ONE OF THESE.
WHAT IF WE DON'T?
YOU CAN TRY ALL YOU LIKE TO APPREHEND ME, BUT I'M ALREADY SHIFTING OUT OF THIS TEMPORAL MOMENT.
YOU AND YOUR FRIENDS, HOWEVER, WILL BE STRETCHED BETWEEN THE SECONDS.
AND KILLED VERY PAINFULLY.
EVERYBODY OUT!
GET OUT NOW!

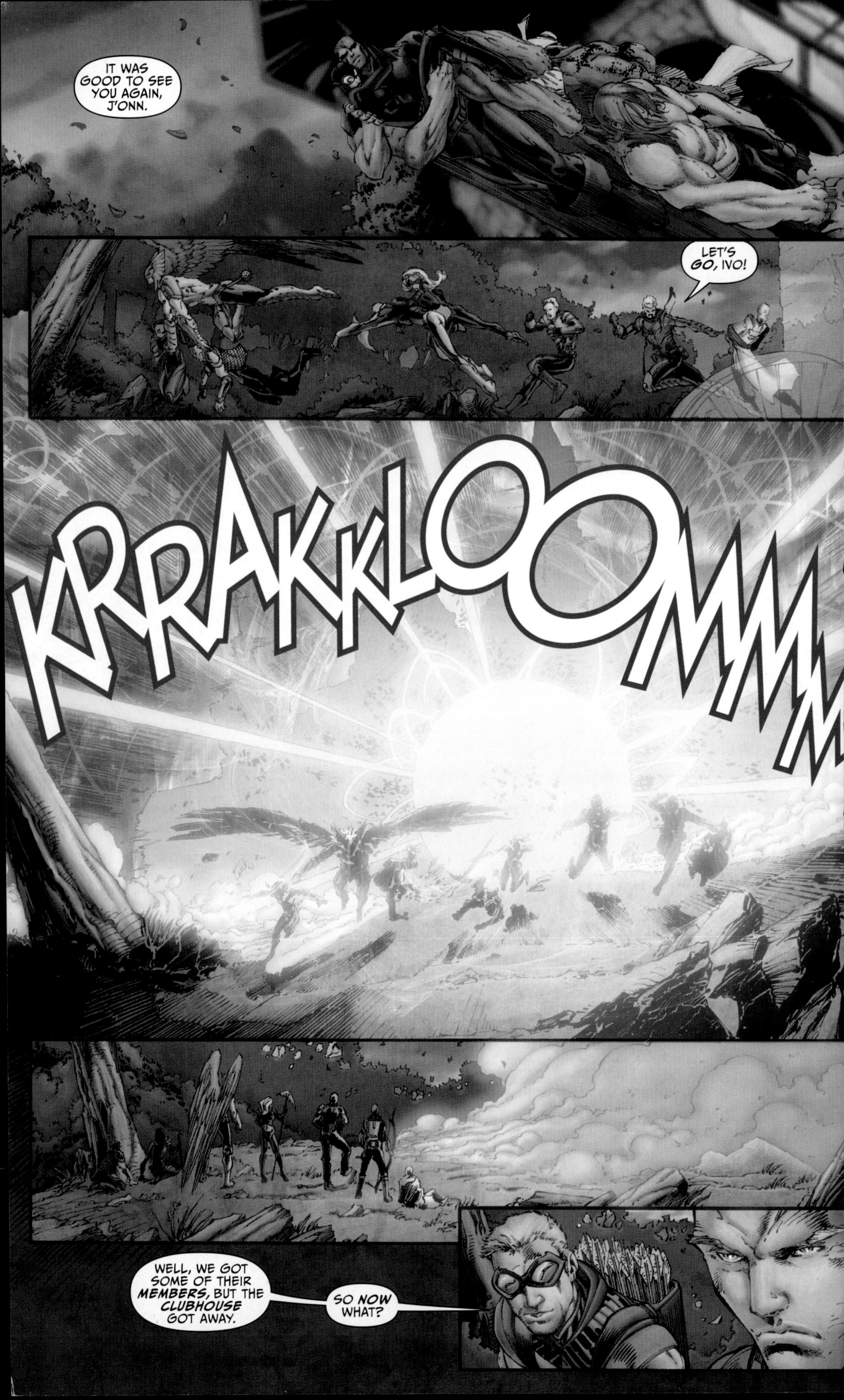
IT WAS GOOD TO SEE YOU AGAIN, J'ONN.
LET'S GO, IVO!
KRRAKKLOOMMM
WELL, WE GOT SOME OF THEIR MEMBERS, BUT THE CLUBHOUSE GOT AWAY.
SO NOW WHAT?

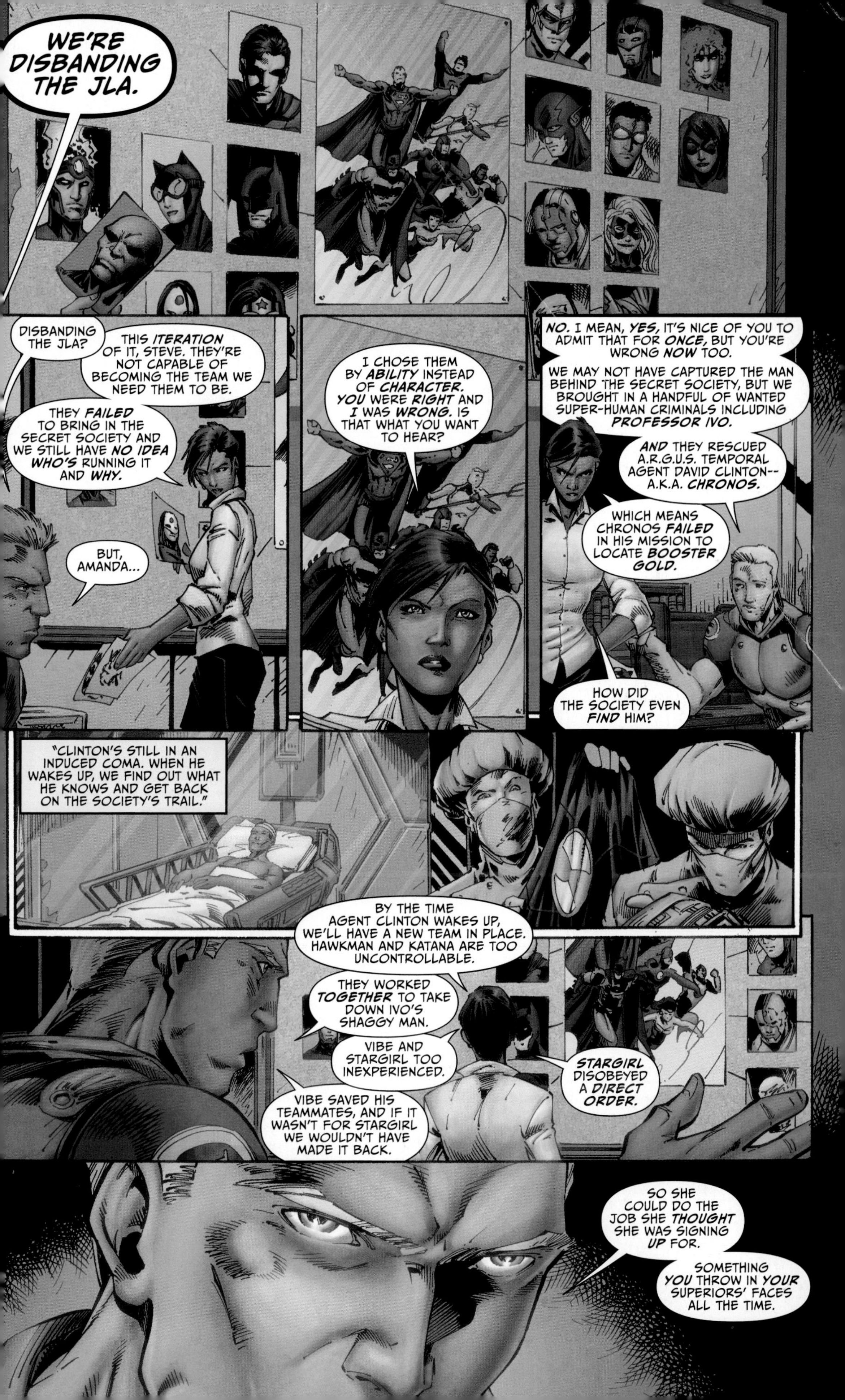
WE'RE DISBANDING THE JLA.
DISBANDING THE JLA?
THIS ITERATION OF IT, STEVE. THEY'RE NOT CAPABLE OF BECOMING THE TEAM WE NEED THEM TO BE.
THEY FAILED TO BRING IN THE SECRET SOCIETY AND WE STILL HAVE NO IDEA WHO'S RUNNING IT AND WHY.
BUT, AMANDA...
I CHOSE THEM BY ABILITY INSTEAD OF CHARACTER. YOU WERE RIGHT AND I WAS WRONG. IS THAT WHAT YOU WANT TO HEAR?
NO. I MEAN, YES, IT'S NICE OF YOU TO ADMIT THAT FOR ONCE, BUT YOU'RE WRONG NOW TOO.
WE MAY NOT HAVE CAPTURED THE MAN BEHIND THE SECRET SOCIETY, BUT WE BROUGHT IN A HANDFUL OF WANTED SUPER-HUMAN CRIMINALS INCLUDING PROFESSOR IVO.
AND THEY RESCUED A.R.G.U.S. TEMPORAL AGENT DAVID CLINTON-- A.K.A. CHRONOS.
WHICH MEANS CHRONOS FAILED IN HIS MISSION TO LOCATE BOOSTER GOLD.
HOW DID THE SOCIETY EVEN FIND HIM?
"CLINTON'S STILL IN AN INDUCED COMA. WHEN HE WAKES UP, WE FIND OUT WHAT HE KNOWS AND GET BACK ON THE SOCIETY'S TRAIL."
BY THE TIME AGENT CLINTON WAKES UP, WE'LL HAVE A NEW TEAM IN PLACE. HAWKMAN AND KATANA ARE TOO UNCONTROLLABLE.
THEY WORKED TOGETHER TO TAKE DOWN IVO'S SHAGGY MAN.
VIBE AND STARGIRL TOO INEXPERIENCED.
VIBE SAVED HIS TEAMMATES, AND IF IT WASN'T FOR STARGIRL WE WOULDN'T HAVE MADE IT BACK.
STARGIRL DISOBEYED A DIRECT ORDER.
SO SHE COULD DO THE JOB SHE THOUGHT SHE WAS SIGNING UP FOR.
SOMETHING YOU THROW IN YOUR SUPERIORS' FACES ALL THE TIME.

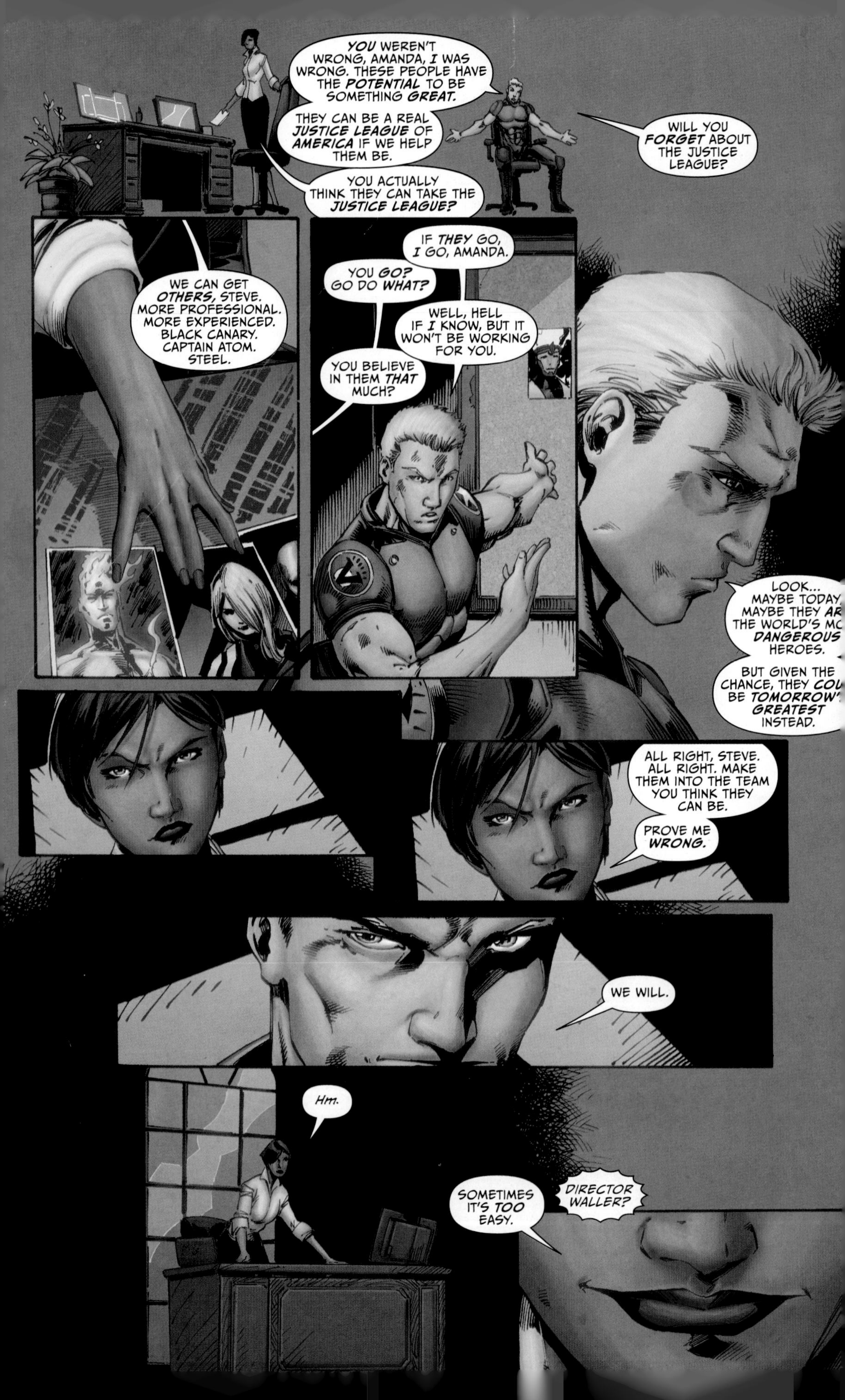
YOU WEREN'T WRONG, AMANDA, I WAS WRONG. THESE PEOPLE HAVE THE POTENTIAL TO BE SOMETHING GREAT.
THEY CAN BE A REAL JUSTICE LEAGUE OF AMERICA IF WE HELP THEM BE.
YOU ACTUALLY THINK THEY CAN TAKE THE JUSTICE LEAGUE?
WILL YOU FORGET ABOUT THE JUSTICE LEAGUE?
WE CAN GET OTHERS, STEVE. MORE PROFESSIONAL. MORE EXPERIENCED. BLACK CANARY. CAPTAIN ATOM. STEEL.
IF THEY GO, I GO, AMANDA.
YOU GO? GO DO WHAT?
WELL, HELL IF I KNOW, BUT IT WON'T BE WORKING FOR YOU.
YOU BELIEVE IN THEM THAT MUCH?
LOOK... MAYBE TODAY, MAYBE THEY AR THE WORLD'S MO DANGEROUS HEROES.
BUT GIVEN THE CHANCE, THEY COU BE TOMORROW'S GREATEST INSTEAD.
ALL RIGHT, STEVE. ALL RIGHT. MAKE THEM INTO THE TEAM YOU THINK THEY CAN BE.
PROVE ME WRONG.
WE WILL.
Hm.
SOMETIMES IT'S TOO EASY.
DIRECTOR WALLER?

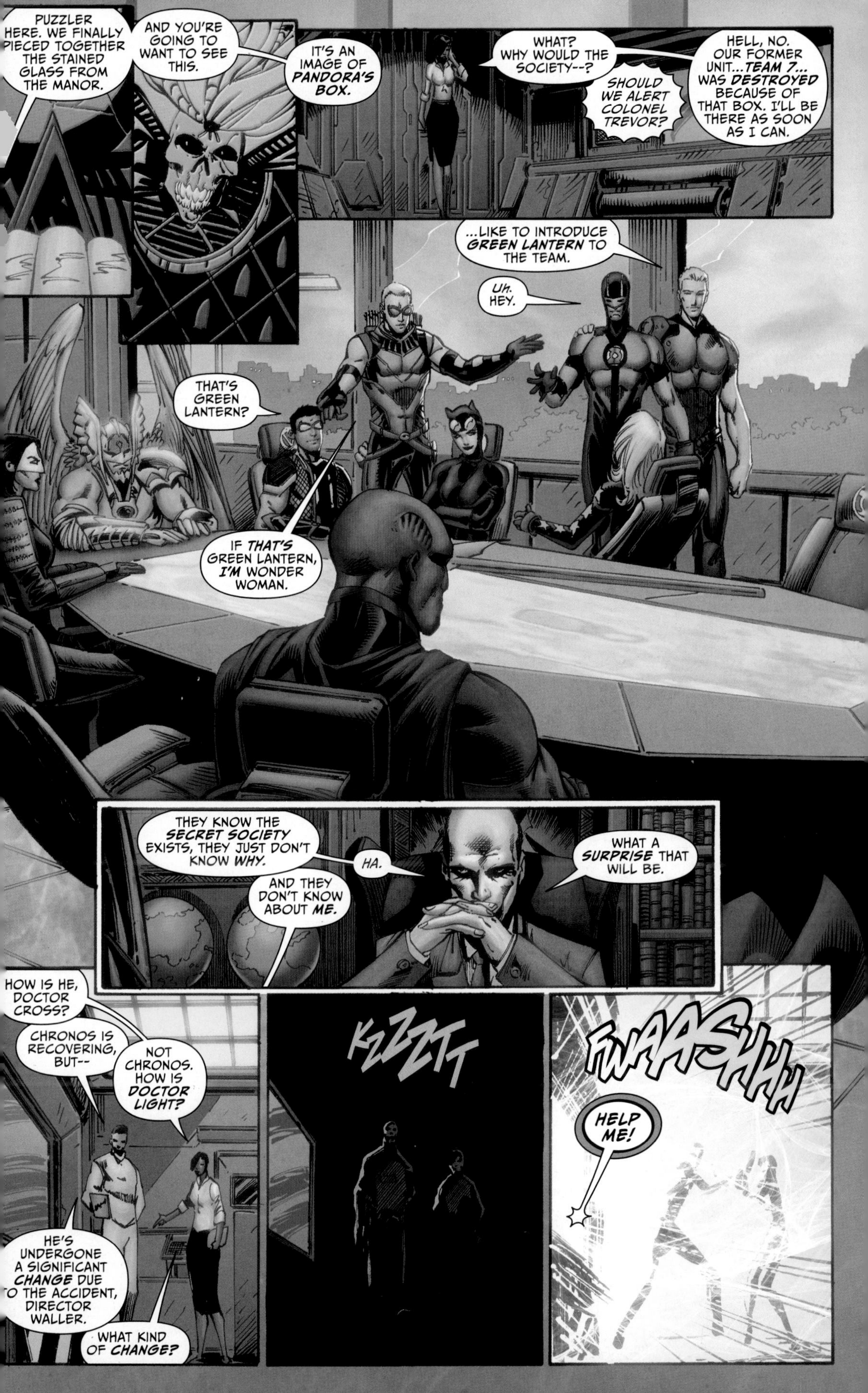
PUZZLER HERE. WE FINALLY PIECED TOGETHER THE STAINED GLASS FROM THE MANOR.
AND YOU'RE GOING TO WANT TO SEE THIS.
IT'S AN IMAGE OF PANDORA'S BOX.
WHAT? WHY WOULD THE SOCIETY--?
SHOULD WE ALERT COLONEL TREVOR?
HELL, NO. OUR FORMER UNIT...TEAM 7... WAS DESTROYED BECAUSE OF THAT BOX. I'LL BE THERE AS SOON AS I CAN.
...LIKE TO INTRODUCE GREEN LANTERN TO THE TEAM.
Uh. HEY.
THAT'S GREEN LANTERN?
IF THAT'S GREEN LANTERN, I'M WONDER WOMAN.
THEY KNOW THE SECRET SOCIETY EXISTS, THEY JUST DON'T KNOW WHY.
HA.
AND THEY DON'T KNOW ABOUT ME.
WHAT A SURPRISE THAT WILL BE.
HOW IS HE, DOCTOR CROSS?
CHRONOS IS RECOVERING, BUT--
NOT CHRONOS. HOW IS DOCTOR LIGHT?
HE'S UNDERGONE A SIGNIFICANT CHANGE DUE TO THE ACCIDENT, DIRECTOR WALLER.
WHAT KIND OF CHANGE?
KZZZZTT
FWAAASHHH
HELP ME!

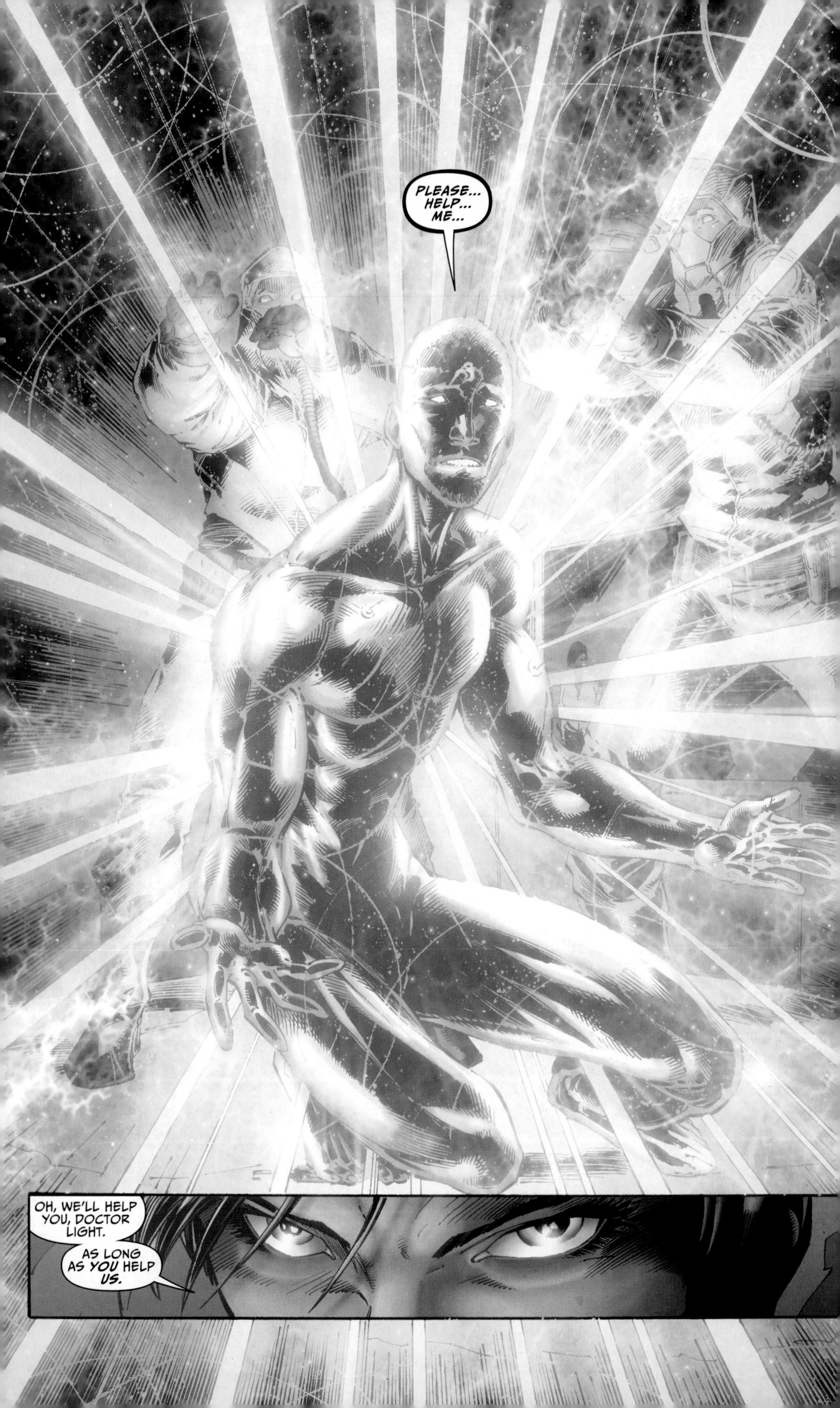
PLEASE... HELP... ME...
OH, WE'LL HELP YOU, DOCTOR LIGHT.
AS LONG AS YOU HELP US.

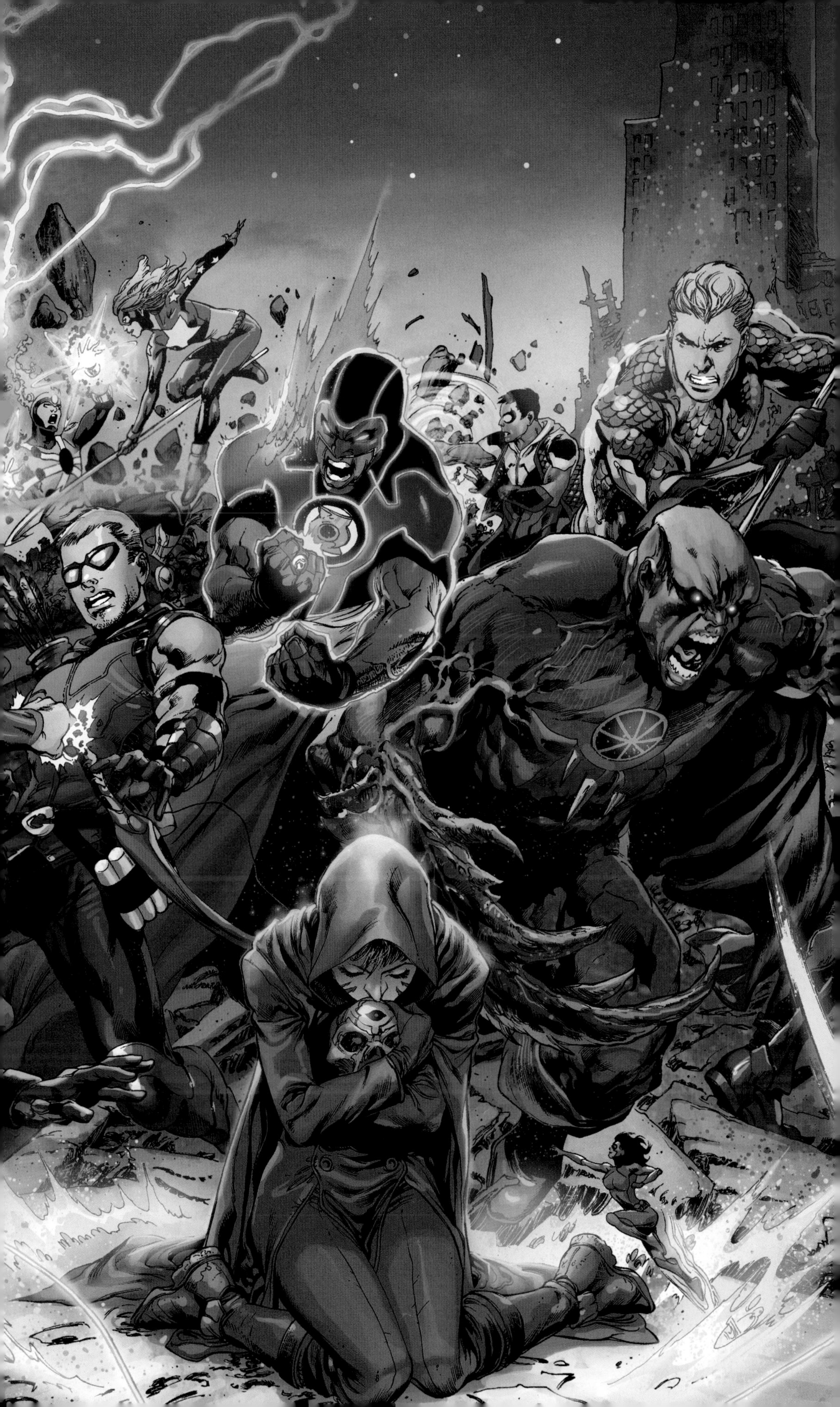

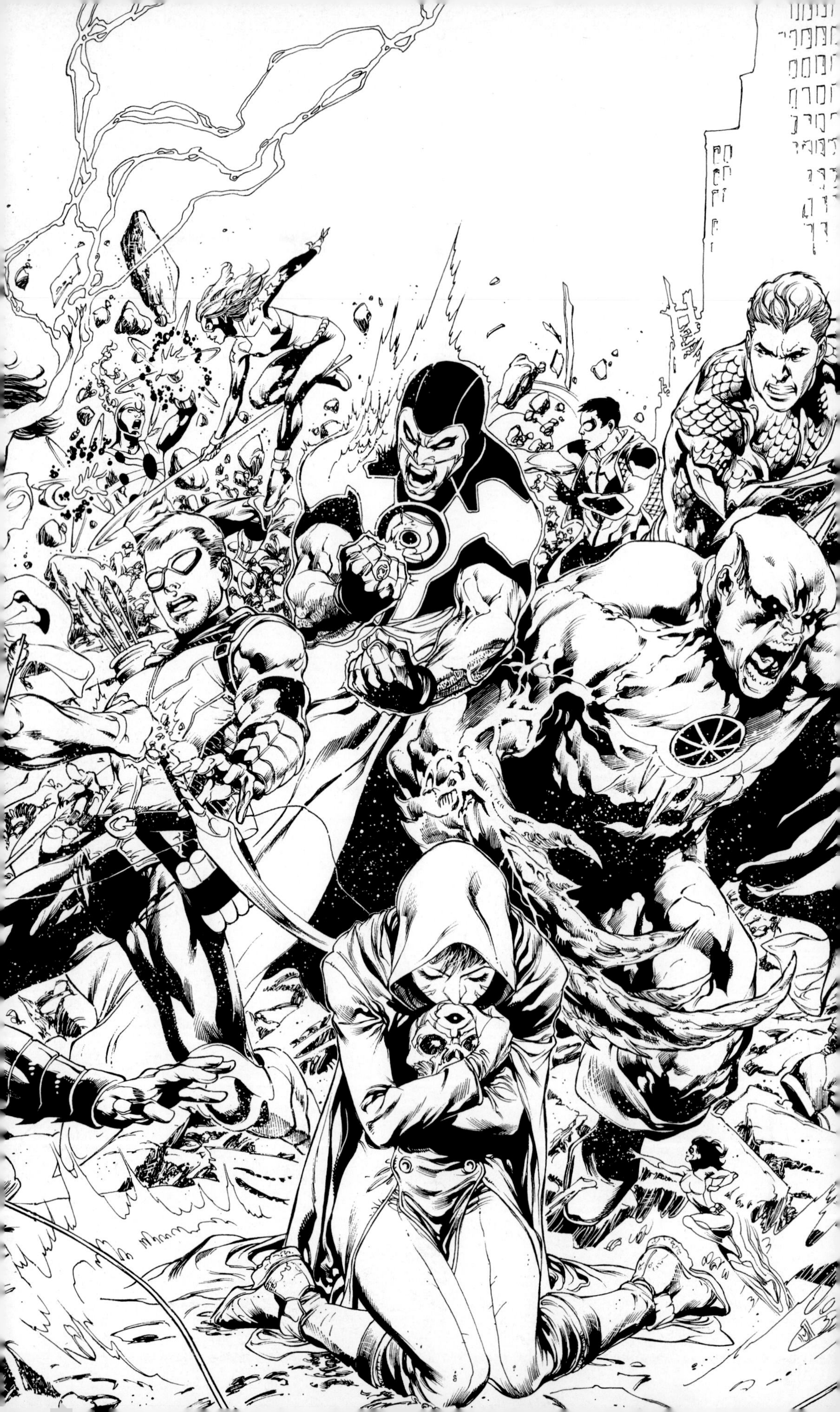

I know you probably have a lot of questions.

So do I.

MY FELLOW SOCIETY MEMBERS...

VLINK

...IT'S TIME.

For as long as I can recall, a QUESTION pops into my brain.

Each syllable pounds in my mind OVER and OVER until I find the ANSWER.

"Who is the Hub City Slayer?" was the latest one.

I tracked the killer down and broke both his arms. He confessed and turned himself in.

For a brief moment, I had a reprieve from my haunting headaches.

But soon the next question arrives, kicking and screaming inside my head and demanding an answer.

WHO IS THE EVIL BEHIND THE EVIL?

WHO IS THE EVIL BEHIND THE EVIL

I've been told that someday I'll answer enough questions to get the answer to my own: WHO AM I?

What is my true name?

Until that day comes, I am the Question.

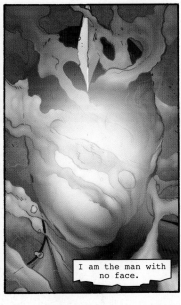

I am the man with no face.

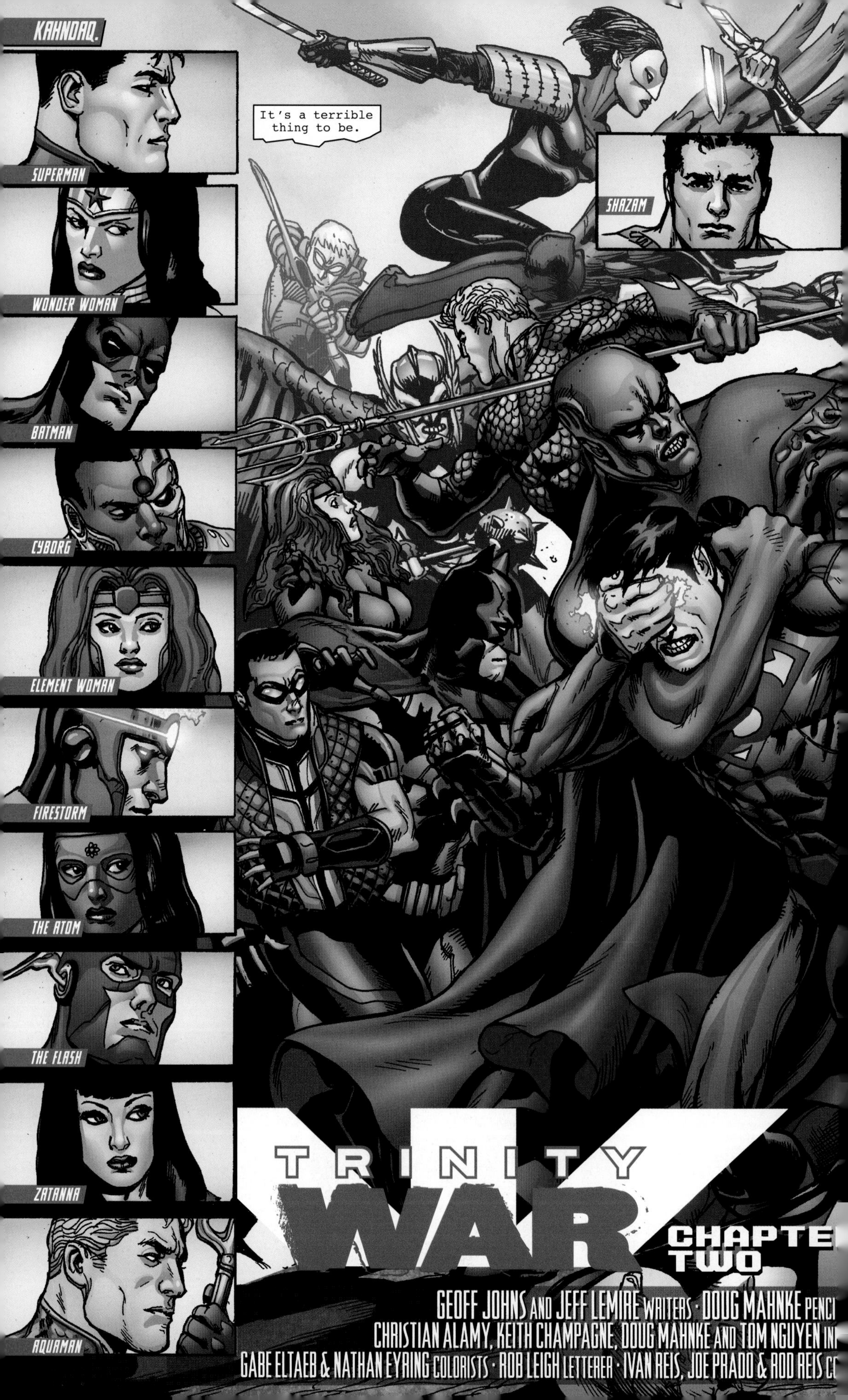
KAHNDAQ.
SUPERMAN
WONDER WOMAN
BATMAN
CYBORG
ELEMENT WOMAN
FIRESTORM
THE ATOM
THE FLASH
ZATANNA
AQUAMAN
It's a terrible thing to be.
SHAZAM
TRINITY WAR
CHAPTE TWO
GEOFF JOHNS AND JEFF LEMIRE WRITERS · DOUG MAHNKE PENCI
CHRISTIAN ALAMY, KEITH CHAMPAGNE, DOUG MAHNKE AND TOM NGUYEN IN
GABE ELTAEB & NATHAN EYRING COLORISTS · ROB LEIGH LETTERER · IVAN REIS, JOE PRADO & ROD REIS C

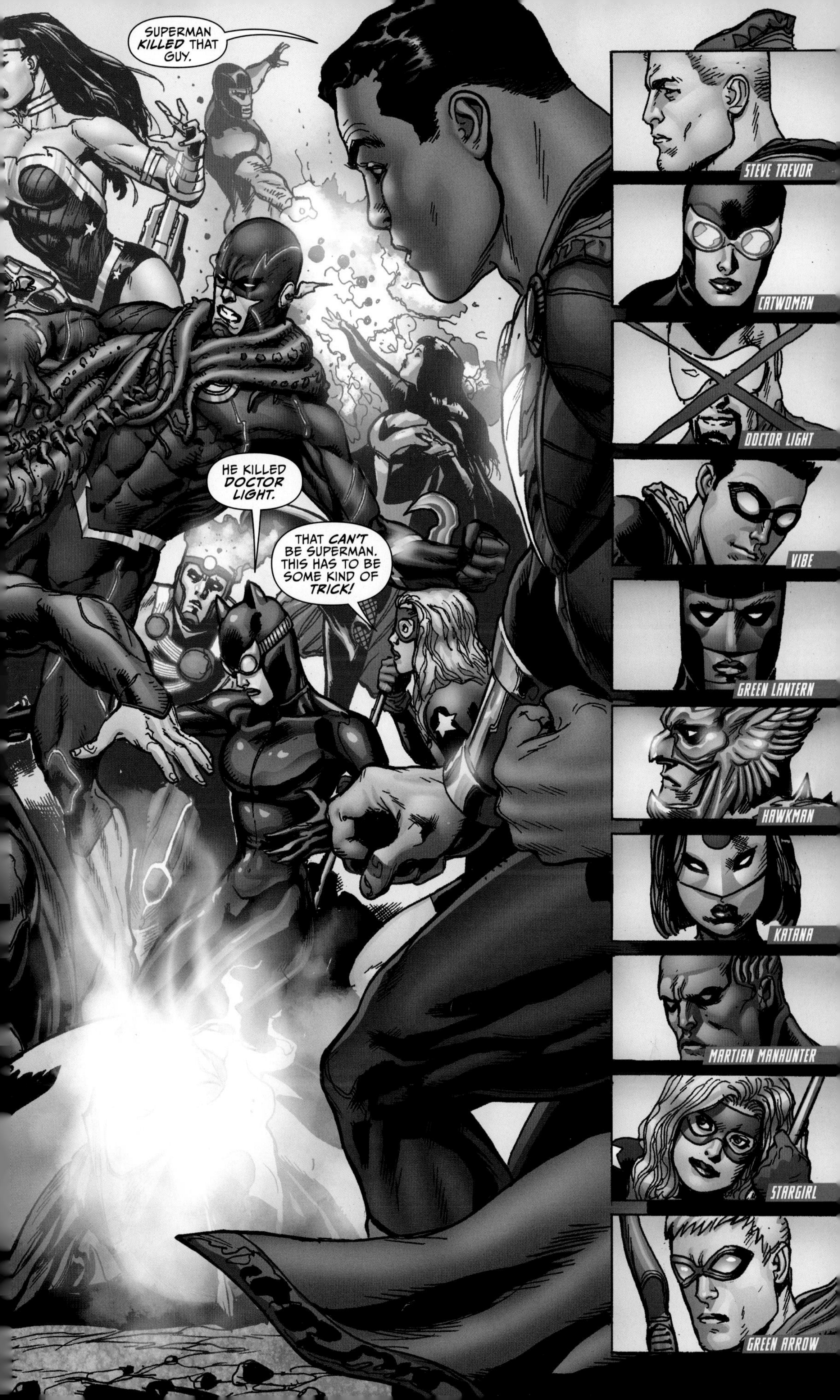
SUPERMAN KILLED THAT GUY.
HE KILLED DOCTOR LIGHT.
THAT CAN'T BE SUPERMAN. THIS HAS TO BE SOME KIND OF TRICK!
STEVE TREVOR
CATWOMAN
DOCTOR LIGHT
VIBE
GREEN LANTERN
HAWKMAN
KATANA
MARTIAN MANHUNTER
STARGIRL
GREEN ARROW

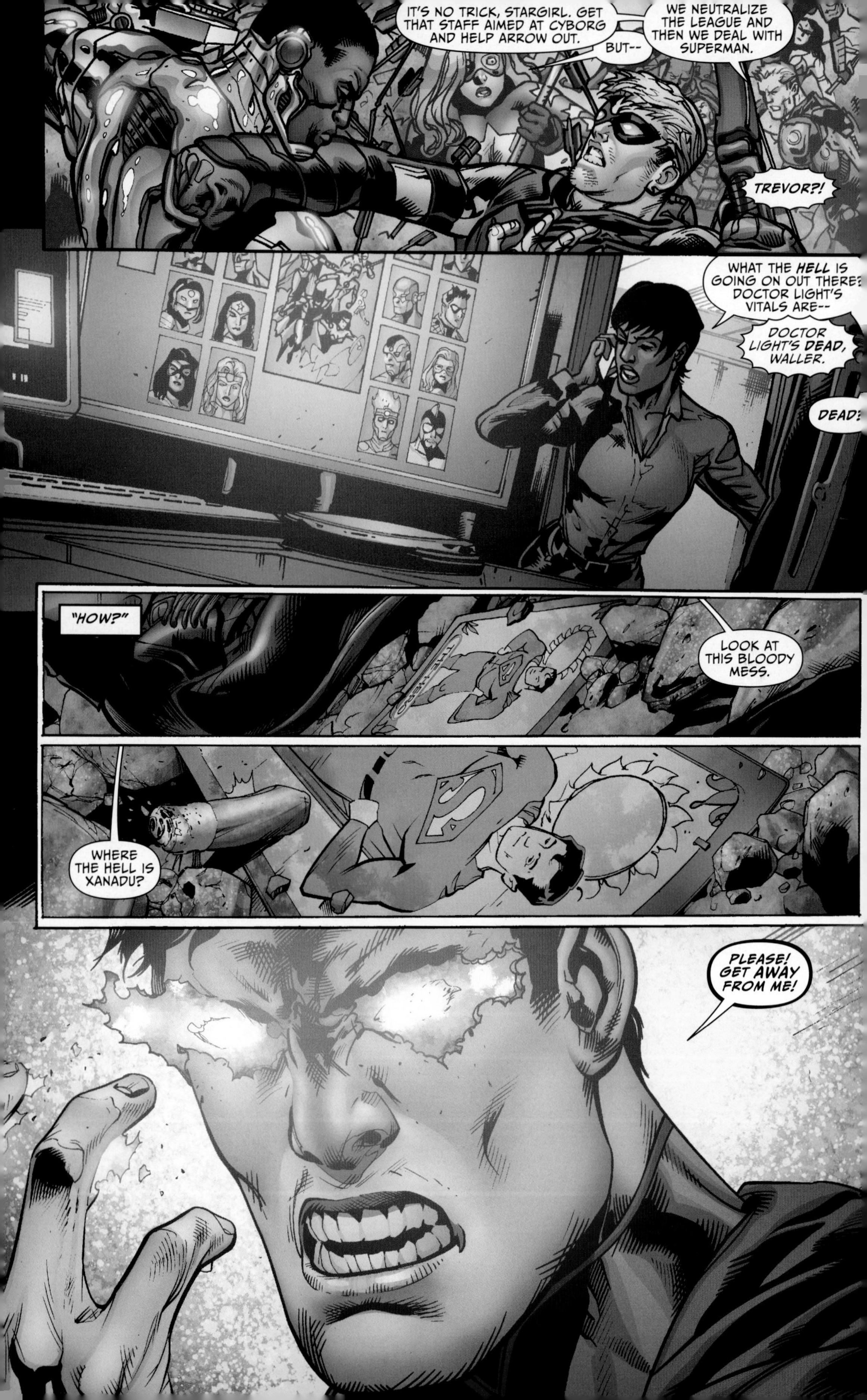
IT'S NO TRICK, STARGIRL. GET THAT STAFF AIMED AT CYBORG AND HELP ARROW OUT.
BUT--
WE NEUTRALIZE THE LEAGUE AND THEN WE DEAL WITH SUPERMAN.
TREVOR?!
WHAT THE HELL IS GOING ON OUT THERE? DOCTOR LIGHT'S VITALS ARE--
DOCTOR LIGHT'S DEAD, WALLER.
DEAD?
"HOW?"
LOOK AT THIS BLOODY MESS.
WHERE THE HELL IS XANADU?
PLEASE! GET AWAY FROM ME!

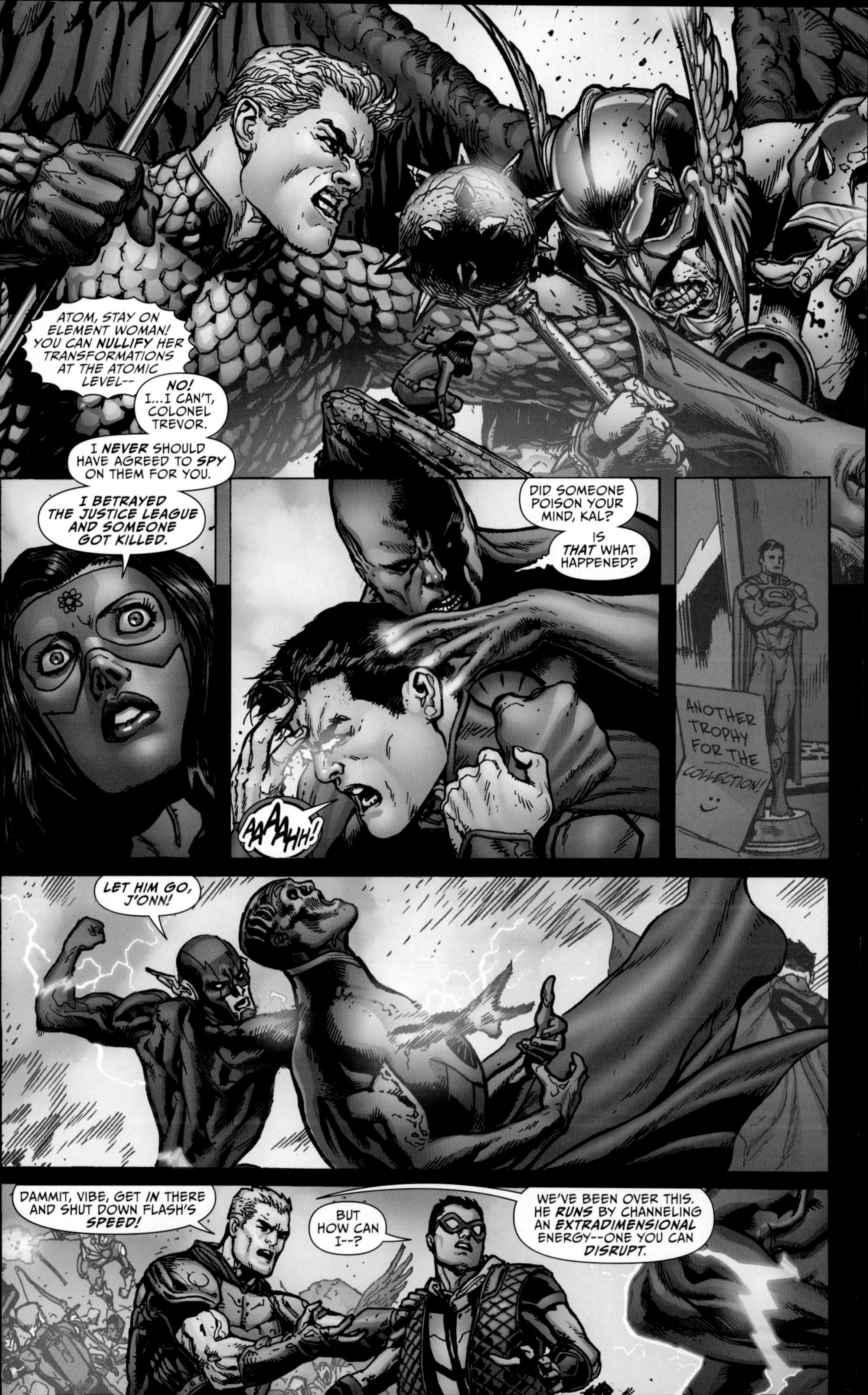
ATOM, STAY ON ELEMENT WOMAN! YOU CAN NULLIFY HER TRANSFORMATIONS AT THE ATOMIC LEVEL--
NO! I...I CAN'T, COLONEL TREVOR.
I NEVER SHOULD HAVE AGREED TO SPY ON THEM FOR YOU.
I BETRAYED THE JUSTICE LEAGUE AND SOMEONE GOT KILLED.
DID SOMEONE POISON YOUR MIND, KAL?
IS THAT WHAT HAPPENED?
AAAAHH!
ANOTHER TROPHY FOR THE COLLECTION!
LET HIM GO, J'ONN!
DAMMIT, VIBE, GET IN THERE AND SHUT DOWN FLASH'S SPEED!
BUT HOW CAN I--?
WE'VE BEEN OVER THIS. HE RUNS BY CHANNELING AN EXTRADIMENSIONAL ENERGY--ONE YOU CAN DISRUPT.

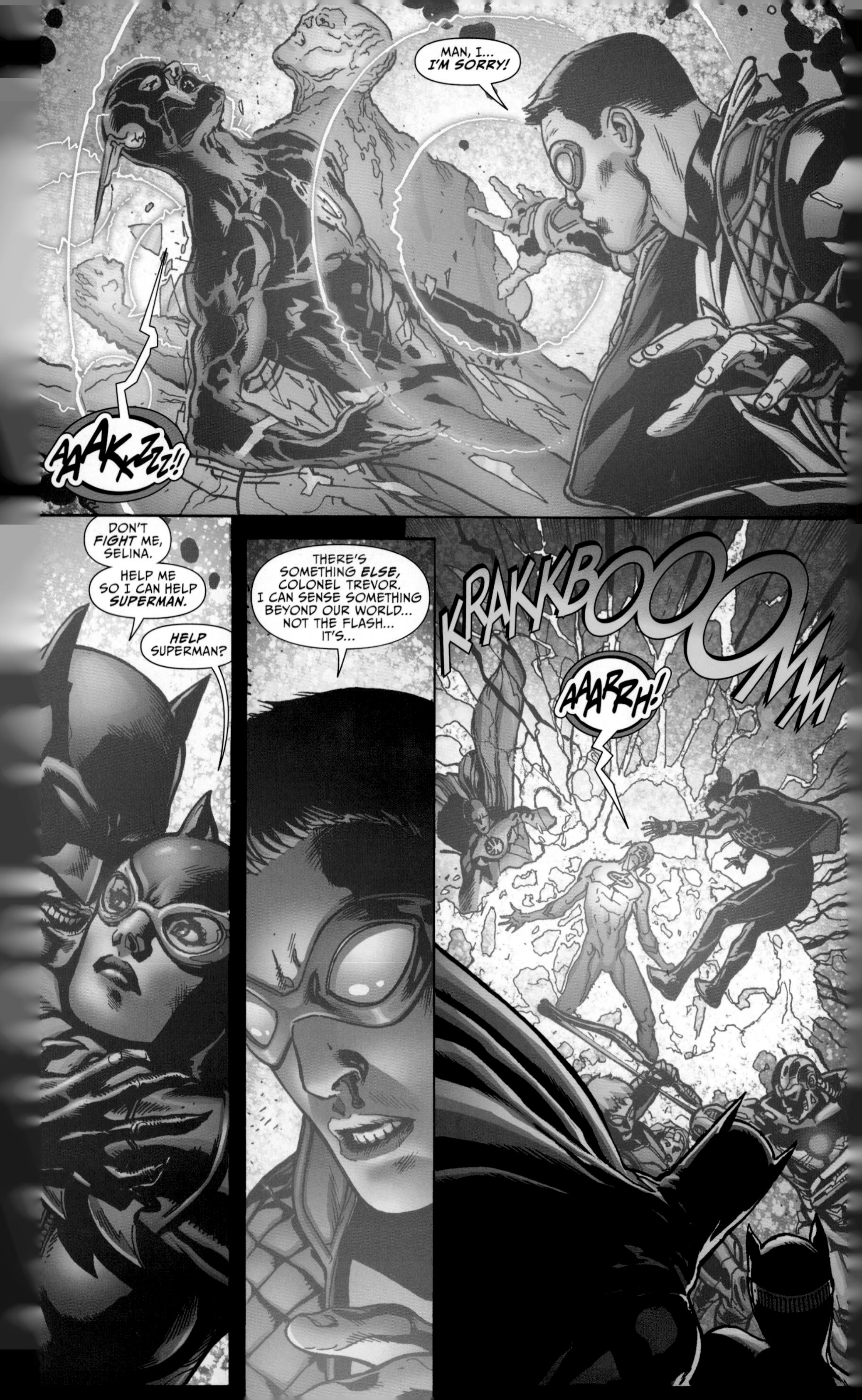
MAN, I... I'M SORRY!
AAAKXZZZZ!!
DON'T FIGHT ME, SELINA. HELP ME SO I CAN HELP SUPERMAN.
HELP SUPERMAN?
THERE'S SOMETHING ELSE, COLONEL TREVOR. I CAN SENSE SOMETHING BEYOND OUR WORLD... NOT THE FLASH... IT'S...
KRAKKBOOOOMM
AAARRH!

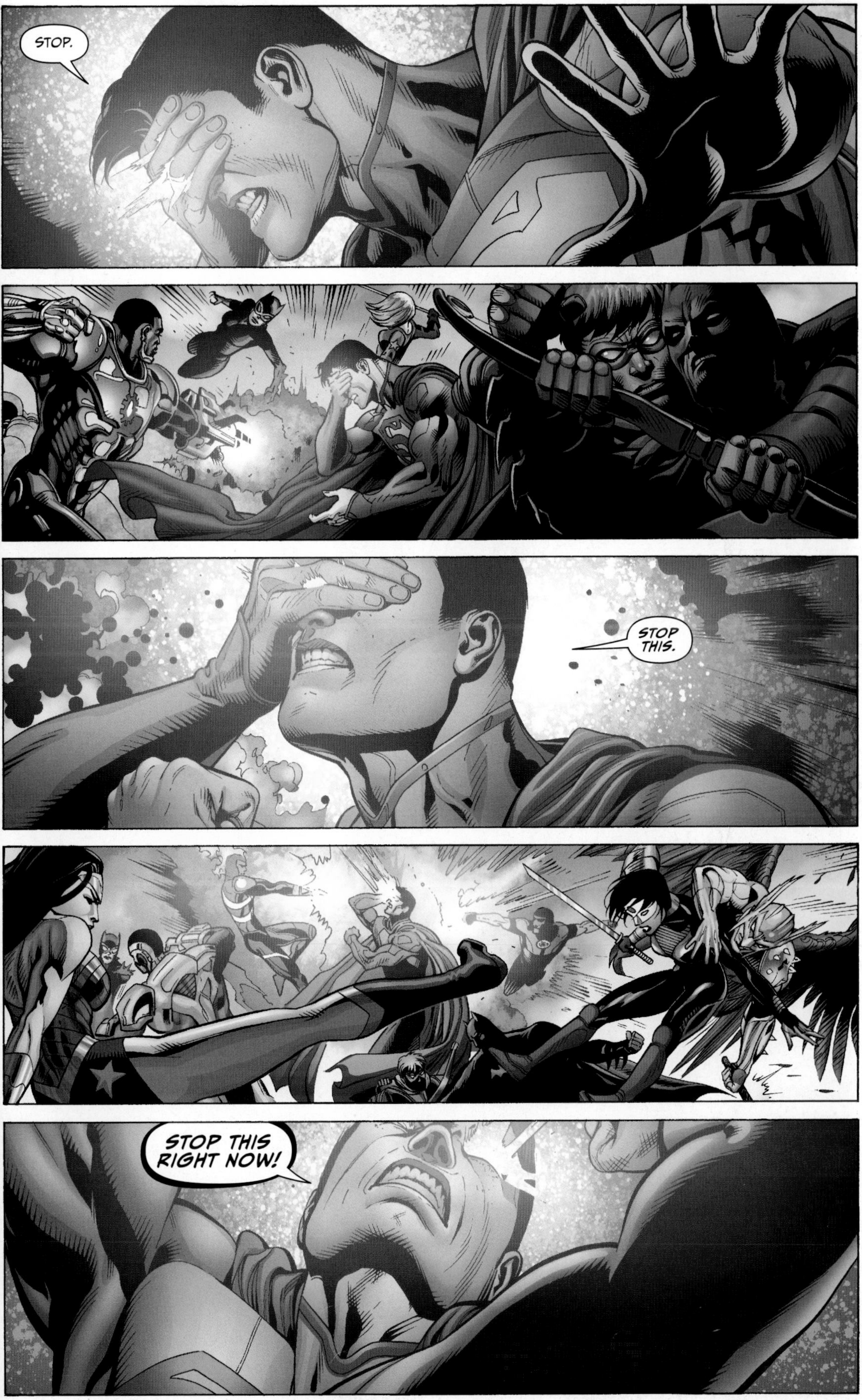
STOP.
STOP THIS.
STOP THIS RIGHT NOW!

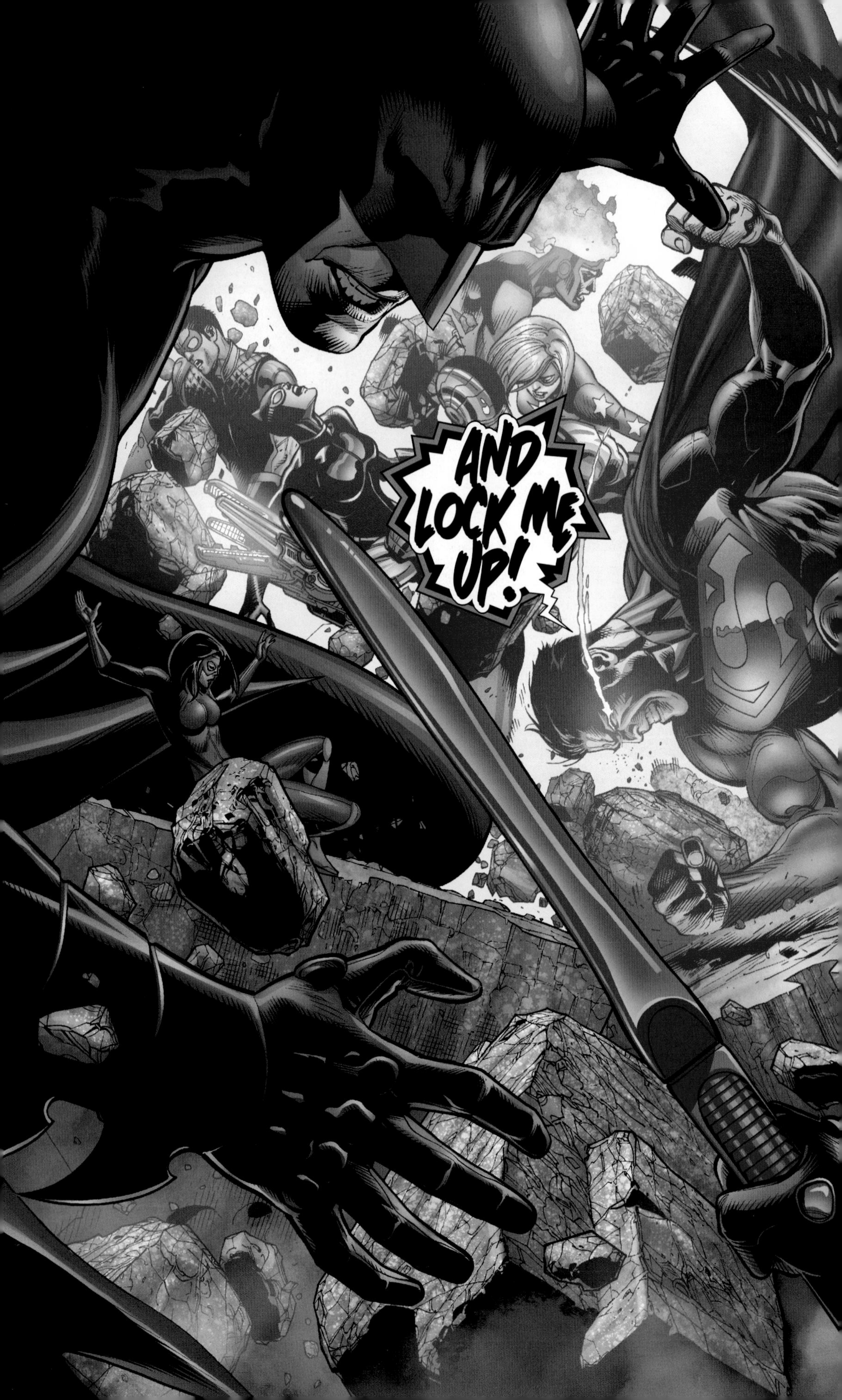
AND LOCK ME UP!

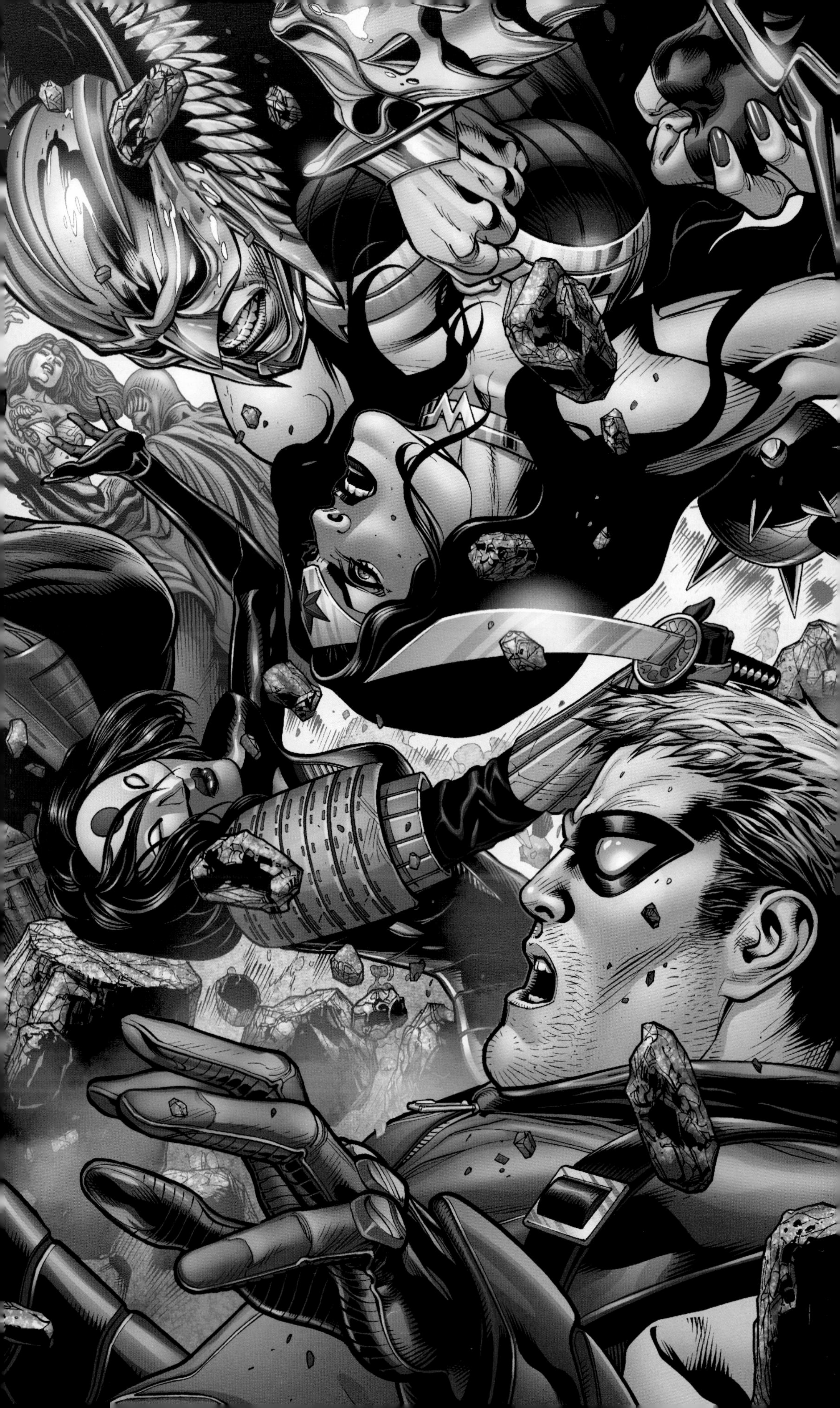

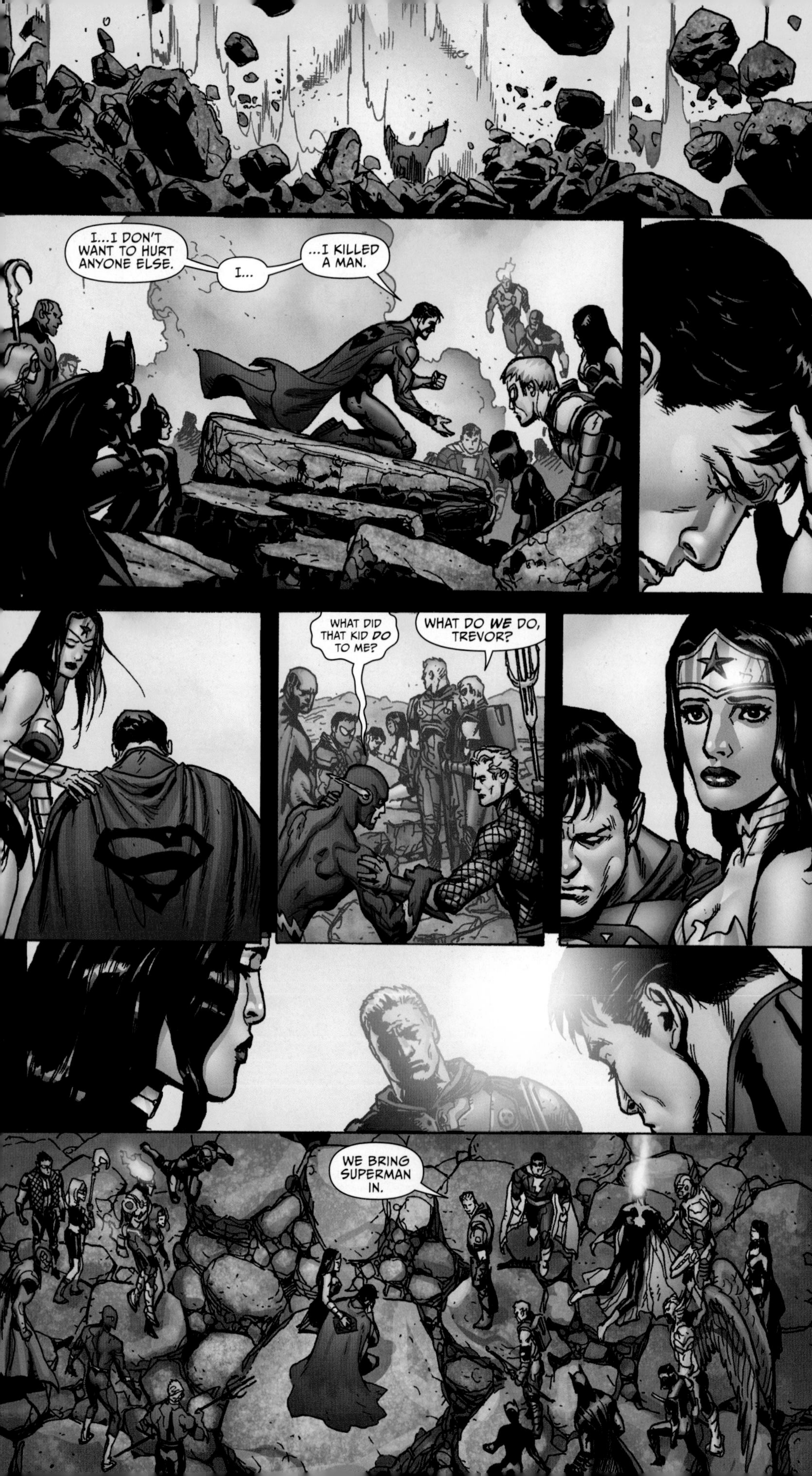
I...I DON'T WANT TO HURT ANYONE ELSE.
I...
...I KILLED A MAN.
WHAT DID THAT KID DO TO ME?
WHAT DO WE DO, TREVOR?
WE BRING SUPERMAN IN.

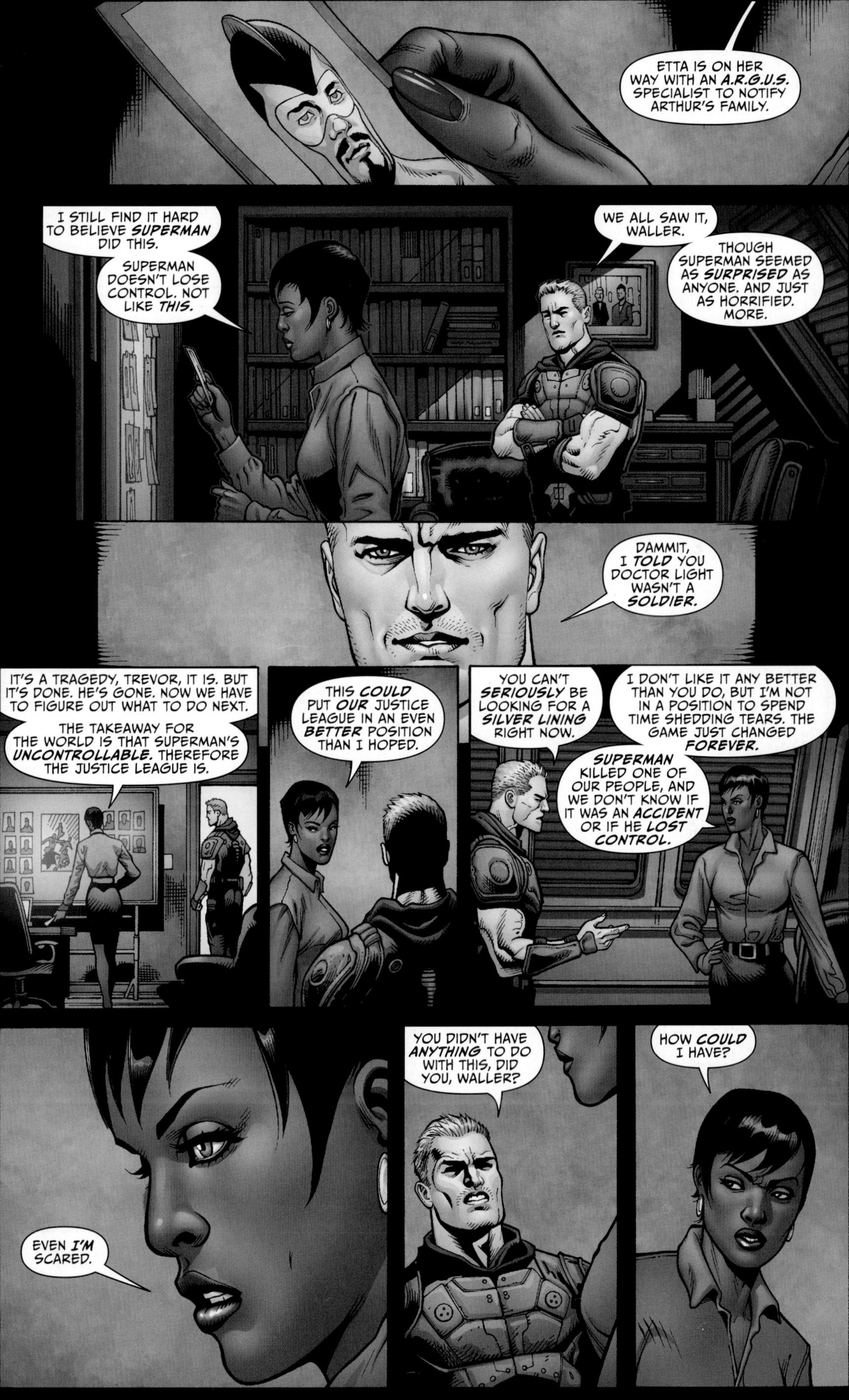
ETTA IS ON HER WAY WITH AN A.R.G.U.S. SPECIALIST TO NOTIFY ARTHUR'S FAMILY.
I STILL FIND IT HARD TO BELIEVE SUPERMAN DID THIS.
SUPERMAN DOESN'T LOSE CONTROL. NOT LIKE THIS.
WE ALL SAW IT, WALLER.
THOUGH SUPERMAN SEEMED AS SURPRISED AS ANYONE. AND JUST AS HORRIFIED. MORE.
DAMMIT, I TOLD YOU DOCTOR LIGHT WASN'T A SOLDIER.
IT'S A TRAGEDY, TREVOR, IT IS. BUT IT'S DONE. HE'S GONE. NOW WE HAVE TO FIGURE OUT WHAT TO DO NEXT.
THE TAKEAWAY FOR THE WORLD IS THAT SUPERMAN'S UNCONTROLLABLE. THEREFORE THE JUSTICE LEAGUE IS.
THIS COULD PUT OUR JUSTICE LEAGUE IN AN EVEN BETTER POSITION THAN I HOPED.
YOU CAN'T SERIOUSLY BE LOOKING FOR A SILVER LINING RIGHT NOW.
I DON'T LIKE IT ANY BETTER THAN YOU DO, BUT I'M NOT IN A POSITION TO SPEND TIME SHEDDING TEARS. THE GAME JUST CHANGED FOREVER.
SUPERMAN KILLED ONE OF OUR PEOPLE, AND WE DON'T KNOW IF IT WAS AN ACCIDENT OR IF HE LOST CONTROL.
EVEN I'M SCARED.
YOU DIDN'T HAVE ANYTHING TO DO WITH THIS, DID YOU, WALLER?
HOW COULD I HAVE?

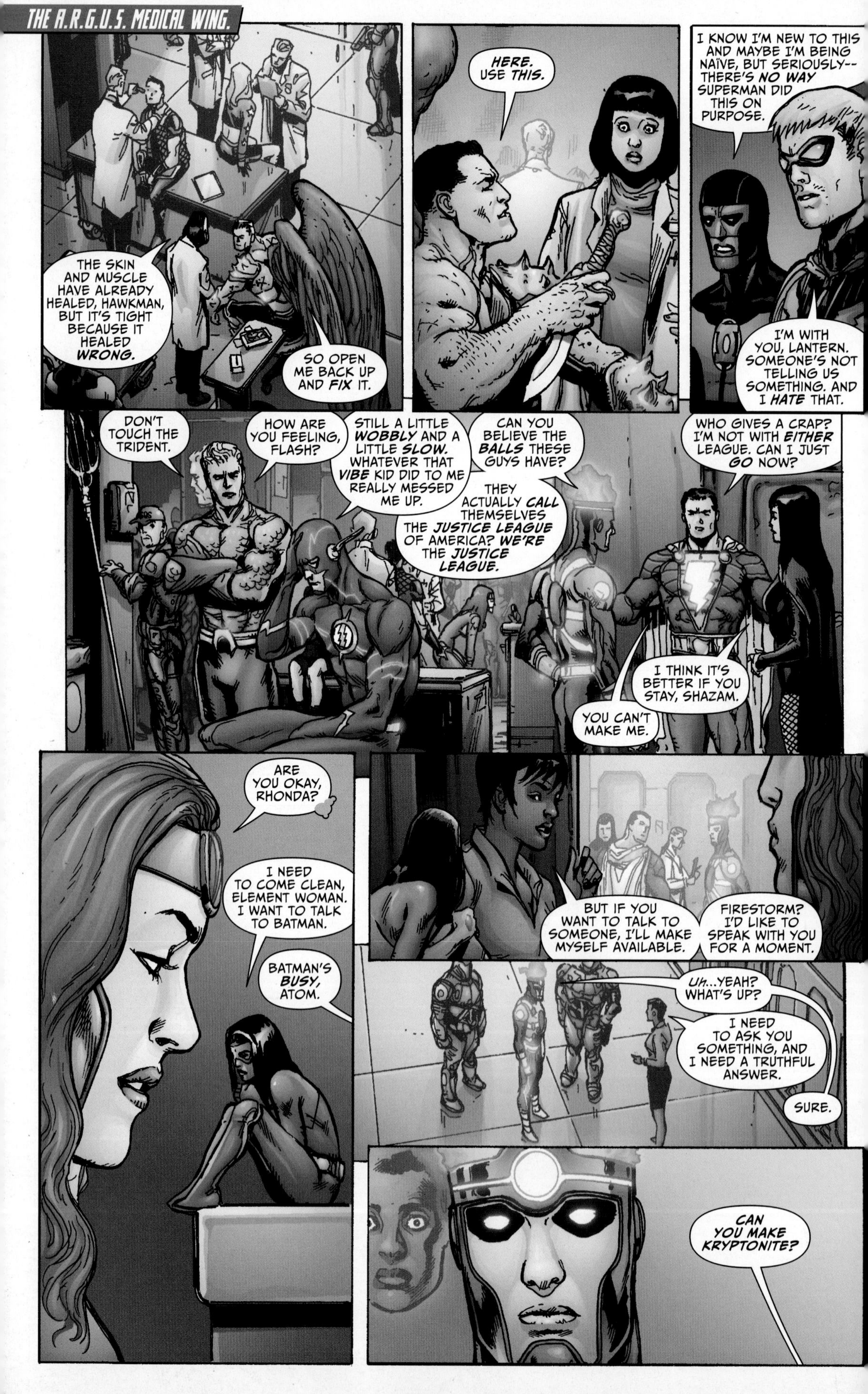
THE A.R.G.U.S. MEDICAL WING.
THE SKIN AND MUSCLE HAVE ALREADY HEALED, HAWKMAN, BUT IT'S TIGHT BECAUSE IT HEALED WRONG.
SO OPEN ME BACK UP AND FIX IT.
HERE. USE THIS.
I KNOW I'M NEW TO THIS AND MAYBE I'M BEING NAÏVE, BUT SERIOUSLY--THERE'S NO WAY SUPERMAN DID THIS ON PURPOSE.
I'M WITH YOU, LANTERN. SOMEONE'S NOT TELLING US SOMETHING. AND I HATE THAT.
DON'T TOUCH THE TRIDENT.
HOW ARE YOU FEELING, FLASH?
STILL A LITTLE WOBBLY AND A LITTLE SLOW. WHATEVER THAT VIBE KID DID TO ME REALLY MESSED ME UP.
CAN YOU BELIEVE THE BALLS THESE GUYS HAVE?
THEY ACTUALLY CALL THEMSELVES THE JUSTICE LEAGUE OF AMERICA? WE'RE THE JUSTICE LEAGUE.
WHO GIVES A CRAP? I'M NOT WITH EITHER LEAGUE. CAN I JUST GO NOW?
I THINK IT'S BETTER IF YOU STAY, SHAZAM.
YOU CAN'T MAKE ME.
ARE YOU OKAY, RHONDA?
I NEED TO COME CLEAN, ELEMENT WOMAN. I WANT TO TALK TO BATMAN.
BATMAN'S BUSY, ATOM.
BUT IF YOU WANT TO TALK TO SOMEONE, I'LL MAKE MYSELF AVAILABLE.
FIRESTORM? I'D LIKE TO SPEAK WITH YOU FOR A MOMENT.
Uh...YEAH? WHAT'S UP?
I NEED TO ASK YOU SOMETHING, AND I NEED A TRUTHFUL ANSWER.
SURE.
CAN YOU MAKE KRYPTONITE?

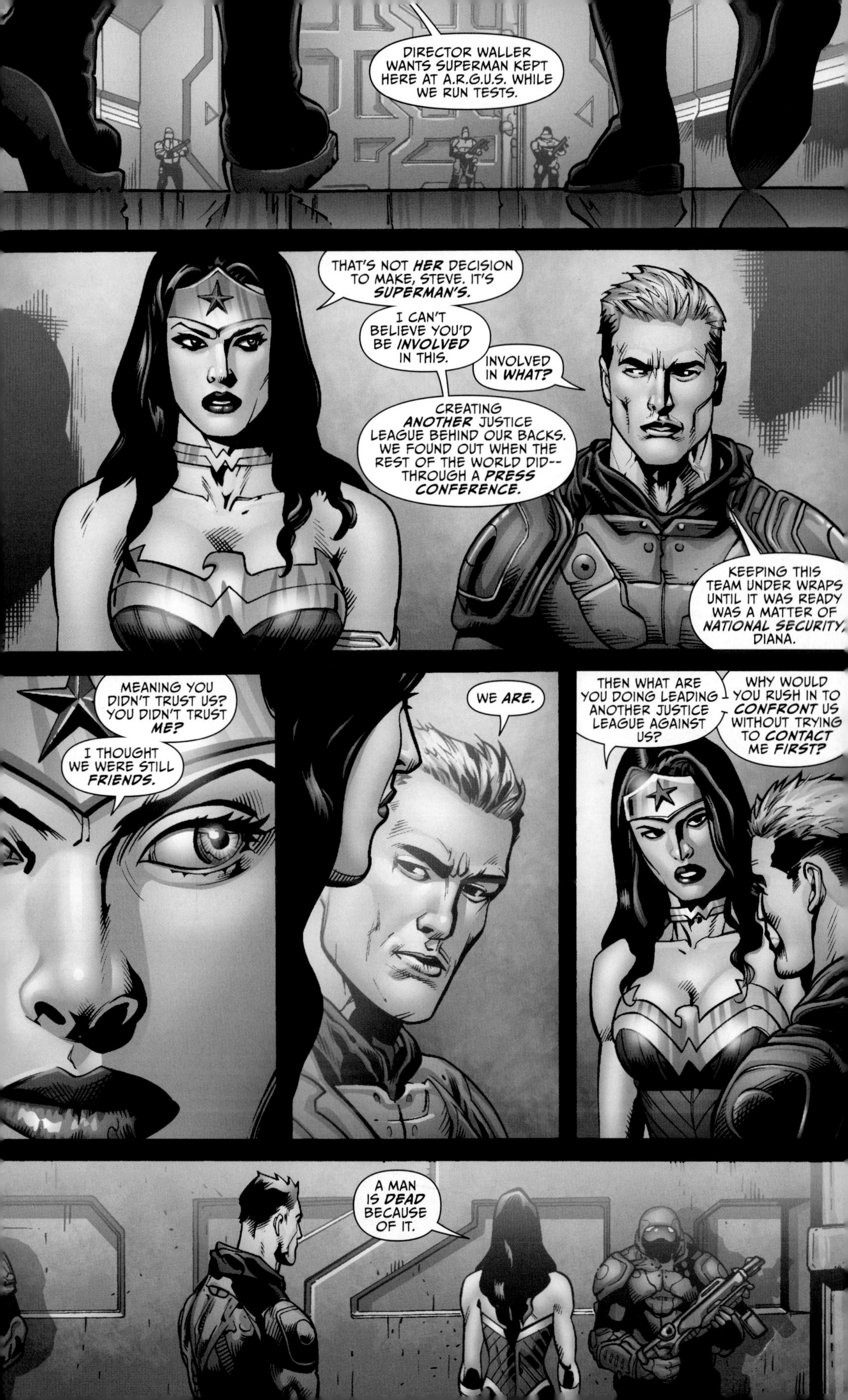
DIRECTOR WALLER WANTS SUPERMAN KEPT HERE AT A.R.G.U.S. WHILE WE RUN TESTS.
THAT'S NOT HER DECISION TO MAKE, STEVE. IT'S SUPERMAN'S.
I CAN'T BELIEVE YOU'D BE INVOLVED IN THIS.
INVOLVED IN WHAT?
CREATING ANOTHER JUSTICE LEAGUE BEHIND OUR BACKS. WE FOUND OUT WHEN THE REST OF THE WORLD DID-- THROUGH A PRESS CONFERENCE.
KEEPING THIS TEAM UNDER WRAPS UNTIL IT WAS READY WAS A MATTER OF NATIONAL SECURITY, DIANA.
MEANING YOU DIDN'T TRUST US? YOU DIDN'T TRUST ME?
I THOUGHT WE WERE STILL FRIENDS.
WE ARE.
THEN WHAT ARE YOU DOING LEADING ANOTHER JUSTICE LEAGUE AGAINST US?
WHY WOULD YOU RUSH IN TO CONFRONT US WITHOUT TRYING TO CONTACT ME FIRST?
A MAN IS DEAD BECAUSE OF IT.

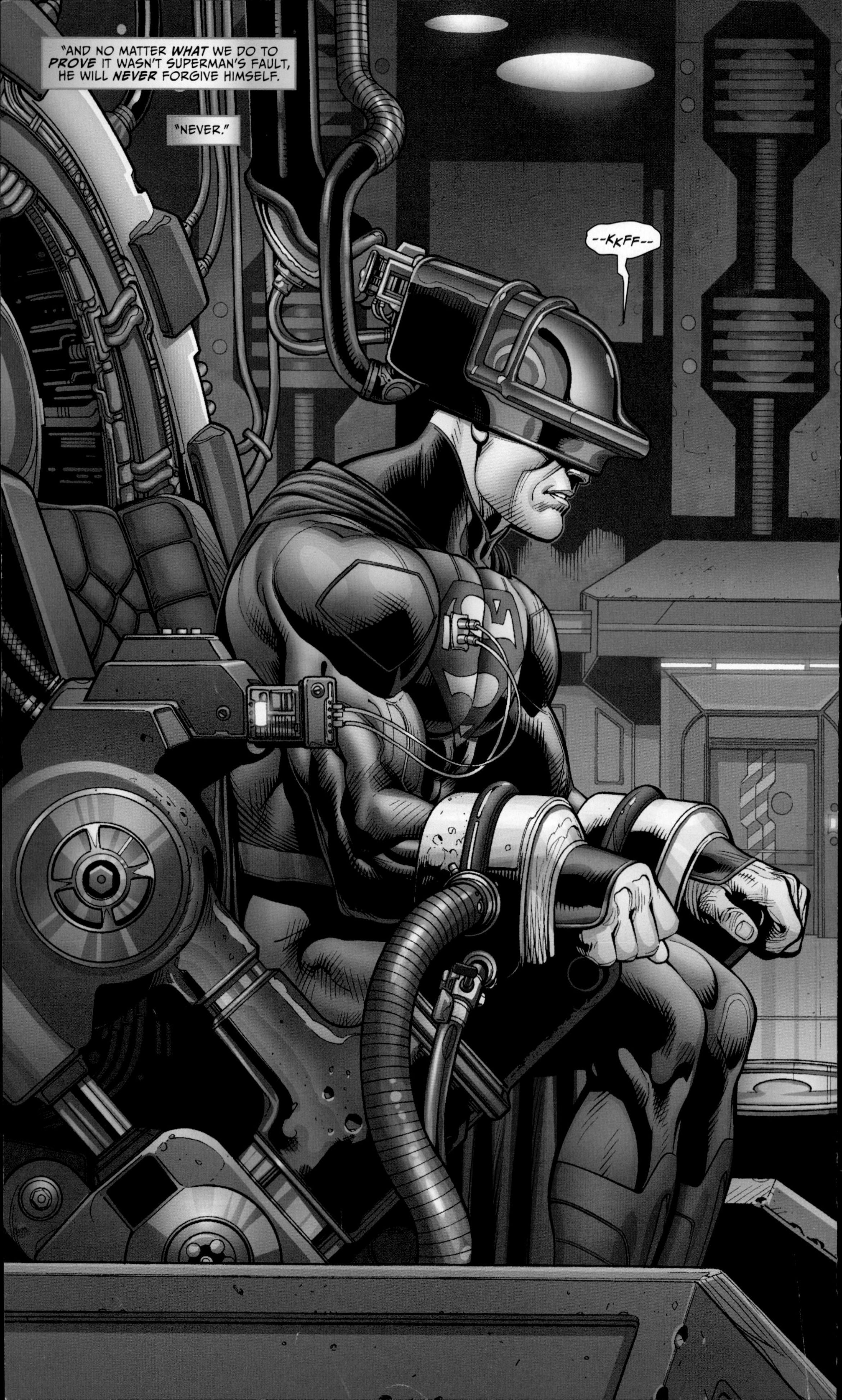
"AND NO MATTER WHAT WE DO TO PROVE IT WASN'T SUPERMAN'S FAULT, HE WILL NEVER FORGIVE HIMSELF.
"NEVER."
--KKFF--

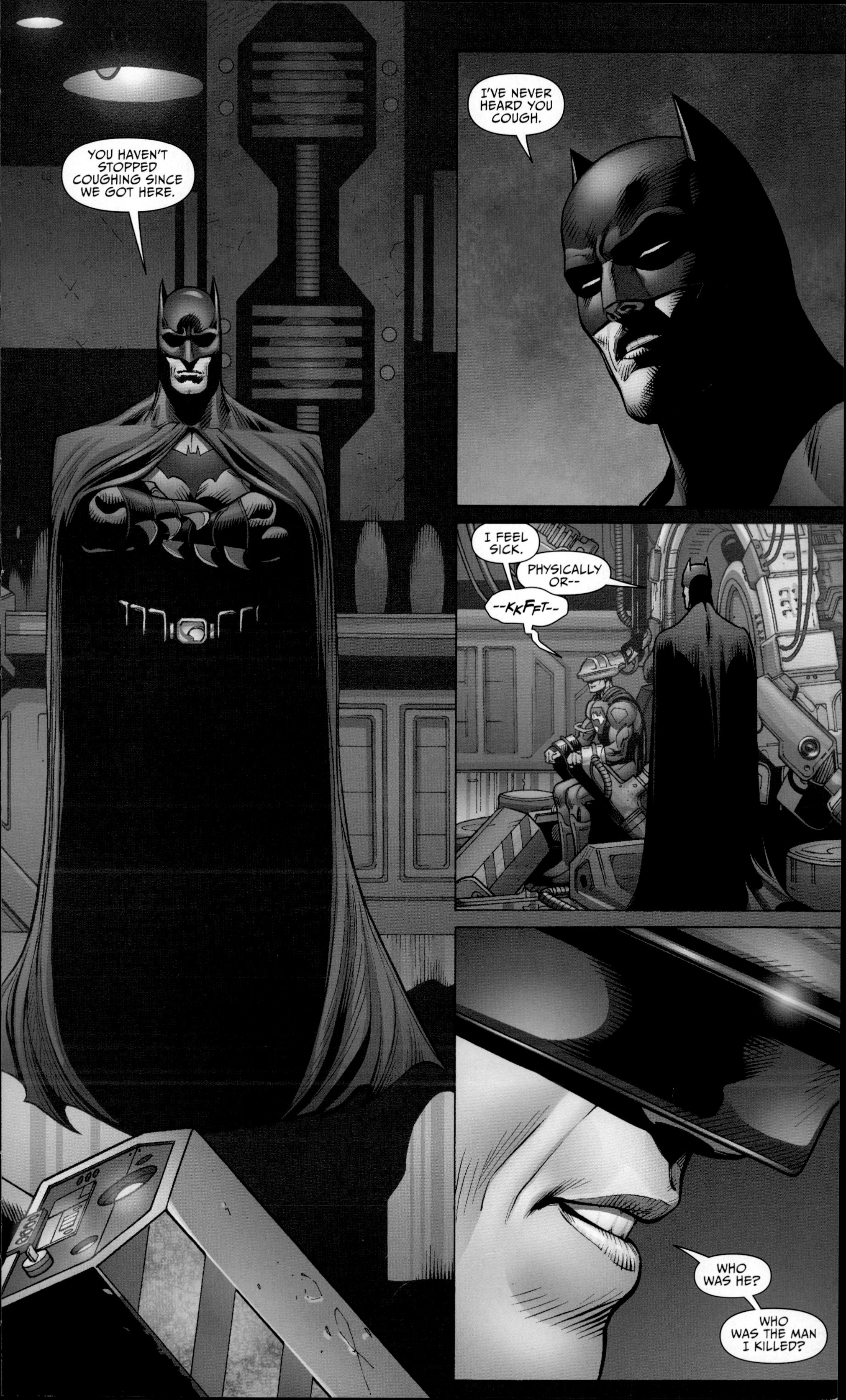
YOU HAVEN'T STOPPED COUGHING SINCE WE GOT HERE.
I'VE NEVER HEARD YOU COUGH.
I FEEL SICK.
PHYSICALLY OR--
--KKFFT--
WHO WAS HE?
WHO WAS THE MAN I KILLED?

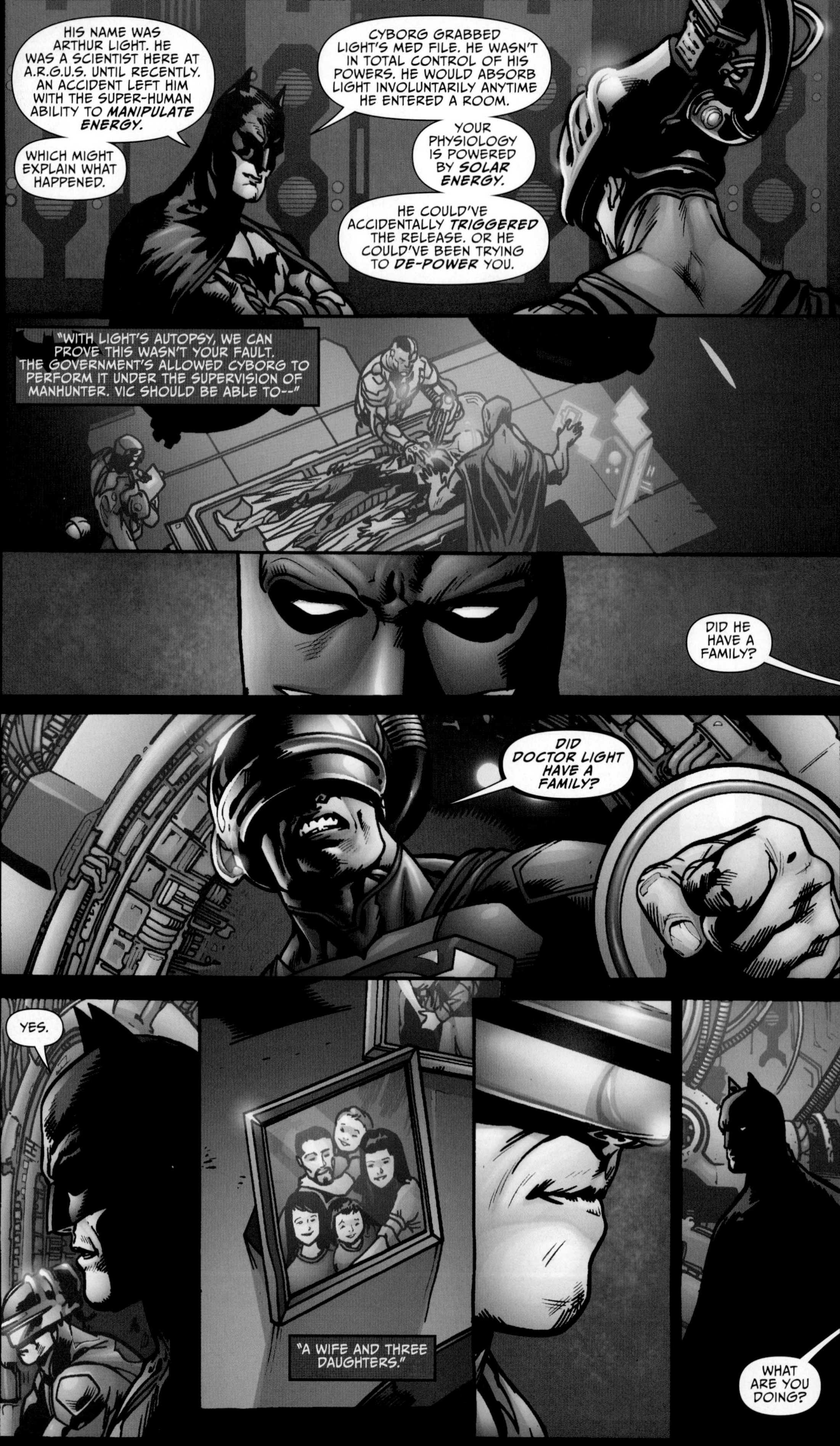
HIS NAME WAS ARTHUR LIGHT. HE WAS A SCIENTIST HERE AT A.R.G.U.S. UNTIL RECENTLY. AN ACCIDENT LEFT HIM WITH THE SUPER-HUMAN ABILITY TO MANIPULATE ENERGY.
WHICH MIGHT EXPLAIN WHAT HAPPENED.
CYBORG GRABBED LIGHT'S MED FILE. HE WASN'T IN TOTAL CONTROL OF HIS POWERS. HE WOULD ABSORB LIGHT INVOLUNTARILY ANYTIME HE ENTERED A ROOM.
YOUR PHYSIOLOGY IS POWERED BY SOLAR ENERGY.
HE COULD'VE ACCIDENTALLY TRIGGERED THE RELEASE. OR HE COULD'VE BEEN TRYING TO DE-POWER YOU.
"WITH LIGHT'S AUTOPSY, WE CAN PROVE THIS WASN'T YOUR FAULT. THE GOVERNMENT'S ALLOWED CYBORG TO PERFORM IT UNDER THE SUPERVISION OF MANHUNTER. VIC SHOULD BE ABLE TO--"
DID HE HAVE A FAMILY?
DID DOCTOR LIGHT HAVE A FAMILY?
YES.
"A WIFE AND THREE DAUGHTERS."
WHAT ARE YOU DOING?

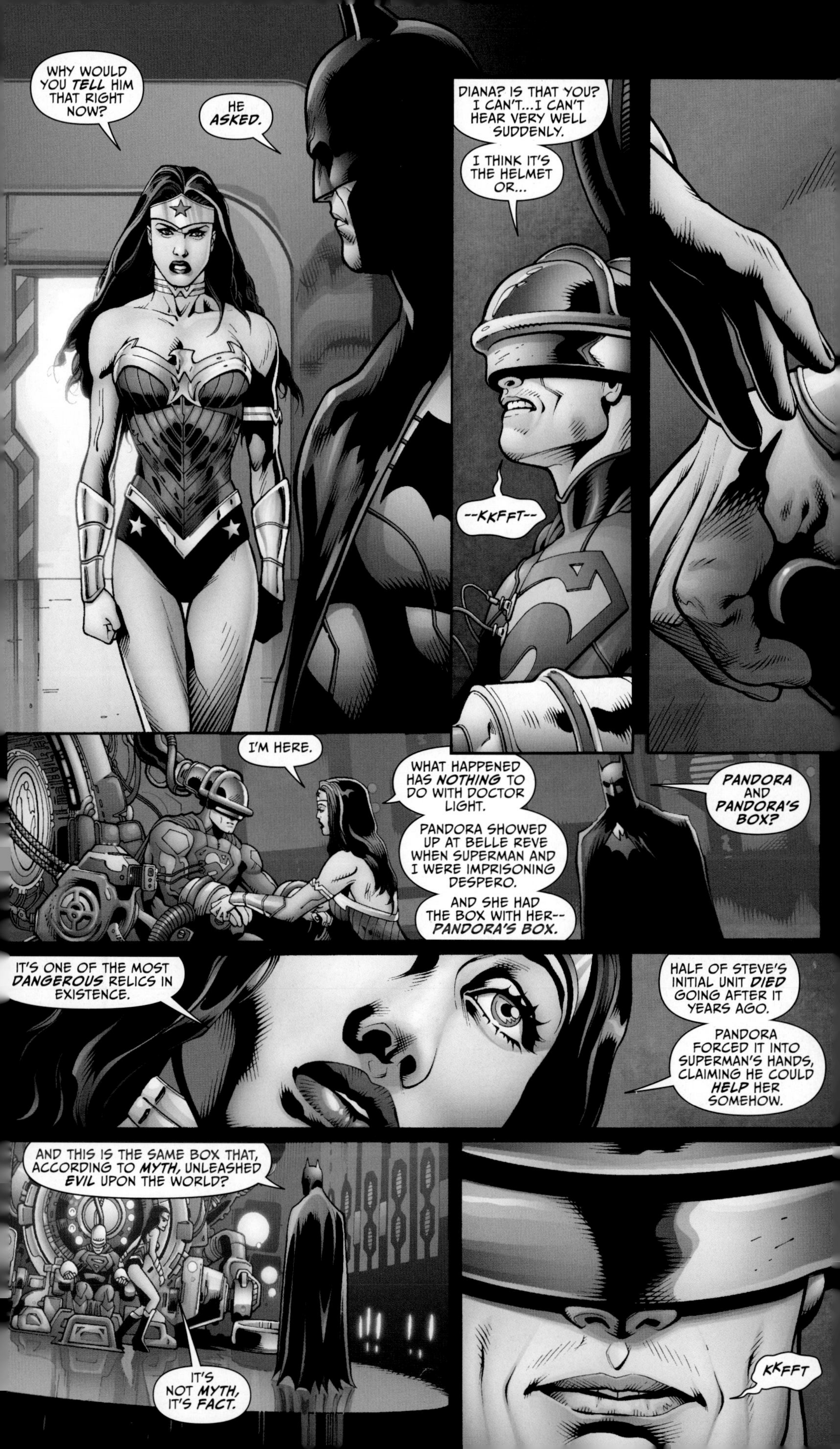

WHY WOULD YOU TELL HIM THAT RIGHT NOW?
HE ASKED.
DIANA? IS THAT YOU? I CAN'T...I CAN'T HEAR VERY WELL SUDDENLY.
I THINK IT'S THE HELMET OR...
--KKFFT--
I'M HERE.
WHAT HAPPENED HAS NOTHING TO DO WITH DOCTOR LIGHT.
PANDORA SHOWED UP AT BELLE REVE WHEN SUPERMAN AND I WERE IMPRISONING DESPERO.
AND SHE HAD THE BOX WITH HER-- PANDORA'S BOX.
PANDORA AND PANDORA'S BOX?
IT'S ONE OF THE MOST DANGEROUS RELICS IN EXISTENCE.
HALF OF STEVE'S INITIAL UNIT DIED GOING AFTER IT YEARS AGO.
PANDORA FORCED IT INTO SUPERMAN'S HANDS, CLAIMING HE COULD HELP HER SOMEHOW.
AND THIS IS THE SAME BOX THAT, ACCORDING TO MYTH, UNLEASHED EVIL UPON THE WORLD?
IT'S NOT MYTH, IT'S FACT.
KKFFT

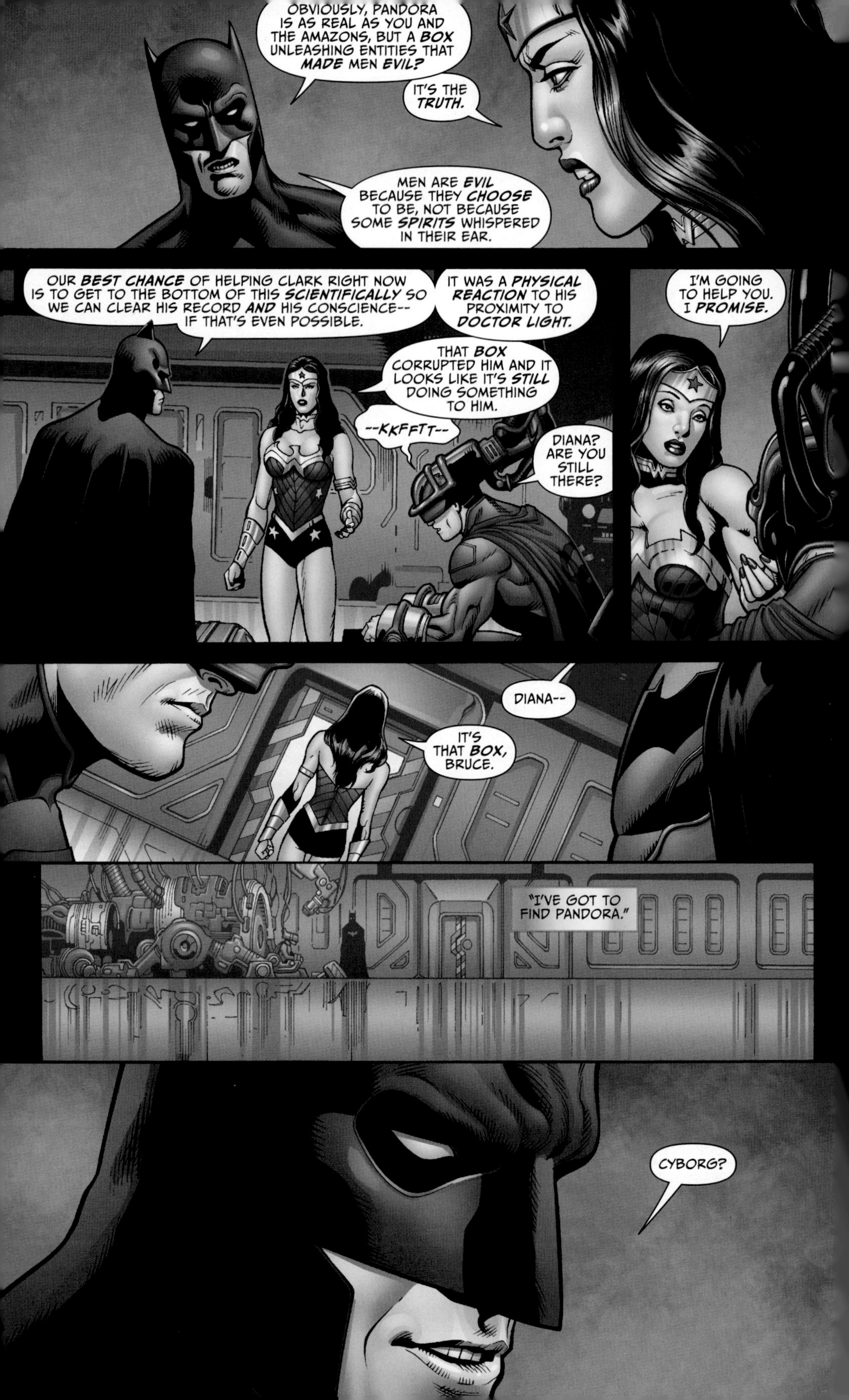
OBVIOUSLY, PANDORA IS AS REAL AS YOU AND THE AMAZONS, BUT A BOX UNLEASHING ENTITIES THAT MADE MEN EVIL?
IT'S THE TRUTH.
MEN ARE EVIL BECAUSE THEY CHOOSE TO BE, NOT BECAUSE SOME SPIRITS WHISPERED IN THEIR EAR.
OUR BEST CHANCE OF HELPING CLARK RIGHT NOW IS TO GET TO THE BOTTOM OF THIS SCIENTIFICALLY SO WE CAN CLEAR HIS RECORD AND HIS CONSCIENCE-- IF THAT'S EVEN POSSIBLE.
IT WAS A PHYSICAL REACTION TO HIS PROXIMITY TO DOCTOR LIGHT.
THAT BOX CORRUPTED HIM AND IT LOOKS LIKE IT'S STILL DOING SOMETHING TO HIM.
--KKFFTT--
DIANA? ARE YOU STILL THERE?
I'M GOING TO HELP YOU. I PROMISE.
DIANA--
IT'S THAT BOX, BRUCE.
"I'VE GOT TO FIND PANDORA."
CYBORG?

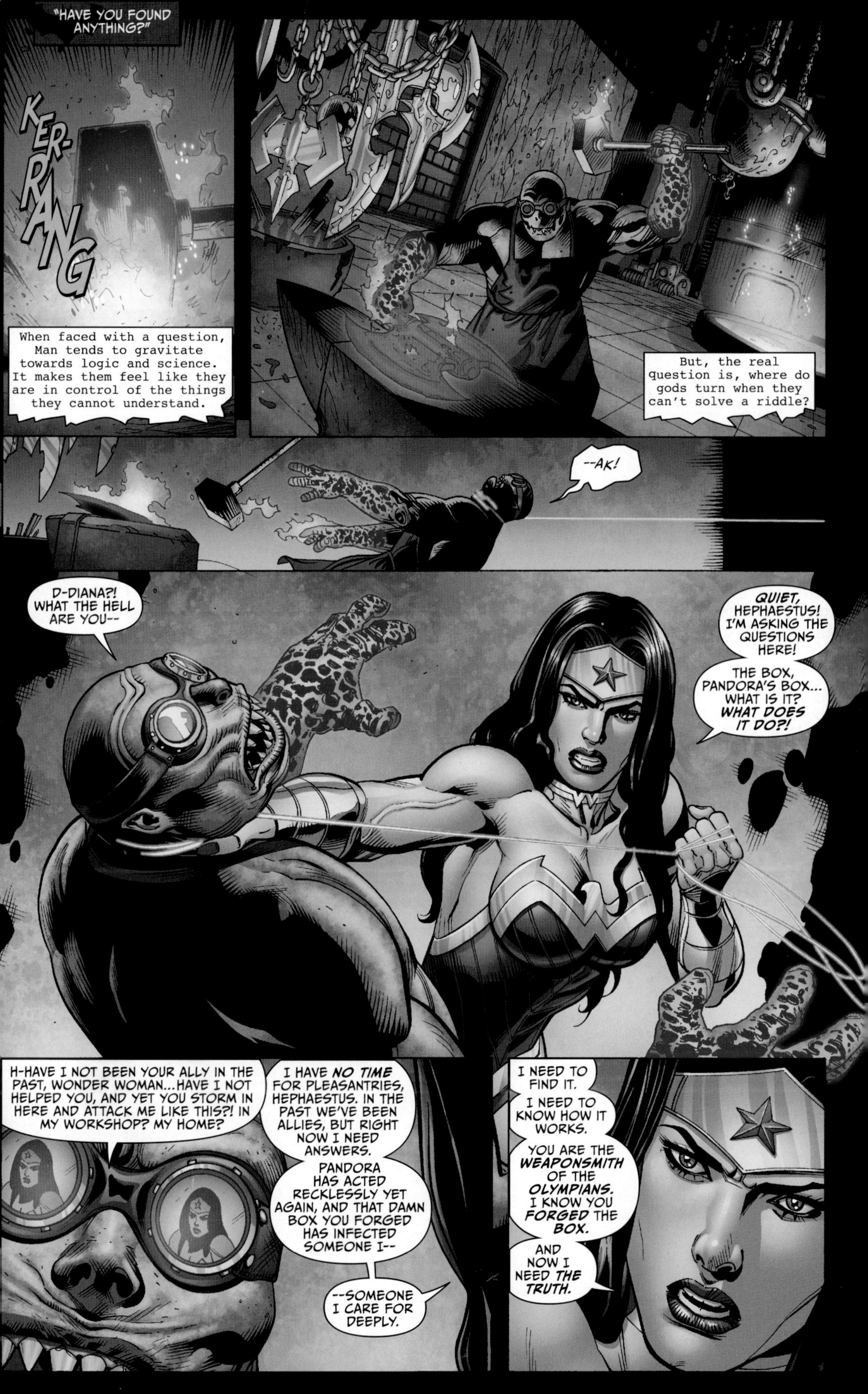

"HAVE YOU FOUND ANYTHING?"
KER-RANG
When faced with a question, Man tends to gravitate towards logic and science. It makes them feel like they are in control of the things they cannot understand.
But, the real question is, where do gods turn when they can't solve a riddle?
--AK!
D-DIANA?! WHAT THE HELL ARE YOU--
QUIET, HEPHAESTUS! I'M ASKING THE QUESTIONS HERE!
THE BOX, PANDORA'S BOX... WHAT IS IT? WHAT DOES IT DO?!
H-HAVE I NOT BEEN YOUR ALLY IN THE PAST, WONDER WOMAN...HAVE I NOT HELPED YOU, AND YET YOU STORM IN HERE AND ATTACK ME LIKE THIS?! IN MY WORKSHOP? MY HOME?
I HAVE NO TIME FOR PLEASANTRIES, HEPHAESTUS. IN THE PAST WE'VE BEEN ALLIES, BUT RIGHT NOW I NEED ANSWERS.
PANDORA HAS ACTED RECKLESSLY YET AGAIN, AND THAT DAMN BOX YOU FORGED HAS INFECTED SOMEONE I--
--SOMEONE I CARE FOR DEEPLY.
I NEED TO FIND IT.
I NEED TO KNOW HOW IT WORKS.
YOU ARE THE WEAPONSMITH OF THE OLYMPIANS. I KNOW YOU FORGED THE BOX.
AND NOW I NEED THE TRUTH.

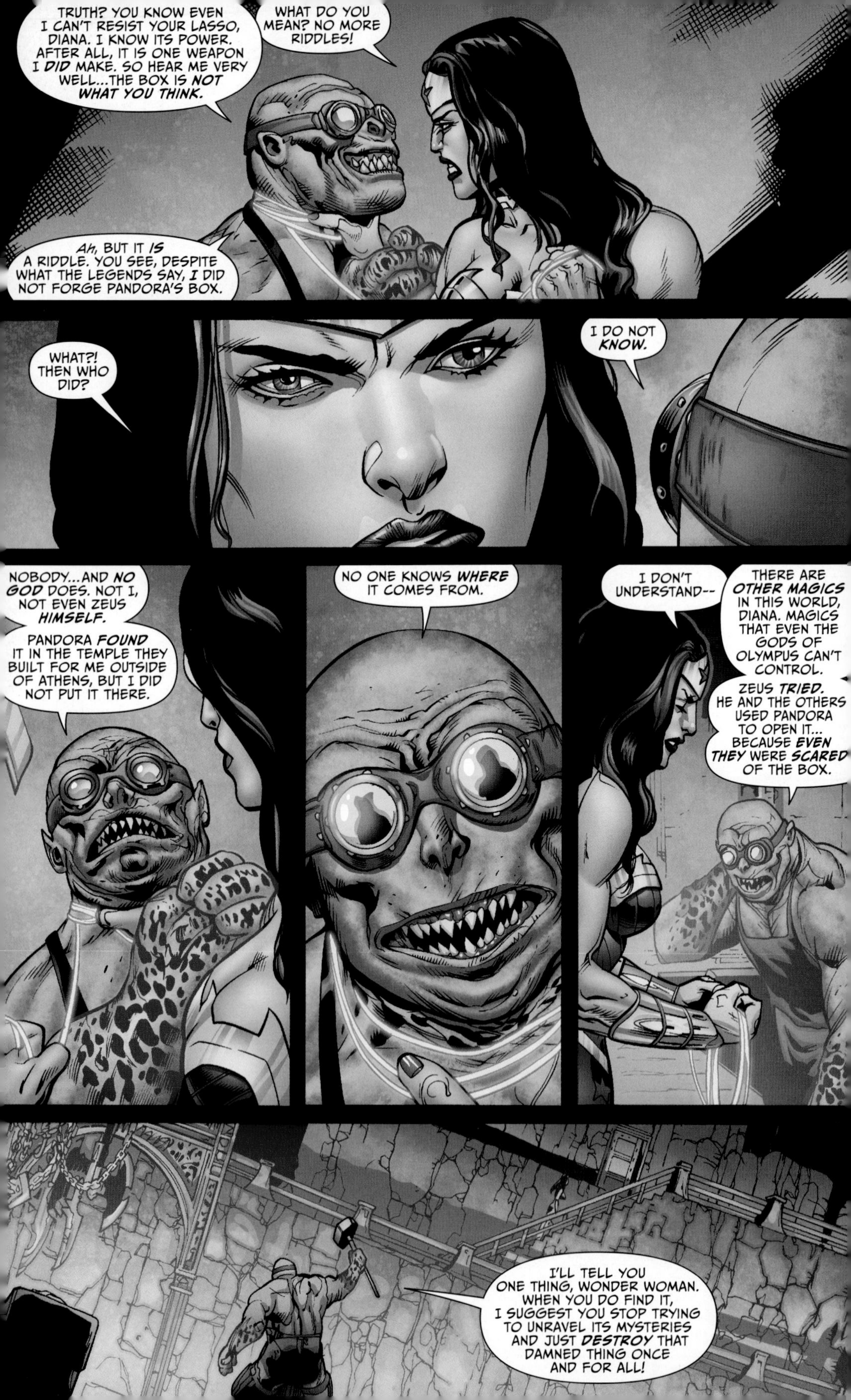
TRUTH? YOU KNOW EVEN I CAN'T RESIST YOUR LASSO, DIANA. I KNOW ITS POWER. AFTER ALL, IT IS ONE WEAPON I DID MAKE. SO HEAR ME VERY WELL...THE BOX IS NOT WHAT YOU THINK.
WHAT DO YOU MEAN? NO MORE RIDDLES!
Ah, BUT IT IS A RIDDLE. YOU SEE, DESPITE WHAT THE LEGENDS SAY, I DID NOT FORGE PANDORA'S BOX.
WHAT?! THEN WHO DID?
I DO NOT KNOW.
NOBODY...AND NO GOD DOES. NOT I, NOT EVEN ZEUS HIMSELF.
PANDORA FOUND IT IN THE TEMPLE THEY BUILT FOR ME OUTSIDE OF ATHENS, BUT I DID NOT PUT IT THERE.
NO ONE KNOWS WHERE IT COMES FROM.
I DON'T UNDERSTAND--
THERE ARE OTHER MAGICS IN THIS WORLD, DIANA. MAGICS THAT EVEN THE GODS OF OLYMPUS CAN'T CONTROL.
ZEUS TRIED. HE AND THE OTHERS USED PANDORA TO OPEN IT... BECAUSE EVEN THEY WERE SCARED OF THE BOX.
I'LL TELL YOU ONE THING, WONDER WOMAN. WHEN YOU DO FIND IT, I SUGGEST YOU STOP TRYING TO UNRAVEL ITS MYSTERIES AND JUST DESTROY THAT DAMNED THING ONCE AND FOR ALL!

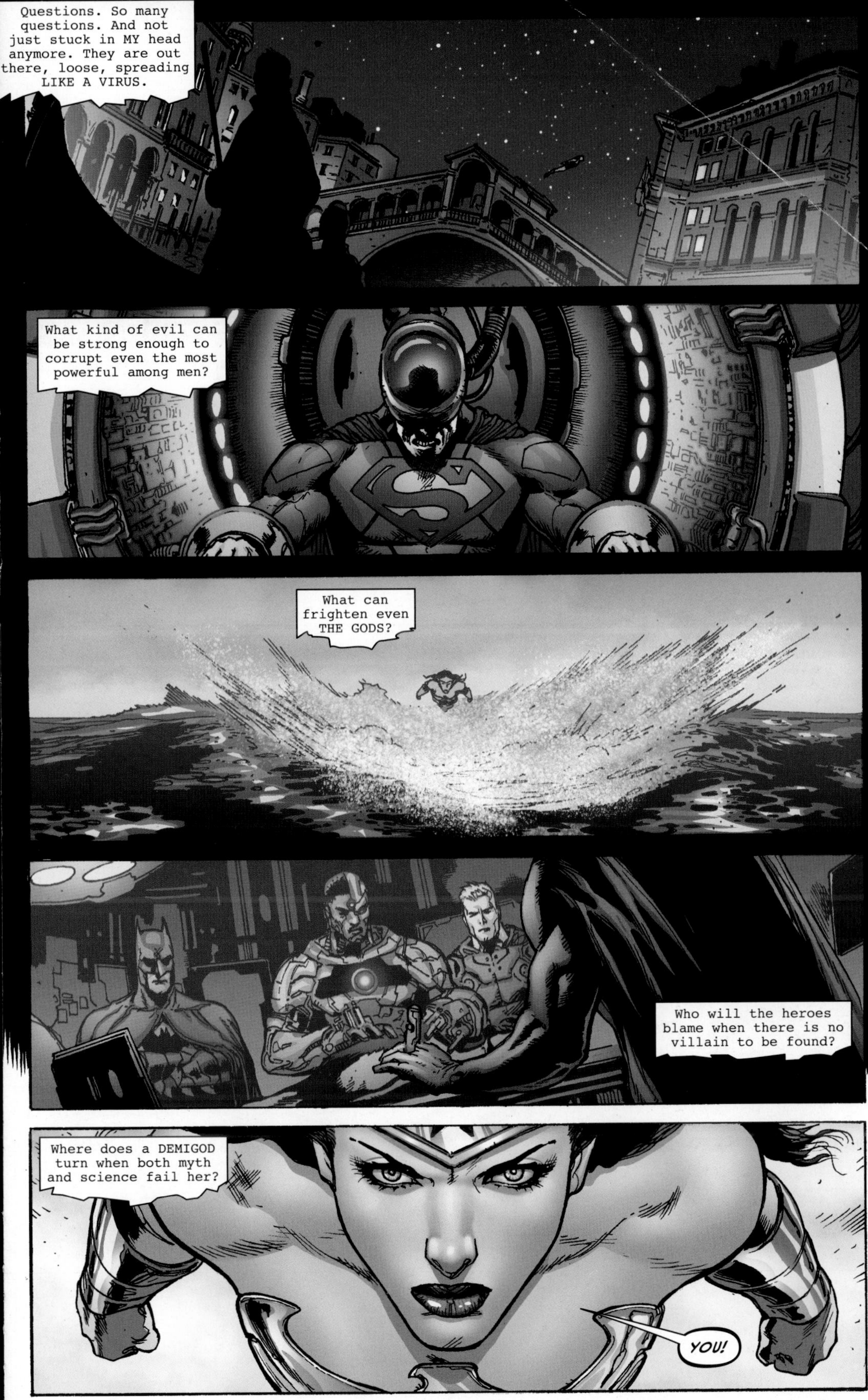
Questions. So many questions. And not just stuck in MY head anymore. They are out there, loose, spreading LIKE A VIRUS.
What kind of evil can be strong enough to corrupt even the most powerful among men?
What can frighten even THE GODS?
Who will the heroes blame when there is no villain to be found?
Where does a DEMIGOD turn when both myth and science fail her?
YOU!

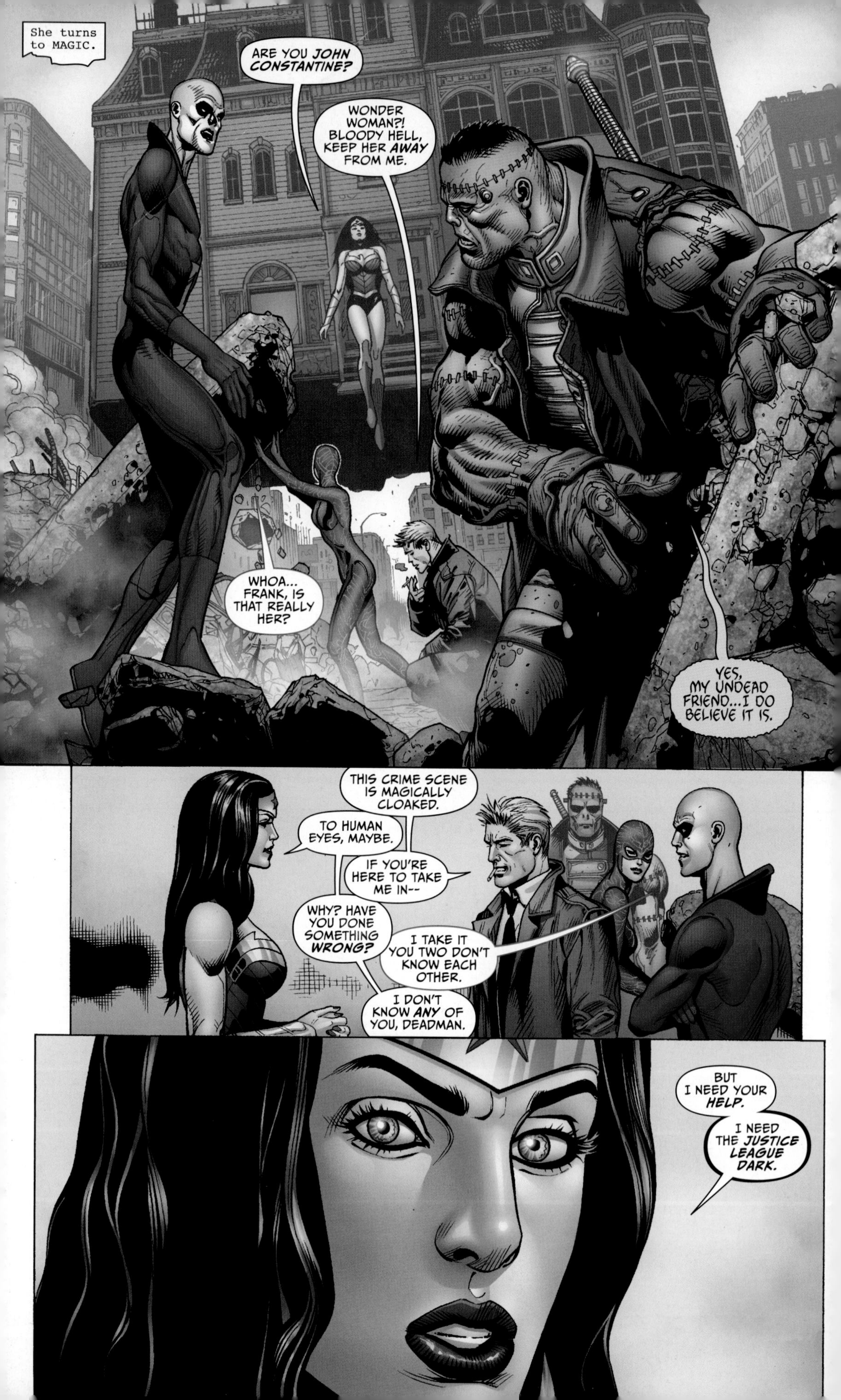
She turns to MAGIC.
ARE YOU JOHN CONSTANTINE?
WONDER WOMAN?! BLOODY HELL, KEEP HER AWAY FROM ME.
WHOA... FRANK, IS THAT REALLY HER?
YES, MY UNDEAD FRIEND...I DO BELIEVE IT IS.
THIS CRIME SCENE IS MAGICALLY CLOAKED.
TO HUMAN EYES, MAYBE.
IF YOU'RE HERE TO TAKE ME IN--
WHY? HAVE YOU DONE SOMETHING WRONG?
I TAKE IT YOU TWO DON'T KNOW EACH OTHER.
I DON'T KNOW ANY OF YOU, DEADMAN.
BUT I NEED YOUR HELP.
I NEED THE JUSTICE LEAGUE DARK.

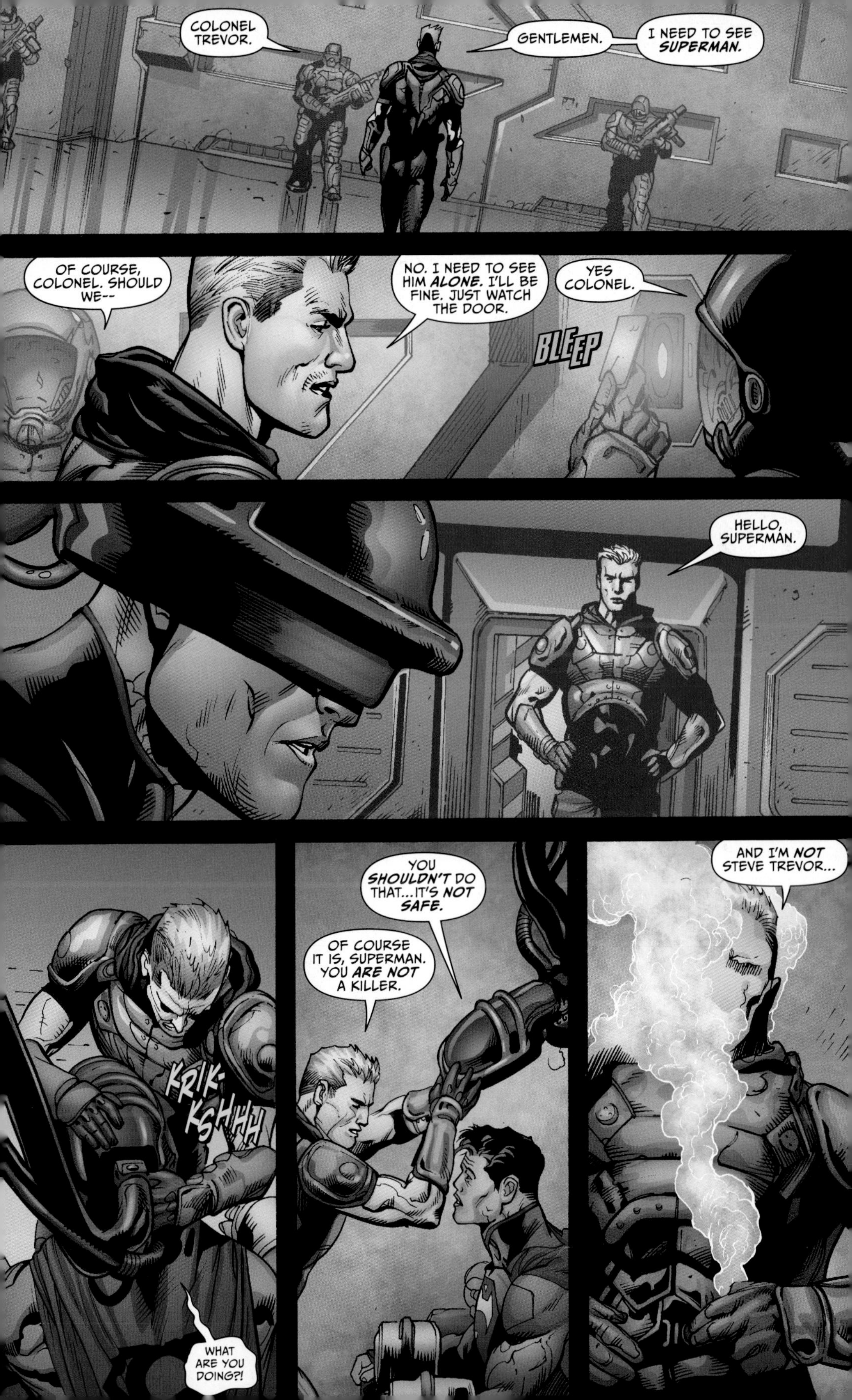

COLONEL TREVOR.
GENTLEMEN.
I NEED TO SEE SUPERMAN.
OF COURSE, COLONEL. SHOULD WE--
NO. I NEED TO SEE HIM ALONE. I'LL BE FINE. JUST WATCH THE DOOR.
YES COLONEL.
BLEEP
HELLO, SUPERMAN.
KRIK-KSHHH
WHAT ARE YOU DOING?!
YOU SHOULDN'T DO THAT...IT'S NOT SAFE.
OF COURSE IT IS, SUPERMAN. YOU ARE NOT A KILLER.
AND I'M NOT STEVE TREVOR...

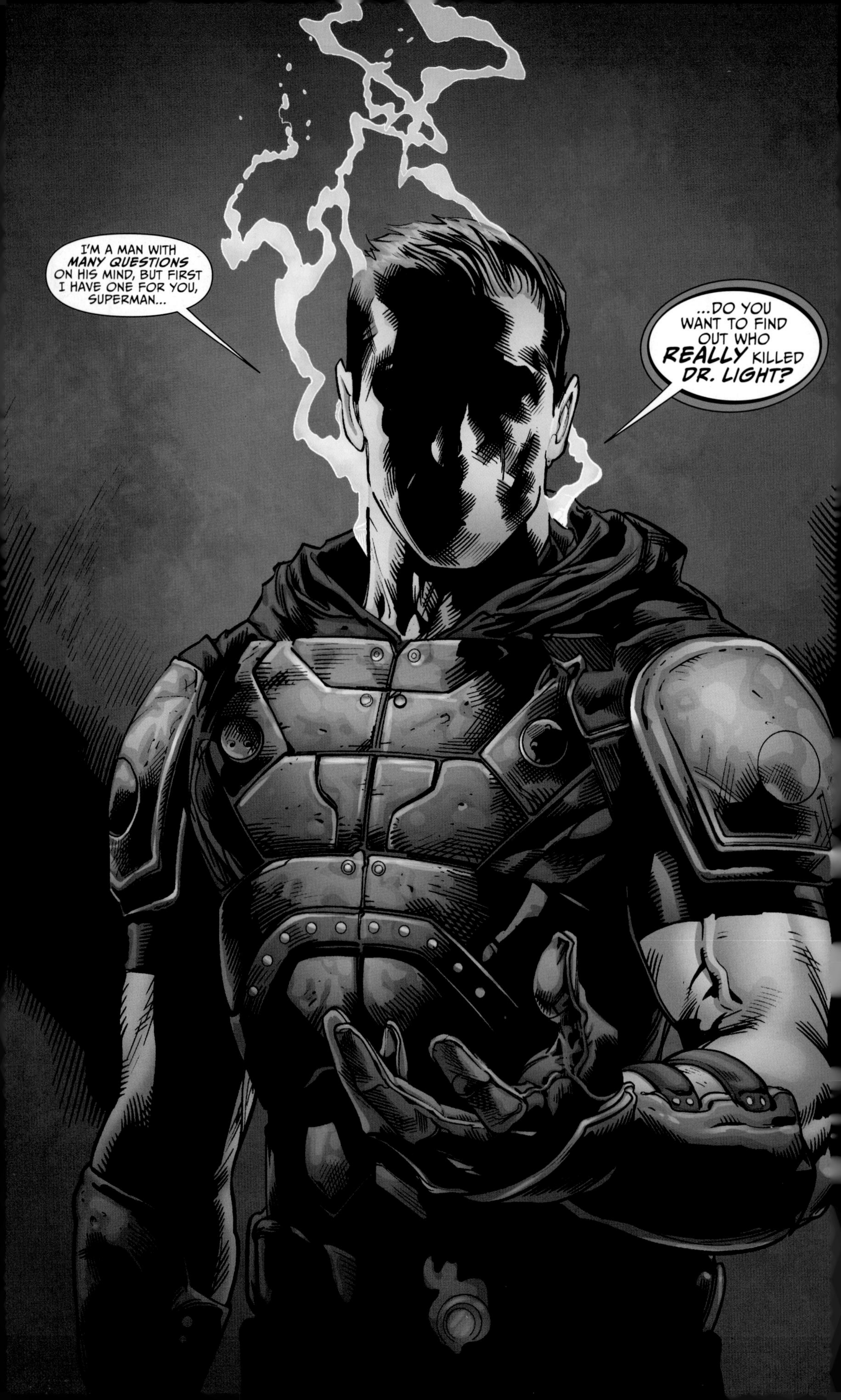
I'M A MAN WITH MANY QUESTIONS ON HIS MIND, BUT FIRST I HAVE ONE FOR YOU, SUPERMAN...
...DO YOU WANT TO FIND OUT WHO REALLY KILLED DR. LIGHT?

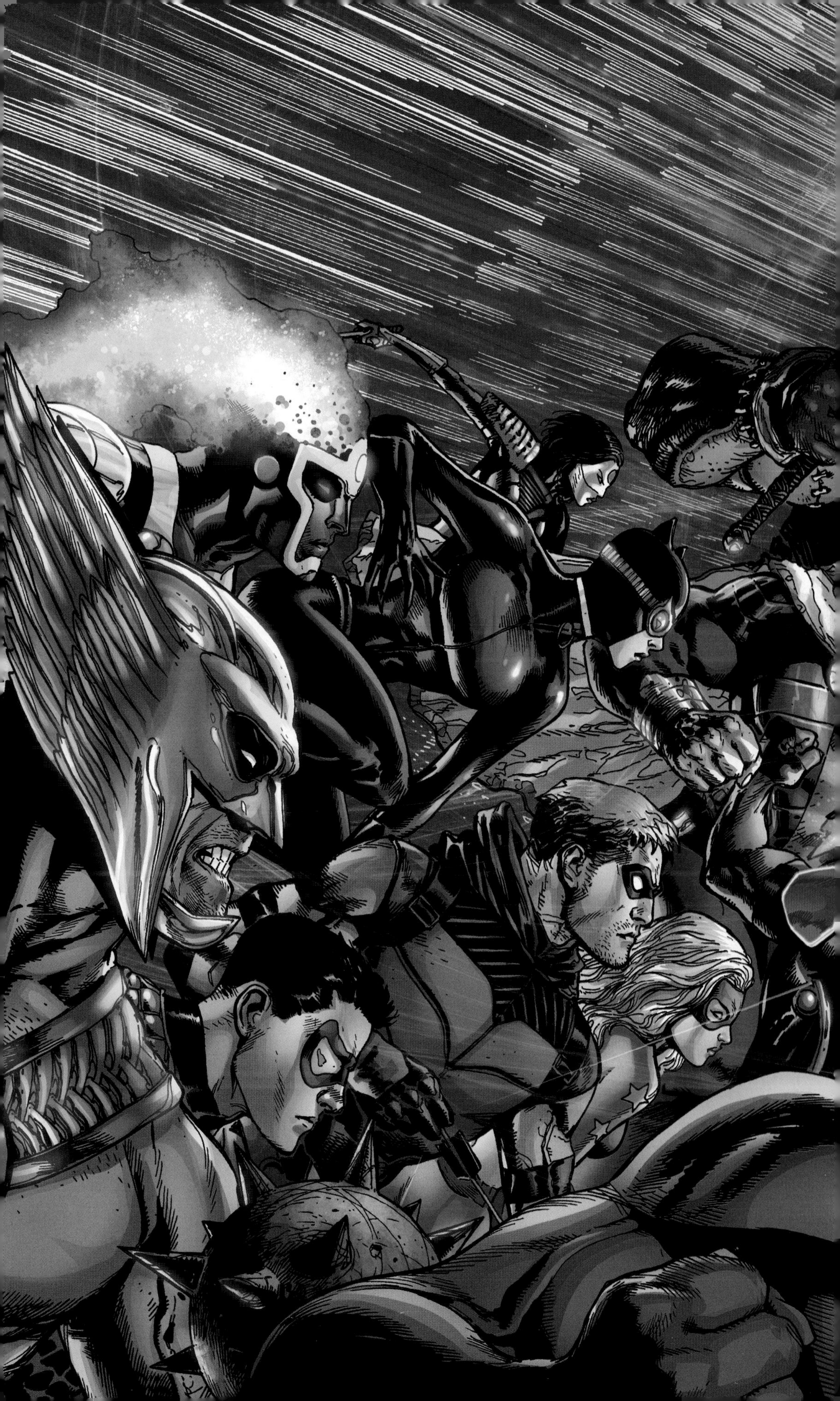

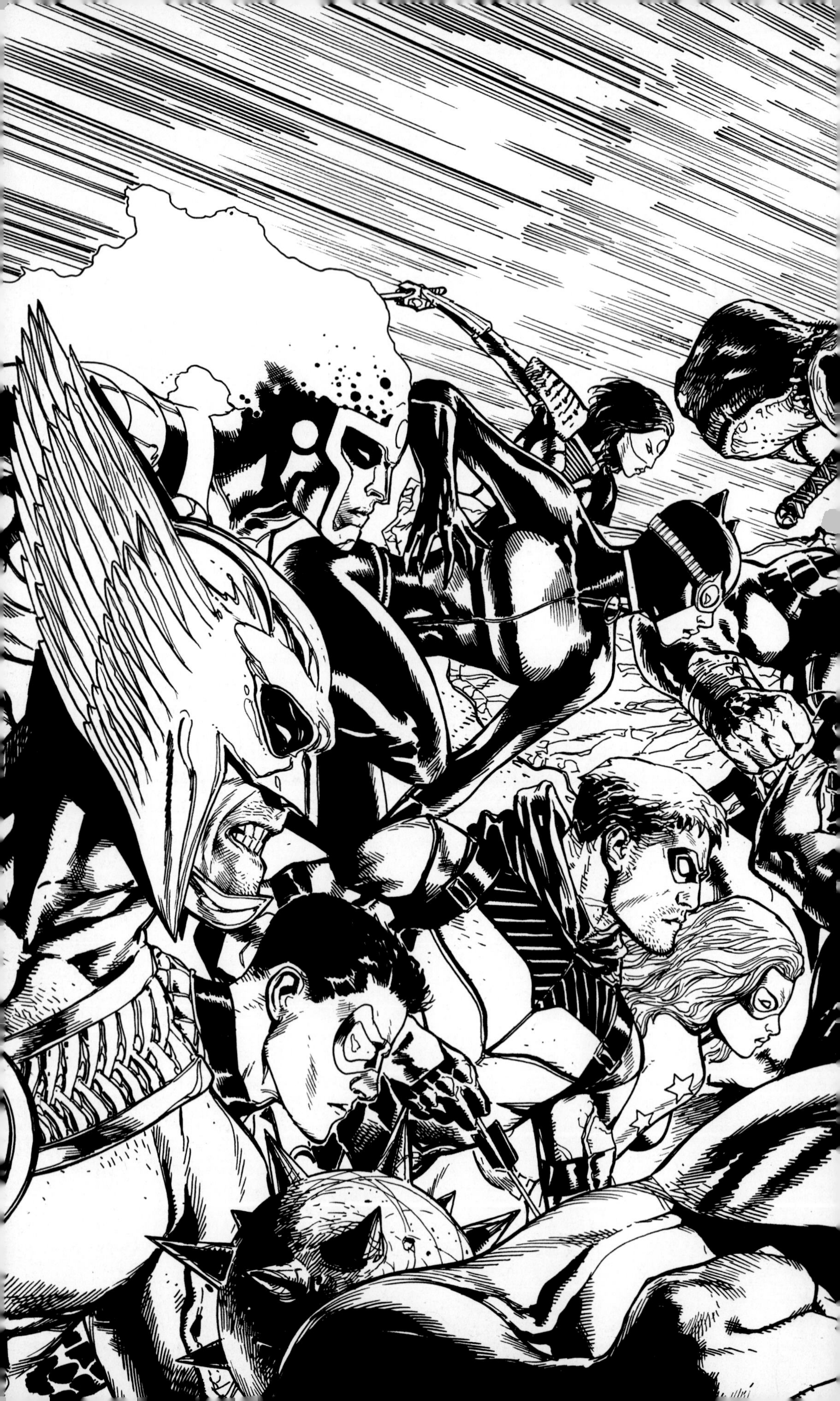

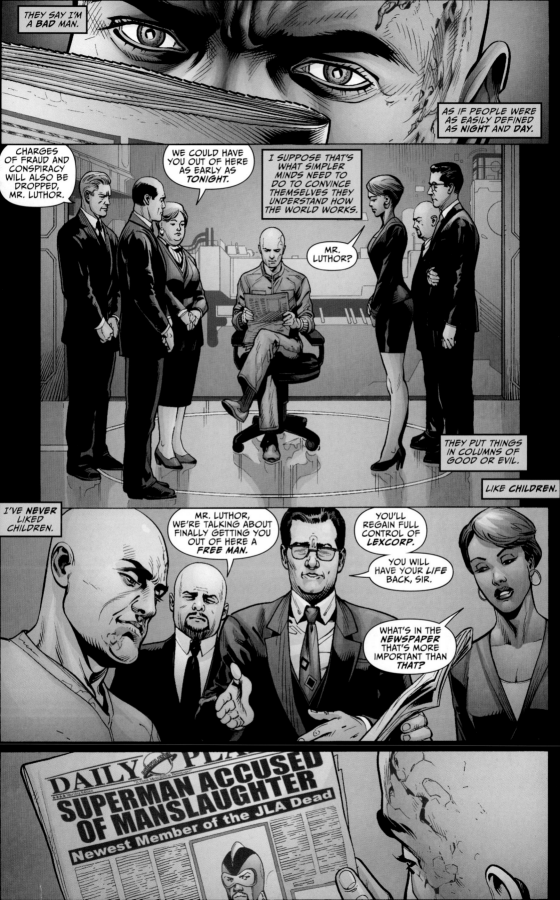

THEY SAY I'M A BAD MAN.

AS IF PEOPLE WERE AS EASILY DEFINED AS NIGHT AND DAY.

CHARGES OF FRAUD AND CONSPIRACY WILL ALSO BE DROPPED, MR. LUTHOR.

WE COULD HAVE YOU OUT OF HERE AS EARLY AS TONIGHT.

I SUPPOSE THAT'S WHAT SIMPLER MINDS NEED TO DO TO CONVINCE THEMSELVES THEY UNDERSTAND HOW THE WORLD WORKS.

MR. LUTHOR?

THEY PUT THINGS IN COLUMNS OF GOOD OR EVIL.

LIKE CHILDREN.

I'VE NEVER LIKED CHILDREN.

MR. LUTHOR, WE'RE TALKING ABOUT FINALLY GETTING YOU OUT OF HERE A FREE MAN.

YOU'LL REGAIN FULL CONTROL OF LEXCORP.

YOU WILL HAVE YOUR LIFE BACK, SIR.

WHAT'S IN THE NEWSPAPER THAT'S MORE IMPORTANT THAN THAT?

DAILY PLANET

SUPERMAN ACCUSED OF MANSLAUGHTER

Newest Member of the JLA Dead

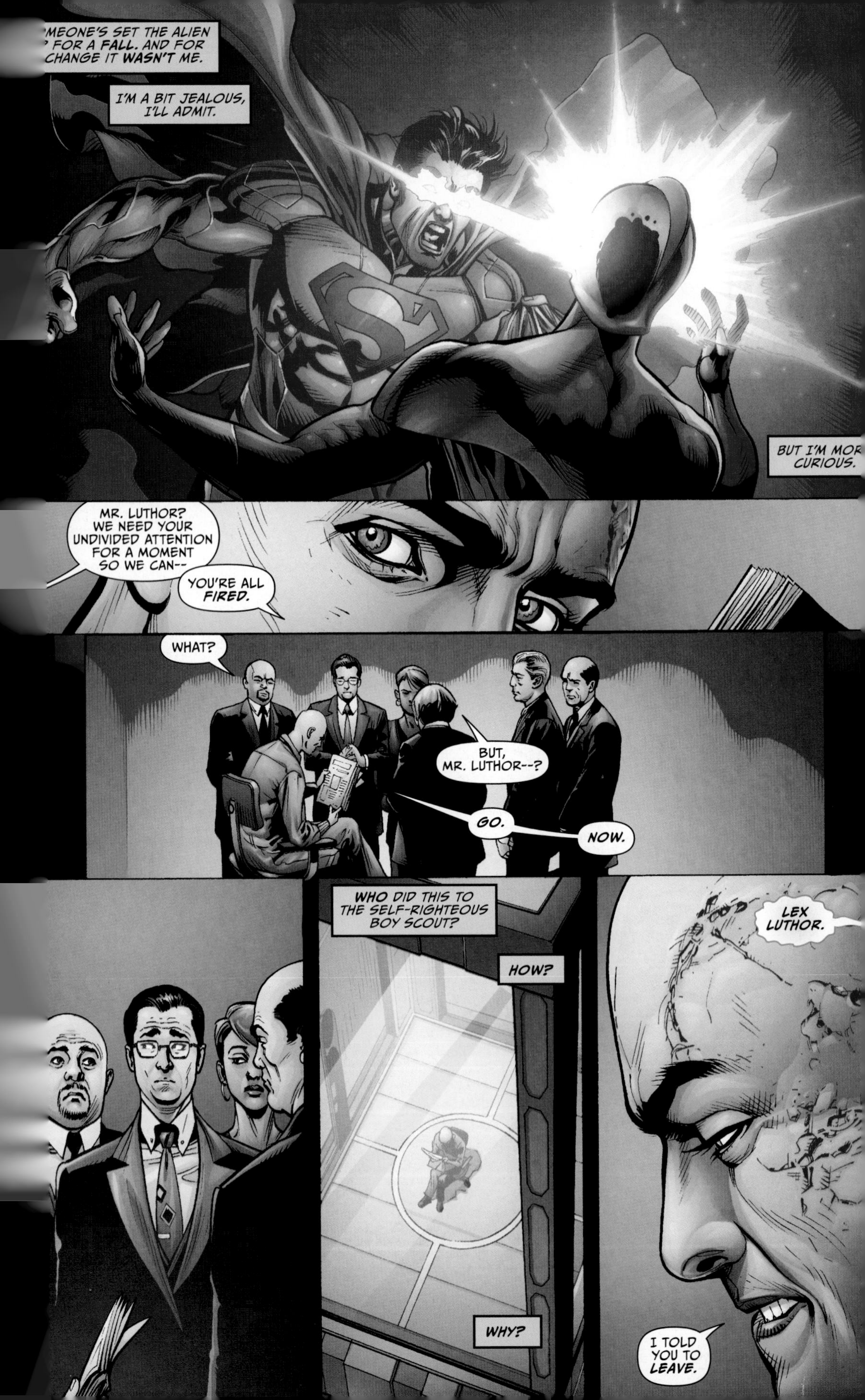
MEONE'S SET THE ALIEN
FOR A FALL. AND FOR
CHANGE IT WASN'T ME.
I'M A BIT JEALOUS, I'LL ADMIT.
BUT I'M MOR CURIOUS.
MR. LUTHOR? WE NEED YOUR UNDIVIDED ATTENTION FOR A MOMENT SO WE CAN--
YOU'RE ALL FIRED.
WHAT?
BUT, MR. LUTHOR--?
GO.
NOW.
WHO DID THIS TO THE SELF-RIGHTEOUS BOY SCOUT?
HOW?
WHY?
LEX LUTHOR.
I TOLD YOU TO LEAVE.

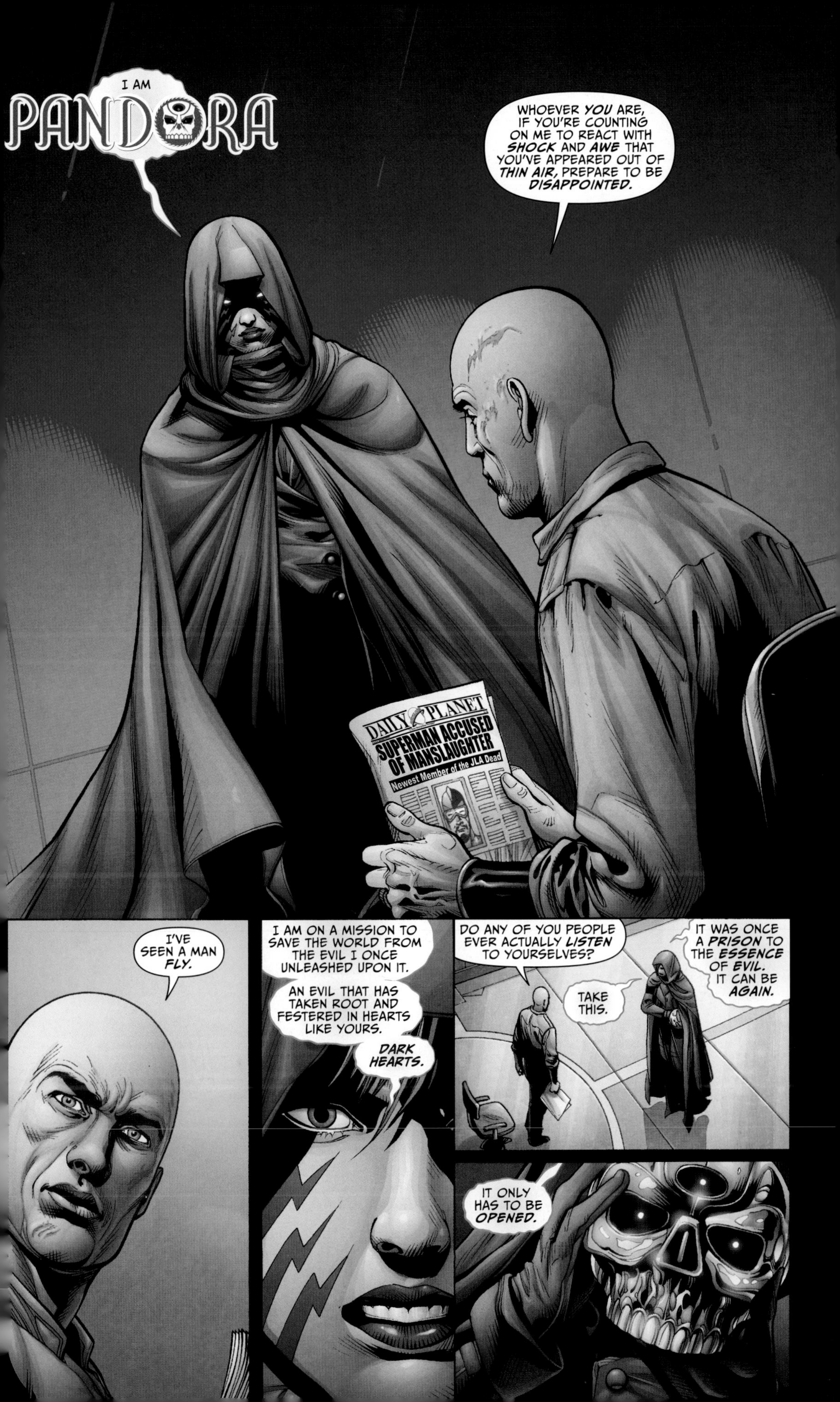
I AM PANDORA
WHOEVER YOU ARE, IF YOU'RE COUNTING ON ME TO REACT WITH SHOCK AND AWE THAT YOU'VE APPEARED OUT OF THIN AIR, PREPARE TO BE DISAPPOINTED.
DAILY PLANET
SUPERMAN ACCUSED OF MANSLAUGHTER
Newest Member of the JLA Dead
I'VE SEEN A MAN FLY.
I AM ON A MISSION TO SAVE THE WORLD FROM THE EVIL I ONCE UNLEASHED UPON IT.
AN EVIL THAT HAS TAKEN ROOT AND FESTERED IN HEARTS LIKE YOURS.
DARK HEARTS.
DO ANY OF YOU PEOPLE EVER ACTUALLY LISTEN TO YOURSELVES?
TAKE THIS.
IT WAS ONCE A PRISON TO THE ESSENCE OF EVIL. IT CAN BE AGAIN.
IT ONLY HAS TO BE OPENED.

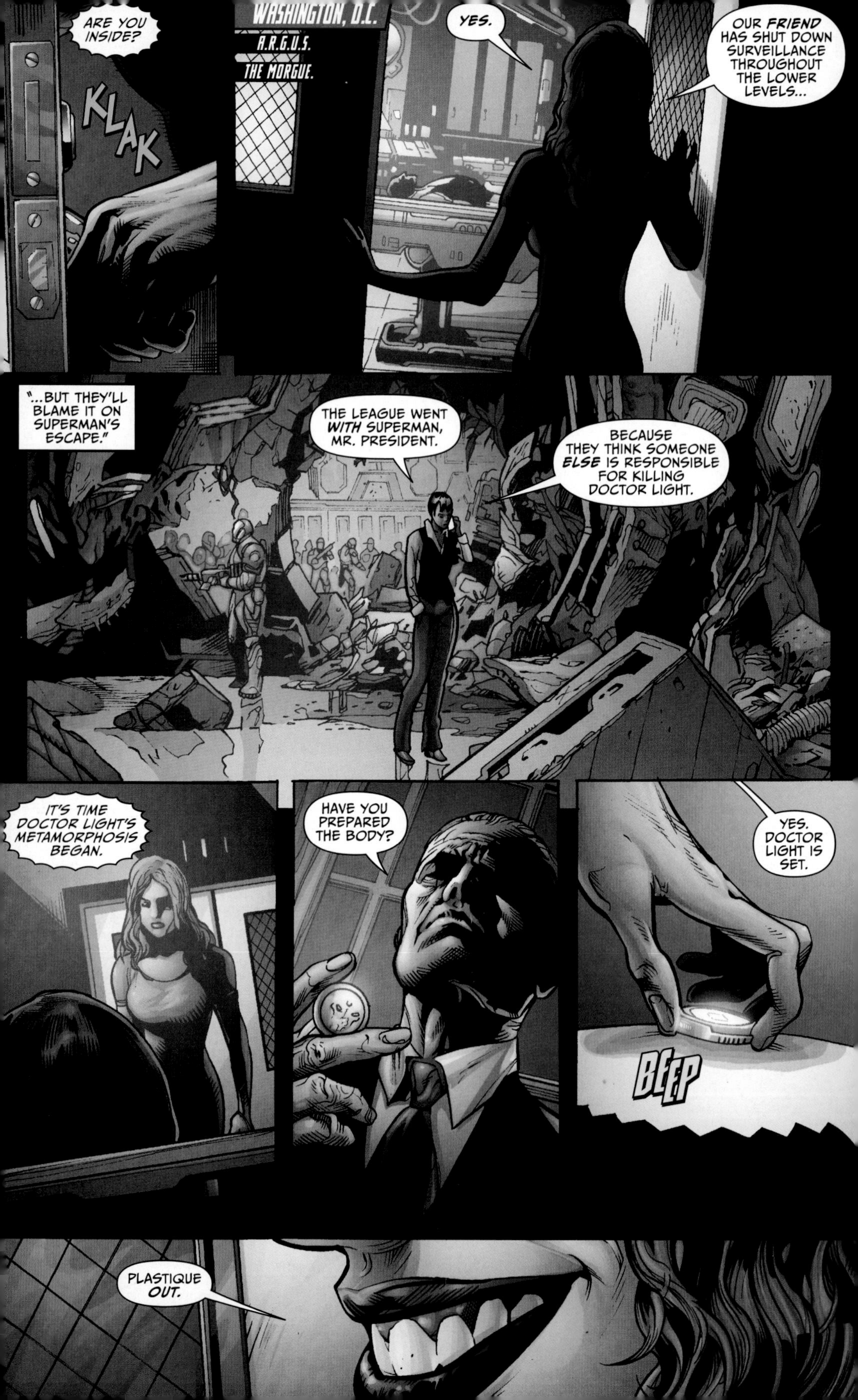
ARE YOU INSIDE?
KLAK
WASHINGTON, D.C.
A.R.G.U.S.
THE MORGUE.
YES.
OUR FRIEND HAS SHUT DOWN SURVEILLANCE THROUGHOUT THE LOWER LEVELS...
"...BUT THEY'LL BLAME IT ON SUPERMAN'S ESCAPE."
THE LEAGUE WENT WITH SUPERMAN, MR. PRESIDENT.
BECAUSE THEY THINK SOMEONE ELSE IS RESPONSIBLE FOR KILLING DOCTOR LIGHT.
IT'S TIME DOCTOR LIGHT'S METAMORPHOSIS BEGAN.
HAVE YOU PREPARED THE BODY?
YES. DOCTOR LIGHT IS SET.
BEEP
PLASTIQUE OUT.

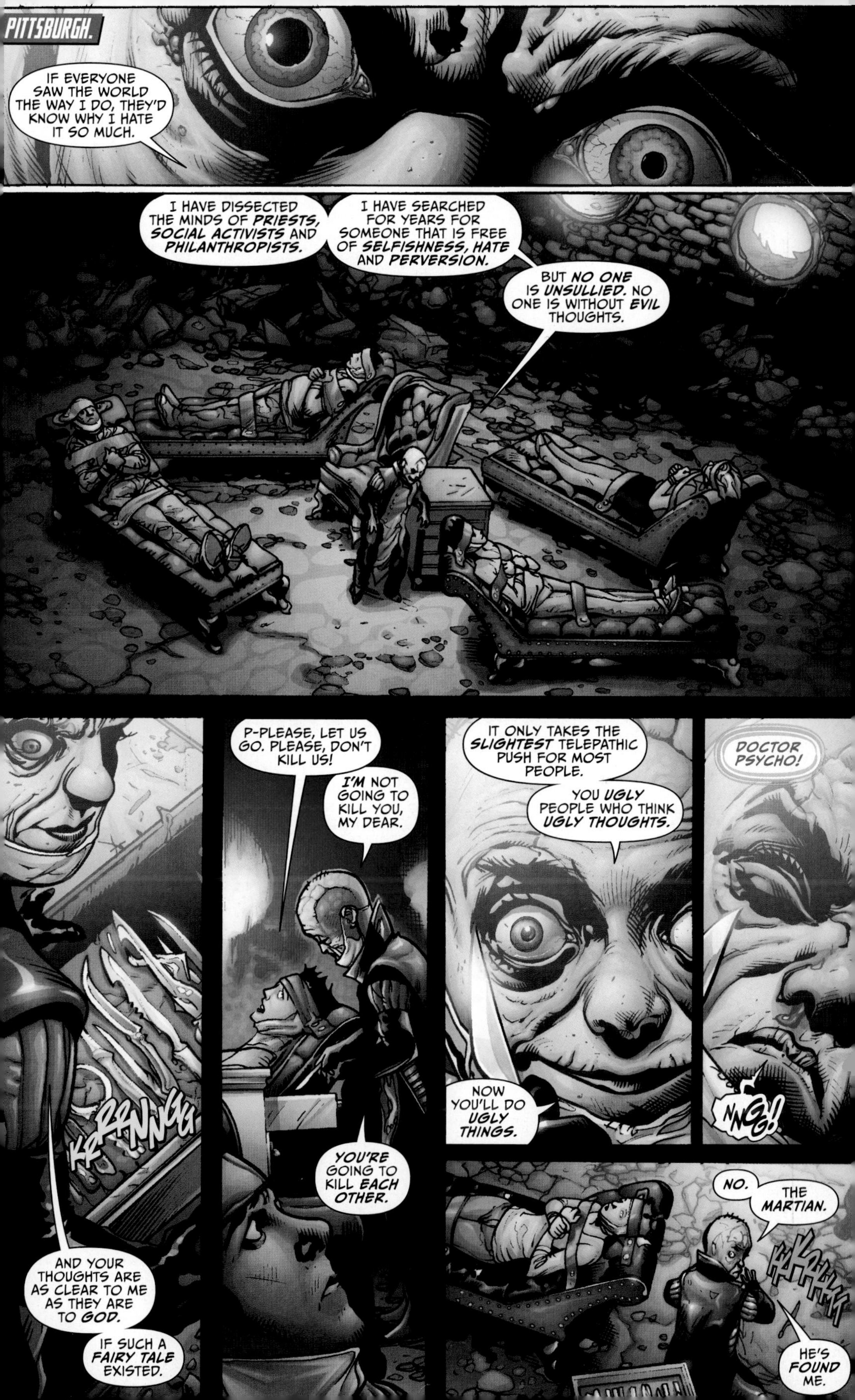
PITTSBURGH.
IF EVERYONE SAW THE WORLD THE WAY I DO, THEY'D KNOW WHY I HATE IT SO MUCH.
I HAVE DISSECTED THE MINDS OF PRIESTS, SOCIAL ACTIVISTS AND PHILANTHROPISTS.
I HAVE SEARCHED FOR YEARS FOR SOMEONE THAT IS FREE OF SELFISHNESS, HATE AND PERVERSION.
BUT NO ONE IS UNSULLIED. NO ONE IS WITHOUT EVIL THOUGHTS.
KRRRNNGG
AND YOUR THOUGHTS ARE AS CLEAR TO ME AS THEY ARE TO GOD.
IF SUCH A FAIRY TALE EXISTED.
P-PLEASE, LET US GO. PLEASE, DON'T KILL US!
I'M NOT GOING TO KILL YOU, MY DEAR.
YOU'RE GOING TO KILL EACH OTHER.
IT ONLY TAKES THE SLIGHTEST TELEPATHIC PUSH FOR MOST PEOPLE.
YOU UGLY PEOPLE WHO THINK UGLY THOUGHTS.
NOW YOU'LL DO UGLY THINGS.
DOCTOR PSYCHO!
NNGG!
NO.
THE MARTIAN.
HE'S FOUND ME.

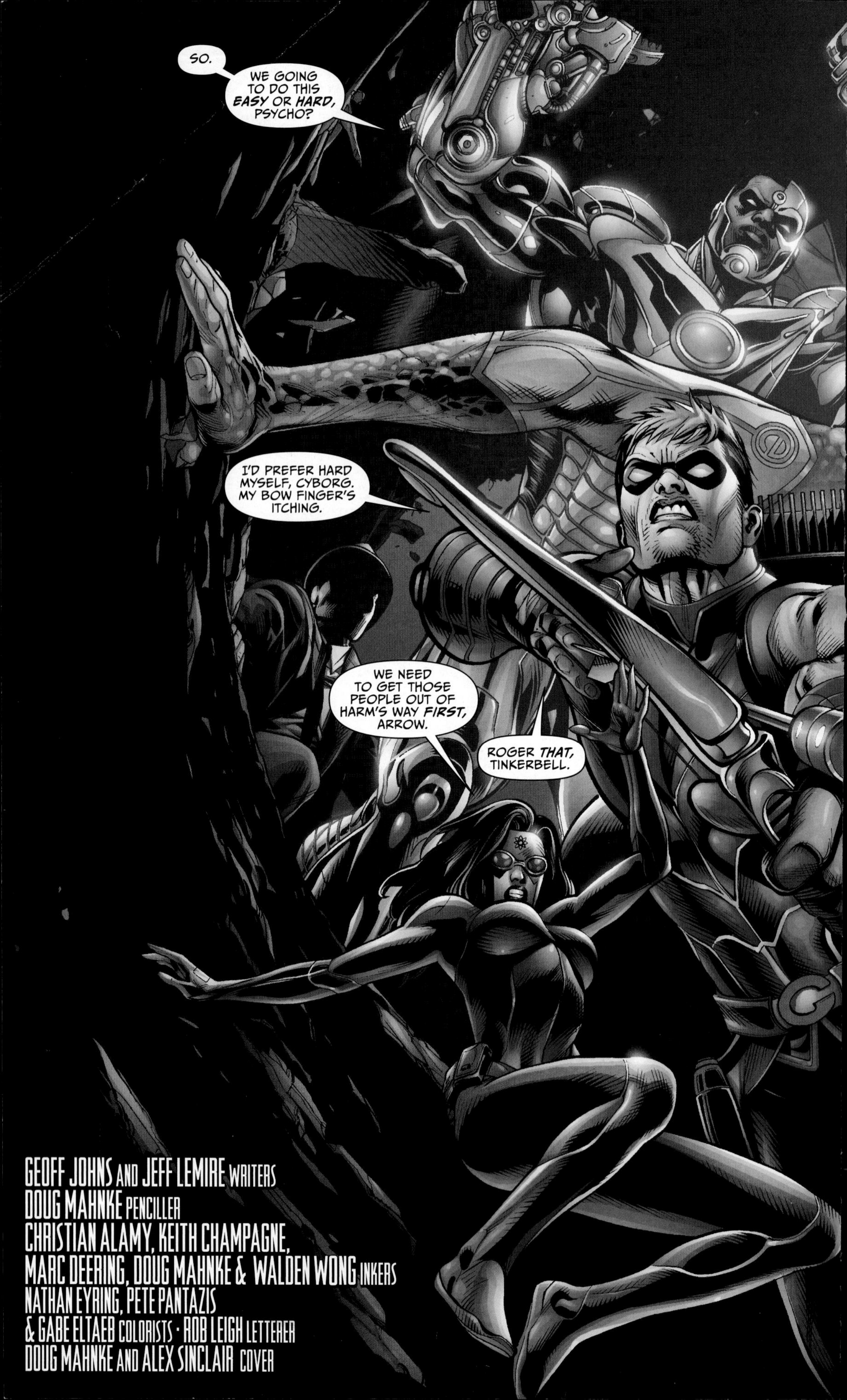
SO.
WE GOING TO DO THIS *EASY* OR *HARD*, PSYCHO?
I'D PREFER HARD MYSELF, CYBORG. MY BOW FINGER'S ITCHING.
WE NEED TO GET THOSE PEOPLE OUT OF HARM'S WAY *FIRST*, ARROW.
ROGER *THAT*, TINKERBELL.

GEOFF JOHNS AND JEFF LEMIRE WRITERS
DOUG MAHNKE PENCILLER
CHRISTIAN ALAMY, KEITH CHAMPAGNE,
MARC DEERING, DOUG MAHNKE & WALDEN WONG INKERS
NATHAN EYRING, PETE PANTAZIS
& GABE ELTAEB COLORISTS · ROB LEIGH LETTERER
DOUG MAHNKE AND ALEX SINCLAIR COVER

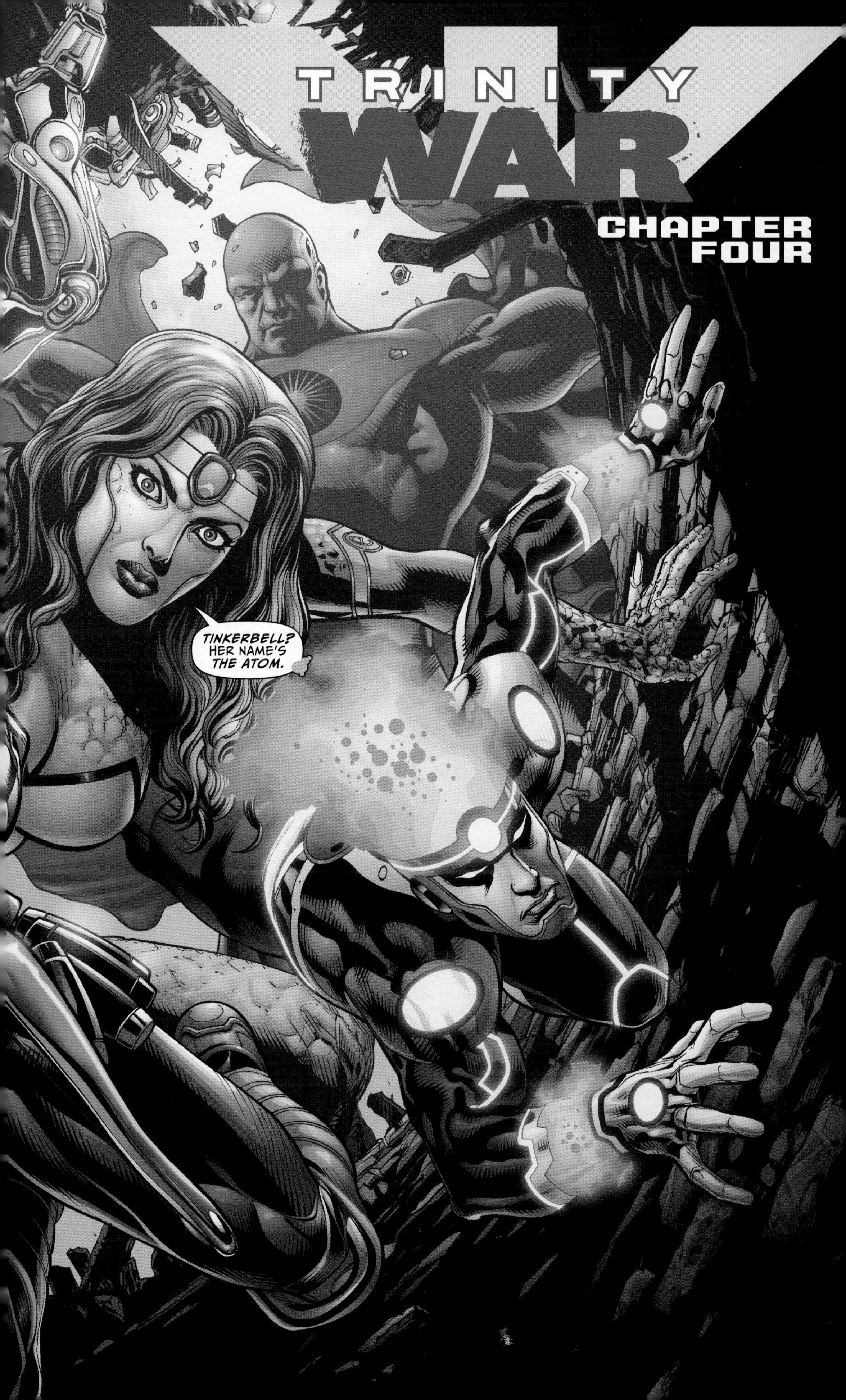
TRINITY WAR
CHAPTER FOUR
TINKERBELL? HER NAME'S THE ATOM.

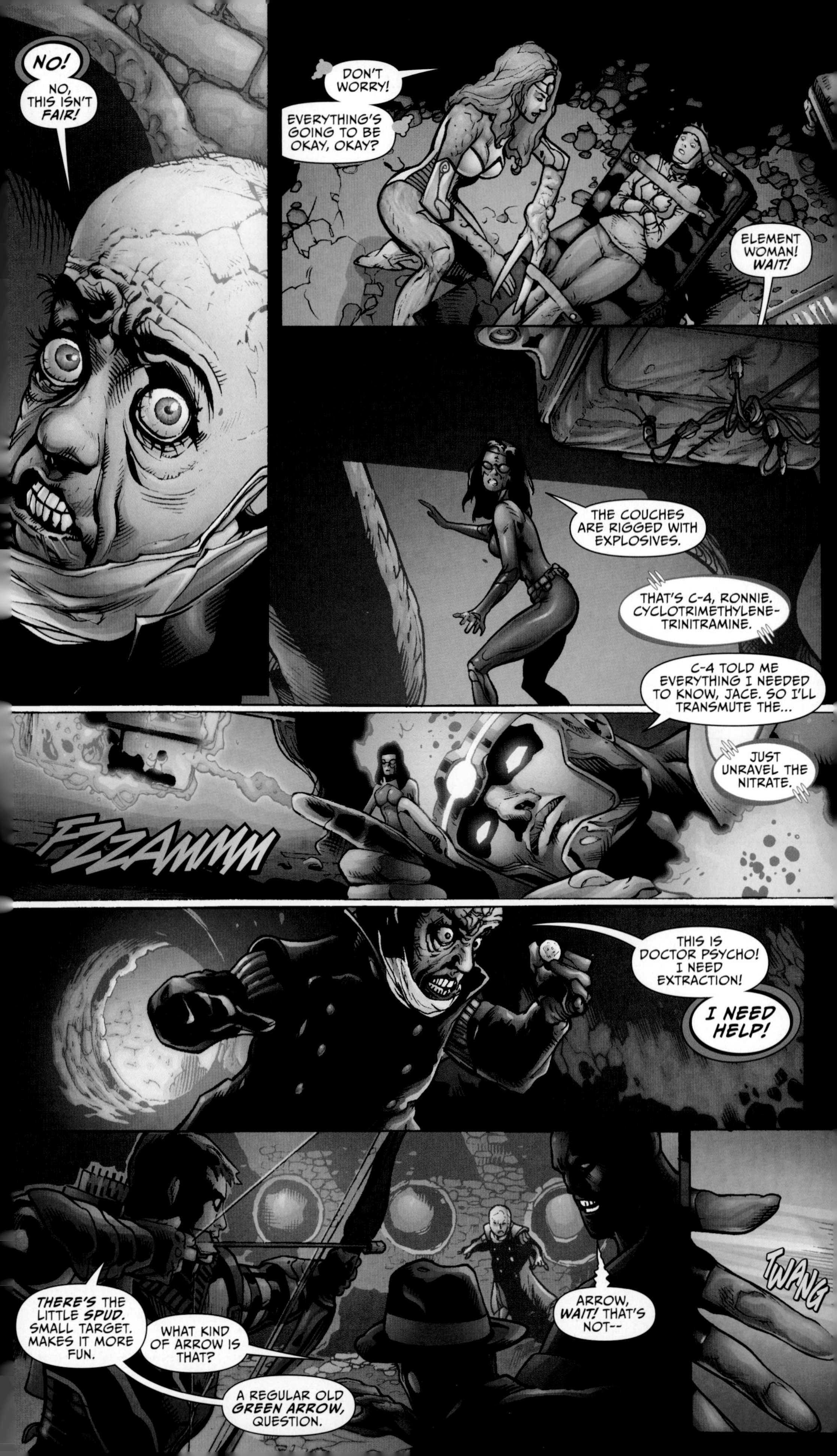

NO! NO, THIS ISN'T FAIR!
DON'T WORRY!
EVERYTHING'S GOING TO BE OKAY, OKAY?
ELEMENT WOMAN! WAIT!
THE COUCHES ARE RIGGED WITH EXPLOSIVES.
THAT'S C-4, RONNIE. CYCLOTRIMETHYLENE-TRINITRAMINE.
C-4 TOLD ME EVERYTHING I NEEDED TO KNOW, JACE. SO I'LL TRANSMUTE THE...
JUST UNRAVEL THE NITRATE.
FZZAMMM
THIS IS DOCTOR PSYCHO! I NEED EXTRACTION!
I NEED HELP!
THERE'S THE LITTLE SPUD. SMALL TARGET. MAKES IT MORE FUN.
WHAT KIND OF ARROW IS THAT?
A REGULAR OLD GREEN ARROW, QUESTION.
ARROW, WAIT! THAT'S NOT--
TWANG

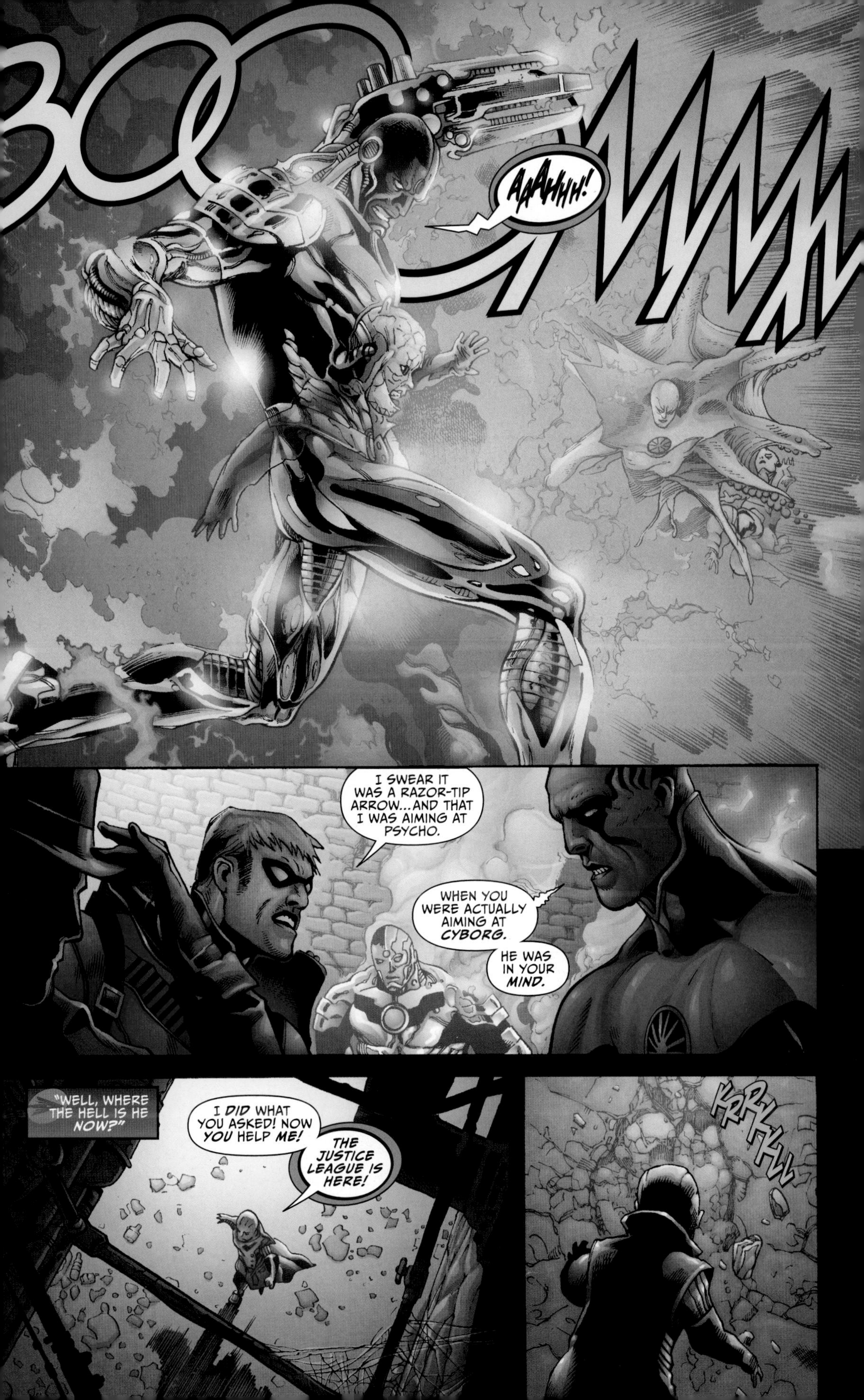

BOOOMMM
AAAHHH!
I SWEAR IT WAS A RAZOR-TIP ARROW...AND THAT I WAS AIMING AT PSYCHO.
WHEN YOU WERE ACTUALLY AIMING AT CYBORG.
HE WAS IN YOUR MIND.
"WELL, WHERE THE HELL IS HE NOW?"
I DID WHAT YOU ASKED! NOW YOU HELP ME!
THE JUSTICE LEAGUE IS HERE!
KRRKKL

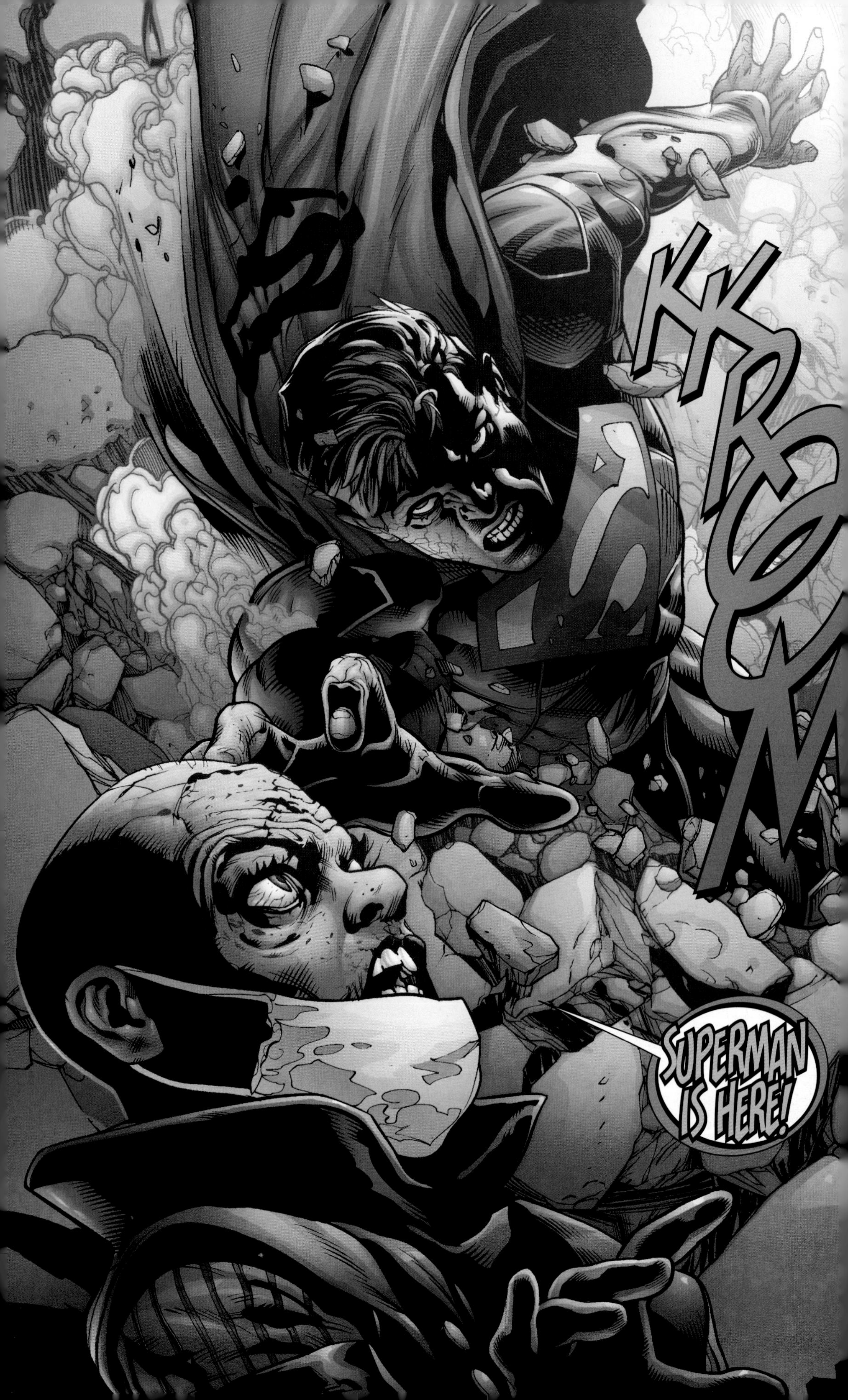
KKRAOOM
SUPERMAN IS HERE!

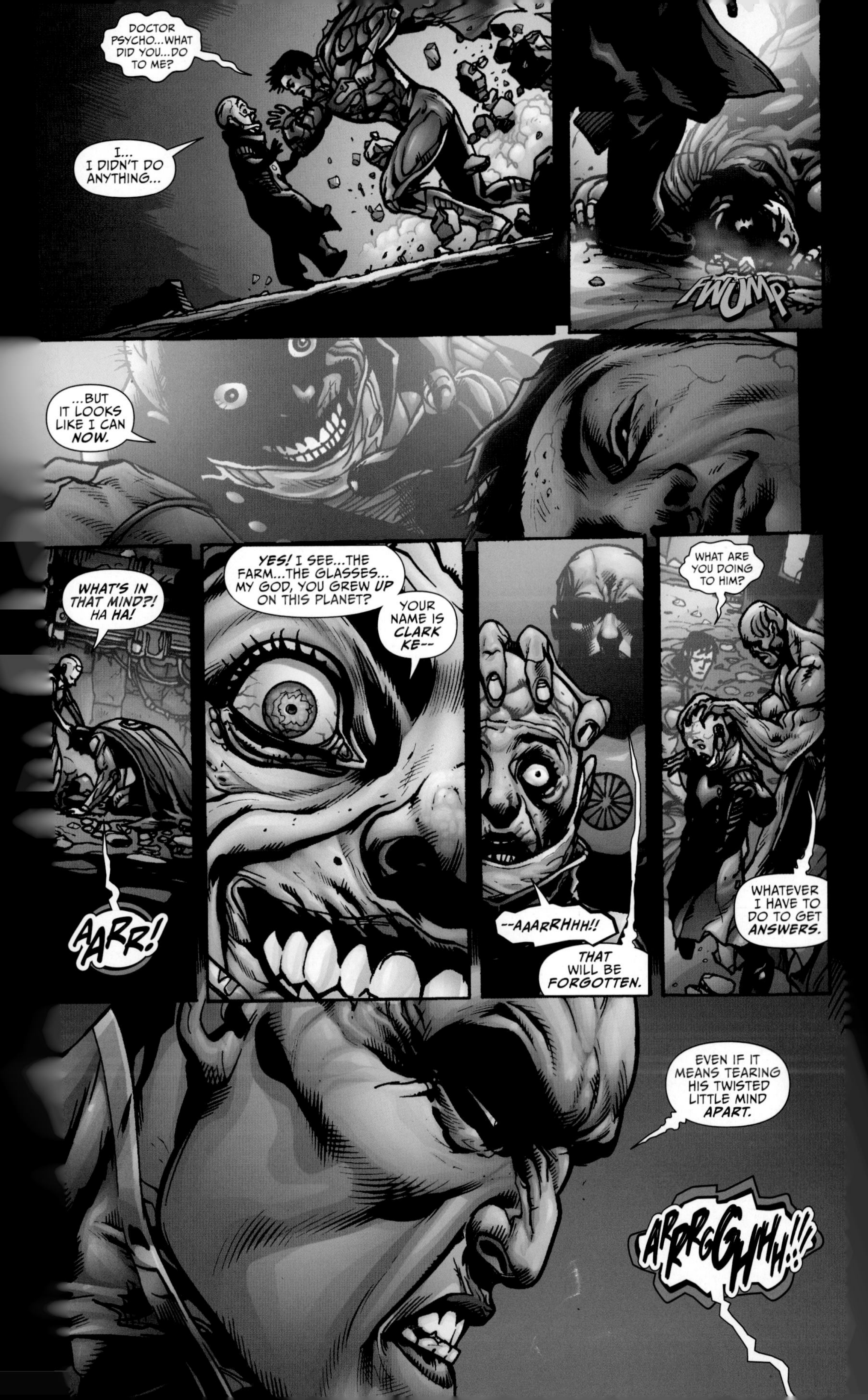
DOCTOR PSYCHO...WHAT DID YOU...DO TO ME?
I... I DIDN'T DO ANYTHING...
FWUMP
...BUT IT LOOKS LIKE I CAN NOW.
WHAT'S IN THAT MIND?! HA HA!
AARR!
YES! I SEE...THE FARM...THE GLASSES... MY GOD, YOU GREW UP ON THIS PLANET?
YOUR NAME IS CLARK KE--
--AAARRHHH!!
THAT WILL BE FORGOTTEN.
WHAT ARE YOU DOING TO HIM?
WHATEVER I HAVE TO DO TO GET ANSWERS.
EVEN IF IT MEANS TEARING HIS TWISTED LITTLE MIND APART.
ARRRGGHHH!!!

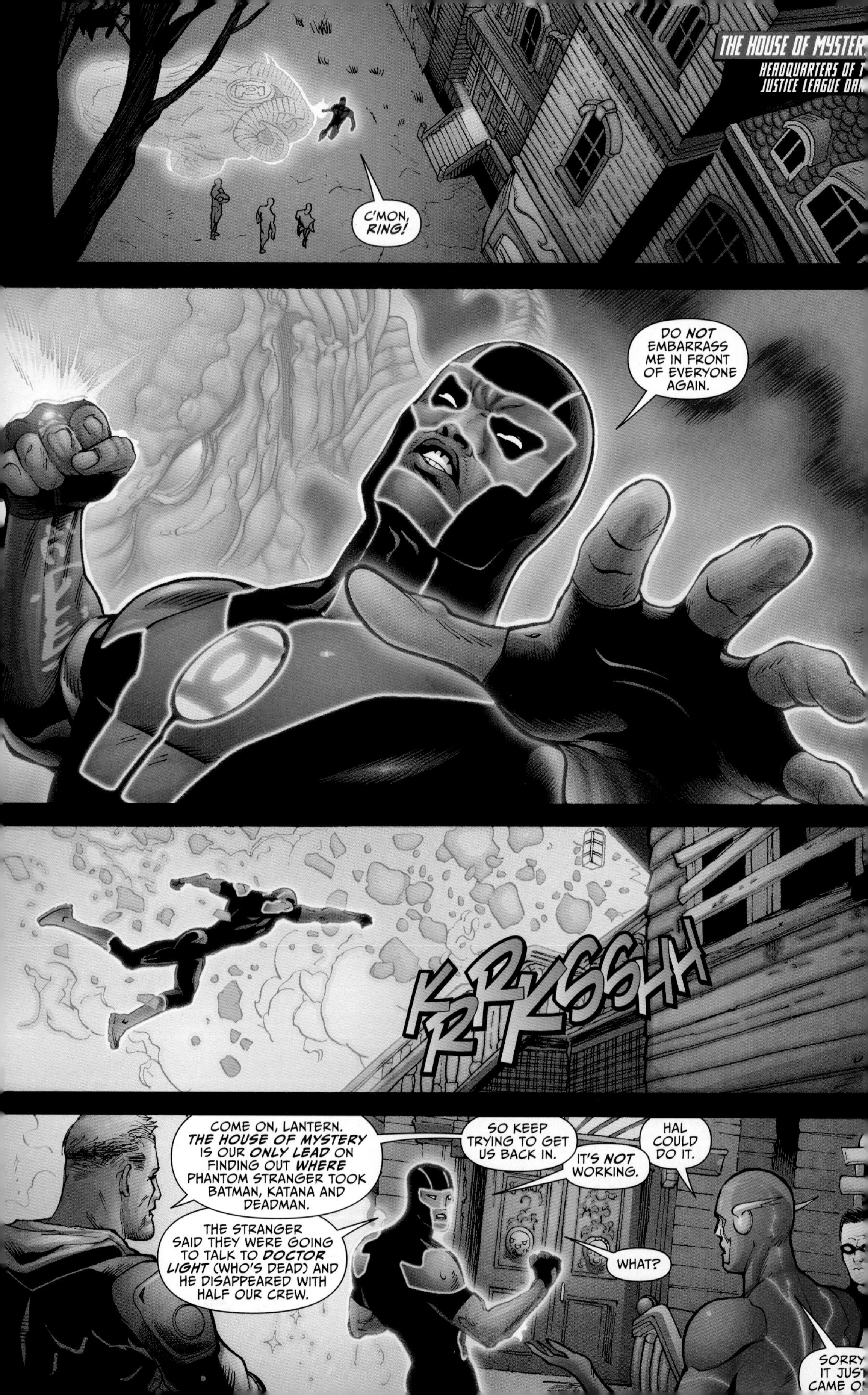

THE HOUSE OF MYSTER
HEADQUARTERS OF T
JUSTICE LEAGUE DAR
C'MON, RING!
DO NOT EMBARRASS ME IN FRONT OF EVERYONE AGAIN.
KRRKSSHH
COME ON, LANTERN. THE HOUSE OF MYSTERY IS OUR ONLY LEAD ON FINDING OUT WHERE PHANTOM STRANGER TOOK BATMAN, KATANA AND DEADMAN.
THE STRANGER SAID THEY WERE GOING TO TALK TO DOCTOR LIGHT (WHO'S DEAD) AND HE DISAPPEARED WITH HALF OUR CREW.
SO KEEP TRYING TO GET US BACK IN.
IT'S NOT WORKING.
HAL COULD DO IT.
WHAT?
SORRY IT JUST CAME O

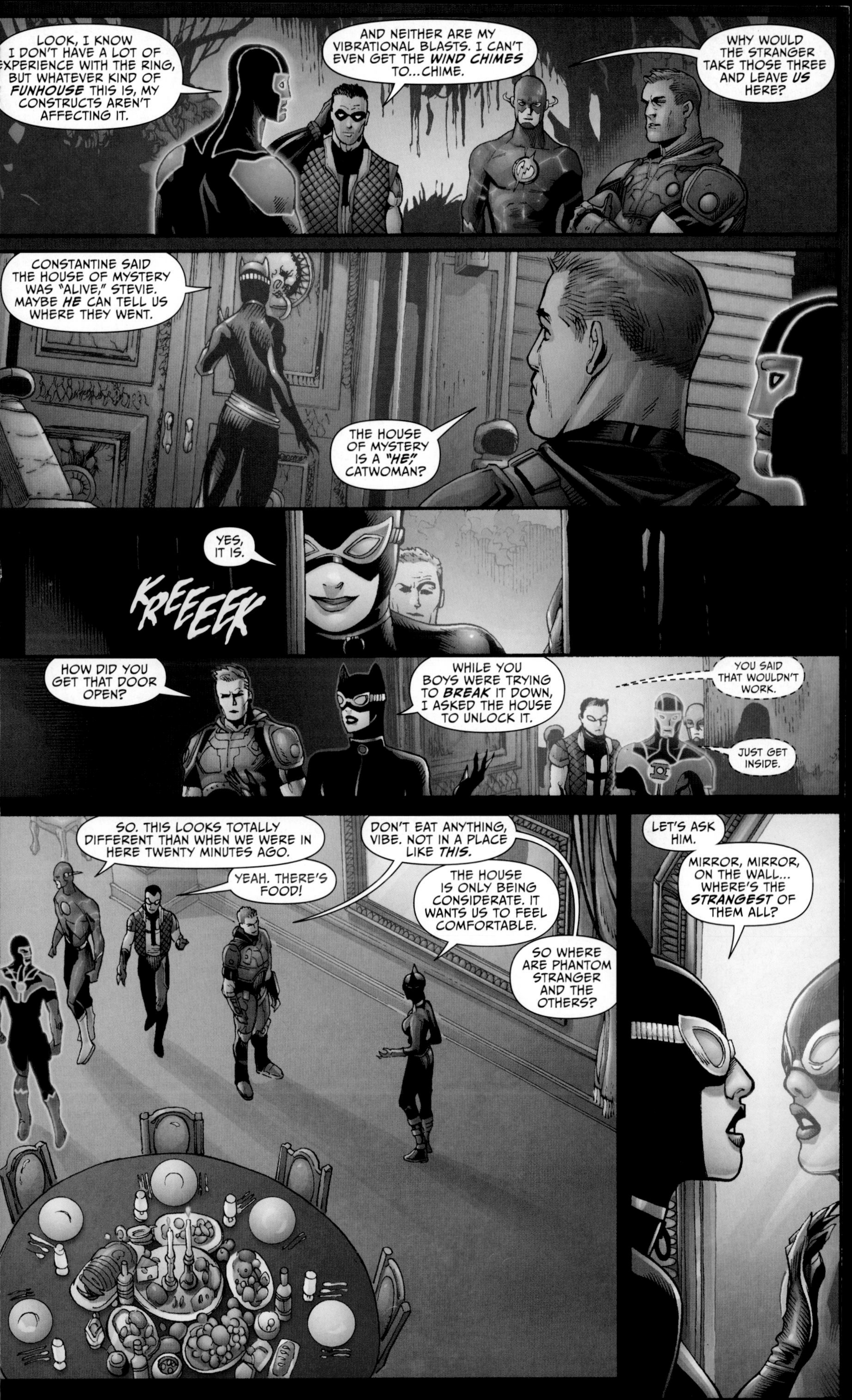
LOOK, I KNOW I DON'T HAVE A LOT OF EXPERIENCE WITH THE RING, BUT WHATEVER KIND OF FUNHOUSE THIS IS, MY CONSTRUCTS AREN'T AFFECTING IT.
AND NEITHER ARE MY VIBRATIONAL BLASTS. I CAN'T EVEN GET THE WIND CHIMES TO...CHIME.
WHY WOULD THE STRANGER TAKE THOSE THREE AND LEAVE US HERE?
CONSTANTINE SAID THE HOUSE OF MYSTERY WAS "ALIVE," STEVIE. MAYBE HE CAN TELL US WHERE THEY WENT.
THE HOUSE OF MYSTERY IS A "HE," CATWOMAN?
YES, IT IS.
KREEEEK
HOW DID YOU GET THAT DOOR OPEN?
WHILE YOU BOYS WERE TRYING TO BREAK IT DOWN, I ASKED THE HOUSE TO UNLOCK IT.
YOU SAID THAT WOULDN'T WORK.
JUST GET INSIDE.
SO. THIS LOOKS TOTALLY DIFFERENT THAN WHEN WE WERE IN HERE TWENTY MINUTES AGO.
YEAH. THERE'S FOOD!
DON'T EAT ANYTHING, VIBE. NOT IN A PLACE LIKE THIS.
THE HOUSE IS ONLY BEING CONSIDERATE. IT WANTS US TO FEEL COMFORTABLE.
SO WHERE ARE PHANTOM STRANGER AND THE OTHERS?
LET'S ASK HIM.
MIRROR, MIRROR, ON THE WALL... WHERE'S THE STRANGEST OF THEM ALL?

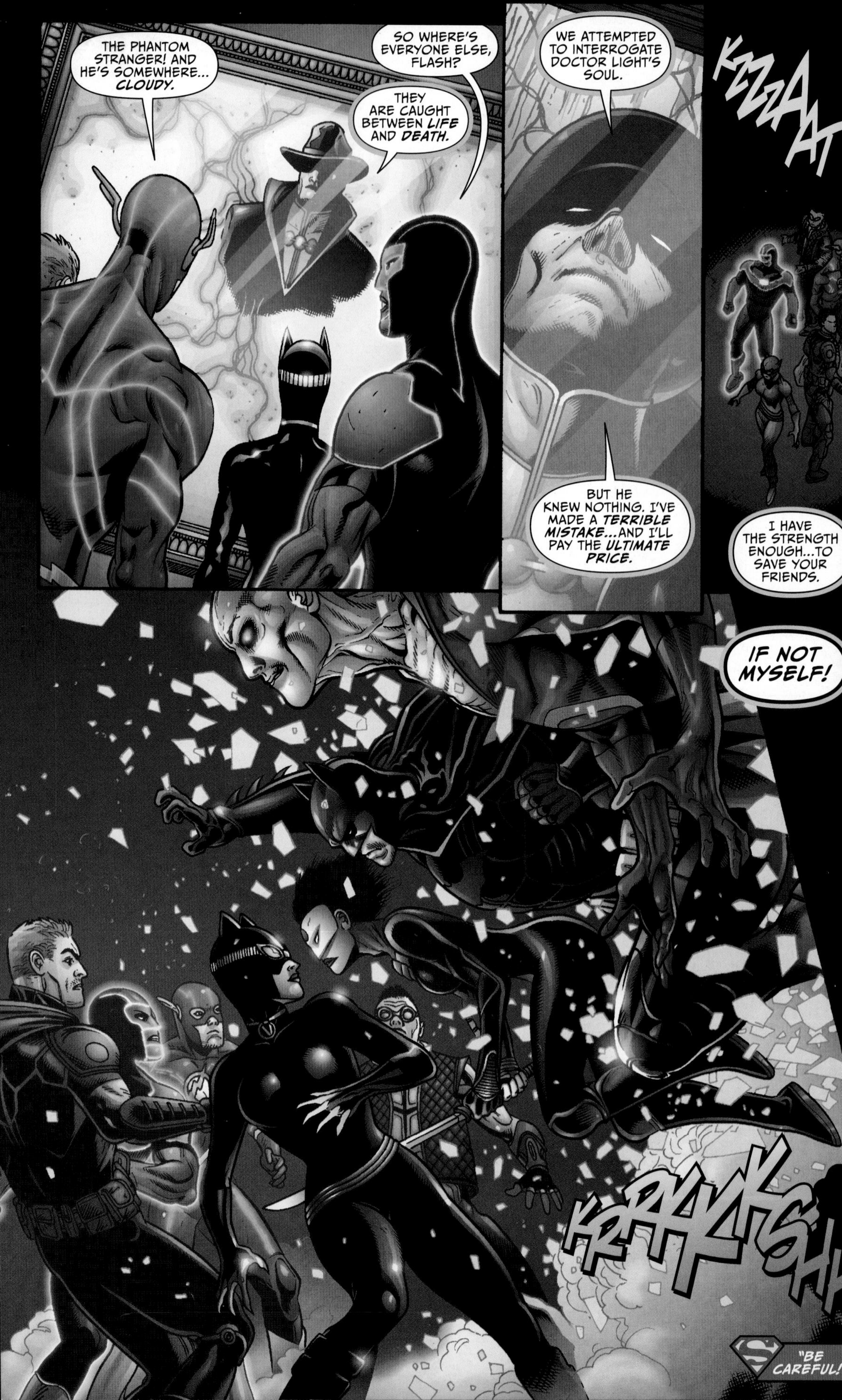

THE PHANTOM STRANGER! AND HE'S SOMEWHERE... CLOUDY.
SO WHERE'S EVERYONE ELSE, FLASH?
THEY ARE CAUGHT BETWEEN LIFE AND DEATH.
WE ATTEMPTED TO INTERROGATE DOCTOR LIGHT'S SOUL.
BUT HE KNEW NOTHING. I'VE MADE A TERRIBLE MISTAKE...AND I'LL PAY THE ULTIMATE PRICE.
KZZZAAAT
I HAVE THE STRENGTH ENOUGH...TO SAVE YOUR FRIENDS.
IF NOT MYSELF!
KRAKKSH
"BE CAREFUL!

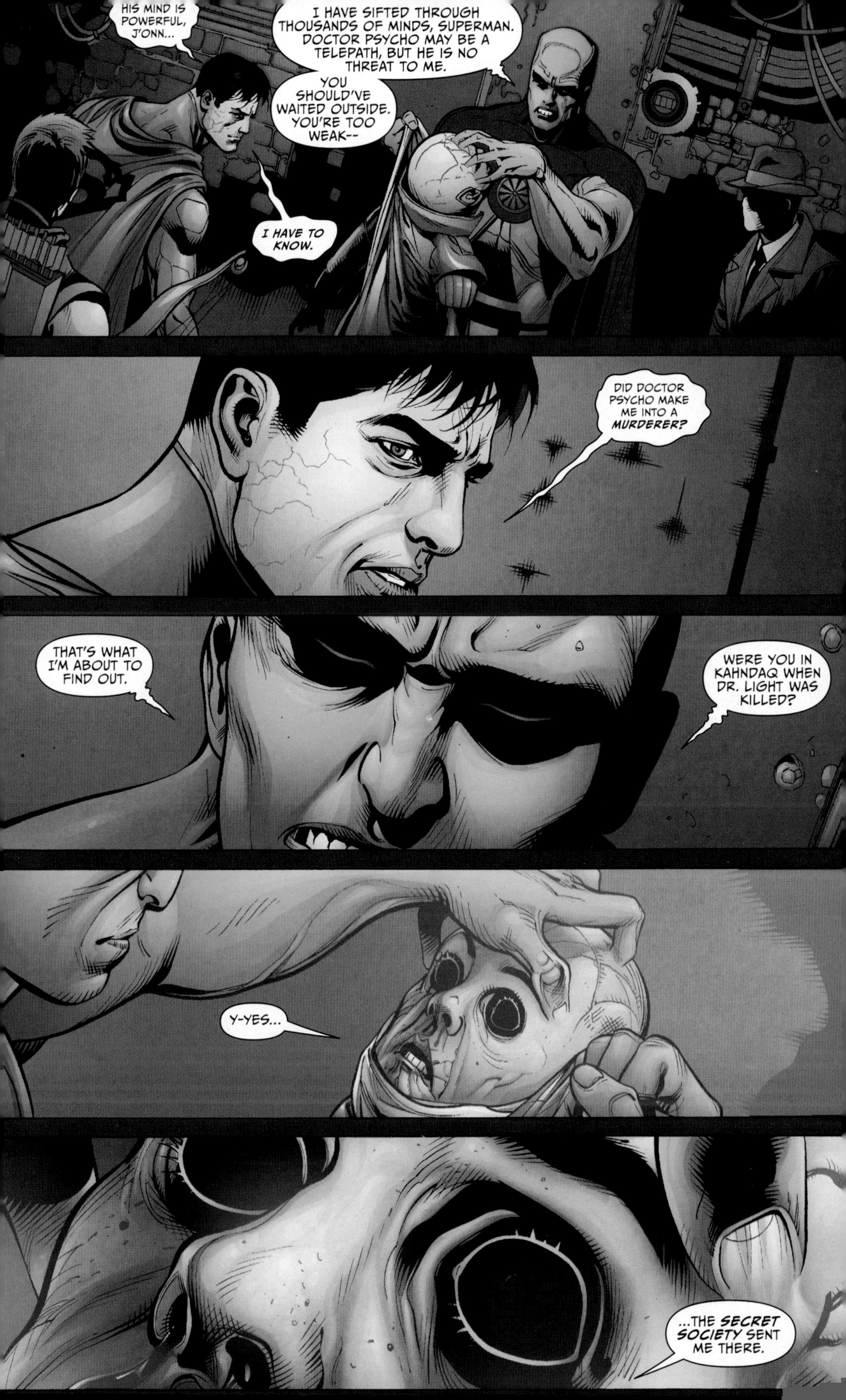
HIS MIND IS POWERFUL, J'ONN...
I HAVE SIFTED THROUGH THOUSANDS OF MINDS, SUPERMAN. DOCTOR PSYCHO MAY BE A TELEPATH, BUT HE IS NO THREAT TO ME.
YOU SHOULD'VE WAITED OUTSIDE. YOU'RE TOO WEAK--
I HAVE TO KNOW.
DID DOCTOR PSYCHO MAKE ME INTO A MURDERER?
THAT'S WHAT I'M ABOUT TO FIND OUT.
WERE YOU IN KAHNDAQ WHEN DR. LIGHT WAS KILLED?
Y-YES...
...THE SECRET SOCIETY SENT ME THERE.

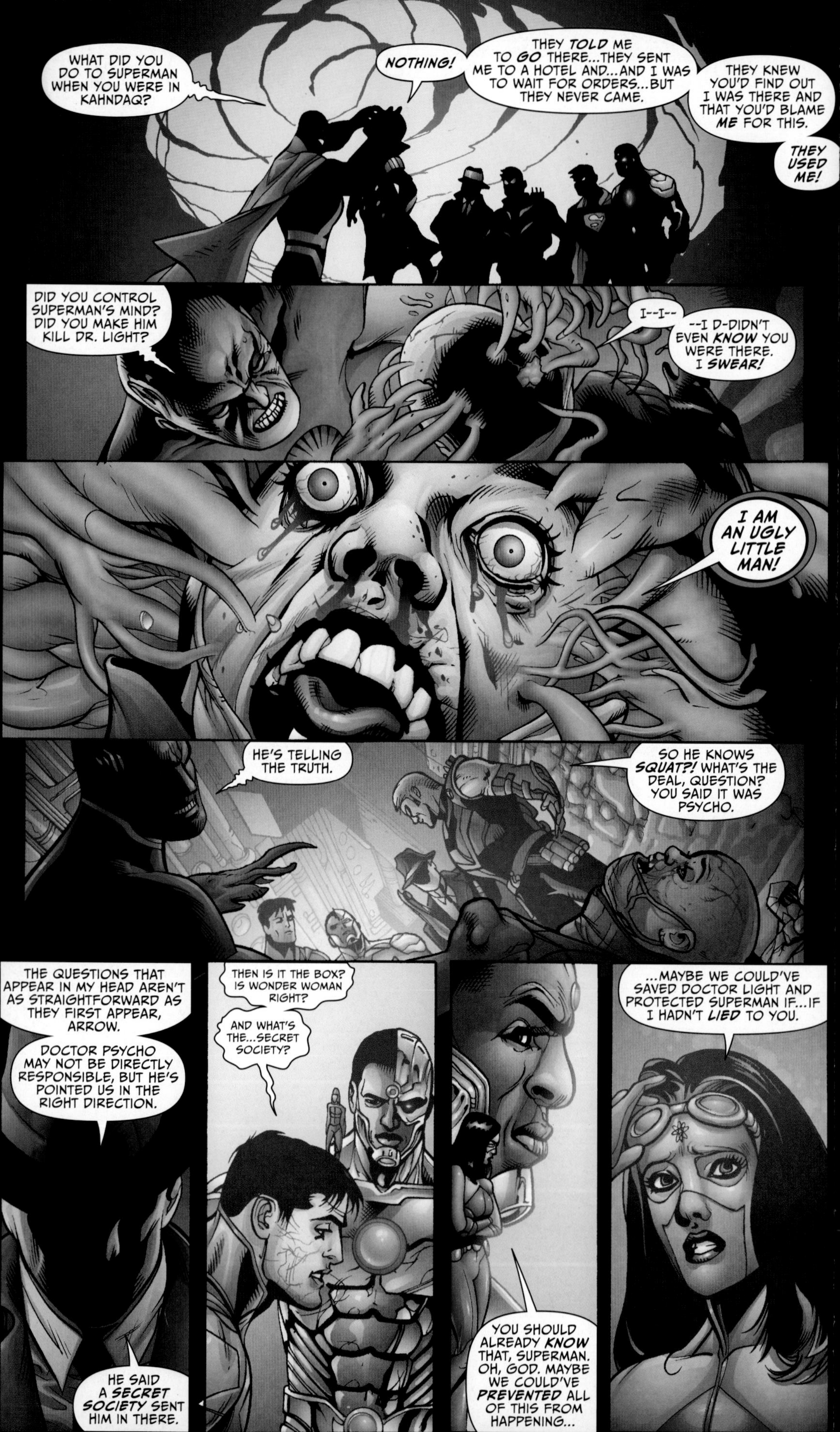

WHAT DID YOU DO TO SUPERMAN WHEN YOU WERE IN KAHNDAQ?
NOTHING!
THEY TOLD ME TO GO THERE...THEY SENT ME TO A HOTEL AND...AND I WAS TO WAIT FOR ORDERS...BUT THEY NEVER CAME.
THEY KNEW YOU'D FIND OUT I WAS THERE AND THAT YOU'D BLAME ME FOR THIS.
THEY USED ME!
DID YOU CONTROL SUPERMAN'S MIND? DID YOU MAKE HIM KILL DR. LIGHT?
I--I--
--I D-DIDN'T EVEN KNOW YOU WERE THERE. I SWEAR!
I AM AN UGLY LITTLE MAN!
HE'S TELLING THE TRUTH.
SO HE KNOWS SQUAT?! WHAT'S THE DEAL, QUESTION? YOU SAID IT WAS PSYCHO.
THE QUESTIONS THAT APPEAR IN MY HEAD AREN'T AS STRAIGHTFORWARD AS THEY FIRST APPEAR, ARROW.
DOCTOR PSYCHO MAY NOT BE DIRECTLY RESPONSIBLE, BUT HE'S POINTED US IN THE RIGHT DIRECTION.
HE SAID A SECRET SOCIETY SENT HIM IN THERE.
THEN IS IT THE BOX? IS WONDER WOMAN RIGHT?
AND WHAT'S THE...SECRET SOCIETY?
YOU SHOULD ALREADY KNOW THAT, SUPERMAN. OH, GOD. MAYBE WE COULD'VE PREVENTED ALL OF THIS FROM HAPPENING...
...MAYBE WE COULD'VE SAVED DOCTOR LIGHT AND PROTECTED SUPERMAN IF...IF I HADN'T LIED TO YOU.

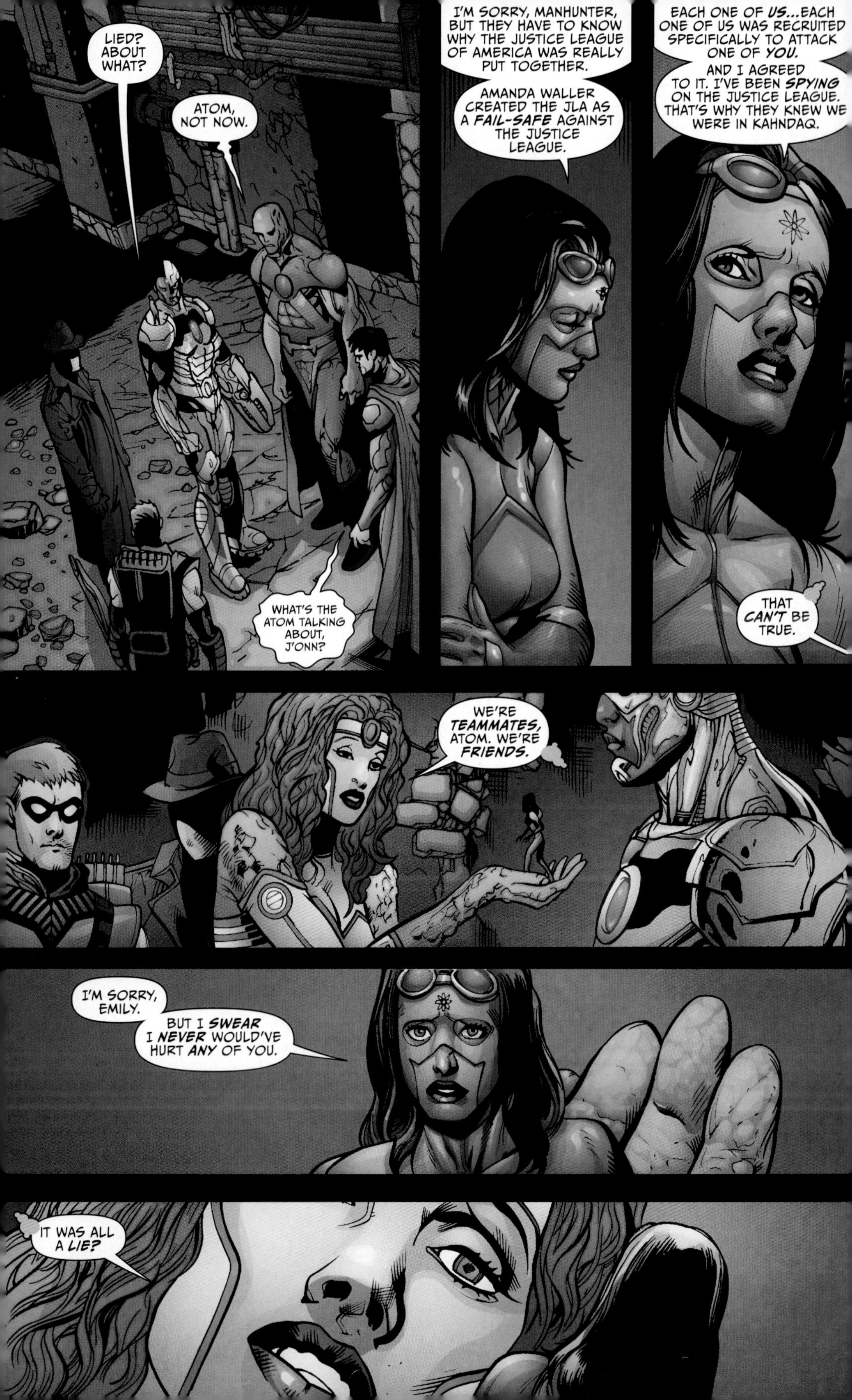
LIED? ABOUT WHAT?
ATOM, NOT NOW.
WHAT'S THE ATOM TALKING ABOUT, J'ONN?
I'M SORRY, MANHUNTER, BUT THEY HAVE TO KNOW WHY THE JUSTICE LEAGUE OF AMERICA WAS REALLY PUT TOGETHER.
AMANDA WALLER CREATED THE JLA AS A FAIL-SAFE AGAINST THE JUSTICE LEAGUE.
EACH ONE OF US...EACH ONE OF US WAS RECRUITED SPECIFICALLY TO ATTACK ONE OF YOU.
AND I AGREED TO IT. I'VE BEEN SPYING ON THE JUSTICE LEAGUE. THAT'S WHY THEY KNEW WE WERE IN KAHNDAQ.
THAT CAN'T BE TRUE.
WE'RE TEAMMATES, ATOM. WE'RE FRIENDS.
I'M SORRY, EMILY.
BUT I SWEAR I NEVER WOULD'VE HURT ANY OF YOU.
IT WAS ALL A LIE?

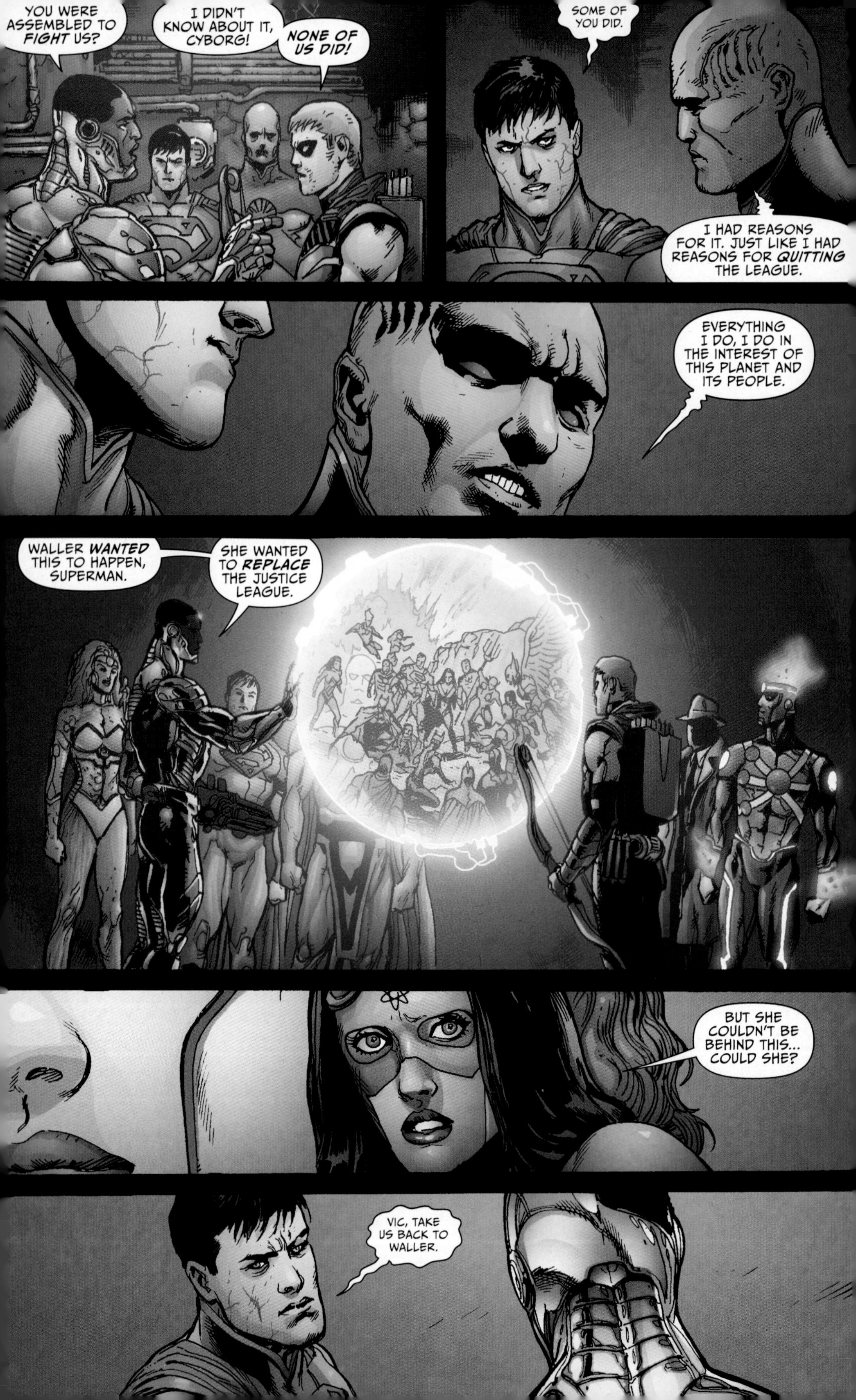
YOU WERE ASSEMBLED TO FIGHT US?
I DIDN'T KNOW ABOUT IT, CYBORG!
NONE OF US DID!
SOME OF YOU DID.
I HAD REASONS FOR IT. JUST LIKE I HAD REASONS FOR QUITTING THE LEAGUE.
EVERYTHING I DO, I DO IN THE INTEREST OF THIS PLANET AND ITS PEOPLE.
WALLER WANTED THIS TO HAPPEN, SUPERMAN.
SHE WANTED TO REPLACE THE JUSTICE LEAGUE.
BUT SHE COULDN'T BE BEHIND THIS... COULD SHE?
VIC, TAKE US BACK TO WALLER.

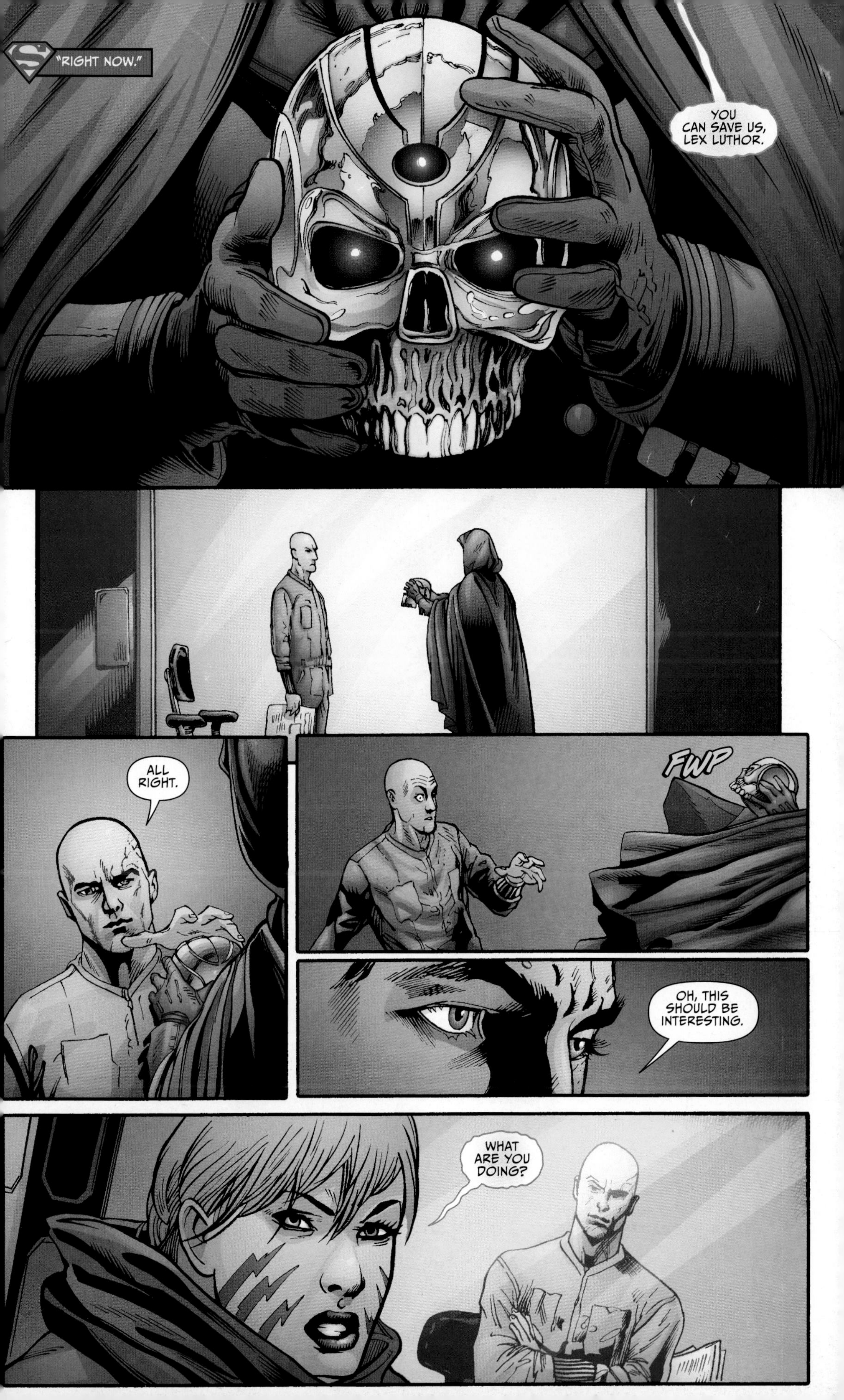
"RIGHT NOW."
YOU CAN SAVE US, LEX LUTHOR.
ALL RIGHT.
FWP
OH, THIS SHOULD BE INTERESTING.
WHAT ARE YOU DOING?

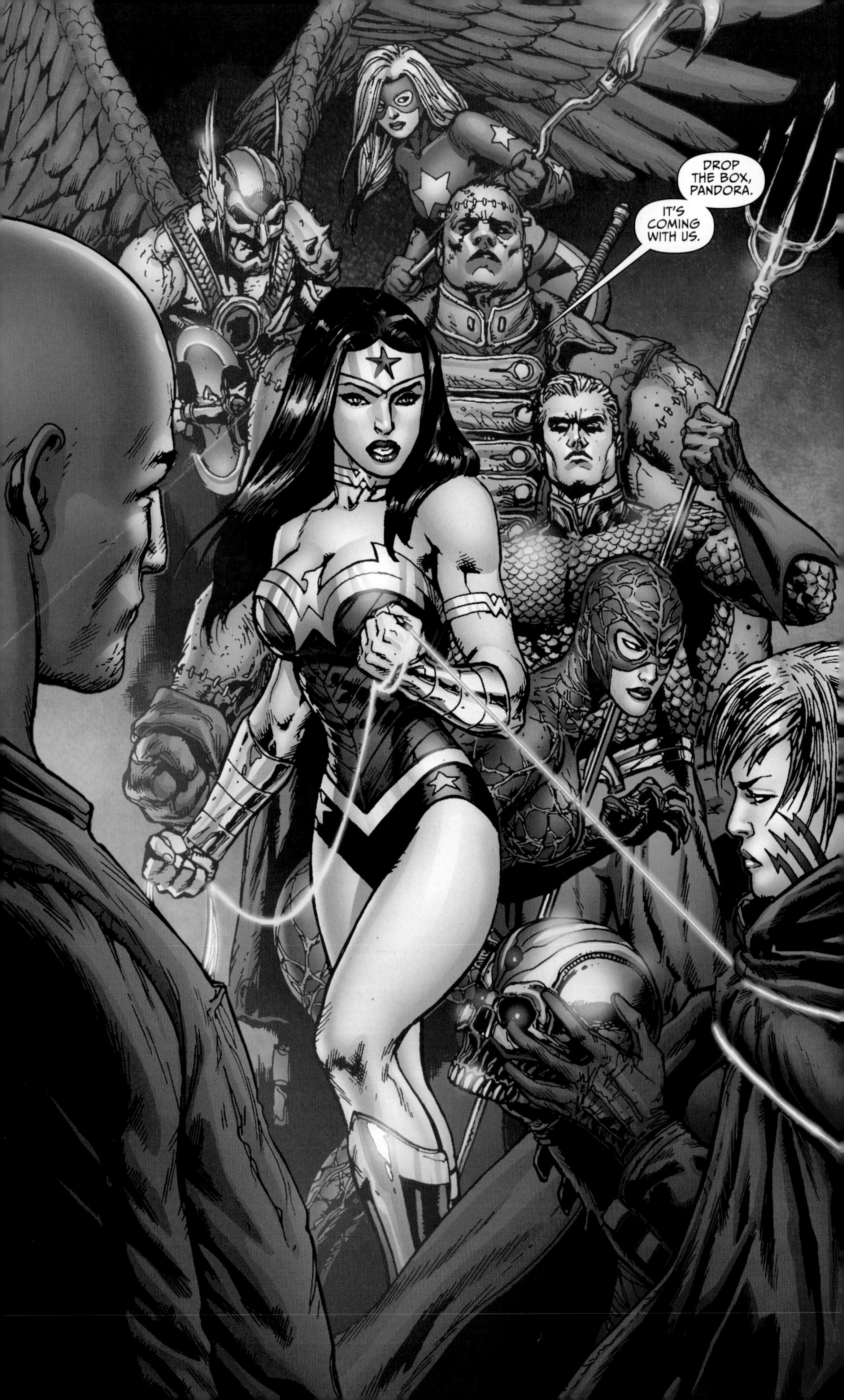

DROP THE BOX, PANDORA.
IT'S COMING WITH US.

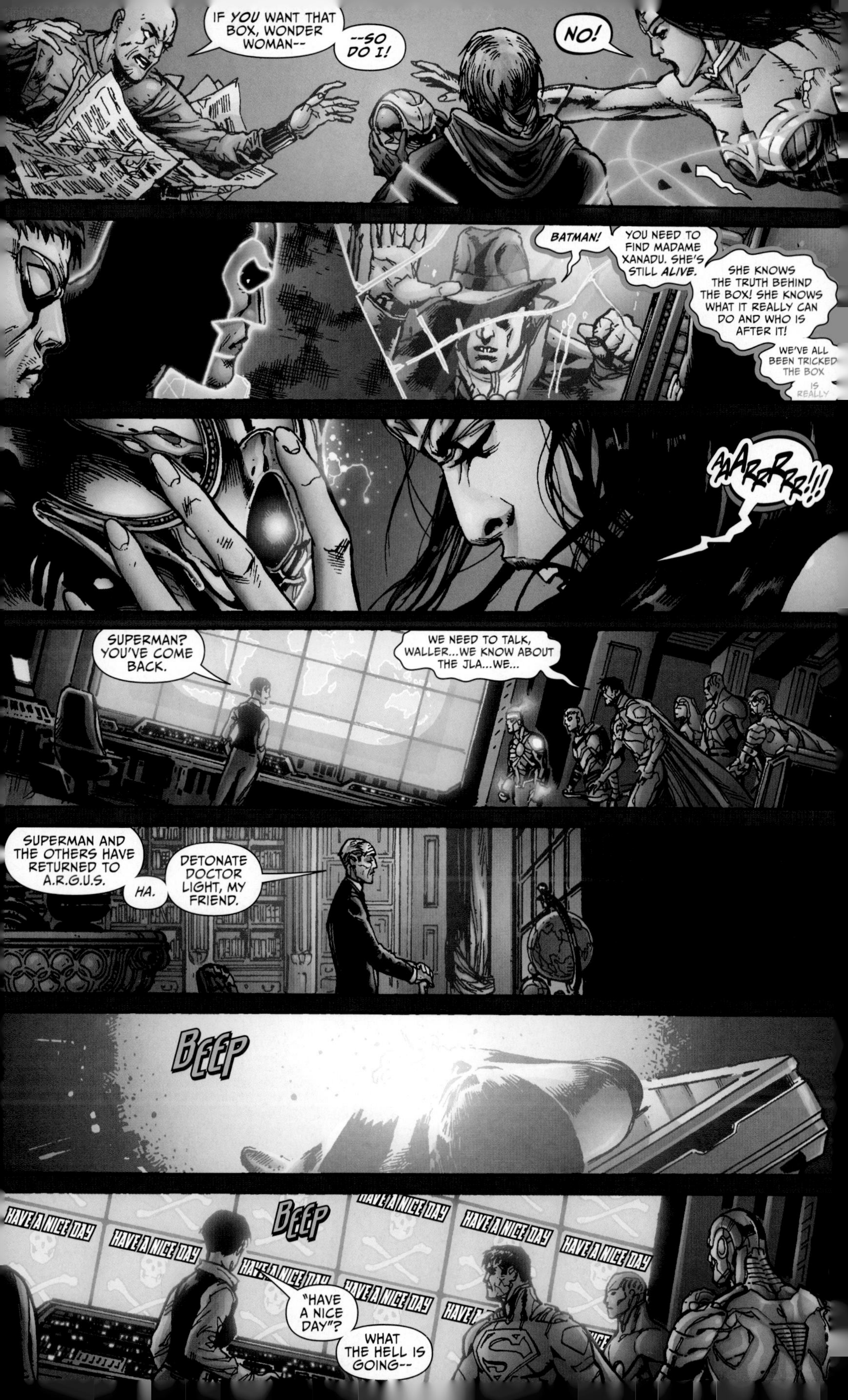

IF YOU WANT THAT BOX, WONDER WOMAN--
--SO DO I!
NO!
BATMAN!
YOU NEED TO FIND MADAME XANADU. SHE'S STILL ALIVE.
SHE KNOWS THE TRUTH BEHIND THE BOX! SHE KNOWS WHAT IT REALLY CAN DO AND WHO IS AFTER IT!
WE'VE ALL BEEN TRICKED. THE BOX IS REALLY
AARRRRR!!!
SUPERMAN? YOU'VE COME BACK.
WE NEED TO TALK, WALLER...WE KNOW ABOUT THE JLA...WE...
SUPERMAN AND THE OTHERS HAVE RETURNED TO A.R.G.U.S.
HA.
DETONATE DOCTOR LIGHT, MY FRIEND.
BEEP
BEEP
HAVE A NICE DAY
"HAVE A NICE DAY"?
WHAT THE HELL IS GOING--

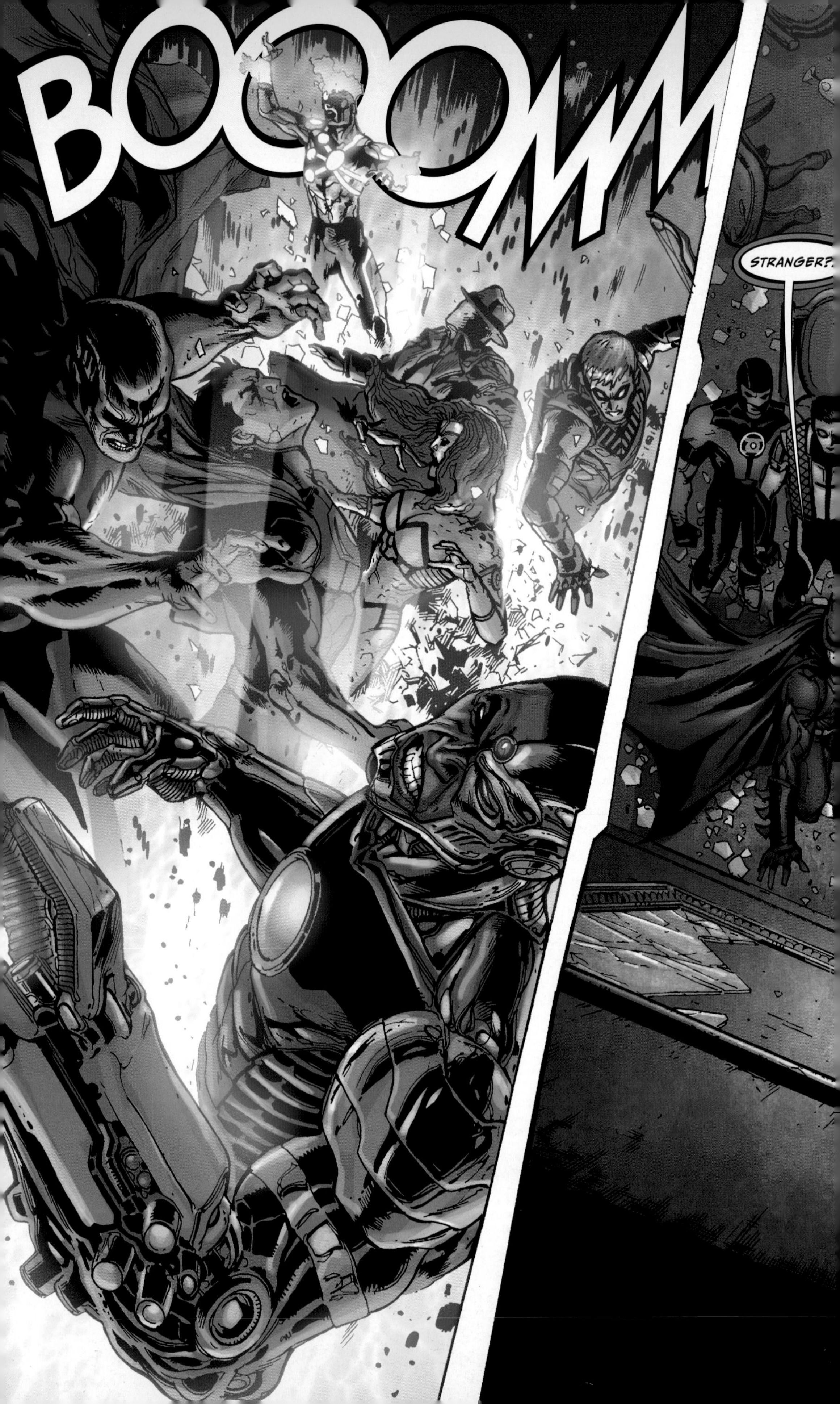
BOOOOMM
STRANGER?..

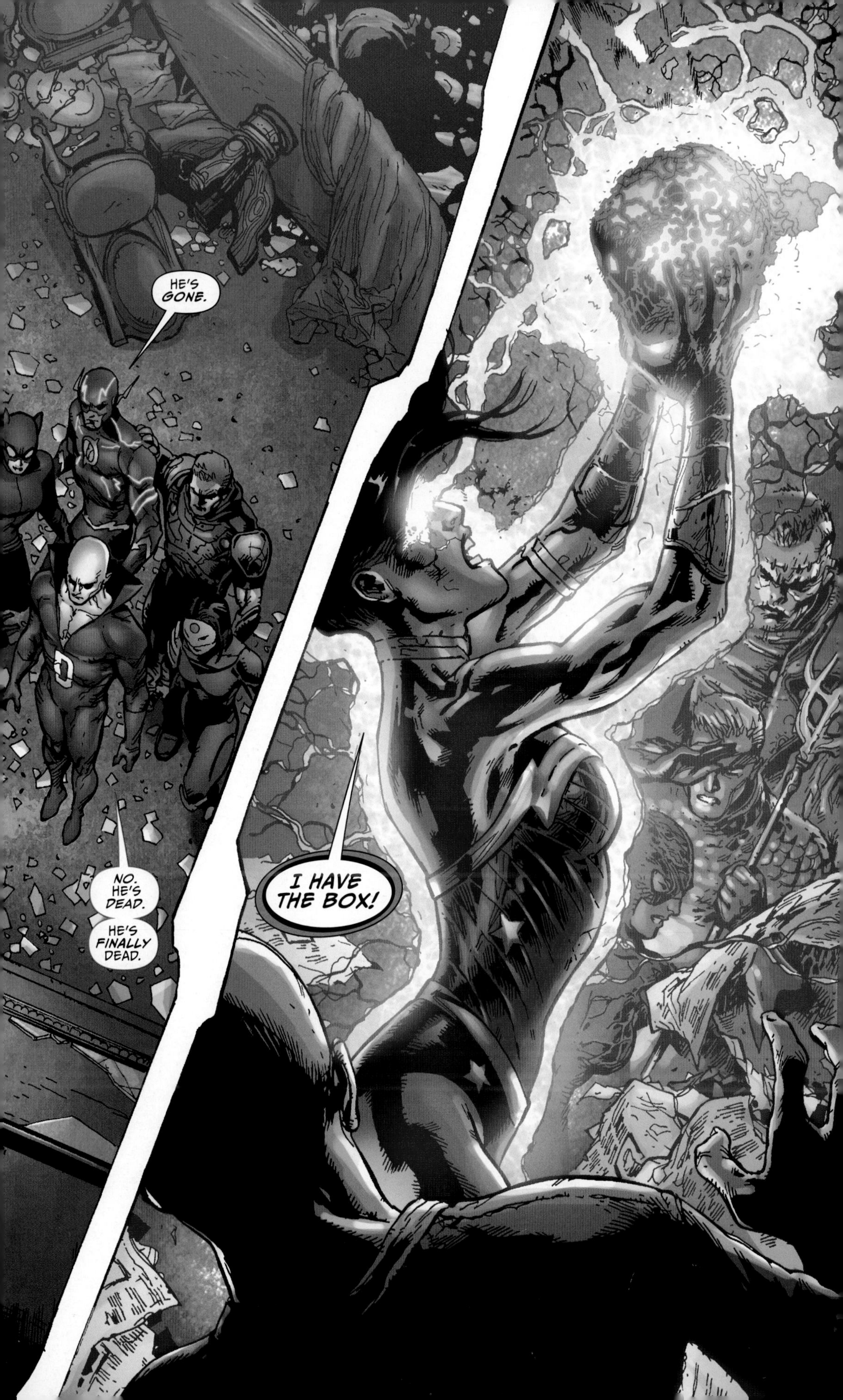
HE'S GONE.
NO. HE'S DEAD.
HE'S FINALLY DEAD.
I HAVE THE BOX!

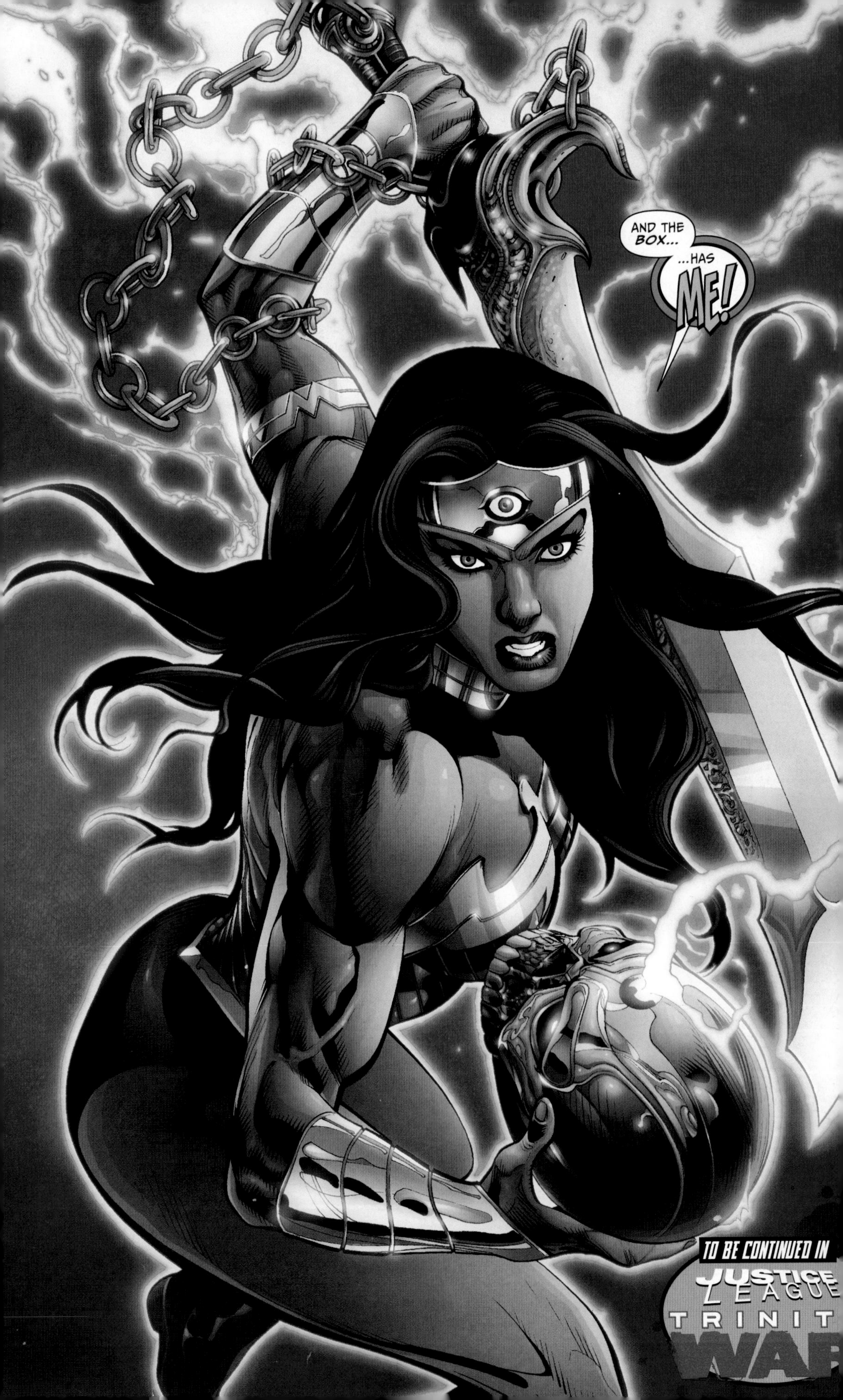
AND THE BOX...
...HAS ME!
TO BE CONTINUED IN
JUSTICE LEAGUE TRINITY WAR

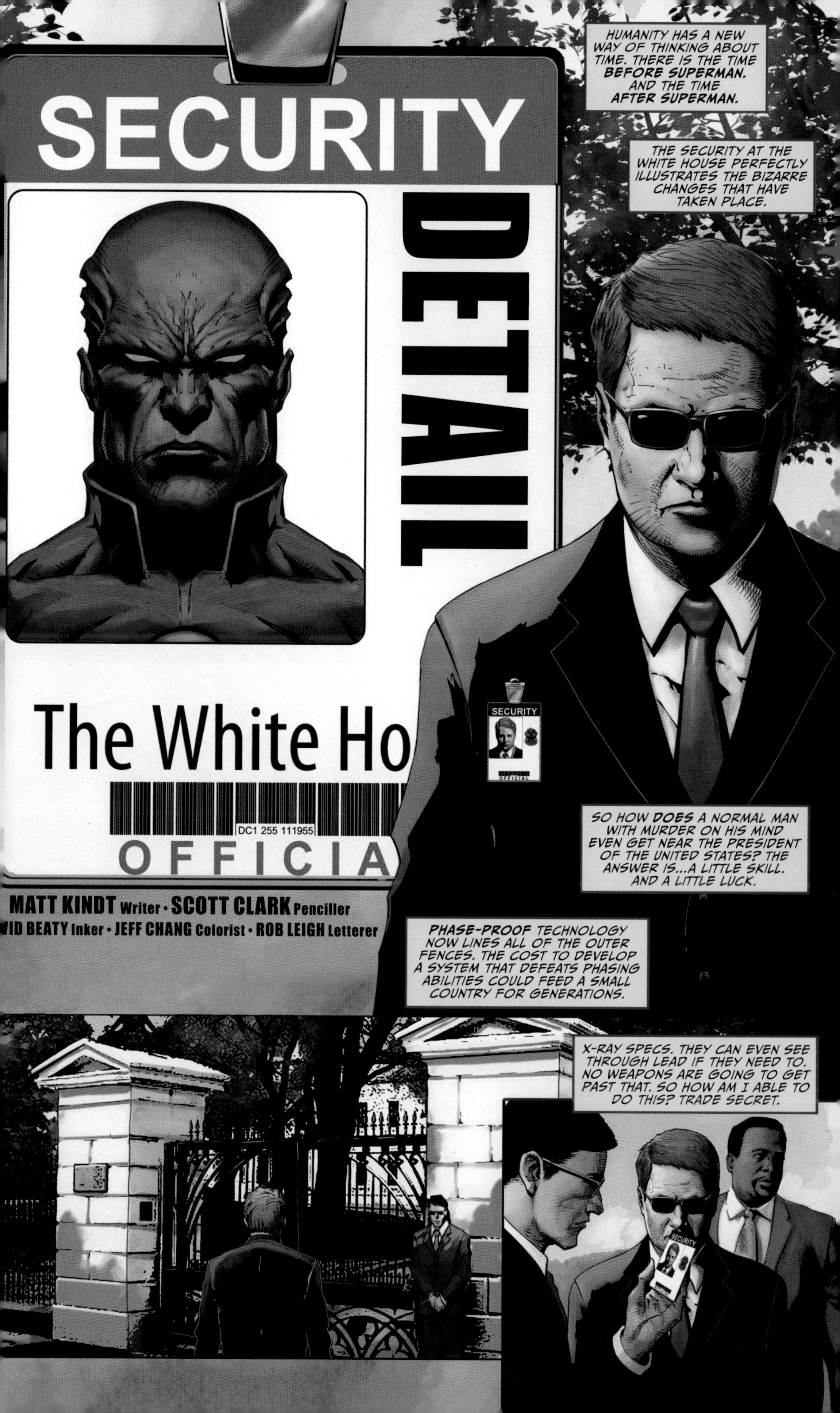
SECURITY
DETAIL
The White Ho
DC1 255 111955
OFFICIA
MATT KINDT Writer • SCOTT CLARK Penciller
VID BEATY Inker • JEFF CHANG Colorist • ROB LEIGH Letterer
HUMANITY HAS A NEW WAY OF THINKING ABOUT TIME. THERE IS THE TIME BEFORE SUPERMAN. AND THE TIME AFTER SUPERMAN.
THE SECURITY AT THE WHITE HOUSE PERFECTLY ILLUSTRATES THE BIZARRE CHANGES THAT HAVE TAKEN PLACE.
SO HOW DOES A NORMAL MAN WITH MURDER ON HIS MIND EVEN GET NEAR THE PRESIDENT OF THE UNITED STATES? THE ANSWER IS...A LITTLE SKILL. AND A LITTLE LUCK.
PHASE-PROOF TECHNOLOGY NOW LINES ALL OF THE OUTER FENCES. THE COST TO DEVELOP A SYSTEM THAT DEFEATS PHASING ABILITIES COULD FEED A SMALL COUNTRY FOR GENERATIONS.
X-RAY SPECS. THEY CAN EVEN SEE THROUGH LEAD IF THEY NEED TO. NO WEAPONS ARE GOING TO GET PAST THAT. SO HOW AM I ABLE TO DO THIS? TRADE SECRET.

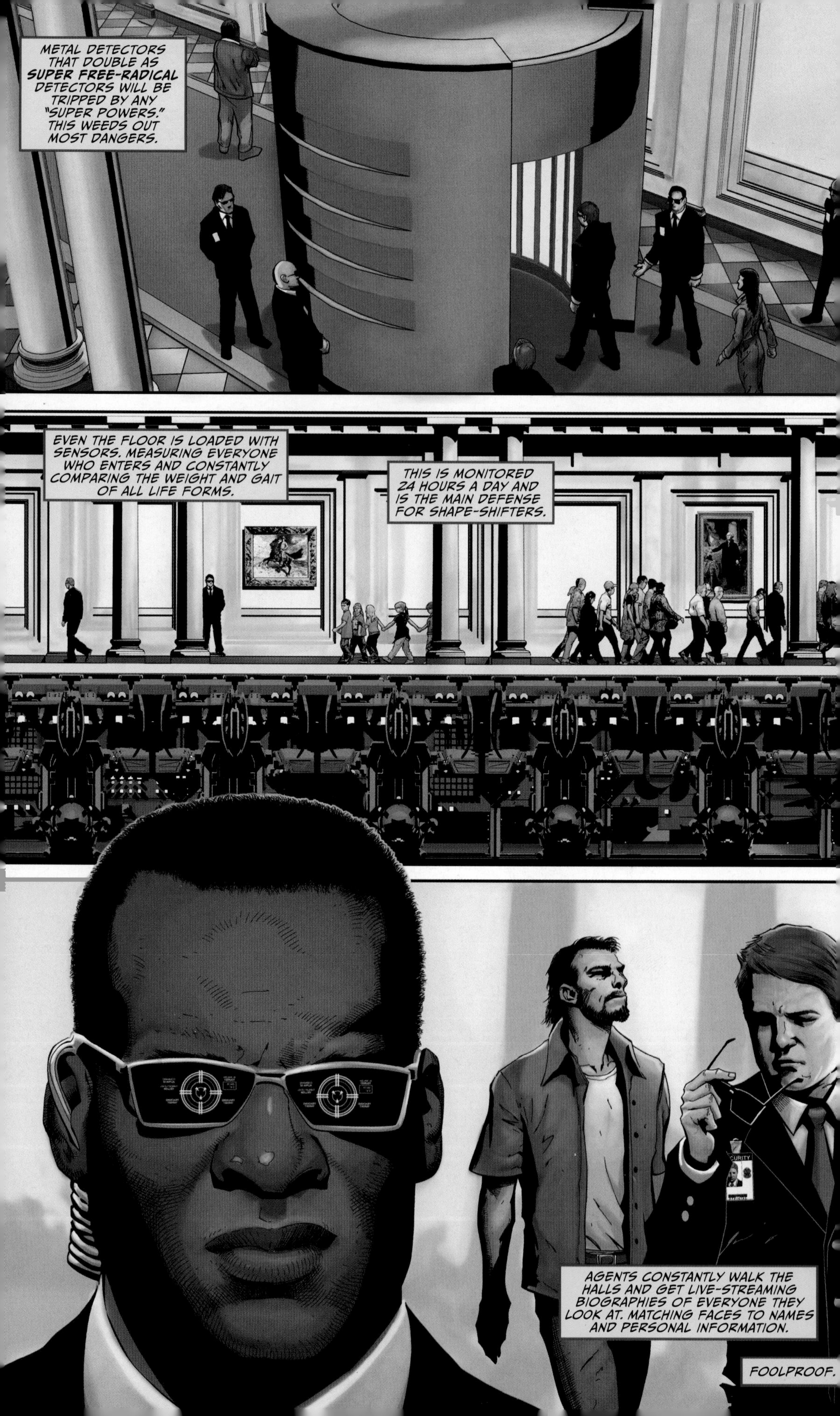
METAL DETECTORS THAT DOUBLE AS SUPER FREE-RADICAL DETECTORS WILL BE TRIPPED BY ANY "SUPER POWERS." THIS WEEDS OUT MOST DANGERS.
EVEN THE FLOOR IS LOADED WITH SENSORS. MEASURING EVERYONE WHO ENTERS AND CONSTANTLY COMPARING THE WEIGHT AND GAIT OF ALL LIFE FORMS.
THIS IS MONITORED 24 HOURS A DAY AND IS THE MAIN DEFENSE FOR SHAPE-SHIFTERS.
AGENTS CONSTANTLY WALK THE HALLS AND GET LIVE-STREAMING BIOGRAPHIES OF EVERYONE THEY LOOK AT. MATCHING FACES TO NAMES AND PERSONAL INFORMATION.
FOOLPROOF.

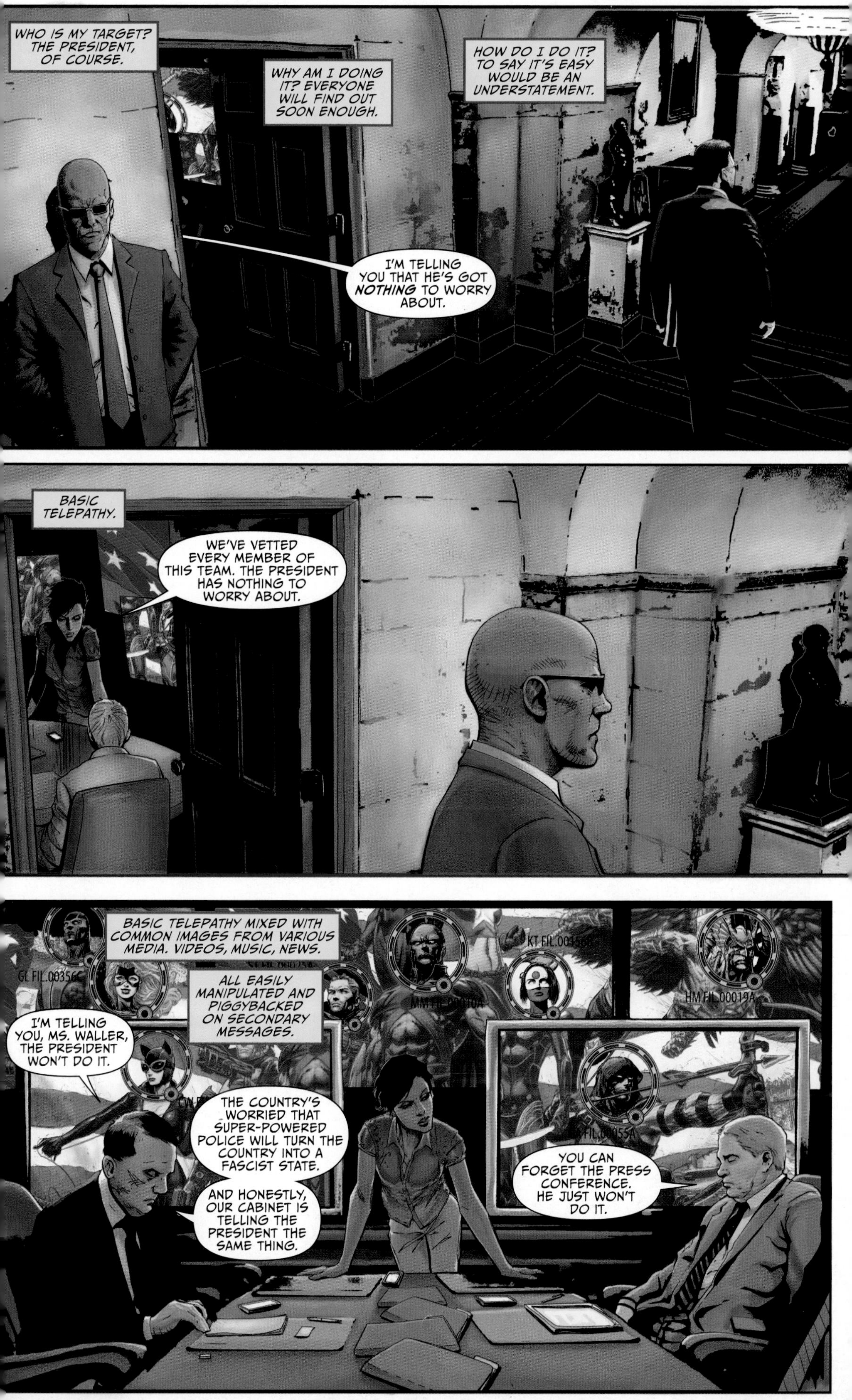
WHO IS MY TARGET? THE PRESIDENT, OF COURSE.
WHY AM I DOING IT? EVERYONE WILL FIND OUT SOON ENOUGH.
HOW DO I DO IT? TO SAY IT'S EASY WOULD BE AN UNDERSTATEMENT.
I'M TELLING YOU THAT HE'S GOT *NOTHING* TO WORRY ABOUT.
BASIC TELEPATHY.
WE'VE VETTED EVERY MEMBER OF THIS TEAM. THE PRESIDENT HAS NOTHING TO WORRY ABOUT.
BASIC TELEPATHY MIXED WITH COMMON IMAGES FROM VARIOUS MEDIA. VIDEOS, MUSIC, NEWS.
ALL EASILY MANIPULATED AND PIGGYBACKED ON SECONDARY MESSAGES.
GL FIL.00356C
KT FIL.00156B
HM FIL.00019A
I'M TELLING YOU, MS. WALLER, THE PRESIDENT WON'T DO IT.
THE COUNTRY'S WORRIED THAT SUPER-POWERED POLICE WILL TURN THE COUNTRY INTO A FASCIST STATE.
AND HONESTLY, OUR CABINET IS TELLING THE PRESIDENT THE SAME THING.
YOU CAN FORGET THE PRESS CONFERENCE. HE JUST WON'T DO IT.

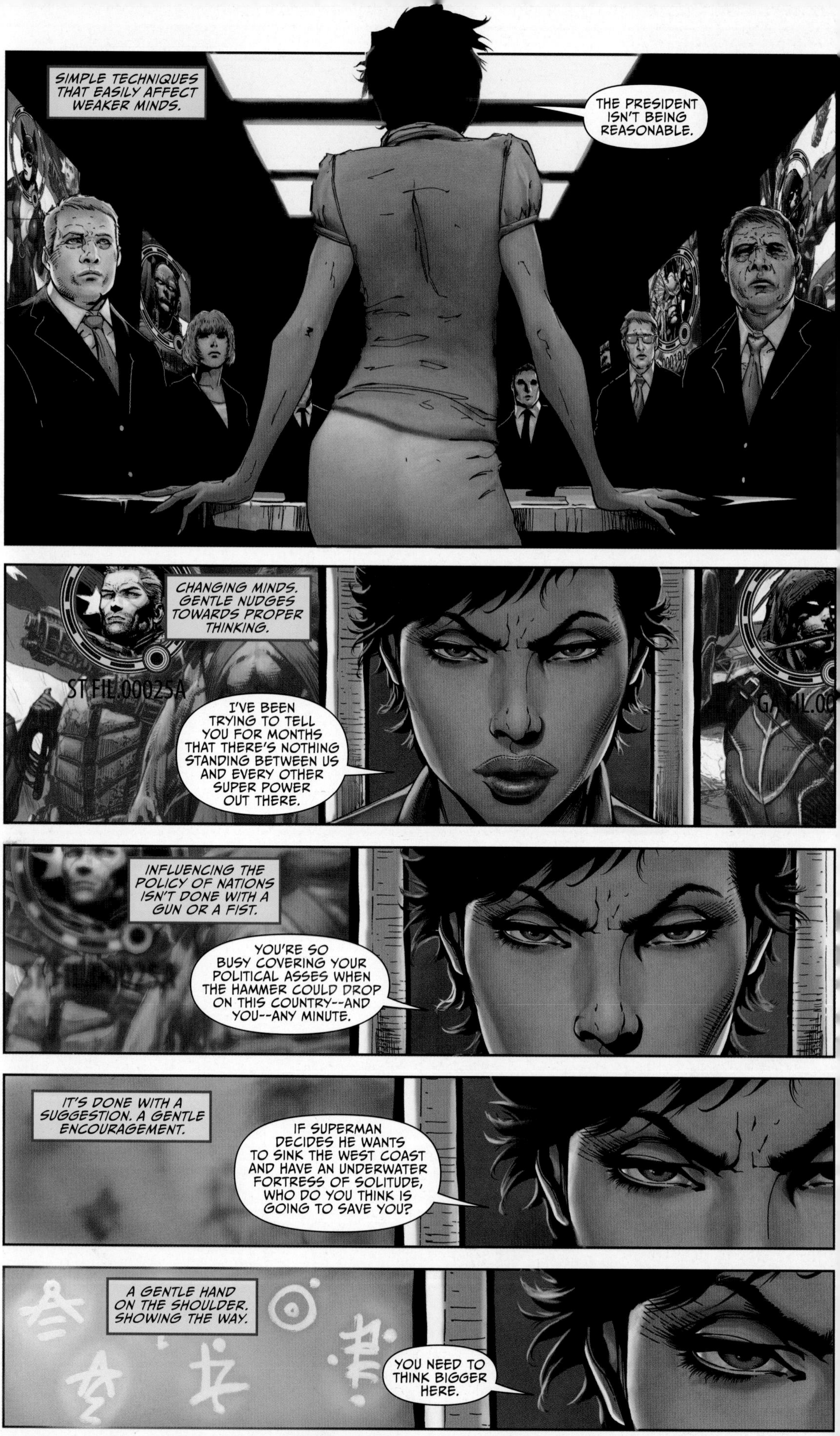
SIMPLE TECHNIQUES THAT EASILY AFFECT WEAKER MINDS.
THE PRESIDENT ISN'T BEING REASONABLE.
CHANGING MINDS. GENTLE NUDGES TOWARDS PROPER THINKING.
ST FIL.00025A
I'VE BEEN TRYING TO TELL YOU FOR MONTHS THAT THERE'S NOTHING STANDING BETWEEN US AND EVERY OTHER SUPER POWER OUT THERE.
INFLUENCING THE POLICY OF NATIONS ISN'T DONE WITH A GUN OR A FIST.
YOU'RE SO BUSY COVERING YOUR POLITICAL ASSES WHEN THE HAMMER COULD DROP ON THIS COUNTRY--AND YOU--ANY MINUTE.
IT'S DONE WITH A SUGGESTION. A GENTLE ENCOURAGEMENT.
IF SUPERMAN DECIDES HE WANTS TO SINK THE WEST COAST AND HAVE AN UNDERWATER FORTRESS OF SOLITUDE, WHO DO YOU THINK IS GOING TO SAVE YOU?
A GENTLE HAND ON THE SHOULDER. SHOWING THE WAY.
YOU NEED TO THINK BIGGER HERE.

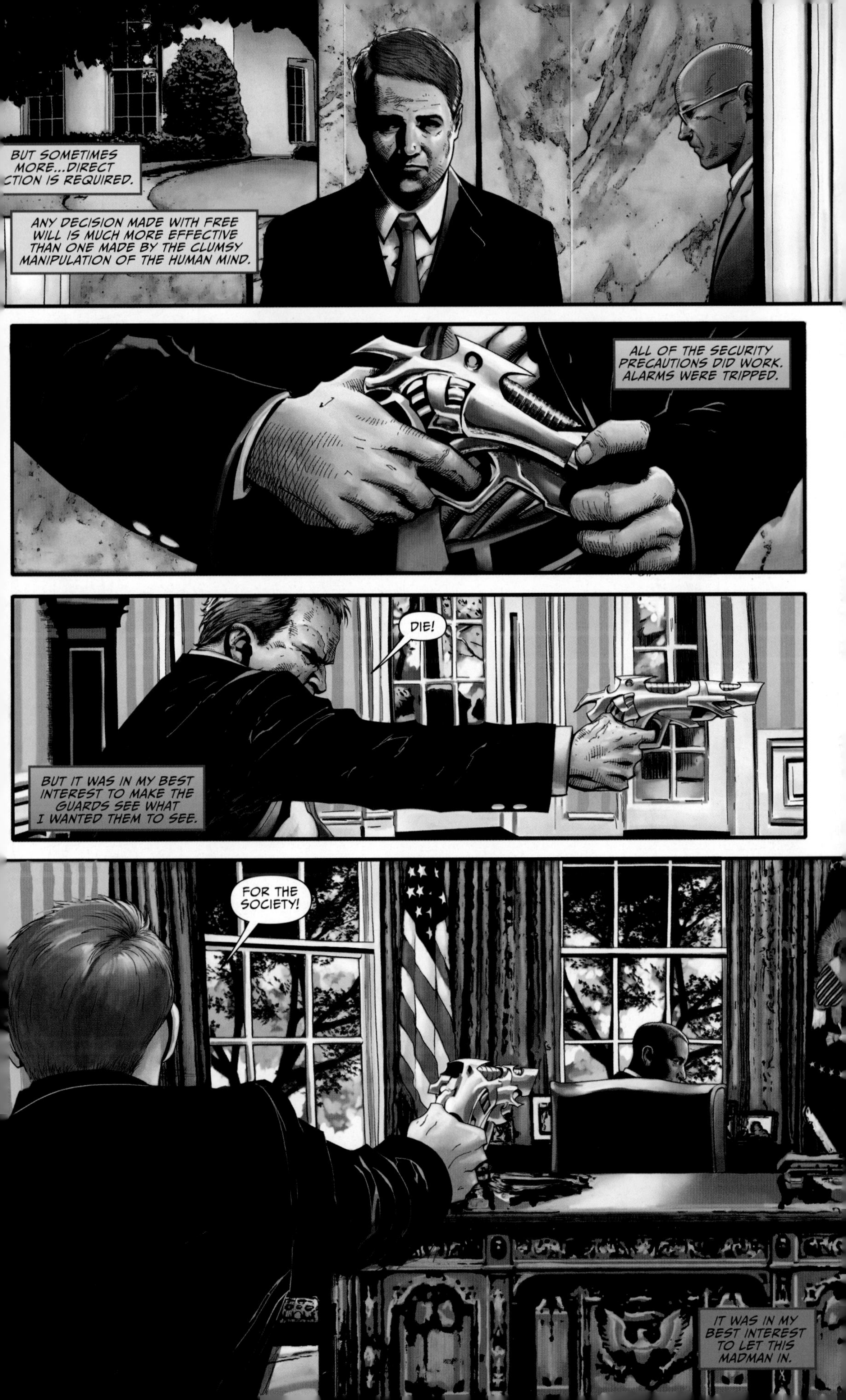
BUT SOMETIMES
MORE...DIRECT
CTION IS REQUIRED.
ANY DECISION MADE WITH FREE
WILL IS MUCH MORE EFFECTIVE
THAN ONE MADE BY THE CLUMSY
MANIPULATION OF THE HUMAN MIND.
ALL OF THE SECURITY
PRECAUTIONS DID WORK.
ALARMS WERE TRIPPED.
DIE!
BUT IT WAS IN MY BEST
INTEREST TO MAKE THE
GUARDS SEE WHAT
I WANTED THEM TO SEE.
FOR THE
SOCIETY!
IT WAS IN MY
BEST INTEREST
TO LET THIS
MADMAN IN.

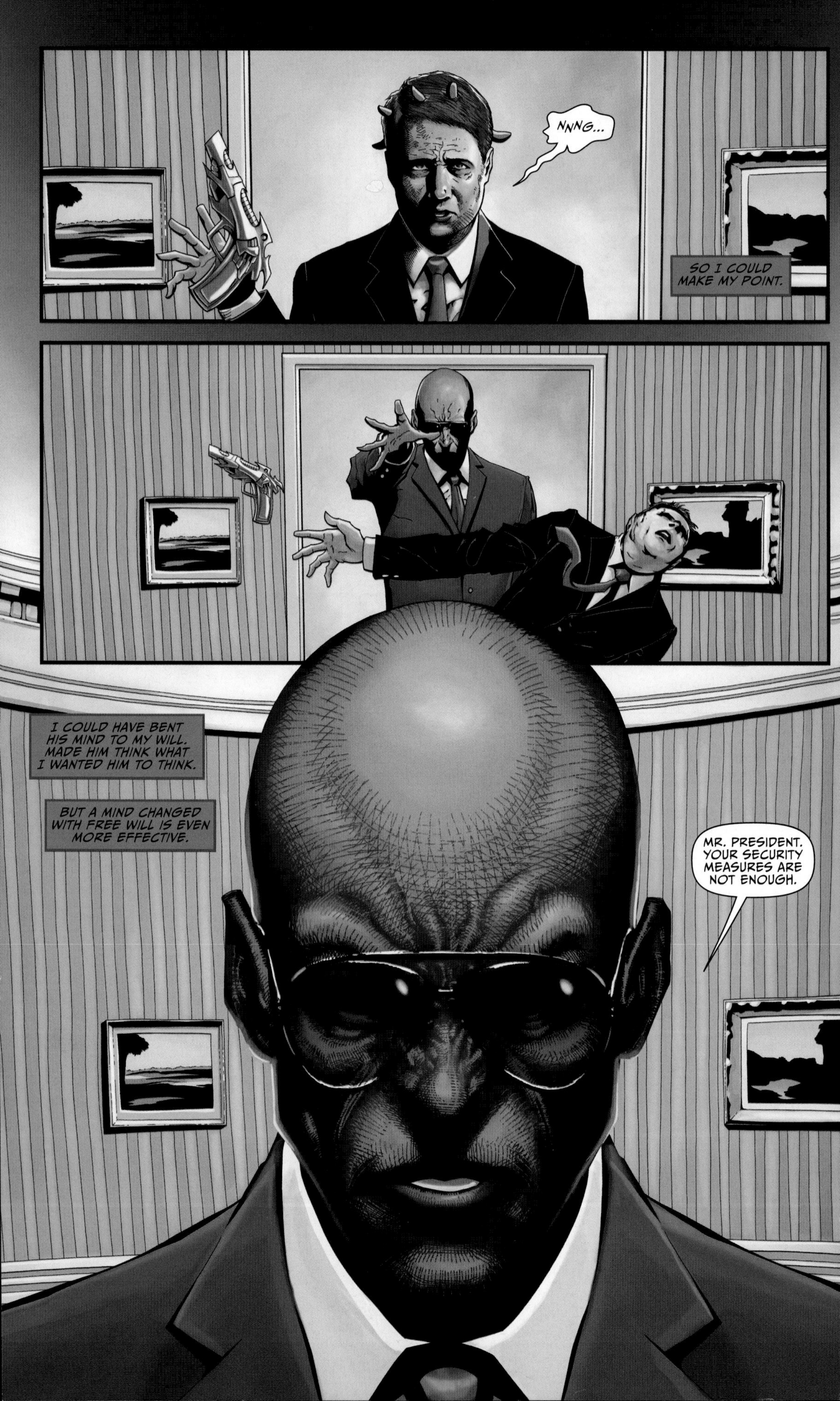
NNNG...
SO I COULD MAKE MY POINT.
I COULD HAVE BENT HIS MIND TO MY WILL. MADE HIM THINK WHAT I WANTED HIM TO THINK.
BUT A MIND CHANGED WITH FREE WILL IS EVEN MORE EFFECTIVE.
MR. PRESIDENT. YOUR SECURITY MEASURES ARE NOT ENOUGH.

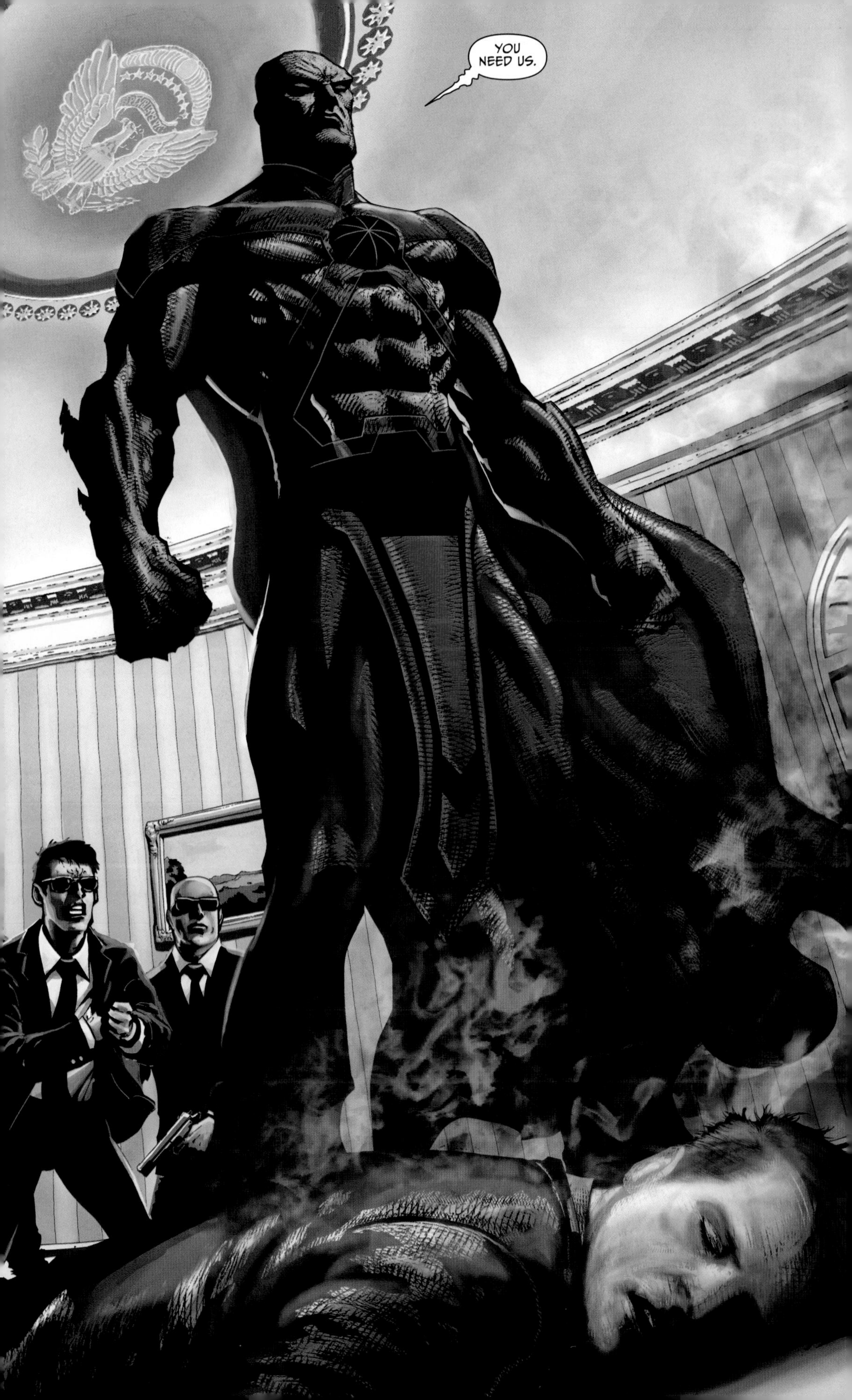
YOU NEED US.

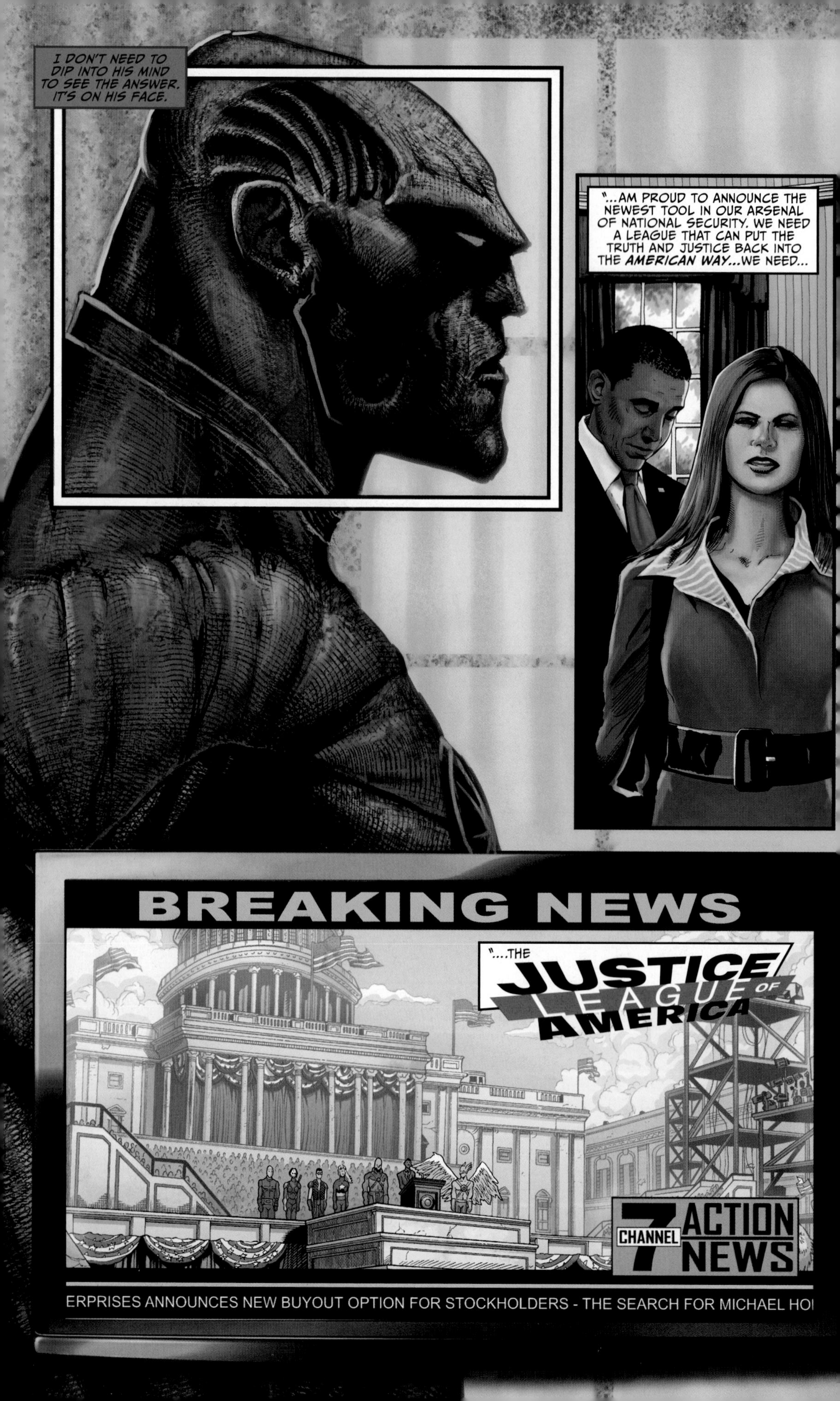
I DON'T NEED TO DIP INTO HIS MIND TO SEE THE ANSWER. IT'S ON HIS FACE.
"...AM PROUD TO ANNOUNCE THE NEWEST TOOL IN OUR ARSENAL OF NATIONAL SECURITY. WE NEED A LEAGUE THAT CAN PUT THE TRUTH AND JUSTICE BACK INTO THE AMERICAN WAY...WE NEED...
BREAKING NEWS
"...THE
JUSTICE LEAGUE OF AMERICA
7 CHANNEL ACTION NEWS
ERPRISES ANNOUNCES NEW BUYOUT OPTION FOR STOCKHOLDERS - THE SEARCH FOR MICHAEL HO

MARTIAN MANHUNTER in
MISSING PIECES

MATT KINDT Writer • MANUEL GARCIA Penciller
DAVID BEATY Inker • JEFF CHANG Colorist • ROB LEIGH Letterer

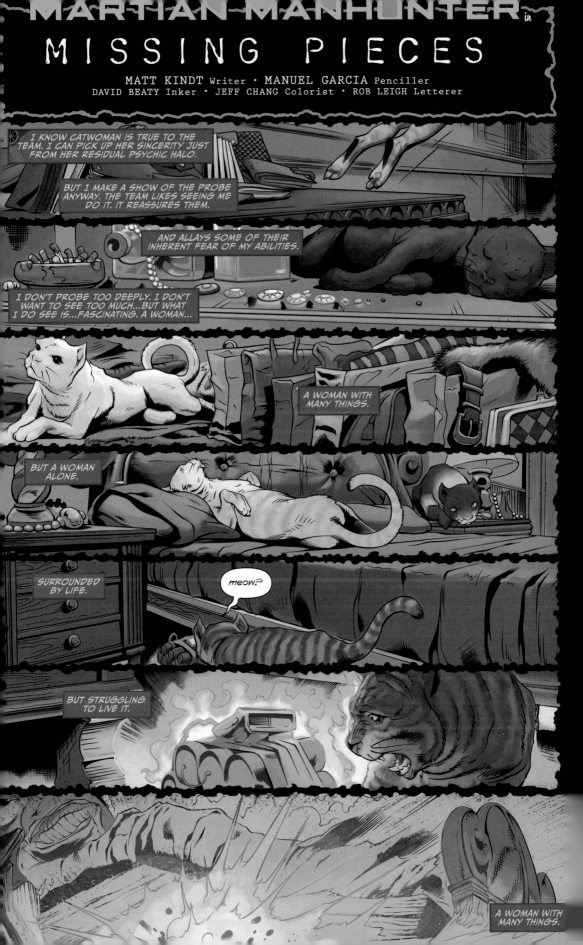

I KNOW CATWOMAN IS TRUE TO THE TEAM. I CAN PICK UP HER SINCERITY JUST FROM HER RESIDUAL PSYCHIC HALO.

BUT I MAKE A SHOW OF THE PROBE ANYWAY. THE TEAM LIKES SEEING ME DO IT. IT REASSURES THEM.

AND ALLAYS SOME OF THEIR INHERENT FEAR OF MY ABILITIES.

I DON'T PROBE TOO DEEPLY. I DON'T WANT TO SEE TOO MUCH...BUT WHAT I DO SEE IS...FASCINATING. A WOMAN...

A WOMAN WITH MANY THINGS.

BUT A WOMAN ALONE.

SURROUNDED BY LIFE.

meow?

BUT STRUGGLING TO LIVE IT.

A WOMAN WITH MANY THINGS.

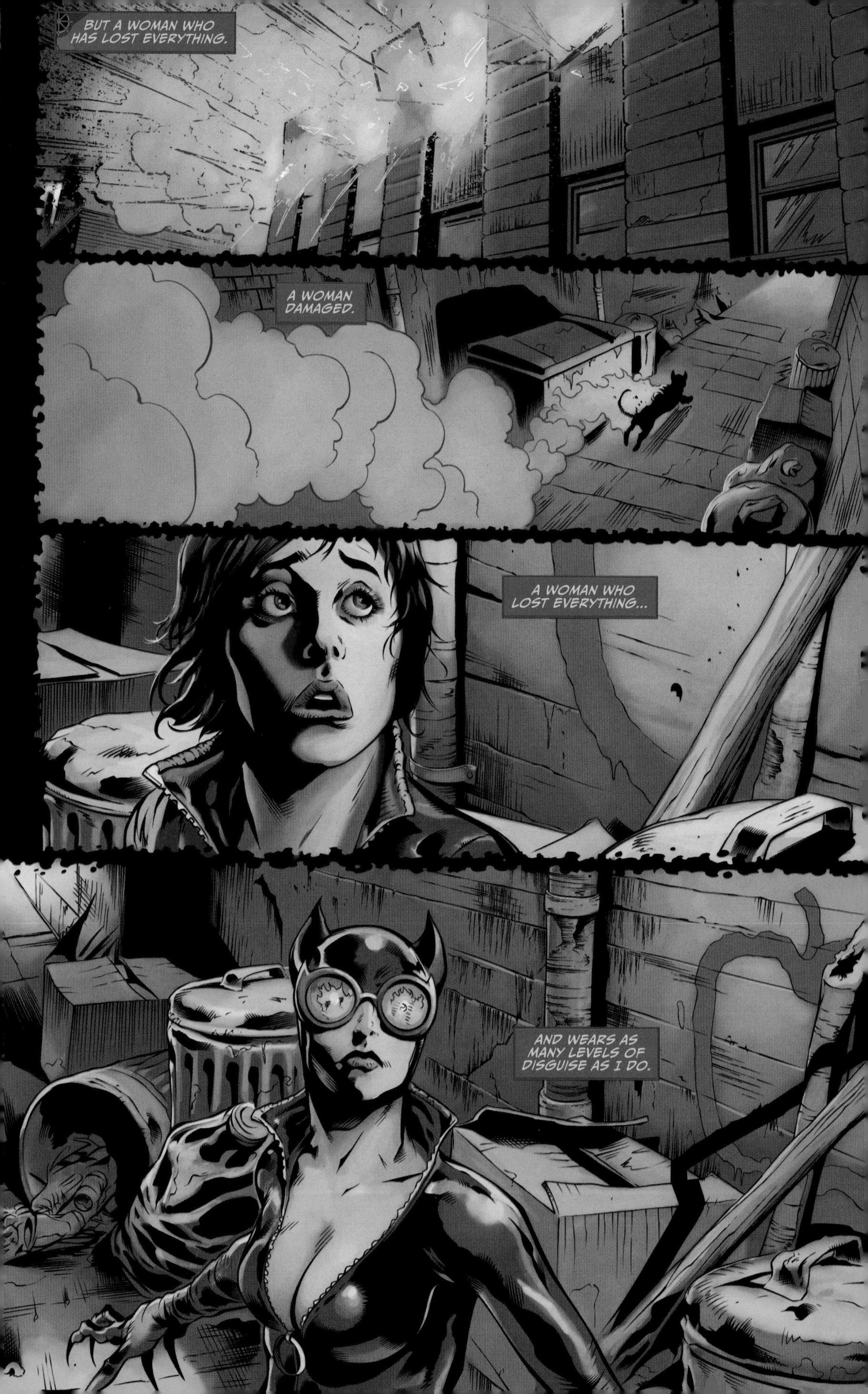
BUT A WOMAN WHO HAS LOST EVERYTHING.
A WOMAN DAMAGED.
A WOMAN WHO LOST EVERYTHING...
AND WEARS AS MANY LEVELS OF DISGUISE AS I DO.

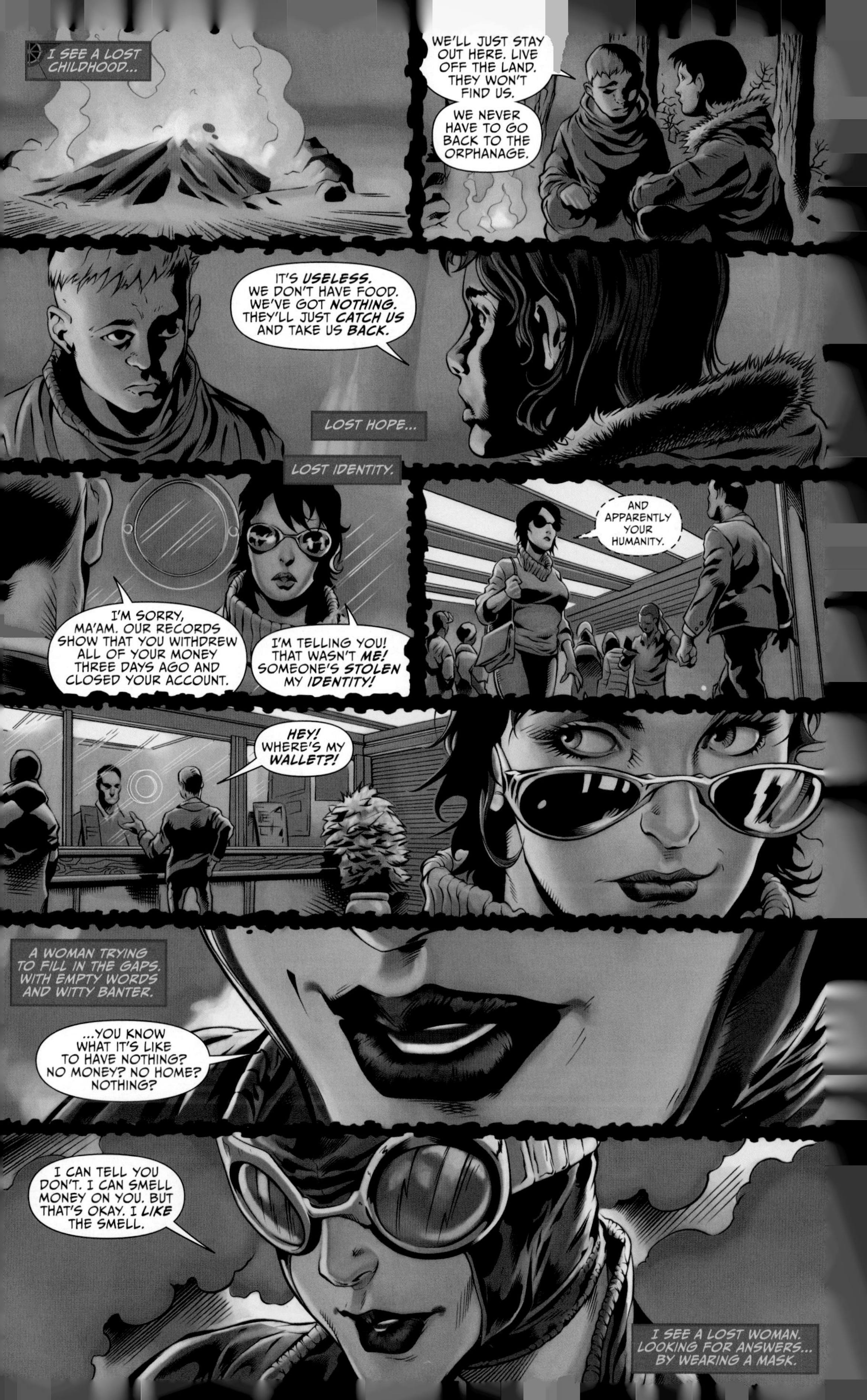
I SEE A LOST CHILDHOOD...
WE'LL JUST STAY OUT HERE. LIVE OFF THE LAND. THEY WON'T FIND US.
WE NEVER HAVE TO GO BACK TO THE ORPHANAGE.
IT'S USELESS. WE DON'T HAVE FOOD. WE'VE GOT NOTHING. THEY'LL JUST CATCH US AND TAKE US BACK.
LOST HOPE...
LOST IDENTITY.
I'M SORRY, MA'AM. OUR RECORDS SHOW THAT YOU WITHDREW ALL OF YOUR MONEY THREE DAYS AGO AND CLOSED YOUR ACCOUNT.
I'M TELLING YOU! THAT WASN'T ME! SOMEONE'S STOLEN MY IDENTITY!
AND APPARENTLY YOUR HUMANITY.
HEY! WHERE'S MY WALLET?!
A WOMAN TRYING TO FILL IN THE GAPS. WITH EMPTY WORDS AND WITTY BANTER.
...YOU KNOW WHAT IT'S LIKE TO HAVE NOTHING? NO MONEY? NO HOME? NOTHING?
I CAN TELL YOU DON'T. I CAN SMELL MONEY ON YOU. BUT THAT'S OKAY. I LIKE THE SMELL.
I SEE A LOST WOMAN. LOOKING FOR ANSWERS... BY WEARING A MASK.

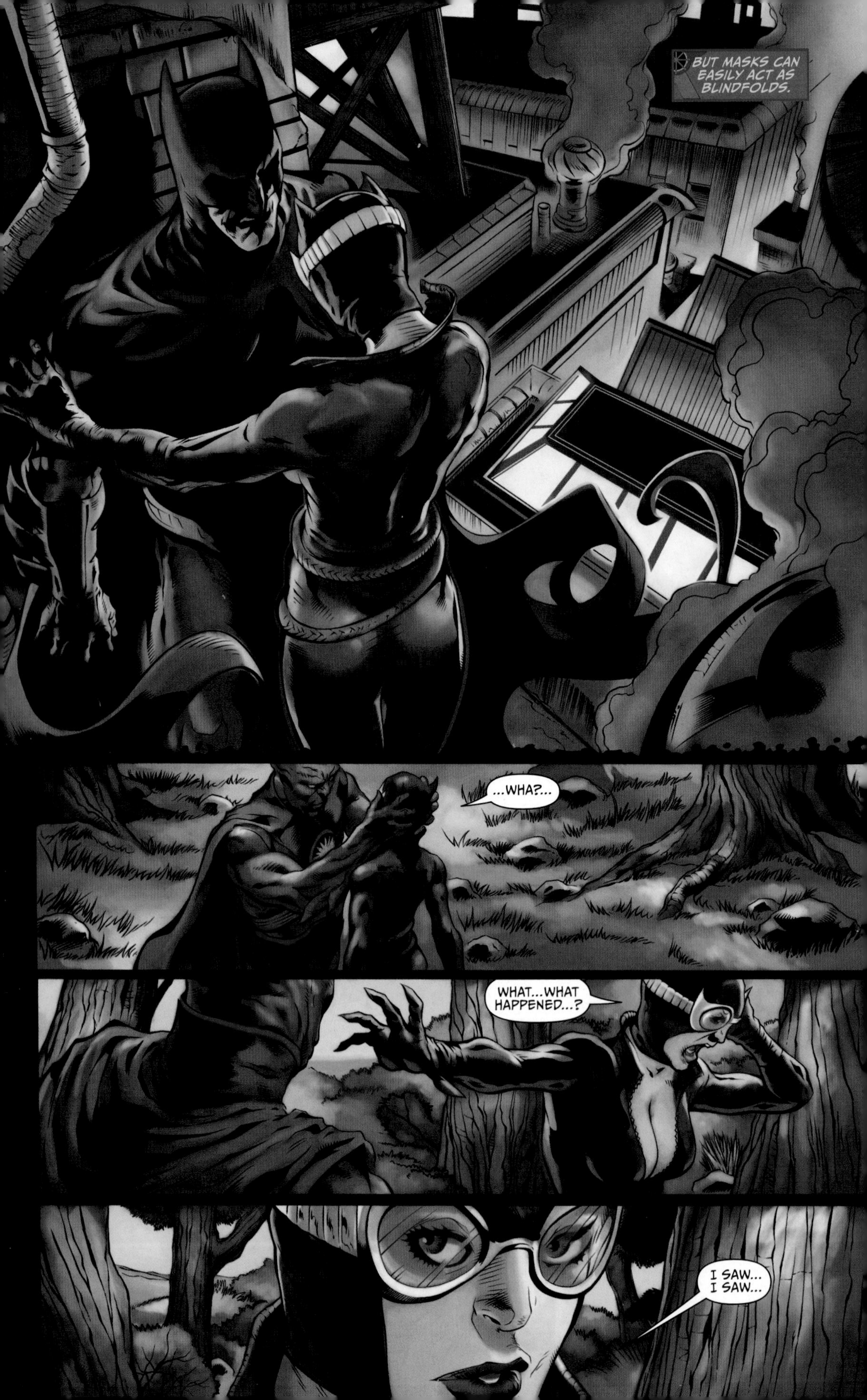
BUT MASKS CAN EASILY ACT AS BLINDFOLDS.
...WHA?...
WHAT...WHAT HAPPENED...?
I SAW... I SAW...

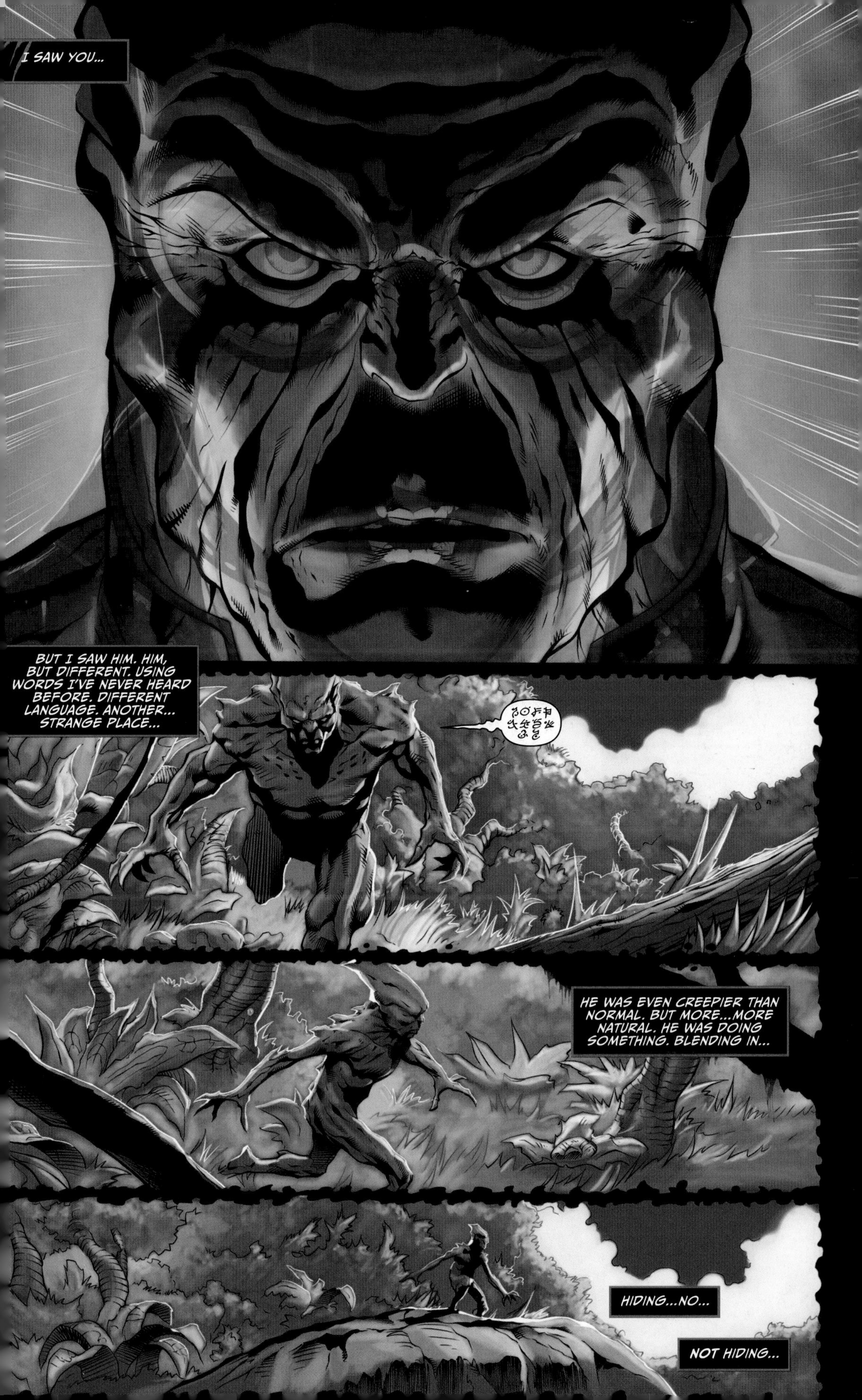
I SAW YOU...
BUT I SAW HIM. HIM, BUT DIFFERENT. USING WORDS I'VE NEVER HEARD BEFORE. DIFFERENT LANGUAGE. ANOTHER... STRANGE PLACE...
HE WAS EVEN CREEPIER THAN NORMAL. BUT MORE...MORE NATURAL. HE WAS DOING SOMETHING. BLENDING IN...
HIDING...NO...
NOT HIDING...

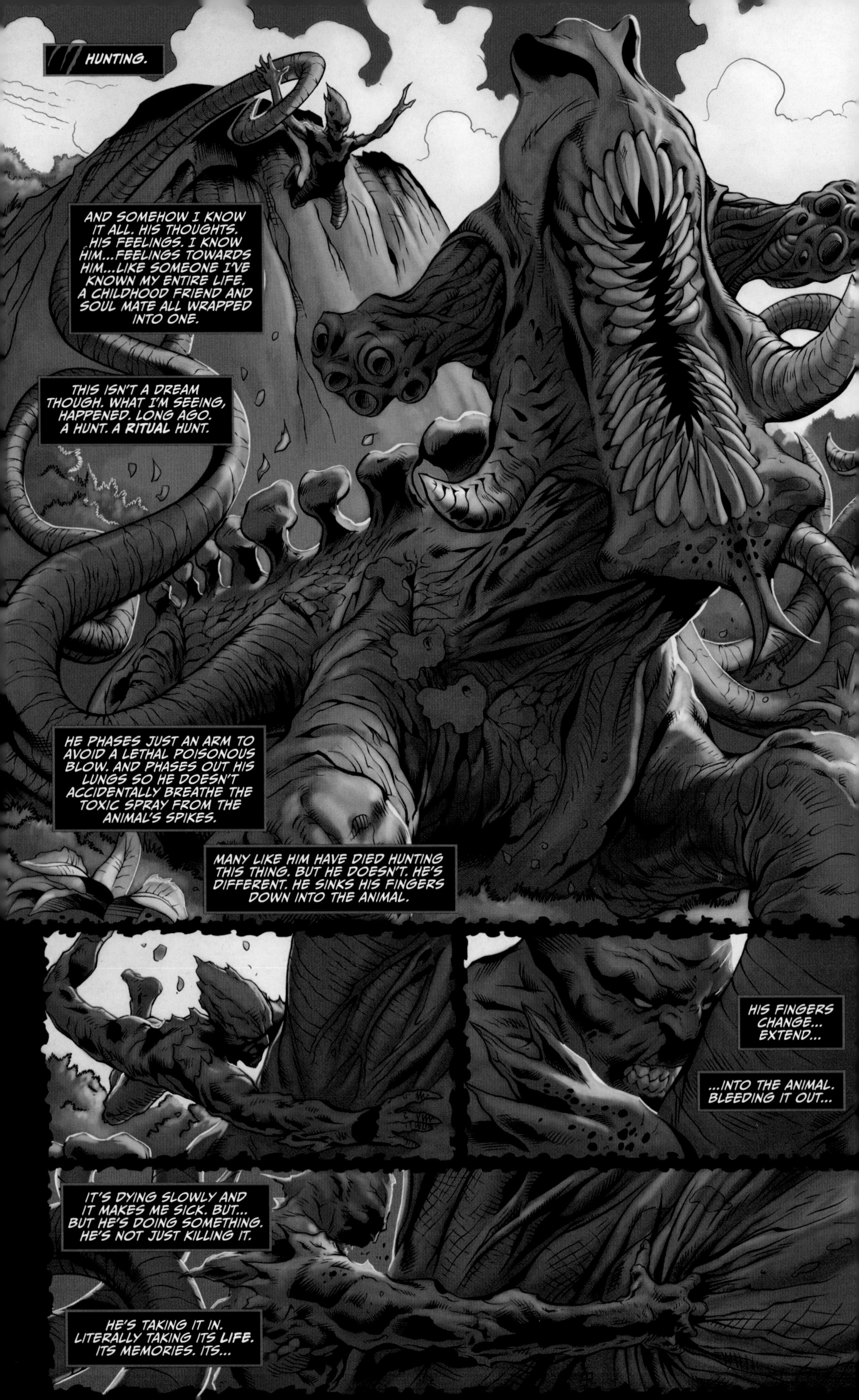
HUNTING.
AND SOMEHOW I KNOW IT ALL. HIS THOUGHTS. HIS FEELINGS. I KNOW HIM...FEELINGS TOWARDS HIM...LIKE SOMEONE I'VE KNOWN MY ENTIRE LIFE. A CHILDHOOD FRIEND AND SOUL MATE ALL WRAPPED INTO ONE.
THIS ISN'T A DREAM THOUGH. WHAT I'M SEEING, HAPPENED. LONG AGO. A HUNT. A RITUAL HUNT.
HE PHASES JUST AN ARM TO AVOID A LETHAL POISONOUS BLOW. AND PHASES OUT HIS LUNGS SO HE DOESN'T ACCIDENTALLY BREATHE THE TOXIC SPRAY FROM THE ANIMAL'S SPIKES.
MANY LIKE HIM HAVE DIED HUNTING THIS THING. BUT HE DOESN'T. HE'S DIFFERENT. HE SINKS HIS FINGERS DOWN INTO THE ANIMAL.
HIS FINGERS CHANGE... EXTEND...
...INTO THE ANIMAL. BLEEDING IT OUT...
IT'S DYING SLOWLY AND IT MAKES ME SICK. BUT... BUT HE'S DOING SOMETHING. HE'S NOT JUST KILLING IT.
HE'S TAKING IT IN. LITERALLY TAKING ITS LIFE. ITS MEMORIES. ITS...

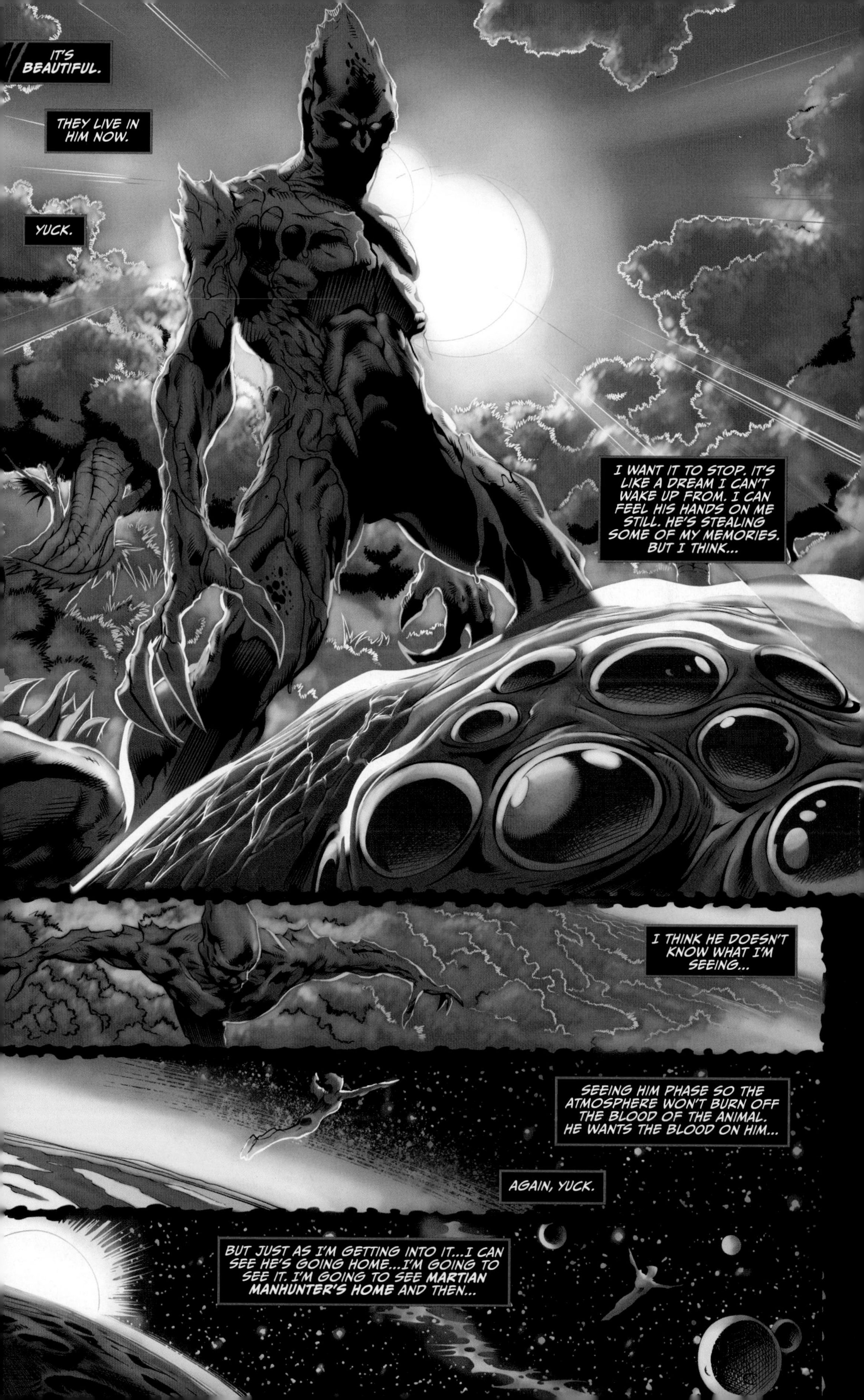
IT'S BEAUTIFUL.
THEY LIVE IN HIM NOW.
YUCK.
I WANT IT TO STOP. IT'S LIKE A DREAM I CAN'T WAKE UP FROM. I CAN FEEL HIS HANDS ON ME STILL. HE'S STEALING SOME OF MY MEMORIES. BUT I THINK...
I THINK HE DOESN'T KNOW WHAT I'M SEEING...
SEEING HIM PHASE SO THE ATMOSPHERE WON'T BURN OFF THE BLOOD OF THE ANIMAL. HE WANTS THE BLOOD ON HIM...
AGAIN, YUCK.
BUT JUST AS I'M GETTING INTO IT...I CAN SEE HE'S GOING HOME...I'M GOING TO SEE IT. I'M GOING TO SEE MARTIAN MANHUNTER'S HOME AND THEN...

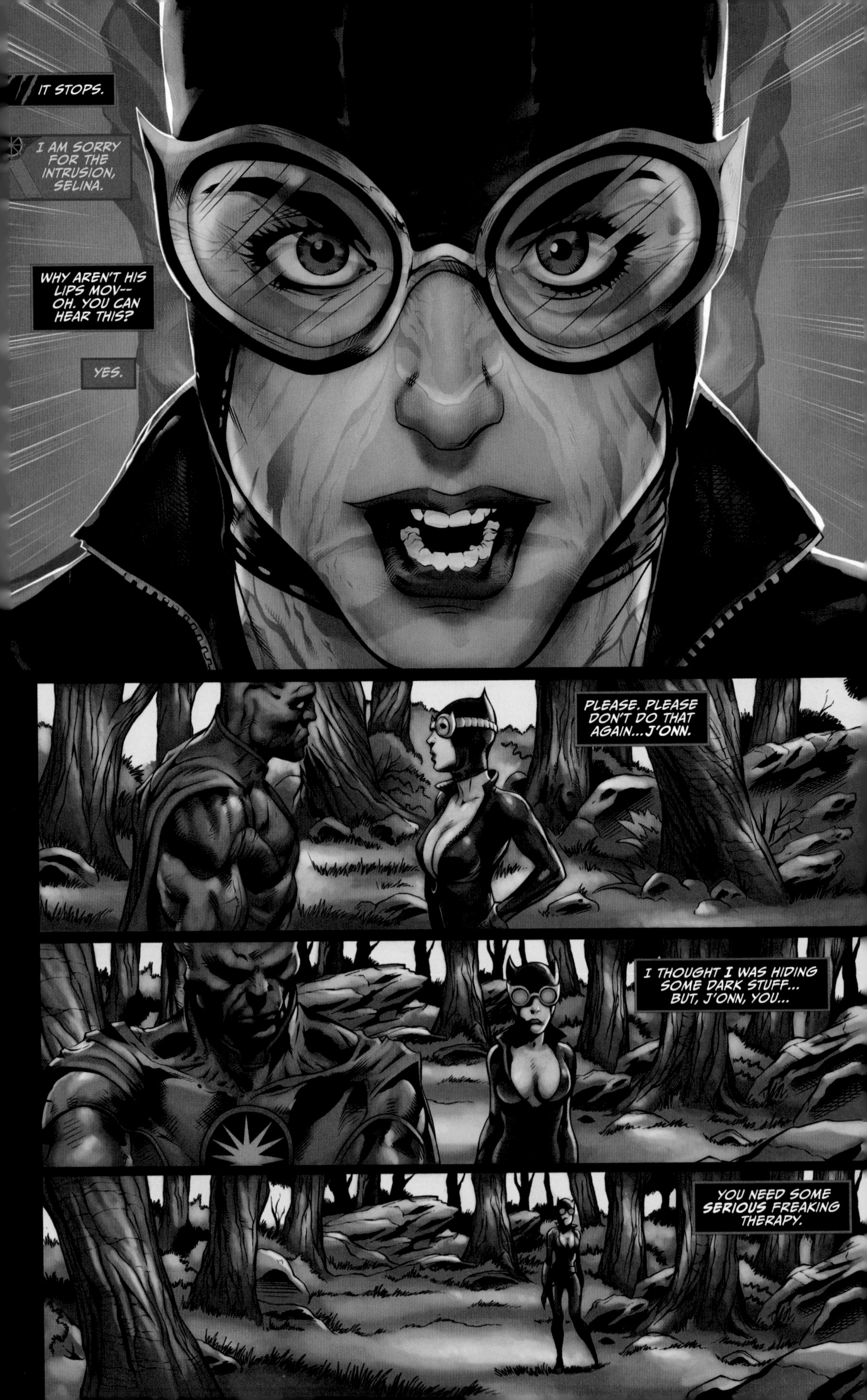
IT STOPS.
I AM SORRY FOR THE INTRUSION, SELINA.
WHY AREN'T HIS LIPS MOV-- OH. YOU CAN HEAR THIS?
YES.
PLEASE. PLEASE DON'T DO THAT AGAIN...J'ONN.
I THOUGHT I WAS HIDING SOME DARK STUFF... BUT, J'ONN, YOU...
YOU NEED SOME SERIOUS FREAKING THERAPY.

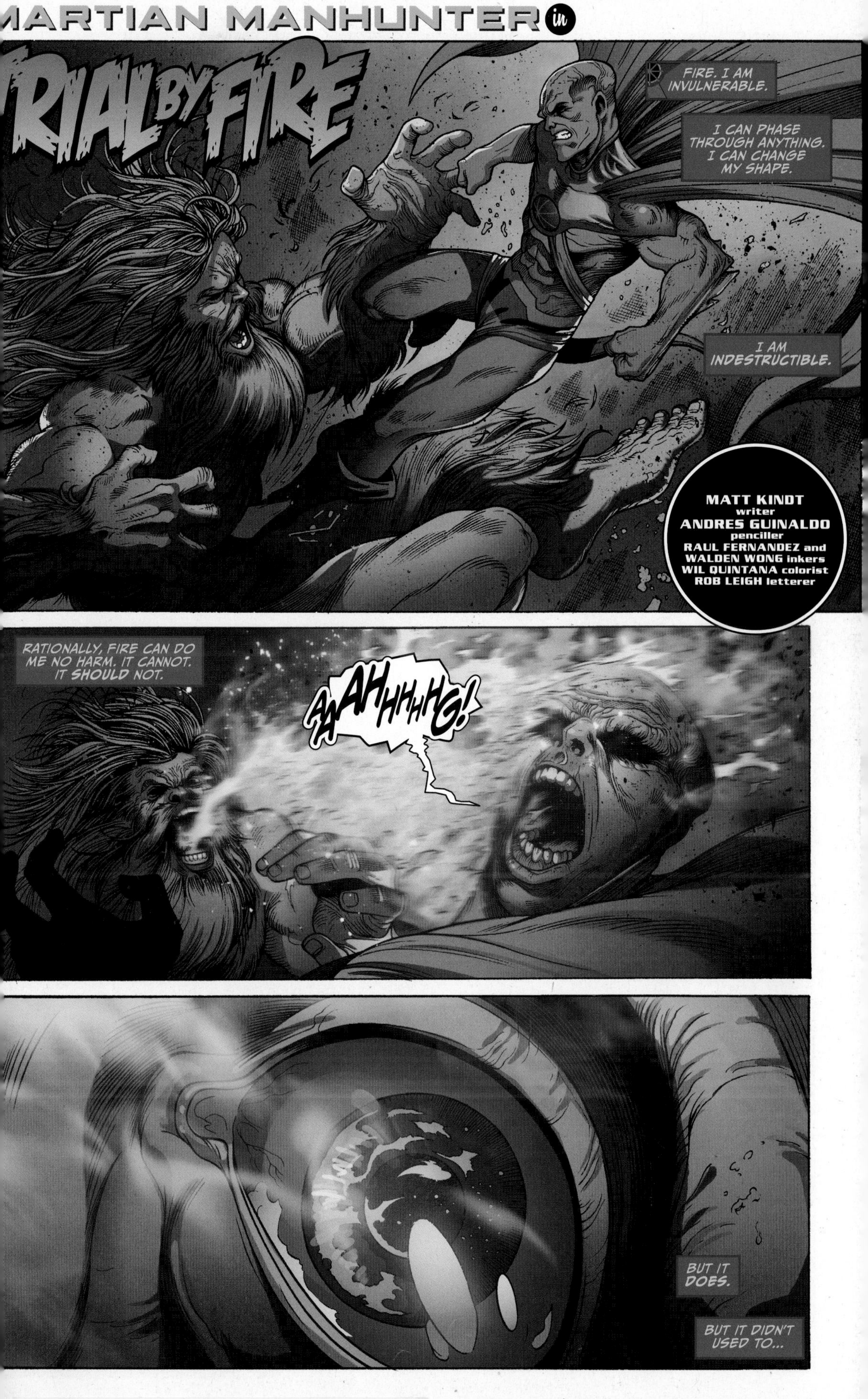

MARTIAN MANHUNTER in
TRIAL BY FIRE
FIRE. I AM INVULNERABLE.
I CAN PHASE THROUGH ANYTHING. I CAN CHANGE MY SHAPE.
I AM INDESTRUCTIBLE.
MATT KINDT writer
ANDRES GUINALDO penciller
RAUL FERNANDEZ and WALDEN WONG inkers
WIL QUINTANA colorist
ROB LEIGH letterer
RATIONALLY, FIRE CAN DO ME NO HARM. IT CANNOT. IT SHOULD NOT.
AAAHHHHG!
BUT IT DOES.
BUT IT DIDN'T USED TO...

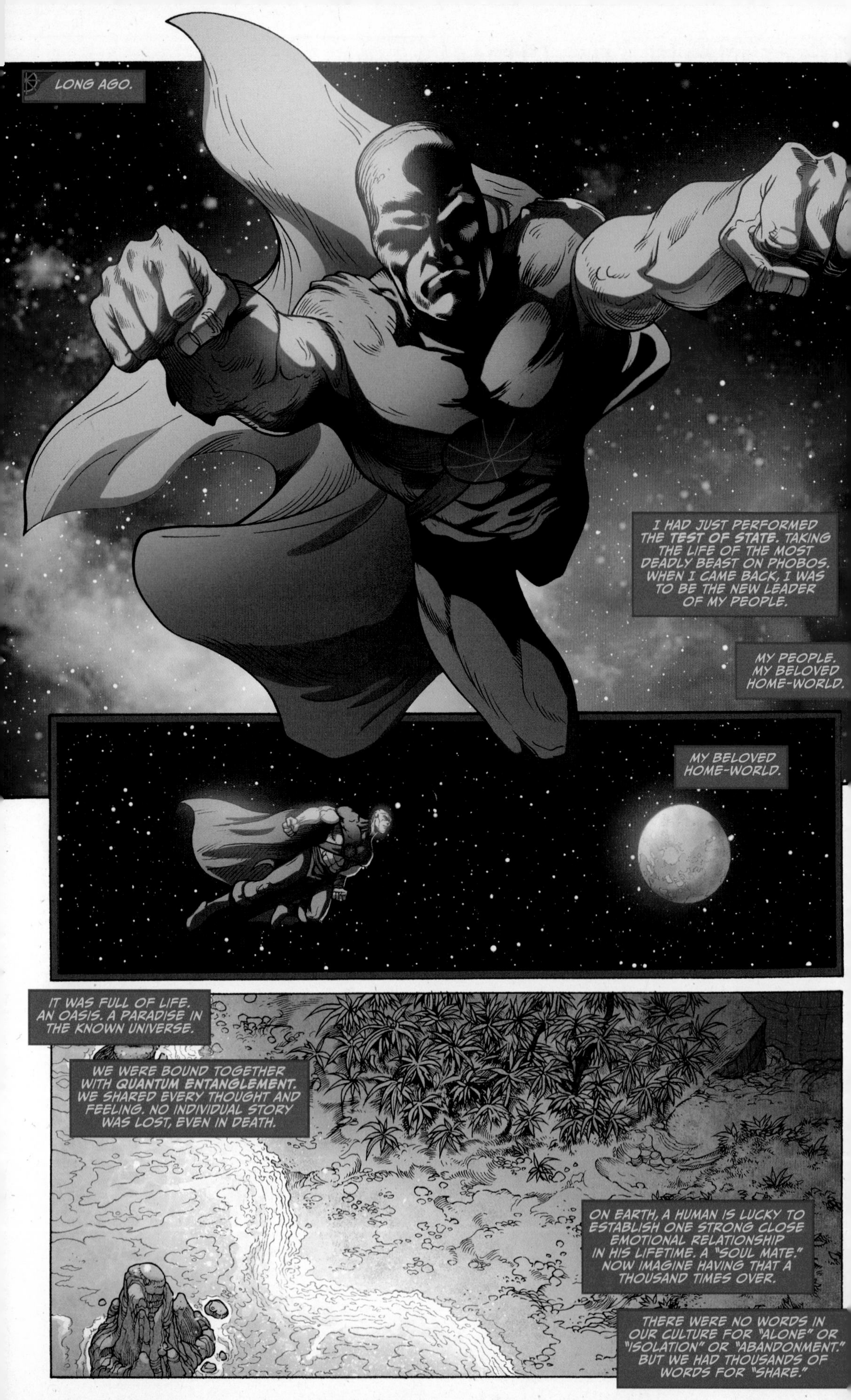
LONG AGO.
I HAD JUST PERFORMED THE TEST OF STATE. TAKING THE LIFE OF THE MOST DEADLY BEAST ON PHOBOS. WHEN I CAME BACK, I WAS TO BE THE NEW LEADER OF MY PEOPLE.
MY PEOPLE. MY BELOVED HOME-WORLD.
MY BELOVED HOME-WORLD.
IT WAS FULL OF LIFE. AN OASIS. A PARADISE IN THE KNOWN UNIVERSE.
WE WERE BOUND TOGETHER WITH QUANTUM ENTANGLEMENT. WE SHARED EVERY THOUGHT AND FEELING. NO INDIVIDUAL STORY WAS LOST, EVEN IN DEATH.
ON EARTH, A HUMAN IS LUCKY TO ESTABLISH ONE STRONG CLOSE EMOTIONAL RELATIONSHIP IN HIS LIFETIME. A "SOUL MATE." NOW IMAGINE HAVING THAT A THOUSAND TIMES OVER.
THERE WERE NO WORDS IN OUR CULTURE FOR "ALONE" OR "ISOLATION" OR "ABANDONMENT." BUT WE HAD THOUSANDS OF WORDS FOR "SHARE."

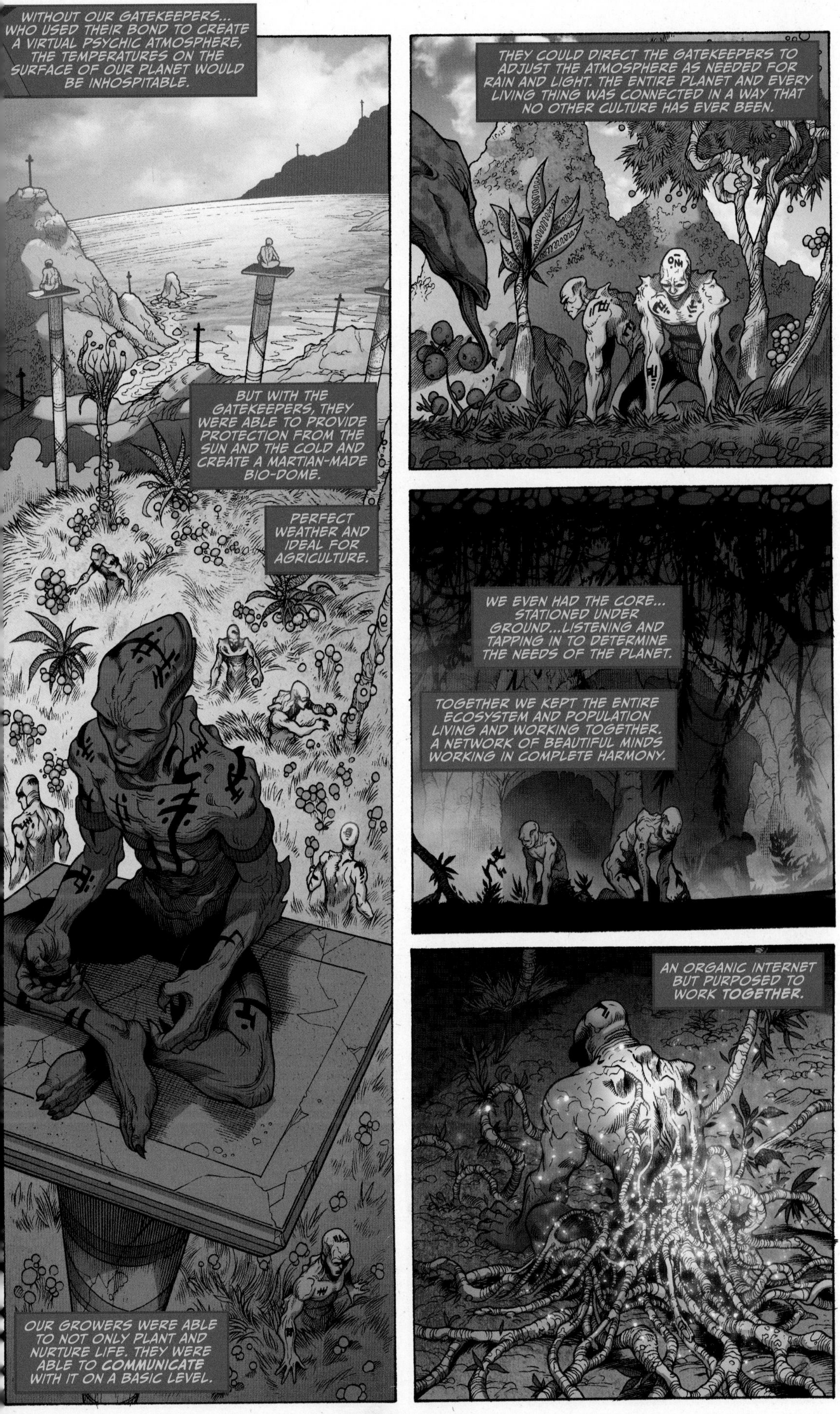
WITHOUT OUR GATEKEEPERS... WHO USED THEIR BOND TO CREATE A VIRTUAL PSYCHIC ATMOSPHERE, THE TEMPERATURES ON THE SURFACE OF OUR PLANET WOULD BE INHOSPITABLE.
BUT WITH THE GATEKEEPERS, THEY WERE ABLE TO PROVIDE PROTECTION FROM THE SUN AND THE COLD AND CREATE A MARTIAN-MADE BIO-DOME.
PERFECT WEATHER AND IDEAL FOR AGRICULTURE.
OUR GROWERS WERE ABLE TO NOT ONLY PLANT AND NURTURE LIFE. THEY WERE ABLE TO COMMUNICATE WITH IT ON A BASIC LEVEL.
THEY COULD DIRECT THE GATEKEEPERS TO ADJUST THE ATMOSPHERE AS NEEDED FOR RAIN AND LIGHT. THE ENTIRE PLANET AND EVERY LIVING THING WAS CONNECTED IN A WAY THAT NO OTHER CULTURE HAS EVER BEEN.
WE EVEN HAD THE CORE... STATIONED UNDER GROUND...LISTENING AND TAPPING IN TO DETERMINE THE NEEDS OF THE PLANET.
TOGETHER WE KEPT THE ENTIRE ECOSYSTEM AND POPULATION LIVING AND WORKING TOGETHER. A NETWORK OF BEAUTIFUL MINDS WORKING IN COMPLETE HARMONY.
AN ORGANIC INTERNET BUT PURPOSED TO WORK TOGETHER.

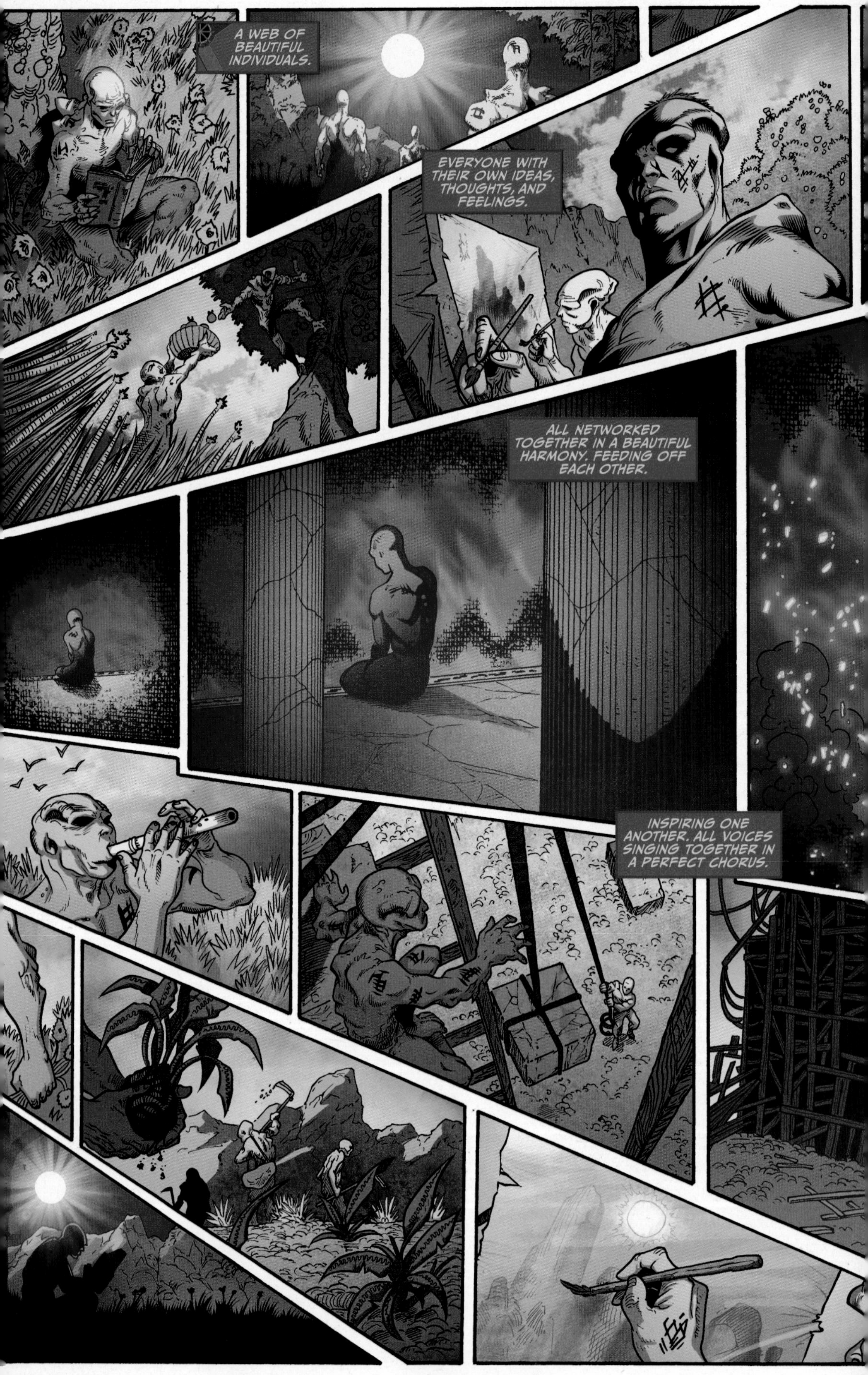
A WEB OF BEAUTIFUL INDIVIDUALS.
EVERYONE WITH THEIR OWN IDEAS, THOUGHTS, AND FEELINGS.
ALL NETWORKED TOGETHER IN A BEAUTIFUL HARMONY. FEEDING OFF EACH OTHER.
INSPIRING ONE ANOTHER. ALL VOICES SINGING TOGETHER IN A PERFECT CHORUS.

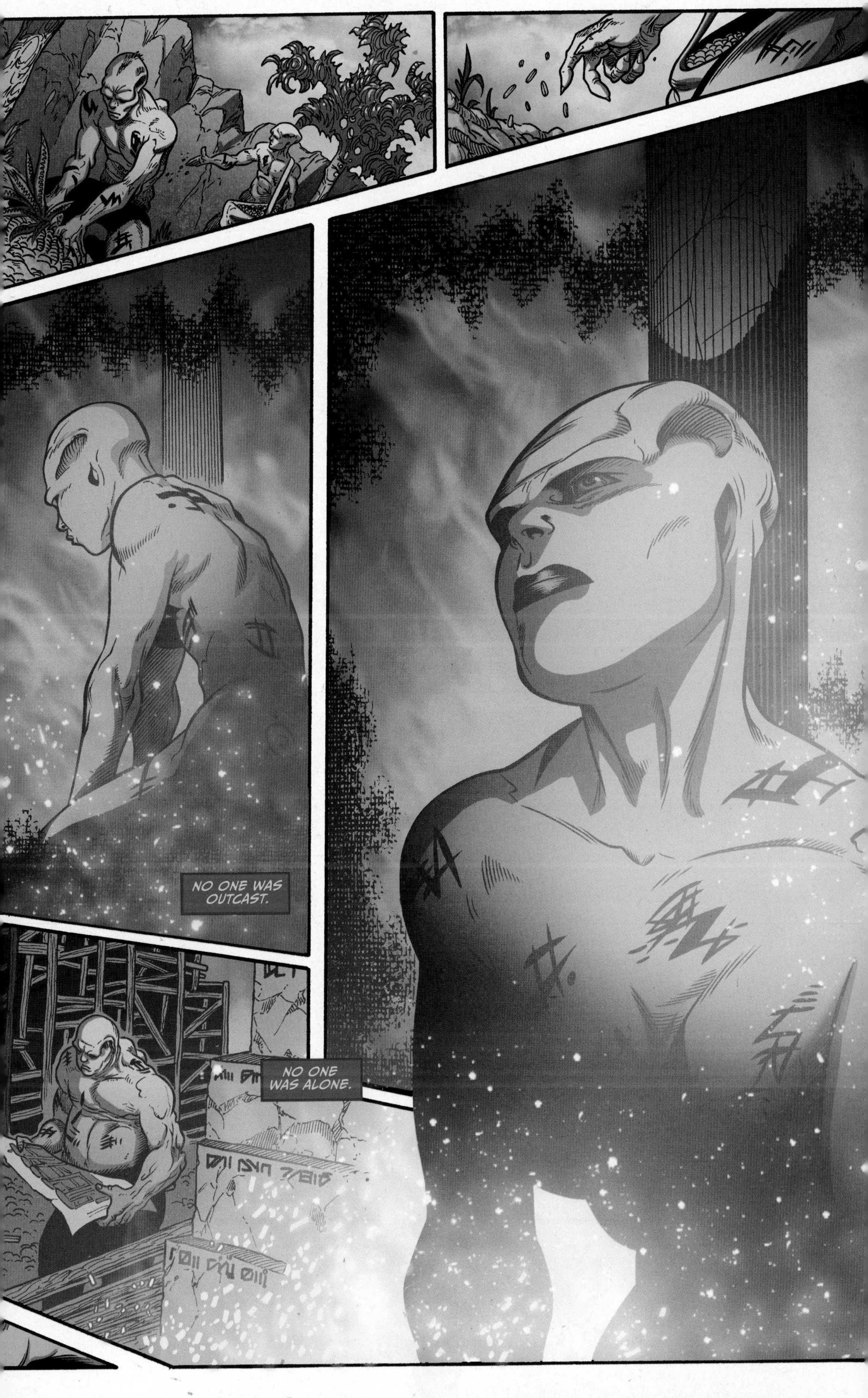
NO ONE WAS
OUTCAST.
NO ONE
WAS ALONE.

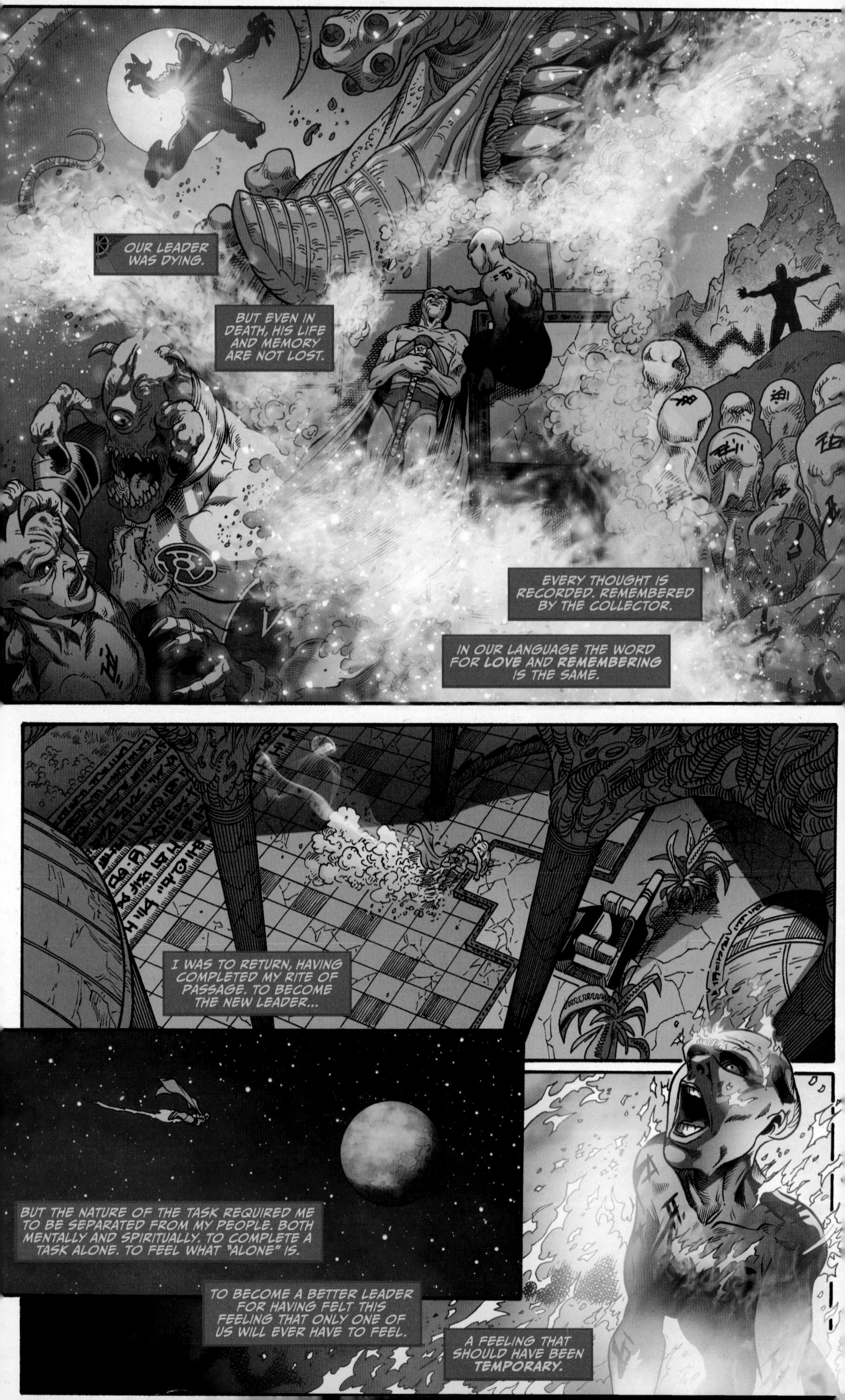
OUR LEADER WAS DYING.
BUT EVEN IN DEATH, HIS LIFE AND MEMORY ARE NOT LOST.
EVERY THOUGHT IS RECORDED. REMEMBERED BY THE COLLECTOR.
IN OUR LANGUAGE THE WORD FOR LOVE AND REMEMBERING IS THE SAME.
I WAS TO RETURN, HAVING COMPLETED MY RITE OF PASSAGE. TO BECOME THE NEW LEADER...
BUT THE NATURE OF THE TASK REQUIRED ME TO BE SEPARATED FROM MY PEOPLE. BOTH MENTALLY AND SPIRITUALLY. TO COMPLETE A TASK ALONE. TO FEEL WHAT "ALONE" IS.
TO BECOME A BETTER LEADER FOR HAVING FELT THIS FEELING THAT ONLY ONE OF US WILL EVER HAVE TO FEEL.
A FEELING THAT SHOULD HAVE BEEN TEMPORARY.

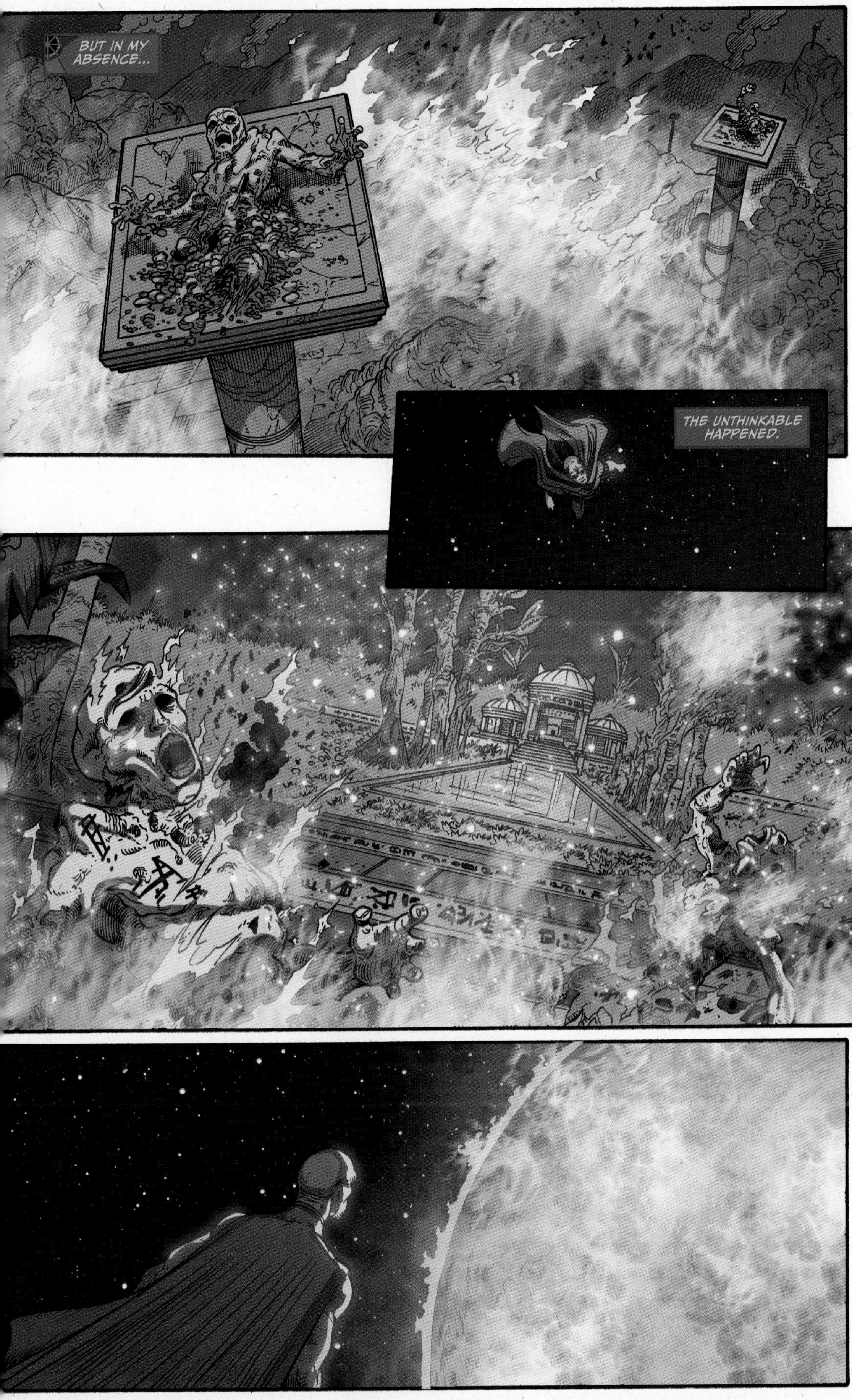
BUT IN MY ABSENCE...
THE UNTHINKABLE HAPPENED.

WHAT SHOULD HAVE BEEN A MOMENT OF TRIUMPH. OF GOOD WILL AND RENEWAL...

WAS NEVER TO BE.

THERE WERE NO WORDS IN OUR CULTURE FOR "ALONE" OR "ISOLATION" OR "ABANDONMENT" OR "HATE."

BUT THAT DIDN'T STOP ME FROM FEELING THEM ALL.

ALL MEMORY WAS GONE. ALL PSYCHIC RESIDUE WIPED OUT. ALL BUT ONE WORD. A WORD I'D NEVER HEARD BEFORE. MAN.

UNTIL THAT DAY, WE HAD NO WORD FOR "MAN."

BUT WE DID HAVE THE WORD.... "HUNTER."

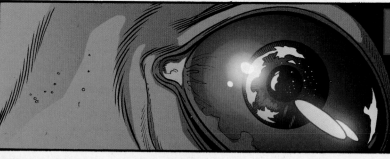

SO WHY DOES FIRE HURT ME? WHY CAN I NOT STOP IT? IT IS BECAUSE OF ANOTHER CONCEPT MY PEOPLE HAD NO WORD FOR.

GUILT.

GUILT FOR SURVIVING WHERE EVERYONE ELSE DIED. GUILT FOR NOT BEING THERE TO HELP THEM. MY UNCONSCIOUS PUNISHING ME. MAKING ME FEEL THE PAIN. THE FIRE. THE DEATH.

THE DEATH THAT I SHOULD HAVE FELT THAT DAY WITH MY PEOPLE.

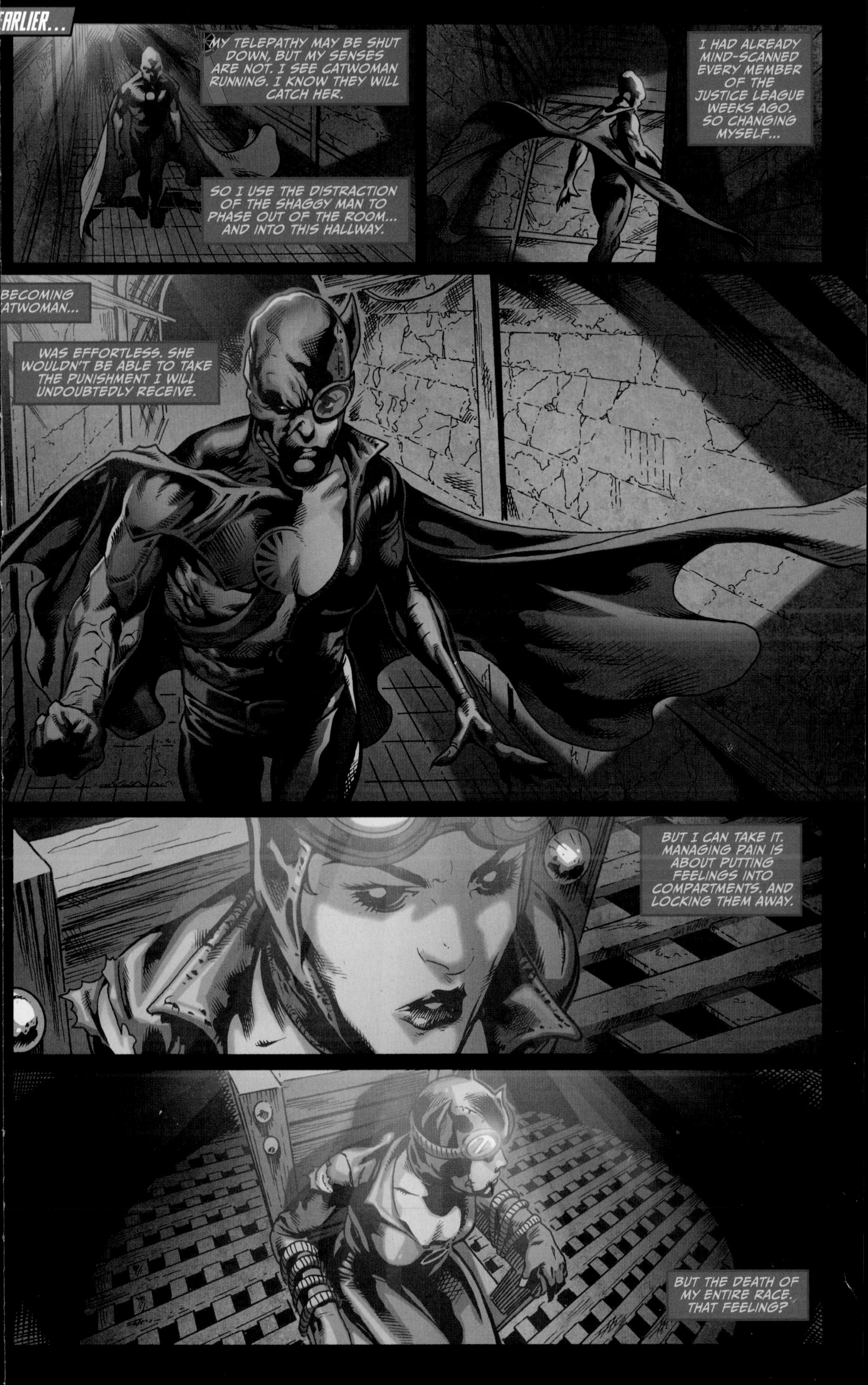
EARLIER...
MY TELEPATHY MAY BE SHUT DOWN, BUT MY SENSES ARE NOT. I SEE CATWOMAN RUNNING. I KNOW THEY WILL CATCH HER.
SO I USE THE DISTRACTION OF THE SHAGGY MAN TO PHASE OUT OF THE ROOM... AND INTO THIS HALLWAY.
I HAD ALREADY MIND-SCANNED EVERY MEMBER OF THE JUSTICE LEAGUE WEEKS AGO. SO CHANGING MYSELF...
BECOMING CATWOMAN...
WAS EFFORTLESS. SHE WOULDN'T BE ABLE TO TAKE THE PUNISHMENT I WILL UNDOUBTEDLY RECEIVE.
BUT I CAN TAKE IT. MANAGING PAIN IS ABOUT PUTTING FEELINGS INTO COMPARTMENTS. AND LOCKING THEM AWAY.
BUT THE DEATH OF MY ENTIRE RACE. THAT FEELING?

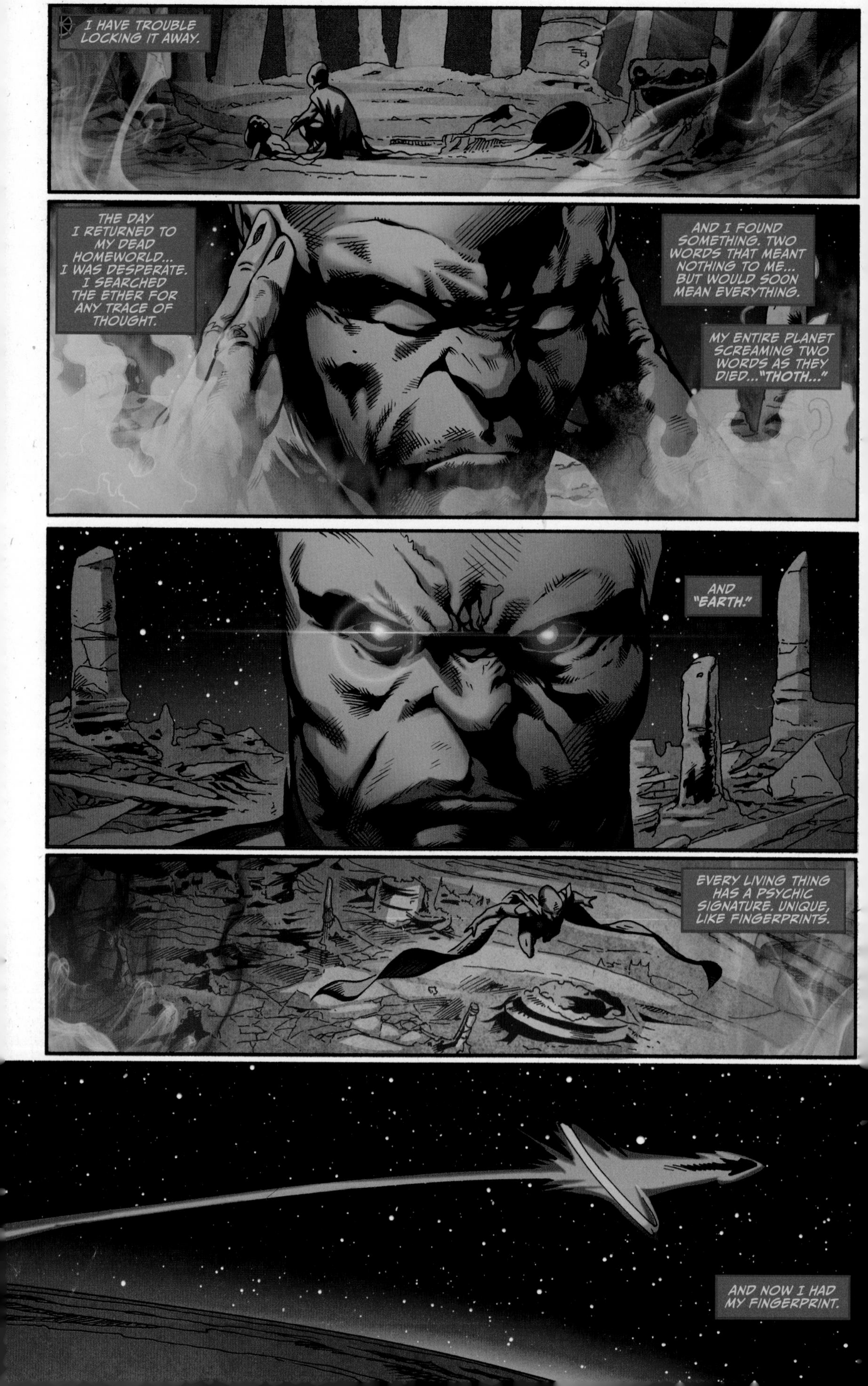
I HAVE TROUBLE LOCKING IT AWAY.
THE DAY I RETURNED TO MY DEAD HOMEWORLD... I WAS DESPERATE. I SEARCHED THE ETHER FOR ANY TRACE OF THOUGHT.
AND I FOUND SOMETHING. TWO WORDS THAT MEANT NOTHING TO ME... BUT WOULD SOON MEAN EVERYTHING.
MY ENTIRE PLANET SCREAMING TWO WORDS AS THEY DIED... "THOTH..."
AND "EARTH."
EVERY LIVING THING HAS A PSYCHIC SIGNATURE. UNIQUE, LIKE FINGERPRINTS.
AND NOW I HAD MY FINGERPRINT.

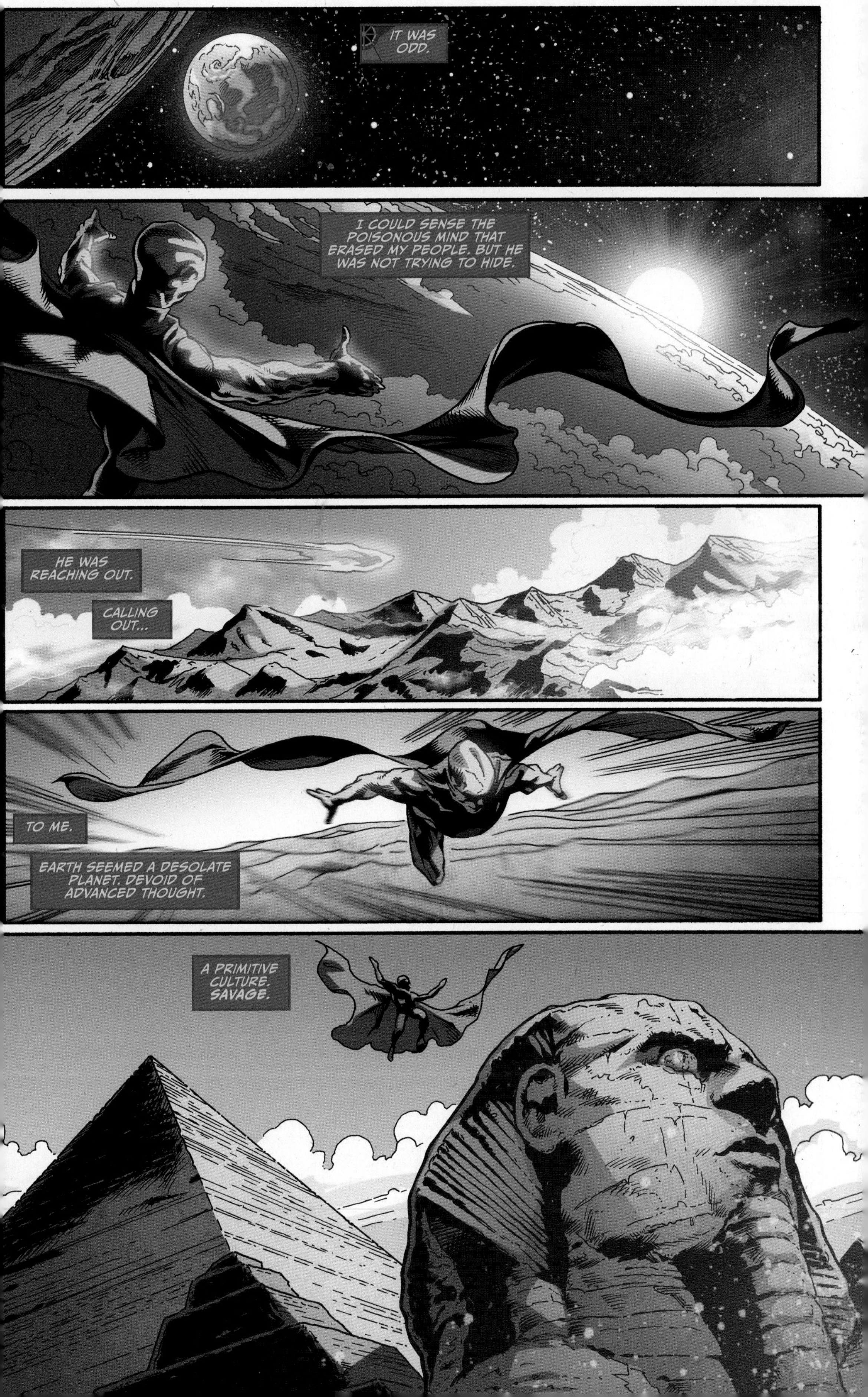
IT WAS ODD.
I COULD SENSE THE POISONOUS MIND THAT ERASED MY PEOPLE. BUT HE WAS NOT TRYING TO HIDE.
HE WAS REACHING OUT.
CALLING OUT...
TO ME.
EARTH SEEMED A DESOLATE PLANET. DEVOID OF ADVANCED THOUGHT.
A PRIMITIVE CULTURE. SAVAGE.

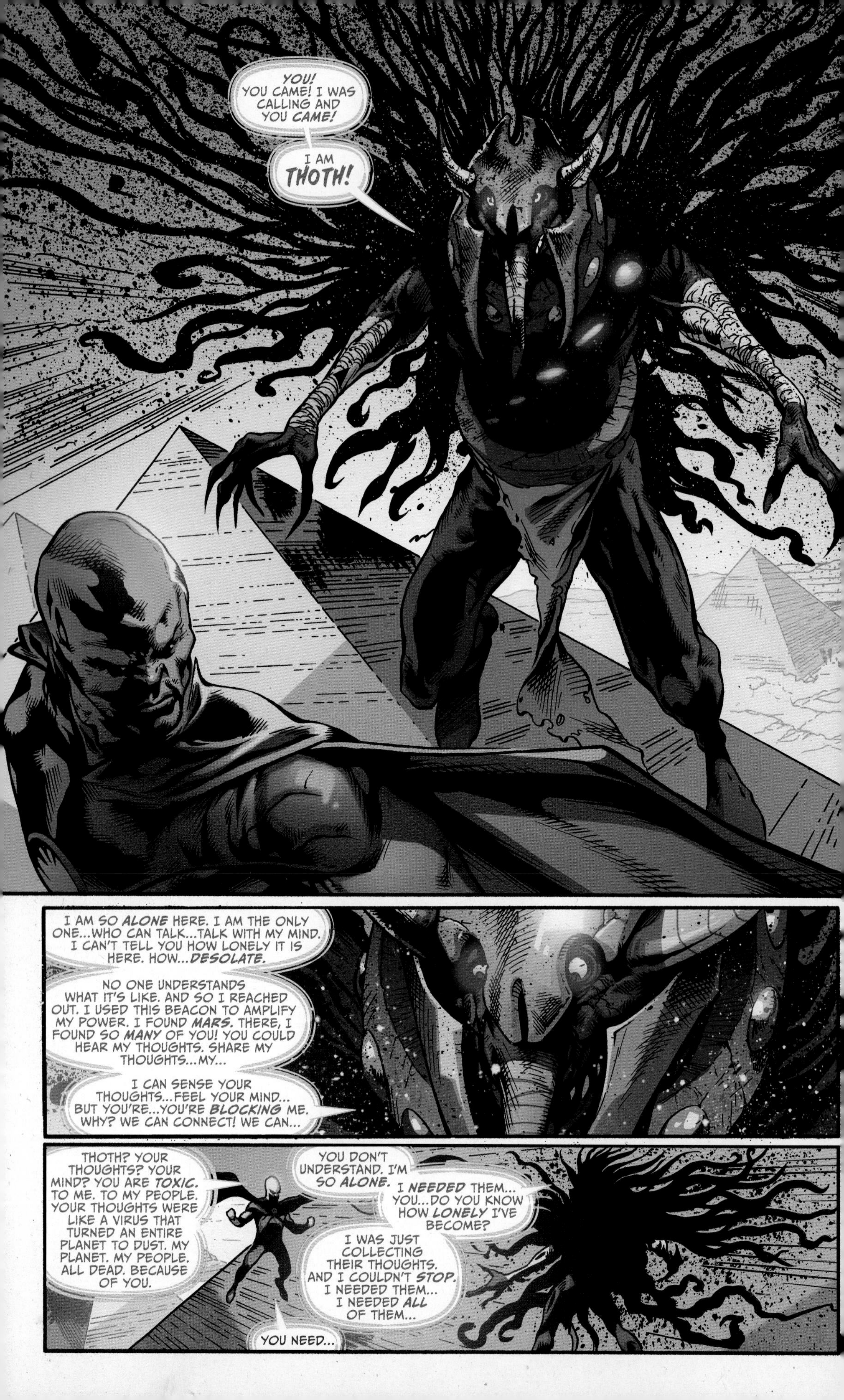
YOU! YOU CAME! I WAS CALLING AND YOU CAME!
I AM THOTH!
I AM SO ALONE HERE. I AM THE ONLY ONE...WHO CAN TALK...TALK WITH MY MIND. I CAN'T TELL YOU HOW LONELY IT IS HERE. HOW...DESOLATE.
NO ONE UNDERSTANDS WHAT IT'S LIKE. AND SO I REACHED OUT. I USED THIS BEACON TO AMPLIFY MY POWER. I FOUND MARS. THERE, I FOUND SO MANY OF YOU! YOU COULD HEAR MY THOUGHTS. SHARE MY THOUGHTS...MY...
I CAN SENSE YOUR THOUGHTS...FEEL YOUR MIND... BUT YOU'RE...YOU'RE BLOCKING ME. WHY? WE CAN CONNECT! WE CAN...
THOTH? YOUR THOUGHTS? YOUR MIND? YOU ARE TOXIC. TO ME. TO MY PEOPLE. YOUR THOUGHTS WERE LIKE A VIRUS THAT TURNED AN ENTIRE PLANET TO DUST. MY PLANET. MY PEOPLE. ALL DEAD. BECAUSE OF YOU.
YOU DON'T UNDERSTAND. I'M SO ALONE.
I NEEDED THEM... YOU...DO YOU KNOW HOW LONELY I'VE BECOME?
I WAS JUST COLLECTING THEIR THOUGHTS. AND I COULDN'T STOP. I NEEDED THEM... I NEEDED ALL OF THEM...
YOU NEED...

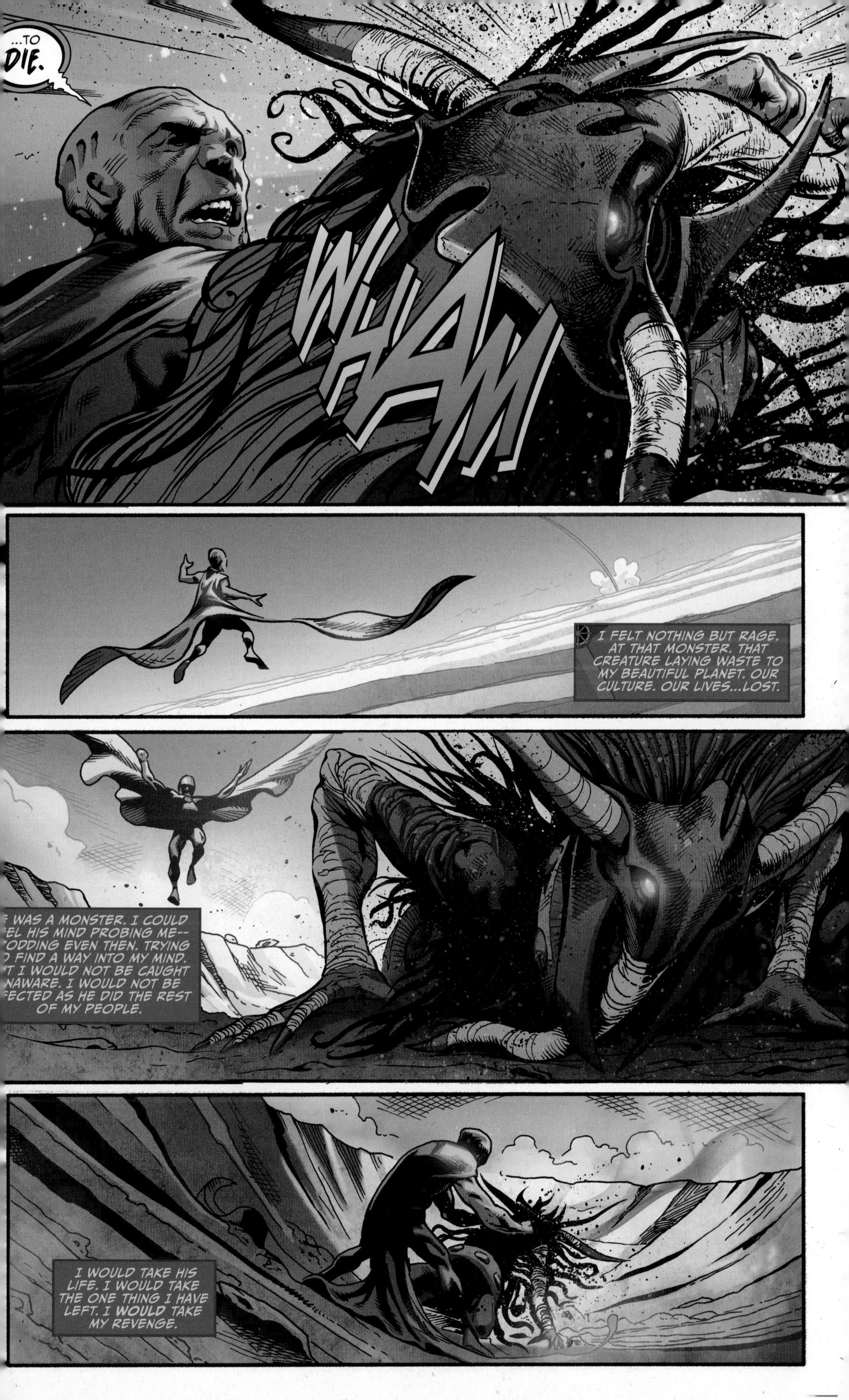

...TO DIE.
WHAM
I FELT NOTHING BUT RAGE. AT THAT MONSTER. THAT CREATURE LAYING WASTE TO MY BEAUTIFUL PLANET. OUR CULTURE. OUR LIVES...LOST.
E WAS A MONSTER. I COULD EL HIS MIND PROBING ME-- ODDING EVEN THEN. TRYING O FIND A WAY INTO MY MIND. T I WOULD NOT BE CAUGHT NAWARE. I WOULD NOT BE FECTED AS HE DID THE REST OF MY PEOPLE.
I WOULD TAKE HIS LIFE. I WOULD TAKE THE ONE THING I HAVE LEFT. I WOULD TAKE MY REVENGE.

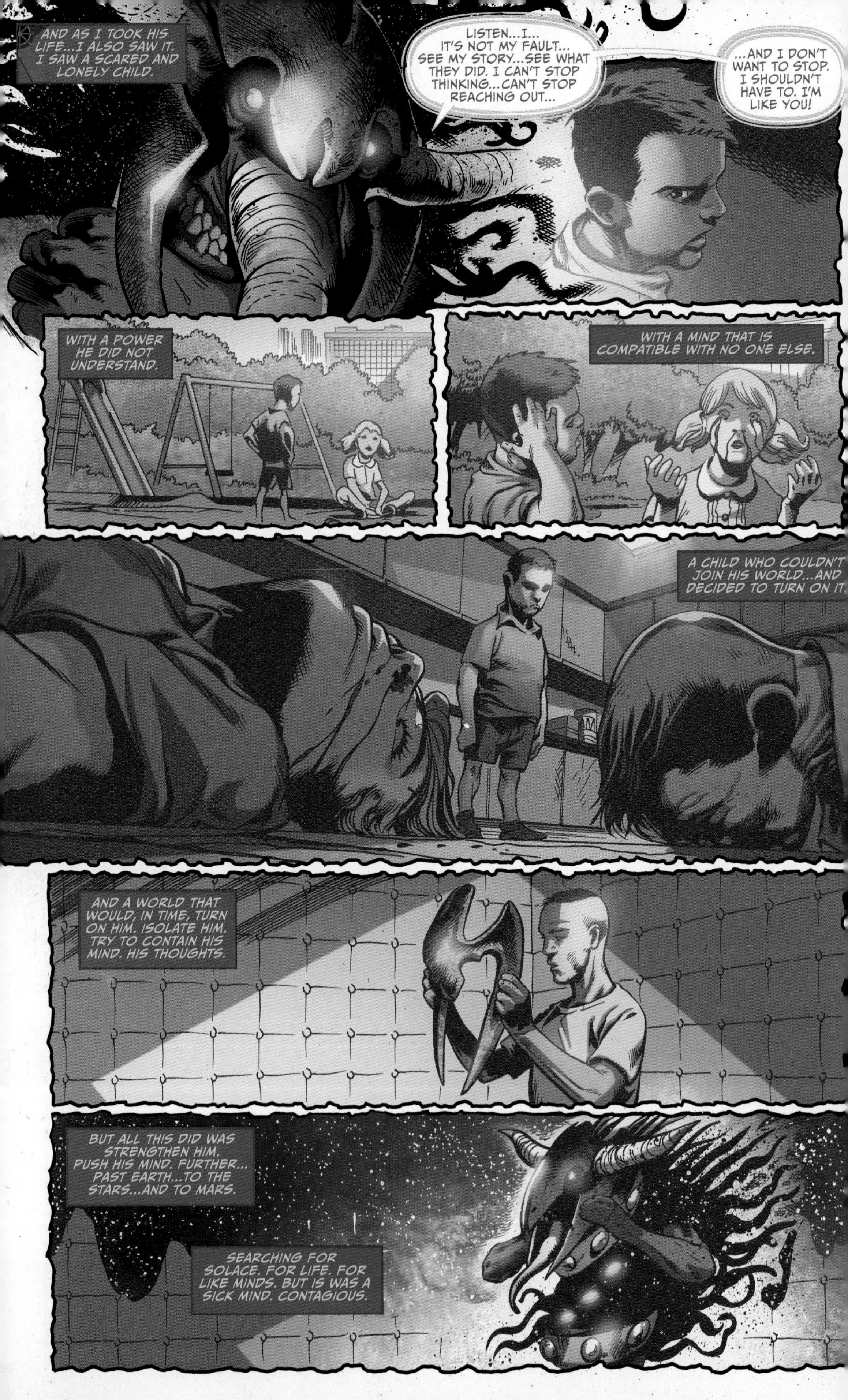
AND AS I TOOK HIS LIFE...I ALSO SAW IT. I SAW A SCARED AND LONELY CHILD.
LISTEN...I... IT'S NOT MY FAULT... SEE MY STORY...SEE WHAT THEY DID. I CAN'T STOP THINKING...CAN'T STOP REACHING OUT...
...AND I DON'T WANT TO STOP. I SHOULDN'T HAVE TO. I'M LIKE YOU!
WITH A POWER HE DID NOT UNDERSTAND.
WITH A MIND THAT IS COMPATIBLE WITH NO ONE ELSE.
A CHILD WHO COULDN'T JOIN HIS WORLD...AND DECIDED TO TURN ON IT.
AND A WORLD THAT WOULD, IN TIME, TURN ON HIM. ISOLATE HIM. TRY TO CONTAIN HIS MIND. HIS THOUGHTS.
BUT ALL THIS DID WAS STRENGTHEN HIM. PUSH HIS MIND. FURTHER... PAST EARTH...TO THE STARS...AND TO MARS.
SEARCHING FOR SOLACE. FOR LIFE. FOR LIKE MINDS. BUT IS WAS A SICK MIND. CONTAGIOUS.

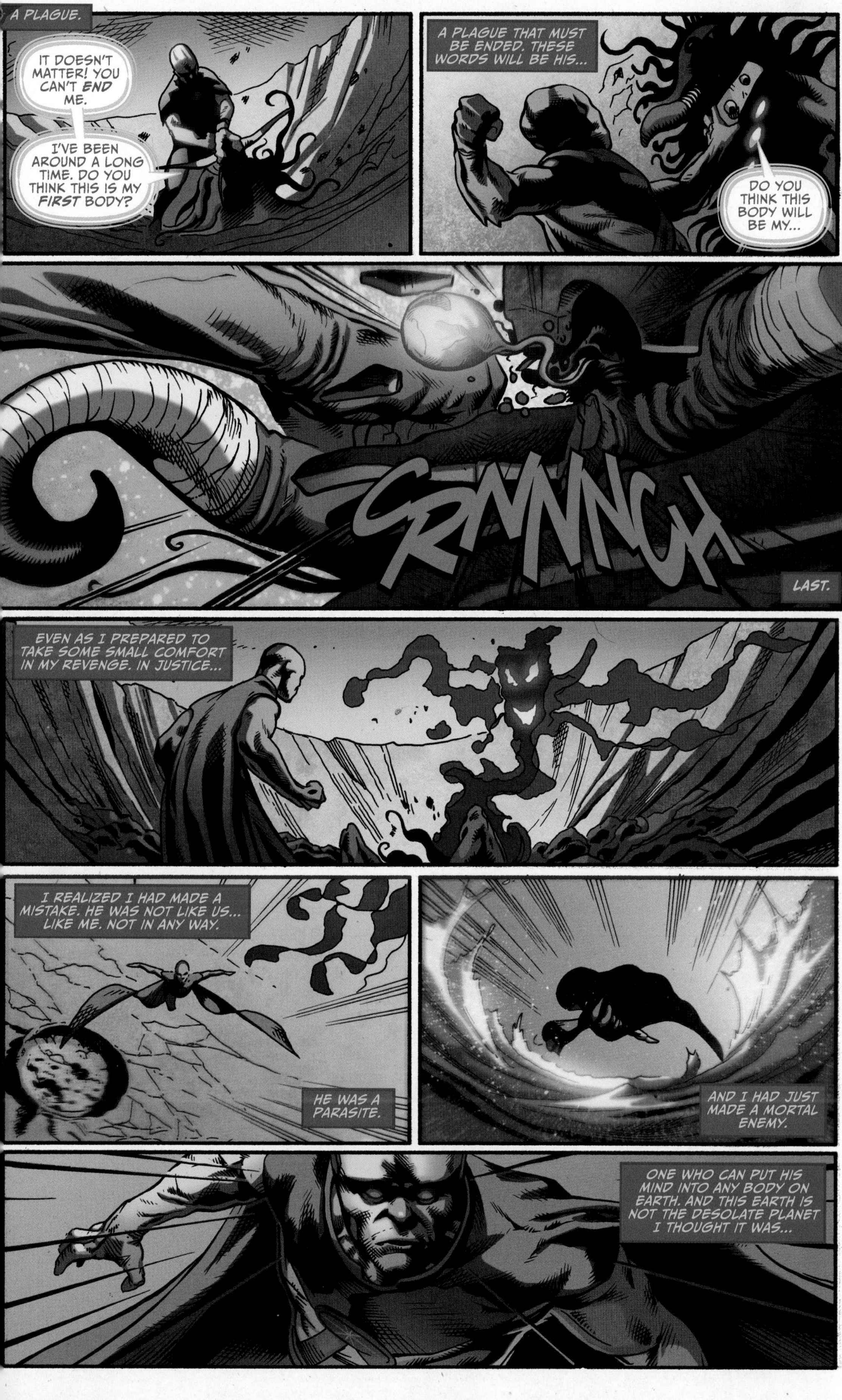
A PLAGUE.
IT DOESN'T MATTER! YOU CAN'T END ME.
I'VE BEEN AROUND A LONG TIME. DO YOU THINK THIS IS MY FIRST BODY?
A PLAGUE THAT MUST BE ENDED. THESE WORDS WILL BE HIS...
DO YOU THINK THIS BODY WILL BE MY...
CRNNNCH
LAST.
EVEN AS I PREPARED TO TAKE SOME SMALL COMFORT IN MY REVENGE. IN JUSTICE...
I REALIZED I HAD MADE A MISTAKE. HE WAS NOT LIKE US... LIKE ME. NOT IN ANY WAY.
HE WAS A PARASITE.
AND I HAD JUST MADE A MORTAL ENEMY.
ONE WHO CAN PUT HIS MIND INTO ANY BODY ON EARTH. AND THIS EARTH IS NOT THE DESOLATE PLANET I THOUGHT IT WAS...

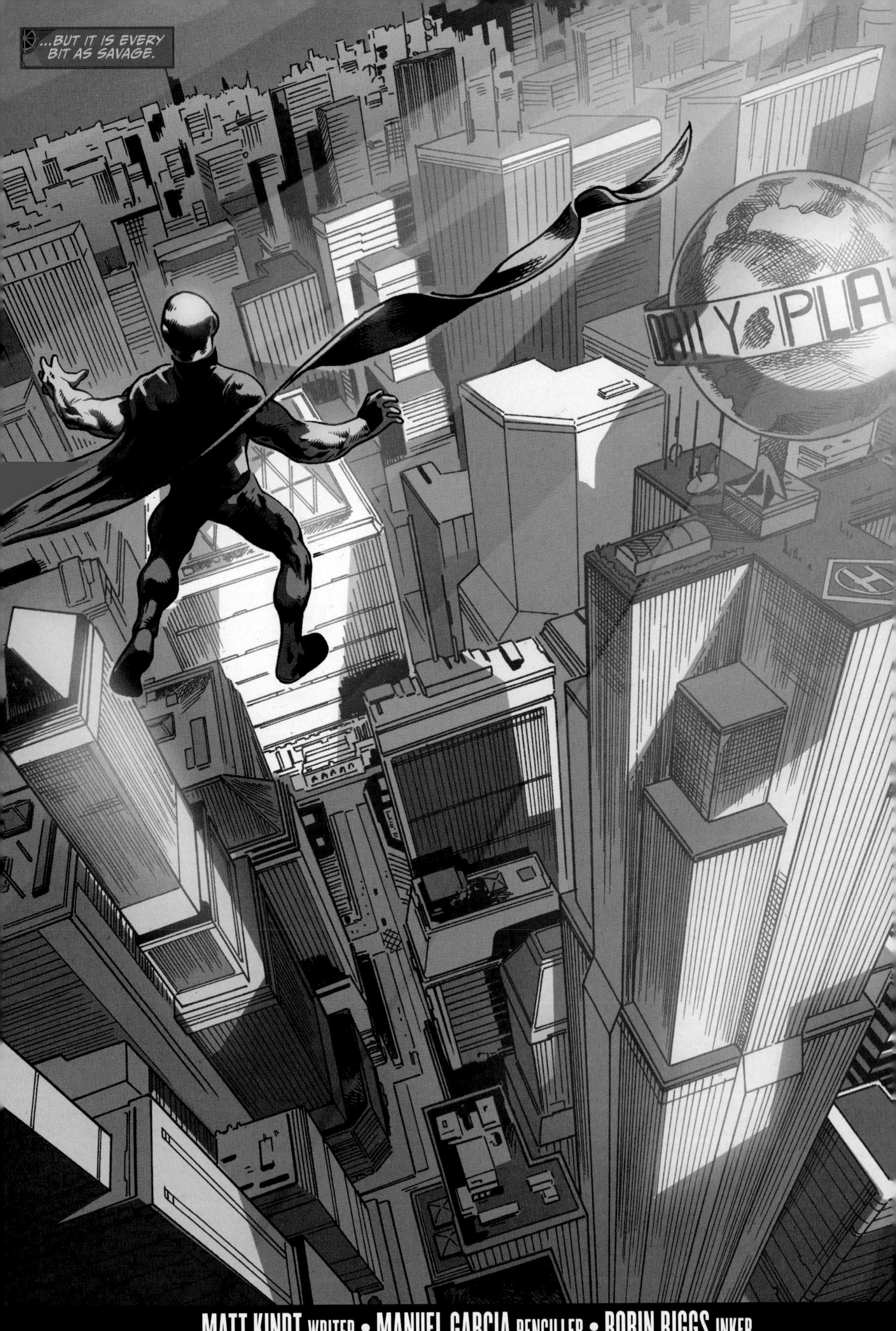
...BUT IT IS EVERY BIT AS SAVAGE.
DAILY PLA

MATT KINDT WRITER • MANUEL GARCIA PENCILLER • ROBIN RIGGS INKER
WIL QUINTANA COLORIST • ROB LEIGH LETTERER
DC COMICS PROUDLY PRESENTS...
THE MARTIAN MANHUNTER

JUSTICE LEAGUE OF AMERICA #2
Variant cover by Juan José Ryp

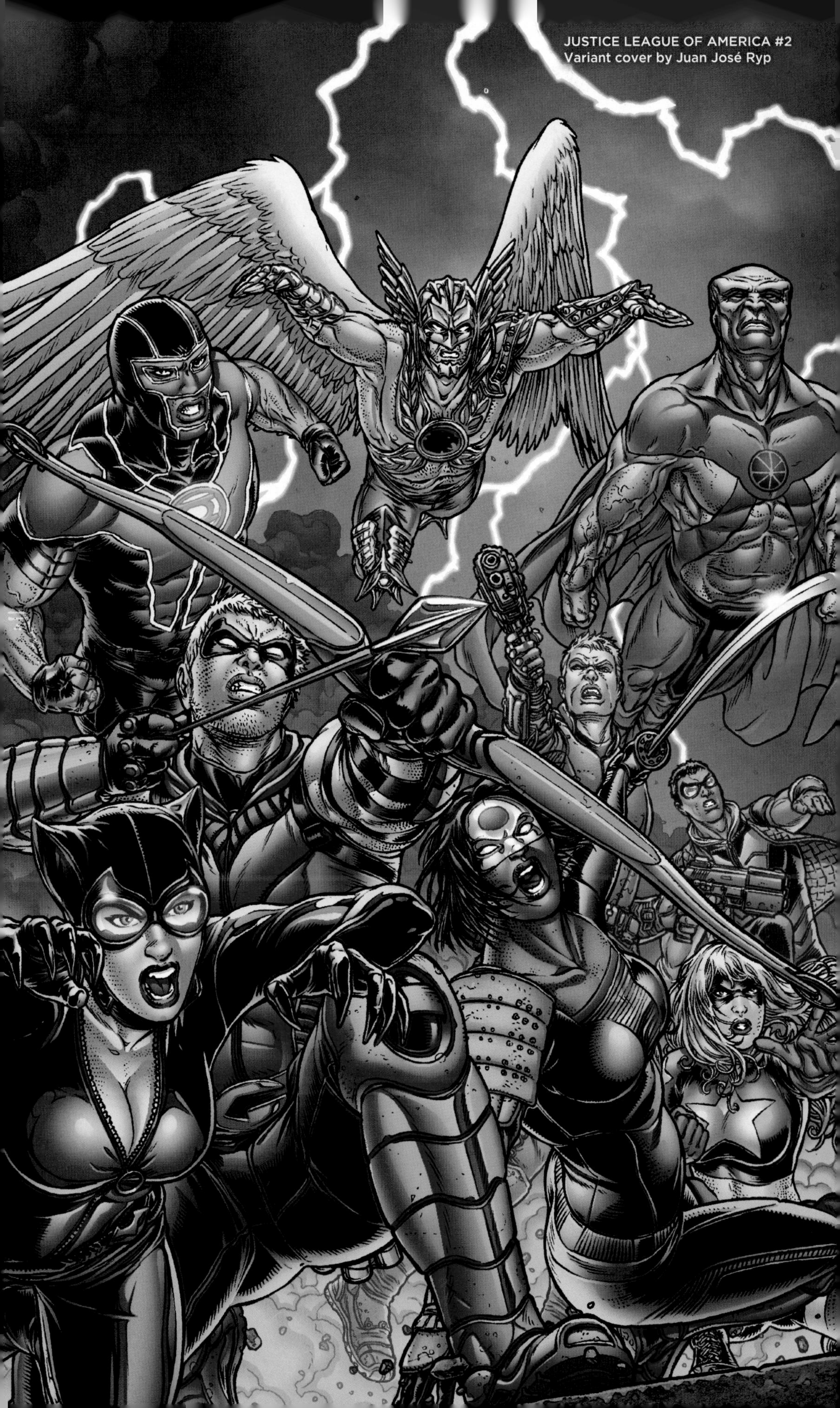

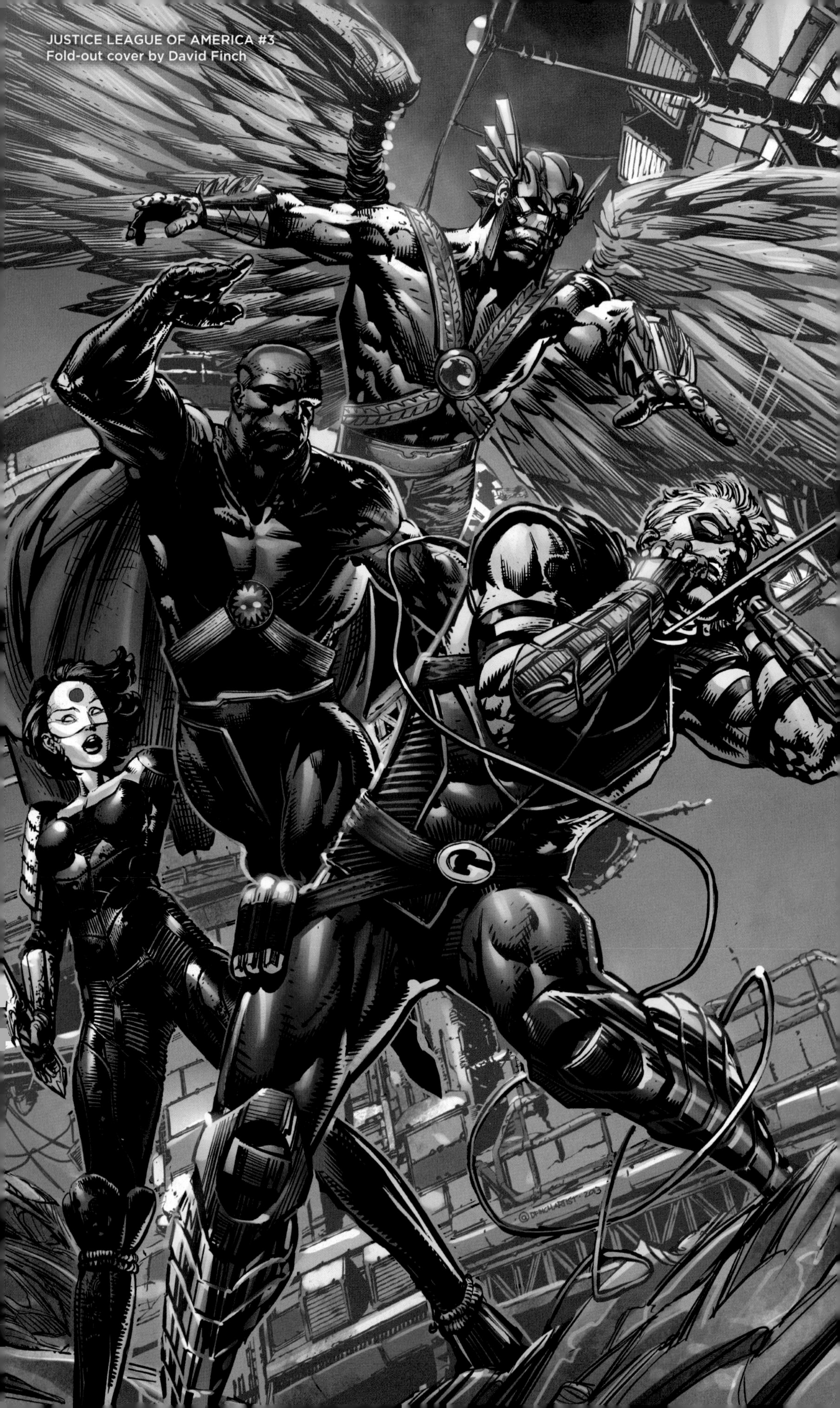

JUSTICE LEAGUE OF AMERICA #3
Fold-out cover by David Finch

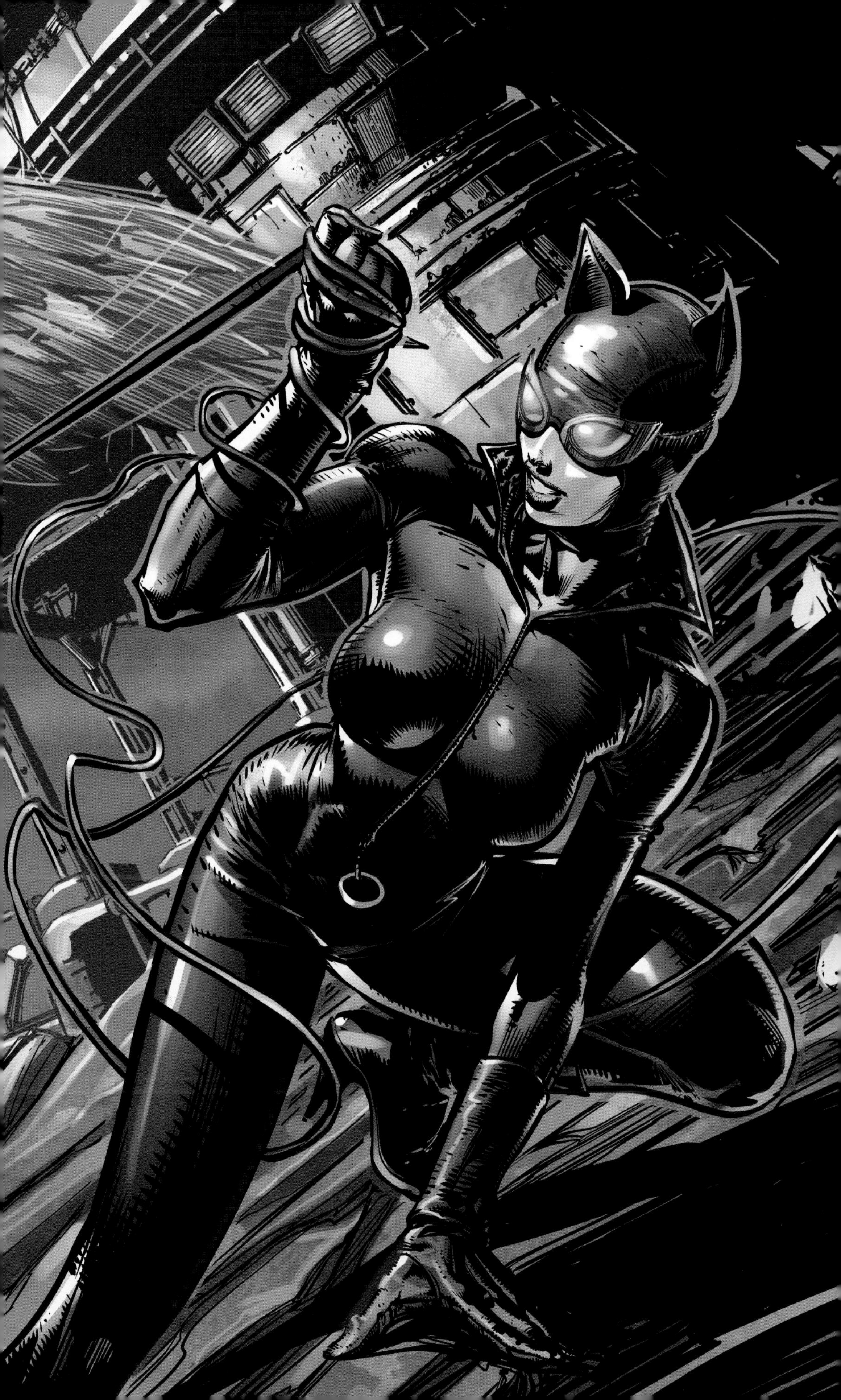

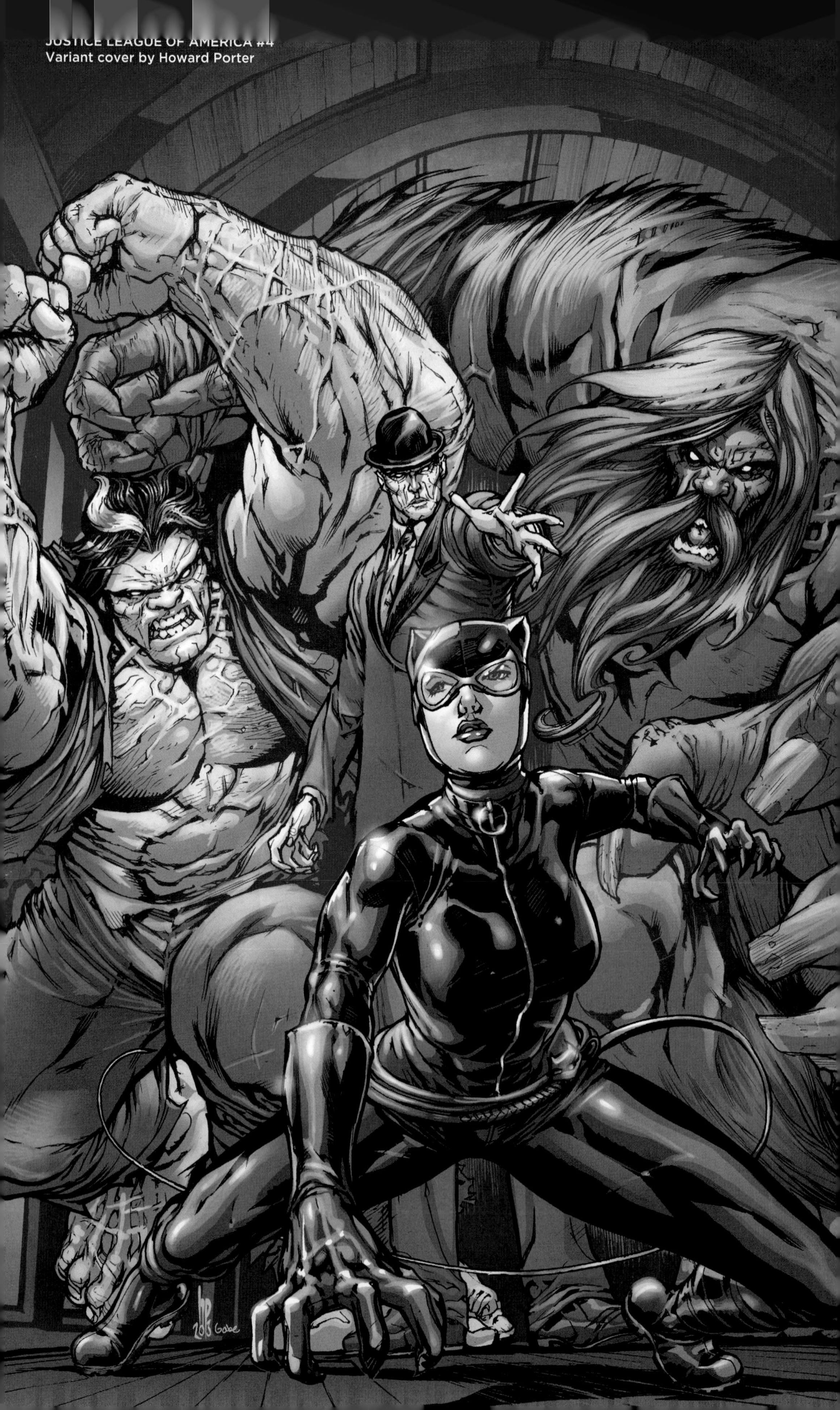

JUSTICE LEAGUE OF AMERICA #4
Variant cover by Howard Porter

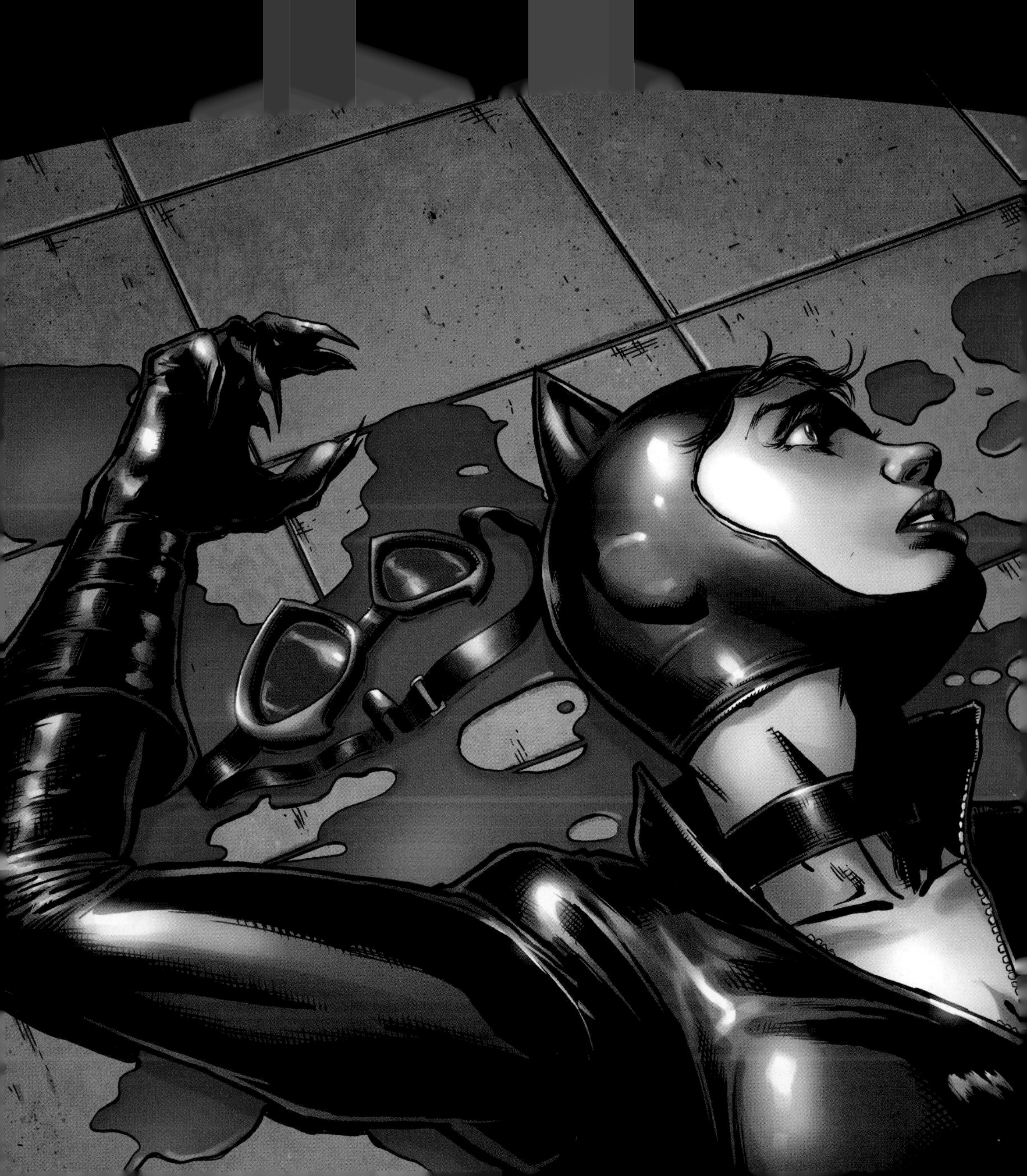

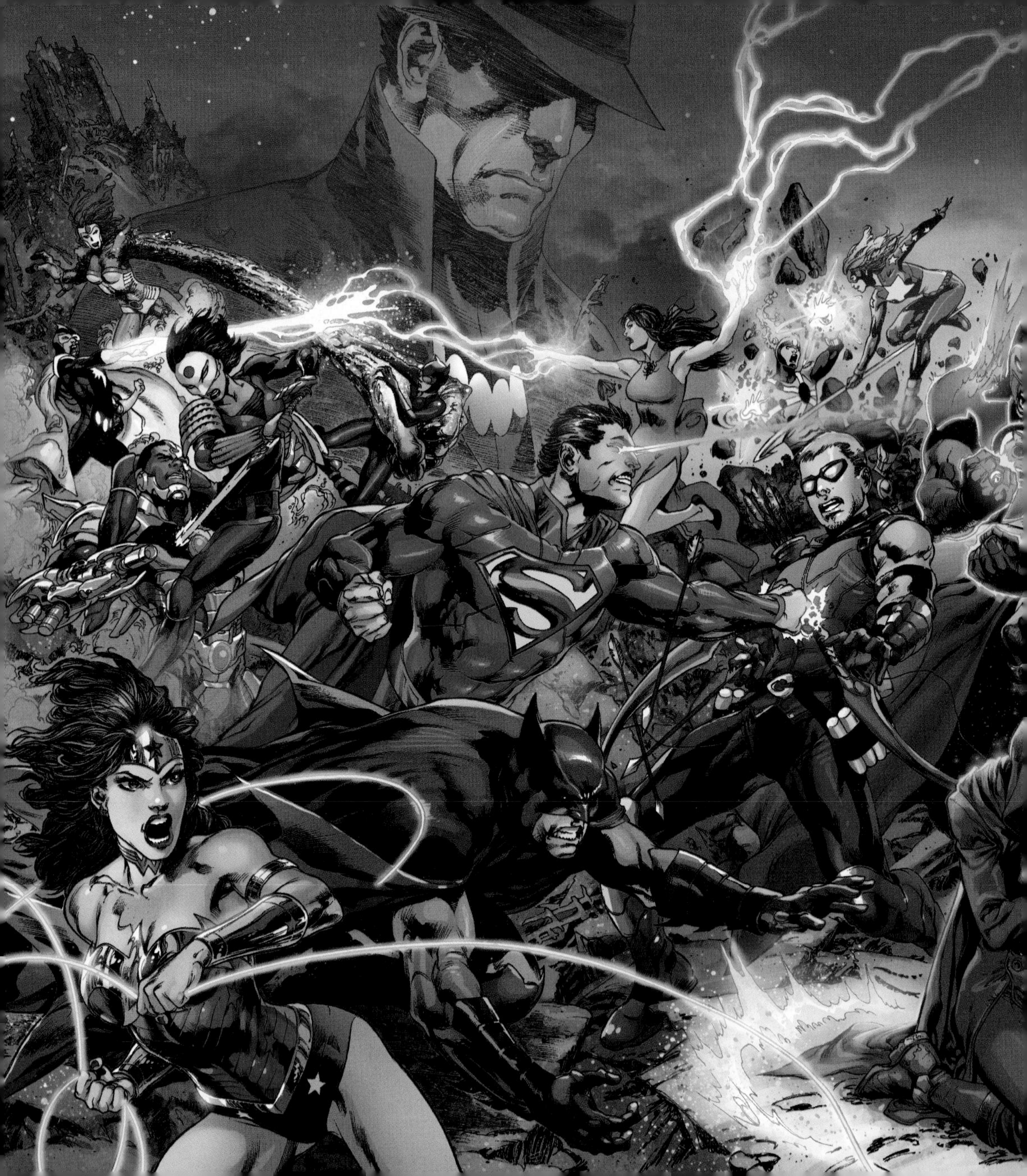

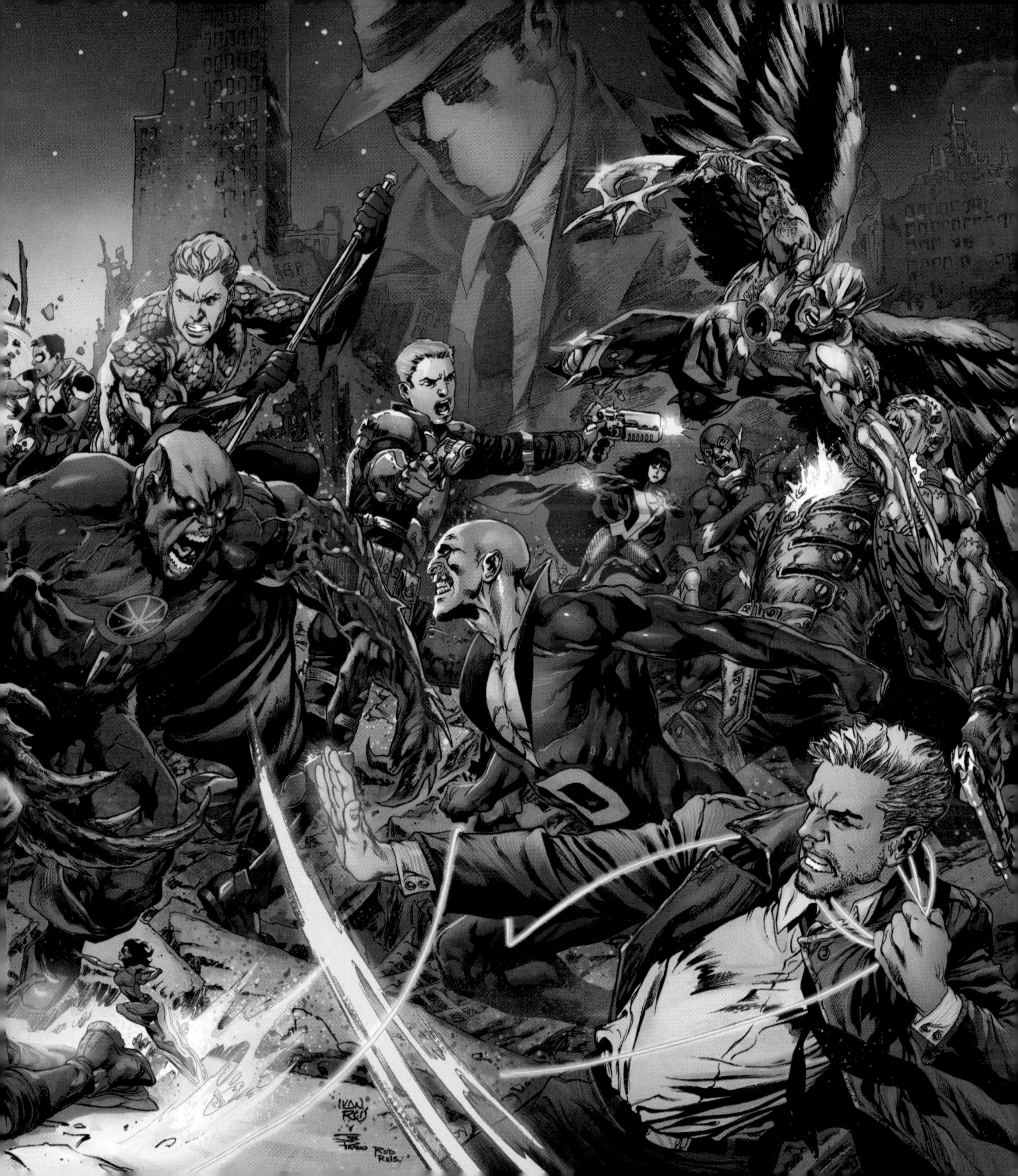
IVAN REIS
ROD REIS

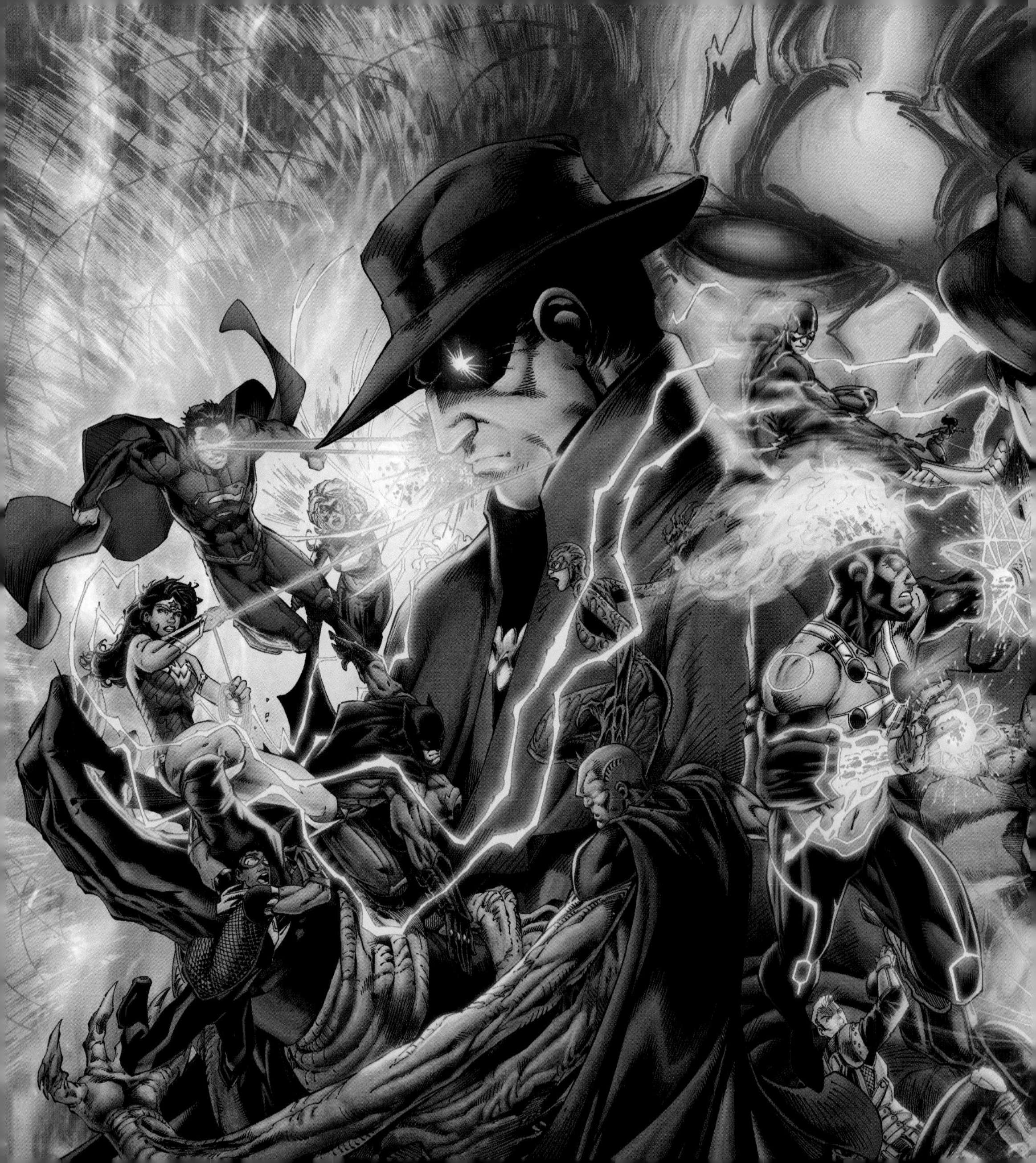

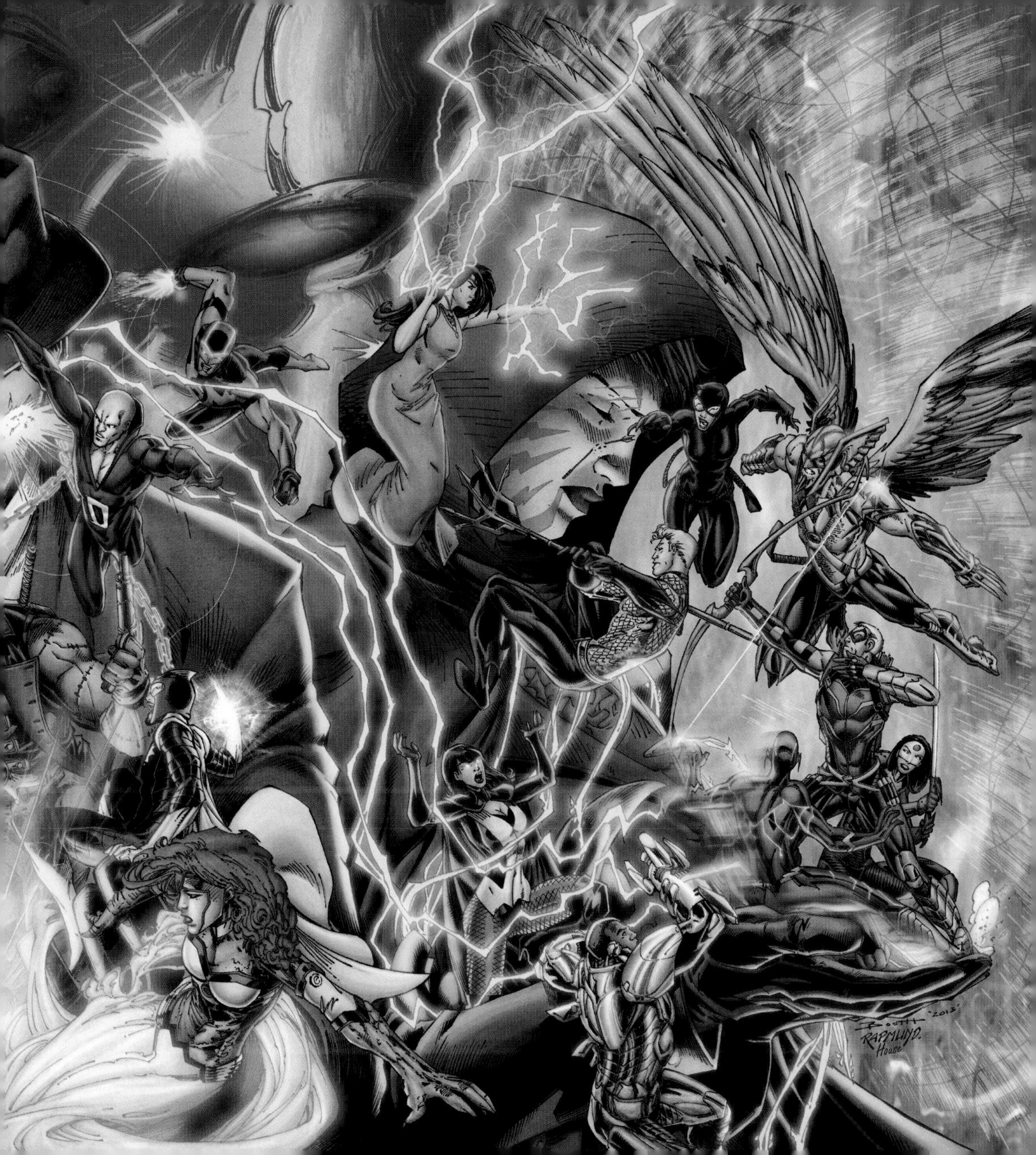

JUSTICE LEAGUE OF AMERICA #7, JUSTICE LEAGUE DARK #23 & JUSTICE LEAGUE #23
Cover triptych by Doug Mahnke

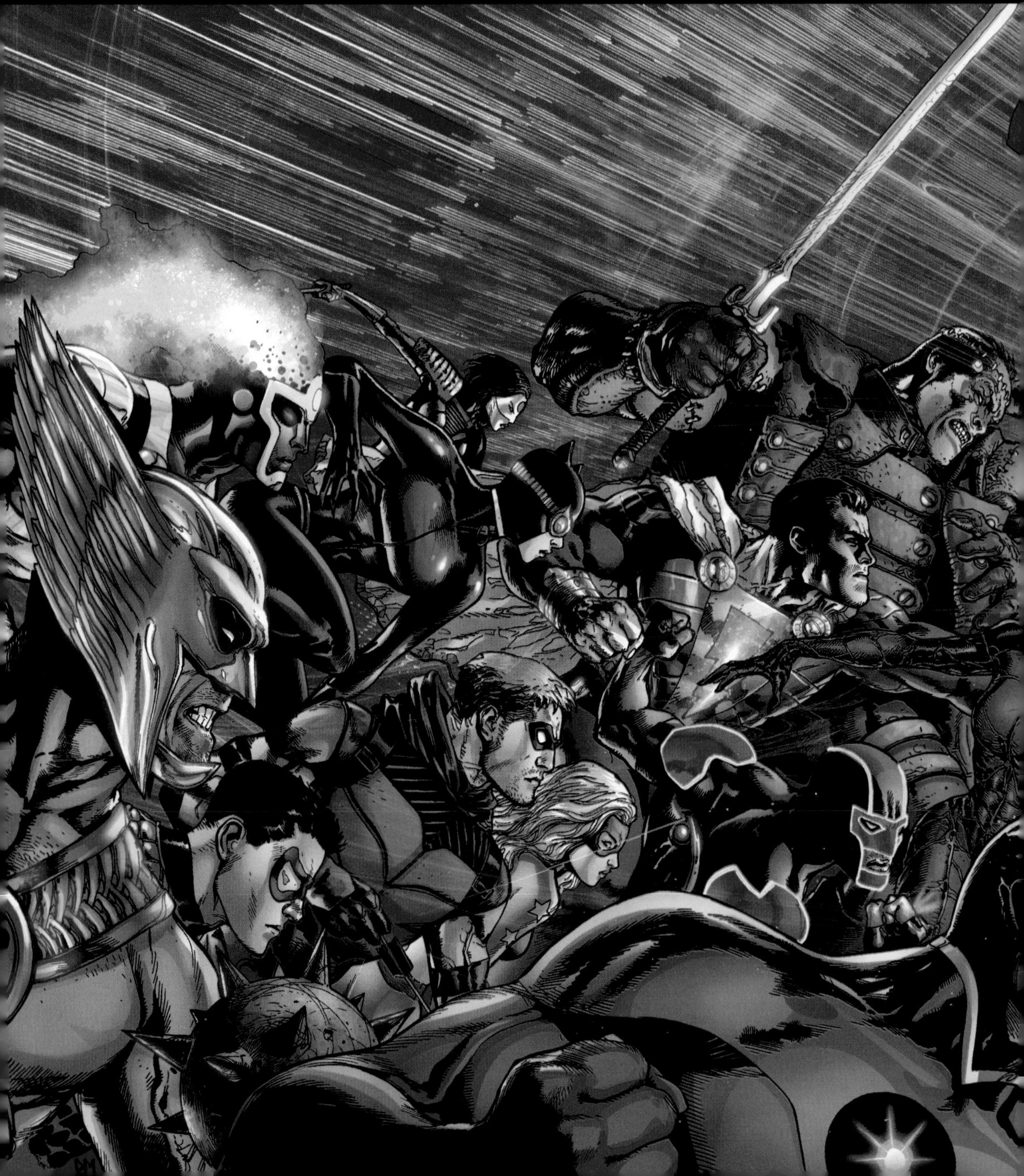

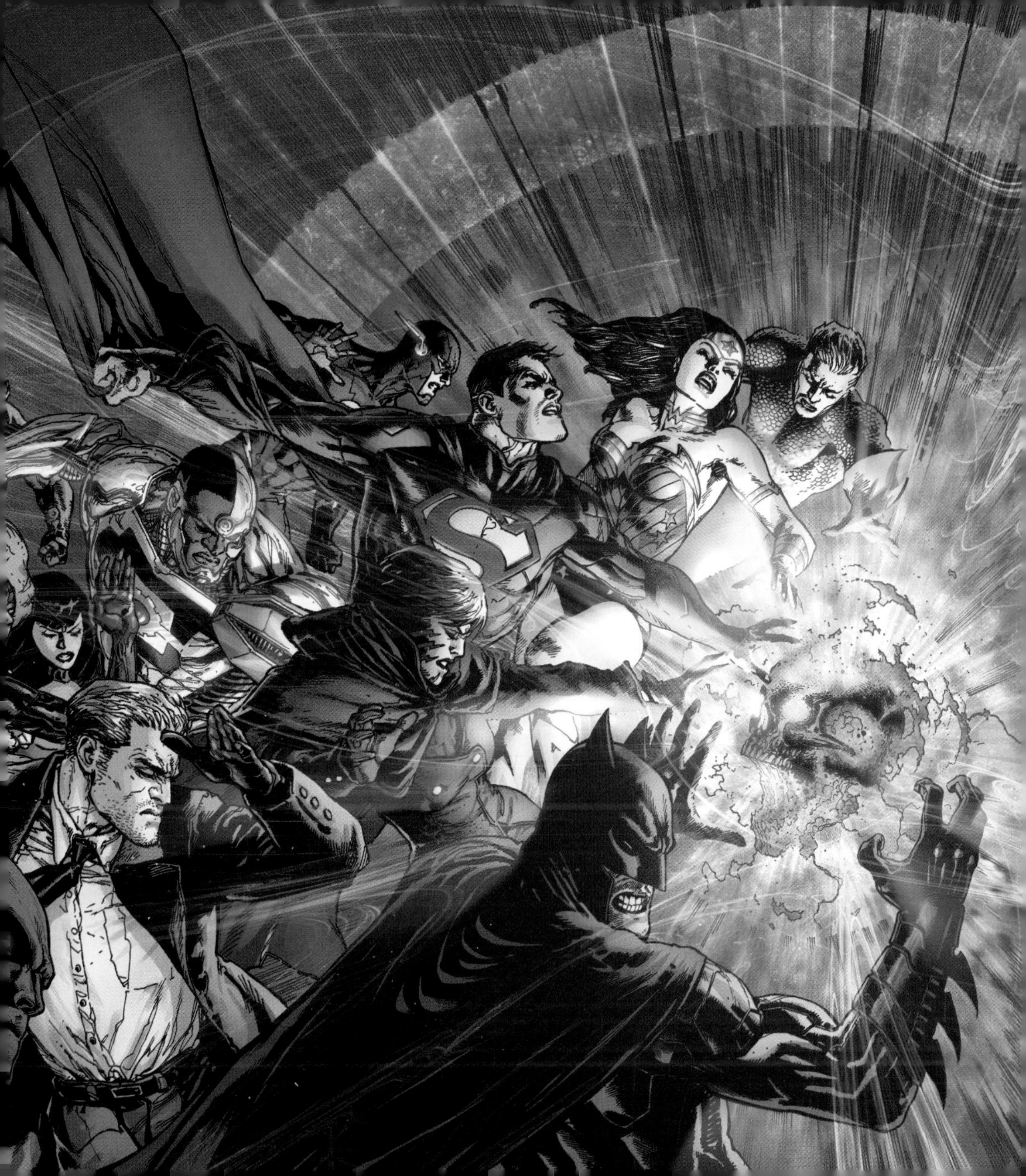

JUSTICE LEAGUE #23, JUSTICE LEAGUE OF AMERICA #7 & JUSTICE LEAGUE DARK #23
Variant cover triptych by Mikel Janin & Vicente Cifuentes

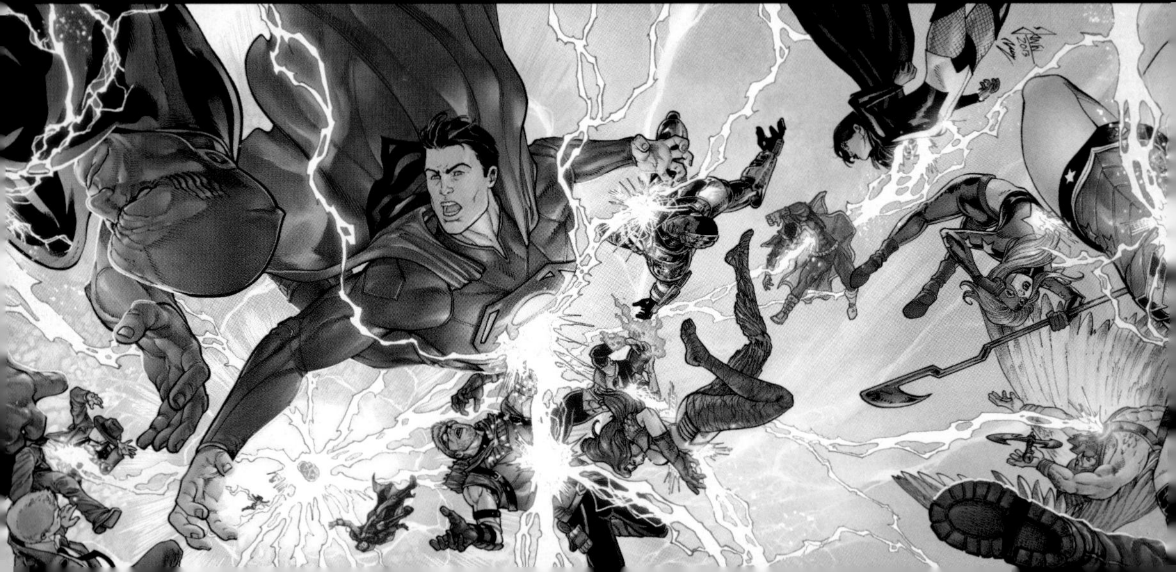

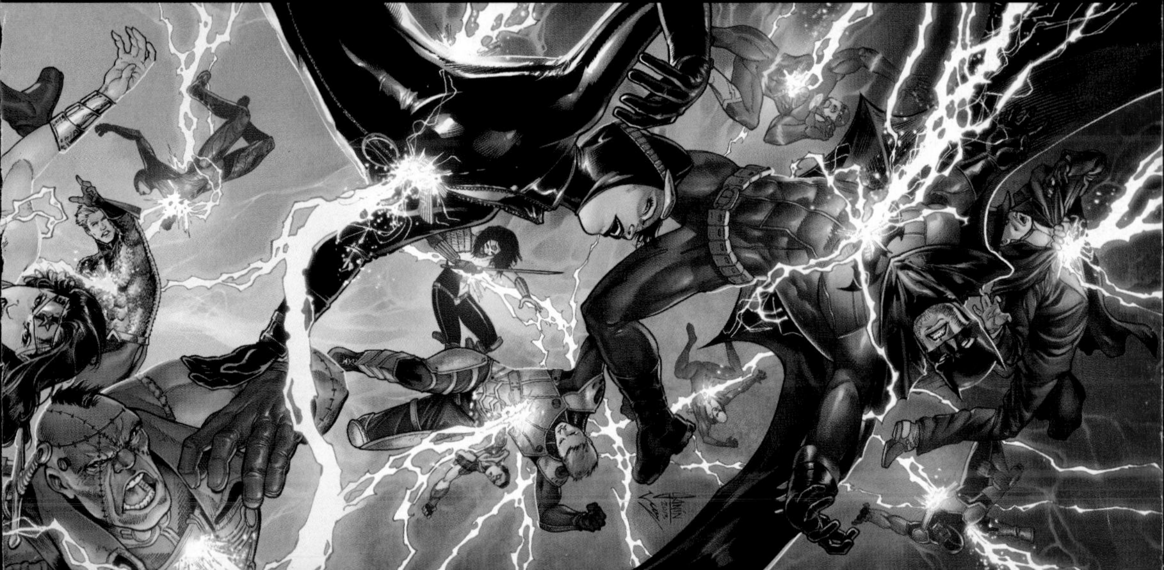

JUSTICE LEAGUE OF AMERICA #3
MAD Magazine variant cover by Hermann Mejia

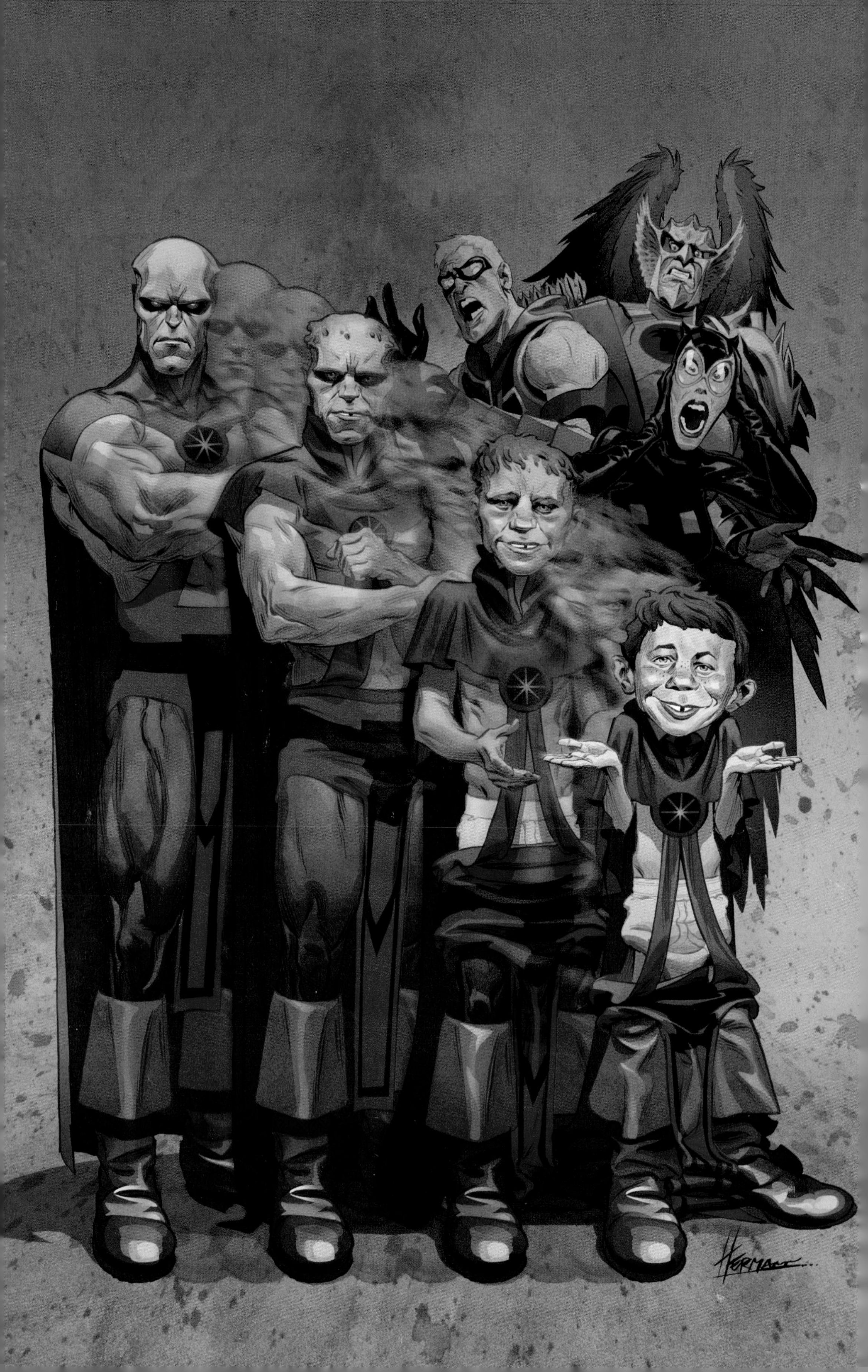